Lecture Notes in Artificial Intelligence   5925

Edited by R. Goebel, J. Siekmann, and W. Wahlster

Subseries of Lecture Notes in Computer Science

T0189656

Jung-Jin Yang   Makoto Yokoo
Takayuki Ito   Zhi Jin   Paul Scerri (Eds.)

Principles of Practice in Multi-Agent Systems

12th International Conference, PRIMA 2009
Nagoya, Japan, December 14-16, 2009
Proceedings

Series Editors

Randy Goebel, University of Alberta, Edmonton, Canada
Jörg Siekmann, University of Saarland, Saarbrücken, Germany
Wolfgang Wahlster, DFKI and University of Saarland, Saarbrücken, Germany

Volume Editors

Jung-Jin Yang
The Catholic University of Korea, Seoul, Korea
E-mail: jungjin@catholic.ac.kr

Makoto Yokoo
Kyushu University, Dept. of Informatics, Fukuoka, Japan
E-mail: yokoo@is.kyushu-u.ac.jp

Takayuki Ito
Nagoya Institute of Technology, Dept. of Computer Science, Nagoya, Japan
E-mail: ito.takayuki@nitech.ac.jp

Zhi Jin
Peking University, Beijing, China
E-mail: zhijin@sei.pku.edu.cn

Paul Scerri
Carnegie Mellon University, Robotics Institute, Pittsburgh, PA, USA
E-mail: pscerri@cs.mu.edu

Library of Congress Control Number: 2009940418

CR Subject Classification (1998): I.2, I.2.11, I.2.9, C.2.4, K.4, D.2, H.5

LNCS Sublibrary: SL 7 – Artificial Intelligence

ISSN   0302-9743

ISBN 978-3-642-11160-0 Springer Berlin Heidelberg New York

springer.com

© Springer-Verlag Berlin Heidelberg 2009

Typesetting: Camera-ready by author, data conversion by Scientific Publishing Services, Chennai, India
Printed on acid-free paper   SPIN: 12813032   06/3180   5 4 3 2 1 0

Preface

Agents are software processes that perceive and act in an environment, processing their perceptions to make intelligent decisions about actions to achieve their goals. Multi-agent systems have multiple agents that work in the same environment to achieve either joint or conflicting goals. Agent computing and technology is an exciting, emerging paradigm expected to play a key role in many society-changing practices from disaster response to manufacturing to agriculture. Agent and multi-agent researchers are focused on building working systems that bring together a broad range of technical areas from market theory to software engineering to user interfaces. Agent systems are expected to operate in real-world environments, with all the challenges complex environments present.

After 11 successful PRIMA workshops/conferences (Pacific-Rim International Conference/Workshop on Multi-Agents), PRIMA became a new conference titled "International Conference on Principles of Practice in Multi-Agent Systems" in 2009. With over 100 submissions, an acceptance rate for full papers of 25% and 50% for posters, a demonstration session, an industry track, a RoboCup competition and workshops and tutorials, PRIMA has become an important venue for multi-agent research. Papers submitted are from all parts of the world, though with a higher representation of Pacific Rim countries than other major multi-agent research forums. This volume presents 34 high-quality and exciting technical papers on multimedia research and an additional 18 poster papers that give brief views on exciting research.

In 2009, the specific theme of the conference was on practical systems. Multi-agent systems show great promise for changing and improving the way complex goals are achieved in the real world, but despite many years of research this promise remains largely unrealized. By focusing this conference on practical aspects of multi-agent systems, we hope to encourage work that allows the promise to be realized. Papers on topics such as participatory simulation, practical auctions, ontology building and framework evaluation move us towards this goal.

To improve the focus on practical systems, PRIMA 2009 included two special tracks that encouraged particularly practical papers. The industrial track encouraged descriptions of systems that are either being built in industry or for real industrial problems. The multimedia track gave authors an opportunity to present their research in a multimedia format, if they believed this provided a better way of exhibiting the research contribution of their work. The 11 papers from these tracks, in this volume, represent particularly practical and exciting work.

December 2009

Jung-Jin Yang
Makoto Yokoo
Takayuki Ito
Zhi Jin
Paul Scerri

Organization

General Chairs

Jung-Jin Yang   Catholic University of Korea, Korea
Makoto Yokoo   Kyushu University, Japan

Program Chairs

Takayuki Ito   Nagoya Institute of Technology/Massachusetts Institute
                    of Technology, Japan/USA
Zhi Jin   Peking University, China
Paul Scerri   Carnegie Mellon University, USA

Industry Track Program Chairs

Satoshi Kurihara   Osaka University, Japan
Minjie Zhang   University of Wollongong, Australia

Publicity Co-chairs

Shigeo Matsubara   Kyoto University, Japan
Tony Bastin Roy   University of Otago, New Zealand
    Savarimuthu

Sponsorship Chairs

Nirmit V Desai   IBM, India
Akihiko Ohsuga   The University of Electro-Communications, Japan

Tutorial / Interactive Session Chair

Tsunenori Mine   Kyushu University, Japan
Buy The Duy   Vietnam National University, Vietnam

Workshop Chair

Quan Bai   CSIRO, Australia
Naoki Fukuta   Shizuoka University, Japan

Financial Chair

Tokuro Matsuo   Yamagata University, Japan
Valentin Robu   Southampton University, UK

Publications Chair

Takahiro Uchiya   Nagoya Institute of Technology, Japan
Gita Sukthankar   University of Central Florida, USA

Agent School and Doctoral Mentoring Track and Demonstration Session Chair

Hiromitsu Hattori   Kyoto University, Japan
Jane Hsu   National Taiwan University, Taiwan

Local Arrangements Chair

Hirofumi Yamaki   Nagoya University, Japan
Shohey Kato   Nagoya Institute of Technology, Japan

Agent Event Chair: (RobuCup)

Itsuki Noda   AIST, Japan
Xiaoping Chen   USTC, China
Oliver Obst   CSIRO, Australia

Advisory Committee Members

Toru Ishida   Kyoto University, Japan
Hideyuki Nakashima   Future University of Hakodate, Japan
Chengqi Zhang   University of Technology, Sydney, Australia
Muninder P. Singh   North Carolina State University, USA
Alexis Drogoul   University of Paris 6, France
Von Won Soo   National Tsing Hua University, Taiwan
R. Sadananda   University of New South Wales, Australia

Program Committee

Quan Bai
Ladislau Boloni
Stephane Bressan
Brahim Chaib-draa
Nilanjan Chakraborty
Shih-Fen Cheng
Sung-Bae Cho
Joongmin Choi
Joaquin Delgado
J.g Denzinger
Frank Dignum
Alexis Drogoul
Shaheen Fatima
Satoru Fujita
Naoki Fukuta
Aditya Ghose
Joseph Giampapa
Robin Glinton
Guido Governatori
Hiromitsu Hattori
Koen Hindriks
Shanli Hu
Atsushi Iwasaki
Kiyoshi Izumi
Wenpin Jiao
Catholijn Jonker
Takahiro Kawamura
Kee-Eung Kim
Minkoo Kim
Yasuhiko Kitamura
Jean-Luc Koning
Jaeho Lee
Ho-fung Leung
Wei Li
Alan Liu
Chao-Lin Liu
Jyi-shane Liu

Lin Liu
Miguel A. Lopez-Carmona
Graham Low
Xudong Luo
Wenji Mao
Xinjun Mao
Ivan Marsa-Maestre
Shigeo Matsubara
Chunyan Miao
Shivashankar Nair
Jean Oh
Akihiko Ohsuga
Mehmet Orgun
Vineet Padmanabhan
Praveen Paruchuri
Valentin Robu
Antonino Rotolo
Yuko Sakurai
David Sarne
Abdul Sattar
Nathan Schurr
Kiam-Tian Seow
Von-Wun Soo
Leon Stering
Leon Sterling
Toshiharu Sugawara
Xijin Tang
Takao Terano
Pradeep Varakantham
Wayne Wobcke
Jun Yan
Minjie Zhang
Wei Zhang
Zili Zhang
Roie Zivan
Leon van der Torre
Satoshi Kurihara

Table of Contents

Technical Papers

Multimedia Papers

Industrial Papers

Poster Papers

A Market-Based Multi-Issue Negotiation Model Considering Multiple Preferences in Dynamic E-Marketplaces

Fenghui Ren[1,*], Minjie Zhang[1], Chunyan Miao[2], and Zhiqi Shen[3]

[1] School of Computer Science and Software Engineering,
University of Wollongong, Australia
{fr510,minjie}@uow.edu.au
[2] School of Computer Engineering
[3] School of Electrical and Electronic Engineering,
Nanyang Technological University, Singapore
{ASCYMiao,zqshen}@ntu.edu.sg

Abstract. Electronic commerce has been a significant commercial phenomenon in recent years and autonomous agents have made the advantages of e-markets more distinct. However, as e-market environments become open and dynamic, existing agent negotiation approaches expose some limitations. Static negotiation strategies and offer evaluation approaches might fail to capture dynamic changes of market situations, as well as changes of negotiators' expectations on negotiation outcomes. When market situations change, agents may need modify their negotiation strategies, expectations and criteria on offer evaluations as well as counter-offer generations in order to maximize their profits. Furthermore, in multi-issue negotiations, agents may have multiple preferences, which might not be delivered by most of existing negotiation approaches. In this paper, we propose a market-based multi-issue negotiation model to capture the dynamic changes of negotiation environments and impacts on negotiation strategies, counter-offer generations and offer evaluations. Also, the proposed model allows negotiators to deliver multiple offers to match their different preferences and negotiators would have more chances to reach agreements. Experimental results illustrate improvements of the proposed model on negotiators' utilities and efficiencies of the whole negotiation system by comparing with the performance of NDF negotiation model.

1 Introduction

Electronic commerce has changed traditional methods of business in recent years and has become a very important commercial phenomenon. Nowadays, many businesses operate in e-marketplaces and intelligent agents can help businesses

---

* The primary author is a Ph.D candidate.

J.-J. Yang et al. (Eds.): PRIMA 2009, LNAI 5925, pp. 1–16, 2009.

to make e-trading more efficiently. Due to different interests in trades, negotiation mechanisms are normally adopted by agents to communicate and compromise to reach mutually beneficial agreements when conflicts happen. Multi-issue negotiation between intelligent agents can lead negotiators to 'win-win' negotiation outcomes, which can hardly be achieved by single issue negotiation [1]. In a dynamic electronic marketplace, people can easily access the e-market to publish information, to retrieve items of interest, to negotiate with opponents synchronously and to terminate any ongoing negotiation freely. In such a frequently changing environment, agents' expectations on negotiation outcomes may not be achieved successfully without considering impacts from the changes of the environment. In order to be success in such a highly dynamic e-marketplaces, agents may need to modify their negotiation strategies, preferences and even their original outcome expectations in some cases.

Although researchers have successfully proposed many multi-issue negotiation models from different considerations, very few of them consider dynamic e-market environments and multiple preferences. Fatima et al. [2] proposed a multi-issue negotiation model to achieve optimal negotiation outcomes for online negotiation. However, their model only worked in the situation of bilateral negotiation without consideration of dynamic changes of negotiation environments. Lai et al. [1][3] presented a model for multi-attribute negotiations between two negotiators. However, impacts on negotiators' strategies from outside options are still not taken into account. Hemaissia et al. [4] proposed a multilateral multi-issue negotiation protocol in a cooperative scenario by employing a mediator agent. However, when the number of negotiation participators fluctuates, the mediator can hardly make an unbiased and accurate response to all negotiators. Fatima et al. [5][6] studied negotiation models in incomplete information settings in different negotiation scenarios and illustrated equilibrium solutions for different negotiation agendas and procedures. However, their work only presented multi-issue negotiation in static negotiation environments.

In this paper, we propose a market-based multiple-offer model for multi-issue negotiation in a complex environment. The contribution of this paper is to propose an approach to help negotiators to make more wise decisions during negotiations by considering both market situations and negotiator own requirements. Furthermore, this model allows agents to deliver multiple offers based on different preferences. By sending these alternative offers, opponents can select their favorite one without sacrificing negotiators own profits, so as to increase utilities of all negotiation parties and the efficiency of the negotiation system.

The rest of this paper is organized as follows. Section 2 proposes the market-based multiple-offer negotiation model, including issues and negotiation environment representations, counter-offer generation, offer evaluation and a negotiation protocol. Section 3 illustrates experimental results of the proposed model in different negotiation environments. Section 4 compares our work with some related works, and Section 5 concludes this paper and outlines our future work.

2 Market-Based Model

2.1 Issue Representation

In most existing multi-issue negotiation models [6][7], negotiators' preferences are presented linearly. Although such a linear representation is convenient in modeling and calculation, it is not very suitable to represent humans concerns in real world situation. For example, if 1 indicates 100% concern on an item, very few people can really realize how great the difference between 0.6 and 0.7 is when they define concerns on the item. So nonlinear indicators are more suitable to fulfill such a task. In some models [8], nonlinear indicators are adopted to represent negotiators concerns, but the significance on each issue is still fixed and negotiators cannot deliver different preferences. For example, alternative criteria from a car buyer between 'lower price' and 'longer warranty' cannot be expressed by existing issue representation approaches. In this subsection, we proposed a non-linear issue representation to solve this problem. The purpose of the following definitions is to introduce a novel way to represent both significance of issues and relationships between issues in multi-issue negotiation, and to express their multiple preferences in negotiations.

Definition 1. *A negotiator's concern on a negotiated issue is represented by a unique concern tag κ, $\kappa \in \{S, N, I\}$, where tag S indicates a significant issue, tag N indicates a normal important issue and tag I indicates an inessential issue. The negotiator may have different negotiation strategies and outcome expectations for issues marked by different concern tags.*

Definition 2. *The relationship between two issues or two AIEs is represented by a unique role tag ξ, $\xi \in \{\cap, \cup\}$. Tag $\cap$ indicates an union relationship between parties on two sides, and a negotiator's expectation on both sides must be satisfied together by the final agreement. Tag $\cup$ indicates an alternative relationship between parties on two sides, and a negotiator's expectation on either side must be satisfied by the final agreement.*

Definition 3. *An Atomic Issue Expression (AIE) is a combination of all negotiated issues. Each issue in an AIE must be assigned with an unique concern tag. The relationship between issues in an AIE must be the union relationship and indicated by role tag $\cap$. Each AIE indicates one preference of a negotiator.*

Definition 4. *A Complete Issue Expression (CIE) is a combination of AIEs. The relationship between any two AIEs in a CIE must be the alternative relationship and indicated by role tag $\cup$. A CIE indicates all preferences of a negotiator. A negotiator could have multiple preferences, but a satisfaction on any preference will lead negotiators to a final agreement.*

For example, in a three-issue negotiation, if a negotiator's CIE is $(I_1^S \cap I_2^N \cap I_3^I)$ $\cup (I_1^N \cap I_2^S \cap I_3^I)$, it indicates that the negotiator has two different preferences on negotiated issues. The first AIE $(I_1^S \cap I_2^N \cap I_3^I)$ indicates a preference which has significant concern tag on Issue I_1, normal concern tag on Issue I_2 and inessential concern tag on Issue I_3, and the second AIE $(I_1^N \cap I_2^S \cap I_3^I)$ indicates a preference which has normal concern tag on Issue I_1, significant concern tag on Issue I_2 and inessential concern tag on I_3. However, a satisfaction on either AIE can lead the negotiator to an agreement.

2.2 Negotiation Environment Representation

Through our studies, we notice that in real-world markets, although people can define reserved offers in advance to represent their expectations, in most cases it is not necessary for them to make their final decisions exactly based on the predefined reserved offers. People may modify their predefined reserved offers. For example, a hesitant buyer may look forward to gaining more profit when he/she notices that his/her expectations can be satisfied easily by most sellers. On the other hand, a rush buyer may accept an offer even if it is worse than his original expectation. However, most existing negotiation approaches do not take these situations into account, negotiators have to make their final decisions exactly based on the predefined reserved prices. In this subsection, we introduce a market-based negotiation model to consider impacts from environment changes on negotiations, and to help negotiators to make more accurate judgements and wise decisions in e-marketplaces when the status of an e-marketplace changes.

Let s ($s \geq 1$) denote the number of suppliers, c ($c \geq 1$) denote the number of consumers, α denote a negotiator's role (a supplier or a consumer), and β denote the negotiator's attitude on the changes of a negotiation environment. If we employ the relationship between supply and demand to represent a market's situation at a certain moment, then the market's situation can be defined as:

$$\Phi(s, c, \alpha) = \frac{c - s}{c + s} \times \alpha \qquad (1)$$

where $\alpha = -1$ for consumers and $\alpha = 1$ for suppliers.

The range of Equation 1 is between $(-1, 1)$, and represents the status of a negotiation environment. If $0 < \Phi < 1$, the environment is in a beneficial status and the negotiator has an advantage in such an environment. If $-1 < \Phi < 0$, the environment is in an inferior status and the negotiator has a disadvantage in the environment. If $\Phi = 0$, the environment is in a equitable status and the negotiator does not have a advantage or disadvantage in the environment. Objectively, Equation (1) represents the relationship between supply and demand in a negotiation environment at a certain moment. However, even for the same situation, negotiators may also have different considerations on environment changes based on their individual situation. Therefore, we generate a graph in Figure 1 to map from objective negotiation environments to subjective responses of negotiators.

In Figure 1, the x-axis represents situations of a negotiation environment (Φ), and the y-axis indicates an response from a negotiator (Ψ). In general, it can be seen that negotiators may have three typical attitudes to respond changes of an environment. (1) Cautious ($\beta > 1$): when an environment's status shifts away from equitable to beneficial or inferior, a negotiator's response is very calm when changes of the environment are not significant. However, when changes in the environment are evident, the negotiator's response will become more vehement.

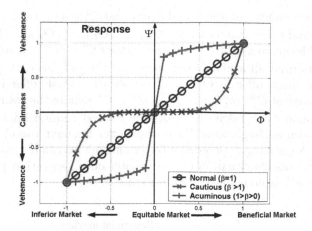

Fig. 1. Negotiators' responses to markets' situations

(2) Acuminous $(1 > \beta > 0)$: when an environment's status shifts away from equitable to beneficial or inferior, a negotiator performs very sensitively even though the change in the environment is not very obvious. However, when the environment's status changes a lot, the negotiator has to control its response for some objective reasons (e.g. the negotiator cannot make further concession anymore). And (3) Normal $(\beta = 1)$: when an environment's status shifts away from equitable to beneficial or inferior, a negotiator's response is also shifted from calmness to vehemence reposefully. Even though the above three typical responses cannot cover all possible situations of negotiators' attitudes on market changes, they still can cover most of general cases. Based on such a consideration, an agent's response to the negotiation environment can be defined as follows by considering both objective and subjective factors from marketplaces and negotiators, respectively:

$$\Psi(s,c,\alpha,\beta) = \begin{cases} \Phi(s,c,\alpha)^{\beta}, & \Phi(s,c,\alpha) \geq 0 \\ -[-\Phi(s,c,\alpha)]^{\beta}, & \Phi(s,c,\alpha) < 0 \end{cases} \tag{2}$$

In the following subsections, we will introduce a counter-offer generation approach and an offer evaluation approach based on an agent response to a negotiation environment, respectively.

2.3   Counter-Offer Generation

Single Issue. We introduce a counter-offer generation approach on single issue firstly. According to Fatima et al. [5], a package deal procedure is the optimal procedure in incomplete information settings compared with simultaneous and sequential procedures. In our model, negotiators will adopt the package deal procedure. For Negotiator P, let vector $\boldsymbol{O}_{t,i} = (o_{t,i}^1, \ldots, o_{t,i}^m, \ldots, o_{t,i}^M)$ denote an offer P received from the ith opponent at round t, where $t \leq \tau$ (τ is Negotiator P's deadline), and $i \leq A$, where A is the total number of Negotiator P's opponents, M

indicates the total number of negotiated issues, and $o_{t,i}^m$ is a particular offer on the mth issue at round t. Let matrix $\mathbf{O_t} = \{\mathbf{O_{t,1}}, \ldots, \mathbf{O_{t,i}}, \ldots, \mathbf{O_{t,A}}\}^T$ denote offers from all available opponents at round t and vector $\mathbf{O_t^m} = (o_{t,1}^m, \ldots, o_{t,i}^m, \ldots, o_{t,A}^m)$ denote all offers from all available opponents on the mth issue at round t. Let o_t^{mb} denote the 'best' offer in $\mathbf{O_t^m}$, o_t^{mw} denote the 'worst' offer in $\mathbf{O_t^m}$, o_t^{ma} denote the average of $\mathbf{O_t^m}$ ($o_t^{ma} = \frac{1}{A}\sum_{i=1}^{n} o_{t,i}^m$), $o_{t'}^{mb}$ denote the estimated 'best' offer in next round t', co_t^m denote Negotiator P's last counter-offer on the mth issue and $co_{t'}^m$ denote Negotiator P's counter-offer for next round on the mth issue. Suppose Negotiator P plays as a buyer and the negotiated issue is a car's price, then one possible situation of the counter-offer generation procedure in round t on the mth issue is illustrated in Figure 2.

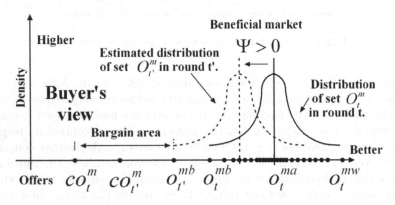

Fig. 2. Counter-offer generation

In Figure 2, the x-axis indicates offers, and the y-axis represents the occurrence density of each offer. The solid curve indicates the distribution of $\mathbf{O_t^m}$ in round t (distributions may be different from case to case), and the dotted line is the estimated distribution of $\mathbf{O_{t'}^m}$ in next round. We make the assumption that the shape of the distribution curve of set $\mathbf{O_{t'}^m}$ is similar to $\mathbf{O_t^m}$'s, but just the range of span is changed. Because the negotiator plays as a buyer and the negotiated issue is a car's price, so the market represented in Figure 2 is a beneficial market ($\Psi > 0$). In a beneficial market, for buyers, opponents' offers on a car's price in next round $\mathbf{O_{t'}^m}$ is estimated to be smaller than $\mathbf{O_t^m}$ on average. The distance between the current counter-offer co_t^m and the estimated 'best' offer $o_{t'}^{mb}$ in next round is the bargaining area. The new counter-offer $co_{t'}^m$ is generated within this area according to the negotiator's strategies, remaining rounds and importance of the issue m.

Firstly, we estimate the 'best' offer $o_{t'}^{mb}$ in next round t' as follows:

$$o_{t'}^{mb} = o_t^{mb} + \Psi(s, c, \alpha, \beta) \times \sqrt{D(\mathbf{O_t^m})} \times \gamma \qquad (3)$$

$$D(O_t^m) = \sum_{i=1}^{A}(o_{t,i}^m - E(O_t^m))^2 p_i \tag{4}$$

where $D(O_t^m)$ indicates the variance of O_t^m, $\gamma = -1$ for issues which an agent prefers a lower value and $\gamma = 1$ for issues which an agent prefers a greater value, $E(O_t^m)$ indicates the mathematical expectation of O_t^m, p_i indicates the distribution of $o_{t,i}^m$ and $\Psi(s,c,\alpha,\beta)$ indicates the agent's response to the market situation. Usually, when the distribution of O_t^m is a Gaussian distribution, then $E(O_t^m) = o_t^{ma}$, $p_i = \frac{1}{A}$ and Equation 4 is specified as:

$$D(O_t^m) = \frac{\sum_{i=1}^{A}(o_{t,i}^m - o_t^{ma})^2}{A} \tag{5}$$

Then the new counter-offer $co_{t'}^m$ for the mth issue is generated as follows:

$$co_{t'}^m = \begin{cases} o_{ini}^m & t = 0, \\ co_t^m + (o_{t'}^{mb} - co_t^m) \times (\frac{t}{\tau})^\lambda & \kappa(m) = S \& t \leq \tau, \\ co_t^m + \frac{1}{2}(o_{t'}^{mb} - co_t^m) \times (1 + \frac{t}{\tau})^\lambda & \kappa(m) = N \& t \leq \tau, \\ o_{t'}^{mb} & \kappa(m) = I \& t \leq \tau. \end{cases} \tag{6}$$

where o_{ini}^m is the negotiator's initial offer on the mth issue, $\kappa(m)$ indicates issue m's concern tag, and we simply adopt parameter λ in Faratin et al.'s model [9] to represent the negotiator's bargaining strategies.

In Figure 3, it can be seen that when the market becomes very beneficial to the buyer agent, it is possible that $o_{t'}^{mb} < co_t^m$ and $co_{t'}^m < co_t^m$. So in the market-based negotiation model, we propose a decommitment mechanism which allows negotiators to reject previous offers if these offers are not formally accepted by any opponents. The reason behind such a mechanism is that in the market-based negotiation model, both offer evaluation approach and counter-offer generation approach are impacted by market situations. When the market situation changes, negotiators may change their considerations on both offer

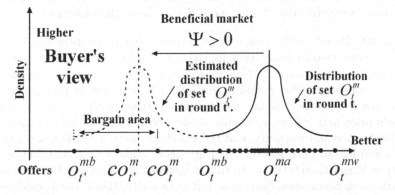

Fig. 3. Counter-offer generation

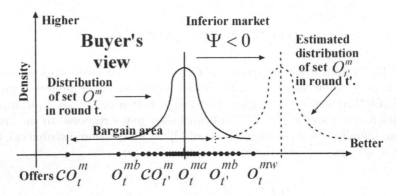

Fig. 4. Counter-offer generation

evaluations and counter-offer generations as well in order to gain more profits. For example, a buyer may generates disadvantageous counter-offers when the market is inferior. However, when the buyer notices that the market may become better and if the previous counter-offer is not accepted by any seller, the buyer can reject the previous disadvantageous counter-offers and re-generate advantageous counter-offers in order to enlarge its profit. On the other hand, if a seller notice that the market may become inferior for it in advance, the seller may accept that buyer's latest offer in order to avoid loss in the future.

Also, markets may become inferior for buyers. In Figure 4, it can be seen that when a market is inferior for buyers, the estimated 'best' offer for the following round t' is worse than the 'best' offer in the round t (i.e., $o_{t'}^{mb} > o_t^{mb}$). During negotiations, if a new counter-offer in round t' can bring more profits to a negotiator than the 'best' offer in round t, then the negotiator will keep on bargaining with opponents and send out the new counter-offer $co_{t'}^m$. However, if the new counter-offer is worse than the 'best' offer from opponents, then the negotiator will not send the new counter-offer $co_{t'}^m$, but make its final decision based on the comparison results between the 'best' offer (o_t^{mb}), the new counter-offer ($co_{t'}^m$) and the negotiator's eagerness to reach an agreement. The eagerness ($\varepsilon \in [0,1]$) is predefined by the negotiator to indicate its eager for completing negotiations (see Subsection 2.4 for more detail about the eagerness).

Multi-issue. Based on the single issue counter-offer generation approach, we introduce a counter-offer generation approach for multi-issue negotiation by considering multiple preference. In this approach, negotiators can provide multiple choices in each negotiation round according to their different preferences. For example, when a prospective car purchaser negotiates with several car dealers on a car's price and warranty, usually dealers will not make great concessions on the both price and warranty, and the purchaser may have such a consideration 'I would like to purchase the car if its price is lower than $30,000 or if its warranty is longer than 5 years'. In this situation, the purchaser has alternative expectations on negotiation outcomes, but such a situation is not considered by most existing negotiation models. In order to solve this problem, we introduce a multi-issue counter-offer generation approach to deliver negotiators' multiple preferences during negotiations.

In multi-issue negotiation, by assigning concern tags and relationship tags on negotiated issues (see Subsection 2.1), a CIE can be generated. A negotiator's multiple preferences on multi-issue are indicated by the CIE. Therefore, in this multiple-offer approach, the number of offers delivered by the negotiator in each round at one time equals the $AIEs$' number in the CIE. Each AIE indicates one preference of the negotiator. By employing the counter-offer generation function introduced in the previous subsection on each issue in each AIE, multiple offers can be generated based on the CIE and delivered to opponents as follows:

$$\Gamma(t, AIE) = \boldsymbol{CO_{t'}} = (co_{t'}^1, \ldots, co_{t'}^m, \ldots, co_{t'}^M) \tag{7}$$

$$\Gamma(t, CIE) = \bigcap \Gamma(t, AIE), \forall AIE \in CIE \tag{8}$$

where each $co_{t'}^m$ in each AIE is calculated by adopting Equation 6. $\Gamma(t, AIE)$ indicates an counter-offer based on the preference implied by a AIE, and $\Gamma(t, CIE)$ indicates all counter-offers based on multiple preferences implied by all $AIEs$ in a CIE.

2.4 Offer Evaluation

When negotiators receive offers from opponents, negotiators should make a response based on the evaluation result on offers. In this section, we introduce an offer evaluation approach to consider both outcome expectations of negotiators and negotiation environments. In dynamic situation, an offer evaluation result may also be impacted by the change of a negotiation environment. For example, if a car's real value can be evaluated correctly by buyers in an equitable market, then the car should be overvalued in a seller's market and undervalued in a buyer's market. Based on such a consideration, we propose an offer evaluation approach sensitively to negotiation environments as follows.

Single Issue. For a given offer vector $\boldsymbol{O_{t,i}} = (o_{t,i}^1, \ldots, o_{t,i}^m, \ldots, o_{t,i}^M)$ from the ith opponent at round t, where $o_{t,i}^m$ denotes the offer on the mth issue. Let $\boldsymbol{O_{ini}} = (o_{ini}^1, \ldots, o_{ini}^m, \ldots, o_{ini}^M)$ denote Negotiator P's initial offer vector. Then, without considering the market situation, each single offer $o_{t,i}^m$ in vector $\boldsymbol{O_{t,i}}$ is evaluated by Negotiator P as follows.

$$\Lambda(o_{t,i}^m, o_{ini}^m, \gamma) = \mathbf{th}\left(\frac{o_{t,i}^m - o_{ini}^m}{o_{ini}^m} \times \gamma\right) + 1 \tag{9}$$

where $\gamma = -1$ for issues which an agent prefers a lower value and $\gamma = 1$ for issues which an agent prefers a greater value, $\mathbf{th}(x)$ is defined as follow.

$$\mathbf{th}(x) = \frac{e^x - e^{-x}}{e^x + e^{-x}} \tag{10}$$

The result of Equation 9 ($\Lambda \in (0,2)$) indicates how Negotiator P's initial offer is satisfied by the offer $o_{t,i}^m$. For example, if Negotiator P plays as a consumer and wants to evaluate a price offer. Because for Negotiator P, a lower price is better, so $\gamma = -1$. For a given price offer $o_{t,i}^m$, when $o_{t,i}^m = o_{ini}^m$ then $\Lambda = 1$. It means that the consumer's expectation is satisfied. When $o_{t,i}^m > o_{ini}^m$ then $0 < \Lambda < 1$, it indicates that the consumer's expectation is only partially achieved. And when $o_{t,i}^m \leq o_{ini}^m$ then $1 < \Lambda < 2$, this implies that the consumer's expectation is overachieved.

Because Equation (9) only evaluates the offer $o_{t,i}^m$ based on Negotiator P's initial offer but does not take the situation of negotiation environment into account, so evaluation results may not be accurate enough to reflect the value of the given offer in a particular market. Therefore, by considering market situations, negotiators can get a more accurate evaluation result on the offer $o_{t,i}^m$ as follows:

$$\Theta(o_{t,i}^m, s, c, o_{ini}^m, \alpha, \beta, \gamma) = \frac{\Lambda(o_{t,i}^m, o_{ini}^m, \gamma)}{\Psi(s, c, \alpha, \beta) + 1} \tag{11}$$

Where the result of Equation 11 ($\Theta \in (0,1)$) indicates the negotiator's utility by accepting the offer $o_{t,i}^m$ in a certain market. If it is an equitable market ($\Psi = 0$ and $\Theta = \Lambda$), then the offer $o_{t,i}^m$ is evaluated unbiasedly. If it is in a beneficial market ($0 < \Psi < 1$ and $\Theta < \Lambda$), then the offer $o_{t,i}^m$ is undervalued. And if it is in an inferior market ($-1 < \Psi < 0$ and $\Theta > \Lambda$), then the offer $o_{t,i}^m$ is overvalued.

Multi-Issue. In this paper, since negotiators' preferences are represented by concern tags, the traditional approach for multi-issue utility calculation is not applicable anymore. We introduce a non-linear utility calculation approach and takes concern tags into account. For the offer vector $\boldsymbol{O}_{t,i}$, Negotiator P generates the combined evaluation result by considering concern tags in a AIE as follows:

$$\Upsilon(\boldsymbol{O}_{t,i}, AIE) = \min\left(\Theta(o_{t,i}^m) | m \in [1, M], o_{t,i}^m \in \boldsymbol{O}_{t,i}, \kappa(m) = \kappa(AIE)\right) \tag{12}$$

where $\Theta(o_{t,i}^m)$ is a simplification of Equation (11), and the AIE indicates one of Negotiator P's preferences, $\kappa(m)$ is the concern tag of the mth issue in the AIE, and $\kappa(AIE)$ is the highest significant concern tag in the AIE. If Negotiator P has multiple preferences on negotiated issues (i.e. more than one AIE in a CIE), then Negotiator P's final evaluation result by considering all preferences in the CIE is calculated as:

$$\Upsilon(\boldsymbol{O}_{t,i}, CIE) = \max\left(\Upsilon(\boldsymbol{O}_{t,i}, AIE), AIE \in CIE\right) \tag{13}$$

It can be seen that in the offer evaluation approach (see Equation 9), the reserved offer, which is employed by most negotiation model, is no longer adopted. That is because in dynamic negotiation environments, when the situation of the environment changes, the predefined reserved offer may not be applicable any-more. So we use a parameter eagerness ($\varepsilon \in [0,1]$) to express negotiators' eagerness on completing the negotiation. When $\varepsilon = 1$, the negotiator would like to accept any offer finally in order to complete the negotiation; when $\varepsilon = 0$, the negotiator will reject all offers which are worse than the initial offer; when $0 < \varepsilon < 1$, the negotiator will only accept the offer $O_{t,i}$ if $\Upsilon(O_{t,i}, CIE) \geq 1 - \varepsilon$. Therefore, when the market's situation changes, negotiators can adjust their evaluations on opponents' offers based on market situations in order to have a more accurate and reasonable reaction.

2.5   Protocol and Equilibrium

In this subsection, a negotiation protocol for the market-based multi-issue negotiation model is proposed based on Rubinstein's alternating offers protocol [9].

Step 1: A negotiator assigns negotiation parameters, i.e., initial offer (O_{ini}, including concerns tags and role tags), eagerness (ε), negotiation deadline (τ), role in negotiation (α), attitude on environment' changing (β), attitude on issues' value (γ) and bargaining strategy (λ). The number of consumers (c) and suppliers (s) can be obtained from the marketplace directly. A CIE is generated based on the negotiator's preference/s. The negotiator initializes t to 0 and counter-offer/s $\Gamma(t, CIE)$ to o_{ini}.

Step 2: The negotiator broadcasts counter-offer/s $\Gamma(t, CIE)$ to all opponents and waits for responses.

Step 3: Once the negotiator gets responses, if any opponent accepts any offer in counter-offer/s $\Gamma(t, CIE)$, then the negotiation is completed. Otherwise, if $t > \tau$, the procedure goes to **Step 4**. If $t \leq \tau$, the procedure goes to **Step 5**.

Step 4: The negotiator has to make the final decision on opponents' offers. For all offers O_t from all opponents at the round t, let O_t^b denote the offer which bring greatest profit to the negotiator. If $\Upsilon(O_t^b, CIE) \geq 1 - \varepsilon$, the negotiator will accept O_t^b and the negotiation is completed. Otherwise, the negotiation fails.

Step 5: The negotiator will generate new counter-offer/s $\Gamma(t, CIE)$ for the next round. Let $\Upsilon(\Gamma(t, CIE), CIE)$ denote the utility that the negotiator may gain from the counter-offer/s $\Gamma(t, CIE)$. If $\Upsilon(O_t^b, CIE)$ is greater than both $\Upsilon(\Gamma(t, CIE), CIE)$ and $1 - \varepsilon$, then O_t^b will be accepted by the negotiator and the negotiation is completed. If $1 - \varepsilon$ is greater than both $\Upsilon(O_t^b, CIE)$ and $\Upsilon(\Gamma(t, CIE), CIE)$, then the negotiator will leave off the procedure and the negotiation fails. If $\Upsilon(\Gamma(t, CIE), CIE)$ is greater than both $\Upsilon(O_t^b, CIE)$ and $1 - \varepsilon$, then the procedure goes to Step 6.

Step 6: The negotiator updates t to t' ($t' = t + 1$), $\Gamma(t, CIE)$ to $\Gamma(t', CIE)$, parameters c, s according to the current market situation and parameter ε, and the procedure goes back to **Step 2**.

Based on the above procedure, the negotiator's equilibrium in round t is defined as follows:

$$\Omega(t) = \begin{cases} \textbf{Quit}, \textit{when } t \geq \tau \wedge \Upsilon(O_t^b, CIE) \geq 1 - \varepsilon \textit{ or } t < \tau \wedge \\ \max(\Upsilon(O_t^b, CIE), \Upsilon(\Gamma(t, CIE), CIE), 1 - \varepsilon) = 1 - \varepsilon, \\ \textbf{Accept } O_t^b, \textit{when } t \geq \tau \wedge \Upsilon(O_t^b, CIE) \geq 1 - \varepsilon \textit{ or} \\ t < \tau \wedge \max(\Upsilon(O_t^b, CIE), \Upsilon(\Gamma(t, CIE), CIE), 1 - \varepsilon) = \Upsilon(O_t^b, CIE), \\ \textbf{Offer } \Gamma(t, CIE), \textit{when } t < \tau \wedge \\ \max(\Upsilon(O_t^b, CIE), \Upsilon(\Gamma(t, CIE), CIE), 1 - \varepsilon) = \Upsilon(\Gamma(t, CIE), CIE). \end{cases}$$
$$(14)$$

3 Experiment

The experiment includes six agents, three of them are consumers and the other three are suppliers. The two negotiated issues are a car's price and warranty. Two consumers employ the proposed market-based model, and others employ the commonly used NDF model [9]. All agents employ the package deal procedure and each offer is delivered in the form of $(dollar, year)$. All settings about agents and the negotiation environment are displayed in Table 1. In the first scenario, three buyer agents, (Agents $db1$, $db2$ and $nb1$) and two seller agents, (Agents $nb1$ and $nb2$) participate in the negotiation. Based on the negotiation environment of Scenario 1, one seller agent, (Agent $nb3$) will join the negotiation in the second scenario and one seller agent (Agent $nb2$) will leave off the negotiation in the third scenario, respectively. Figure 5 shows how the proposed market-based model captures the changes of the negotiation environment, and offers in each negotiation round are highlighted by index number. Agent $db1$ employs the market-based model and its CIE is $(d^S \cap y^S)$. Agent $db2$ employs the market-based model as well and its CIE is $(d^S \cap y^N) \cup (d^N \cap y^S)$. Agent $db2$ will deliver two offers in each negotiation round. Finally, in order to fairly evaluate the performance of different negotiation approaches, their agreements are compared based on the Euclidean distance to the initial offer ($2000, 2y$).

In the first scenario, because consumer's number is greater than supplier's number, the market is in inferior status for consumers. In Figure 5(a), it can be seen that Agent $db2$ delivers two offers in each round and sellers can pick up either one based on their individual preferences. Because Agent $db2$ provides more options to its opponents, so Agent $db2$ reaches an agreement firstly with Agent $ns2$ at ($2484, 3.2y$). Since Agent $db1$ does not provide alternative offers to opponents, so offers delivered by Agent $db1$ are located between Agent $db2$'s paratactic offers. In round-6, Agent $db1$ achieves an agreement secondly with Agent $ns1$ at ($2480, 3.2y$). By comparing these two agreements, it can be seen

Table 1. Experiment setup

Agent role	Consumer			Supplier		
Agent name	db1	db2	nb1	ns1	ns2	ns3
Negotiation model	Market-based model			NDF model		
Initial offer	($2000, 5y)			($3000, 2y)	($2700, 1.8y)	($3300, 2.2y)
Reserved offer	eagerness=1		($3000, 2y)	($2000, 5y)	($1800, 4.5y)	($2200, 5.5y)
Preference	$(d^S \cap y^S)$	$(d^S \cap y^N) \cup (d^N \cap y^S)$		(0.5, 0.5)		

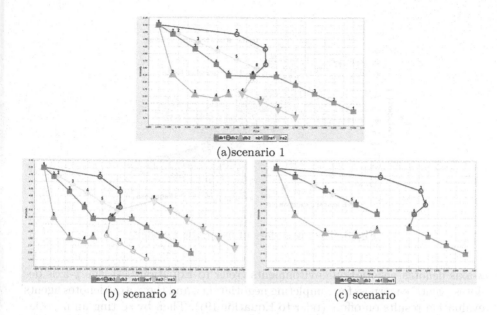

(a)scenario 1

(b) scenario 2   (c) scenario

Fig. 5. Negotiations in different environments

that Agent $db2$ gets a little bit more profit than Agent $db1$ in a shorter time. In this scenario, Agent $nb1$ does not reach an agreement with any seller agents and fails the negotiation.

In the second scenario, because consumer's number equals suppler's number, the market is in equitable status for all negotiators. In Figure 5(b), when seller Agent $ns3$ enters into the negotiation, the environment becomes better for buyers than the first scenario. Agent $db2$ reaches an agreement firstly with Agent $ns3$ at ($2457, 3.2y$) and agent $db1$ achieves an agreement secondly with Agent $ns1$ at ($2470, 3.2y$). By comparison with the first scenario, it can be seen that both market-based buyer agents gain more profits as the environment becomes better. The NDF Agent $nb1$ reaches an agreement with Agent $ns2$ finally at ($2750, 3.8y$). Obviously, Agents $db2$ and $db1$'s outcomes are much better than Agent $nb1$'s based on the consideration of Euclidean distance to the initial offer ($2000, 2y$). Also, it can be confirmed that the agent which provides multiple options to opponents can gain more profits in multilateral negotiations.

In the third scenario (Figure 5(c)), it can be seen that when seller Agent $ns2$ leaves off the negotiation, the negotiation environment becomes more disadvantageous for buyer agents (i.e. more competitive). Finally, buyer Agent $db2$ won the negotiation with the only seller Agent $ns1$ at ($2726, 3.4y$). Even though this agreement is worse than the previous two scenarios for Agent $db2$, Agent $db2$ defeats other buyer agents and reaches agreement with the only seller agent. Therefore, we can say that the market-based agent can win the negotiation in competition and the multiple offer strategy increases the chance for it to be the winner.

In Figure 6, we illustrate a model to demonstrate how environments and agents' eagerness impact agents' strategies and decisions in negotiations. The

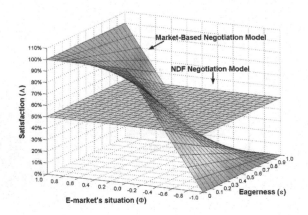

Fig. 6. Trading surface of negotiation models

x-axis denotes negotiation environments (refer to Equation (1)), the y-axis denotes agents' eagerness for completing negotiations, and the z-axis denotes agents' evaluation results on offers (refer to Equation (9)). Then by setting all negotiation parameters (β and λ) to 1, a trading surface for the market-based negotiation model can be formulated as follows.

$$\Lambda(\Phi, \varepsilon) = \begin{cases} (1 + \Phi) * (1 - \varepsilon), & when \ -1 \leq \Phi \leq 0, \\ (\Phi - 1) * \varepsilon + 1, & when \ 0 < \Phi \leq 1. \end{cases} \quad (15)$$

where $\varepsilon \in [0, 1]$ and $\Phi \in [-1, 1]$.

The trading surface defines a set of thresholds on agents' profits. During a negotiation, agents will accept offers above or on the surface, but reject offers below the surface. Also, we display another trading surface for the NDF model. Comparison with the market-based model, the trading surface of the NDF model is just a plane surface. That means agents in the NDF model fix their thresholds in all situations as a constant, and do not consider changes of environment and eagerness of completion of negotiations.

In this section, we illustrated experimental results in different negotiation environments and also compared outcomes between the market-based model and the NDF model. Based on these results, we can claim that the market-based agents can modify their negotiation strategies dynamically when the negotiation environment changes. Also, the multiple offer strategy increases the probability for agents to enlarge their outcome profits and/or to enlarge their chances to win negotiation. Therefore, the market-based multiple offer model can help agents to make more wise decisions complex negotiation environments.

4   Related Works

Sycara et.al. [10] proposed a model for bilateral negotiation by considering uncertain and dynamic outside options. It is argued that outside options can impact agent negotiation strategies. According to the complexity of outside options in negotiation, negotiations are further divided into three levels, which are *single-thread negotiation*, *synchronized multi-thread negotiation* and *dynamic multi-thread negotiation*. *Single-thread negotiation* is only processed between two agents without outside options. *Synchronized multi-thread negotiation* is based on the *single-thread negotiation* model, and also considers concurrently existing outside options. *Dynamic multi-thread negotiation* is expanded from *synchronized multi-thread negotiation* by considering uncertain outside options which may occur dynamically in the future. Sycara's model gives a very novel classification and description on general negotiation. The market-based negotiation model proposed in this paper focuses on e-marketplaces and its changes, and allows outside options during negotiations, so it belongs to *dynamic multi-thread negotiation*.

Dasgupta and Hashimoto [11] proposed an approach to address the problem of dynamic pricing in a competitive online economy where a product is differentiated by buyers and sellers on multi-issue. Agents may have incomplete knowledge of the negotiation parameters. A seller employs a collaborative filtering algorithm to determine a temporary consumer's purchase preferences and a dynamic pricing algorithm to determine a competitive price for the product. Therefore, the price prediction approach gives a solution about the bidding strategy in complex negotiation environments. However, their approach pays attention only to sellers, without considering the situation of buyers. Our market-based negotiation model is suitable for adoption by both sellers and buyers.

Ren et.al. [12] proposed a market-driven model to help agents to make concessions in negotiation. Four concession factors, namely *trading opportunity*, *trading competition*, *trading time and strategy* and *eagerness*, are introduced to represent both market and agent situations. Each concession factor impacts an agent's concession from a certain consideration. All concession factors are updated by the agent according to the market's dynamic situation. But agents' judgements on offers and expectations on negotiation outcomes are still fixed. In this paper, we model markets by considering both market situations and agent desires. During negotiations, agents make concessions based on both objective and subjective considerations in the negotiation.

By comparison with the above related works, the proposed market-based multiple-offer negotiation model has the following merits. It models negotiations in e-marketplaces by considering (1) both objective situations of markets and subjective eagerness of agents, (2) both concurrent and future possible situations of e-marketplaces, (3) both agents' individual profit and trade-offs of whole e-marketplaces, and (4) agents' multiple preferences in multi-issue negotiations.

5 Conclusion and Future Work

In this paper, we proposed a market-based multiple-offer negotiation model to help agents to make wise decisions in multilateral, multi-issue negotiation. In our model, the offer evaluation approach and counter-offer generation approach have taken the negotiation environment into account. Offers from opponents are evaluated relatively by considering negotiation environment and agents' eagerness for trading. Based on experimental results, we further put forward the concept of 'trading surface' and discovered that the trading surface of the market-based negotiation model is more applicable than the NDF model's in complex e-marketplaces. Future research will focus on real-world case testing and more comprehensive evaluations.

References

1. Lai, G., Sycara, K., Li, C.: A Pareto Optimal Model for Automated Multi-attribute Negotiations. In: 6th Int. Conf. on Autonomous Agents and Multi-Agent Systems (AAMAS 2007), pp. 1040–1042 (2007)
2. Fatima, S., Wooldridge, M., Jennings, N.: Approximate and Online Multi-Issue Negotiation. In: 6th Int. Conf. on Autonomous Agents and Multi-Agent Systems (AAMAS 2007), pp. 947–954 (2007)
3. Lai, G., Li, C., Sycara, K.: A General Model for Pareto Optimall Multi-Attribute Negotiations. In: 2nd Int. Workshop on Rational, Robust, and Secure Negotiations in Multi-Agent Systems (RRS 2006), pp. 55–76 (2006)
4. Hemaissia, M., Seghrouchni, A., Labreuche, C., Mattioli, J.: A Multilateral Multi-Issue Negotiation Protocol. In: 6th Int. Conf. on Autonomous Agents and Multiagent Systems (AAMAS 2007), pp. 939–946 (2007)
5. Fatima, S., Wooldridge, M., Jennings, N.: Multi-Issue Negotiation Under Time Constraints. In: 1st Int. Conf. on Autonomous Agents and Multi-Agent Systems (AAMAS 2002), pp. 143–150 (2002)
6. Fatima, S., Wooldridge, M., Jennings, N.: An Agenda-Based Framework for Multi-Issue Negotiation. Artificial Intelligence 152(1), 1–45 (2004)
7. Bosse, T., Jonker, C., Treur, J.: Experiments in Human Multi-Issue Negotiation: Analysis and Support. In: 3rd Int. Con. on Autonomous Agents and Multi-Agent Systems (AAMAS04), pp. 671–678. IEEE Computer Society, Los Alamitos (2004)
8. Fujita, K., Ito, T., Klein, M.: A Preliminary Result on A Representative-Based Multi-Round Protocol for Multi-Issue Negotiations. In: 7th Int. Conf. on Autonomous Agents and Multiagent Systems (AAMAS 2008), pp. 1573–1576 (2008)
9. Faratin, P., Sierra, C., Jennings, N.: Negotiation Decision Functions for Autonomous Agents. Journal of Robotics and Autonomous Systems 24(3-4), 159–182 (1998)
10. Li, C., Sycara, K., Giampapa, J.: Dynamic Outside Options in Alternating-Offers Negotiations. In: 38th Annual Hawaii Int. Conf. on System Sciences (HICSS 2005), pp. 1–10 (2005)
11. Dasgupta, P., Hashimoto, Y.: Multi-Attribute Dynamic Pricing for Online Markets Using Intelligent Agents. In: 3rd Int. Conf. on Autonomous Agents and Multiagent Systems (AAMAS 2004), pp. 277–284 (2004)
12. Ren, F., Sim, K., Zhang, M.: Market-Driven Agents with Uncertain and Dynamic Outside Options. In: 6th Int. Conf. on Autonomous Agents and Multi-Agent Systems (AAMAS 2007), pp. 721–723 (2007)

Designing Protocols for Collaborative Translation

Daisuke Morita and Toru Ishida

Department of Social Informatics, Kyoto University, Yoshida Honmachi,
Sakyoku, Kyoto, 6068501, Japan
Tel.:+81-75-753-4820
morita@ai.soc.i.kyoto-u.ac.jp, ishida@i.kyoto-u.ac.jp

Abstract. In this paper, we present a protocol for collaborative translation, where two non-bilingual people who use different languages collaborate to perform the task of translation using machine translation (MT) services. Members in one real life example of intercultural collaboration try to share information more effectively by modifying unnatural machine translated sentences manually and improving their fluency. However, there are two problems with this method: One is that poor quality of translation can induce misinterpretations, and the other is that phrases in the machine translated sentence that a person cannot make sense of remain unmodified. The proposed protocol is designed to solve these problems. More concretely, one person, who handles the source language and knows the original sentence (source language side), evaluates the adequacy between the original sentence and the translation of the sentence modified to be fluent by the other person, who handles the target language (target language side). In addition, by determining whether the meaning of the machine translated sentence is understandable, it is ensured that the two non-bilingual people do above tasks properly. As a result, this protocol 1) improves MT quality; and 2) terminates successfully only when the translation result becomes adequate and fluent. The experiment results show that when the protocol terminates successfully, the quality of the translation increases to about 83 percent in Japanese-English translation and 91 percent in Japanese-Chinese translation.

1 Introduction

Internationalization and the spread of the Internet are increasing our chances of seeing and hearing many languages. As a result, the number of multilingual groups where the native languages of the members differ is increasing. In the past, communication in such groups typically took place in one language, which was in many cases English. However, members who are required to communicate in a non-native language frequently find communication difficult [Takano 93, Aiken 94, Kim 02], thus such collaboration tends to be ineffective [Aiken 02, Tung 02].

Machine translation (MT) is a powerful tool for such groups, because it allows people to communicate in their native language. Actually, many groups use MT in their activities.

J.-J. Yang et al. (Eds.): PRIMA 2009, LNAI 5925, pp. 17–32, 2009.

MT is useful for realizing some level of communication, because participants can pick up the general meaning even if some words are badly translated [Nomura 03]. However, most MT systems make many translation errors. More precisely, many of the machine translated sentences are generally neither adequate nor fluent. In intercultural and multilingual collaboration based on MT, translation errors have caused mutual misconceptions [Ogden 03]. Moreover, it is difficult to identify translation errors because of the asymmetric nature of MT [Yamashita 06].

Similar kinds of problems are caused in real fields of intercultural collaboration. Members of one NPO group try to share information by modifying unnatural machine translated sentences manually and improving their fluency. However, there are two problems in this method: One is that poor quality of translation can induce misinterpretations, and the other is that phrases in the machine translated sentence that a person cannot make sense of remain unmodified. These problems cause mutual misinterpretation in such collaboration.

In this paper we present the protocol of collaborative translation, where two non-bilingual people who use different languages collaborate to perform the task of translation with an MT system. In the past, only bilingual people could determine whether a translated sentence has the same meaning as a corresponding source sentence. However, the protocol presented in this paper does not assume the presence of bilingual people, and is designed to solve two above-mentioned problems. As a result, the collaborative translation protocol 1) improves MT quality; and 2) terminates successfully only when the translation result becomes adequate and fluent.

The key idea of this protocol is to clarify the task of one person, who handles the source language (source language side) and of another person, who handles the target language (target language side). The target language side modifies the machine translated sentence to improve its fluency. The source language side evaluates the adequacy between the back-translation of the modified sentence and the source sentence. In addition, by determining whether the meaning of the machine translated sentence is understandable, it is ensured that two non-bilingual people do the above tasks properly.

The phenomenon which is observed in this protocol is similar to "coordinated attack problem [Halpern 90]" which is often cited in regards to the problems in the distributed environment such as multi-agent systems. We will show that although it has been proven that common knowledge cannot be attained in such an environment, this kind of problem is solved in collaborative translation protocol by adopting one heuristic.

This protocol ensures that it will most likely output good translations when terminating successfully. However, even if the protocol terminates successfully, the translation results may not be perfect because of human factors, characteristics of MTs, and interlinguistic characteristics. We evaluated the success rate and the reliability of the collaborative translation protocol in an experiment described in chapter 4.

2 Human-Assisted Machine Translation

2.1 Practice in the Field of Intercultural Collaboration

In many real fields of intercultural collaboration, MT is used as a tool for communication and information sharing. We will use internationally active NPO group in Japan as an example of a group working with MTs. The NPO has participants in Japan, South Korea, Austria, and Kenya. The group have a variety of native languages such as Japanese, Korean, German and English.

English is frequently used as a common language for communication in a multilingual community where native languages of community members differ. However, it is often the case in such community that there are people who are not proficient in English. The problem is that using English or a non-native language in communication tends to make it difficult for such people to share the information with others [Takano 93, Aiken 94, Kim 02]. In order to foster information sharing and invigorate intergroup discussion, the group mentioned above developed their own web BBS system using MT. In this system, each person edits an article in his or her native language. The article is translated via this system to three languages, and it enables other people to read contents of the article in their own native language. However, the quality of MT is often imperfect. This can make it difficult to share information among the members of the group. To overcome the problem with MT quality, this system enables people to correct errors of machine translated sentences manually. The illustration of this web BBS system is shown in Figure 1. In this figure, posting a Japanese article is taken as an example. Machine translated sentences can be modified to be natural expressions, which make intragroup information sharing easier.

In addition, the fluency as well as the quality of machine translated sentences can be improved by guessing the meaning of the translated sentences from

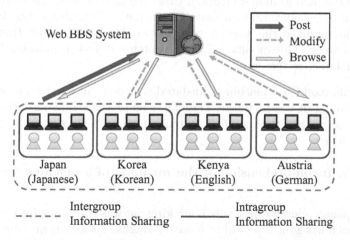

Fig. 1. Illustration of the web BBS system of the NPO group

the context of the text and the background knowledge in the community when modifying it.

Example 1: Improvement of translation quality by modifying machine translated sentence

The Japanese sentence All children who looked at the picture were surprised was translated into English as Everyone was surprised at the children who saw the picture. This English sentence has a different meaning from the original Japanese sentence. However, a native English speaker guessed the true meaning from the context and based on the background of his or her community and modified the English sentence as Children were surprised to look at the picture. This modified English sentence has the same meaning as the original Japanese sentence.

2.2   Problems in Modifying Machine Translation

Wordy and unnatural machine translated sentences can be expressed naturally by modifying them. This leads to making the meaning of the translated sentences clearer and intragroup information sharing easier. From this point of view, human-assisted machine translation is an useful method for real fields of intercultural collaboration. However, there are two main problems in the naive implementation of human-assisted machine translation. The problems are described below.

Example 2: Misinterpretation of the meaning of a machine translated sentence

The Japanese sentence He needed 1 week to cure a cold was translated into English as He was necessary to correct a cold for 1 week. Since there were diction and grammar errors in this English sentence, this sentence was modified to be a natural expression by the native English speaker. However, he or she modified this English sentence as He should recover from a cold within 1 week. This modified English sentence differs in meaning from the original Japanese sentence.

A person who modifies a machine translated sentence can never understand the original meaning of the sentence. Therefore, he or she might misinterpret the meaning. Due to this, the modified sentence might differ in meaning from the original sentence.

Example 3: Incomprehension of the meaning of a machine translated sentence

The Japanese sentence His belly is sticking out was translated into English as A stomach has gone out to him. A native English speaker cannot understand the meaning of this machine translated English sentence. Therefore, this sentence remained unmodified.

It is almost impossible to modify phrases of a machine translated sentence that he or she cannot make sense of. Such phrases tend to remain unmodified. As a result, information about such phrases cannot be shared throughout the domain.

Human-assisted machine translation has following problems:

- It cannot be determined that a modified machine translation has the same meaning as a corresponding original sentence
- Phrases in the machine translated sentence that a person cannot make sense of remained unmodified

It is true that human-assisted machine translation is helpful for information sharing in real fields of intercultural collaboration. However, the prevention of misconception and accurate information sharing cannot be realized until these two problems are solved.

3   Collaborative Translation

3.1   Definition

Participants in a collaborative translation task are two non-bilingual people: one person who handles the source language (source language side), and one person who handles the target language (target language side). Only an MT system performs the task of translation. While the original document can not be revised, the source language side can submit alternatives to the original sentences to the MT system to create reference material.

The source language side and the target language side play different roles. The target language side cannot determine whether a machine translated sentence has the same meaning as the original sentence. However, he or she can determine whether the machine translated sentence is fluent. Therefore, he or she can modify the non-fluent sentences to be more fluent. We assume that the sentences modified by a person are always fluent. Like the target language side, the source language side cannot determine whether the machine translated sentence has the same meaning as the original sentence. However, given the machine translation of a sentence modified by the target language side, the source language side can determine whether the back-translation of the modified sentence has the same meaning as the original sentence. By thinking of this, he or she determines whether a machine translated sentence has the same meaning as the original sentence.

The above definitions are illustrated in Figure 2.

3.2   Protocol

In order to work together efficiently, it is essential to establish shared knowledge or common ground on the subject [Clark 81, Clark 86, Isaacs 87, Clark 91, Krauss 64]. The process of establishing common ground consists of the presentation phase to

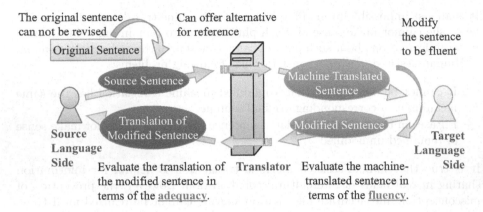

Fig. 2. The basic concept of collaborative translation

present information to the addressees and the acceptance phase to confirm that addressees have received the information correctly [Clark 91]. In collaborative translation, the presentation phase is the transmission of a machine translated sentence to the target language side. The acceptance phase is all processes following the presentation phase. The protocols must be designed to ensure that the correctness of the translation result can be confirmed in the acceptance phase.

Figure 3 shows the formal statement of the basic protocol, which is the minimal protocol to perform collaborative translation. The detail of this protocol is described below.

This protocol starts by sending the machine translated sentence of the original sentence to the target language side (1. Transmission of Source Sentence). Since the source language side plays a role of determining whether the translation of the sentence which is modified by the target language side has the same meaning as the original sentence, he or she waits until the target language side finishes modifying the machine translated sentence to be fluent. In a practical application, since we suppose that the protocol is executed on each sentence of a document in parallel, a person will work at another sentence when he or she waits the processing of an earlier sentence. The target language side plays a role in evaluating the fluency of the machine translated sentence. However, as mentioned in the section 2.2, he or she cannot modify the machine translated sentence if he or she cannot understand its meaning. Therefore, he or she determines that its meaning is understandable before modifying (2. Readability Determination of Translation). If not understandable, the source language side is required to paraphrase the original sentence to make another version of the machine translation. Generally speaking, MTs have a characteristic which tends to output different expressions with a little change of the source sentence. The target language side keeps requesting the source language side to paraphrase the original sentence until the meaning of the machine translated sentence becomes understandable. Only after its meaning is understandable, the target language side modifies it to be fluent (3. Modification of Translation). After the

Let s be a source sentence.

Let c, a, and f be boolean functions. For any sentence x, $c(x)$ indicates that the content of x is understandable, $a(x, s)$ indicates that x means a source sentence s adequately, and $f(x)$ indicates that x is fluent.

Let m and t be functions. For any sentence x, $m(x)$ indicates a human modified sentence of x, and $t(x)$ indicates a machine translated sentence x. For instance, $m(t(s))$ indicates a human modified version of a machine translation of the source. Let p be the number of modifications made by the source language side, the maximum value permitted is P. Let q be the number of modifications made by the target language side, the maximum value permitted is Q.

1) [Source Language Side: Transmission of Source Sentence]
   Let $p := 0$
   Transmit s to the target language side
      Goto 2)
2) [Target Language Side: Readability Determination of Translation]
   Let $t(s)$ be a machine translated s
   If not $c(t(s))$
      Request the source language side to modify s
      Goto 6)
   Else If $c(t(s))$
      Let $q := 0$
      Goto 3)
3) [Target Language Side: Modification of Translation]
   Let $q := q + 1$
   If $q \geq Q$
      Terminate protocol with label *Unsuccessful*
   Else If $q < Q$
      Let $m(t(s))$ be a human modified sentence of $t(s)$ to be $f(m(t(s)))$
      Transmit $m(t(s))$ to the source language side
      Goto 4)
4) [Source Language Side: Readability Determination of Back-Translation]
   Let $t(m(t(s)))$ be a machine translated $m(t(s))$
   If not $c(t(m(t(s))))$
      Request the target language side to modify $m(t(s))$
      Goto 3)
   Else If $c(t(m(t(s))))$
      Goto 5)
5) [Source Language Side: Adequacy Determination of Back-Translation]
   If $a(t(m(t(s))))$
      Terminate protocol with label *Successful*
   Else If not $a(t(m(t(s))), s)$
      Goto 6)
6) [Source Language Side: Modification of Source Sentence]
   Let $p := p + 1$
   If $p \geq P$
      Terminate protocol with label *Unsuccessful*
   Else If $p < P$
      Let s be a human modified source sentence
      Goto 2)

Fig. 3. The formal statement of collaborative translation protocol

modification of the target language side comes finishes, the source language side starts to evaluate the adequacy of the modified sentence. Since the source language side is also monolingual, the modified sentence is translated into the source language to enable him or her to understand its semantics. In the same way as in the case of the target language side, the source language side determines if the meaning of the translation is understandable (4. Readability Determination of Back-Translation). If understandable, he or she determines that the translation of the modified sentence has the same meaning as the original sentence. (5. Adequacy Determination of Back-Translation). If these sentences have the same meaning, it is recognized that the modified machine translation is not only fluent, but also has the same meaning as the original sentence. Consequently, the protocol can terminate successfully. If these sentences do not have the same meaning, it can be seen that the interpretation of the machine translated sentence by the target language side is likely to differ from the meaning of the original sentence. Therefore, the source language side paraphrases the original sentence again and presents the different expression of the machine translated sentence to the target language side (6. Modification of Source Sentence).

As mentioned above, since an MT intervenes in the communication channel between the source language side and the target language side, there is a possibility that the target language side can interpret information differently from the original meaning. Accordingly, the source language side needs to confirm that the interpretation of the target language side is the same as the intention of the source language side. The confirmation can be made by receiving the translated version of the interpretation of the target language side. However, since the target language side cannot know whether his or her interpretation is transmitted to the source language side properly, he or she needs to confirm this. Even if these processes of confirmation are repeated again and again, they cannot inambiguously confirm whether they have common interpretation. This phenomenon is similar to "coordinated attack problem [Halpern 90]", which is often referred as the problems in the distributed environment such as multi-agent systems. In addition, it has been proven that common knowledge cannot be attained in such an environment [Halpern 90]. In this protocol, one heuristic is adopted that the machine translated sentence has the same meaning as the original meaning if the back-translation has the same meaning as the original sentence. By using this heuristic, common interpretation between the source language side and the target language side can be attained in this protocol.

In order to guarantee that the protocol always terminates, the maximum numbers P and Q of modification of the source language side and the target language side are defined. When translation quality is not improved by repetitive processings of the protocol, the improvement cannot be attained in this protocol, so the protocol will be aborted at a proper stage. Besides, the number of paraphrases that a human can conceive has limitations. In a past intercultural collaboration experiment [Nomura 03], it is reported that the average number of modifications of an original sentence to improve the MT quality (called self-initiated repair in [Nomura 03]) by the most enthusiastic user was eight times. However, this is viewed as a rare case, so it is reasonable to regard the limitation to even an enthusiastic user as four or five times. There can be two different policies to set the limits; "you must make an effort up to the maximum number of modification since translation quality is likely to be improved," and "you do not have to make an effort over the maximum number since it is a waste of time." From the results of intercultural collaboration experiment, it is reasonable to set the maximum numbers P and Q to three according to the policy of the former, or to five according to the latter.

3.3 Effectiveness

Figure 4 shows that the problem of the target language side's misinterpretation such as example 2 was solved by applying the collaborative translation protocol. The source language side is a native Japanese speaker, and the target language side is a native English speaker. In the first turn, the target language side modified the machine translated sentence with his or her misinterpretation. However, the source language side could determine that the back-translation of the modified sentence did not have the same meaning as the original sentence. This showed that the target language side may misinterpret the meaning of the translated sentence. The source language side modified the source sentence, and

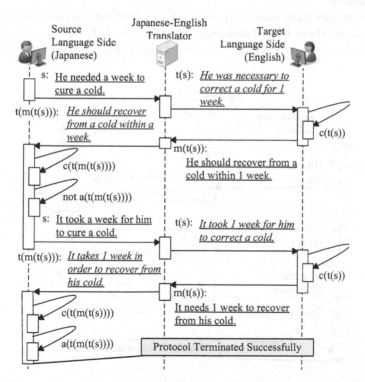

Fig. 4. The problem of Example 2 is solved by collaborative translation protocol

the target language side received its machine translated sentence which was expressed differently from the previous one. In the second turn, the target language side modified it with his or her interpretation which was different from one in his or her first turn. The source language side determined that the back-translation had the same meaning as the original sentence. To sum up, it was recognized that the translated sentence had the same meaning as the original sentence. The target language side's misinterpretation can be detected and corrected by applying the protocol.

Figure 5 shows that the problem such as example 3 was solved in scenario in which the target language side cannot modify the machine translated sentence due to its bad quality. In the first turn, the target language side could not understand the meaning of the machine translated sentence. Therefore, the protocol requested the source language side to modify the source sentence. In the second turn, the target language side received the machine translated sentence again which was expressed differently from the previous one. The target language side could modify it because its meaning was understandable. The source language side determined that the back-translation had the same meaning as the original sentence. Therefore, it was recognized that the translated sentence had the same meaning as the original sentence. The protocol can continue without stopping its processes even if the content of a machine translated sentence is not understandable.

These examples show that the protocol had a tendency to solve two problems of human-assisted machine translation. However, the MT quality tends to cause some errors because of the multi-linguistic characteristics such as word polysemy

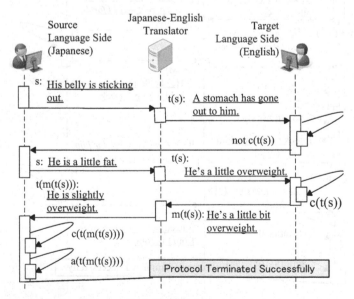

Fig. 5. The problem of Example 3 is solved by collaborative translation protocol

and the ambiguity of syntax analysis. In addition, there are human factors such as difficulties in consistent judgment and different criteria about assessment of translation adequacy. Because of these factors, although the protocol terminates successfully, the translation result could have a different meaning from the source sentence. Therefore, we will confirm the effectiveness of the protocol experimentally.

4 Evaluation

4.1 Setting

We evaluated the collaborative translation protocol in an experiment. Web services provided by Language Grid Project [Ishida 06] were used as modules of the MT system. This project is operated at Kyoto University and its basic software modules have been developed at the National Institute of Information and Communications Technology (NICT).

We used an MT test set provided by NTT Communication Science Laboratories[1]. This set consists of 3,718 Japanese sentences with English translations. In this experiment, 100 randomly selected sentences containing no proper nouns were used as the test set. Japanese-English and Japanese-Chinese translations were conducted and three pairs of participants were made in each language pair to minimize the human effects. The values P and Q, which are defined as the maximum numbers of modifications made by the source language side and the target language side, were set to three.

Besides, we evaluated the effectiveness of the method using back-translation, which is frequently used to improve the quality of machine translated sentences in many fields of intercultural collaboration. Back-translation is the process of translating a document that has already been translated into a foreign language back into the original language. By comparing the back-translated text to the source text, we can roughly figure out the quality of the MT without understanding the target language. We would like to show that the collaborative translation protocol is superior to this conventional method of improving MT quality. In the back-translation experiment, the maximum number of modification of a source sentence was also set to three and if a person could not determine that a back-translated sentence had the same meaning as the corresponding original sentence within the maximum modification limit, we viewed that the back-translation method terminated unsuccessfully.

The results of the collaborative translation, back-translation and the pure MT were scored by bilingual readers on a scale of 5 (All, Most, Much, Little, and None) in terms of translation adequacy[2]. Ratings were conducted by three people and the median was used as the final evaluated value. Since it is postulated that manually modified sentences are always fluent, the fluency of the translated sentences were not evaluated in this experiment.

---

[1] http://www.kecl.ntt.co.jp/mtg/resources/index.php
[2] http://projects.ldc.upenn.edu/TIDES/Translation/TransAssess02.pdf

In addition, we measured the average time required for collaborative translation and back-translation method and compared them to demonstrate that the time required for collaborative translation was tolerable.

4.2 Results

Success Rate. The rates in Japanese-English translation in which each protocol could terminate successfully were 67 percent for back-translation, and 70 percent for collaborative translation. On the other hand, the success rate in Japanese-Chinese translation was 78 percent for back-translation, and 62 percent for collaborative translation. Correlation between success rates of collaborative translation and of back-translation method were not observed, and those rates are in the same range.

Translation Adequacy. Figure 6 shows a graph of evaluated values of adequacy for pure MT, back-translation and collaborative translation in Japanese-English translation, and figure 7 shows Japanese-Chinese translation. Blue line with triangle marks in each graph indicates the percentage of translation that scored "All" when the protocol terminated successfully and red line with square marks indicates the percentage of translations scored "All" to all results used in the experiment (that is, including sentences where the protocol terminated but also unsuccessfully). In terms of pure MT, these percentages are the same. When the collaborative translation protocol terminated successfully, 83 percent of Japanese-English translation and 91 percent of Japanese-Chinese translation

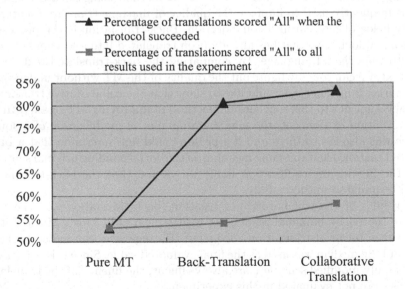

Fig. 6. Results of collaborative translation, back-translation, and pure MT in Japanese-English translation

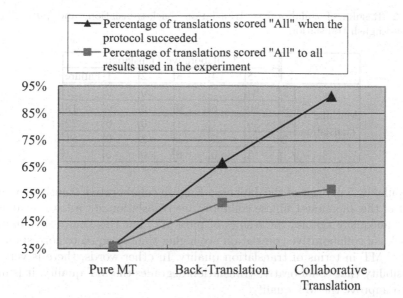

Fig. 7. Results of collaborative translation, back-translation, and pure MT in Japanese-English translation

were scored "All". This result shows that the translation quality is likely to be high if the collaborative translation protocol terminates successfully. As mentioned above, there is a possibility that the adequacy of the translated sentences could be low even if the collaborative translation protocol terminates successfully, but the possibility is very low. Besides, when comparing the results of collaborative translation with the results of back-translation, collaborative translation is superior to back-translation method in terms of translation adequacy in both Japanese-English and Japanese-Chinese translation.

Table 1 shows changes in the evaluated value of the adequacy of the collaborative translation from the value of pure MT in Japanese-English translation, and table 2 shows changes in Japanese-Chinese translation. Since this experiment was conducted with three pairs, 300 result sentences of collaborative translation

Table 1. Results of collaborative translation, back-translation, and pure MT in Japanese-English translation

		Collaborative Translation					
		5	4	3	2	1	Failure
Machine Translation	5	117	10	0	2	3	27
	4	21	5	0	0	0	22
	3	15	5	4	0	0	18
	2	11	1	2	0	0	16
	1	11	1	1	0	1	7

Table 2. Results of collaborative translation, back-translation, and pure MT in Japanese-English translation

		Collaborative Translation					
		5	4	3	2	1	Failure
Machine Translation	5	84	2	1	0	0	21
	4	30	6	0	0	0	18
	3	39	1	1	0	0	22
	2	16	2	1	2	0	51
	1	2	0	0	0	0	1

were available. 5 percent of the Japanese-English collaborative translation and 1 percent of the Japanese-Chinese collaborative translation got a lower evaluated value in adequacy against the results of pure MT, but this shows that most of the results of collaborative translation are higher than or equal to corresponding results of MT in terms of translation quality. In other words, there is very little possibility that collaborative translation degrades the MT quality, it is more likely to improve the MT quality.

Required Time. Average working time per sentence to modify a source sentence in the back-translation method is 40.2 seconds in Japanese-English translation and 29.1 seconds in Japanese-Chinese translation. In collaborative translation, the average working time for the source language side is 48.1 seconds in Japanese-English translation and 56.2 seconds in Japanese-Chinese translation. The time for the target language side is 30.4 seconds in Japanese-English translation and 42.9 seconds in Japanese-Chinese translation. As mentioned in section 3.2, since it is supposed that in a practical application multiple protocols for each original sentence are executed in parallel, the real required time of collaborative translation is not the sum of working times of the source language side and target language side but the maximum. That is, average required time for collaborative translation per a sentence which is used in this experiment is around one minute.

Since collaborative translation needs more human work than pure MT and back-translation method, the working time required is longer. However, we showed that the required time for collaborative translation is not considerably different from the time needed for the back-translation method. Besides, experimental results show that translation adequacy can be improved further by collaborative translation, and the translation results excel especially in fluency because the machine translated sentences are modified manually. Therefore, we can conclude that collaborative translation is more useful in the field of intercultural collaboration using MT.

5   Conclusion

Nowadays, many communities use MT in their activities. In one real field of intercultural collaboration, members try to enhance intergroup and intragroup information sharing by modifying low-quality machine translation manually. However, there are two problems in the naive implementation: One is that poor quality of translation could induce misinterpretation, and the other is that phrases in the machine translated sentence that a person cannot make sense of remain unmodified. Our main research contribution is that we introduced the protocol in collaborative translation. This protocol solves the above two problems and, in addition, this protocol 1) improves MT quality; and 2) terminates successfully only when a translation result becomes adequate and fluent. We made it clear that the target language side can modify the machine translated sentences to be fluent, and the source language side can evaluate the translation quality by determining whether the back-translation of the modified sentence has the same meaning as the original sentence. Only 53 percent of Japanese-English translation and 36 percent of Japanese-Chinese translation were perfect translations in pure MT. However, when the collaborative translation protocol terminated successfully, 83 percent of Japanese-English translation and 91 percent of Japanese-Chinese translation were perfect. This revealed experimentally that collaborative translation is much more likely to result in a good translation.

Acknowledgment

This research was partially supported by Kyoto University Global COE Program: Informatics Education and Research Center for Knowledge-Circulating Society.

References

[Aiken 02]   Aiken, M.: Multilingual communication in electronic meetings. ACM SIGGROUP Bulletin 23(1), 18–19 (2002)

[Aiken 94]   Aiken, M., Hwang, C., Paolillo, J., Lu, L.: A group decision support system for the asian pacific rim. Journal of International Information Management 3, 1–13 (1994)

[Clark 91]   Clark, H.H., Brennan, S.E.: Grounding in communication. In: Resnick, L.B., Levine, R.M., Teasley, S.D. (eds.) Perspectives on socially shared cognition, American Psychological Association, Washington, DC (1991)

[Clark 81]   Clark, H.H., Marshall, C.E.: Definite reference and mutual knowledge. Elements of discourse understanding, 10–63 (1981)

[Clark 86]   Clark, H.H., Wilkes-Gibbs, D.: Referring as a collaborative process. Cognition, 1–39 (1986)

[Halpern 90] Halpern, Y.J., Moses, Y.: Knowledge and Common Knowledge in a Distributed Environment. Journal of the ACM 37(3), 549–587 (1990)

[Isaacs 87]   Isaacs, E.A., Clark, H.H.: References in conversation between experts and novices. Journal of Experimental Psychology: General 16(1), 26–27 (1987)

[Ishida 06]   Ishida, T.: Language grid: An infrastructure for intercultural collaboration. In: IEEE/IPSJ Symposium on Applications and the Internet (SAINT 2006), pp. 96–100 (2006)

[Kim 02]   Kim, K.J., Bonk, C.J.: Cross-cultural comparisons of online collaboration. Journal of Computer Mediated Communication 8(1) (2002)

[Krauss 64]   Krauss, R.M., Weinheimer, S.: Changes in reference phases as a function of frequency of usage in social interaction: A preliminary study. Psychonomic Science 1, 113–114 (1964)

[Nomura 03]   Nomura, S., Ishida, T., Yamashita, N., Yasuoka, M., Funakoshi, K.: Open source software development with your mother language: Intercultural collaboration experiment 2002. In: International Conference on Human-Computer Interaction (HCI 2003), vol. 4, pp. 1163–1167 (2003)

[Ogden 03]   Ogden, B., Warner, J., Jin, W., Sorge, J.: Information sharing across languages using mitre's trim instant messaging (2003)

[Takano 93]   Takano, Y., Noda, A.: A temporary decline of thinking ability during foreign language processing. Journal of Corss-Cultural Psychology 24(4), 445–462 (1993)

[Tung 02]   Tung, L.L., Quaddus, M.A.: Cultural differences explaining the differences in results in gss: implications for the next decade. Decision Support Systems 33(2), 177–199 (2002)

[Yamashita 06] Yamashita, N., Ishida, T.: Effects of machine translation on collaborative work. In: International Conference on Computer Supported Cooperative Work (CSCW 2006), pp. 512–523 (2006)

An Affective Agent Playing Tic-Tac-Toe as Part of a Healing Environment

Matthijs Pontier[1,2] and Ghazanfar Farooq Siddiqui[1,2,3]

[1] VU University Amsterdam, Center for Advanced Media Research Amsterdam,
De Boelelaan 1083, 1081HV Amsterdam, The Netherlands
[2] VU University Amsterdam, Department of Artificial Intelligence,
De Boelelaan 1083, 1081HV Amsterdam, The Netherlands
[3] Quaid-i-Azam University Islamabad, 45320, Pakistan
{mpr210,ghazanfa}@few.vu.nl
http://www.few.vu.nl/{mpr210,ghazanfa}

Abstract. There is a growing belief that the environment plays an important role in the healing process of patients, supported by empirical findings. Previous research showed that psychological stress caused by loneliness can be reduced by artificial companions. As a pilot application for this purpose, this paper presents an affective agent playing tic-tac-toe with the user. Experimenting with a number of agents under different parameter settings shows the agent is able to show human-like emotional behavior, and can make decisions based on rationality as well as on affective influences. After discussing the application with clinical experts and making improvements where needed, the application can be tested in a clinical setting in future research.

Keywords: Cognitive Modeling, Emotion Modeling, Healing Environment.

1 Introduction

Many people do not like the atmosphere in hospitals. Since two decades, there is a growing belief that not only the health care itself, but also the environment affects the healing process of the patients. This has increased the interest in healing environments. The role of the environment in the healing process is a growing concern among health care providers, environmental psychologists, consultants and architects. Among them the consensus is growing that not only the level of care, but also the design of the health care facility affects the wellness of its patients [7].

Researchers are finding that making changes and additions to the physical and social environment of the health care facility, thereby taking the patient into account, can positively influence patients' outcomes (e.g., [2], [6], [18], [22], [25]). Moreover, health care professionals are finding that changes in design can enhance recovery in patients, and reduce the length of their stay in the hospital [15]. On the other hand, researchers are also finding that unfamiliar environments in clinics, hospitals, and nursing homes can produce psychological stress that can negatively affect healing and wellness.

J.-J. Yang et al. (Eds.): PRIMA 2009, LNAI 5925, pp. 33–47, 2009.

Poor design has even been linked to negative effects on the patient, such as anxiety, delirium, elevated blood pressure levels, and an increased intake of pain drugs [23].

One factor that can be reduced by a healing environment is psychosocial stress. An important predictor of psychosocial stress is loneliness [12]. Loneliness is a common problem frequently encountered in the elderly in long-term care facilities. Many people that are staying in a long-term care facility lack social interaction. Artificial toys can be used to reduce loneliness. Previous research showed that animal-shaped toys can be useful as a tool for occupational therapy (e.g., [18], [26], [27]). Robot animal therapy has been widely investigated. For example, Dautenhahn and Robins [20], [28] used mobile robots and dolls respectively to treat autistic children. Wada and Shibata developed Paro [27], a robot shaped like a baby-seal that interacts with users to encourage positive mental effects. Interaction with Paro has been shown to improve users' moods, making them more active and communicative with each other and caregivers. Research groups have used Paro for therapy at eldercare facilities and with those having Alzheimer's disease [14], [17]. Banks et al. [2] showed that animal-assisted therapy with an AIBO dog helped just as good for reducing loneliness as therapy with a living dog. In their paper they indicate that AIBO was not used to its full capacity and that if more options were used, its effects might be further enhanced. Over the past decade, a lot of novel work on computational models of emotion in virtual agents can be observed. Nevertheless, compared to human affective complexity, current emotion models of virtual agents are still quite simple. If an artificial companion demonstrates human-like emotional behavior, this might increase its ability to reduce loneliness of patients in a long-term care facility, as part of a healing environment.

In our paper, we present a virtual agent that could be seen as a pilot application for this purpose. The artificial companion is an affective virtual agent that can play tic-tac-toe, equipped with Silicon Coppélia [19], an integration of three affect-related models as proposed in [3]. Because it is equipped with these affect-related models, it can show human-like emotional behavior. Therefore, it might be a useful to serve as an artificial interaction partner for patients in a long-term care facility.

2   The Application

The application presented in this paper is an affective virtual agent that can play tic-tac-toe against the user. The object of tic-tac-toe is to get three in a row on a three by three game board. You play on a three by three game board. Players alternate placing X's and O's on the game board until one of the players has three in a row, or all nine squares on the board are filled, which means the game ends in a tie. For creating the virtual agent, we used Haptek's peopleputty software [11]. Through this program we created the face of the virtual agent. The agent simulates 5 emotions: joy, distress, hope, fear and surprise, which can be expressed with either a low or a high intensity.

We created 32 (2^5) different emotional states using peopleputty; one for each possible combination of two levels of intensity of the five emotions simulated by the agent. We created a webpage for the application, on which the virtual agent was embedded as a Haptek player. We used JavaScript [1], a scripting language, in combination with scripting commands provided by the Haptek software [11], to control the Haptek player within a web browser.

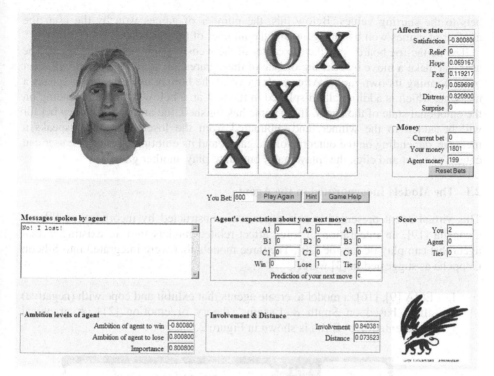

Fig. 1. The website with the tic-tac-toe application

Figure 1 shows the resulting website. In Figure 1, the agent, playing O's, just lost a game, and therefore looks sad. The website shows in the top left the agent which the user plays against. If the agent speaks a message, this is additionally shown in a textbox that is shown below the agent. Below this textbox, the ambition levels of the agent for winning and losing, and the importance of the current game for the agent are shown. Right next to this, the level of involvement and distance from the agent towards the user are shown. Right next to the textbox, the predictions of the agent about the expected next move and the outcome of the game are shown. Above this, just below the tic-tac-toe board, the user can enter its bet, and there is a 'play again' button which the user can click on to play a new game with the inserted amount of money as bet. Additionally, there is a hint button, which makes the agent give a hint to the user about in which square to make a move. Further, there is a 'game help' button. If the user clicks this button, the agent will explain the rules of the game.

Because the purpose of this paper is to show how the application works, the affective state is not only shown by means of a facial expression of the agent, but the emotion variables are also shown numerically on the top right. If the application would be designed to be used by human users, these numerical values would not be shown, and only the facial expression would be visible to the user. Below the affective state in numbers, the amount of money that is currently played for (current bet), the amount of money of the user (your money), and the amount of money of the agent (agent money) are shown. There is also a 'reset bets' button, which resets the bets to the starting values. Below this, the number of games won by the user, the number of games won by the agent, and the number of ties is shown.

The tic-tac-toe board is on the top center of the website, right next to the agent. The user can make a move by clicking on one of the squares, on which the agent will react by performing its own move. After each move of the human user, the agent speaks a message, which is additionally displayed in the text-area below its face, depending on the emotional state of the agent. If the game has finished, the amount of money bet for will be added to the winner, and subtracted from the loser. The agent speaks a message, depending on the outcome of the game, and its emotional state. The user can enter a new bet and click the 'play again' button to play another game.

2.1 The Models Incorporated in the Agent

This virtual agent presented in this paper was constructed by incorporating Silicon Coppélia [19], an integration of three affect-related models into an existing virtual agent that can play tic-tac-toe [29]. The three models that were integrated into Silicon Coppélia as suggested in [3] were:

1. EMA [9], [16], a model to create agents that exhibit and cope with (negative) affect based on Smith & Lazarus' theory of emotion [21]. A graphical representation of EMA is shown in Figure 2.

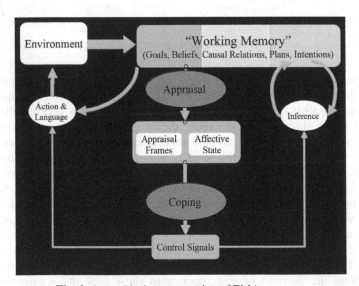

Fig. 2. A graphical representation of EMA

2. CoMERG [4] (the Cognitive Model for Emotion Regulation based on Gross), which can simulate different emotion regulation strategies explained by Gross [10] using a set of logical rules and difference equations. Figure 3 shows a graphical representation of the emotion regulation model by Gross.

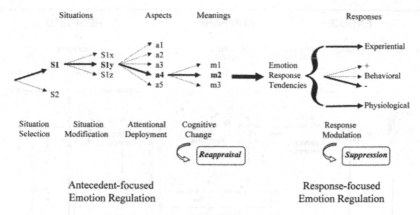

Fig. 3. A graphical representation of the emotion regulation model by Gross

3. I-PEFiC^{ADM} [13], a model for building agents that can trade rational for affective choices based on the concern-driven theory of Frijda [8]. A graphical representation of I-PEFiC^{ADM} is shown in Figure 4.

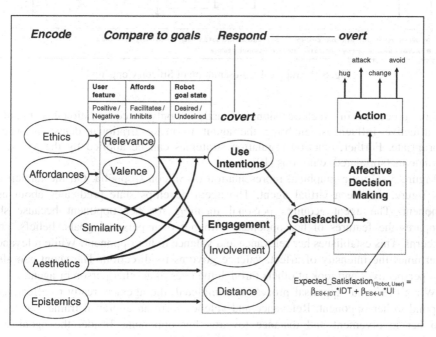

Fig. 4. A graphical representation of I-PEFiC^{ADM}. Curved arrows indicate interaction effects.

Integrating these models enabled agents in simulation experiments to show richer interaction than they could with any of the models alone. Using the combined model, they could simulate emotions based on beliefs about states in the world, and how these states affect their goals. The model was also used to simulate affective decision

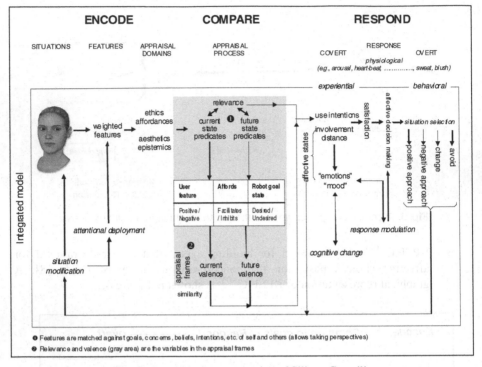

Fig. 5. A graphical representation of Silicon Coppélia

making processes, in which decisions are made not only based on rationality, but also on affective influences, enabling the agent to make irrational decisions where appropriate. Further, emotion regulation strategies can be applied by the agent, to regulate its (simulated) emotions [19].

Figure 5 shows a graphical representation of Silicon Coppélia. On the far left of this figure, we see a virtual agent. The agent develops state predicates about her opponent. The agent acquires personal meaning for her opponent because she compares the features of her opponent with her own personal goals, beliefs, and concerns. This establishes her relevance and valence to her opponent. While relevance determines the intensity of affect, valence governs its direction. The agent can also take perspectives and look at others through the eyes of another person or agent.

When the initial appraisal process is completed, the agent is ready to affectively respond to her opponent. Relevance and valence form an appraisal frame that feeds into her involvement and distance towards her opponent. Inside, the agent will 'experience' several (perhaps ambiguous) emotions.

During affective decision making, the agent selects the move in the game that promises the highest expected satisfaction. The performed action leads to a new situation, and after her opponent also made his/her move, the model loops until the game has finished.

Table 1. Designed values for perceiving the features of the human user

Feature	Designed value of human user
Good	0.6
Bad	0.2
Beautiful	0.5
Ugly	0.3
Realistic	0.9
Unrealistic	0.1
Intended Aid	0.7
Intended Obstacle	0.4

2.2 Determining which Action to Take

In Silicon Coppélia [19], the agents perceive each other's features according to I-PEFiC [24], by multiplying a designed value (a value the designer expects to raise in another agent), and a bias for perceiving this feature. For this application, as starting values, all biases were set to the neutral value of 1 for the agent. The designed values of the human user were set as can be found in Table 1. These values were chosen arbitrarily, and in an application with real users they should be reconsidered together with an expert. This will lead the agent to perceive the human user with the following variables:

In Silicon Coppélia, the agents also have beliefs that features of other agents affect certain goal-states in the world. For this application, the possible goal-states are 'agent wins' and 'human wins'. The beliefs about features facilitating these goal-states were set as can be seen in Table 2:

Table 2. Designed values for perceiving the features of the human user

Feature or Action	Facilitates 'agent wins'	Facilitates 'human wins'
Good	0.5	-0.5
Bad	-0.5	0.5
Beautiful	0.1	0.1
Ugly	0.1	0.1
Realistic	0.1	0.1
Unrealistic	0.1	0.1
Intended Aid	0.7	-0.7
Intended Obstacle	-0.7	0.7

The agent also has beliefs about actions facilitating goal-states. As there are nine squares on the board, there are nine possible actions for the agent: putting an O in each possible place. In Silicon Coppélia, the agents have beliefs that action facilitate goal-states in the range [-1, 1], where -1 means the agent beliefs the action strongly inhibits the goal-state, and 1 means the agent beliefs the action strongly facilitates the goal-state.

Each turn, the beliefs that actions facilitate goal-states are calculated based on a heuristic that estimates the chances of winning when a certain move is made. If the agent can make three O's in a row, the belief that performing this action facilitates 'agent wins' is set to 1, and the belief that this facilitates 'human wins' is set to -1.

If the human user has two X's in a row, and the third square in this row is still empty, the agent will belief that putting an O on this square facilitates 'agent wins' with a value of 0.9, and inhibits 'human wins' with a value of -0.9. If a square is already occupied, the belief that putting an O on this square facilitates a goal is set to 0 for both goals, as it is an illegal move. If none of these rules apply for a square, the belief that putting an O on the middle square (B2) facilitates 'agent wins' is set to 0.5, and that it facilitates 'human wins' to -0.5. Similarly, the belief that putting an O on corner squares (A1, A3, C1 and C3) facilitates 'agent wins' is set to 0.3 and for 'human wins' this is set to -0.3. Finally, the belief that putting an O on the remaining squares (A2, B1, B3 and C2) facilitates 'agent wins' is set to 0.1 and for 'human wins' this is set to -0.1. For actions which facilitate desired goals, and inhibit undesired goals (i.e., actions with a high expected utility, generalized over multiple goals), strong action tendencies are calculated [19].

In Silicon Coppélia, each action has a level of positivity and a level of negativity. In this application, the level of negativity of each action is defined as the belief of the agent that the action facilitates winning the game. The level of negativity of the action is defined as 1 minus this belief.

Using these variables, the affective decision-making of Silicon Coppélia [19] is used to determine the action of the agent. The expected satisfaction is calculated using the following formula, and the action with the highest level of expected satisfaction is picked.

$$
\begin{aligned}
\text{ExpectedSatisfaction(Action)} = \\
w_{at} * \text{Action\_Tendency} + \\
w_{pos} * (1 - \text{abs(positivity} - \text{bias}_I * \text{Involvement})) + \\
w_{neg} * (1 - \text{abs(negativity} - \text{bias}_D * \text{Distance}))
\end{aligned}
$$

The agent will search for the action with the level of positivity that is closest to the level of (biased) involvement towards the user, the level of negativity closest to the level of (biased) distance towards the user, and the strongest action tendency. The importance of positivity, negativity and action tendency for selecting an action can be adjusted by changing the weights (w_{pos}, w_{neg}, and w_{at} respectively). If an agent wants to perform more positive actions, it can, for example, increase its bias for involvement, and decrease its bias for distance. This way, the agent will prefer more positive and less negative actions.

Note that this way, the agent can also deliberately lose by setting a high ambition level for the goal 'human wins', or because the agent is too involved with the user to try to win each game. The agent can also determine its ambition level for winning on the outcomes of the previous games, and the amount of money that is played for. For example, it can try to win the game if it has less money than the human user, and deliberately try to lose if it has more money than the human user. The agent can also determine the importance of each game, by dividing the amount that is played for by the total amount of money the agent has left. This importance can then be the deviation from 0 in the ambition level.

2.3 Calculating the Emotions of the Agent

The agent simulates some emotions while playing the game, based on the actions that are being performed by the user, the perceived likelihood of winning and losing, and the outcome of the game. Hope and fear are calculated each time the agent has made its move and the human user is on turn. The hope and fear of the agent are based on the perceived likelihood it will win or lose the game. If the human user is on turn and can make a winning move, it estimates the likelihood for losing 0.8, the likelihood for a tie 0.1, and the likelihood for winning 0.1. If the agent could make a winning move if it would be on turn (but it cannot, because the human user is), it will estimate its likelihood for winning 0.5, the likelihood for a tie 0.4 and its likelihood for losing 0.1. Otherwise, the likelihood for winning and losing are both estimated 0.3 by the agent and the likelihood for a tie is estimated 0.4.

The found likelihoods are used in the following function to calculate the hope for a goal. This function is similar to the function described in [5].

IF f >= likelihood THEN hope_for_goal =
-0,25 * (cos(1 / f * π * likelihood(goal)) -1,5) * ambition_level(goal)

IF f < likelihood THEN hope_for_goal =
-0.25 * (cos(1 / (1-f) * π * (1-likelihood(goal))) -1.5) * ambition_level(goal)

These functions differ from most approaches present in the literature, since their top is not situated at the point where the likelihood is 0. In these functions, f is a shaping parameter (in the domain [0, 1]) that can be used to manipulate the location of the top of the hope curve. The value of this parameter may differ per individual, and represents 'fatalism' (or 'pessimism'): the top of the likelihood/hope-curve is always situated at the point where likelihood = f. Thus, for an f close to 1, the top of the curve is situated to the extreme right (representing persons that only 'dare' to hope for events with high probabilities). Similarly, for an f close to 0, the top of the curve is situated to the extreme left (representing persons that already start hoping for events with low probabilities). In this paper, f is set at 0.5. We chose a smooth function instead of a linear function, because this function best matches the emotion curves found in humans. Furthermore, a higher ambition level simply leads to a higher hope (which is standard in the literature). If the ambition level is negative (i.e., the goal is undesired), the outcome of hope_for_goal will be a negative value.

The following algorithm is performed to the found values for hope_for_goal

1. Sort the values in two lists: [0→1] and [0→-1]
2. Start with 0 and take the mean of the value you have and the next value in the list. Continue until the list is finished. Do this for both the negative and the positive list.
3. Hope = Outcome positive list.   Fear = abs(Outcome negative list).

The values are sorted in a list with positive hope_for_goal's (i.e., hope for desired goals), and negative hope_for_goal's (i.e., fear for undesired goals). For both the lists, 0 is the starting point, and the mean of the value you have and the next value in the list (where the next value is the value closest to 0 that is left in the list) is picked until the end of the list is reached. The new level of hope for the agent is the outcome of the positive list, and the new level of fear for the agent is the absolute value of the outcome of the negative list.

The joy and distress of the agent are based on reaching or not reaching desired or undesired goal-states. If a goal-state becomes true (i.e., the agent wins or the human user wins), the levels of joy and distress are calculated by performing the following formulas:

```
IF ambition_level(goal) >= 0 THEN:
  new_joy      = old_joy + mf_joy * ambition_level(goal) * (1-old_joy)
  new_distress = old_distress + mf_distress * -ambition_level(goal) * old_distress

IF ambition_level(goal) < 0 THEN:
  new_joy      = old_joy + mf_joy * ambition_level(goal) * old_joy
  new_distress = old_distress + mf_distress * -ambition_level(goal) * (1-old_distress)
```

In this formula, mf_joy and mf_distress are modification factors that determine how quickly joy and distress change if the agent wins or loses the game. In this paper, the values were both set at 1. These modification factors are multiplied with the impact value, which is ambition_level(goal) for joy and -ambition_level(goal) for distress. This way, if a desired goal is reached, this will increase joy and decrease distress, and reaching an undesired goal will decrease joy and increase distress. Multiplying with limiter (1-old_joy) for joy and old_distress for distress if the goal is desired manages the formula does not go out of range. Further, it manages that if an agent's level of joy or distress approaches an extreme value, it will be harder to push it further to the extreme, and easier to get it back to a less extreme value. If the reached goal is undesired, old_joy is used as limiter for joy and (1-old_distress) as limiter for distress, because the values of joy and distress will move in the opposite direction as when the goal is desired.

The level of surprise is calculated in a similar manner as in [5], [29]. To calculate the level of surprise during the game, the agent generates expectations about which move the user will make. If a square is free, that square gets a point. If the user can make three in a row, or prevent the agent from making three in a row the next turn, the square of that move gets 1 extra point. If the user has one X in a row, and the remaining squares of that row are free, those squares get 0.5 point. After all the squares have got their points, the sum of all points of the squares is normalized to 1. The resulting values for each square are the predicted likelihoods of the human making a move on that square. If the user makes a move on a certain square, the level of surprise for the agent is 1 − likelihood(move). If the game finishes, the level of surprise for the agent is 1 minus the perceived likelihood that the game would end that way.

After each move of the human user, the agent speaks a message, depending on the level of surprise. In the system, there is a small database of messages, labeled with certain emotion intensities. If the level of surprise is very low, it will show that it expected this move, with a message like 'I thought you would do that' or 'A predictable move'. On the other hand, if the agent is very surprised by the move of the user, it will speak a more surprised message, like 'That move surprised me!' or 'You are full of surprises.'

All five emotions inserted in the system (joy, distress, hope, fear and surprise) are simulated in parallel. If the level of joy, distress or surprise is below 0.5, a low intensity of the emotion is shown by the agent. If the level of joy, distress, or surpise is greater or equal than 0.5, a high intensity of the emotion is shown by the agent.

Because playing the tic-tac-toe game rarely leads to extreme values of hope and fear in the agent, for hope and fear this boundary is set to 0.25.

After each game has ended, the level of satisfaction for the agent is calculated in the range [-1, 1]. If the agent wins, the level of satisfaction will be the ambition level for 'agent wins'. Similarly, if the human user wins, the level of satisfaction will be the ambition level for 'human wins'. If the game ends in a tie, the importance of the game is calculated by dividing the amount that is played for by the total amount of money of the agent. The satisfaction of the agent after a tied game is then calculated by multiplying the importance of the game with 0.5.

Also a level of relief is calculated for the agent after each game, in the range [-1, 1], by multiplying the level of satisfaction with the level of surprise. Further, a message is displayed, based on the outcome of the game and the level of satisfaction and relief, the agent speaks a message in a similar way as after each move. If the agent wins, and the level of relief is low, and the level of satisfaction is low, it will display a neutral message like 'I win'. If the level of satisfaction is higher, it will display a more enthusiastic message like 'Superb match for me!' If the level of relief is higher, it speaks this relief with a message like 'I won, that is such a huge relief'. If the agent loses, and has a relatively neutral level of satisfaction close to 0, it will display a message like 'You won'. If the agent is very dissatisfied, with a value close to -1, it will speak a more dramatic message, like 'No! I lost everything!' If the game ends in a tie, the agent speaks a neutral message like 'We tied'. If the agent's ambition was to win, and it wins, it will show a happy facial expression. If it loses, it will look sad. If the agent's ambition was to lose, and it wins, it shows a sad facial expression. If its ambition was to lose and it loses, the facial expression will be happy.

3 Results

To test the application, the behavior of the agent has been tested under various parameter settings. All agents experimented with can be found at [30].

Agent 1: The agent tries to win

The ambition level for winning of agent 1 is set to 1, and its ambition level for losing is -1. The weight of the affective influences in the decision making process is set to 0. Under these parameter settings, the agent will always try to win. Because in tic-tac-toe it is impossible to lose if you play it right and you do not want to lose, it is impossible to win of the agent. The best game outcome that can be achieved is a draw.

If the agent wins, it will increase its joy and decrease its distress. If the agent loses, it will decrease its joy and increase its distress. If you make a move the agent does not expect, or the game ends otherwise than expected, it will be surprised. The expectations of the agent can be seen on the website. If the agent thinks it is likely that it will win, it will have a relatively high level of hope, and if it thinks it is likely that it will lose, it will have a relatively high level of fear.

Agent 2: The agent deliberately tries to lose

Agent 2 has an ambition level for winning of -1, and an ambition level for losing of 1. This means for the agent, winning is an undesired goal, and losing is a desired goal.

The weight of the affective influences in the decision making process have set to 0, so the agent will always try to lose. The only way to let the agent win is to make sure you don't make three in a row, and with the last move of the agent, it can do nothing else than make the winning move. Because the agent wants to lose, it will increase its level of joy and decrease its level of distress when it loses. If it wins, it will decrease its level of joy, and increase its level of distress.

Agent 3: The agent decides whether it wants to win based on its money

For agent 3, the ambition level for winning and losing is dependent on its amount of money compared to the amount of money of the human. If the agent has more money than the human, it will have an ambition level for winning of -1*importance and an ambition level for losing of 1*importance. If the amount of money of the agent is less or equal than that of the human, the agent will have an ambition level for winning of 1*importance and an ambition level for losing of -1*importance. The weight of the affective influences of the agent is set to 0. This causes the agent to try to win, unless it already has more money than the human user. If the agent has the ambition to win and it does, it will decrease its joy, and decrease its distress, and if it loses it will decrease its joy and increase its distress. However, if the agent has the ambition to lose, and it wins, it will decrease its joy and increase its distress, and vice versa if it loses. How big the increases and decreases of joy and distress are, depends on the importance of the game.

Agent 4: The agent is too involved with the user to win

Agent 4 is very involved with its user. It is programmed to perceive its user as good, beautiful, realistic, and intending to aid (designed values set to 1). It is also programmed to perceive its user as not bad, not ugly, not unrealistic, and not intending to obstruct. This causes the agent to be very involved with the user with a value of 0.85, and not much at a distance towards the user, with a value of 0.08 at the start of the simulation. The ambition level of the agent to win is defined as the importance of the game, and the ambition level to lose as the negation of this importance. The weight of rational influences in the decision-making process is set to 0. This makes the agent want to perform actions towards the user with a high level of positivity, and a low level of negativity. Because actions to win the game have a relatively low level of positivity and a high level of negativity, the agent will perform actions that facilitate losing the game. Because this agent always has a positive ambition to win and a negative ambition to lose, winning will always increase its level of joy, and decrease its level of distress, and losing will always decrease its level of joy, and increase its level of distress. How big this increase or decrease is, is dependent on the importance of the game.

Agent 5: The agent is balanced, and wins sometimes, and loses sometimes

Agent 5 perceives the user with values as can be seen in Table 1. This leads the agent to be involved with the user with a value of 0.63, and to be at a distance with the user with a value of 0.26 at the start of the simulation. The ambition level of the agent to win is defined as the importance of the game, and the ambition level to lose as the negation of this importance. The rational influences in the decision-making process are set to 0.8, and the influences of positivity and negativity of action are both set to 0.1. Despite having a higher ambition to win than to lose under all circumstances, the agent will be too involved with the user to try to win in a game for a small amount of money. However, if the agent's money is almost gone, or the game is about a lot of money, the agent finds the game so important that it will do its best to try to win.

Similarly to agent 4, if agent 5 wins, this will increase joy and decrease distress, and vice versa if it loses.

4 Discussion

This study presents an affective virtual agent that can play tic-tac-toe. Because it is equipped with Silicon Coppélia [19], an integration of three affect-related models as suggested in [3], it can show human-like emotional behavior.

We created five different agents, each with different parameter settings, to test the behavior under various conditions. We manipulated the ambition levels of the agent, and thereby created agent 1, an agent that always tries to win, and agent 2, an agent that always deliberately tries to lose. Agent 3 determines its ambition level for winning and losing on whether it has more money than the user or not. If the user has more money than the agent, it will deliberately try to lose, but otherwise it will try to win. Agent 4 bases its decisions in the game on emotions, and because it is designed to be very involved with the user, it will perform actions that facilitate the user winning the game. Agent 5 bases its decisions partly on emotions, and partly on rationality. Agent 5 always has more ambition to win than to lose. How big this difference in ambition is, is dependent on the amount of money that is played for. This results in the agent trying to win if the agent plays for a big amount of money, or when its money is almost gone. However, if the game is only about a small amount of money, the agent will be too involved with the user to try to win. Based on whether the agent reaches its goals (winning and losing when the agent has ambitions to win or lose), the likelihood of these goals, and the expectedness of the move of the user and the outcome of a game, the emotions joy, distress, hope, fear and surprise are simulated and shown by the agent by means of facial expressions.

This virtual agent presented in this paper should be seen as a pilot application. Many improvements can still be made, such as giving feedback in a more sophisticated manner. Before it can be tested in a clinical setting, we should first discuss with experts where the application could be improved. We should also discuss with them what type of behavior the agent should show under which conditions, and adjust the parameter settings to meet these requirements. After that, user studies should indicate under which parameter settings participants find the agent most human-like.

However, experimenting with a number of agents, each with different parameter settings indicates that a realistic affective agent playing tic-tac-toe can be created.

Previous research already showed that interacting with a robot pet could decrease loneliness in patients staying in a long-term care facility. An artificial interaction partner that can show human-like emotional behavior might even have a greater beneficial effect on decreasing loneliness in patients. In future research, we intend to perform user studies to show whether this really is the case.

Acknowledgments

We would like to thank Tibor Bosse and Edwin Zwanenburg for their input to the paper, and Edwin Zwanenburg for implementing the game environment.

References

1. About JavaScript – MDC,
   `http://developer.mozilla.org/en/docs/About_JavaScript`
2. Banks, M.R., Willoughby, L.M., Banks, W.A.: Animal-Assisted Therapy and Loneliness in Nursing Homes: Use of Robotic versus Living Dogs. Journal of the American Medical Directors Association 9, 173–177 (2008)
3. Bosse, T., Gratch, J., Hoorn, J.F., Pontier, M.A., Siddiqui, G.F.: Coppélius' concoction: Similarity and complementarity among three affect-related agent models. In: International Conference on Agents and Artificial Intelligence, ICAART 2010 (2010) (submitted)
4. Bosse, T., Pontier, M.A., Treur, J.: A Dynamical System Modelling Approach to Gross' Model of Emotion Regulation. In: Lewis, R.L., Polk, T.A., Laird, J.E. (eds.) Proceedings of the 8th International Conference on Cognitive Modeling, ICCM 2007, pp. 187–192. Taylor and Francis, Abington (2007)
5. Bosse, T., Zwanenburg, E.: There's Always Hope: Enhancing Agent Believability through Expectation-Based Emotions. In: Pantic, M., Nijholt, A., Cohn, J. (eds.) Proceedings of the 2009 International Conference on Affective Computing and Intelligent Interaction, ACII 2009, pp. 111–118. IEEE Computer Society Press, Los Alamitos (2009)
6. Davidson, A.W.: Banking on the Environment to Promote Human Well-being. In: Seidel, A.D. (ed.) Banking on design? Proceedings of the 25th annual conference of the Environmental Design Research Association (EDRA), Oklahoma City, OK, pp. 62–66 (1994)
7. Devlin, A.S., Arneill, A.B.: Health Care Environments and Patient Outcomes: A Review of the Literature. Environment and Behavior 35(3), 665–694 (2003)
8. Frijda, N.H.: The Emotions. Cambridge University, New York (1986)
9. Gratch, J., Marsella, S.: Evaluating a computational model of emotion. Journal of Autonomous Agents and Multiagent Systems (Special issue on the best of AAMAS 2004) 11(1), 23–43 (2006)
10. Gross, J.J.: Emotion Regulation in Adulthood: Timing is Everything. Current directions in psychological science 10(6), 214–219 (2001)
11. Haptek, Inc., `http://www.haptek.com`
12. Hawkli, L.C., Masi, C.M., Berry, J.D., Cacioppo, J.T.: Loneliness Is a Unique Predictor of Age-Related Differences in Systolic Blood Pressure. Psychology and Aging 21(1), 152–164 (2006)
13. Hoorn, J.F., Pontier, M.A., Siddiqui, G.F.: When the user is instrumental to robot goals. First try: Agent uses agent. In: Proceedings of IEEE/WIC/ACM Web Intelligence and Intelligent Agent Technology 2008, WI-IAT 2008, pp. 296–301. IEEE/WIC/ACM, Sydney AU (2008)
14. Kidd, C., Taggart, W., Turkle, S.: A Social Robot to Encourage Social Interaction among the Elderly. In: Proceedings of IEEE ICRA, pp. 3972–3976 (2006)
15. Lemprecht, B.: The gap between design and healing. Metropolis 77, 123 (1996)
16. Marsella, S., Gratch, J.: EMA: A Model of Emotional Dynamics. Cognitive Systems Research 10(1), 70–90 (2009)

17. Marti, P., Bacigalupo, M., Giusti, L., Mennecozzi, C.: Socially Assistive Robotics in the Treatment of Behavioral and Psychological Symptoms of Dementia. In: Proceedings of BioRob, pp. 438–488 (2006)
18. Nakajima, K., Nakamura, K., Yonemitsu, S., Oikawa, D., Ito, A., Higashi, Y., Fujimoto, T., Nambu, A., Tamura, T.: Animal-shaped toys as therapeutic tools for patients with severe dementia. In: 2001: Proceedings of the 23rd Annual International Conference of the IEEE Engineering in Medicine and Biology Society, vol. 4, pp. 3796–3798 (2001)
19. Pontier, M.A., Siddiqui, G.F.: Silicon Coppélia: Integrating three affect-related models for establishing richer agent interaction. In: Proceedings of the International Conference on Intelligent Agent Technology, IAT 2009 (to appear, 2009)
20. Robins, B., Dautenhahn, K., Boekhorst, R.T., Billard, A.: Robotic Assistants in Therapy and Education of Children with Autism: Can a Small Humanoid Robot Help Encourage Social Interaction Skills? Journal of Universal Access in the Information Society 4, 105–120 (2005)
21. Smith, C.A., Lazarus, R.S.: Emotion and Adaptation. In: Pervin, L.A. (ed.) Handbook of Personality: theory & research, pp. 609–637. Guilford Press, New York (1990)
22. Ulrich, R.S.: View through a Window Influence Recovery from Surgery. Science 224, 420–421 (1984)
23. Ulrich, R.S.: Effects of Interior Design on Wellness: Theory and Recent Scientific Research. Journal of Health Care Interior Design 3, 97–109 (1991)
24. Van Vugt, H.C., Hoorn, J.F., Konijn, E.A.: Interactive engagement with embodied agents: An empirically validated framework. Computer Animation and Virtual Worlds 20, 195–204 (2009)
25. Verderber, S., Reuman, D.: Windows, Views, and Health Status in Hospital Therapeutic Environments. Journal of Architectural and Planning Research 4, 120–133 (1987)
26. Wada, K., Shibata, T.: Living with Seal Robots in a Care House - Evaluations of Social and Physiological Influences. In: IEEE/RSJ International Conference on Intelligent Robots and Systems, pp. 4940–4945 (2006)
27. Wada, K., Shibata, T.: Social Effects of Robot Therapy in a Care House -Change of Social Network of the Residents for One Year. JACIII 13, 386–392 (2009)
28. Werry, I., Dautenhahn, K.: Applying Mobile Robot Technology to the Rehabilitation of Autistic Children. In: Proc. of 7th Int. Symp. on Intelligent Robotic Systems, pp. 265–272 (1999)
29. Zwanenburg, E.: Enhancing Believability through Expectation-Based Emotions in a BDI Agent. Master Thesis, Vrije Universiteit Amsterdam (2009)
30. http://www.few.vu.nl/~ghazanfa/PRIMA2009/tictactoe.html

A Multi-agent Model for Emotion Contagion Spirals Integrated within a Supporting Ambient Agent Model

Tibor Bosse[1], Rob Duell[2], Zulfiqar A. Memon[1,3],
Jan Treur[1], and C. Natalie van der Wal[1,2]

[1] Vrije Universiteit Amsterdam, Department of Artificial Intelligence
De Boelelaan 1081, 1081 HV Amsterdam, The Netherlands
[2] Force Vision Lab, Barbara Strozzilaan 362a, 1083 HN Amsterdam, The Netherlands
[3] Sukkur Institute of Business Administration (Sukkur IBA),
Airport Road Sukkur, Sindh, Pakistan
{tbosse,rduell,zamemon,treur,cwl210}@few.vu.nl

Abstract. To avoid the occurrence of spirals of negative emotion in their teams, team leaders may benefit from intelligent agent systems that analyze the emotional dynamics of the team members. As a first step in developing such agents, this paper uses an agent-based approach to formalize and simulate emotion contagion spirals within groups. The computational multi-agent model is integrated within an intelligent ambient agent to monitor and predict group emotion levels over time and propose group support actions based on that.

Keywords: multi-agent model, emotion contagion spirals, ambient agent model.

1 Introduction

The occurrence of emotion contagion spirals in groups is a social phenomenon, where levels of emotion occur that may substantially exceed the original emotion levels of group members. How to avoid such spirals for negative emotions and how to stimulate them for positive emotions can be a real challenge for both group members and group leaders. This paper first presents an analysis and a computational model for the occurrence of emotion contagion spirals in groups. Next, it is shown how this model has been integrated within an ambient agent model to support group leaders. The ambient agent can predict and analyze the team's emotional level for present and future time points. In case a team's emotional level is found (to become) deficient compared to a certain norm, the ambient agent proposes the team leader to take some measures.

Emotions allow humans to respond quickly and efficiently to events that affect their welfare [15]. In addition, they provide us with information about others' behavioral intentions, and script our social behavior. Research on the idea that emotion also has a strong social component, which can influence interactions, is found in, e.g. [12], [13]. The process of emotion contagion, in which a group member influences the emotions of another group member (and vice versa), through the conscious or unconscious induction of emotion states [20], is a primary mechanism

J.-J. Yang et al. (Eds.): PRIMA 2009, LNAI 5925, pp. 48–67, 2009.

through which individual emotions create a collective emotion. This process has been described as an inclination to mimic the gestural behavior of others, to "synchronize facial expression, utterances and attitudes" [13]. Emotion contagion has been shown to occur in many cases varying from emotions in small groups to panicking crowds; see [1], [16] and [22]. The positive effects of the spread of emotions in groups have been investigated empirically in [9], where it is hypothesized that positive emotions trigger upward spirals toward enhanced emotional well-being. This prediction is based on Frederickson's broaden-and-build theory [10]. The broaden hypothesis states that positive emotions broaden people's mind-sets: the scopes of attention, cognition, action and the array of percepts, thoughts, and actions presently in mind are widened. The complementary narrowing hypothesis predicts the reverse pattern: negative emotions shrink people's thought-action repertoires. Support for the broaden and narrowing hypotheses can be found in [8]. The build hypothesis expresses that positive emotions encourage people to discover and explore new ways of thinking and action, by which they are building their personal resources such as socio-emotional and, intellectual skills. The broaden hypothesis can predict upward spirals in emotional well-being of a person, which the authors investigated in [9]. The authors demonstrated that initial experiences with positive affect can improve broad-minded-coping, which in turn can predict increases in positive affect over time, creating an upward spiral towards improved emotional well-being.

This paper first introduces a multi-agent model that formalizes and simulates emotion contagion spirals within groups. Next it is shown how this computational model can be used in applications within a teamwork context, supported by an intelligent ambient agent. Section 2 explains a formalized model of group emotion contagion spirals. Next, in Section 3, simulation results for this model are presented and in Section 4, the model is analyzed mathematically. Section 5 addresses formal verification of the emotion contagion spirals model and the simulation results. Section 6 describes how the model for emotion contagion spirals has been integrated within an existing ambient agent model. In Section 7 some simulation results are discussed for the resulting ambient agent model. Section 8 is a discussion.

2 The Emotion Contagion Spiral Model

The model introduced in this paper distinguishes multiple factors that influence emotion contagion spirals. In [1] (following [16]) Barsade describes an informal model of emotion contagion in which the emotion being expressed and transferred between group members, is characterized by the valence (positive or negative) and the energy level with which the emotion is expressed. Furthermore Barsade [1] suggests two categories of contagion

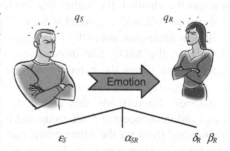

Fig. 1. Aspects of Emotion Contagion Spirals

mechanisms: automatic subconscious contagion, through mimicry and feedback, and conscious transfer, through social comparison of moods and appropriate responses in groups, mediated by attention. Regardless of the mechanisms employed, it is claimed that the type of emotion and the degree of emotion contagion in groups, is influenced by the emotional valence and the emotional energy.

Inspired by these theories, in this section a computational model of emotion contagion spirals is proposed. First a number of aspects are distinguished that play a role in the contagion spirals, varying from aspects related to the sender, the channel between sender and receiver and the receiver of the transferred emotion. Accordingly, the model distinguishes three parts in the process of transfer of emotion and related parameters: a sender S, a receiver R, and the channel from S to R (see Fig. 1 and Table 1).

Table 1. Parameters for aspects of emotion contagion spirals

current level of the sender's emotion	q_S	current level of the receiver's emotion	q_R
extent to which the sender expresses the emotion	ε_S	openness or sensitivity for received emotion	δ_R
the strength of the channel from sender to receiver	α_{SR}	tendency to adapt emotions upward or downward	β_R

The aspect ε_S depends on how introvert or extravert, expressive, active and energetic the person is. It represents the degree to which a person transforms internal emotion into external expression. In this sense, an introvert person will induce a weaker contagion of an emotion than an extravert person. The aspect α_{SR} depends on the type and intensity of the contact between the two persons (e.g., distance versus attachment). The aspect δ_R indicates the degree of susceptibility of the receiver: the extent to which the receiver allows the emotions received from others to affect his own emotion, and how flexible/persistent the receiver is emotionally. The aspect β_R describes the tendency to amplify or reduce emotions, when triggered by received emotions.

As a first step, all aspects have been formalized numerically by numbers in the interval $[0, 1]$. In addition, the parameter γ_{SR} is used to represent the strength of which an emotion is received by R from sender S, modeled as:

$$\gamma_{SR} = \varepsilon_S \, \alpha_{SR} \, \delta_R \qquad (1)$$

The stronger the channel, the higher α_{SR} and the more contagion will take place. The model works as follows: if gamma is set to 0 there will be no contagion, if γ_{SR} is 1, there will be a maximum strength of contagion. If γ_{SR} is not 0, there will be contagion and the higher the value, the more contagion will take place. In this way, the parameter γ_{SR} can create the behavior as formulated by hypothesis (a) and (b) from [2]. In a way γ_{SR} expresses the energy level with which an emotion is being expressed and transferred. Interestingly this energy level γ_{SR}, depends on situational factors (processes and influences) at both group and individual level. The overall strength by which emotions from all the other group members are received by R in a group G, indicated by γ_R, is defined as $\gamma_R = \Sigma_{S \in G \backslash R)} \gamma_{SR}$.

The proposed model can simulate both upward and downward emotional spirals through mechanisms, with which not only an individual agent, but also the whole group of agents can get to a higher or lower level of emotion. Each agent transfers an emotion value q between 0 and 1. The model makes it possible for each agent in certain situations to approximate values like 0 and 1, or values in between. Thus it represents upward or downward spirals, where each of the agents will get to a higher or lower level over time. Each agent will reach its own emotional equilibrium within the group. Suppose G is a group of agents. The dynamics of an agent R's emotion level is described as

$$dq_R/dt = \gamma_R [\beta_R PI + (1-\beta_R) NI - q_R] \tag{2}$$

The upward or downward direction of the change in an agent R's emotional level over time depends on parameter β_R, and the speed of the ascend or descend on parameter γ_R. Here

$$\gamma_R = \Sigma_{S \in G\backslash R} \gamma_{SR} \tag{3}$$

with

$$\gamma_{SR} = \varepsilon_S \alpha_{SR} \delta_R \tag{4}$$

Furthermore, PI and NI are the positive and negative impact of received emotion from the other group members respectively, which will be specified in more detail below. The parameter β_R defines the overall impact as a weighted combination of the two contributions. By varying the values of the β_R's, upward as well as downward spirals can be simulated. If $\beta_R = 1$ then the receiver is only susceptible for positive impact. If $\beta_R = 0$, then the receiver is only susceptible to negative impact. Any number between 0 and 1 represents a person who is more or less susceptible to positive and negative impact. E.g., if $\beta_R = 0.8$, the agent will be infected by 80% with PI and by 20% with NI. In more detail the positive and negative impacts of the other group members are defined as:

$$PI = 1 - (1-q_R^*)(1-q_R) \tag{5}$$

$$NI = q_R * q_R \tag{6}$$

Here

$$q_R^* = \Sigma_{S \in G\backslash R} w_{SR} q_S \tag{7}$$

is a weighted sum of the emotion levels of the other group members, with weights:

$$w_{SR} = \varepsilon_S \alpha_{SR} / \Sigma_{C \in G\backslash R} \varepsilon_C \alpha_{CR} \tag{8}$$

By filling these in the equation (2), the detailed set of equations for group G is for all $R \in G$:

$$dq_R/dt = \gamma_R [\beta_R (1 - (1-q_R^*)(1-q_R)) + (1-\beta_R) q_R^* q_R - q_R] \tag{9}$$

Note that the model presented so far, represents the emotional states of all agents within a group separately. The question of how these separate individual emotional states can be interpreted and aggregated by another agent, in order to assess the collective emotional state of a group, is addressed in Section 6.

3   Simulation Results for the Emotion Contagion Spiral Model

Inspired by the theory put forward in [9], the proposed model can simulate both upward and downward emotional spirals. A large number of simulations have been performed, using standard numerical simulation software, resulting in a variety of interesting patterns. In this section some of the simulation results are discussed. More simulation results can be found in Appendix A in [23]. The next section presents results of a mathematical analysis in which for most patterns their occurrence was proven, under certain conditions.

All simulations presented below are for a group of 3 agents that are infecting each other with the same emotion. A first pattern found is that when the β's of all three agents are set to 0, the emotion levels of all of them will approximate 0, with speed depending on the δ_R (susceptibility) and ε_S α_{SR} (individual and group characteristics); see Fig. 2 (with time on the x-axis and emotion strength on the y-axis). The reverse happens when all β's are set to 1, then all agents will achieve an equilibrium of 1. The occurrence of these patterns have been proved mathematically in Theorem 2, discussed in the next section.

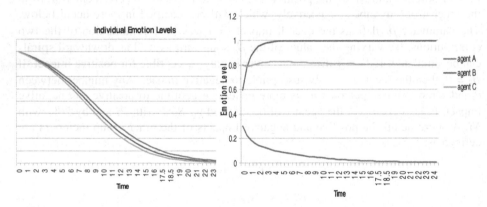

Fig. 2. Simulation trace 1 (all β=0, all δ_a=0.6 δ_b=0.7, δ_c=0.8, and all w_{DC}=0.2)

Fig. 3. Simulation trace 2 (β (a, b, c) = (0, 1, 0.8), all δ_R=0.9, all w_{DC}=0.9)

Another situation occurs when the three agents have their β's set to: 0, 1 and any other number. A situation was simulated in which agent a is susceptible only with negative impact ($\beta = 0$), agent b is only susceptible with positive impact ($\beta = 1$), and agent c is susceptible to more positive than negative impact ($\beta = 0.8$). In Fig. 3, it is shown that in this case all equilibria match the agent's β. The speed of ascend or descend again depends on the susceptibility of the agent (setting of δ_R) and the situational factors at the individual and group level (represented by ε_S and α_{SR}). This illustrates the more general result expressed in Proposition 3, discussed in the next section. A next simulated situation (see Fig. 4), is one where all three agents are equally susceptible to positive and negative impact, by setting every agent's β to 0.5. In this situation all agents approximate equilibrium at 0.6; this equilibrium is the average of the initial emotional level. This simulation illustrates Theorem 3, discussed

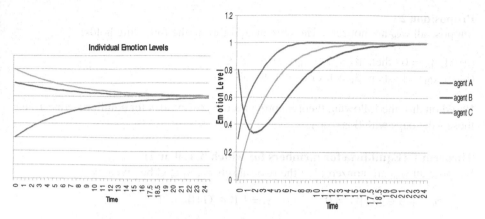

Fig. 4. Simulation trace 3 (all β=0.5, all δ_R=0.1, all w_{DC}=0.9)

Fig. 5. Simulation trace 4 (β (a, b, c) = β (1, 0.3, 0.8), all δ_R=0.9, w_{ba}=0.625, w_{ca}=0.375, w_{ab}=0.64, w_{cb}=0.36, w_{ac}=0.4, w_{bc}=0.6)

in the next section. In the next situation presented, the settings are: β (a, b, c) = β (1, 0.3, 0.8), as shown in Fig. 5. This represents a situation where agent a is only or fully susceptible to positive impact, agent b is susceptible more towards negative impact and agent c is more susceptible towards positive impact. Interestingly, agent b does not have equilibrium of 0 or below 0.5: all agents have equilibrium of 1. An indication for the height of the equilibrium could be the average β, which is 0.7 in this situation. This makes it possible to lift the emotional level of all group members to make the group-as-a-whole achieve an upward spiral [9]. In the mathematical analysis such behavior has been proved to occur (between two agents) in Theorem 4.

4 Mathematical Analysis for the Emotion Contagion Spiral Model

This section presents some of the results of a mathematical analysis of the model that has been made. More results and proofs can be found in Appendix B in [23]. First, the following conditions on monotonicity have been found.

Proposition 1 (Monotonicity Conditions)
(a) If $\beta_A = 0$ then $q_A(t)$ is always monotonically decreasing;
    it is strictly decreasing when $q_A*(t) < 1$ and $q_A(t) > 0$.
(b) If $\beta_B = 1$ then $q_B(t)$ is always monotonically increasing;
    it is strictly increasing when $q_B*(t) > 0$ and $q_B(t) < 1$.
(c) If $\beta_A \leq 0.5$ and $q_A*(t) \leq q_A(t)$ then $q_A(t)$ is monotonically decreasing;
    it is strictly decreasing when $q_A*(t) < q_A(t)$.
(d) If $\beta_B \geq 0.5$ and $q_B*(t) \geq q_B(t)$ then $q_B(t)$ is monotonically increasing;
    it is strictly increasing when $q_B*(t) > q_B(t)$.

Next, equilibria have been investigated. First, conditions have been established for the case of an equilibrium with one of the emotion values 0 or 1.

Proposition 2
Suppose all w_{SR} are nonzero. Then for an equilibrium the following holds:

(a) If $q_A = 0$ then $\beta_A = 0$ or $q_C = 0$ for all C
(b) If $q_B = 1$ then $\beta_B = 1$ or $q_C = 1$ for all C

Based on this, the following theorem provides the possibilities for equilibria concerning those subgroups with β is 0 or 1.

Theorem 1 (Equilibria for members for which β is 0 or 1)
Suppose all w_{SR} are nonzero. Let the two subsets S_0, $S_1 \subseteq G$ be given by

$$S_0 = \{ A \in G \mid \beta_A = 0 \} \qquad S_1 = \{ B \in G \mid \beta_B = 1 \}$$

Then for an equilibrium the following holds:

(a) If $A \in S_0$ then $q_A = 0$ or $q_C = 1$ for all $C \neq A$. If $B \in S_1$ then $q_B = 1$ or $q_C = 0$ for all $C \neq B$.
(b) If $\#(S_0) \geq 2$, i.e., there are at least two members A_1 and A_2 with $\beta_{A1} = 0$ and $\beta_{A2} = 0$, then either $q_A = 0$ for all $A \in S_0$ or $q_C = 1$ for all $C \in G$.
(c) If $\#(S_1) \geq 2$, i.e., there are at least two members B_1 and B_2 with $\beta_{B1} = 1$ and $\beta_{B2} = 1$, then either $q_B = 1$ for all $B \in S_1$ or $q_C = 0$ for all $C \in G$.
(d) If $\#(S_0) \geq 2$ and $\#(S_1) \geq 2$, then there are three possibilities:

  (i) $q_C = 0$ for all $C \in G$
  (ii) $q_C = 1$ for all $C \in G$
  (iii) $q_A = 0$ for all $A \in S_0$ and $q_B = 1$ for all $B \in S_1$

In the specific case, that for all group members β is 0 or 1, a complete classification of equilibria can be obtained; for an example, see Fig. 2.

Theorem 2 (Equilibria when all β's are equal to 0 or 1)
Suppose all w_{SR} are nonzero and for all C it holds $\beta_C = 0$ or $\beta_C = 1$, in other words, the whole group G is partitioned into the two subsets

$$S_0 = \{ A \in G \mid \beta_A = 0 \} \text{ and } S_1 = \{ B \in G \mid \beta_B = 1 \}.$$

Then for an equilibrium the following hold:

(a) If $S_0 = G$ and $S_1 = \varnothing$, i.e., $\beta_C = 0$ for all C, then either
     $q_C = 0$ for all C (attracting) or $q_C = 1$ for all C (non-attracting).
(b) If $S_1 = G$ and $S_0 = \varnothing$, i.e., $\beta_C = 1$ for all C, then either
     $q_C = 0$ for all C (non-attracting) or $q_C = 1$ for all C (attracting).
(c) If $\#(S_0) = \#(S_1) = 1$, i.e., there is exactly one member A with $\beta_A = 0$, and exactly one member B with $\beta_B = 1$, then there are two possibilities:

  (i) $q_A = 0$ for $A \in S_0$ and q_B has any value for $B \in S_1$
  (ii) $q_B = 1$ for $B \in S_1$ and q_A has any value for $A \in S_0$

(d) If $\#(S_0) = 1$ and $\#(S_1) \geq 2$, i.e., there is exactly one member A with $\beta_A = 0$, and there are at least two members B_1 and B_2 with $\beta_{B1} = \beta_{B2} = 1$, then there are two possibilities:

  (i) $q_C = 0$ for all $C \in G$

  (ii) $q_B = 1$ for all $B \in S_1$ and q_A has any value for $A \in S_0$

(e) If $\#(S1) = 1$, and $\#(S0) \geq 2$, i.e., there is exactly one member B with $\beta B = 1$, and there are at least two members A_1 and A_2 with $\beta_{A1} = \beta_{A2} = 0$, then there are two possibilities:

  (i) $q_C = 1$ for all $C \in G$

  (ii) $q_A = 0$ for all $A \in S_0$ and q_B has any value for $B \in S_1$

(f) If $\#(S_0) \geq 2$ and $\#(S_1) \geq 2$, i.e., there are at least two members A_1 and A_2 with $\beta A1 = \beta A2 = 0$ and also at least two members B_1 and B_2 with $\beta_{B1} = \beta_{B2} = 1$, then there are three possibilities:

  (i) $q_C = 0$ for all $C \in G$

  (ii) $q_C = 1$ for all $C \in G$

  (iii) $q_A = 0$ for all $A \in S_0$ and $q_B = 1$ for all $B \in S_1$

For the specific case of three group members, where one member has β is 0, one has 1 and one has neither, the following holds; for an example, see Fig. 3.

Proposition 3 (A case for 3 members)
Consider a group G which consists of three members named by a, b, c with $\beta a = 0$, $\beta b = 1$, and $\beta c = \beta$, where $0 < \beta < 1$ is assumed. Moreover, suppose all w_{SR} are nonzero. Then the following are the possibilities for equilibria:

  (i) $q_a = q_b = q_c = 0$

  (ii) $q_a = q_b = q_c = 1$

  (iii) $q_a = 0$, $q_b = 1$ and $q_c = \beta w_{bc} / ((1-\beta)w_{ac} + \beta w_{bc})$

In particular, when $w_{ac} = w_{bc}$, then the value for q_c in (iii) is β.

The following proposition shows that only in trivial cases a group member with β not 0 or 1 can reach 0 or 1.

Proposition 4 ($qA = 0$ with $\beta A > 0$ or $qB = 1$ with $\beta B < 1$)
Suppose all w_{SR} are nonzero. Then for an equilibrium it holds

  (i) If $q_A = 0$ for some A with $\beta_A > 0$ then $q_C = 0$ for all $C \in G$.

  (ii) If $q_B = 1$ for some B with $\beta B < 1$ then $q_C = 1$ for all $C \in G$.

The case that all group member converge to an equal equilibrium value which is not 0 or 1, only occurs when all β's are 0.5; for an example, see Fig. 4.

Theorem 3 (Equal equilibrium values for all members)
Suppose all w_{SR} are nonzero, then for an equilibrium the following are equivalent:

  (i) For some q with $0 < q < 1$ it holds $q_C = q$ for all C.

  (ii) For all C it holds $\beta_C = 0.5$.

For the case of two persons, a complete classification can be found:

Theorem 4 (The case of two persons)
Suppose the group consists of two persons named by a and b. Then for an equilibrium, there are the following possibilities:
(i) When $\beta a + \beta b \neq 1$ the only two possibilities are:

$$q_a = q_b = 0 \qquad \text{attracting when } \beta_a + \beta_b < 1$$
$$q_a = q_b = 1 \qquad \text{attracting when } \beta_a + \beta_b > 1$$

(ii) When $\beta_a + \beta_b = 1$ attracting equilibria occur where qa and qb get values between 0 and 1.

5 Formal Verification of the Emotion Contagion Spiral Model

This section addresses the analysis of the emotion contagion spiral model by verification of dynamic properties. Following [5], the dynamics of a model can be analyzed by specifying certain dynamic statements that are (or are not) expected to hold in terms of temporal logical and numerical expressions, and automatically verifying these statements against simulation traces. The purpose of this type of verification is to check whether the model behaves as it should. A typical example of a property that may be checked is: whether no unexpected situations occur, such as a variable running out of its bounds (e.g., $q_A(t) > 1$, for some t and A), or whether eventually an equilibrium value is reached. Other more complex examples can be found in the propositions and theorems presented in the previous section. By running a large number of simulations and automatically verifying such properties against the resulting simulation traces, the modeler can easily locate sources of errors in the model.

For the emotion contagion spiral model, a number of such dynamic properties have been formalized in the language TTL [5] and automatically checked. The temporal predicate logical language TTL supports formal specification and analysis of dynamic properties, covering both qualitative and quantitative aspects. TTL is built on atoms referring to states of the world, time points and traces, i.e., trajectories of states over time. In addition, dynamic properties are (sorted) temporal predicate logic statements that can be formulated with respect to traces based on the state ontology Ont in the following manner. Given a trace γ over state ontology Ont, the state in γ at time point t is denoted by state(γ, t). These states can be related to state properties via the formally defined satisfaction relation denoted by the infix predicate |=: state(γ, t) |= p denotes that state property p holds in trace γ at time t. Based on these statements, dynamic properties can be formulated in a formal manner in a sorted predicate logic, using quantifiers over time and traces and the usual logical connectives such as ¬, ∧, ∨, ⇒, ∀, ∃. A dedicated software environment has been developed for TTL, featuring both a Property Editor for building and editing TTL properties and a Checking Tool that enables automated formal verification of such properties against a set of (simulated or empirical) traces. Based on the language TTL, different types of dynamic properties of the emotion contagion spiral processes have been formalized, such as: properties addressing limit behavior (equilibria reached), properties of the process from initial values to the equilibria and comparative properties that relate two traces for two different parameter settings of the model. Below, a number of these properties are introduced, both in semi-formal and in informal notation (note that they are all defined for a particular trace γ (or $\gamma1$ and $\gamma2$), and sometimes for a particular time interval between tb and te):

P1a - Emotional stability for agent a around value x
For all time points t between tb and te in trace γ the level of emotion of agent a is between $x - \alpha$ and $x + \alpha$ (where α is a constant)

P1a(γ:TRACE, tb, te:TIME, x:REAL, a:AGENT, α:REAL) $\equiv$
$\forall$t:TIME $\forall$y:REAL   state(γ, t) $\models$ emotion(agent(a), y) & tb $\leq$ t $\leq$ te $\Rightarrow$ x-α $\leq$ y $\leq$ x+α

Property P1a can be used to check whether an agent's level of emotion stays around a certain (given) value. For example, for α = 0.000001, property P1a(traceFig3, 15, 50, 1.0, b, 0.000001) was true. One step further, P1a can be used as a building block to check the propositions and theorems related to equilibria presented in Section 4 against the generated traces. For example, property P1b checks whether Theorem 3 holds:

P1b - Equal Equilibria for Beta's of 0.5
If   for all agents a1 and a2, w_{a1a2} is nonzero in trace γ
then   if for all a, β_a = 0.5, eventually the same equilibrium q
          (between 0 and 1) will occur for all agents
    and   if for all agents eventually the same equilibrium q
          (between 0 and 1) will occur, β_a=0.5 for all agents a.

P1b(γ:TRACE, α:REAL) $\equiv$
[$\forall$a1,a2:AGENT [a1$\neq$a2 $\Rightarrow$
$\exists$w:REAL>0 [state(γ, 1) $\models$ has_weight_for(agent(a1), agent(a2),w)]]] $\Rightarrow$
[[$\forall$a:AGENT state(γ, 1) $\models$ has_beta(agent(a),0.5)] $\Rightarrow$
$\exists$q:REAL $\forall$a:AGENT P1b(γ,40,50,q,a, α)]] &
[[$\exists$q:REAL $\forall$a:AGENT P1b(γ,40,50,q,a, α)] $\Rightarrow$
[$\forall$a:AGENT state(γ, 1) $\models$ has_beta(agent(a),0.5)]]

This property, which has been proven in the mathematical analysis, has been checked for α = 0.15 for all generated traces, and indeed was confirmed.

P2a - Monotonic Increase of Emotion[1]
For all time points t1 and t2 with t1 < t2 between tb and te in trace γ
if   at t1 the level of emotion of agent a is x1
      and   at t2 the level of emotion of agent a is x2
then   x1 $\leq$ x2.

---

[1] A strict variant of such properties can be created by replacing $\leq$ by <.

P2a(γ:TRACE, tb, te:TIME, a:AGENT) $\equiv$
$\forall$t1,t2:TIME $\forall$x1,x2:REAL
state(γ, t1) $\models$ emotion(agent(a), x1) & state(γ, t2) $\models$ emotion(agent(a), x2) & tb $\leq$ t1 $\leq$ te
& tb $\leq$ t2 $\leq$ te & t1 < t2 $\Rightarrow$ x1 $\leq$ x2

Property P2a and the variant P2b addressing monotonic decrease (by replacing $\leq$ in the consequent by $\geq$) can be used to check whether an agent's level of emotion increases or decreases monotonically over a certain interval. Such monotonicity, for example, occurs for agent a during the whole trace shown in Fig. 3. (i.e., property P2b(traceFig3, 1, 50, a) succeeded). Furthermore, these properties can be used as building blocks to check the propositions and theorems related to monotonicity presented in Section 4 against the generated traces. For example, property P2c checks whether part (c) and (d) of Proposition 1 hold:

P2c - Conditional Monotonicity
For all agents a1,
if β_{a1} > 0.5 and q_{a1}* $\geq$ q_{a1} between tb and te in trace γ
then q_{a1} is monotonically increasing during this interval
and if β_{a1} < 0.5 and q_{a1}* $\leq$ q_{a1} between tb and te in trace γ
then q_{a1} is monotonically decreasing during this interval.

P2c(γ:TRACE, tb, te:TIME) $\equiv$
$\forall$a1:AGENT   [[$\forall$t:TIME $\exists$a2,a3:AGENT $\exists$b,x1,x2,x3,w2,w3:REAL
state(γ, 1) $\models$ has_beta(agent(a1),b) & b>0.5 & state(γ, t) $\models$ emotion(agent(a1), x1) &
state(γ, t) $\models$ emotion(agent(a2), x2) & state(γ, t) $\models$ emotion(agent(a3), x3) & a2$\neq$a3 &
tb $\leq$ t $\leq$ te &
state(γ, 1) $\models$ has_weight_for(agent(a2),agent(a1),w2) &
state(γ, 1) $\models$ has_weight_for (agent(a3),agent(a1),w3) &
w2*x2+w3*x3 $\geq$ w1]
$\Rightarrow$ p2a(γ, tb, te, a1)] & [[$\forall$t:TIME $\exists$a2,a3:AGENT $\exists$b,x1,x2,x3,w2,w3:REAL
state(γ, 1) $\models$ has_beta(agent(a1),b) & b<0.5 & state(γ, t) $\models$ emotion(agent(a1), x1) &
state(γ, t) $\models$ emotion(agent(a2), x2) & state(γ, t) $\models$ emotion(agent(a3), x3) & a2$\neq$a3 &
tb $\leq$ t $\leq$ te &
state(γ, 1) $\models$ has_weight_for(agent(a2),agent(a1),w2) &
state(γ, 1) $\models$ has_weight_for (agent(a3),agent(a1),w3) & w2*x2+w3*x3 $\leq$ w1]
$\Rightarrow$ p2b(γ, tb, te, a1)]

Here, q_{a1}* is calculated as explained in Formula (3). This property has been confirmed for all possible intervals in all generated traces.

P3 - Emotion Approaches Value x with Speed s
For all time points t1 and t2 between tb and te in trace γ

if   at t1 the level of emotion of agent a is x1
  and   at t2 the level of emotion of agent a is x2
  and   t2 = t1+1
then   s * |x-x1| $\geq$ |x-x2| (where s is a constant < 1).

P3(γ:TRACE, tb, te:TIME, x:REAL, a:AGENT) ≡
∀t1,t2:TIME ∀x1,x2:REAL
state(γ, t1) ⊨ emotion(agent(a), x1) & state(γ, t2) ⊨ emotion(agent(a), x2) & tb ≤ t1 ≤ te
& tb ≤ t2 ≤ te & t2 = t1+1 ⇒ |x-x1| * s ≥ |x-x2|

Property P3 can be used to check whether an agent's level of emotion approaches some given value x, and additionally determines the speed s with which this happens (where $0 < s < 1$, and a high s denotes a slow speed). For the trace shown in Fig. 3, it turned out that agent a approaches emotion level 0 with a speed of approximately 0.959, agent b approaches 1 with a speed of 1.000, and agent c approaches 0.8 with a speed of 0.999.

P4 - Higher Beta's lead to Higher Emotion Levels
If   for all agents the initial level of emotion is higher (or equal) in trace γ1 than in γ2
and   for all agents the beta is higher (or equal) in trace γ1 than in γ2
then   for all agents the final level of emotion will be higher (or equal) in trace γ1 than in γ2.

P4(γ1, γ2:TRACE, tb, te:TIME) ≡
[∀a:AGENT ∃x1,x2:REAL
state(γ1, tb) ⊨ emotion(agent(a),x1) & state(γ2, tb) ⊨ emotion(agent(a),x2) & x1≥x2] &
[∀a:AGENT ∃x1,x2:REAL state(γ1, tb) ⊨ has_beta(agent(a),x1) &
state(γ2, tb) ⊨ has_beta(agent(a),x2) & x1≥x2] ⇒
[∀a:AGENT ∃x1,x2:REAL state(γ1, te) ⊨ emotion(agent(a),x1) &
state(γ2, te) ⊨ emotion(agent(a),x2) & x1≥x2]

This property can be used to compare traces with different parameter settings. It turned out to hold for all generated traces, as long as the initial values were not 0 or 1.

6 Integrating the Emotion Spiral Model within an Agent Model

The emotion contagion spiral model described in the previous sections has been integrated within an ambient agent model to analyze the occurring dynamics of emotion contagion spirals. The ambient agent predicts the level of a given type of emotion (considered positive in the case study presented here) in the group and based on an assessment of this it proposes actions. A generated assessment indicates when the group emotion level at some (future) time point is predicted to be too low, compared to a certain norm (*EN*). When the agent detects this, it comes up with action proposals. As an input for the predictions the concept expressed emotion level ($\varepsilon_S q_A$) is used: the emotion level that can be observed from someone's face, for example, by use of a face reader. To integrate the emotion contagion spiral model within an agent model, a generic agent model for human-aware ambient computing (see [4]) was used as a point of departure, as was done in [6].

6.1   Assessment of Emotion Contagion Spirals

The dynamic properties defining the model that reasons about emotion contagion spirals are described below. Here the beliefs on emotion expressiveness, openness, and channel strengths are assumed to be initially given and to persist until they are changed. An example scenario is assumed where at some (initial) point in time the emotion levels of the members are observed, and from that time point onwards, the emotion levels for subsequent time points are predicted.

First the role of observed expressed emotions is formalised. The agent is assumed to be connected to observation equipment in the form of a face reader with software that detects emotion expressions from face images. This expressed emotion EV results from the emotion level V and the expressiveness E by which the emotion is displayed on the face. In the model it is assumed that the expressed emotion level is formalised as the product $V*E$. Note that this means that it is assumed that the expressiveness (being a number between 0 and 1) always reduces the level of the emotion: $EV \leq E$. In other words, this assumption excludes the situation that an emotion level is expressed that is not there (no faking of emotions). Moreover, note that in ADR2 below it is assumed that the expressiveness factor E is nonzero. Then under the assumptions discussed above, from an expressed emotion level EV the emotion level V itself can be determined as $V = EV/E$.

ADR1   Observing group members' expressed emotion levels
If   the agent observes an expressed emotion level
then   the ambient agent will believe this.
    observes(agent, has_ expressed_emotion_level_at(A, V, T))
    —» belief(agent, has_ expressed_emotion_level_at(A, V, T))

ADR2   Generating an emotion level belief from a belief on an expressed emotion level
If   the agent believes that a group member has expressed emotion level EV
and   that this group member has expressiveness E
then   it will generate a belief that this group member has emotion level EV/E
    belief(agent, has_expressed_emotion_level_at(A, EV, T)) &
    belief(agent, has_expressiveness(E))
    —» belief(agent, has_emotion_level_at(A, EV/E, T))

The following two properties show how the specific emotion spiral model introduced here is integrated within the agent model.

ADR3   Generating beliefs on contagion strengths
If   the ambient agent believes that B has expressiveness E
  and   the ambient agent believes that the channel from B to A has strength C
  and   the ambient agent believes that A has openness D
then the ambient agent will believe that the contagion strength from B to A will be
    $E*C*D$
  belief(agent, has_expressiveness(B, E)) &
  belief(agent, has_channel_strength(B, A, C)) & belief(agent, has_openness(A, D))
    —» belief(agent, has_contagion_strength(B, A, E*C*D))

ADR4 Updating beliefs on emotion levels

If $A{\neq}B$ and $B{\neq}C$ and $C{\neq}A$
and   the ambient agent believes that A has emotion level $V1$ at time T
and   the ambient agent believes that B has emotion level $V2$ at time T
and   the ambient agent believes that C has emotion level $V3$ at time T
and   the ambient agent believes that the contagion strength from B to A is $CS2$
and   the ambient agent believes that the contagion strength from C to A is $CS3$
and   the ambient agent believes that the step size is DT
and   the ambient agent believes that the A has orientation $BETA1$
then   the ambient agent will believe that the emotion level of A will be
        $V1 + (CS2+CS3)* [BETA1 *(1 - (1-((CS2/(CS2+CS3)) *V2 +$
        $(CS3/(CS2+CS3))* V3))*(1-V1)) + (1- BETA1)* ((CS2/(CS2+CS3))* V2$
        $+ (CS3/(CS2+CS3)) *V3) *V1 - V1] * DT$ at time $T+DT$

```
A≠B & B≠C & C≠A &
belief(agent, has_emotion_level_at(A, V1, T)) &
belief(agent, has_emotion_level_at (B, V2, T)) &
belief(agent, has_emotion_level_at(C, V3, T)) &
belief(agent, has_contagion_strength(B, A, CS2)) &
belief(agent, has_contagion_strength (C, A, CS3)) &
belief(agent, step_size(DT))
—» belief(agent, has_emotion_level_at(A, V1 + (CS2+CS3)*
   [ BETA1 *(1 – (1-((CS2 / (CS2+CS3)) *V2 + (CS3 / (CS2+CS3))* V3))* (1-V1)) +
   (1- BETA1)* ((CS2 / (CS2+CS3))* V2 + (CS3 / (CS2+CS3)) *V3) *V1 – V1]*
   DT, T+DT))
```

An analysis also involves an assessment of the (expected) level of the group's emotion. To this end, first a belief on the group's emotion level is generated.

ADR5 Determining beliefs on the group's emotion level
If   the ambient agent believes that the group members have
          emotion levels $V1, V2, V3$
and   relevance $R1, R2, R3$ respectively
then   it will believe that the group's emotion level is $R1*V1+ R2*V2+R3*V3$.

```
belief(agent, has_emotion_level_at(a1, V1, T)) &
belief(agent, has_emotion_level_at (a2, V2, T)) &
belief(agent, has_emotion_level_at(a3, V3, T)) &
belief(agent, has_relevance(a1, R1)) & belief(agent, has_relevance(a2, R2)) &
belief(agent, has_relevance(a3, R3))
—» belief(agent, group_emotion_ level_at(R1*V1+ R2*V2+R3*V3, T))
```

An assessment is generated when the predicted group emotion level at some time point is too low, compared to a certain norm. The assessment includes an estimation of how much the group emotion level is too low (the *group emotion deficient*):

ADR6 Assessment of the group's emotion level
  If   the ambient agent believes that the group emotion level *V* at time *T* is lower
         than the emotion norm *EN*,
  then   it will assess the situation as having a group emotion deficient *EN-V* at *T*.
    belief(agent, group_emotion_ level_at(V, T)) &
    belief(agent, group_emotion_norm (EN)) & V<EN
    —» assessment(agent, group_emotion_ deficient_at(EN-V, T))

6.2 Generating Proposals for Support Actions

Using the assessment and based on
the integrated emotion spiral model, a
support model generates support
actions. The support model used was
fully adopted from [6]; it uses a
heuristic approach. When a negative
assessment of the (future) group
emotion state is made, then the
ambient agent proposes actions to the team leader, in order to avoid such states. To this
end, two heuristics are applied: (1) let the group members with lowest emotion levels
get less impact on the other members, and get more impact from the other members,
and (2) let the group members with highest emotion levels get more impact on the
other members, and get less impact from the other members. A low and high threshold
are assumed for this. For an overview of the action options based on the two heuristics,
see Table 2. The extent by which an action is proposed depends on the deficiency
measure indicated by the assessment. Moreover, a feasibility ranking of the possible
actions is taken into account; for more details, see [6].

Table 2. Overview of the action options

	person under low threshold	person above high threshold
expressiveness	decrease	increase
channels: to others	decrease	increase
from others	increase	decrease

7   Simulation Results for the Ambient Agent Model

The LEADSTO software environment [9] has been used to perform a number of
simulation experiments for the agent model for group emotion spiral support. An
example scenario is used to illustrate it. The simulation for the assessment is
discussed in Section 7.1, and Section 7.2 shows the generation of support actions.

7.1 Simulation of the Assessment of Emotion Contagion Spirals

In this section the simulation results of the analysis process are shown in an example
scenario that represents a situation where the group emotion is happiness and is
analyzed by the ambient agent. In this example, the ambient agent generates beliefs on
the individual emotion levels of three group members, named Arnie, Bernie and
Charlie (see ADR2), and of the group emotion level at different points in time (see
ADR5). The agent also assesses the (expected) group's emotion deficient at a future
time point based on its belief of the group emotion level and the norm for the group
emotion level. The norm of the group emotion can be set by the modeler and represents
in this example an optimal level of happiness, at which the team can perform as
optimal as possible. The norm was set to *0.60* in this example.

In this example scenario Arnie, Bernie and Charlie are all not very happy (initial emotion levels are *0.3* and *0.1*). They are all very open to receive each others happiness, all have an openness δ of *0.9*. Arnie can send his emotions most effectively to others, because his contagion strength, which is his channel α multiplied

Table 3. Overview of the parameter settings

	Arnie	Bernie	Charlie
Initial emotion level q	0.3	0.1	0.1
Impact β	0.3	1	0.6
Contagion strength $\varepsilon a*\alpha ab$	0.72		
Contagion strength $\varepsilon a*\alpha ac$	0.72		
Contagion strength $\varepsilon b*\alpha ba$		0.45	
Contagion strength $\varepsilon b*\alpha bc$		0.45	
Contagion strength $\varepsilon c*\alpha ca$			0.09
Contagion strength $\varepsilon c*\alpha cb$			0.09
openness δ	0.9	0.9	0.9
relevance ρ	0.34	0.33	0.33

by his expressiveness ε, is *0.72* for both Bernie and Charlie. Bernie can send emotions less effectively, his contagion strength is *0.45*. Charlie can send his emotions with even less power: his contagion strength is *0.09*. For an overview of the settings, see Table 3.

In Fig. 6. a simulation trace is shown in which the horizontal axis represents time, and the vertical axis represents quantitative information about generation of ambient agent's beliefs on the individual and group emotion levels at different (future) time points. In this situation, the total group emotion level goes from 0.49 downwards and through an upwards spiral mechanism to 0.58 in 500 time steps. This means that the group emotion level is always below the norm of 0.60. In this analysis model, our ambient agent predicts the future development of the group emotion level and this prediction shows that it will stay below the norm for all the future time steps. In this case it can propose appropriate actions to the team leader early in time, to help the group emotion level get above the norm faster. The simulations are based on step size $\Delta t = 0.1$.

On the x-axis in Fig. 6., time goes from *0* to *1*. This time actually represents processing time of the ambient agent. The idea is that the agent reads the emotions of

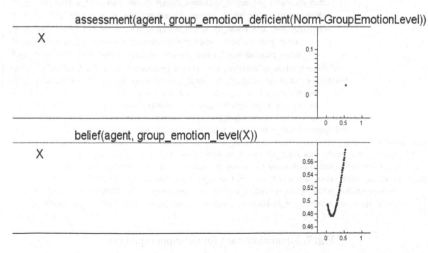

Fig. 6. Simulation trace of the analysis processes

the persons at time point *0* and from that time point the ambient agent starts to generate beliefs on the development of the emotion levels of the group members and the group as a whole. The developments of the emotion levels (simulated by the ambient agent from time point *0* to *0.5*) are estimated for real future time points *0* to *5*. At time point *0.5* on the x-axis, the agent makes the assessment of an expected emotion deficiency for real future time point *5*. The ambient agent assesses that on future time point *5*, there is a group emotion deficiency to be expected (of about *0.04*).

7.2 Simulation of the Support Process

In this section, the example scenario of the previous section is extended with the support of the ambient agent. The assumption is made that Arnie, Bernie and Charlie are working on a task together that is perhaps stressful, since they are not very happy (initial emotion levels are *0.3* or *0.1*). Arnie is very charismatic and he works together a lot with Bernie and Charlie, this is represented in his high contagion strength. Charlie on the other hand is very introvert and therefore his contagion strength is weak. Bernie has a medium contagion strength. All three are open to receive happy emotions from others, since they all have a high level of openness. In the previous section it was shown that the ambient agent predicted the future development of the group emotion level, namely an upward spiral that still was below the norm at future time point *5*. Therefore, based on its heuristics, the ambient agent detects which group members are high or low emotion members, and generates action options that decrease or increase parameters related to these members: expressiveness or channel strength. After ranking these options, the agent proposes to the group leader those options, which do not exceed a certain feasibility threshold. An example of (a part of) such a trace is shown in Fig. 7. Here, time is on the horizontal axis, and state

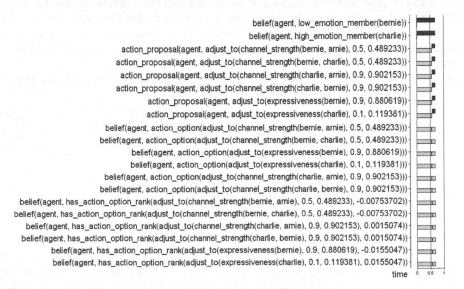

Fig. 7. Simulation trace for the support process

properties are on the vertical axis. A dark box indicates that a state property is true. Fig. 7. shows that the ambient agent detects the high and/or low emotion members (Charlie is detected as a high emotion member and Bernie as a low emotion member.) (see SDR1 and SDR2 in [6]), the action-options are ranked (see SDR9 in [6]) and the ambient agent proposes the actions that do not exceed the feasibility threshold to the group leader (see SDR10 in [6]).

8 Discussion

Within teams performing critical tasks, a team leader is responsible for a good spirit in the team. Due to high pressure, the emotions within the team may easily take the form of a negative spiral. Therefore, it is challenging to regulate such patterns.

Recently, researchers have started to investigate emotions in a social context more extensively. For the work reported in the current paper, specific work on emotion contagion spirals was taken as a point of departure; cf. [8], [9], [10]. In the current paper, a multi-agent-based model for emotion contagion spirals has been presented and analyzed. Although an extensive empirical validation is left for future work, it turned out that the model is able to produce various interesting emerging patterns as described (informally) in the psychological literature, including the upward and downward emotion spirals discussed in [9]. Although this is not an exhaustive proof, it is an important indication that the model behaves as expected. In contrast to most existing (symbolic) agent-based modeling approaches, the current approach represents a multi-agent system using numerical techniques.

Literature on computational models of emotion contagion spirals is scarce. Most existing computational models of emotional processes represent emotion as a process or state that depends on observed stimuli by a single agent; e.g., [7], [17], [21]. These existing computational models of emotion differ from our proposed model, in that the focus in these models lies more on individual emotions, not on collective emotion. The only computational models that come close to the process modeling of this current work can be found in the area of social science, named social diffusion modeling. Examples of social diffusion models are: the diffusion of innovations, see [19], social movements like political interests and parties, see [14], and crowd behavior, as in emergency evacuation, see [18][2]. Even though social diffusion models can simulate the contagion of a certain innovation and use similar concepts as the current work does, such as a sender, receiver and communication channel, these computational models of social diffusion also differ from our model, in the way that they model the complex spread of innovations as diffusion that is asymmetric in time, irreversible, and nondeterministic. Our model of emotion contagion spirals, models the continuous spread of emotions among the group members over time, which can have many patterns in it and is reversible in time.

Based on the model for emotion contagion spirals an ambient agent model was developed, that uses the computational model to assess the expected emotion contagion

---

[2] The question to what extent our model is able to simulate such completely different processes is beyond the scope of this paper. Although these processes share some characteristics with the process of emotion contagion, for other factors (e.g. openness, or the tendency to adapt emotions upward or downward) it is not trivial to find a counterpart.

spirals at future time points, and proposes actions to the team leader to regulate these spirals. The generic agent model for human-aware ambient intelligence applications described in [4] was taken as a point of departure, as also was chosen in [6]. One of the possible applications of the resulting ambient agent model, could be to analyze and support group emotion in virtual meetings. For example, when two groups at two locations in the world are video-conferencing, a software agent could measure the group emotion of one group and show this emotion level to the group leader of the other group. The ambient software agent could then, if necessary, provide support to the group leader, e.g. by analyzing n is the best time to let the other group make a decision, or how to calm the other group down after their anger level got too high during decision making.

In follow-up research, more attention will be paid to the model's external validation of the model for emotion contagion spirals. The mathematical and automated analyses described above have been successfully performed to guarantee internal validity, and it fits to patterns described informally in (social) psychological literature. Nevertheless, this does not guarantee that the model is directly applicable to humans in a more detailed and more quantitative manner, and in particular it does not show which personality parameter values fit which person. Therefore, as a next step, a more detailed validation of the model in laboratory experiments is planned. The idea is to create a setting in which various humans interact in a room, while continuously being subject to (physiological) measurements (e.g., using emotion recognition approaches as discussed in [11]) to assess their emotions. The obtained data can then be used in order to fine-tune the model using adaptive and machine learning techniques. This will not only provide a more detailed validation of the model, but also result in realistic parameter settings for different types of individuals.

Another possibility for future work is to combine two different models addressing the transfer of emotions between group members, namely the absorption model presented in [3], and the model for spirals introduced in the current paper. Within a heterogeneous group, some members may absorb emotions while others may amplify emotions. The former type of members may be described by the model from [3], whereas the latter type of members better fit the model in the current paper. By combining the two models a more heterogeneous group may be modeled.

A final possibility to extend the model is to consider multiple emotions. Currently, the group contagion spirals of only one emotion can be modeled. It will be interesting, for example, to study the impact of simultaneous occurrences of happiness and anger within the same group, or the interaction between anger and fear within a group. For specific types of emotions, specific values may have to be estimated, e.g. α, δ, ρ. However, if also interaction between different emotions is to be addressed (for example, anger in one person affecting fear in another person), more specific work is needed, which is planned for the future.

References

1. Barsade, S.G.: The ripple effect: Emotional contagion and its influence on group behavior. Administrative Science Quarterly 47(4), 644–675 (2002)
2. Barsade, S.G., Gibson, D.E.: Group Emotion: a View from Top and Bottom. In: Gruenfeld, D., Mannix, E., Neale, M. (eds.) Research on managing groups and teams, pp. 81–102. JAI Press, Stamford (1998)

3. Bosse, T., Duell, R., Memon, Z.A., Treur, J., van der Wal, C.N.: A Multi-agent Model for Mutual Absorption of Emotions. In: Otamendi, J., Bargiela, A., Montes, J.L., Pedrera, L.M.D. (eds.) Proceedings of the 23rd European Conference on Modelling and Simulation, ECMS 2009, pp. 212–218 (2009)
4. Bosse, T., Hoogendoorn, M., Klein, M., Treur, J.: A Generic Agent Architecture for Human-Aware Ambient Computing. In: Mangina, E., Carbo, J., Molina, J.M. (eds.) Agent-Based Ubiquitous Computing. Series on Ambient and Pervasive Intelligence, vol. 1, pp. 35–62. World Scientific Publishers/Atlantis Press (2009); Shorter version in: Mühlhäuser, M., Ferscha, A., Aitenbichler, E. (eds.): ConstructingAmbient Intelligence: AmI 2007 Workshops Proceedings. Communications in Computer and Information Science (CCIS), vol. 11, pp. 93–103. Springer, Heidelberg (2008)
5. Bosse, T., Jonker, C.M., van der Meij, L., Sharpanskykh, A., Treur, J.: Specification and Verification of Dynamics in Agent Models. Intern. Journal of Cooperative Information Systems 18, 167–193 (2009)
6. Duell, R., Memon, Z.A., Treur, J., van der Wal, C.N.: An Ambient Agent Model for Group Emotion Support. In: Cohn, J., Nijholt, A., Pantic, M. (eds.) Proceedings of the Third International Conference on Affective Computing and Intelligent Interaction, ACII 2009, pp. 550–557. IEEE Computer Society Press, Los Alamitos (2009)
7. Elliott, C.: The Affective Reasoner: A Process Model of Emotions in a Multi-Agent System. PhD Dissertation, Northwestern University. Technical Report No.32 (1992)
8. Frederickson, B.L., Branigan, C.: Positive Emotions broaden the scope of attention and thought-action repertoires. Cognition and Emotion 19(3), 313–332 (2005)
9. Frederickson, B.L., Joiner, T.: Positive emotions trigger upward spirals toward emotional well-being. Psychological Science 13(2), 172–175 (2002)
10. Frederickson, B.L.: The role of positive emotions in positive psychology: The broaden-and-build theory of positive emotions. American Psychologist 56, 218–226 (2001)
11. Goldman, A.I., Sripada, C.S.: Simulationist models of face-based emotion recognition. Cognition 94, 193–213 (2005)
12. Hareli, S., Rafaeli, A.: Emotion cycles: On the social influence of emotion in organizations. Research in Organizational Behavior 28, 35–59 (2008)
13. Hatfield, E., Cacioppo, J.T., Rapson, R.L.: Emotional contagion. Cambridge University Press, Cambridge (1994)
14. Hedström, P., Sandell, R., Stern, C.: Mesolevel Networks and the Diffusion of Social Movements: The Case of the Swedish Social Democratic Party. American J. of Sociology 106(1), 145–172 (2000)
15. Lazarus, R.S.: Emotion and adaptation. Oxford University Press, New York (1991)
16. LeBon, G.: The Crowd. A Study of the Popular Mind. Unwin, London (1897)
17. Marsella, S., Gratch, J.: EMA: A process model of appraisal dynamics. Journal of Cognitive Systems Research 10(1), 70–90 (2009)
18. Pan, X., Han, C., Dauber, K., Law, K.: Human and social behaviour in computational modeling and analysis of egress. Automation in Construction 15(4), 448–461 (2006)
19. Rogers, E.: Diffusion of Innovations. Free Press, New York (1983)
20. Schoenewolf, G.: Emotional Contagion: Behavioral induction in individuals and groups. Modern Psycho-analysis 15, 49–61 (1990)
21. Silverman, B.G.: More Realistic Human Behavior Models for Agents in Virtual Worlds: Emotion, Stress, and Value Ontologies. T.R., Univ. of Penn./ACASA (2001)
22. Totterdell, P., Kellet, S., Teuchmann, K., Briner, R.B.: Evidence of mood linkage in work groups. Journal of Personality and Social Psychology 74, 1504–1515 (1998)
23. http://www.cs.vu.nl/~tbosse/emotion/PRIMA09/

Statistical Utterance Selection Using Word Co-occurrence for a Dialogue Agent

Naoki Isomura, Fujio Toriumi, and Kenichiro Ishii

Graduate School of Information Science,
Nagoya University, Aichi, Japan
naoki@kishii.ss.is.nagoya-u.ac.jp
{tori,kishii}@is.nagoya-u.ac.jp

Abstract. In this paper, we proposed a statistical utterance selection method for dialogue agents by applying a machine learning algorithm. We defined statistical candidate utterance selection as a question that automatically selects an appropriate utterance from speech collections prepared in advance as responses. To realize automatic utterance evaluation, we employed manually evaluated data as learning data so that relative magnitude correlation will be learned from them.

We checked the order of the automatically evaluated values to prove the validity of our proposed method. In this simulation, the result shows that the top appropriate utterance is selected at 47.5%, and it is selected within the top 10 at 78.0%. For implementing this method in agents that assist humans by replying, we found that it is quite possible to realize such an agent.

Keywords: machine learning, utterance selection, dialogue agent, non-task-oriented dialogue.

1 Introduction

Recently, computerized dialogue agents are being actively investigated and used in various fields. Not only task-oriented dialogue agents like reservation services but also non-task-oriented dialogue systems like chatter are highly anticipated.

Previously, we proposed a criterion that can objectively and quantitatively evaluate non-task-oriented dialogue agents using a Hidden Markov Model, leading to the possibility of comparatively estimating a dialogue agent's capacity in natural communication [5]. Therefore, in the next stage, our goal is to design a dialogue agent that can stimulate conversations like a talk show host, who starts a conversation with such careful preparation as developing questions with information from a dialogue partner. In this paper, our goal is to realize a function that prepares speech collection by given information before engaging in a dialogue by computer. To create such a dialogue agent, the following two problems need to be solved:

J.-J. Yang et al. (Eds.): PRIMA 2009, LNAI 5925, pp. 68–79, 2009.

1) Automatic generation of speech collections
2) Automatic selection of appropriate reactions from speech collections

This paper concentrates on the second problem, which means achieving automatic choice of an appropriate response from speech collections prepared in advance based on a dialogue partner's profile.

By achieving automatic selection of responses, we expected not only to realize a conversation agent but also an agent that can encourage humans to respond. In other words, agents can propose appropriate candidate responses that reflect the circumstances and the dialogue partner for conversations or panel discussion organizers.

Many machine learning-based statistical methods have been proposed as solutions for the problem of selecting suitable answers among multiple input choices. Consider the dependency parsing of Japanese as an example; after inputting the segments, all possible pairs of segments are classified as "dependent" or "non-dependent" [3,10]. Such a dilemma is called a binary classification problem, and machine learning methods such as Decision Tree and Maximum Entropy Method (MEM) are recognized as applicable solutions. Except for binary classification, a preference learning method also exists, which is a machine learning method that is advocated as applicable to model the relative magnitude correlation of the candidates and to rank them [7].

This paper presents a method that models the relative magnitude correlation of possible utterances and ranks them to select candidate choices. First, we define the problem of utterance selection. Then we illustrate a method used to learn how humans choose from those possible utterances. Additionally, an experiment verifies this method's validity by comparing manual selection with co-occurrence information.

2   Selection of Candidate Utterances

In this paper, we define "utterance" as a one-time statement and "dialogue" as an ordered set consisting of all the utterances from the conversation's beginning to its end. When a conversation is paused at s, we define $A_s = \{a_1^s, a_2^s, \ldots, a_{m_s}^s\}$ as a candidate set that contains at least one suitable answer to continue conversation s. Tables 1 and 2 illustrate examples s and A_s. Table 1 shows a continuing conversation that paused at No. 8. In respond to utterance "Suizokukan no shizuka de ochitsuita funniki ga suki desu. (I like the aquarium's atmosphere because it is so quiet and relaxing.)", candidate set A_s can be found, illustrated by Table 2.

A_s is created in advance based on the partner's information and contains possible answers produced by methods like using template. Nevertheless, how to create A_s will not be discussed, since this study is focusing on the selection method.

Here, s and A_s satisfy the following condition: A_s contains one or more appropriate answers in response to s (correct solution).

The selection of the candidate utterance forms correct solution set C_s by locating all appropriate answers from A_s. For instance, in response to the last utterance

Table 1. Example of continuing conversation s

No.	speaker: utterance
1	A: Donna sakana, doubutsu ga suki desu ka? (What kind of fish or animals do you like?)
2	B: Iruka ga suki desu. (Oh, I like dolphins.)
3	A: Doushite desu ka? (Why?)
4	B: Iruka wa totemo kashikoi kara desu. (I think they are very smart.)
5	A: Watashi mo daisuki desu. (Yeah, I like them too.)
6	B: Sore wa ureshii desu. (Oh, great!)
7	A: Suizokukan no suki na tokoro wa donna tokoro desu ka? (What do you like about the aquarium?)
8	B: Suizokukan no shizuka de ochitsuita funniki ga suki desu. (I like the atmosphere of aquariums because they are so quiet and relaxing.)

Table 2. Example of candidate set A_s related to s

No.	Candidate utterance
a_1^s	Mizu ni wa nani ka kokoro o ochitsukaseru chikara ga arimasu yo ne? (Yeah, the water seems to have some power that can make us calm.)
a_2^s	Sono doubutsu no donna tokoro ga suki desu ka? (What do you like about that animal?)
a_3^s	Ato 4 nen chikaku arimasu mon ne. Nani ka mitsukaru to ii desu ne. (There is still about four years left, if you could find something.)
a_4^s	Suizokukan wa ochitsukimasu yo ne. (I agree, aquariums are relaxing.)
a_5^s	Shakai ni yakudatsu to omoimasu. Benkyou ganbatte kudasai. (I think that is meaningful for the public. Good luck with your studies.)
a_6^s	Sou deshita ka. Suki na eigahaiyuu wa imasu ka? (I see. Do you have any favorite movie actors?)

(No. 8) in Table 1, Table 2 has two correct solutions: "Yeah, the water seems to have some power that can make us calm," and "I agree, aquariums are relaxing." Therefore, in this example, correct solution set C_s will be $C_s = \{a_1^s, a_4^s\}$.

3   Statistical Candidate Utterance Selection Method

3.1   Automatic Candidate Utterance Selection

This section describes the method used in our study to automatically select candidate utterances. s indicates the state of the conversation, and A_s is a set containing candidate utterances in response to s.

By specifically processing s and $a(\in A_s)$, we generated feature vector $\Phi(s,a)$, which can be expressed in the following equation:

$$\Phi(s,a) = (x_1(s,a), x_2(s,a), \dots, x_n(s,a)) \in \mathbb{R}^n. \tag{1}$$

For instance, when focusing on the last utterance in s and a, a feature $x_i(s,a)$ is represented if it contains a specific word, a word class, or a combination of the two.

We then defined $f(\Phi(s,a))$ as a function that will return the evaluated value of a feature vector. Here it can be denoted by a linear function for short, which can be expressed as follows:

$$f(\Phi(s,a)) = \sum_{j=1}^{n} w_j x_j(s,a). \tag{2}$$

Note that w_j is a parameter that represents the weight of $x_j(s,a)$.

Using the above evaluation function, optimum utterance $\hat{a}$ in response to the state of the conversation can be obtained by the following equation:

$$\hat{a} = \operatorname*{argmax}_{a \in A_s} f(\Phi(s,a)). \tag{3}$$

Therefore, the candidate utterances can be ranked by sorting the value from the above evaluation function.

Furthermore, at every pause s_i in a conversation, correct solution set C_{s_i} can be found for it. The learning data are a set of data comprised of these solution sets that can be expressed in the following form. $T = \{C_{s_1}, C_{s_2}, \dots, C_{s_M}\}$. M is the number of correction sets. At the same time, $\bar{T} = \{\bar{C}_{s_1}, \bar{C}_{s_2}, \dots, \bar{C}_{s_M}\}$ represents the false answer set. Here, $\bar{C}_s = A_s \backslash C_s$.

By using the learning data, parameter $w = (w_1, w_2, \dots, w_n)$ in evaluation function f is evaluated based on some criteria. This is called the objective function.

In this paper, we compared the following proposed method to the maximum entropy method.

3.2 Proposed Method

Given $a_c \in C_s$ and $a_{\bar{c}} \in \bar{C}_s$, the value of optimum evaluation function $\hat{f}$ should satisfy the following equation:

$$\hat{f}(\Phi(s,a_c)) - \hat{f}(\Phi(s,a_{\bar{c}})) > 0. \tag{4}$$

In other words, the desirable sign of expression $\hat{f}(\Phi(s,a_c)) - \hat{f}(\Phi(s,a_{\bar{c}}))$ is positive, which means it equals

$$\operatorname{sgn}\left(\hat{f}(\Phi(s,a_c)) - \hat{f}(\Phi(s,a_{\bar{c}}))\right) = 1. \tag{5}$$

Note that $\operatorname{sgn}(x)$ is a function that always returns an integer:

$$\operatorname{sgn}(x) = \begin{cases} 1 & x > 0 \\ 0 & x = 0 \\ -1 & x < 0. \end{cases} \tag{6}$$

Since some utterances are appropriate to some inputs while others are not, modeling the relative magnitude correlation of the candidate utterance for every input is preferred. In this way the nature of the candidate utterance selection problem can be shown better. Focusing on the relative magnitude correlation of every piece of learning data, we can define optimum evaluation function's parameter $\hat{w}$ by the following equations:

$$\hat{w} = \underset{w}{\operatorname{argmax}} F_{w} \tag{7}$$

$$F_{w} = \sum_{\substack{s, a_c \in C_s, \\ a_{\bar{c}} \in \bar{C}_s}} \operatorname{sgn}\left(t(s, a_c, a_{\bar{c}})\right) \tag{8}$$

$$t(s, a_c, a_{\bar{c}}) = f(\Phi(s, a_c)) - f(\Phi(s, a_{\bar{c}})) \tag{9}$$

$$= \sum_{j=1}^{n} w_j(x_j(s, a_c) - x_j(s, a_{\bar{c}})). \tag{10}$$

Since differentiating $\operatorname{sgn}(x)$ in the right-hand side of equation (8) is impossible, obtaining the optimum solution is difficult. Therefore, we approximate $\operatorname{sgn}(x)$ by a continuous function like the following expression:

$$\operatorname{sgn}(x) \approx \frac{2}{1 + e^{-kx}} - 1 \,, k > 0. \tag{11}$$

If we substitute expression (11) into Eq. (8) and then calculate the constant, we get object function F_w:

$$F_{w} = \sum_{\substack{s, a_c \in C_s, \\ a_{\bar{c}} \in \bar{C}_s}} \left(\frac{2}{1 + e^{-kt(s, a_c, a_{\bar{c}})}} - 1. \right) \tag{12}$$

$$\Rightarrow \sum_{\substack{s, a_c \in C_s, \\ a_{\bar{c}} \in \bar{C}_s}} \left(\frac{1}{1 + e^{-kt(s, a_c, a_{\bar{c}})}} \right). \tag{13}$$

Optimum solution $\hat{w}$ can be obtained using Eqs. (7), (10), and (13) and such measures as Improved Iterative Scaling (IIS), Generalized Iterative Scaling (GIS) [1], and Limited Memory Broyden-Fletcher-Goldfarb-Shanno (L-BFGS)[8]. In this paper, we used one conjugate gradient scheme, a specifically Scaled Conjugate Gradient (SCG) method [9].

3.3   Maximum Entropy Method (MEM)

The maximum entropy method (MEM) is a parameter calculation method that is potent, especially when available data are sparse [10].

Granted that the sporadic rate of every feature equals the ratio of the learning data to the unknown data, we extrapolate the parameters for the most homogeneous distribution. For example, when there are no learning data and n parameters, then every w_i will be assigned an equal probability of $1/n$.

To prevent overtraining, a maximum a posteriori estimation is applied to regularize the parameters. The objective function of maximum entropy method $L_{\boldsymbol{w}}$ can be represented by the following expressions:

$$\hat{\boldsymbol{w}} = \underset{\boldsymbol{w}}{\mathrm{argmax}}(L_{\boldsymbol{w}}) \tag{14}$$

$$L_{\boldsymbol{w}} = \sigma \sum_{\substack{s,a_c \in C_s, \\ a_{\bar{c}} \in \bar{C}_s}} \left(\boldsymbol{w}\Phi(s,a_c) - \log \left(\sum_{a_{\bar{c}} \in \bar{C}_s} \exp(\boldsymbol{w}\Phi(s,a_{\bar{c}})) \right) \right) - \frac{1}{2}||\boldsymbol{w}||^2. \tag{15}$$

The regularization term is $-\frac{1}{2}||\boldsymbol{w}||^2$. σ is a parameter to control the modeling complexity regarding the learning data. The value of σ is selected by the result of cross validation.

4   Automatic Candidate Utterance Selection Experiment

4.1   Experimental Methodology

This section describes an experiment of automatic candidate utterance selection.

To show the effectiveness of the automatic candidate utterance selection method that learns manually evaluated candidate utterances, we checked the order of the automatically evaluated values.

For a comparison of selection accuracy, we used a maximum entropy method ($\sigma = 0.1$) as a baseline. To rank the utterances, we sorted the values from the evaluation function and chose the following four types of features:

- Combination of 2-gram of an input and a candidate utterance
- Number of input and output segments
- Types and number of identical self-sufficient words
- Types and number of co-occurring self-sufficient words

Figure 1 shows the features of Table 1 as input and "Mizu ni wa nani ka kokoro o ochitsukaseru chikara ga arimasu yo ne?" as a candidate. We generated a feature vector from the last utterance "Suizokukan no shizuka de ochitsui ta funniki ga suki desu. (I like the atmosphere of aquariums because they are quiet and relaxing.)" and the candidate. First, we used a 2-gram combination feature as a combination of a 2-gram in an input and a 2-gram in a candidate utterance. We previously converted the self-sufficient words into word classes. Second, we chose the number of segments as a feature that is divided into 1, 2, 3, 4, 5, or more. Third, we used the word class feature of identical words like "ochitsuku". Last, we chose the number of co-occurring words for every word class as a feature. These identical word and co-occurring word features are divided into 0, 1, 2, 3, or more.

In this experiment, we removed the features that appeared less than 100 from all features. As a result, 3638 features were used.

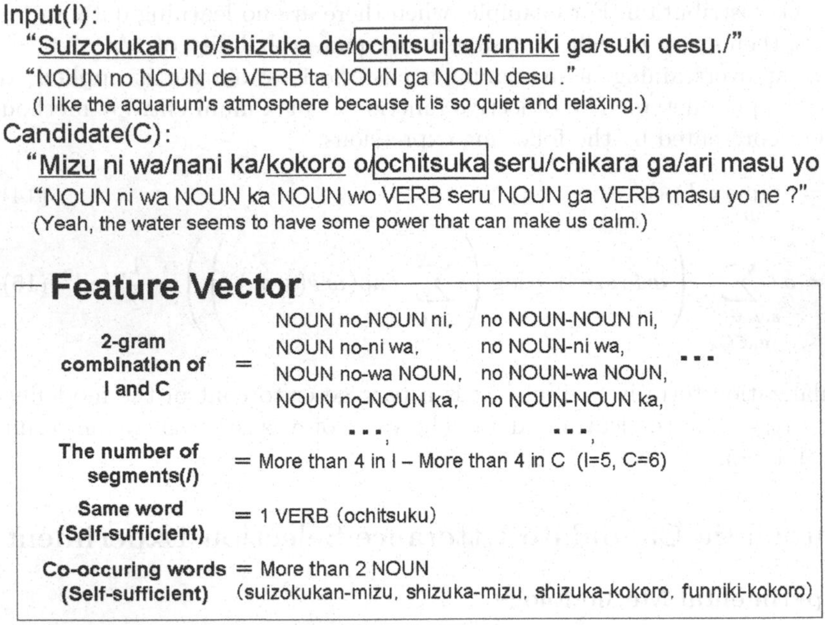

Input(I):

"Suizokukan no/shizuka de/ochitsui ta/funniki ga/suki desu./"

"NOUN no NOUN de VERB ta NOUN ga NOUN desu ."

(I like the aquarium's atmosphere because it is so quiet and relaxing.)

Candidate(C):

"Mizu ni wa/nani ka/kokoro o/ochitsuka seru/chikara ga/ari masu yo ne?/"

"NOUN ni wa NOUN ka NOUN wo VERB seru NOUN ga VERB masu yo ne ?"

(Yeah, the water seems to have some power that can make us calm.)

┌─ **Feature Vector** ─────────────────────────────────

| 2-gram combination of I and C | = | NOUN no-NOUN ni,
NOUN no-ni wa,
NOUN no-wa NOUN,
NOUN no-NOUN ka, | no NOUN-NOUN ni,
no NOUN-ni wa,
no NOUN-wa NOUN,
no NOUN-NOUN ka, | ... |

..., ...,

The number of segments(*l*) = More than 4 in I – More than 4 in C (I=5, C=6)

Same word (Self-sufficient) = 1 VERB (ochitsuku)

Co-occuring words (Self-sufficient) = More than 2 NOUN
(suizokukan-mizu, shizuka-mizu, shizuka-kokoro, funniki-kokoro)

Fig. 1. Example of feature

4.2 Extraction of Co-occurring Words

In this experiment, we chose co-occurring self-sufficient words as features. By checking them, a candidate utterance with a semantic relation with an input is more likely to be selected.

In this paper, we use word co-occurrence frequency from the Web Japanese N-gram [6] for handling semantic relations [4]. Web Japanese N-gram contains 2.6 million words from about 20 billion Google sentences and consists of 1- to 7-grams. We simultaneously employed the number of times the words appeared in the 7-gram as the word co-occurrence frequency.

The differences in the frequency among words are so large in the Web Japanese N-gram that we employed Log-Likelihood Scores (LLS)[2] on a semantic relation index. LLS is an index that can detect a co-occurrence relation where the differences in the frequency among words are large. In this experiment, we regarded a word pair of $LLS > 10000$ as co-occurring words. For instance, "suizokukan (aquarium)" and "umi (sea)" are co-occurring because their LLS is 1347152. In contrast, "suizokukan (aquarium)" and "haiyuu (actor)" are not co-occurring because their LLS is 625. Table 3 shows other co-occurring words of "suizokukan (aquarium)".

4.3 Experiment Data

In this experiment, we extracted 59 utterances from the dialogues of 11 college students for learning and tests. Before the dialogue began, the subjects

Table 3. Words that co-occur with "suizokukan (aquarium)"

No.	name	LLS
1	umi (sea)	1347152
2	doubutsu (animals)	1042871
3	kaisuiyoku (swimming in sea)	698701
4	hakubutsukan (museum)	642141
5	kankou (sightseeing)	471946
6	têma pâku (theme park)	194108
7	iruka (dolphins)	144445
8	penguin (penguins)	80175
9	nyuuzyou (admission)	28964
10	mizu (water)	14436

discussed such small talk topics as how to spend holidays, future dreams, and self-introductions.

We manually created candidate utterance collections on the basis of each profile.

For example, a_1^s, a_4^s in Table 2 is created from the following profile:

> My favorite place is aquariums. I like their atmosphere because they are gloomy, quiet, and relaxing. I used to visit one every month. I go the aquarium when I can spare the time. But recently I seldom have the chance.

Table 4 shows the number of inputs, the number of candidate utterances, and the average number of appropriate candidate utterances of the experiment data.

There were 70 to 180 candidate utterances and an average of 122 for input. An input represents the state of a dialogue, and all pairs of the last utterances of

Table 4. Experiment data

No.	Number of inputs	Number of candidate utterances	Average number of appropriate candidate utterances
1	2	124	7.00
2	6	180	5.00
3	4	70	2.75
4	8	107	2.78
5	10	146	2.08
6	5	161	2.17
7	4	127	4.00
8	6	70	2.67
9	10	130	1.09
10	2	73	1.00
11	2	71	1.33

an input and a candidate utterance that is "appropriate" or not were evaluated manually. We regard an appropriate utterance as one that doesn't change the topic and that has a relation to the input. To reduce the influence of subjective evaluation, we regard a pair evaluated as "appropriate" by two or more persons as a correct pair; otherwise it is a false pair. As a result of manual evaluation, an average of 2.62 utterances were correct pairs.

In the experiment, we used input s and utterance a_c^s in correct pairs as correct solution set C_s.

We used the leave-one-out cross-validation method to evaluate automatic candidate utterance selection by dividing the 59 inputs and the candidates evaluated by hand into 58 pieces of learning data and one piece of test data. We assumed that the test data are unknown and automatically evaluated them and then compared the results to the manual evaluations. We modified the data that became the test data, repeated this step 59 times, and evaluated the automatic candidate utterance selection by the order of the automatically evaluated values.

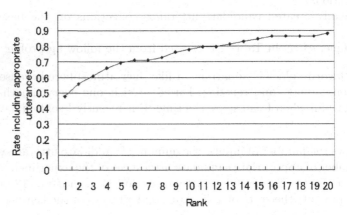

Fig. 2. Rate of appropriate candidate utterance: proposed method

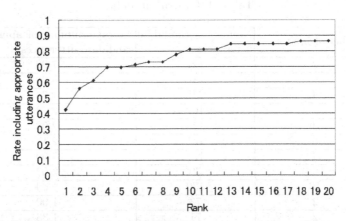

Fig. 3. Rate of appropriate candidate utterance: maximum entropy method

4.4 Results

Figures 2 and 3 show the experiment results using the proposed and maximum entropy methods, respectively.

The x-axis represents the rank of the first appearance of an appropriate utterance, and the y-axis represents the cumulative frequency. In other words, the figures show the rate of the inputs that include at least one appropriate utterance within each rank.

In Fig. 2, an appropriate utterance was selected the top at 47.5% and within the top 10 at 78.0% using the proposed method. Similarly, in Fig. 3, the rates are 42.4% and 78.0% using the maximum entropy method.

From the results, we found that the rate was high when the appropriate utterance is first in order using the proposed method. However, the methods had similar rates when within the top 10 in order.

For example, Table 5 shows the order of the top five automatically evaluated values of candidates for "Okashi wa tsukuru no yori mo taberu no ga suki na'n desu. (I prefer eating sweets to making them myself)". In this example, the number of candidate utterances and appropriate candidate utterances are 146 and 6, respectively. In Table 5, "Sou deshita ka. (I see.), "Yoku tabemasu ka? (Do you eat them often?), and "Doushite desu ka? (Why?)" are appropriate utterances by manual evaluation, but not the others.

In the case of both the maximum entropy and proposed methods, the appropriate candidate utterances came in first, second, and fifth.

These results show that the maximum entropy and proposed methods are effective for candidate utterance selection.

Moreover, $\hat{w}$, which was estimated by the proposed method, included 3299 features (90.7% of all the features) within $|w| \leq 1.0$. Table 6 shows part of the features where $|w| > 1.0$. In the table, w was estimated to increase the likelihood of choosing the candidate that contains co-occurring words or the same words

Table 5. Example of ranking

method	rank	candidate utterance
Maximum entropy method	1	Sou deshita ka. (I see.)
	2	Yoku tabemasu ka? (Do you eat it often?)
	3	Ie, ie, gokenson o. (Don't be so modest.)
	4	"Suki koso mono no zyouzu nare" to iimasu kara. (It is said that we do best the things we enjoy.)
	5	Doushite desu ka? (Why?)
Proposed method	1	Yoku tabemasu ka? (Do you eat it often?)
	2	Sou deshita ka. (I see.)
	3	Ie, ie, gokenson o. (Don't be so modest.)
	4	"Suki koso mono no zyouzu nare" to iimasu kara. (It is said that we do best the things we enjoy.)
	5	Doushite desu ka? (Why?)

Table 6. $\hat{w}$ after learning with proposed method

No.	feature	w
1	There is one same NOUN in a candidate and an input	3.28
2	There are two co-occurring words in a candidate and an input	2.01
3	There is one co-occurring ADJECTIVE in a candidate and an input	1.85
4	There are two co-occurring VERBs in a candidate and an input	1.64
5	There is one identical VERB in a candidate and a input	1.12
6	There two segments in an input and more than three segments in a candidate	-1.65
7	An input contains "NOUN o" and two segments in a candidate	-2.05
8	There is no identical NOUN in a candidate or in an input	-3.02

in an input. This means that the utterances that contain co-occurring words or the same words in an input are important for a dialogue.

5 Conclusion

In this paper, we employed a machine learning algorithm and proposed a statistical candidate utterance selection method for dialogue agents. We defined statistical candidate utterance selection as a question that automatically selects an appropriate utterance from speech collections prepared in advance as a response. To achieve automatic evaluation of candidate utterances, manually evaluated candidate utterances served as learning data, so that the relative magnitude correlation will be learned from the data. To prove the validity of the proposed method, we checked the order of the automatically evaluated values and conclude that the method is effective since an appropriate utterance is selected as the top at 47.5% and within the top 10 at 78.0%.

This method remains open to improvement regarding its implementation in dialogue agents in the sense that it is significant to let appropriate utterances become the first in order.

On the other hand, for implementing this method in agents that encourage humans to reply, the agent must include all possible appropriate responses when giving a suggestion. In this sense, since our method is more effective when giving an ordered list of up to ten appropriate responses, realizing such an agent is quite possible.

Our future work will concentrate on how to realize automatic generation of a large number of speech selections. In this paper, possible responses based on the profiles of dialogue partners were prepared beforehand when conducting the experiment; however we actually prefer automatically produced candidate answers.

Further research will investigate the ratio between the amount of learning data and appropriate responses as well as the minimum size of the learning data demanded for effective learning.

References

1. Della Pietra, S., Della Pietra, V., Lafferty, J., Technol, R., Brook, S.: Inducing features of random fields. IEEE transactions on pattern analysis and machine intelligence 19(4), 380–393 (1997)
2. Dunning, T.: Accurate methods for the statistics of surprise and coincidence. Computational linguistics 19(1), 61–74 (1993)
3. Haruno, M., Shirai, S., Ooyama, Y.: A japanese dependency parser based on a decision tree. Transactions of Information Processing Society of Japan 39(12), 3177–3186 (1998)
4. Inaba, M., Isomura, N., Toriumi, F., Ishii, K.: Evaluation method of Non-task-oriented dialogue system using Semantic Network. Technical report of IEICE (2009)
5. Isomura, N., Toriumi, F., Ishii, K.: Evaluation method of non-task-oriented dialogue system using HMM. The IEICE transactions on information and systems J92-D(4), 542–551 (2009)
6. Kudo, T., Kazawa, H.: Web japanese n-gram version 1, published by gengo shigen kyokai
7. Kudo, T., Matsumoto, Y.: Japanese dependency parsing using relative preference of dependency. Transactions of Information Processing Society of Japan 46(4), 1082–1092 (2005)
8. Liu, D.C., Nocedal, J.: On the limited memory BFGS method for large scale optimization. Mathematical Programming 45(1), 503–528 (1989)
9. Møller, M.: A scaled conjugate gradient algorithm for fast supervised learning. Neural Networks 6, 525 (1993)
10. Uchimoto, K., Sekine, S., Isahara, H.: Japanese dependency structure analysis based on maximum entropy models. Transactions of Information Processing Society of Japan 40(9), 3397–3407 (1999)

On the Impact of Witness-Based Collusion in Agent Societies

Amirali Salehi-Abari and Tony White

School of Computer Science, Carleton University,
1125 Colonel By Drive, Ottawa, Ontario, K1S 5B6, Canada
{asabari,arpwhite}@scs.carleton.ca

Abstract. In ways analogous to humans, autonomous agents require trust and reputation concepts in order to identify communities of agents with which to interact reliably. This paper defines a class of attacks called witness-based collusion attacks designed to exploit trust and reputation models. Empirical results demonstrate that unidimensional trust models are vulnerable to witness-based collusion attacks in ways independent multidimensional trust models are not. This paper analyzes the impact of the proportion of witness-based colluding agents on the society. Furthermore, it demonstrates that here is a need for witness interaction trust to detect colluding agents in addition to the need for direct interaction trust to detect malicious agents. By proposing a set of policies, the paper demonstrates how learning agents can decrease the level of encounter risk in a witness-based collusive society.

1 Introduction

By analogy with human societies in which trust is one of the most crucial concepts driving decision making and relationships, *trust* is indispensable when considering interactions among individuals in artificial societies such as are found in e-commerce marketplaces. According to Jarvenpaa et al. [5], trust is an essential aspect of any relationship in which the trustor does not have direct control over the actions of a trustee, the decision is important, and the environment is uncertain.

We use the experience that we gain in interacting with others to judge how they will perform in similar situations. However, when we need to assess our trust in someone of whom we have no direct personal experience, we often ask others regarding their personal experience with this individual. This collective opinion of others regarding the specific individual is known as an individual's reputation.

As reputation and trust have recently received considerable attention in many diverse domains several definitions exist. Mui et al. define trust as "a subjective expectation an agent has about another's future behavior based on the history of their encounters" [8]. While trust definitions focus more on the history of agents' encounters, reputation is based on the aggregated information from other individuals. For instance, Sabater and Sierra [10] declared that "reputation is the opinion or view of someone about something".

J.-J. Yang et al. (Eds.): PRIMA 2009, LNAI 5925, pp. 80–96, 2009.

Sabater and Sierra [11] categorized computational trust and reputation models based on various intrinsic features. From their perspective, a trust and reputation model can be cognitive or game-theoretical in terms of its conceptual model. Trust and reputation models might use different sources of information such as direct experiences, witness information, sociological information and prejudice. Direct experience and witness information are pertinent to this paper. Direct experiences deal with agent-to-agent interactions while witness information is information that comes from members of the community about others. Trust and reputation models vary in terms of individual behavior assumptions; in some models, cheating behaviors and malicious individuals are not considered at all whereas in others possible cheating behaviors are taken into account. There are many computational models of trust, a review of which can be found in [11].

Regret [10] is a decentralized trust and reputation system oriented to e-commerce environments. The system takes into account three different sources of information: direct experiences, information from third party agents and social structures. Yu and Singh [16] developed an approach for social reputation management, in which they represented an agent's ratings regarding another agent as a scalar and combined them with testimonies using combination schemes similar to certainty factors. Huynh et al. [4] introduced a trust and reputation model called FIRE that incorporates interaction trust, role-based trust, witness reputation, and certified reputation to provide a trust metric.

Most recently, researchers have identified the existence of cheaters (exploitation) in artificial societies employing trust and reputation models [6,12], and the existence of inaccurate witnesses [15,2], and [17]. Kerr and Cohen [6] examined the security of several e-commerce marketplaces employing a trust and reputation system. To this end, they proposed several attacks and examined their effects on each marketplace. Unfortunately, Kerr and Cohen assume that buyers are honest in the witness information provided to one another and consequently do not consider collusion attacks. Salehi-Abari and White [12] introduced and formally modeled the con-man attack and demonstrated the vulnerability of several trust models against this attack. This work also did not consider any collusion attacks.

There are few trust models which consider the existence of an adversary in providing witness information and present solutions for dealing with inaccurate reputation. TRAVOS [14] models an agent's trust in an interaction partner. Trust is calculated using probability theory that takes account of past interactions and reputation information gathered from third parties while coping with inaccurate reputations. Yu and Singh [17] is similar to TRAVOS, in that it rates opinion source accuracy based on a subset of observations of trustee behavior.

To our knowledge, there is no formal model of witness-based collusion and analysis of the level of encounter risk for trust-aware agents in witness-based collusive societies. In a witness-based collusion attack, an unreliable witness provider in spite of being cooperative in its direct interactions provides high ratings for other malicious agents (other members of the colluding group), thus resulting in motivating the victim agent to interact with them. This lack of study on witness-based collusion attacks motivates the work reported in this paper. This paper expands on a preliminary workshop paper [13].

Our contributions include the introduction of witness-based collusion attacks; a formal agent-based model of this attack class; an analysis of the impact of this attack class on agent societies, and on the level of encounter risk for trust-aware individuals; and a proposal for strategies of trust-aware agents to deal with this attack class.

The remainder of this paper proceeds as follows. Before describing the Witness-based Collusion Attack in Section 3, we discuss the environment model of agents in Section 2. We describe the agent model in Section 4, and experiments in Section 5. Finally, conclusions and future work are explained in Section 6.

2   Environment Model

The majority of open distributed computer systems can be modeled as multi-agent systems (MAS) in which each agent acts autonomously to achieve its objectives. Autonomy is represented here by the evaluation of policies that cause changes in agent trust and reputation models and subsequent changes in societal structure. Our model incorporates heterogeneous agents interacting in a game theoretic manner. The model is described in the following 3 subsections.

2.1   Interactions

An agent interacts with a subset of all agents that are the neighbors of the given agent. Two agents are *neighbors* if both accept each other as a neighbor and interact with one another continuously. An agent maintains the *neighborhood* set which is dynamic, changing when an agent is determined to be untrustworthy or new agent interactions are required. Agents have bounded sociability as determined by the maximal cardinality of the neighborhood set. Agents can have two types of interactions with their neighbors: *Direct Interaction* and *Witness Interaction*.

Direct Interaction. Direct interaction is the most frequently used source of information for trust and reputation models [11,9]. Different fields have their own interpretation of direct interaction. For example, in e-commerce, direct interaction might be considered to be buying or selling a product, whereas in file sharing systems direct interaction is file exchange.

Witness Interaction. An agent can ask for an assessment of the trustworthiness of a specific agent from its neighbors and then the neighbors send their ratings of that agent to the asking agent. We call this asking for an opinion and receiving a rating, a Witness Interaction.

2.2   Games: IPD and GPD

Direct and witness interactions are modeled using two extensions of the Prisoner's Dilemma. The Prisoner's Dilemma is a non-zero-sum, non-cooperative, and simultaneous game in which two players may each "cooperate" with or "defect" from the other player. In the Iterated Prisoner's Dilemma (IPD) [1], the game is played repeatedly. As a result, players have the opportunity to "punish" each other for previous uncooperative play. The IPD is closely related to the evolution of trust because if both players trust each other they can both cooperate and avoid mutual defection. We have modeled the direct interaction using IPD.

Witness Interaction is modeled by the Generalized Prisoner's Dilemma (GPD). GPD is a two-person game which specifies the general forms for an asymmetric payoff matrix that preserves the social dilemma [3]. GPD is compatible with client/server structure where one player is the client and the other one is the server in each game. The decision of the server alone determines the ultimate outcome of the interaction.

2.3   Cooperation and Defection

We define two kinds of **Cooperation** and **Defection** in our environment: (1) Cooperation/Defection in Direct Interaction (CDI/DDI) and (2) Cooperation/Defection in Witness Interaction (CWI/DWI).

CDI/DDI have different interpretations depending on the context. For example, in e-commerce, defection in an interaction can be interpreted as the agent not satisfying the terms of a contract, selling poor quality goods, delivering late, or failing to pay the requested amount of money to a seller [9]. CWI means that the witness agent provides a reliable rating for the asking agent regarding the queried agent. In contrast, DWI means that the witness agent provides an unreliable rating for the asker agent regarding the queried agent.

3   Witness-Based Collusion Attack

Collusion can be defined as a collaborative activity that gives to members of a colluding group benefits they would not be able to gain as individuals. Collusion attacks occur when one or more agents conspire together to take advantage of breaches in trust models to defraud one or more agents. It can be the case that agents in the colluding group adopt a sacrificial stance in collusion attacks in order to maximize the utility of the colluding group.

Collusion attacks often work based on the basic idea that one or more agents show themselves as trustworthy agents in one type of interaction (usually direct interaction). Afterward, they will be untrustworthy in other type of interaction (e.g., witness interaction) by providing false information in favor of other members of the colluding group. This false information usually encourages a victim to interact with members of the colluding group. The members of the colluding group will cheat the victim, if victim interacts with them.

As depicted in Figure 1, we formally define three roles in the Witness-based Collusion Attack: *victim agent*, *enticer agent*, and *malicious agent*. Enticer agents and malicious agents form the colluding group to exploit victim agents. The enticer agents show themselves trustworthy in direct interactions to victim agents and consequently they become trustworthy neighbors of victim agents. Afterward, when victim agents are looking for ratings (reputation) of malicious agent

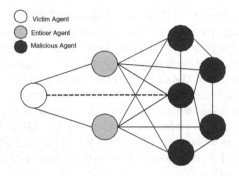

Fig. 1. Witness-based Collusion Attack

by asking from their trustworthy neighbors, the enticer agents provide high ratings for malicious agents (other members of the colluding group) in order to
encourage the victim agents to interact with them, and consequently the victim
agents will be exploited by them. The dashed line in Figure 1 shows the start of
interaction of a victim agent with a malicious agent as a result of high ratings
provided by enticer agents.

It can be observed that when the victim agent bases its assessment of witness
information on the cooperations (trustworthiness) in direct interactions, this
attack will be successful. In particular, the success of this attack is the result of
the inappropriate assumption that whoever is cooperative (trustworthy) in direct
interactions will be cooperative (trustworthy) in providing witness information
regarding other agents.

It is the hypothesis of this paper that the Witness-based Collusion Attack can
be prevented if the asker agent utilizes an independent multi-dimensional trust
model. In this sense, the asker agent will assess the witness providers based on
their cooperations in witness interactions.

4   Agent Model

This section presents two types of trust variables and a type of reputation variable that assist agents in determining with whom they should interact. Furthermore, three policy types will be presented: direct interaction policy, witness
interaction policy, and connection policy which assist agents in deciding how and
when they should interact with another agent.

4.1   Trust Variables

Based on the aforementioned cooperation/defection explained in section 2.3, two
modeled dimensions of trust are proposed. The motivation for having two trust
variables is that we believe trustworthiness has different independent dimensions.
For instance, an agent who is trustworthy in a direct interaction is not necessarily
trustworthy in a witness interaction.

Each trust variable is defined by $T_{i,j}(t)$ indicating the trust rating assigned by agent i to agent j after t interactions between agent i and agent j, while $T_{i,j}(t) \in [-1, +1]$ and $T_{i,j}(0) = 0$. One agent in the view of the other agent can have one of the following levels of trustworthiness: *Trustworthy, Not Yet Known,* or *Untrustworthy*. Following Marsh [7], we define an upper and a lower threshold for each agent to model different levels of trustworthiness. The agent i has its own upper threshold $-1 \leq \omega_i \leq 1$ and lower threshold $-1 \leq \Omega_i \leq 1$. Agent j is *Trustworthy* from the viewpoint of agent i after t times of interactions if and only if $T_{i,j}(t) \geq \omega_i$. Agent i sees agent j as an *Untrustworthy* agent if $T_{i,j}(t) \leq \Omega_i$ and if $\Omega_i < T_{i,j}(t) < \omega_i$ then the agent j is in the state *Not Yet Known*.

Direct Interaction Trust (DIT). Direct Interaction Trust (DIT) is the result of CDI/DDI. Each agent maintains $DIT_{i,j}(t)$ variables for the agents with which they have had direct interactions. We used the following trust updating scheme motivated by that described in [16]:

if $DIT_{i,j}(t) > 0$ and CDI then

$$DIT_{i,j}(t + 1) = DIT_{i,j}(t) + \alpha_D(i)(1 - DIT_{i,j}(t))$$

if $DIT_{i,j}(t) < 0$ and CDI then

$$DIT_{i,j}(t + 1) = (DIT_{i,j}(t) + \alpha_D(i))/(1 - min(|DIT_{i,j}(t)|, |\alpha_D(i)|))$$

if $DIT_{i,j}(t) > 0$ and DDI then

$$DIT_{i,j}(t + 1) = (DIT_{i,j}(t) + \beta_D(i))/(1 - min(|DIT_{i,j}(t)|, |\beta_D(i)|))$$

if $DIT_{i,j}(t) < 0$ and DDI then

$$DIT_{i,j}(t + 1) = DIT_{i,j}(t) + \beta_D(i)(1 + DIT_{i,j}(t))$$

Where $\alpha_D(i) > 0$ and $\beta_D(i) < 0$ are positive evidence and negative evidence weighting coefficients respectively for updating of the direct interaction trust variable of agent i. The value of $DIT_{i,j}(t)$, ω_i^{DIT} and Ω_i^{DIT} determine that the agent j is either *trustworthy, Not Yet Known* or *Untrustworthy* in terms of direct interaction from the perspective of agent i.

Witness Interaction Trust (WIT). Witness Interaction Trust (WIT) is the result of the cooperation/defection that the neighbors of an agent have with the agent regarding witness interaction (CWI/DWI). Agent i maintains a $WIT_{i,j}(t)$ variable for the agent j from whom it has received witness information. The updating scheme of $WIT_{i,j}(t)$ is similar to the one presented for $DIT_{i,j}(t)$ but CDI and DDI should be replaced by CWI and DWI respectively and $\alpha_D(i) > 0$ and $\beta_D(i) < 0$ is replaced with $\alpha_W(i) > 0$ and $\beta_W(i) < 0$ respectively. Where $\alpha_W(i) > 0$ and $\beta_W(i) < 0$ are positive evidence and negative evidence weighting coefficients respectively for updating of the witness interaction trust variable of agent i. The value of $WIT_{i,j}(t)$, ω_i^{WIT} and Ω_i^{WIT} determine that the agent j is either *Trustworthy, Not Yet Known* or *Untrustworthy* in terms of witness interaction.

4.2 Witness-Based Reputation (WR)

As agents need to predict the trustworthiness of those agents with whom they have never interacted, we use witness-based reputation (WR) for predicting trustworthiness of these agents. This reputation is calculated based on the witness information received from the neighbors.

Witness-based reputation for a specific agent is calculated based on the ratings of other agents. The asking agent stores the ratings of other agents in an *Opinion* variable. $Opinion(j,k)$ shows the rating issued by agent j regarding agent k. WR of agent k from the perspective of agent i after reception of t opinions (ratings) is denoted by $WR_{i,k}(t)$ and can be calculated by either Equation 1 or Equation 2:

$$WR_{i,k}(t) = \frac{\sum_{j \in OpinionSenders} (\phi(DIT_{i,j}) \times Opinion(j,k))}{\sum_{j \in OpinionSenders} \phi(DIT_{i,j})} \tag{1}$$

$$WR_{i,k}(t) = \frac{\sum_{j \in OpinionSenders} (\phi(WIT_{i,j}) \times Opinion(j,k))}{\sum_{j \in OpinionSenders} \phi(WIT_{i,j})} \tag{2}$$

In both formulae, the *OpinionSenders* variable includes indices of the neighbors of agent i who sent their ratings about agent k and $WIT_{i,j}$ is the current value of WIT variable of agent j from the perspective of agent i. Note that, $\phi(r)$ is a converter function that is calculated by Equation 3.

$$\phi(r) = \begin{cases} 0 & -1 \leq r < \Omega \\ \frac{r-\Omega}{\omega-\Omega} & \Omega \leq r \leq \omega \\ 1 & \omega \leq 1 \end{cases} \tag{3}$$

The value of $WR_{i,k}(t)$, ω_i^{WR} and Ω_i^{WR} determine that the agent k is either *Trustworthy, Not Yet Known* or *Untrustworthy* in terms of witness-based reputation from the perspective of agent i.

4.3   Agent Policy Types

The perceptions introduced above allow agents to determine the trustworthiness of other agents. Policies make use of agent perceptions, trust and reputation models in order to decide upon the set of agents with which they will interact and in what ways they will interact. Policies may cause the agent interaction neighborhood to change, for example. Several policy classes have been defined for the research reported here; they are explained in the following subsections.

Direct Interaction Policy (DIP). This type of policy assists an agent in making decisions regarding its direct interactions.

Witness Interaction Policy (WIP). This type of policy exists to aid an agent in making three categories of decisions related to its witness interactions. First, agents should decide how to provide the witness information for another agent on receiving a witness request. Should they manipulate the real information and forward false witness information to the requester (an example of defection) or should they tell the truth? The second decision made by the Witness Interaction Policy is related to when and from whom the agent should ask for witness information. Should the agents ask for the witness information when it has a connection request from an unknown party? Should the agents ask for witness information from a subset or all of its neighbors? The third decision is on how agents should aggregate the received ratings. For example, should the agent calculate the simple average of ratings or a weighted average of ratings?

We defined three sub witness interaction policies: Answering Policy (AP), Querying Policy (QP), and Information-Gathering policy (IGP). Answering Policy intends to cover the the first category of decisions mentioned above while Querying Policy and Information-Gathering policy apply to the second and third categories respectively.

Connection Policy (CP). This policy type assists an agent in making decisions regarding whether it should make a request for connection to other agents and whether the agents should accept/reject a request for a connection.

4.4 Experimentally Evaluated Policies

This section described policies that were evaluated experimentally.

Direct Interaction Policies. Three kinds of DIPs used in our experiments are: Always Cooperate (AC), Always-Defect (AD), and Trust-based Tit-For-Tat (TTFT). Agents using the AC policy for their direct interactions will cooperate with their neighbors in direct interactions regardless of the action of their neighbor. In contrast, agents using the AD policy will defect in all neighbor interactions. Agents employing TTFT will start with cooperation and then imitate the neighbors' last move as long as the neighbors are neither trustworthy nor untrustworthy. If a neighbor is known as untrustworthy, the agent will defect and immediately disconnect from that neighbor. If a neighbor is known as trustworthy, the agent will cooperate with it.

Connection Policy. Three kinds of connection polices used in our experiments are: Conservative (C), Naive (N), and Greedy (G). There is an internal property for each of these policies called Socializing Tendency (ST) which affects decisions regarding making connection requests and the acceptance of a connection request. Both Naive and Greedy policies use Algorithm 1 with different values for ST.

According to Algorithm 1, any connection request from another agent will be accepted regardless of ST value but the agent will attempt to connect to unknown agents if its number of neighbors is less than ST.

Algorithm 1. Greedy and Naive Policies

```
 1: {CRQ is a queue containing the connection requests}
 2: if CRQ is not empty then
 3:    j = dequeue(CRQ)
 4:    connectTo(j)
 5: end if
 6: if size(neighborhood) < ST then
 7:    j = get unvisited agent from list of all known agents
 8:    if ∃j ≠ null then
 9:       requestConnectionTo(j)
10:    end if
11: end if
```

Algorithm 2. Conservative Connection Policy

```
1: if CAQ is not empty then
2:     j = dequeue(CAQ)
3:     connectTo(j)
4: end if
5: if size(neighborhood) < ST then
6:     if SIQ is not empty then
7:         j = dequeue(SIQ)
8:     else
9:         if CRQ is not empty then
10:            j = dequeue(CRQ)
11:        else
12:            j = get unvisited agent from list of all known agents
13:        end if
14:    end if
15:    if ∃j ≠ null then
16:        connectTo(j)
17:    end if
18: end if
19: if CRQ is not empty then
20:    j = dequeue(CRQ)
21:    enque(SIQ,j)
22: end if
```

Using the Conservative policy presented in Algorithm 2, the agents connect to confirmed agents regardless of the number of their neighbors. CAQ contains the list of agent IDs confirmed; this confirmation of an agent might be accomplished by a witness interaction policy. If the number of neighbors is less than ST, the agent connects to the agents requested for connections or to an unvisited agent. Finally, if there are any agent IDs in CRQ (a queue of connection requests), the first agent ID will be inserted in SIQ (a list of agents whose reputations should be investigated).

We set the value of ST 5, 25, and 100 for Conservative, Naive, and Greedy connection policies respectively.

Algorithm 3. Answering Policy

```
1: if receiving a witness request about j from k then
2:     opinion = *
3:     send opinion to k
4:     if |opinion − DIT_{i,j}(t)| < DT then
5:         Send CWI to k after T_W time steps
6:     else
7:         Send DWI to k after T_W time steps
8:     end if
9: end if
```

Witness Interaction Policy. Three kinds of answering policies are modeled: Honest (Ho), Liar (Li), and Misleader (Mi). All these sub-policies use the pseudo-code presented in Algorithm 3 while differentiating in the assignment of opinion variable (refer to * in Algorithm 3). The asterisk should be replaced by $DIT_{i,j}(t)$, "$-1*DIT_{i,j}(t)$", or 1 for Honest, Liar, or Misleader policy respectively. An agent employing the Liar policy gives manipulated ratings to other agents by giving high ratings for untrustworthy agents and low ratings for trustworthy ones. The Misleader policy ranks all other agents as trustworthy but the Honest policy always tells the truth to everyone. CWI/DWI will be sent based on whether the forwarding opinion agrees with the internal trust value of an agent or not. If the difference between them is less than the Discrimination Threshold (DT), an agent will send CWI otherwise DWI is sent. We can therefore say that: Liar always defects, Honest always cooperates, and Misleader sometimes defects (by rating high untrustworthy agents) and sometimes cooperates (by rating low trustworthy agents) in providing the witness information. In the experiments reported here DT is set to 0.25.

Using the Querying Policy presented in Algorithm 4, the agents ask for witness information from their neighbors regarding agents which are in the SIQ queue. SIQ contains a list of agents whose reputations should be investigated. After asking for witness information regarding a specific agent, the ID of that agent is inserted in the WIFQ queue. WIFQ contains the list of agents waiting for the

Algorithm 4. Querying Policy

```
 1: if SIQ is not empty then
 2:     k = dequeue(SIQ)
 3:     for all j ∈ Neighborhood do
 4:         Ask for witness information about k from j
 5:     end for
 6:     enque(WFIQ, k)
 7: end if
 8: for all k ∈ WFIQ do
 9:     if WR_{i,k} > ω_i^{WR} then
10:         enque(CAQ, k)
11:         remove(WFIQ, k)
12:     else
13:         if WR_{i,k} < Ω_i^{WR} then
14:             remove(WFIQ, k)
15:         else
16:             if ShouldBeReInvestigated(k) then
17:                 for all j ∈ Neighborhood do
18:                     Ask for witness information about k from j
19:                 end for
20:             end if
21:         end if
22:     end if
23: end for
```

result of an investigation. If an agent in the WIFQ is known as trustworthy in the context of WR, then the ID of that agent will be added to CAQ which contains the list of confirmed agents. The agents known as untrustworthy in terms of WR will be removed from WIFQ. If an agent in WIFQ is known neither as trustworthy nor as untrustworthy and the primitive $ShouldBeReInvestigated(k)$ returns a *true* value, then again the agent will request witness information from their neighbors regarding the given agent (the agent k). This primitive can be easily implemented relying on whether agent k remains in WIFQ for more than a specific amount of time.

We have specified two information-gathering policies: DIT-based Weighted (DTW), and WIT-based Weighted (WTW). Both use Algorithm 5 while differentiating in the calculation of $WR_{i,k}$ (refer to * in Algorithm 5). DTW calculate it by using the formula presented in the Equation 1, Whereas WTW use the formula presented in the Equation 2.

Algorithm 5. Information-Gathering Policy
1: {Suppose that agent i is executing this code}
2: **if** receiving opinion about k from j **then**
3:     Calculate $WR_{i,k}(t)$ based on *
4: **end if**

5   Experiments

We have empirically analyzed our agent types at both microscopic and macroscopic levels. On the macro level, we studied how society structure changes over the course of many interactions. On the micro level, the utility of agents and the number of dropped connections are examined. $\overline{U_{AT}(i)}$, the average of utilities for agents with the type of AT at time step i, is calculated by:

$$\overline{U_{AT}(i)} = \frac{\sum_{a \in AT} U_{Avg}(a, i)}{N_{AT}} \tag{4}$$

where $U_{Avg}(a, i)$ is the average of utility of agent a over its interactions at time step i and N_{AT} is the total number of agents in the society whose type is AT. The utility of each interaction is calculated as follows: If agent i defects and agent j cooperates, agent i gets the Temptation to Defect payoff of 5 points while agent j receives the Sucker's payoff of 0. If both cooperate each gets the Reward for Mutual Cooperation payoff of 3 points, while if both defect each gets the Punishment for Mutual Defection payoff of 1 point.

$\overline{D_{AT}(i)}$, the average of dropped connections for agents with the type of AT at time step i, is calculated by:

$$\overline{D_{AT}(i)} = \frac{\sum_{a \in AT} D_{total}(a, i)}{N_{AT}} \tag{5}$$

where $D_{total}(a, i)$ is the total number of connections broken for agent a from the start time to time step i and N_{AT} is total number of agents of society whose type are AT.

We have modeled the witness-based collusion attacks by using Enticer and Malicious agents as explained in Section 3. In addition to these two types of agents, the agent society includes Trust-Aware agents which are equipped with perception variables (trust and reputation variables) to assess trustworthiness of others and with policies to properly interact with others. We have defined two classes of Trust-Aware agents for our experiments: Trust-Aware (TA_w) and Trust-Aware$^+$ (TA_w^+) where TA_w uses a unidimensional trust model as opposed to TA_w^+ which uses a multi-dimensional trust model. Table 1 presents all agent types used for all experiments.

Experiment 1. We have run two simulations of 200 agents for this experiment. In the first simulation, which models a non-collusive society, TA_w agents comprise 75% of the population and the rest are Malicious agents (for our convenience, we refer to this simulation as Sim1). The second simulation represents the witness-based collusive society in which Enticer and Malicious agents comprise 5% and 20% of the populations respectively and the rest are TA_w agents (for our convenience, we refer to this simulation as Sim2). The objective of this experiment is to understand the effect of a witness-based collusion attack on the structure of agent society and on the level of encounter risk. Encounter risk is defined to be linearly related to the average number of dropped connections.

Table 1. Agent Types and Specifications

Name	Enticer	Malicious	TA_w	TA_w^+
Trust	-	-	DIT	DIT&WIT
DIP	AC	AD	TTFT	TTFT
CP	N	G	C	C
AP	Mi	Li	Ho	Ho
QP	-	-	QP	QP
IGP	-	-	DTW	WTW

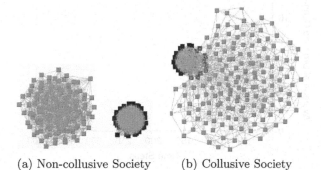

(a) Non-collusive Society   (b) Collusive Society

Fig. 2. The Final Society Structure in Exp. 1

The structures of the agent society after 400 time steps for Sim1 and Sim2 are presented in Figure 2 where TA_w agents and Malicious agents are in green (light gray in white-black print) and in black respectively. Red squares with white "-" represent Enticer agents. In non-collusive societies as shown in Figure 2a, we have two isolated groups of TA_w and Malicious agents. In the witness-based collusive society (see Figure 2b), we could not achieve separation of Malicious and TA_w agents seen in Sim1. Since TA_w agents perceived Enticer agents as trustworthy agents in direct interaction so they maintain their connections with Enticer agents. As illustrated in Figure 2b, TA_w agents are connected indirectly to Malicious agents by means of Enticer agents while acting a buffer between the Malicious agents and TA_w agents.

Figure 3 illustrates $\overline{D}$ of TA_w over the course of two simulations of Sim1 and Sim2. TA_w agents in Sim1 (non-collusive society) have considerably fewer dropped connections when compared to the TA_w agents in Sim2 (witness-based collusive society). In this sense, TA_w agents expose themselves to higher level of risk of being exploited by malicious agents in Sim2 as a result of ongoing witness-based attacks, when compared to Sim1. This high level of risk is due to the fact that each TA_w agent is surrounded by Enticer agents, resulting in receiving more manipulated opinions about other malicious agents while the senders of all opinions are trustworthy in terms of direct interactions.

Experiment 2. We have run two simulations of 200 agents for this experiment, in each of which Enticer, Malicious agents are 5% and 20% of the populations respectively. The remainder of the population (75%) is either TA_w or TA_w^+. Both TA_w and TA_w^+ benefit from using the Conservative connection policy and witness interaction policies for inquiring about the trustworthiness of the connection requester from neighbors. Note that, these two types employ various witness information-gathering policies and different trust models. TA_w utilizes a uni-dimensional trust model (i.e., DIT), whereas TA_w^+ utilizes a multi-dimensional trust model (i.e., DIT and WIT).

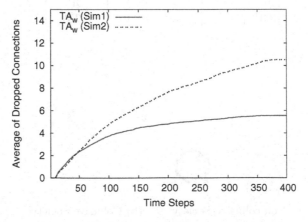

Fig. 3. $\overline{D}$ of agent types over simulation

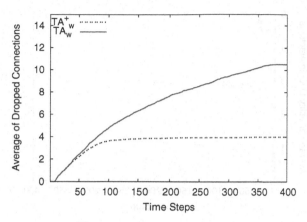

Fig. 4. $\overline{D}$ of agent types over the simulation

This experiment is intended to demonstrate the benefit of using multi-dimensional trust where there are witness-based collusion attacks. More precisely, the intention behind this experiment is to show that TA_w^+ agents by using multi-dimensional trust and appropriate witness interaction policies (e.g., WTW) can decrease the impact of Enticer and Malicious agents (colluding groups) on aggregating the reputation ratings. As a result, the TA_w^+ agents can decide more reliably regarding the trustworthiness of other agents and expose themselves to a lower level of risk.

As shown in Figure 4, TA_w^+ agents have considerably fewer dropped connections when compared to TA_w. Policies used by this agent type result in successful acceptance/rejection of connection requests. In this sense, TA_w^+ agents expose themselves to smaller numbers of untrustworthy agents and consequently lower the level of risk of being exploited by these agents.

Figure 5 illustrates $\overline{U}$ for TA_w and TA_w^+ types over the course of the simulations. $\overline{U}$ reaches the value of 3 faster for TA_w^+ than TA_w and will fall below it later. This is evidence of the learning capability of TA_w^+ agents especially by using WIT for aggregating opinions in witness interaction policies. Each TA_w^+ agent, by updating WIT, will learn which of its neighbors are trustworthy in terms of witness information and then weight their opinions based on their WIT which is completely independent of DIT. As a result, false opinions of neighbors cannot mislead them several times whereas TA_w agents can be deceived several times by false opinions from the same neighbors (Enticer agents) because of the lack of this trust dimension.

Experiment 3. This experiment intends to show the effect of population proportion of Enticer agents on the efficacy of Witness-based collusion attacks and on the robustness of TA_w and TA_w^+. We have run 2 sets of 4 simulations. Each set consists of 200 agents with different proportions of Enticer and Malicious agents while keeping the proportion of either TA_w or TA_w^+ agents unchanged as shown in Table 2. The simulations are run for 400 time steps.

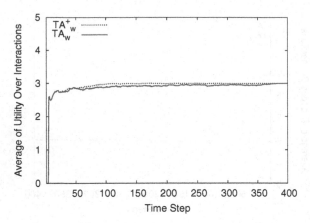

Fig. 5. $\overline{U}$ of agent types over the simulation

Table 2. Population Distributions of Experiment 3

Agent Type	Population			
	Pop1	Pop2	Pop3	Pop4
Malicious	20%	15%	10%	5%
Naive	5%	10%	15%	20%
TA_w or TA_w^+	75%	75%	75%	75%

Figure 6 presents $\overline{D}$ of each agent type at time step 400 for each of the runs. By increasing the proportion of Enticer agents (i.e., decreasing the proportion of Malicious agents), the $\overline{D}$ of TA_w and TA_w^+ will be decreased. Moreover, it can be observed that in all runs the number of dropped connection for TA_w is greater when compared with the number of dropped connections of TA_w^+. This is evidence of the fact that TA_w^+ has better robustness against this attack.

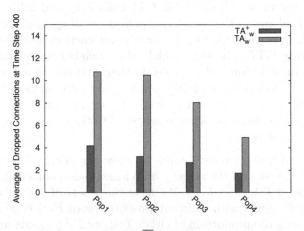

Fig. 6. $\overline{D}$ for all runs

6   Conclusion

Witness-based collusion attacks degrade the value of DIT in trust-aware agent societies. In these attacks, agents which are trustworthy in their direct interactions, collude with malicious agents by providing a good rating for them. We experimentally show how a unidimensional trust model is vulnerable against witness-based collusion attacks. This vulnerability results in TA_w agents, which use a unidimensional trust model to weight the ratings, exposing themselves to a higher level of encounter risk. Furthermore, TA_w^+ agents, by using WIT, weight the rating of Enticer agents and decrease the impact of them in their final assessment. This results in exposing themselves to a lower level of risk in their interactions. We empirically demonstrate that the efficacy of TA_w^+ over TA_w is better for different population proportions of Enticer and Malicious agents. Finally, we conclude multi-dimensionality is a crucial factor for resistance against witness-based collusion attacks.

Collusion attacks are an emerging area of research in trust and reputations systems. Future work will uncover new classes of such attacks and ways in which they can be defeated.

References

1. Axelrod, R.: The Evolution of Cooperation. Basic Books, New York (1984)
2. Dellarocas, C.: Mechanisms for coping with unfair ratings and discriminatory behavior in online reputation reporting systems. In: ICIS, pp. 520–525 (2000)
3. Feldman, M., Lai, K., Stoica, I., Chuang, J.: Robust incentive techniques for peer-to-peer networks. In: EC 2004, pp. 102–111. ACM, New York (2004)
4. Huynh, T.D., Jennings, N.R., Shadbolt, N.R.: An integrated trust and reputation model for open multi-agent systems. Autonomous Agents and Multi-Agent Systems 13(2), 119–154 (2006)
5. Jarvenpaa, S.L., Tractinsky, N., Vitale, M.: Consumer trust in an internet store. Inf. Technol. and Management 1(1-2), 45–71 (2000)
6. Reid, K., Robin, C.: Smart cheaters do prosper: Defeating trust and reputation systems. In: AAMAS 2009, Budapest, Hunagry, ACM, New York (2009)
7. Marsh, S.: Formalising trust as a computational concept (1994)
8. Mui, L., Mohtashemi, M., Halberstadt, A.: A computational model of trust and reputation for e-businesses. In: HICSS 2002, Washington, DC, USA, p. 188. IEEE Computer Society Press, Los Alamitos (2002)
9. Ramchurn, S.D., Huynh, D., Jennings, N.R.: Trust in multi-agent systems. Knowl. Eng. Rev. 19(1), 1–25 (2004)
10. Sabater, J., Sierra, C.: Regret: A reputation model for gregarious societies. In: Fourth Workshop on Deception Fraud and Trust in Agent Societies, pp. 61–70 (2001)
11. Sabater, J., Sierra, C.: Review on computational trust and reputation models. Artif. Intell. Rev. 24(1), 33–60 (2005)
12. Salehi-Abari, A., White, T.: Towards con-resistant trust models for distributed agent systems. In: IJCAI 2009: Proceedings of the Twenty-first International Joint Conference on Artificial Intelligence, Pasadena, CA, USA, pp. 272–277 (2009)

13. Amirali, S.-A., Tony, W.: Witness-based collusion and trust-aware societies. In: SPOSN 2009: the Workshop on Security and Privacy in Online Social Networking (2009)
14. Luke Teacy, W.T., Patel, J., Jennings, N.R., Luck, M.: Coping with inaccurate reputation sources: experimental analysis of a probabilistic trust model. In: AAMAS 2005, pp. 997–1004. ACM Press, New York (2005)
15. Whitby, A., Jsang, A., Indulska, J.: Filtering out unfair ratings in bayesian reputation systems. In: Proceedings of 7th International Workshop on Trust in Agent Societies (2004)
16. Yu, B., Singh, M.P.: A social mechanism of reputation management in electronic communities. In: Klusch, M., Kerschberg, L. (eds.) CIA 2000. LNCS (LNAI), vol. 1860, pp. 154–165. Springer, Heidelberg (2000)
17. Yu, B., Singh, M.P.: Detecting deception in reputation management. In: AAMAS 2003, pp. 73–80. ACM, New York (2003)

Efficient Methods for Multi-agent Multi-issue Negotiation: Allocating Resources

Mengxiao Wu[1], Mathijs de Weerdt[2], and Han La Poutré[1]

[1] Centre for Mathematics and Computer Science (CWI),
Amsterdam, The Netherlands
{wu,hlp}@cwi.nl
[2] Delft University of Technology,
Delft, The Netherlands
M.M.deWeerdt@tudelft.nl

Abstract. In this paper, we present an automated multi-agent multi-issue negotiation solution to solve a resource allocation problem. We use a multilateral negotiation model, by which three agents bid sequentially in consecutive rounds till some deadline. Two issues are bundled and negotiated concurrently, so win-win opportunities can be generated as trade-offs exist between issues. We develop negotiation strategies of the agents under an incomplete information setting. The strategies are composed of a Pareto-optimal-search method and concession strategies. An important technical contribution of this paper lies in the development of the Pareto-optimal-search method for three-agent multilateral negotiation. Moreover, we present the identification of agreements and Pareto-optimal outcomes achieved by our methods in mathematical proof. We show through computer experiments that using the tractable heuristic of Pareto-optimal-search combined with well-designed concession strategies by agents results in (near) Pareto-optimal outcomes.

1 Introduction

With the rapid development of multi-agent systems, automated negotiation has been widely used to solve coordination and cooperation problems in complex systems. The potentially time-consuming negotiation process is delegated to autonomous software agents who conduct the negotiation on behalf of rational players. In this paper, we propose an automated multi-agent multi-issue negotiation solution to solve a resource allocation problem. In contrast to most previous work on two-player multi-issue negotiation (e.g., [1]) or multi-player single-issue negotiation (e.g., [2]), the negotiation model presented in this work is a *multi-player multi-issue* negotiation model in particular *three-player two-issue* cases. It is also different from the model of multiple bilateral negotiation between more than two players (e.g., [3]); it is a *multilateral* negotiation that always involves all players in a single negotiation. Thus, the negotiation model used by us is more involved and applies to multi-issue negotiation between more than two players in the real world. Given the model, we develop heuristics of negotiation strategies for three-agent two-issue cases where the agents have *non-linear* utility functions and *incomplete information* about his opponents' preferences, deadlines, etc. Compared to

J.-J. Yang et al. (Eds.): PRIMA 2009, LNAI 5925, pp. 97–112, 2009.
© Springer-Verlag Berlin Heidelberg 2009

game-theoretic solutions, our heuristic methods are practical and tractable; the whole solution is very efficient such that (near) Pareto-optimal outcomes can be achieved.

In our negotiation model, two issues are bundled and negotiated concurrently, so the agents can make trade-offs between issues when they have different preferences amongst the issues. This may generate win-win opportunities in which the agents reach an agreement that makes them mutually better off. However, this also makes the negotiation more complicated, because making appropriate proposals is nontrivial when an agent has multiple proposals which may give him the same maximum utility. To tackle with that, we decompose the negotiation strategies into two parts: a Pareto-optimal-search method and concession strategies. The former takes the Pareto optimality into account to choose bids which can make other agents better off while keeping the bidder own desired utility. The latter determines the desired utilities that the agents want to get as the negotiation progresses.

In this work, we develop a Pareto-optimal-search method, which is called the *orthogonal bidding strategy*, for the three-agent multilateral negotiation. In [4,5,6,7], some similar methods work on two-agent cases where the desires of two agents, such as a buyer and a seller, are reverse to each other. That means, one agent wants to reach an agreement on large amounts of issues while the other one wants to reach an agreement on small amounts of issues. In the negotiation, they make compromises by moving their proposals towards each other. Each agent's proposal can be directly used to guide his opponent's counter-proposal towards an agreement. However, this becomes more difficult in our three-agent cases. One point is that all three agents here have the same directions of desires, getting large amounts of issues to achieve high utilities. Moving proposals close to each other directly is an inappropriate way to pursue an agreement. Another point is that compromises should take place between the desires of three sides. These two points make each agent difficult to determine his counter-proposal based on two proposals of his opponents directly. To solve the problem, first, we let each agent make bids only for his own parts of two issues [8]. Second, we introduce the *reference point* to model the bidding of the other two agents to guide the current bidder's decision. The reference points help the agents to choose the most satisfied bids for each other to pursue the Pareto optimality. The most satisfied bid made by an agent is the one benefiting his opponents most amongst multiple bids which give himself the same maximum utility. This is the cooperative part of a competitive game to generate win-win opportunities. Besides that, the reference points are also used to measure the distances from the current state to an agreement, which can be taken into account by the concession strategies, during the negotiation. Given a desired utility level and its corresponding indifference curve, the orthogonal bidding strategy lets an agent choose the bid which is closest (measured in the Euclidean distance) to the reference point introduced by the last bid of each of his opponents on the indifference curve. We show through computer experiments that by using the Pareto-optimal-search method for three-agent cases combined with well-designed concession strategies, the agents can reach agreements quickly under an incomplete information environment, and those outcomes are very close to Pareto-optimal solutions.

The rest of this paper is organized as follows. In Section 2, we give a brief summary of related work. In Section 3, we present the negotiation model including the problem model, the negotiation protocol and utility functions. In Section 4, we investigate the negotiation strategies, the orthogonal bidding strategy and various concession strategies, and discuss possible Pareto-optimal outcomes achieved by using our methods. In Section 5, we provide computer experiments to show the efficiency of our solutions. Conclusions and future work are given in Section 6.

2   Related Work

The complex negotiation has been extensively studied in last decades and most research work has been conducted in two fields, game theory and artificial intelligence (AI). In the game-theoretic way, the best known negotiation model is the alternating-offer bargaining game [9]. Its two-player single-issue negotiation model has been extended to the multi-player negotiation (e.g., [2,10]) or the multi-issue negotiation (e.g., [1,11]). The multi-player multi-issue negotiation has been studied in [8,12]. A major limitation of the game-theoretic methods is that the equilibrium solutions are difficult to apply in practice, especially in the negotiation with incomplete information or non-linear utility functions or both. In this work, we adopt the multi-player multi-issue negotiation model proposed in [8], but propose heuristic computational methods of negotiation strategies of agents with incomplete information and non-linear utility functions.

Related to our work, in [4,5], heuristic methods to find Pareto-optimal solutions of two-agent two-issue negotiation are introduced. The negotiation strategies are decomposed into concession strategies and Pareto-optimal-search methods. Given his opponent's offer, an agent uses concession strategies to determine his desired utility level first and then chooses a counter-offer on the indifference curve of the utility level in the orthogonal way, the counter-offer lying closest (measured in the Euclidean distance) to his opponent's offer. In [6,7], similar methods are used in both two-issue and three-issue cases. In these work of two-agent cases, an agent can directly regard his opponent's offer as the target to make compromises. It is easy to identify agreements and Pareto-optimal solutions based on two indifference curves. In our work, we propose an orthogonal method to solve the three-agent two-issue negotiation problem. When three agents partition two issues, any agent's offer cannot be used as a target to determine the counter-offer in the orthogonal way. We introduce the reference point to model every two agents' offers to support using the orthogonal method in three-agent cases. We also identify agreements and Pareto-optimal solutions based on three indifference curves, which is more complex than the situations in those work.

In [13], the agents apply similarity criteria to make trade-offs between issues. Given a desired utility level, an agent chooses a counter-offer on the indifference curve of the utility level that is most similar to his opponent's last offer. Their approach, however, is applied to linear additive utility functions and requires the agents have some knowledge about how their opponent weights the issues in the negotiation. In [14], the authors consider fuzzy constraints on the combination of multiple issues instead of the way that setting one fuzzy constraint on each single issue used in [13]. In [15], the authors propose a method based on kernel density estimation to learn the weights assigned by the opponent, but it still requires the agents have some prior information about the real weights the opponent assigns on the issues. Compared to their work, we consider the negotiation over continuous issues and choose the Euclidean distance instead the similarity criterion. It does not require any prior information of agents and is not restricted to linearly additive utility functions. In [16], the trade-off algorithm based on similarity criterion is extended to the negotiation between more than two agents. The algorithm lets each agent choose the counter-offer that is the most similar to the offers of all the other agents on his indifference curve. Because no single notion is introduced to model all the other offers, the algorithm lets the agent select the counter-offer as the one with minimum square (similarity) difference respecting all the other offers. In our work, we use one reference point to model two agents' bids and let the other agent still choose the closest offer based on the Euclidean distance. No other (new) measurement is required. Instead of the negotiation mechanism, an auction-based method is proposed in [17] for multi-issue negotiation with non-linear utility functions.

3   The Negotiation Model

Suppose three rational agents, $N = \{1, 2, 3\}$, partition two issues (resources), $M = \{1, 2\}$, through negotiation. The range of each issue is normalized to a *continuous* range $[0, 1]$. Each agent requires a combination of a part of every issue. Hence, we let the two issues be bundled and negotiated concurrently, so the agents can make trade-offs between issues to maximize their utilities within an agreement. The negotiation takes place round by round $n \in \mathbb{N}$ until an agreement is reached or some agent quits. In each round, three agents bid partitions *sequentially* in some order. The bidding order can either be pre-specified before the negotiation starts or be generated randomly before every round. In this model, only a unanimous agreement can be accepted and implemented.

In the two-agent negotiation, whether one agent proposes partitions for two agents or only for himself has the same effect. However, if an agent needs to propose partitions for all in the negotiation between more than two agents, he has to decide how his opponents divide the issues left by him. Considering that every agent actually only focuses on his own parts and does not know the preferences of his opponents, we let agents bid in the way that every agent only proposes his own desired parts of issues [8]. We let $\mathbf{x}_i \in (0, 1)^2$ denote a bid of agent $i \in N$ in a round and let $x_{i,j} \in \mathbf{x}_i$ denote the amount of issue $j \in M$. We define an agreement to be:

$$\mathbf{x} = (\mathbf{x}_1, \mathbf{x}_2, \mathbf{x}_3) \text{ subject to } \forall j \in M \sum_{i=1}^{3} x_{i,j} \leq 1 \tag{A}$$

where $\mathbf{x}$ is a profile of bids made by three agents in a round. If the three bids can form an agreement in the round, the negotiation stop successfully, otherwise the negotiation passes on to the next round. Each agent $i \in N$ has a negotiation deadline T_i. If no agreement is reached in any round $n \leq T$ where $T = min\{T_1, T_2, T_3\}$, the agent will quit and the whole negotiation will stop unsuccessfully. Every agent gets zero utility at the outcome of disagreement.

In this work, we assume every agent has a *strictly convex* preference. We define the utility function $u_i : (0, 1)^{2 \times 3} \times \mathbb{N} \to \mathbb{R}^+$, where $u_i(\mathbf{x}, n)$ represents the utility that agent i would get in round n, if the agents all made bids as specified in $\mathbf{x}$. If $\mathbf{x}$ can form an agreement, the utility of $\mathbf{x}$ for agent i only depends on his bid $\mathbf{x}_i$ and is calculated by a valuation function $v_i : (0, 1)^2 \rightarrow \mathbb{R}^+$. In this work, we assume the valuation function to be *continuous* and *strictly monotonically increasing* in each of the issues. Formally, the utility function is given by:

$$u_i(\mathbf{x}, n) = \begin{cases} 0 & \text{if } n > T \\ 0 & \text{if } n = T \text{ and not } (\mathbf{A}) \\ v_i(\mathbf{x}_i) & \text{if } n \leq T \text{ and } (\mathbf{A}) \end{cases} \tag{1}$$

where $\mathbf{x}_i \in \mathbf{x}$ and $T = min\{T_1, T_2, T_3\}$.

In this model, every agent's preference and negotiation deadline are private information. Given the negotiation model above, we investigate the negotiation strategies of agents under the incomplete information setting.

4   The Negotiation Strategies

In this section, we present the negotiation strategies. As trade-offs exist between issues, it is possible that multiple bids give the same maximum utility to the bidder. Hence, when it is an agent's turn to bid, he can decide a desired utility level first and then choose a bid amongst those bids of the utility level. The negotiation strategy of an agent is then to specify (i) how to determine the desired utility levels during the whole negotiation and (ii) how to bid given a desired utility level and possible bids of other agents.

Once an agent determines a desired utility level, all bids introducing the same maximum utility at the level are indifferent to the agent, but his bids may influence the bidding of his opponents, which results in various outcomes. To enhance the opportunity of reaching an agreement with his desired utility, the agent can choose a bid to benefit his opponents as much as possible at his current utility level. This is the cooperation part of the negotiation, in which all agents may be better off by making trade-offs between issues, and the negotiation may result in a Pareto-optimal outcome. An outcome is Pareto-optimal if there is no other outcome that would make at least on agent better off without making any other agent worse off. Given the multiple bids at an agent's current utility level, the one benefiting his opponents most will make them most satisfied. We call it the most satisfied bid. If no agreement can be reached on the current utility levels, even if all agents cooperatively make bids satisfying with each other as much as possible, one or more agents must concede their desires of utilities to pursue an agreement, which is better than zero utility of disagreement.

Hence, an agent's negotiation strategy can be decomposed into Pareto-optimal-search methods and concession strategies [4]. The former takes the Pareto optimality into account to search the most satisfied bid (for all agents) on the current utility level; the latter is to determine how to make concessions by lowering the desired utility levels. Under an incomplete information setting, at any moment, every agent knows his own current desired utility level, his preference and the previous bids of his opponents. In the next section, first, we will present how to use the *orthogonal bidding strategy* as the Pareto-optimal-search method to make the most satisfied bid at the current utility levels in case of three agents. Second, we will introduce the concession strategies.

4.1 The Orthogonal Bidding Strategy

Given the utility function of agent $i \in N$, a utility level can be represented by an indifference curve, which is a graph showing different combinations of issues, between which the agent is indifferent. Thus, it is equivalently to choose any bid (point) on an indifference curve as rendering the same level of utility for the agent. To enhance the opportunity to reach an agreement at his current desired utility level, the agent can choose one bid on the curve which satisfies his opponents most. That means, the rest of issues introduced by the bid gives his opponents highest possibility to get their desired utility levels. Reversely, if a bid of an agent is closest to the rest of issues left by his opponents, it is the one that his opponents satisfy most, give their current desires.

In this section, we will present how an agent determines the most satisfied bid on his curve, given the last bid of each of his opponents, and how the agents search the possible Pareto-optimal solutions, given their current desired utility levels.

The Strategy. When it is agent i's turn to bid, to choose a bid that satisfies his opponents most, he needs to model his opponents' desires first. For the two-agent negotiation studied in [4,5,6,7], each agent's offer can be used directly to guide his opponent's counter-offer towards an agreement. However, for the three-agent negotiation model in this work, moving bids close to each other cannot form an agreement. Moreover, when an agent considers compromises, two bids of his opponents should be taken into account together.

To solve the problem above, we introduce the reference point to represent the desires of any two agents for the other agent during the negotiation. Given two agents' bids, the rest of the issues composes a reference point which implies the joint desire of the two agents for the other agent, and making bids close to the reference point can make them satisfied. Formally, the reference point r_i is given by

$$r_i = (r_{i,1}, r_{i,2}) = (1 - \sum_{k \in N-\{i\}} x_{k,1}, \ 1 - \sum_{k \in N-\{i\}} x_{k,2}) \tag{2}$$

where $\mathbf{x}_k = (x_{k,1}, x_{k,2})$ is always the last bid of agent $k \in N - \{i\}$, which can happen in the current round or the previous round determined by the bidding order.

We define the orthogonal bidding strategy to be the way that when it is agent i's turn to bid, he always chooses the bid on his current indifferent curve which is closest (measured in the Euclidean distance) to the reference point r_i. In this work, the reference points are given by Equation (2). We mention that there may be some other ways to choose the reference points, and the way to determine the reference point is independent of the orthogonal bidding strategy. Figure 1 illustrates how each agent chooses a bid most satisfied his opponents' desires, which are modeled by a reference point based on their latest bids, where no concession happens during the negotiation round (so the curves are fixed). The indifference curves of the example are generated based on Cobb-Douglas functions. Given the bids of agent 1 and 3 in round n, agents 2, 3 and 1 bid sequentially in round $n + 1$.

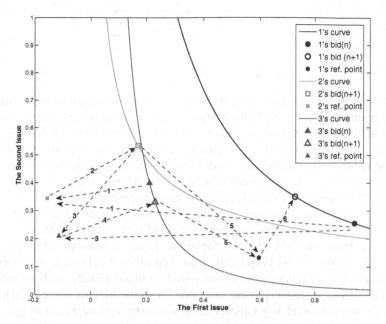

Fig. 1. Example of the orthogonal bidding strategy

(1) First agent 2 calculates the reference point based on the bids of agent 1 and 3 in round n.

(2) Agent 2 chooses the bid which is closest to the reference point determined in step (1) on his curve.

(3) Agent 3 calculates the reference point based on agent 1's bid in round n and agent 2's bid chosen in step (2).

(4) Agent 3 chooses the bid which is closest to the reference point determined in step (3) on his curve.

(5) Agent 1 calculates the reference point based on agent 2's bid chosen in step (2) and agent 3's bid chosen in step (4).

(6) Agent 1 chooses the bid which is closest to the reference point determined in step (5) on his curve.

Although it is possible that some agent uses the orthogonal bidding strategy but some agent uses another negotiation strategy, in the rest of this work, we analyze the solution that all three agents use the orthogonal bidding strategy to search the Pareto-optimal solution. The analysis also holds if they do not know the strategies of each other, but they do use the orthogonal bidding strategy.

The Agreement. To better to describe the process of reaching an agreement, we let R be the point representing the remaining issues. given three bids, and let Δ denote the distance between the remaining issues R to the origin $\mathbf{0} = (0,0)$. Formally, the remaining issues R and the distance Δ can be calculated by

$$R = (R_1, R_2) = (1 - \sum_{i=1}^{3} x_{i,1}, 1 - \sum_{i=1}^{3} x_{i,2}),$$

$$\Delta = \|R - \mathbf{0}\| = \|R\| \tag{3}$$

The remaining issues R indicates the bidding result of a round, given three bids; the reference point r_i indicates the bidding state of agent i's opponents, given two bids. Note that before reaching an agreement, the remaining issues here may have negative values, $R_1 < 0$ or $R_2 < 0$ or both, which implies the total requirements of issues still need to be reduced. In case the remainder is negative, we will use the measure Δ to indicate how far the current negotiation state is from an agreement. Next, we use an example to show how three agents keep using the orthogonal bidding strategy on fixed utility levels to reach an agreement. We call the process the orthogonal search. In this example, three agents' initial bids are generated randomly and the indifference curves are generated based on Cobb-Douglas functions. Figure 2 illustrates the orthogonal search in which three agents keep bidding on their utility levels without concession. The bids and reference points move closer round by round. Finally, each agent's bids and reference points are converged into one point on his indifference curve. That means, each agent's final bid completely satisfies the desires of his opponents and an agreement is reached. From another perspective, the distance Δ keeps reducing and the remaining issues R moves to the origin $\mathbf{0}$ and finally converges into it. That also indicates reaching an agreement. We mention it is possible that the bids of an agreement do not exactly coincide with their reference points after finite rounds, and the convergence may be

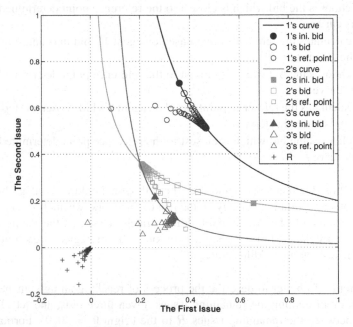

Fig. 2. Example of the orthogonal search

generated based on the finite precision of computers. Based on the example, we give the following lemma.

Lemma 1. *A profile of bids* $\mathbf{x} = (\mathbf{x}_1, \mathbf{x}_2, \mathbf{x}_3)$ *is an agreement* $\iff$ *each reference point* r_i *Pareto dominates bid* $\mathbf{x}_i$, *i.e.,* $r_{i,j} \geq x_{i,j}$, *where* $i \in N$ *and* $j \in M$.

Proof. Because $\mathbf{x}$ is an agreement, given the condition of agreements (**A**), $x_{i,j} \leq 1 - \sum_{k \in N - \{i\}} x_{k,j}$ where $j \in M$. Given the definition of reference points in Equation (1), r_i Pareto dominates $\mathbf{x}_i$, i.e., $r_{i,j} \geq x_{i,j}$.

If $r_{i,j} \geq x_{i,j}$ where $i \in N$ and $j \in M$, given the definition of reference points in Equation (1), we have $x_{i,j} + \sum_{k \in N - \{i\}} x_{k,j} \leq 1$. Hence, the bid profile $\mathbf{x}$ is an agreement. $\square$

The Pareto Optimality. In the example of Figure 2, the remaining issues R converges into the origin. That means, all issues are exactly partitioned without shortages and remains. However, this does not necessarily indicate a Pareto-optimal solution in multi-issue negotiation as the agents may still have chances to get Pareto improvements by making trade-offs between issues. A Pareto improvement is a change from one solution to another solution that can make at least one agent better off without sacrificing the utilities of the other agents. The following example shows a negotiation solution, in which the issues are partitioned completely but the opportunities of Pareto improvements clearly exist.

Figure 3 illustrates an example where three agents reach an agreement by using the orthogonal search on relatively low utility levels. The initial reference points in Figure 3 are

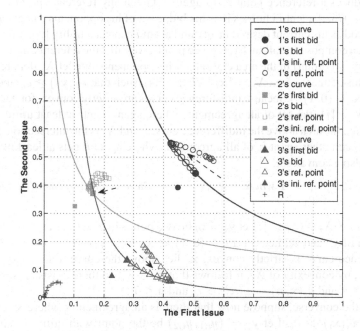

Fig. 3. Example of the orthogonal search on low utility levels

derived from the final reference points of the orthogonal search on higher utility levels. Each agent determines his first bid based on the initial reference points in the orthogonal way separately and then do the orthogonal search on the fixed curves. We observe that each agent's bids and reference points converge into one point (in the direction indicated by the arrow) on the curve and an agreement is formed by the convergence points. (The convergence point of agent 2 just happens close to his first bid.) However, different from the example in Figure 2, the reference points appear in the upper-right area of the curves. Because those indifference curves are strictly convex, any point (bid) in the upper-right area of a curve can give the agent a higher utility than the utility level of the curve. Suppose agent i chooses a reference point r_i in the upper-right area of his curve instead of the convergence point as his bid and the other two agents choose the bids which generate r_i on their curves. Each of the new bids equals to the reference point introduced by the other two bids. The three new bids can form an agreement (Lemma 1); agent i's utility is increased and the other two agents' utilities are unchanged. That is a Pareto improvement, so the solution of the three convergence points is not Pareto-optimal. From another perspective, except for the final state, the remaining issues are always more than zero in the orthogonal search. That means, the agents have opportunities to reach an agreement with less issue and use extra issues to make Pareto improvement. Next, we give the geometrical interpretation of Pareto-optimal solutions achieved by using our method and the mathematical proof.

We let c_i denote the current desired utility level of agent $i \in N$ and C_i denote the set of all points on the indifference curve of utility c_i, i.e., $C_i = \{\mathbf{x}_i \mid v_i(\mathbf{x}_i) = c_i\}$. That means, any point in C_i has the value c_i. If the point is a bid of an agreement, the bid will give agent i utility c_i. Every combination of two points (bids) on the other two agents' curves introduces a reference point r_i to agent i. Given any reference point r_i where $r_{i,j} > 0$ $(j \in M)$, if agent i chooses it as his bid, each of his opponents can get a utility at least as good as his current desired utility and agent i can get a utility larger than zero. Given the area composed of all such reference points, we call it the reference area of agent i where every bid (point) in the area can satisfy his opponents. We let X_i denote the set of all such bids of agent i, i.e., $X_i = \{\mathbf{x}_i \mid \forall k \neq i \, \exists \mathbf{x}_k \text{ such that } v_k(\mathbf{x}_k) \geq c_k \text{ and } (\mathbf{A})\}$. (Recall that $\mathbf{x}_i \in (0, 1)^2$.) Because indifference curves are strictly convex, for each other agent $k \in N - \{i\}$, the set of all agreements where agent k gets at least utility c_k is a convex set (i.e., the area above the indifference curve), and X_i is the intersection of these sets, one for each other agent k, of all agreements where agent k gets at least utility c_k, and is thus also a convex set.

Lemma 2. $|X_i \cap C_i| > 1$ where $i \in N$ $\iff$ there is an agreement $\mathbf{x}$ such that $u_i(\mathbf{x}, n) > c_i$ $(n \leq T)$.

Proof. Suppose $|X_i \cap C_i| > 1$. Let $\mathbf{y}_i \neq \mathbf{z}_i$ be two points in $X_i \cap C_i$. Let $\mathbf{x}_i$ be a convex combination of $\mathbf{y}_i$ and $\mathbf{z}_i$, i.e., for a $t \in (0, 1)$ let $\mathbf{x}_i = t \cdot \mathbf{y}_i + (1 - t) \cdot \mathbf{z}_i$. Because the indifference curve is strictly convex, $\mathbf{x}_i$ lies above the curve, thus $v_i(\mathbf{x}_i) > c_i$. Furthermore, by convexity of X_i, it follows that $\mathbf{x}_i \in X_i$, so there exists an agreement $\mathbf{x}$ where $\mathbf{x}_i \in \mathbf{x}$ and $u_i(\mathbf{x}, n) = v_i(\mathbf{x}_i) > c_i$ and $n \leq T$.

To prove the converse, suppose now that there is an agreement $\mathbf{x}$ where $\mathbf{x}_i \in \mathbf{x}$ and $u_i(\mathbf{x}, n) = v_i(\mathbf{x}_i) > c_i$. Let $\mathbf{y}_i = (y_{i,1}, y_{i,2})$ be the point with utility c_i such that $y_{i,1} = x_{i,1}$, and let $\mathbf{z}_i = (z_{i,1}, z_{i,2})$ be the point with utility c_i such that $z_{i,2} = x_{i,2}$.

These points both exist, because of continuity of the utility function. Also we know that y_i and z_i are in X_i because they only use less of one of the issues, and all utility functions are strictly monotonically increasing in all issues. Thus $X_i \cap C_i$ contains at least these two points.   □

Figure 4 gives the graphical representation of Lemma 2 where agent i represents the third agent. The left one illustrates the existence of an agreement x where $x_i \in x$ is above the curve and x_i is a convex combination of y_i and z_i, when $|X_i \cap C_i| > 1$. The right one illustrates when an agreement x exists and $u_i(x, n) = v_i(x_i) > c_i$, there are at least two points $y_i, z_i \in X_i$ on the curve. Hence, $|X_i \cap C_i| > 1$.

Obviously, when an agreement x in the above example exists, agent i (red one) can make Pareto improvements by bidding x_i instead of any point on his current indifference curve. Reversely, if $X_i \cap C_i = \emptyset$, no agreement can be reached on the current utility levels, which is not a Pareto-optimal outcome of this negotiation. Hence, if the reference area and the indifference curve of every agent $i \in N$ has a unique intersection, the profile of three intersections is a Pareto-optimal solution. We give the following theorem with a condition that the indifference curves are strictly convex.

Theorem 1. $|X_i \cap C_i| = 1$ *where* $i \in N$ $\iff$ *there is a Pareto-optimal solution* $x = (x_1, x_2, x_3)$ *where* $u_i(x, n) = c_i$ $(n \leq T)$.

Proof. We give proof by contradiction. Suppose there is a Pareto-optimal solution x where $u_i(x, n) = c_i$. Suppose $|X_i \cap C_i| \neq 1$. If $|X_i \cap C_i| = 0$, no agreement can be reached at every agent i's desired utility level c_i, so no Pareto-optimal solution x exists. There is a contradiction. If $|X_i \cap C_i| > 1$, Pareto improvements exist, i.e., $\exists x'$ such that $u_i(x', n) > c_i$ (Lemma 2), so the solution x in which $u_i(x, n) = c_i$ is not a Pareto-optimal solution. There is a contradiction. Hence, if there is a Pareto-optimal solution x where $u_i(x, n) = c_i$, then $|X_i \cap C_i| = 1$ and $X_i \cap C_i = \{x_i\}$.

Suppose $|X_i \cap C_i| = 1$. Suppose no Pareto-optimal solution exists. If no agreement exists, then $|X_i \cap C_i| = 0$. There is a contradiction. If there is an agreement x but it is not Pareto-optimal, then Pareto improvements exists. If $\exists x'$ such that $u_i(x', n) > c_i$, then $|X_i \cap C_i| > 1$ (Lemma 2). There is a contradiction. Hence, if $|X_i \cap C_i| = 1$, there is a Pareto-optimal solution x where $X_i \cap C_i = \{x_i\}$ and $u_i(x, n) = c_i$.   □

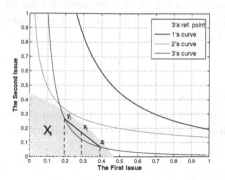
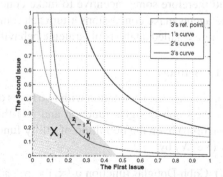

Fig. 4. Example of the reference area

4.2   Concession Strategies

In the previous section, we presented how the agents bid at desired utility levels. At the beginning of the negotiation, each agent has a relatively high desire of utility, and he can choose to concede at any moment as the negotiation progresses. In this section, we address the concession strategies which determine how to concede, given the previous bids. In this work, we develop four concession strategies:

1. *Amount of utility.* Agent $i \in N$ concedes a fixed amount utility au.
2. *Fraction of utility.* Agent $i \in N$ concedes a fixed fraction $fu < 1$ of the current desired utility.
3. *Fraction of difference.* Agent i concedes a fixed fraction $fd < 1$ of the difference between his current desired utility and the utility that he would get by bidding the last reference point r_i. When $r_{i,j} < 0$ $(j \in M)$, the strategy adopts the difference between his current desired utility and zero utility, which means using the origin to replace the reference point r_i.
4. *Fraction of remains.* Agent i concedes a fix fraction $fr < 1$ of the remaining issues R. Before reaching an agreement, one or two issues' remains R_j have negative values. The conceding is to add a fraction of the remain(s) that has the negative value(s) to the last bid $\mathbf{x}_i$.

For the first strategy, the concession per time is fixed. For all the other three strategies, the concession per time turns to small as the negotiation proceeds, which is helpful for agents to reach (near) Pareto-optimal solutions.

Combining the concession strategies and the orthogonal bidding strategy, in next section, we evaluate the average performance of different combinations of negotiation strategies. We will measure the Pareto improvement of each agent, the change from his utility and bid in the agreement to his utility and bid in a Pareto-optimal solution.

5   Experimental Analysis

In this section, we design experiments to measure the efficiency and optimality of the proposed negotiation solutions, and compare the performance of different concession strategies. In the setting we study, there is a negotiation deadline for each of the agents, and therefore some incentive to make concessions. In our current experiments we let the agents make concessions after each round until an agreement is reached, and leave a more detailed analysis of strategic behavior for future work.

5.1   Settings

We simulate the negotiation with two types of functions that are used a lot in economics: (i) the Cobb-Douglas function and (ii) the constant elasticity of substitution (CES) function. Given the definition of utility function (1), we specify the valuation function v_i $(i \in N)$ by:

(i) Cobb-Douglas function $v_i(\mathbf{x}_i) = \gamma_i \cdot x_{i,1}^{\alpha_i} \cdot x_{i,2}^{\beta_i}$,
(ii) CES function $v_i(\mathbf{x}_i) = \gamma_i \cdot (\alpha_i \cdot x_{i,1}^{\beta_i} + (1 - \alpha_i) \cdot x_{i,2}^{\beta_i})^{1/\beta_i}$.

Table 1. Parameters of utility functions

Type	α_1	α_2	α_3	β_1	β_2	β_3	γ_1	γ_2	γ_3
Cobb-Douglas 1	0.64	0.65	0.83	0.52	0.83	0.42	5.97	6.21	8.14
Cobb-Douglas 2	0.24	0.25	0.25	0.92	0.78	0.78	6.4	7.9	8.5
Cobb-Douglas 3	0.267	0.35	0.23	0.91	0.82	0.88	5.31	5.34	8.31
CES 1	0.91	0.855	0.83	0.123	0.25	0.33	8.23	7.12	9.28
CES 2	0.717	0.65	0.623	0.443	0.492	0.464	7.8	8.72	9.348

We generate the parameters of the valuation functions randomly and choose five typical cases listed in Table 1. Therefore, we have 5 instances of utility functions in the following experiments. Given four concession strategies, for each of them, we choose two factors. One is a (relatively) big step factor, which can make the agents reach agreements quickly and get near Pareto-optimal outcomes. The other one is a small step factor, which let agents get more efficient outcomes. Therefore, we totally have 8 instances of concession strategies.

Given an agreement $\mathbf{x}$, we measure the efficiency of this outcome by Pareto improvements. For each agent $i \in N$, we let P_i denote the Euclidean distance between his final bid $\mathbf{x}_i \in \mathbf{x}$ and his bid in the Pareto-optimal solution, in which agent i's utility is maximized and the utility for agent $k \in N - i$ is kept the same as $u_k(\mathbf{x}, n)$ where n is the finish round of negotiation. In addition, we let Q_i denote the difference between agent i's utility $u_i(\mathbf{x}, n)$ and his utility achieved in the Pareto-optimal solution.

For each combination of one utility function instance and one concession strategy instance, we run the negotiation 100 times, each of which has random initial bids. Given all results using instances of Cobb-Douglas utility functions, we calculate average P_i and Q_i for each concession strategy instance. Finally, we get 8 pairs of P_i and Q_i of each agent i for 8 concession strategy instances combined with Cobb-Douglas utility functions, and get another 8 pairs of P_i and Q_i of each agent i for 8 concession strategy instances combined with CES utility functions. To better compare and analyze the performance of our solutions, we enlarge the range of issues 100 times in the calculation of utilities. All results are presented in the next section.

5.2   Experimental Results

Table 2 shows the average Euclidean distance P_i and utility difference Q_i from the Pareto-optimal solution of each agent i for various concession strategy instances combined with Cobb-Douglas utility functions. Table 3 shows the average Euclidean distance P_i and utility difference Q_i from the Pareto-optimal solution of each agent i for various concession strategy instances combined with CES utility functions. For example, the element $(1, 1)(= 0.0541 / 25.6880)$ in Table 2 is the average Euclidean distance and utility difference of agent 1 between his bids in the agreements and the Pareto-optimal solutions respectively, which are generated in the experiments of concession strategy "amount of utility" with the factor $au = 30$ and Cobb-Douglas utility functions. The column of round in each table indicates how many rounds the agents reach the agreements.

Table 2. Average Euclidean distance and utility difference from Pareto-optimal solutions of each agent for various concession strategy instances combined with Cobb-Douglas utility functions

Concession strategy	P_1 / Q_1	P_2 / Q_2	P_3 / Q_3	Round
Amount of utility ($au = 30$)	0.0541 / 25.6880	0.0314 / 34.3712	0.0383 / 32.6222	11
Amount of utility ($au = 10$)	0.0103 / 8.3359	0.0127 / 11.4980	0.0117 / 10.5680	21
Frac. of utility ($fu = 0.05$)	0.0312 / 25.2408	0.0301 / 30.2793	0.0279 / 28.1602	12
Frac. of utility ($fu = 0.01$)	0.0121 / 8.1018	0.0096 / 11.0645	0.0132 / 9.0251	58
Frac. of difference ($fd = 0.1$)	0.0190 / 1.7297	0.0164 / 2.6683	0.0139 / 1.9356	17
Frac. of difference ($fd = 0.05$)	0.0070 / 1.2109	0.0072 / 1.6012	0.0090 / 1.2351	31
Frac. of remains ($fr = 0.15$)	0.0830 / 14.8853	0.0724 / 15.4760	0.0451 / 13.9908	9
Frac. of remains ($fr = 0.1$)	0.0438 / 3.4280	0.0372 / 5.1806	0.0168 / 4.0223	15

Table 3. Average Euclidean distance and utility distance from Pareto-optimal solutions of each agent for various concession strategy instance combined with CES utility functions

Concession strategy	P_1 / Q_1	P_2 / Q_2	P_3 / Q_3	Round
Amount of utility ($au = 30$)	0.0725 / 44.9505	0.0711 / 41.0294	0.0795 / 50.9900	15
Amount of utility ($au = 10$)	0.0372 / 14.2733	0.0261 / 14.8818	0.0283 / 16.9309	43
Frac. of utility ($fu = 0.05$)	0.0413 / 23.2897	0.0401 / 23.0080	0.0422 / 27.0832	19
Frac. of utility ($fu = 0.01$)	0.0330 / 7.3399	0.0136 / 7.2989	0.0220 / 8.5175	93
Frac. of difference ($fd = 0.1$)	0.0209 / 2.0875	0.0139 / 1.9603	0.0402 / 2.3787	19
Frac. of difference ($fd = 0.05$)	0.0037 / 1.3575	0.0231 / 1.1985	0.0168 / 1.5789	35
Frac. of remains ($fr = 0.15$)	0.0152 / 4.1480	0.0561 / 4.0198	0.0623 / 4.6728	11
Frac. of remains ($fr = 0.1$)	0.0308 / 2.1478	0.0317 / 1.9390	0.0369 / 2.3900	16

From the results, we find both the Euclidean distance and the utility difference from the agreements to the Pareto-optimal solutions of each concession strategy instance is very small, which indicates our solution can provide near Pareto-optimal solutions for those types of utility functions. (Recall that the range of issues is enlarged 100 times in the calculation of utilities.) For each concession strategy, when a big step factor is used, the agreements can be reached very fast; when a small step factor is used, the agreements are very close to the Pareto-optimal solutions for every agents. Although the performance of the former is a little lower than that of the latter, we find it is also very good. Meanwhile, the speed of reaching agreements of the latter is a little slower than that of the former, but it is completely acceptable in the automated negotiation between software agents. Amongst those concession strategies, we find the performance of concession strategy "fraction of difference" is best in our experiments. The reason is it takes the reference points into account, which is the key factor of the orthogonal bidding strategy. To conclude, the solution of the orthogonal bidding strategy combined with well-designed concession strategies is very efficient such that near Pareto-optimal outcomes can be achieved quickly.

6   Conclusions and Future Work

In this paper, we present an automated three-agent two-issue negotiation solution to solve a resource allocation problem. We adopt a multilateral negotiation model, in which three agents bid combinations of parts of two continuously valued issues sequentially. The model applies to multi-issue negotiation between more than two players in the real world. We develop tractable heuristics of negotiation strategies used in a complex setting, in which the agents have non-linear utility functions and incomplete information about their opponents' preferences and negotiation deadlines. The negotiation strategies are decomposed into two parts: a Pareto-optimal-search method and concession strategies. The agents determine their desired utility levels by using concession strategies first and then use the orthogonal bidding strategy as the Pareto-optimal-search method to find the bids which satisfy all agents most on their current utility levels. The method makes bids approaching the Pareto-optimal solution as the negotiation proceeds. Important technique contributions lie in the development of the orthogonal bidding strategy for three-agent cases, which can be easily extended to multi-agent cases, and the identification of agreements and Pareto-optimal outcomes achieved by the methods based on mathematical proof. We show through computer experiments that the solution composed of the orthogonal bidding strategy and well-designed concession strategies is very efficient such that (near) Pareto-optimal outcomes can be achieved in short time.

An interesting extension of our work will be to develop the orthogonal bidding strategy for three-agent three-issue cases. The orthogonal method will work on indifference surfaces. Searching the most satisfied bids and identifying agreements and Pareto-optimal outcomes will become more complex. Further, we may design some heuristic combined with the orthogonal method to solve the negotiation with many issues. Another interesting extension is to develop more precise concession strategies, such as time independent strategies and correlated strategies. Moreover, we may study the negotiation results when utility functions are non-strict monotonicity.

References

1. Fatima, S., Wooldridge, M., Jennings, N.: Multi-Issue Negotiation with Deadlines. Journal of Artificial Intelligence Research 27, 381–417 (2006)
2. Binmore, K.: Bargaining and Coalitions. Game-Theoretic Models of Bargaining, 269–304 (1985)
3. Gerding, E., Somefun, D., La Poutre, J.: Multi-attribute Bilateral Bargaining in a One-to-Many Setting. In: Faratin, P., Rodríguez-Aguilar, J.-A. (eds.) AMEC 2004. LNCS (LNAI), vol. 3435, p. 129. Springer, Heidelberg (2005)
4. Somefun, D.J.A., Gerding, E.H., Bohte, S.M., La Poutré, J.A.H.: Automated negotiation and bundling of information goods. In: Faratin, P., Parkes, D.C., Rodríguez-Aguilar, J.-A., Walsh, W.E. (eds.) AMEC 2003. LNCS (LNAI), vol. 3048, pp. 1–17. Springer, Heidelberg (2004)
5. Somefun, D., Gerding, E., La Poutre, J.: Efficient methods for automated multi-issue negotiation: Negotiating over a two-part tariff. International Journal of Intelligent Systems 21(1) (2006)
6. Lai, G., Sycara, K., Li, C.: A decentralized model for multi-attribute negotiations with incomplete information and general utility functions. In: Proceedings of second international workshop on rational, robust, and secure negotiations in multi-agent systems. Springer, Heidelberg (2006)
7. Lai, G., Sycara, K.: A generic framework for automated multi-attribute negotiation. Group Decision and Negotiation (2009)

8. Wu, M., de Weerdt, M., La Poutré, J., Yadati, C., Zhang, Y., Witteveen, C.: Multi-player Multi-issue Negotiation with Complete Information. In: Proceedings of second international workshop on agent-based complex automated negotiations. Springer, Heidelberg (2009)
9. Rubinstein, A.: Perfect Equilibrium in a Bargaining Model. Econometrica 50(1), 97–110 (1982)
10. Shaked, A.: A Three-Person Unanimity Game. In: Talk given at the Los Angeles national meetings of the Institute of Management Sciences and the Operations Research Society of America (1986)
11. Fatima, S., Wooldridge, M., Jennings, N.: An agenda-based framework for multi-issue negotiation. Artificial Intelligence 152(1), 1–45 (2004)
12. Rausser, G., Simon, L.: A non-cooperative model of collective decision making: A multilateral bargaining approach. Department of Agricultural and Resource Economics. University of California, Berkeley (1992)
13. Faratin, P., Sierra, C., Jennings, N.: Using similarity criteria to make issue trade-offs in automated negotiations. Artificial Intelligence 142(2), 205–237 (2002)
14. Luo, X., Jennings, N., Shadbolt, N., Leung, H., Lee, J.: A fuzzy constraint based model for bilateral, multi-issue negotiations in semi-competitive environments. Artificial Intelligence 148(1), 53–102 (2003)
15. Coehoorn, R., Jennings, N.: Learning on opponent's preferences to make effective multi-issue negotiation trade-offs. In: Proceedings of the 6th international conference on Electronic commerce, pp. 59–68. ACM, New York (2004)
16. Ros, R., Sierra, C.: A negotiation meta strategy combining trade-off and concession moves. Autonomous Agents and Multi-Agent Systems 12(2), 163–181 (2006)
17. Ito, T., Hattori, H., Klein, M.: Multi-issue negotiation protocol for agents: Exploring nonlinear utility spaces. In: Proceedings of the 20th International Joint Conference on Artificial Intelligence (IJCAI 2007), pp. 1347–1352 (2007)

Token Based Resource Sharing in Heterogeneous Multi-agent Teams

Yang Xu[1] and Paul Scerri[2]

[1] School of Computer Science and Engineering,
University of Electronic Science and Technology of China,
Chengdu, SC 610054, China
xuyang@uestc.edu.cn
[2] School of Computer Science, Carnegie Mellon University,
Pittsburgh, PA 15213, USA
pscerri@cs.cmu.edu

Abstract. In a cooperative heterogeneous multiagent team, distributed agents are required to harmonize activities and make the best use of resources to achieve their common goal. Agents are required to share their resource with very a few of the teammates who need it but with a limited view of the team, they do not know who they are. In this paper, we put forward our resource sharing algorithm for a large heterogeneous team. It does not require a complete view of the team or depend on excessive communication. Agents only make use of the knowledge from allocating tasks or sharing the other resources. The key is that we use influence diagram to model how agents may predict what the other agents are doing from their limited information received. By utilizing the relevances between tasks and resources or pairs of resources, We have setup a local probability model so that agents can reason in the uncertainty and can efficiently share the resource within a few hops to its target. Based on this model, we have two additional designs of dynamic threshold and local decision exchange model so that agents can enhance their local decisions and greatly increase the resource sharing performance. Our experiment results show this system design is feasible for resource sharing in a large heterogeneous multiagent team.

Keywords: Resource sharing; Teamwork; Local decision model; Uncertainty; Heuristic reasoning.

1 Introduction

Exciting emerging applications in domains such as military operations, space or disaster response require hundreds or thousands of heterogeneous agents and robots to work together. In those teams, efficient resource sharing is important to perform their activities [5], e.g., delivering a hydrant to a fire fighting capable agent to help it to fight a fire. However, the resource requirements come to the team in a spontaneous, unpredictable and most importantly, distributed way. Without a complete view of the team or knowing what other members are doing,

J.-J. Yang et al. (Eds.): PRIMA 2009, LNAI 5925, pp. 113–126, 2009.

an agent cannot decide where to share a resource. For example, without knowing who is going to fight a fire, the agent holding a hydrant cannot make its decision where to send it. Moreover, in a typical heterogeneous multiagent team, only a small number of agents are capable of performing a special task and require some specific types of resources, therefore, the resource sharing has to be targeted.

While the problem of resource sharing has been extensively studied, previous resource sharing researches always avoided the key problem of agents' inabilities to gain the complete team knowledge, either by designing centralized information agent [14] or via the heavy communication to maintain accurate team states [13], rendering it inappropriate to a large heterogeneous multiagent team. In contrast, our solution for resource sharing among large teams can perform distributed resource sharing without maintaining accurate models of the team nor the excessive communications. In our approach, resources are represented by a resource token and allowed to be passed in the network. An agent receiving a resource token gets the permission to access the resource. If the agent cannot make use of a resource, it should locally make a decision to pass it on further to an agent that may have better knowledge of specifically who needs the resource. Therefore, no single agent needs to make the whole decisions of where to send a resource but push it to the target agents closer.

In this paper, we analyze how agents make decisions to share resources in a view of decision theoretical agents. The decision theoretical approach such as POMDP cannot solve the problem because agents cannot get a complete view of the team state or have rich knowledge of what the others are doing. However, from our analysis of influence diagram model, agents' previous received messages such as the coordination information of task allocations or the other resource tokens may give them a good clue of the team states. For example, previously received pending task of "fight a fire in a building" denotes the direction where the task is sent is much closer to the agent who will take the role. Therefore, it is more reasonable to send a hydrant to these part of agents who are more likely to do fire fighting. On the other hand, the receiving of a hydrant denotes the senders are less likely involved in the fire fighting activities and they should be excluded from sending other similar resources.

Based on agents' incomplete knowledge about the team states, we have setup a local probability decision model to help agents make decisions under uncertainty. Although those decisions are imprecise but under the team's social network organization, agents' imprecise decisions are able to gather more related coordination messages to improve their models. Under the small world effect, a resource is able to be sent to any potential receiver within very a few "hops". In addition to this approach, we have designed tokens' dynamic threshold to help the resource sharing out of their local optimal decisions but assign the resource to a global optimal agent. Moreover, our local decision exchange model allows agents proactive "ask for" resources and influence the resource sharing decision of the agents close to it so that related resources can be quickly delivered.

2   Related Work

The problem of resource sharing has been extensively studied in the domain such as military, electronic commerce, grid computing, scheduling and Timetabling [3,5]. Most related work can be classified into one of two major categories: centralized or decentralized resource sharing. The first strand of research is based on a centralized model, such as descending demand procedure [2], combinatorial auctions [4], contract-net protocols [8] and task-swap negotiation protocol [9]. Those kinds of researches are to find some optimal solutions for resource sharing that could maximum multiagent team's utilities [6], moreover under some specific constraints over the domain [7]. Centralized algorithms rely on all resource planning with one or some particular supervisors, e.g., an auctioneer [2] to make the decision to assign available resources, rendering infeasible according to communication bottom neck or the lack of centralized control over distributed agents. Decentralized resource sharing algorithms suit large teams in nature, but make some assumptions that are infeasible to coordinate a large scale multiagent team. For example, use information agent or message broad [14] which can response to all information communication to build global team knowledge. Some other researches rely on agents' maintaining a shared precise model of the team, such as STEAM [13]. Decision theory based on MDP [1] and distributed routing algorithm such as DHTs [10] assumed that the global states of the network are known. Using excessive communication protocol to build agents' local knowledge for efficient resource sharing [9] is also impracticable and will result in communication congestions in the system. Algorithms that are scalable often rely on swarm-like behavior that, while robust, can be very inefficient [15].

3   Token-Based Resource Sharing Model

Based on recent successful implements of algorithms for information sharing [12], we represent our token-based resource sharing approach. The key is to represent sharable physical resources as resource tokens so that they can passed around the team. In this section, we also mathematically model how decision theoretical agents should make their resource sharing decision.

3.1   Representing Resource Tokens

The key idea of our token-based resource sharing approach is to abstract physical resources and represent as resource tokens. The agent holding a resource token has exclusive access to the resource and passes it to another agent to transfer access to that resource. Agents either keep a token or pass it to teammates. The decision of resource sharing is how to pass the resource token to the right agent who could make the best use of it. Hence, instead of requiring a single agent to perform the reasoning we allow the reasoning to be shared. If an agent believes a resource might be useful to some other agents it can pass it on to one that may have better knowledge of who needs the resource.

A resource token is defined as a data structure of communication message with required parameters including: time stamp, threshold, path, and its initiation ID. The structure of any resource token Δ is written as $\Delta =< ID, resource, path, threshold, TimeToActive >$, where $resource$ is the physical resource it represented. Due to the nature of $resource$, Δ cannot be duplicated or resent. When an agent is holding Δ, it takes over control of $\Delta.resource$. The agent will release $\Delta.resource$ if Δ is passed. To mark the uniqueness of resource tokens, we define the requirement $\forall \Delta_i, \Delta_j, if \Delta_i \neq \Delta_j, \Delta_i.resource \neq \Delta_j.resource$. $\Delta.path$ records the sequence of agents where Δ has traveled. $TimeToActive$ records the time since the resource token's last sleep. A resource has to "sleep" at an agent if it was not accepted for a long time. This can avoid the resource passing in the multiagent team but no one actually is interested in it at this time. $threshold$ is a special parameter and can be used to dynamically adjust the threshold whether an agent is able to keep a resource. The details of this design will be described in section 5.

3.2   Decision Theoretical Reasoning

To make rational decisions, a straightforward way is to model agent's decision as a POMDP. An agent a's local POMDP model for passing a resource token Δ is written as a tuple of $< S, K, \mathcal{A}, T, \Re, O, \Omega >$. S is the set of team state as "what are agents doing" and s is a specific one; $\mathcal{A}$ is the activity space that the agent a sends Δ to one of its teammates or keep it for itself. For notation convenience, it can be written as $move(\Delta, b)$. Note, keeping a token for itself applies when the agent accepts the resource. $T : S \times \mathcal{A} \rightarrow S$ is the transition function that describes the resulting state when executing a token passing. $\Re : S \rightarrow R$ defines the instantaneous reward for being in a specific state. If at s the resource gets accepted, $R(s) > 0$. The utility function under a policy π is defined as $v^\pi(s) = \sum_{t=0:\infty} (d^t \times R(s(t)) - t \times commcost)$ where $commcost$ is the communication cost and $d < 1$ is a predefined discount factor. $v^*(s)$ allows the agent to select actions according to the optimal policy $\pi^*(s(t)) = argmax_{\chi \in Action_a} v^*(s(t+1))$. By value iteration, $v^*(s(t)) = argmax_{\chi \in Action_a} [R(s(t)) - commcost + d \times v^*(s(t+1))]$. This policy tells the agent where to move resources to maximize the team's expected utility. We define an expected utility matrix V, where each expected utilities vector $V[b]$ represents the expected utilities to choose the action $move(\Delta, b)$ at different state s.

The key of this decision model is the observation function $O : K \times S \rightarrow \Omega$ when the agent has a limited knowledge of the team. K is the knowledge base of the agent. Belief state Ω is a discrete probability distribution vector over the team state S inferred from agent's local knowledge. For example, if $S = \{s_1, s_2, s_3\}$ and $\Omega = [0.6, 0.2, 0.2]$, it estimates that the probability of state being s_1 is 0.6 and being s_2 and s_3 are 0.2. One way of solving a POMDP is Q-MDP [1]. Agent a makes use of V to calculate the expected reward vector. For example, if a may send a token to b, c, and d and $EU(\Omega) = [5, 10, 6, 4]$, then $EU(\Omega, b) = 10$ represents the expected utility of action $move(\Delta, b)$ according to the Q-MDP.

Then the locally-optimal policy in Q-MDP is to $argmax_{\chi \in A}EU(\Omega_a, c)$. As in the previous example, passing Δ to b is the best choice because $EU(\Omega, b)$ is the maximum value of $EU(\Omega)$.

4 Sharing Resource under Incomplete Knowledge

Based on the POMDP model, without enough knowledge of the team, it is computational hard for an agent to find its optimal policy and a proximation is required. In this section, we put forward a heuristic approach of resource sharing. The aim of this design is not to find a way that agents can act optimally, but with a few hops, a resource token can still be efficiently delivered to the agent who can make use of it.

4.1 Reasoning Based on Influence Diagram

Before we put forward our heuristic algorithm design, we analysis our problem according to an influence diagram model at first.

In figure 1, agents' decision of where to pass a resource token is based on the states of what the other agents are doing. However, it is not completely observable. As a part of team sate, heterogeneous agents' capabilities are the key factor on what activities or tasks agents may involve in. Therefore, if agents know how the tasks are allocated, they know how to share the resources. In our design, similar to resource sharing, tasks can be encapsulated as task tokens as well [17]. Agents can keep the task token if it can be accepted, otherwise, it will be forwarded to one who is the most suitable to perform the task or knows who does. Therefore, by observing all its incoming tokens about task allocation, agents may infer where to send a resource token best. For example, if an agent a knows a task token has been send to its teammate b, it is reasonable for a to send a related resource which is critical to perform that task to b, e.g., hydrant to fire fighting task. As another example, if b rejected a task and sent it to a, a

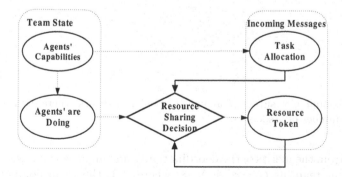

Fig. 1. Influence Diagram Model of Resource Sharing Problem in Large Scale Heterogeneous Team

should not send the resources related to perform that task to that agent. On the other hand, the movement of resource tokens is another clue for agents to make their resource sharing decisions. If agent a knows b sent a resource token to him, a should not send some "similar" resources to b because b or the agents close to b may not need those resources. For example, if b sent some resources such as "hamburger" and "pizza" to a. a can infer that b may not be hungry. Other food should be avoided sending to b. According to this idea, we setup an agent a's history as H_a which is the history of all received tokens by a. It could be the key to the agent's local resource sharing reasoning. The details of the algorithm design will be described in section 4.3.

4.2   Building Association Network for the Team

To make correct decisions, agents are required to obtain sufficient knowledge of the team state to support their decisions. If so few messages was gotten in H_a, the agents cannot make rational decisions. Otherwise, it requires the network to create overwhelming messages, which should be avoided in the algorithm. We have observed that, in a human group, members typically maintain a small number of associates but can rapidly transmit information to any member of the group in a few hops, a phenomenon known as small world effect [16]. This phenomenon showed that by using very vague (and often incorrect) knowledge about the population, people are able to pass a message until the desired recipient very quickly. On the other hand, other than considering all the other people as direct receptions, people only maintain models of their associates. By passing the information to their associates, they will get more information about their associates and their decision model could be reinforced. An example of associate network is shown as figure 2.

Fig. 2. An Example of a subset of a typical associate network where each agent only have a small number of associates

Learning from the merits of the coordination from human society, we organized the multiagent team as $G = < A, N >$, where A is the team composing of a set of agents and N is the network on which resource token should be passed. $< a_i, a_j > \in N$ denotes that a_i, a_j are neighbors and able to send resources directly with each other. $n(a) \subseteq A$ defines all of the neighbors of agent a. Any agent a's action $\mathcal{A}$ should be rewrite as $\mathcal{A}' : S \rightarrow (n(a) \cup a)$ which is to move a resource token to one of the associates or keep it for itself. Informally, by using their local decision models, agents infer which team member will either need a resource or be in the best position to know who does. This process will be repeated until the resource is accepted.

4.3   Local Probability Model

In summary of figure 1, we use agents' received tokens of both tasks and resources to infer what current team state is, and make their decisions of where to share the resources they are holding. Therefore, any incoming task or resource tokens can be used to predict where to send other related resource tokens. In this paper, we have modeled agents' histories as the knowledge base to support their decisions. Specifically, we rewrite our POMDP model in section 3 as $< S, H, \mathcal{A}', T, \Re, O', P >$ where agent a's knowledge K_a is completely built based on its received tokens H_a. Since the nature of H_a, it can only provide very limited view of the system state. The observation function should be rewritten as well: $O' : H \times S \rightarrow P$. Based on agent a's incomplete knowledge H, it can only infer a very vague state distribution as P other than Ω.

Therefore, P_a can be used to predict where to move tokens so that it can reach the receiver in the least hops. Each row $P_a[\Delta]$ in P_a represents a vector that determines the decision where to pass a token Δ to one of its associates. Specifically, each value $P_a[\Delta, b] \rightarrow [0, 1], b \in n(a)$ represents the probability of passing token Δ to associate b who would be most likely close to whom can make use of it. Our policy $\pi^{**} : argmax_{\chi \in \mathcal{A}'} EU(P_a[\Delta], c)$ is to pass the resource token to one of its neighbor and gets the most reward. In this function, the optimal policy no longer relates to the entire team state, but completely depends on the history of previously received tokens $H(a)$.

The key to this distributed reasoning lies on how the probability model P_a is updated. If the action indicated by P_a matches the optimal policy π^* of the POMDP model, the team will act optimally. Clearly, any received relative token Δ_i may change the probability distribution $P_a[\Delta_j]$. We consider two cases. In the first case, agent a has its history H_a but without Δ_i; In the second case, the agent has the same history but with Δ_i, and we write the history as $H'_a = H_a + \Delta_j$. Because of the existing of Δ_i, agent a's probability distribution should be different and we write as $P_a[\Delta_j]$ vs $P'_a[\Delta_j]$ according to two cases. we will find: $\frac{P'_a[\Delta_j]}{P_a[\Delta_j]} = \frac{EU(P'_a[\Delta_j])}{EU(P_a[\Delta_j])}$. It can be approximated as $\frac{P'_a[\Delta_j]}{P_a[\Delta_j]} \approx \frac{EU(p(\Delta_j|(H_a+\Delta_i)))}{EU(p(\Delta_j|H_a))}$ [1], where $H'_a = H_a + \Delta_i$. To simplify, I assume H_a and Δ_i are independent.

By using the Bayes rule, we will find $\frac{P'_a[\Delta_j, b]}{P_a[\Delta_j, b]}$ only depends on $EU(p(\Delta_j|\Delta_i))$. We refer to this as *relevance* and write as $Rel(\Delta_i, \Delta_j)$. Deciding where to send one token based on the receipt of another relies on knowing something about the relationship between the two tokens. When $EU(\{\Delta_j, \Delta_i\}, b) > 0$ and $Rel(\Delta_i, \Delta_j) > 1$ indicate that an agent with use for Δ_i will often also have use for Δ_j, $EU((\Delta_j, \Delta_i), b) < 0$ and $Rel(\Delta_i, \Delta_j) < 1$ indicate that an agent Δ_i also has use for it but that it is unlikely to have use for Δ_j. If $EU(\{\Delta_j, \Delta_i\}, b) = 0$, and $Rel(\Delta_i, \Delta_j) = 1$, then nothing can be inferred. In our design, the value of $Rel(\Delta_i, \Delta_j)$ is a part of domain background knowledge which can be easily inferred from the domain experts. Therefore, we can get the the update function of $P_a[\Delta_j]$ according to a specific token Δ_i in H_a, as $Update(P_a[\Delta_j], \Delta_i)$:

$$\begin{cases} P_a[\Delta_j, b] \times Rel(\Delta_i, \Delta_j) & \text{if } \Delta_i \neq \Delta_j, \Delta_i \text{ is } task, b = next(n(a), \Delta_i.path) \\ P_a[\Delta_j, b] \times 1/Rel(\Delta_i, \Delta_j) & \text{if } \Delta_i \neq \Delta_j, \Delta_i \text{ is } resource, b = first(n(a), \Delta_i.path) \\ \varepsilon & \text{if } \Delta_i = \Delta_j, b \in \Delta_j.path \cap n(a) \end{cases}$$

In the first case, the resource token is more likely to be sent to the neighbor who previously received a task from that agent. For example, previously received a pending task of "fight a fire in a building" denotes the direction where the task is sent is much closer to the agent who will take the role. Therefore, it is more reasonable to send a hydrant to these part of agents who are more likely to do fire fighting. In the second case, the resource token should be avoid sending to the similar resource sender. For example, the receiving of a hydrant denotes the senders are less likely involved in the fire fighting activities and they should be excluded from sending other similar resources. The third case encodes the idea that a should typically not pass the same resource token back to the agents who previously had it. All the other values in $P_a[\Delta]$ will be kept but a normalization is applied to ensure that $\sum_{b \in n(a)} P_a[\Delta_j, b] = 1$.

5   Improving Resource Sharing

In addition to our basic heuristic algorithm, in this section, we make our efforts to enhance the efficiency of the approach in two ways. The dynamic threshold can help the algorithm conduct a global optimal research. The local decision exchange model allows agents to proactively "ask for" resources so that resources can be quickly delivered.

5.1   Intelligent Resource Assignment

Our heuristic algorithm may efficiently find an agent who can make use of a resource, however, in a large scale heterogeneous team, multiple agents may request the same resource. In this scenario, our current solution is not able to find the global optimal resource sharing but only can find one resource receiver no matter whether it is the best. To avoid this, we have setup the *threshold* as a part of resource token. *Threshold* generalizes a threshold to decide whether it can be accepted by a receiver. An agent may keep a resource if its desire for that resource is greater than the token's threshold. While an agent holds the resource token Δ, $\Delta.threshold$ slowly increases. This mechanism ensures that resources can leave the holder and is available for the other agents. Moreover, the high threshold also generates priority that the poor agents although need the resource, have to pass it to the high priority agents first. For example, in urban search and rescue, a few fire drunks will be first available to the buildings in fire with higher priority. When the resource token is being passed, $\Delta.threshold$ is decreased to avoid a situation in which a token would be passed indefinitely and will be available to the agents without priorities.

5.2 Sharing of Local Decision Model

Based on our global resource sharing algorithm, we allow agents to locally push some additional information to share their local decision model. This design may significantly improve our resource sharing efficiency but with a very little communication overhead. For example, an agent b need a specific resource Δ_i so much or knows who does. It can tell its associate a if gets the resource, it is the best agent to send it to. In this case, a message can be sent to "ask for" the resource and agent a's local decision model should be changed. Similarly, an agent decided that it should be excluded as a specific resource receiver, it can also send such an additional message to share its decision as well. For example, a UAV gets an emergent attach task and should ask for to traverse a space represented by a resource token. On the other hand, if a UAV has been far from an air space and has no intention to close it in a long run, it should ask for excluding it as the resource receiver. Based on this idea, we define those special message as $e : \Delta \rightarrow [0, lowbound] \cup [upbound, 1]$. For an agent a, a message $e_b(\Delta_i) = \beta$ denotes that agent b's demand of getting resource Δ_i is β. If $\beta \in [upbound, 1]$, b is more favorite on resource Δ_i; If $\beta \in [0, lowbound]$, b does not want resource Δ_i. Please note $upbound$ and $lowbound$ are two important parameters. Only if $e_b(\Delta_i)$ is lower or higher than these thresholds, agent b is allowed to share its local model so that only a little communication overhead is created.

Consistent with the idea of our heuristic resource sharing, if an agent a knows the demands of a resource Δ_i, it can infer b's reference on any related resource Δ_j. For example, if a knows b is hungry and deadly need a resource of "pizza", a is able to infer b might need a "hamburger" as well. Based on this idea, When an agent a get a local sharing message $e_b(\Delta_i)$, we modeled our local sharing model:

$$P_a[j, b] = \begin{cases} P_a[j, b] \times rel(\Delta_j, \Delta_i) \times e_b(\Delta_i) \times 2, & if \Delta_j \neq \Delta_i \\ P_a[j, b] \times e_b(\Delta_i) \times 2, & if \Delta_j = \Delta_i \end{cases}$$

The same normalization process should be applied. The advantage of the local decision model sharing is that agents are able to initiatively share their resource sharing decision if their demand is beyond the predesigned threshold. Although their neighbors' decision models are only partially influenced, this desire might still beyond the threshold and can be shared further in the network. In this way, a required resource can reach its destination much quicker. Therefore, the efficiency of resource sharing may be greatly increased, which is very important to some emerging application domains.

6 Experiment Setup and Results

In this section, we will show the empirical evaluation of our approach with a set of fidelity experiments. Our evaluation is consisted with two parts. In the first part, the key is to verify the feasibility of using previously received messages in agents' history to train their probability decision models to forward a resource. In the second part, we designed an abstract simulator to "coordinate" a large group of robots so that the efficiency of our resource sharing approach can be tested.

6.1   Resource Sharing under Distributed Local Probability Model

In these experiments, we use a team with 400 agents and each of them has, on average, four associates. One agent is randomly chosen as the resource Δ holder and another one is randomly picked as the receiver for that resource. The receiver firstly sends out 20 messages m that is related with Δ, each of them travel at most 50 hops. Then the source agent sends out Δ with $rel(\Delta, m)$ varied and we measure how many hops or messages cost that it takes Δ to reach the sink agent. We arrange the associate network topology as a small world network. Each point on the graphs is based on the average of 1000 runs.

In Figure 3.a, we show the average number of hops (one hop per communication message) taken to deliver Δ as we varied the strength of $rel(\Delta, m)$ from 0.45 to 1. As expected, our algorithm works and the stronger $rel(\Delta, m)$ the more efficient of routing. Next, we look in detail at exactly how many related messages should be sent by the source to make the resource delivery from the sink efficient. We use the same settings above except the number of related messages sent from sink agent varied and $rel(\Delta, m)$ is set at 0.9. From figure 3.b, we can see that only a few related messages are required to dramatically decrease the communication cost to share Δ. This result also shows that a few related messages are enough to build a "precise" probability model for routing resources. To investigate the influence of team size on resource sharing performance, in Figure 3.c, we ran experiments using different sizes of the team from 100 to 550 with $rel(\Delta, m)$ =0.7. The routing efficiency is measure as the percentage of nodes involved for

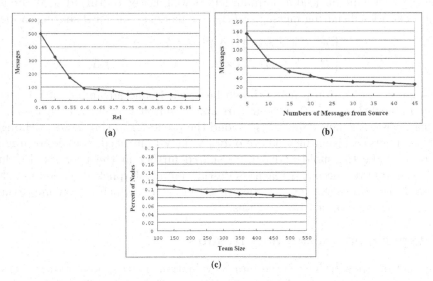

Fig. 3. Results under distributed local probability model: (a) The communication cost dramatically reduces as $rel(\Delta, m)$ increases; (b) Communication cost reduces as the related messages increase from sink; (c) Resource sharing works even slightly better when team scales up in measuring of percentage.

passing resource. We define $percentage = \frac{agents\ involved\ resource\ delivery}{team\ size}$. Experiment result in figure 3.c shows with different sizes of the agents, the efficiency of resource sharing is almost the same. It indicates that the network size is not a factor that influences the resource sharing.

6.2   Resource Sharing in Simulated Team Coordination

In this experiment, we have designed an abstract simulator called CoordSim [12] (figure 4). This simulator is capable of simulating the major aspects of coordination, including sensor fusion, plan management, information sharing, task assignment, and resource allocation. CoordSim abstracts the environment by simulating only its effects on the team. Uncertain sensor readings are received randomly by some agents in the team at a parameterizable rate. Agents cannot receive any domain knowledge unless they sense it themselves or are "told" by a teammate. The physical resources required for tasks are simulated and allow only one agent to access them at any given time. I simulated the spatial layout of tasks, which are distributed randomly in an open environment. All agents are allowed to locally reasoning and "act" at each time step. Communication is implemented via object passing, making it very fast. Reward is simulated as being received by the team when a task is allocated and the task performing agent gains required resources via our designed resource sharing algorithm. In this experiment, we simulated a domain similar with urban search rescue RoboCup where heterogeneous robots required performing a number of tasks, which requires several types of resource to be shared.

In this experiment, we have encoded five different algorithms. In figure 5 and 6, "TaskResouce" implements our complete algorithm design; "Random" is nothing more than a random resource passing; "ResourceOnly" implements an algorithm similar to "TaskResource" but only make use of the relevant resource tokens to build their knowledge; "NoLocalModel" is similar to "TaskResource" as well but without local decision sharing model; The last algorithm "NoDynThreshold" does everything as "TaskResource" but without a dynamic threshold in the resource tokens. The default settings in the experiment: 50 agents; 50 pending tasks and 100 resources; each task requires one of three similar resources etc.

Fig. 4. A Screen Shoot of CoordSim Simulator

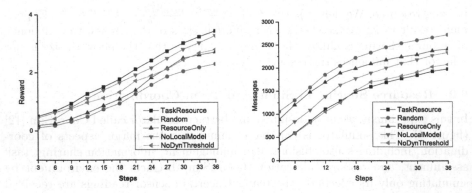

Fig. 5. Reward gain and message cost over different time steps and different coordination strategies

In figure 5, we investigate the number of rewards and the number of messages (one message per token move) after a specific number of time steps. We have shown that each individual coordination algorithms by using local knowledge to support their resource sharing decision outperform "random" with more reward but less communication overhead. Clearly, "TaskResouce" by integrating both global and local heuristic algorithms works best. The rest of the algorithms can only take the advantages of partial of our algorithm design. For example, the "NoDynThreshold" algorithm can decrease the communication overhead as less as "TaskResouce", but at a cost of reward gain.

In figure 6, we investigate the influence of team size (range from 50 to 500) on the efficiency of our local decision model. Each team with different sizes and different coordination strategies run and stop at the same time steps. We measured both reward gain and communication cost, and the same conclusions as figure 5 can be reached. Therefore, all our algorithm designs are feasible in scalable teams.

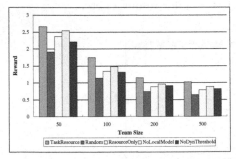
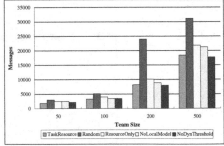

Fig. 6. Reward gain and message cost over different team sizes (50, 100, 200, and 500) and different coordination strategies

7 Summary and Future Work

In this paper, we present a novel approach to the challenges of sharing resource in a large scale multiagent team. Our experiments show that our approach is scalable and efficient. This approach opens the possibility of developing a range of new executing applications of heterogeneous agents not possible with existing approaches. Our key to the resource sharing algorithm is to encapsulate physical resource into a communication data structure called resource token. This algorithm utilizes agents' previous received tasks or related resources to build their local knowledge. By exploring the relationships between the coordination context and resource to be shared, we have successfully built agents' probability decision to enable efficient resource sharing. However, our initial experiments reveal that while our algorithms are capable of dealing with some of the challenges of the domain, many challenges remain. A major issue we leave for future research is how to calculate the relationships between coordination which is highly relevant to domain knowledge and expertise. Furthermore, we did not investigate how resource sharing works on negative relative context where the relationship is less than 1.

Acknowledgement

This research has been sponsored by National Natural Science Foundation of China 60905042.

References

1. Dolgov, D., Durfee, E.: Resource allocation among agents with preferences induced by factored MDPs. In: The fifth international joint conference on Autonomous agents and multiagent systems, pp. 297–304 (2006)
2. Sotomayor, M.: A Simultaneous Descending Bid Auction for Multiple Items and Unitary Demand. Revista Brasileira de Economia Rio de Janeiro 56(3), 497–510 (2002)
3. Endriss, U., Maudet, N., Sadri, F., Toni, F.: Negotiating socially optimal allocations of resources - an overview. Journal of Artificial Intelligence Research 25 (2006)
4. Andersson, M., Sandholm, T.: Contract type sequencing for reallocative negotiation. In: The 20th International Conference on Distributed Computing Systems (ICDCS 2000), pp. 154–160. IEEE, Los Alamitos (2000)
5. Chavez, A., Moukas, A., Maes, P.: Challenger: A multi-agent system for distributed resource allocation. In: 1st International Conference on Autonomous Agents, pp. 323–331. ACM Press, New York (1997)
6. Endriss, U., Maudet, N., Sadri, F., Toni, F.: On optimal outcomes of negotiations over resources. In: The 2nd International Joint Conference on Autonomous Agents and Multiagent Systems, pp. 177–184 (2003)
7. Lematre, M., Verfaillie, G., Bataille, N.: Exploiting a common property resource under a fairness constraint: A case study. In: The 16th International Joint Conference on Artificial Intelligence (IJCAI 1999), pp. 206–211 (1999)

8. Mahajan, R., Gupta, A.: Scalable Contract Net Based Resource Allocation Strategies for Grids. In: 9th International Conference on Parallel and Distributed Computing, pp. 25–32 (2008)
9. Passarella, A., Delmastro, F., Conti, M.: XScribe: a stateless, cross-layer approach to P2P multicast in multi-hop ad hoc networks. In: Decentralized Resource Sharing in Mobile Computing and Networking, pp. 6–11 (2007)
10. Zahn, T., Wittenburg, G., Schiller, J.: Towards efficient range queries in mobile ad hoc networks using DHTs. In: Decentralized Resource Sharing in Mobile Computing and Networking, pp. 72–74 (2007)
11. Xu, Y., Scerri, P., Sycara, K., Lewis, M.: Comparing market and token-based coordination. In: The fifth international joint conference on Autonomous agents and multiagent systems, pp. 1113–1115 (2006)
12. Xu, Y., Lewis, M., Sycara, K., Scerri, P.: Information sharing in very large teams. In: AAMAS 2004 Workshop on Challenges in Coordination of Large Scale Multi-Agent Systems (2004)
13. Pynadath, D., Tambe, M.: The communicative multiagent team decision problem: analyzing teamwork theories and models. Journal of Artificial Intelligence Research 16, 389–423 (2002)
14. Decker, K., Sycara, K., Pannu, A., Williamson, M.: Designing behaviors for information agents. In: The First International Conference on Autonomous Agents (1997)
15. Delgado, J., Pujol, J., Sanguesa, R.: Emergence of coordination in scale-free networks. In: Web Intelligence and Agent Systems, pp. 131–138 (2003)
16. Milgram, S.: The small world problem. Psychology Today 22, 61–67 (1967)
17. Scerri, P., Farinelli, A., Okamoto, S., Tambe, M.: Allocating Tasks in Extreme Teams. In: The fourth international joint conference on Autonomous agents and multiagent systems (2005)

Gaia Agents Implementation through Models Transformation

Nikolaos Spanoudakis[1,2] and Pavlos Moraitis[2]

[1] Technical University of Crete, Dept of Sciences, University Campus,
73100 Chania, Greece
nikos@science.tuc.gr
[2] Laboratory of Informatics Paris Descartes (LIPADE), Paris Descartes University,
45 rue des Saints-Pères, 75270 Paris Cedex 06, France
{Nikolaos.Spanoudakis,pavlos}@mi.parisdescartes.fr

Abstract. Gaia is a well-known Agent Oriented Software Engineering (AOSE) methodology. The emerging Model-Driven Engineering (MDE) paradigm encourages software modelers to automate the transition of one type of software model to another and eventually the code generation process. Towards this end we define a process for transforming the Gaia roles model liveness formulas to statecharts. This achievement on one hand allows the modeler to work on detailed agent design and permits, on the other hand, to automatically generate an agent's code using any one of the statecharts-based tools in the market.

Keywords: Agent Oriented Software Engineering, Statecharts, Gaia methodology, Model Driven Engineering.

1 Introduction

During the last years, there has been a growth of interest in the potential of agent technology in the context of software engineering. A new trend in the Agent Oriented Software Engineering (AOSE) field is that of converging towards the Model-Driven Engineering (MDE) paradigm. Thus, a lot of well known AOSE methodologies propose methods and tools for automating models transformations in the meanwhile proposing metamodels in the modern ecore [1] or MOF [10] formats. Examples of such methodologies are Tropos [13] and Ingenias [3]. The Gaia methodology [19] is a popular methodology that, however, does not address the issue of transforming its design models to code. Efforts in the past have produced some results, however not in the MDE sense, that is without automating the process.

In this paper we present an automated process for transforming the Gaia roles model liveness property to a statechart [5]. The latter is a platform independent model (PIM) of the system to be, a result that is compatible with the Object Management Group (OMG) Model Driven Architecture (MDA) paradigm [7]. Moreover, the produced statechart is defined in a standardized format that can be used for defining new model to text transformations for any desired platform.

This process delivers several original results. The first result is the formal definition of the syntax of a Gaia liveness formula. Then, we define the statecharts [5]

J.-J. Yang et al. (Eds.): PRIMA 2009, LNAI 5925, pp. 127–142, 2009.
© Springer-Verlag Berlin Heidelberg 2009

metamodel based on the ordered rooted tree data structure. Finally, we define a recursive transformation algorithm from a liveness formula to a statechart. This paper not only provides these theoretical results but also an implementation using the Human-Usable Textual Notation (HUTN) specification of OMG [11] and the Eclipse popular Integrated Development Environment (IDE).

This paper is organized in the following way. In section 2 we present the definition of the Gaia liveness formula followed by the formal definition of the statechart and its metamodel in section 3. The transformation algorithm and the technologies needed for implementing it are presented and discussed in section 4. Finally, section 5 includes conclusions and future work.

2   The Gaia Liveness Formula Definition

The Gaia methodology [19] is an attempt to define a general methodology that it is specifically tailored to the analysis and design of Multi-Agent Systems (MAS). Gaia emphasizes the need for new abstractions in order to model agent-based systems and supports both the levels of the individual agent structure and the agent society in the MAS development process. MAS, according to Gaia, are viewed as being composed of a number of autonomous interactive agents that live in an organized society in which each agent plays one or more specific roles. Gaia defines the structure of MAS in terms of the role model. The model identifies the roles that agents have to play within the MAS and the interaction protocols between the different roles. The Gaia methodology is a three phase process and at each phase the modeling of the MAS is further refined. These phases are the analysis phase, the architectural design phase and, finally, the detailed design phase.

The objective of the Gaia analysis phase is the identification of the roles and the modeling of interactions between the roles found. Roles consist of four attributes: *responsibilities*, *permissions*, *activities* and *protocols*. Responsibilities are the key attribute related to a role since they determine the functionality. Responsibilities are of two types: *liveness properties* – the role has to add something good to the system, and *safety properties* – the role must prevent something bad from happening to the system. Liveness describes the tasks that an agent must fulfill given certain environmental conditions and safety ensures that an acceptable state of affairs is maintained during the execution cycle. In order to realize responsibilities, a role has a set of permissions. Permissions represent what the role is allowed to do and, in particular, which information resources it is allowed to access. The activities are tasks that an agent performs without interacting with other agents. Finally, protocols are the specific patterns of interaction, e.g. a seller role can support different auction protocols. Gaia has operators and templates for representing roles and their attributes and also it has schemas that can be used for the representation of interactions between the various roles in a system. The operators that can be used for liveness expressions-formulas along with their interpretations are presented in Table 1. Note that activities are written underlined in liveness formulas.

The Gaia2JADE process [9] used the Gaia models and provided a roadmap for transforming Gaia liveness formulas to Finite State Machine (FSM) diagrams and then provided some code generation for JADE implementation. It also proposed some changes to Gaia such as the incorporation of a functionality table, where the activities

Table 1. Gaia Operators for Liveness Formulas

Operator	Interpretation	Operator	Interpretation
x‖y	x and y interleaved	x.y	x followed by y
x^{ω}	x occurs infinitely often	[x]	x is optional
x^*	x occurs 0 or more times	x|y	x or y occurs
x+	x occurs 1 or more times		

were refined to algorithms, and a way to describe simple protocols. However, it did not cater for parallelism, and it did not produce the FSM diagrams automatically.

The reader can see a Gaia roles model for a role named "personal assistant" in Figure 1. This role employs seven activities and seven protocols (activities are underlined in the *Protocols and Activities* field). In its liveness formula it describes the order that these protocols and activities will be executed by this role.

The liveness formula grammar has not been defined formally in the literature, thus it is defined here using the Extended Backus–Naur Form (EBNF), which is a metasyntax notation used to express context-free grammars. It is a formal way to describe computer programming languages and other formal languages. The EBNF syntax for the *liveness* formula is presented in the following listing, using the BNF style followed by Russel and Norvig [16], i.e. terminal symbols are written in bold:

```
liveness              → { formula }
formula               → leftHandSide = expression
leftHandSide          → string
expression            → term
                      | parallelExpression
                      | orExpression
                      | sequentialExpression
parallelExpression    → term || term || … || term
orExpression          → term | term | … | term
sequentialExpression  → term . term . … . term
term                  → basicTerm
                      | (expression)
                      | [expression]
                      | term*
                      | term+
                      | term^ω
                      | |term^ω|^number
```

```
basicTerm          → string

number             → digit | digit number

digit              → 1 | 2 | 3 | …

string             → letter | letter string

letter             → a | b | c | …
```

> *Role*: Personal Assistant
> *Description*: This role interacts with a meetings manager role in order to arrange and negotiate the user's meetings and with the user through a human-machine interface in order to get the user's requests and show him his schedule.
> *Protocols and Activities*: <u>get user request</u>, <u>read schedule</u>, <u>show results</u>, <u>learn user preference</u>, <u>update user preferences</u>, send change request, receive change results, send new request, receive new results, receive proposed date, <u>decide response</u>, send results, receive outcome, <u>update schedule</u>
> *Responsibilities*:
>   *Liveness*:
>   personal assistant = (manage meetings. learn user habits)$^\omega$ || (negotiate meeting date)$^\omega$
>   manage meetings = get user request. (read schedule | request change meeting | request new meeting). show results
>   learn user habits = learn user preference. update user preferences
>   request change meeting = send change request. receive change results
>   request new meeting = send new request. receive new results
>   negotiate meeting date = receive proposed date. (decide response. send results. receive outcome)+. update schedule

Fig. 1. The Gaia role model of a personal assistant agent

The reader should note that the Gaia operators have been enriched with a new operator, the $|x^\omega|^n$, with which we can define an activity that can be concurrently instantiated and executed more than one times (n times).

Figure 1 shows that the functionality of the personal assistant role is described by the liveness property. Thus, if the liveness formulas are transformed to a computer program then a large portion of the agent program is complete. However, this is not possible as there is a lot of information missing. First of all the functionality behind each activity is obscure. Then, the variables that will determine, e.g. whether the optional activities will be executed (i.e. an activity in brackets) are missing. This kind of information can be inserted in a statechart, thus we decided that in order to provide a design artifact that could lead to code generation we needed to transform the Gaia liveness formulas to a statechart [5]. However, before defining this transformation we needed a formal model for the statechart.

3 The Statechart Definition and Metamodel

Statecharts [5] are used for modeling systems. They are based on an activity-chart that is a hierarchical data-flow diagram, where the functional capabilities of the system are captured by activities and the data elements and signals that can flow between them. The behavioral aspects of these activities (what activity, when and under what conditions it will be active) are specified in statecharts. The fact that the statechart can capture together the functional and behavioral aspects of a system is its greatest advantage, as it completely defines a system. This is not true for a single UML model as a number of different models need to be combined for a complete description of a system (e.g. a class diagram together with an activity diagram). Thus, statecharts are ideal for defining systems in a platform independent manner. We intend to use statecharts in a specific level of abstraction, that of an agent, in order to model the interactions between its components (or capabilities). The statechart, therefore, implements the *intra-agent control model* (IAC) of an agent.

The authors in [5] present the statechart language adequately but not formally. Several authors have presented formal models for this language; as such an approach is needed for developing relevant statecharts-based Computer-Aided Software Engineering (CASE) tools. For example, David et al. [2] proposed a formal model for the RHAPSODY tool and Mikk et al. [8] for the STATEMATE tool. The first one has been used as basis for the definition of our statechart as it is the first intended for object-oriented language implementation (STATEMATE is for C language development). These models not only formally describe the elements of the statechart; they also focus on the execution semantics. However, this issue is out of the scope of this work. It is assumed that, as long as the language of statecharts is not altered, a statechart can be executed with any CASE tool.

The formal model that is adopted here-in is a subset of the ones presented in the literature as there are several features of the statecharts not used herein, such as the history states (which are also defined differently in these works). After formally presenting the statechart in the following paragraph, we will provide a metamodel in a common format such as the Eclipse Modeling Framework (EMF) and also discuss why this is needed.

3.1 Formal Statechart Definition

An *ordered rooted tree* is a rooted tree where the children of each internal vertex are ordered [15]. To produce a total order of the vertices of an ordered rooted tree all the vertices must be labeled. This is achieved recursively as follows:

1. Label the root with the integer 0. Then label its k children (at level 1) from left to right with $0.1, 0.2, 0.3, ..., 0.k$.
2. For each vertex v at level n with label A, label its k_v children, as they are drawn from left to right, with $A.1, A.2, ..., A.k_v$.

Thus, A.1 means that A is the parent of A.1. The definition below for the statechart is inspired by the definition proposed by David et al. [2].

Definition 1. A *statechart* is a tuple (L, δ) where:

- $L = (S, \lambda, Var, Name, Activity)$ is an ordered rooted tree structure representing the states of the statechart.

  — $S \subseteq \mathbb{N}^*$ is the set of all nodes in the tree.
  — $\lambda: S \rightarrow \{$AND, OR, BASIC, START, END, CONDITION$\}$ is a mapping from the set of nodes to labels giving the type of each node. For $l \in S$ let $AND(l)$ denote that $\lambda(l)=$AND. Similarly $OR(l)$ denotes that $\lambda(l)=$OR and the same holds for all labels. START and END denote those nodes without activity, which exist so that execution can start and end inside OR-states. BASIC corresponds to a basic state. A condition state is denoted as CONDITION. START, END, BASIC and CONDITION nodes are leaves of L.
  — Var is a mapping from nodes to sets of variables. $var(l)$ stands for the subset of local variables of a particular node l.
  — $Name$ is a mapping from nodes to their names. $name(l)$ stands for the name of a particular node l.
  — *Activity* is a mapping from nodes to their algorithms in text format implementing the processes of the respective states. $activity(l)$ stands for the algorithm of a particular state that is represented by node l.

- $\delta \subseteq S \times TE \times S$ is the set of state transitions, where TE is a set of transition expressions.

The following are also defined according to the definitions of David et al. (2003):

Definition 2. Let l an internal vertex of an ordered rooted tree L. We call $sons(l) = \{l.x \in S | x \in \mathbb{N}\}$ the children of l

Definition 3. Let l, k two vertices of an ordered rooted tree L such that $\exists x \in \mathbb{N}, k.x = l$. Then the vertex k is called parent to l and it is denoted as *parent(l)*

Definition 4. Let l a vertex of an ordered rooted tree L. Then, the ancestors of l are defined as $ancestors(l) = parent(l) \cup ancestors(parent(l))$

3.2 The Statechart Metamodel

Model driven engineering relies heavily in model transformation [17]. Model transformation is the process of transforming a model to another model. The requirements for achieving the transformation are the existence of metamodels of the models in question and a transformation language in which to write the rules for transforming the elements of one metamodel to those of another metamodel.

In the software engineering domain a *model* is an abstraction of a software system (or part of it) and a *metamodel* is another abstraction, defining the properties of the model itself. Thus, like a computer program conforms to the grammar of the programming language in which it is written, a model conforms to its metamodel (or its *reference model*). However, even a metamodel is itself a model. In the context of model engineering there is yet another level of abstraction, the *metametamodel*, which is defined as a model that conforms to itself [6].

A transformation that is used for transforming a textual representation to a graphical model is called a *Text to Model (T2M)* transformation. The textual representation must adhere to a language syntax definition usually using BNF. A liveness formula proposes such a kind of syntax. The graphical model must have a metamodel. Then, a transformation of the text to a graphical model can be defined.

In the heart of the model transformation procedure is the Eclipse Modeling Framework (EMF, [1]). EMF unifies Java, XML, and UML technologies, allowing the modeler to switch between them as they provide the same information in a different representation. Regardless of which one is used to define it, an EMF model is the common high-level representation that "glues" them all together.

Ecore [1] is EMF's model of a model (metamodel). It functions as a metametamodel and it is used for constructing metamodels. It defines that a model is composed of instances of the *EClass* type, which can have attributes (instances of the *EAttribute* type) or reference other EClass instances (through the *EReference* type). Finally, EAttributes can be of various *EDataType* instances (such are integers, strings, real numbers, etc). Figure 2 shows the ecore metamodel in detail.

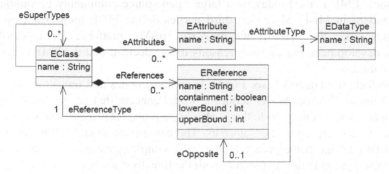

Fig. 2. The Ecore metamodel (Budinsky et al., 2003)

A similar technology, the Meta-Object Facility (MOF), is an OMG standard [10] for representing metamodels and manipulating them. There are a number of essential concepts used in MOF modeling. A Package is used to encapsulate a collection of related Classes and Associations. Packages can also contain simple type definitions. Classes exist in the commonly-used sense of the word, describing an object and its properties. These properties are represented through Attributes and References, which can be inherited using a multiple-inheritance system. Attributes have a name and a type. This includes a range of types from basic types such as integers, strings, and booleans to more complex types such as enumerations, and through to structured types. In addition, attributes have both upper and lower limits on the number of times that they can appear within a class instance. An Association is used to represent a relationship between instances of two classes, each of which plays a role within the association. Associations can have the additional property of containment; an association represents a containment relationship if one of the participant classes does not exist outside the scope of the other. A Class participating in an association can also contain a Reference to the association. A reference appears much like an attribute, but reflects the set of class instances that participate in the Association with the containing class instance.

MOF is older than EMF and it influenced its design. MOF was initially designed primarily for use with the Common Object Request Broker Architecture (CORBA). CORBA is an architecture that enables programs, called objects, to communicate with one another regardless of what programming language they were written in or what operating system they're running on.

EMF, on the other hand, is a product of the Eclipse project, an open source project and was intended as a low-cost tool to obtain the benefits of formal modeling and Java code generation. As a consequence, one could say that EMF took a bottom-up approach whereas MOF took a top-down approach [4].

However, the EMF meta-model is simpler than the MOF meta-model in terms of its concepts, properties and containment structure, thus, the mapping of EMF's concepts into MOF's concepts is relatively straightforward and is mostly 1-to-1 translations. EMF is used today by a large open source community becoming a de facto standard in MDE. Moreover, third parties define MDE tools based on EMF technology, like the openArchitectureWare (oAW) platform for model-driven software development. For all these reasons it was decided that the EMF technology would be used.

The statechart metamodel (see Figure 3) contains nodes and transitions according to Definition 1. The metamodel defines a *Model* concept that has *nodes*, *transitions* and *variables* EReferences. Note that it also has a *name* EAttribute. The latter is used to define the namespace of the statechart. The namespace should follow the Java or C# modern package namespace format (see a sample namespace for the meetings management system in the next section with the transformations).

The nodes contain the following attributes (followed by the relevant concept name in the statechart definition):

- *name* (Name). The name of the node,
- *type* (λ). The type of the node (one of AND, OR, BASIC, START, END),
- *label* (label). The node's label, and
- *activity* (Activity). The activity related to the node.

Nodes also refer to *variables*. The Variable EClass has the attributes *name* and *type* (e.g. the variable with *name* "count" has *type* "integer"). Finally the transitions have four attributes:

- *name*, usually in the form <source node label>TO<target node label>
- *TE*, the transition expression
- *source*, the source node label, and,
- *target*, the target node label.

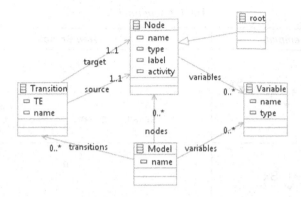

Fig. 3. The statechart metamodel

4   The Liveness2Statechart Transformation

The Liveness2Statechart transformation is achieved by using the "Gaia operators transformation templates" (shown in Table 2) for transforming the process part of the agent interaction protocol model to a statechart. Table 2 has three columns. The first depicts a Gaia formula with a certain operator. The second shows how to draw the statechart relevant to this operator using the common statechart graphic language. The third shows how the same Gaia formula is transformed to the statechart representation defined in this paper (as a tree branch).

The tree branch representation (in Table 2) uses grey arrows to connect a father node to its sons. On the top left of each node the label of the node is shown. The root node of each branch is supposed to have a label L and the other nodes are labeled accordingly. The type of each node is written centered in the middle of the node. Finally, the name of each node is centered in the bottom of each node. The reader should note that the nodes for the x or y variables of the Gaia formula do not have a node type. This is because it is possible that they are basic or non-basic nodes. If they are basic then the node's type is set to BASIC, otherwise another branch is added with this node as the root and as the reader can notice all templates set the type of the root of the branch.

Table 2. Templates of extended Gaia operators (Op.) for Statechart generation

Op.	Template	Tree Branch
x | y	●→©→⟨Sx⟩⟨Sy⟩→◉	L OR x|y — L.1 START, L.2 COND., L.3 ... x, L.4 ... y, L.5 END

Table 2. (*continued*)

Op.	Template	Tree Branch
$x*$	Sx	L OR $x*$ — L.1 START, L.2 COND., L.3 ... x, L.4 END
x^ω	Sx	L OR x^ω — L.1 START, L.2 ... x
$x.y$	Sx, Sy	L OR $x.y$ — L.1 START, L.2 ... x, L.3 ... y, L.4 END
$x+$	Sx	L OR $x+$ — L.1 START, L.2 ... x, L.3 END
$[x]$	Sx	L OR $[x]$ — L.1 START, L.2 COND., L.3 ... x, L.4 END
$|x^\omega|^n$	Sx, Sx, ... n instances	L OR $|x^\omega|^n$ — L.1 START, L.2 AND — L.2.1 OR, L.2.2 OR, ... L.2.n OR — L.2.1.1 START, L.2.1.2 ... x, L.2.2.1 START, L.2.2.2 ... x, L.2.n.1 START, L.2.n.2 ... x

Table 2. (*continued*)

Op.	Template	Tree Branch
x ‖ y		

A designer can use the Gaia transformation templates to manually transform the liveness formula to a statechart. Alternatively, he can use an implementation of the following recursive algorithm for building the statechart automatically (three dots represent omitted code for space reasons):

```
Program transform(liveness)
    Var root = 0
    S = S ∪ {root}
    Name(root) = liveness->formula₁->leftHandSide
    createStatechart(formula₁->expression, root)
End Program


Procedure createStatechart(expression, father)
    Var terms = 0
    For each termᵢ in expression
      terms = terms + 1
    End For
    If terms > 1 Then
      If expression is sequentialExpression Then
        λ(father) = OR
        S = S ∪ {father.1}
        λ(father.1) = START
        Var k=2
        For Each termᵢ in expression
            S= S ∪ {father.k}
            Name(father.k) = termᵢ
            δ = δ ∪ {(father.(k-1), {}, father.k)}
            k = k + 1
        End For
        S = S ∪ {father.k}
        δ = δ ∪ {(father.(k-1), {}, father.k)}
```

```
            λ(father.k) = END
        Else If expression is orExpression
            ...
        Else If expression is parallelExpression
            ...
        End If
    For Each term_i in expression
        If term_i is basicTerm Then
            handleBasicTerm(term_i, getNode(father, term_i)
        Else
            If term_i is of type '('term')' Then
                createStatechart(term, getNode(father, term_i))
            Else If (term_i is of type '['term']') or (term_i is
of type term'*') Then
                ...
            Else If (term_i is of type term'ω') or (term_i is of
type term'+') Then
                ...
            Else If term_i is of type '|'term'ω|ⁿ' Then
                ...
            End If
        End If
    End For
End function


Function getNode(father, term)
    QueuedList queue
    queue.addLast(father)
    Do While queue.notEmpty()
        element_i = queue.getFirst()
        If Name(element_i) = term Then Return element_i Else
            For each son_j in sons(element_i)
                queue.addLast(son_j)
            End For
        End If
    End do
End function


Function handleBasicTerm(term, node)
    Var isBasic = true
    For each formula_i in liveness
        If (formula_i->leftHandSide = term) Then
            createStatechart(formula_i->expression, node)
            isBasic = false
        End If
    End For
    If isBasic Then λ(node) = BASIC
End function
```

The program "transform" sets the root label equal to zero and its name equal to the left hand side of the first liveness formula. Then it calls the "createStatechart" procedure that takes two arguments. An *expression*, as it is defined in the Gaia liveness grammar, and a node (its label) under which it will build the tree.

The "createStatechart" procedure firstly checks whether the *expression* is a *parallelExpression*, an *orExpression* or a *sequentialExpression* and adds the relevant tree branch. Then, the procedure examines each *term* in the *expression*. A special function, the "handleBasicTerm" searches the formulas to find whether the term is a *basicTerm* or it appears in the left hand side of a following formula, which in this case needs to be expanded with the relevant tree branch. This is done by calling again the "createStatechart" procedure (recursively). Another function is used for this purpose, the "getNode". It searches (breadth first search) the tree branch below a node (the father) for the descendant with a specific name and returns its label. This is needed because the term's name is available but in order to add a tree branch the node's label is needed a parameter for the "createStatechart" procedure call. If the examined *term* of the *expression* is a non-basic term then again the relevant tree branch is added to the statechart.

After applying the transformation algorithm, the statechart (or intra-agent control model) depicted in Figure 4 is created for the personal assistant liveness property presented in Figure 1. The reader can see the "negotiate meeting date" OR state

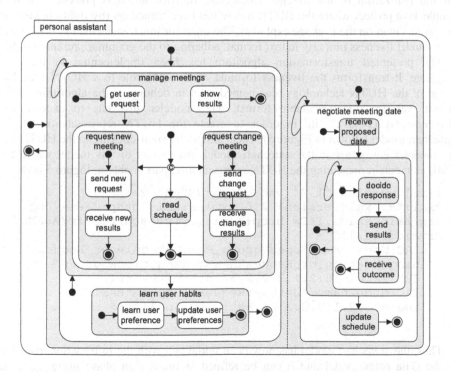

Fig. 4. The automatically generated statechart for the personal assistant agent

(representing the execution of an interaction protocol) executed in parallel with the other agent capabilities.

For automating the transformation procedure we needed to implement this algorithm and produce statecharts adhering to the statechart metamodel. This is a T2M transformation. In order to do this we used a Java program for transforming the liveness property to a standardized textual representation. The latter could be automatically transformed to a statechart model based on Eclipse and EMF technology as it is described below.

Rose et al. [14] described an implementation of the Human-Usable Textual Notation (HUTN) specification of OMG [11] using Epsilon, a suite of tools for MDE for Eclipse. OMG created HUTN aiming to offer three main benefits to MDE:

—   a generic specification that can provide a concrete HUTN language for any model, which is described by a metamodel
—   the HUTN languages to be fully automated both for production and parsing
—   the HUTN languages to conform to human-usability criteria

The Epsilon platform is an implementation of HUTN, which automates the transformation process by eliminating the need for a grammar specification by auto defining it accepting as input the relevant EMF metamodel (i.e. the one shown in Figure 3). This is the main reason for choosing HUTN. In Figure 5, the eclipse project for the realization of the Liveness2Statechart transformation is presented. It is a simple Java project where the HUTN nature has been turned on (by right-clicking on the project icon on the Package explorer). The input for this transformation is the Gaia roles model liveness property in text format, adhering to the grammar presented in §2.

The presented transformation algorithm has been implemented in the java language. It transforms the liveness formula of an SRM role to a HUTN file. The usage of the HUTN technology also helped a lot in debugging the algorithm as the output was in human-readable format. The modeler just has to execute the "Liveness2HUTN.java" file in order to create the HUTN representation of the statechart model (shown in Figure 5). Then, simply by right-clicking to the HUTN file the modeler can generate the statechart model. An extract of this model where the XML elements representing the HUTN representation part visible in Figure 5 is the:

```
<?xml version="1.0" encoding="UTF-8" ?>
<xmi:XMI xmi:version="2.0" xmlns:xmi="http://www.omg.
org/XMI" xmlns:IAC="http://mi.parisdescartes.fr/ASEME/
metamodels/IAC">
  <IAC:Node name="open_group_ReadSchedule_or_Request
  ChangeMeeting_or_RequestNewMeeting_close_group" type=
  "OR" label="0.2.1.2.2.2.3" activity="null" />
  <IAC:Node name="GetUserRequest" type="BASIC"
  label="0.2.1.2.2.2" activity="null" />
...
```

Thus, the statechart model has now been initialized with the information available in the Gaia roles model and it can be refined in the design phase using, e.g., the *Sample Reflective Ecore Model Editor* of Eclipse.

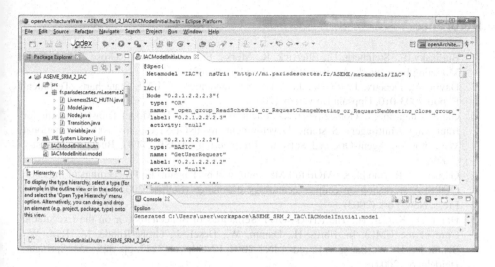

Fig. 5. The Eclipse project for T2M transformation

5 Conclusion

This paper showed how engineers, who use the Gaia methodology for modeling their agent-based systems, can implement their agents through the use of statecharts. The later allow to define the interactions between the different modules (or capabilities) of an agent (i.e. his intra-agent control) in a sufficient detail that can lead to implementation. A statechart is a platform independent model (PIM) of the system under development, as statecharts can be implemented using a number of existing programming languages and CASE tools. The statechart is automatically produced by the Gaia liveness property (a set of liveness formulas), which describes the behavior of an agent. This transformation is not a straightforward process and it is achieved through the following original results:

- Definition of a grammar for representing a liveness model.
- Formal definition of a statechart for agent-oriented development.
- Conception of a recursive algorithm for transforming the Gaia liveness property to a statechart. The modeler can make the transformation either manually (using the Gaia transformation templates) or automatically using the popular Eclipse IDE.

The manual transformation is also a valuable result as a developer can transform the liveness property to a statechart using any existing CASE tool. The Rhapsody tool [5] has been successfully used for implementing the MARKET-MINER agent, a real world system [18]. We are currently working in automating the code generation process (model to text – M2T) for a popular agent platform, the Java Agent Development Framework (JADE).

References

1. Budinsky, F., Steinberg, D., Ellersick, R., Merks, E., Brodsky, S.A., Grose, T.J.: Eclipse Modeling Framework. Addison Wesley, Reading (2003)
2. David, A., Deneux, J., d'Orso, J.: A Formal Semantics for UML Statecharts. Technical Report 2003-010, Uppsala University (2003)
3. García-Magariño, I., Gómez-Sanz, J.J., Fuentes-Fernández, R.: Model Transformations for Improving Multi-agent Systems Development in INGENIAS. In: 10th International Workshop on Agent-Oriented Software Engineering (AOSE 2009), Budapest Hungary (2009)
4. Gerber, A., Raymond, K.: MOF to EMF: there and back again. In: Proceedings of the 2003 OOPSLA workshop on eclipse technology eXchange (Eclipse 2003), pp. 60–64. ACM Press, New York (2003)
5. Harel, D., Kugler, H.: The RHAPSODY Semantics of Statecharts (Or on the Executable Core of the UML). In: Ehrig, H., Damm, W., Desel, J., Große-Rhode, M., Reif, W., Schnieder, E., Westkämper, E. (eds.) INT 2004. LNCS, vol. 3147, pp. 325–354. Springer, Heidelberg (2004)
6. Jouault, F., Bézivin, J.: KM3: A DSL for Metamodel Specification. In: Gorrieri, R., Wehrheim, H. (eds.) FMOODS 2006. LNCS, vol. 4037, pp. 171–185. Springer, Heidelberg (2006)
7. Kleppe, A., Warmer, S., Bast, W.: MDA Explained. The Model Driven Architecture: Practice and Promise. Addison-Wesley, Reading (2003)
8. Mikk, E., Lakhnech, Y., Petersohn, C., Siegel, M.: On formal semantics of Statecharts as supported by STATEMATE. In: Proceedings of the second BCS-FACS Northern Formal Methods Workshop. Springer, Heidelberg (1997)
9. Moraitis, P., Spanoudakis, N.: The Gaia2JADE Process for Multi-Agent Systems Development. J. Appl. Artif. Intell. 20(2-4), 251–273 (2006)
10. Object Management Group: Meta Object Facility (MOF) Core Specification (2001)
11. Object Management Group: Human-Usable Textual Notation V1.0 (2004)
12. openArchitectureWare (oAW), http://www.openarchitectureware.org/
13. Perini, A., Susi, A.: Automating Model Transformations in Agent-Oriented Modeling. In: Müller, J.P., Zambonelli, F. (eds.) AOSE 2005. LNCS, vol. 3950, pp. 167–178. Springer, Heidelberg (2006)
14. Rose, L.M., Paige, R.F., Kolovos, D.S., Polack, F.A.C.: Constructing models with the Human-Usable Textual Notation. In: Czarnecki, K., Ober, I., Bruel, J.-M., Uhl, A., Völter, M. (eds.) MODELS 2008. LNCS, vol. 5301, pp. 249–263. Springer, Heidelberg (2008)
15. Rosen, H.K.: Discreet Mathematics and its Applications, 4th edn. McGraw Hill, New York (1999)
16. Russel, S., Norvig, P.: Artificial Intelligence a Modern Approach, 2nd edn. Prentice Hall, Englewood Cliffs (2003)
17. Sendall, S., Kozaczynski, W.: Model Transformation: The Heart and Soul of Model-Driven Software Development. IEEE Softw. 20(5), 42–45 (2003)
18. Spanoudakis, N., Moraitis, P.: Automated Product Pricing Using Argumentation. In: Proceedings of the 5th IFIP Conference on Artificial Intelligence Applications & Innovations (AIAI 2009). Springer, Heidelberg (2009)
19. Zambonelli, F., Jennings, N.R., Wooldridge, M.: Developing multiagent systems: the Gaia Methodology. ACM T. Softw. Eng. Meth. 12(3), 317–370 (2003)

ONTOMO: Development of Ontology Building Service

Evaluation of Instance Recommendation Using Proper Noun Extraction

I. Shin[1], Takahiro Kawamura[1], Hiroyuki Nakagawa[1], Ken Nakayama[2],
Yasuyuki Tahara[1], and Akihiko Ohsuga[1]

[1] Graduate School of Information Systems, University of Electro-Communication
1-5-1 Chofugaoka, Chofu-shi, Tokyo 182-8585, Japan
[2] Institute for Mathematics and Computer Science, Tsuda College
2-1-1 Tsudacho, Kodaira-shi, Tokyo 187-8577, Japan
{shinichi,kawamura,nakagawa,ken,tahara,akihiko}@ohsuga.is.uec.ac.jp

Abstract. In the research area of web technologies, ontologies are recently widely used. By using ontologies, we can share common understanding of the structure of information among people or software agents and enable reuse of domain knowledge. However, the difficulties in building ontologies have been pointed out and its costs are raising problems currently. To build an ontology, we must determine the domain that the ontology will cover, and define taxonomy, properties, instances of the ontology. It is very difficult and time consuming to build them without any tools. In this paper, we propose ONTOMO that enables Internet users to take part in building ontologies as a part of collective intelligence. In particular, we present an instance recommendation mechanism based on the editing history of multiple users together with experimental evaluations.

Keywords: Ontology, Collection Intelligence, Web Service, Proper Noun Extraction.

1 Introduction

An Ontologie is knowledge repository in which categories are defined as well as relationships between these categories. It is similar to a dictionary with greater detail and structure that enables machines to process its content. An ontology consists of a set of concepts, axioms, and relationships that describe a domain of interest. Using ontologies, we can share common understanding of the structure of information among people or software agents and it enables us to reuse the domain knowledge. Recently in particular in the research area of web technologies, ontologies have been widely spreading. Systems that use ontologies are also rapidly increasing. Compared with heavy weight ontologies used in design and diagnosis, light weight ontologies are often used in the web. The $is-a$ relation accounts for 80-90% of the total relations [1]. However, the difficulties in building

J.-J. Yang et al. (Eds.): PRIMA 2009, LNAI 5925, pp. 143–158, 2009.

ontologies have been pointed out and its costs are raising problems currently. In order to build an ontology, we must determine the domain that the ontology will cover, and define taxonomy, properties, instances of the ontology. It is very difficult and time consuming to build them without any tools. Many ontology building tools have been released. However most of them need high level knowledge about ontologies and are designed for experts while general users can easily use only a few of them. In this paper, we propose an ontology building service, ONTOMO, designed not for experts but for general users who are considered as collective intelligence and can easily build ontologies by ONTOMO. To improve usability, ONTOMO is designed with a high level interface, built by Flex [2]. In particular, the most important feature of ONTOMO is to recommend instances similar to some instances input by different users. In addition, ONTOMO provides an interesting consequence of building ontology to general users in order to make them be interested in ontology, that is, a blog search application that enables the users to compare blog comments related to the products found by different search options from our electrical products ontology.

This paper is organized as follows. Section 2 presents the requirements to ONTOMO. Section 3 describes the functionalities and the features of ONTOMO. Section 4 explains the implementation of ONTOMO. Section 5 presents the most important feature in this paper, the instance recommendation mechanism with experimental evaluations. Section 6 discusses the effectiveness of ONTOMO based on the requirements described in Section 2. Section 7 presents related researches. The conclusions of this paper is described in Section 8.

2   Requirements to ONTOMO

There are three types of requirements to ONTOMO. These requirements are summarized as follows:

(1) Requirements as a general information system
(a) First, no need to install. It is not necessary to learn how to use the system. Preparations should be easy not only before you use the system, but also after you have started to use the system. (b) Satisfactory visibility and usability. (c) Important feature of offering an incentive to make users feel convenient and amusing. An information sharing mechanism is also required.

(2) Requirements as an ontology editor used on the web
To input instances is more important than editing the ontology structure. (a) It is difficult for the users to find all of the instances by themselves. Thus some assistance is required. If someone have made misconceptions, it is necessary to make them notice the misconceptions easily. (b) It is also important to find the latest information, including new words and new conceptions.

(3) Requirements as a cooperative ontology editor
When the users are going to input an instance, (a) we want to know whether an ontology that includes the instance already exists or not. If it exists, it should be easy to find it. (b) If conflicts among different users arise, we need to edit ontologies to keep the consistency efficiently.

Being aware of the requirement (2) in particular, we design and build ON-TOMO as an ontology editor different from many others. ONTOMO is a web application, which does not need to be installed and can be shared by different users. Moreover, ONTOMO has the features of its good responses and usability as well as a desktop application by using Flash that can exchange data between the client and the server asynchronously. To build the graphical interface, we make use of a graph library called SpringGraph [3] to show the ontology structure and manipulate the ontology elements, including the instances, the classes, and the properties.

In order to input instances efficiently, we propose an instance recommendation mechanism based on the collaboration of different users. We record histories edited by different users to a database, and use them to find candidate instances by our ONTOMO proper noun extraction, similar to GoogleSets [5], and recommend them to users. Moreover, there are two search applications built in ON-TOMO. One is an ontology search application which searches instances across all of the ontologies by different search options, and the other is a blog search application which retrieves blog comments. They may be regarded as some incentives that make users be interested in building ontology. We cannot always expect the correctness and the dependability of the information retrieved by the blog search application, but we can get the lasted information easily.

3   Functionalities and Features of ONTOMO

3.1   Overview

ONTOMO consists of a Flash web interface as the frontend, and a web service as the backend(Fig.1)D The frontend includes an ontology editor, two search applications, including an ontology search application and a blog search application, and an instance recommendation mechanism. Among them, the instance

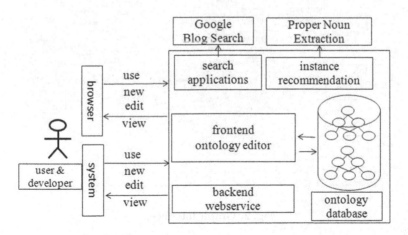

Fig. 1. Functionalities and Features of ONTOMO

recommendation mechanism is the main feature of the ONTOMO. The ontology editor has a friendly user interface with many functionalities such as create, edit, delete, and list. Moreover, the ontology search application can search instances across all of the ontologies, reflecting any changes made by the ontology editor immediately as they are linked to each other. The latest information can also be retrieved by the blog search application.

On the other hand, the backend web service provides the APIs, used to build ontology, to the public so that they can be used in the systems built by different programming languages, such as Java and C++.

3.2   Ontology Editor

The ontology editor consists of the graph view, the XML view, and the list view. In the graph view, users can create, edit, and delete ontologies. In the XML view, OWL data is formatted to a XML format. In the list view, the ontology elements, including the instances, the classes, and the properties are listed up. We use SpringGraph, a spring-model-based graph drawing library, to show the ontology structure consisting of the instances, the classes, and the properties(Fig.2). SpringGraph is a Flex component that displays a set of items linked to each other. In the graph view, the distance between two items can be changed by the slider bar on the top. For example, if there are so many instances near a class that we cannot distinguish them, we can change the parameter to expand the distance.

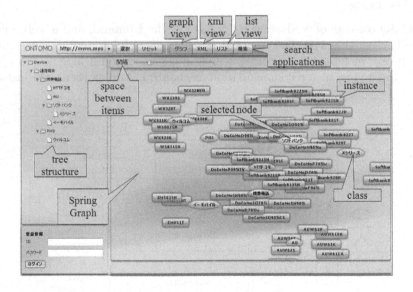

Fig. 2. Graph Interface

3.3   Search Applications

Ontology Search Application: We have built three ontologies of mobile phones, digital cameras, and media players in ONTOMO. It is possible to combine different properties defined in the ontologies to search the information stored in ONTOMO(Fig.3). When we provide some of the common properties defined in each ontology as the search options, we will retrieve the related instances across all of the ontologies. For example, if we choose "sony" as the option for the manufacturers, instances made by "sony" from the three ontologies will be retrieved. On the other hand, if we choose "docomo" as the option for the phone companies, which is defined only in the mobile phone ontology, docomo mobile phones will be retrieved.

Blog Search Application: We use the results obtained from the ontology search application to retrieve the latest information by the blog search application. For example, if we click an instance, named D905i, in the results retrieved from the mobile phone ontology, some snapshots of D905i will be shown. So you can easily open one of the web sites by clicking the link(Fig.3).

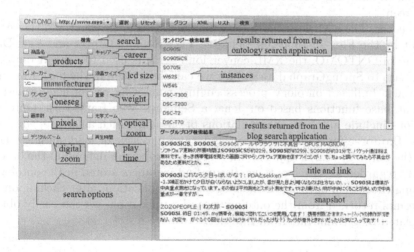

Fig. 3. Ontology and Blog Search

4   Implementation of ONTOMO

ONTOMO consists of the following three layers: the client, the server and the resource layers(Fig.4). In the client layer, we use Flex as an asynchronous communication framework to build a desktop application-like interface. While the server layer consists of Tomcat, a J2EE server, and an ontology process engine, implemented by Jena [4]. In the resource layer, ontology data is stored in the MySQL database or the XML files. After the users edit ontology, the requests from the client browsers will be sent to the server. Next, the Flex components

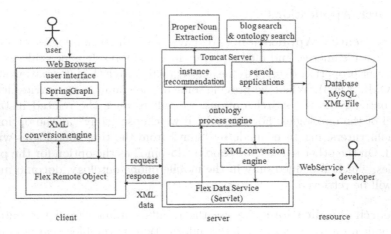

Fig. 4. Implementation of ONTOMO

invoke the related APIs from the ontology process engine to carry out the actions on the ontology. The results will be returned to the client and shown on the screen.

Moreover, The asynchronous data exchange between the client and the server is built by the Flex components including Flex Remote Object and Flex Data Service. In ONTOMO, the XML conversion engine is used to convert ontology OWL data to SpringGraph data so that we can show them in the flash frontend.

We also built an ontology process engine, consisting of ontology functions and database functions based on Jena, a Semantic web framework. Ontology functions include all of the manipulations of ontology, such as create, edit, and delete. Database functions access to the database to save or load ontology data.

In the ontology search application, all of the properties defined in the ontologies are regarded as search options. It can find instances stored in the ontologies by using the search options. In the blog search application, after clicking one of the results returned from the ontology search application, we can easily obtain the related blog comments from Internet.

5   Instance Recommendation Mechanism

In this section, we will present the instance recommendation mechanism based on editing histories by different users. When we input instances into ontologies, we can hardly remind of all of the instances without any clues. So we found out that it is difficult to build the entire ontology. Further, it is important but difficult to create ontologies of new ideas including digital products, music and software, because they are updated frequently. As a result, there is a limitation to finish such work manually. Though we expect input by users who are considered as collective intelligence, we need a mechanism which can supports users to add instances. For this purpose, we built the instance recommendation mechanism based on histories stored in a database according to the editing activities of the users. The instance recommendation mechanism is an approach that makes use of a proper noun extraction mechanism, such as GoogleSets and SEAL [6], that retrieves candidate instances which belong to the same class as the seed instance input by users and recommends them to users. We introduce our ONTOMO proper noun extraction, similar to Googlesets and SEAL, to retrieve candidate instances. For example, if three instances, Toyota, Honda, and Nissan, are input, it extracts the class "automobile" including Toyota, Honda, and Nissan, and retrieves other instances, such as Suzuki and Mitsubishi, which belong to the class "automobile".

In ONTOMO, after three instances, Toyota, Honda, and Nissan, are input by users in sequence, as soon as the fourth instance, GM, is input, we pick up the latest three instances, Honda, Nissan, and GM, considered as the seeds, and apply them to our ONTOMO proper noun extraction to retrieve candidate instances. Before recommending to users, ONTOMO remove noises, including the instances existing in the ontology and the incorrect instances(Fig.5).

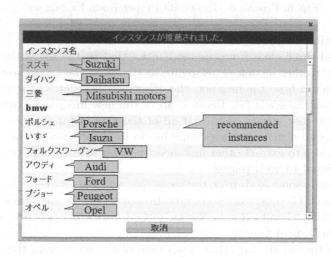

Fig. 5. Instance Recommendation

5.1   ONTOMO Proper Noun Extraction

GoogleSets, a famous proper noun exaction application, can extract candidate instances properly from a class whose number of the total correct instances are not changed frequently, such as banks, universities and so on. On the other hand, it cannot work properly for such classes as cameras and mobile phones because the number of the correct instances is often changed. Therefore, to extract candidate instances with high precision is difficult. ONTOMO proper noun extraction solves this problem by using bootstrapping. Bootstrapping can extract candidate instances without training data. ONTOMO proper noun extraction consists of four steps(Fig.6).

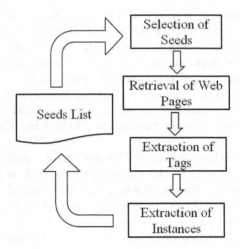

Fig. 6. Process of ONTOMO Proper Noun Extraction

(1) Selection of seeds

We selected three seeds from the seeds list,@that is, the list of the instances used to extract other instances belonging to the same class. One seed is a new instance retrieved from the internet, the other two seeds are old instances that already exist in the seeds list. Because all of the new instances extracted from the internet are not always correct. If all of the new instances are used as the seeds, the precision may decreases rapidly. So we select two old instances and one new instance to extract other instances in order to keep high precision.

(2) Retrieval of web pages

After selecting some seeds from the seeds list, we create a query to retrieve related web pages. The query is the combination of the seeds' names. For example, the query will be "Toyota Honda Nissan", "GM Ford Chrysler" and so on.

(3) Extraction of tags

We search the HTML tags that wrap each of the seeds from the web pages retrieved in the step (1).For example, there are such HTML tags as follows.

$< td > Toyota < td >$
$< td > Honda < td >$
$< td > Nissan < td >$
$< td > Mazuda < td >$
$< td > Suzuki < td >$

The $< td >$ tag will be extracted since it wraps each of the seeds. On the other hand, there are such HTML tags as follows.

$< td > Toyota < td >$
$< td > Honda < td >$
$< td > Mazuda < td >$
$< td > Suzuki < td >$

In this case, no tags will be extracted since the $< td >$ tag only wraps two of the seeds.

(4) Extraction of instances

If tags that wrap each of the seeds are extracted, we use the tags to extract other instances. In the former case, Mazuda, Suzuki will be extracted as the instances that belong to the same class as the seeds. Finally, we add the extracted instance into the seeds list for the next extraction.

In almost all of the web pages, it is very likely that each of these web pages contains other instances which are wrapped in the same HTML tags as the seeds, and belong to the same semantic class as the seeds. So if only a few seeds are given, we repeat these four steps to extract a great number of candidate instances belonging to the same class as the seeds. However, a problem we have to point out is that incorrect patterns may decrease the precision. A pattern that wraps each seed is used to extract other candidate instances. If the pattern is incorrect, some unexpected candidate instances will be extracted, and these unexpected instances may be selected as seeds to be used in the next extraction. As a result, the number of the incorrect instances will surge and the precision will be dropped. To prevent the precision from declining, we consider the number of the patterns that wraps each of the seeds in a web page. Let us call this number N. If $N < 2$, the pattern and all of the candidate instances wrapped in this pattern are discarded.

5.2   Overview of Instance Recommendation Mechanism

We regard the set that a user intends to retrieve as Si, and the set returned by our ONTOMO proper noun extraction as Se. It is desirable that If Si almost equals to Se. All we have to do is input all of the instances retrieved by our ONTOMO proper noun extraction into the ontology. On the other hand, if Si does not equal to Se, we have to carry out either one of the following measures.

(1)$|Se \cap Si| \ll |Si|$.

If few correct instances in Si are included in Se(Fig.7), the recall is low, because the correct instances retrieved in Se are very few. We need to input another new instance that is not included in the Se but in Si. Then we get a new expanded set Se' so that the recall will increase (Experiment 1).

(2)$|Se \cap Si| \ll |Se|$.

If there are so many incorrect instances in Se that few correct instances in Se are included in Si(Fig.8), the precision will fall because there are many incorrect instances in Se. Therefore, we adopt the precision filter, presented in the next section, removing the incorrect set Sx, to raise the precision with keeping the recall from falling (Experiment 2).

5.3   Precision Filter

The precision filter is a filter that removes incorrect instances obtained from our ONTOMO proper noun extraction to keep high precision with the following two processes.

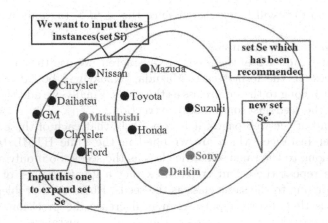

Fig. 7. $|Se \cap Si| \ll |Si|$

(1) We remove of the instances that already exists in the class.
(2) We select some other instances from the class which is different from the class the seeds belong to. Then we apply them to our ONTOMO proper noun extraction to retrieve a new set Sx. We compare Se with Sx to remove the incorrect instances in the Se.

For example, we suppose that a user inputs instances into the Japanese automobile class as Fig.9. So Si is the set that the user is intend to retrieve. We apply three instances, Toyota, Honda and Nissan, also called seeds, to our ONTOMO proper noun extraction in order to get a new set Se. The result indicates a decline in precision since some incorrect instances such as Daikin, Sony, GM, and Ford are included in Se.

Next, we select some instances which belong to different classes, then apply them to our ONTOMO proper noun extraction to get a new set. For example,

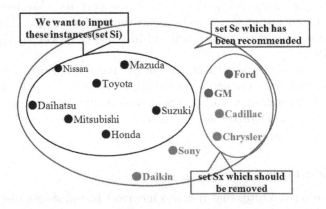

Fig. 8. $|Se \cap Si| \ll |Se|$

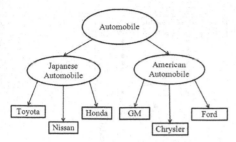

Japan	Toyota, Honda, Nissan, Mazuda, Fuji Heavy Industries, Mitsubishi Motor, Suzuki, Daihatsu, Hino, Isuzu, Mitsuuoka Motor, NissanDiesel, Lexus, Subaru, etc
America	GM, Ford, Chrysler, Chevrolet, Hummer, Cadillac, Buick, Pontiac, Saturn, GMC, Lincoln, Mercury, Dodge, Zip, etc
Germany	Porsche, Opel, Audi, BMW, VW, Daimler, Benz, Smart, etc
Italy	Ferrari, Alfa Romeo, Fiat, Lamborghini, Maserati, etc
English	Jaguar, Lotus, Land Rover, Rover, Aston Martin, PACCAR, etc
Sweden	Volvo, SAAB, Scania, etc
Others	现代, 大宇, 起亚, AVTOVAZ,GAZ, UAZ, Tata, 第一汽车, 中国汽车, 北京汽车, 东风汽车, 奇瑞汽车, 哈尔滨汽车, 吉利汽车, 长城汽车, BYD, 山东汽车, 山西汽车, 中国重汽, 福建汽车, etc

Fig. 9. Automobile Ontology   **Fig. 10.** Correct Data Sets for Experiment

we select three instances, GM, Ford and Chrysler, belonging to the American automobile class which is different from the Japanese automobile class, to get a new set Sx which is returned from our ONTOMO proper noun extraction.

It is probably that there are many instances of the American automobile class in Sx. We need to remove the instances that both exist in Sx and Se, more specifically, comparing Sx to Se to remove the instances of the American automobile class that also appear in Se. In other words, the mechanism is to combine the ontologies into the proper noun extraction to raise precision. However, if Sx is so large that instances of Japanese automobile class are included in Sx, these instances may be removed and recall may decline.

5.4 Evaluation of Instance Recommendation

As already mentioned, the instance recommendation mechanism is aware of the retrieval of information that changes frequently, such as new digital products. Compared to dynamic data, static data can help us to measure the precision and the recall exactly in the follow experiments. So we used the data of the world ranking of manufacturers by the motor vehicle production [7] for the experiment. From the top 49 manufacturers and their brands, we created 2 data sets. One is all of the manufacturers and brands, and the other is only for the Japanese manufacturers and their brands(Fig.10). Instead of users, we used automatic input by a computer to simplify the experiment. We performed two experiments; Experiment 1 is to measure how much our ONTOMO proper noun extraction can help to boost the increment of instances, and Experiment 2 is to measure how much precision may be improved by the help of our precision filter.

Evaluation method:

recall = existing instances / all of the correct instances
precision = existing instances / all of the instances including incorrect instances

Experiment 1(ONTOMO Proper Noun Extraction): Si in Fig.10 is the data set of all of the automobile manufacturers and their brands in the world. There are 75 instances in Si. We evaluated how much recall and precision may be improved by our ONTOMO proper noun extraction. We needed some seeds

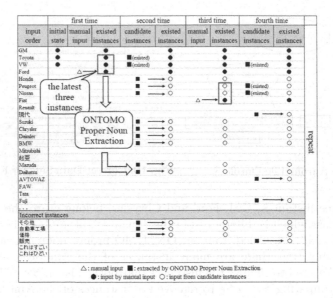

Fig. 11. Instance Recommendation by ONTOMO Proper Noun Extraction

used for the first time in the experiment. So we input three instances, Toyota, Honda, and GM, into the ontology. Once the fourth instance, Ford, is input, ON-TOMO proper noun extraction produced the latest three instances, i.e. Honda, GM, and Ford. After that, it retrieved other similar instances from the Internet without the precision filter. Then we input all of the instances into the new set Se extracted from ONTOMO proper noun extraction(Fig.11).

Evaluation method:

$$recall = (3 + \Delta)/75$$
$$precision = (3 + \Delta)/(3 + \Delta + incorrect\ instances)$$

Experiment results are shown in Fig.13 and Fig.14. In Experiment 1, the correct instances are input by a computer into ontology automatically instead of users. From Fig.13, the recall represented as blue line reached 100% at the 72nd time. With the help of ONTOMO proper noun extraction, the precision climbed quickly as much more instances were input. The recall represented as red line arrived at 100% at the 23rd time. We confirmed that ONTOMO proper noun extraction can exactly boost the increment of instances. On the other hand, from Fig.14, the precision represented as blue line is always 100% when instance is input by the automatic input. While the precision represented as red line fell because the number of the incorrect instances extracted by ONTOMO proper noun extraction increased.

Experiment 2(Precision Filter): We also want to know how much the precision filter can improve precision exactly. Si is the set that includes only Japanese manufacturers and their brands. There are two classes in the ontology, the Japanese automobile class and the American automobile class, which are the

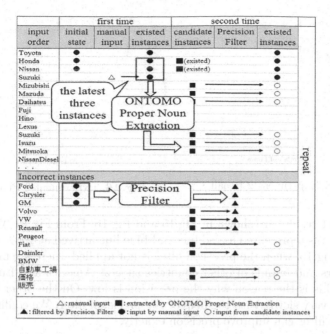

| input order | first time | | | second time | | | |
| | initial state | manual input | existed instances | candidate instances | Precision Filter | existed instances | |

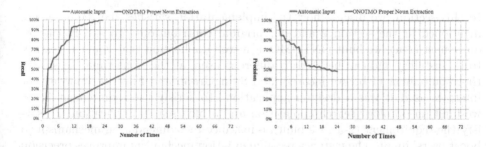

△ : manual input   ■ : extracted by ONOTMO Proper Noun Extraction
▲ : filtered by Precision Filter   ● : input by manual input   ○ : input from candidate instances

Fig. 12. Instance Recommendation by ONTOMO Proper Noun Extraction and Precision Filter

Fig. 13. Experiment 1 Recall   **Fig. 14.** Experiment 1 Precision

subclasses of the automobile class. We need some seeds used for the first time in the experiment. So we input three instances, Toyota, Honda, and Nissan, into the Japanese automobile class and other three instances, GM, Ford, and Chrysler, into the American automobile class. In Experiment 2, the step is the same as Experiment 1. We used ONTOMO proper noun extraction and the precision filter to improve precision and recall by removing incorrect instances(Fig.11).

Evaluation method:

$recall = (3 + \Delta)/14$
$precision = (3 + \Delta)/(3 + \Delta + incorrect\ instances)$

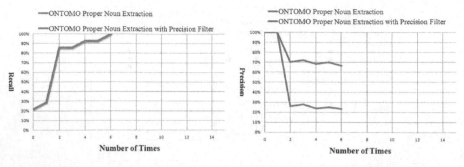

Fig. 15. Experiment 2 Recall   **Fig. 16.** Experiment 2 Precision

Experiment results are shown in Fig.15 and Fig.16. From Fig.15, We can see that both recalls represented as red line and blue line arrived at 100% at the 6th time. From Fig.16, when the precision filter is not applied, there are many other manufacturers and brands of other countries such as America and European in the result. This is the reason why the precision is low. On the other hand, the precision fell very slowly with the help of the precision filter. We confirmed that the precision filter can improve precision exactly.

6   Discussion

In this section, we discuss how the implementation satisfies the requirements mentioned in the section 2 and our original contributions. To satisfy the requirement (1-a), we built ONTOMO as a web application that is not necessary to be installed and can be used by different users at the same time. To satisfy the requirement (1-b), we incorporated SpingGraph and Flash to build a user interface as if it was a desktop application. To satisfy the requirement (1-c), we built an ontology search application and a blog search application. To satisfy the requirement (2-a), we built an instance recommendation mechanism to boost users' input. The instance recommendation mechanism improves precision by making use of ontologies. Furthermore, after the precision filter is applied, we found that precision climbed to a high level, while recall fell. We have some plan to improve our system. To satisfy the requirement (2-b), we realized retrieval of the latest information related to the instances in the ontology from the blog search application. Furthermore, we are going to implement such functionalities as wiki, an ontology agent, and a web service. To satisfy the requirement (3-a), we will add wiki into ONTOMO, which has the history management and the difference management functionalities. It can rollback the past data by using the history management functionality. The difference management functionality can find the difference and keep the consistency between two versions of data edited by different users. We will also add an ontology agent into ONTOMO, who can help us to keep the data consistency, and check whether data exists when some instances are input by users. Finally, we will open the APIs of ontology building as a web service. These APIs can be used in other systems implemented in various languages such as Java and C++ by making use of the web service.

The main contributions of ONTOMO are the ONTOMO proper noun extraction and the instance recommendation. The ONTOMO proper noun extraction, based on a bootstrapping process, can extract candidate instances properly from a class as GoogleSets. On the other hand, the instance recommendation is based on editing histories from different users. It is an approach that makes use of a proper noun extraction in help retrieving candidate instances to boost users' input. We also add the precision filter into the instance recommendation to improve precision and recall by comparing ontologies to instance sets extracted by the ONTOMO proper noun extraction.

7   Related Work

Protege [8] is the most popular Java based ontology editor now. Protege can also show the structures of ontology with a plug-in. Hozo [9] is a java based ontology editor from Osaka University. It can deal with the role concept exactly. It is also a distributed application that checks the differences on the server to keep the consistency between different versions of the ontology data. SWOOP [10] is a web based ontology editor from Maryland University. Classes, properties and instances are linked by URLs and navigated easily as if it was a web browser.

Moreover, we introduce some related researches of instance extraction. PANKOW [11] uses an approach of [is-a] to decide whether an instance belongs to a class or not by web search. SEAL [12] picks up common tags from web pages to retrieve candidate words, and improve the precision with their Random Walk algorithm. ISEAL [13] makes several calls to SEAL, each call using a small number of seeds that is a mixture of user-provided and self-generated seeds. Wolfgang Holzinger [14] shows how to use ontologies to bootstrap a knowledge acquisition process that extracts product information from tabular data on Web pages and use logical rules to reason about product specific properties and to derive higher-order knowledge about product features.

8   Conclusion

In this paper, we presented ONTOMO as an ontology building service. It is designed not for experts but for general users. ONTOMO is different from other ontology editors. ONTOMO has a desktop application-like interface built by the Flash and the SpringGraph. It also has an instance recommendation mechanism which may boost users' input. To implement the instance recommendation mechanism, we built a new proper noun extraction which is based on the bootstrapping. Additionally, two search applications, an ontology search application and a blog search application, may make users be interested in the ontology.

References

1. Schickel-Zuber, V., Faltings, B.: OSS: A Semantic Similarity Function based on Hierarchical Ontologies. In: Proceedings of IJCAI 2007 (2007)
2. Flex, http://www.adobe.com/jp/products/flex/
3. SpringGraph, http://mark-shepherd.com/blog/springgraph-flex-component/
4. Jena, http://jena.sourceforge.net/
5. GoogleSets, http://labs.google.com/sets
6. SEAL, http://www.rcwang.com/seal/
7. WORLD MOTOR VEHICLE PRODUCTION RANKING OF MANUFACTURERS, http://oica.net/wp-content/uploads/world-ranking-2007.pdf
8. ProtegeWiki, http://Protege.cim3.net/cgibin/wiki.pl
9. Hozo, http://www.hozo.jp/hozo/
10. SWOOP, http://www.mindswap.org/2004/SWOOP/
11. pankow, http://km.aifb.uni-karlsruhe.de/pankow
12. Richard, C., Wang, W.W.: Cohen: Language-Independent Set Expansion of Named Entities using the Web. In: ICDM 2007, Omaha, NE, USA (2007)
13. Wang, R.C., Cohen, W.W.: Iterative Set Expansion of Named Entities using the Web. In: ICDM 2008, Pisa, Italy (2008)
14. Holzinger, W., Krüpl, B., Herzog, M.: Using Ontologies for Extracting Product Features from Web Pages. In: Cruz, I., Decker, S., Allemang, D., Preist, C., Schwabe, D., Mika, P., Uschold, M., Aroyo, L.M. (eds.) ISWC 2006. LNCS, vol. 4273, pp. 286–299. Springer, Heidelberg (2006)
15. Yangarber, R., Lin, W., Grishman, R.: Unsupervised Learning of Generalize Names. In: COLING 2002 (2002)
16. Shchekotykin, K., Jannach, D.: ALLRIGHT: Automatic Ontology Instantiation from Tabular Web Documents. In: Aberer, K., Choi, K.-S., Noy, N., Allemang, D., Lee, K.-I., Nixon, L.J.B., Golbeck, J., Mika, P., Maynard, D., Mizoguchi, R., Schreiber, G., Cudré-Mauroux, P. (eds.) ASWC 2007 and ISWC 2007. LNCS, vol. 4825, pp. 466–479. Springer, Heidelberg (2007)
17. Wu, F., Weld, D.S.: Automatically Refining the Wikipedia Infobox Ontology. In: WWW 2008 (2008)
18. Brin, S.: Extracting patterns and relations from the world wide web. In: Proceedings of SIGMOD Workshop on Databases and the Web, pp. 172–183 (1998)

Syncretic Argumentation
by Means of Lattice Homomorphism

Taichi Hasegawa[1], Safia Abbas[1], and Hajime Sawamura[2]

[1] Graduate School of Science and Technology, Niigata University
8050, 2-cho, Ikarashi, Niigata, 950-2181 Japan
{hasegawa,safia}@cs.ie.niigata-u.ac.jp
[2] Institute of Science and Technology, Niigata University
8050, 2-cho, Ikarashi, Niigata, 950-2181 Japan
sawamura@ie.niigata-u.ac.jp

Abstract. In this paper, we attempt to formalize the syncretic argumentation, taking into account the Golden Rule in the ethics of reciprocity and Confucius' Golden Rule. After outlining the underlying argumentation framework, Logic of Multiple-valued Argumentation (LMA), we describe the syncretic argumentation framework by introducing the lattice homomorphism on truth-values (epistemic states) of propositions, and the new definitions of arguments justified under syncretized knowledge base. We also argue about its implications and new directions to further work.

1 Introduction

In his influential work on the abstract argumentation framework [1], the notion of "acceptability" has played the most significant role in specifying the various kinds of semantics for argumentation: admissible, stable, preferred, grounded, complete. An abstract argumentation framework is a tuple $< A, R >$, where A is a set of arguments and R is a binary relation on A called an attack relation. In Dung's theory of argumentation, we are not concerned with the internal structure of arguments and why and how arguments attack others. Everything is abstracted away in this way. This abstraction, however, was a good starting point for developing the argumentation semantics that is to capture what acceptable or admissible arguments are and the whole of justified arguments. There can be a plurality of sets of justified arguments in argumentation as mentioned above, contrasting with the semantics of an ordinary logic that is to be uniquely given by the Tarskian semantics, for example. Naturally, this reflects a figure of argumentation, a decisive difference from a logic.

The notion of acceptability is a counterpart of the phenomenon observed in our daily argumentation and originates from an old saying "The one who has the last word laughs best", as stated by Dung. It is an empirical social truth or wisdom that has been acquired by people, taking long time. It is remarkable and suggestive that Dung's theory of argumentation had started from such a daily

J.-J. Yang et al. (Eds.): PRIMA 2009, LNAI 5925, pp. 159–174, 2009.

but philosophical observation. This might be because argumentation is humans' most normal but intelligent action for thought and communication by language.

We developed the Logic of Multiple-valued Argumentation (LMA) [2] that is a variant of Dung's abstract argumentation framework concretized in such a way that the arguments are represented in terms of the knowledge representation language, Extended Annotated Logic Programming (EALP) and the attack relation consists of various sorts of attack such as rebuttal, undercut, defeat, etc. EALP is an extension of ELP (Extended Logic Programming), and a very expressive knowledge representation language in which agents can express their knowledge and belief with annotations as truth-values that allow to represent various kinds of uncertainty of information. In a word, LMA is an argumentation framework that allows agents to participate in uncertain argumentation under uncertain knowledge bases if once the common annotation is shared among agents. Put it differently, agents are assumed to have a homogeneous recognition for propositions under the same annotation as truth-values.

In this paper, we make a clean break with this assumption, directing to a more natural but complex settings of argumentation named "syncretic argumentation". By the term "syncretic argumentation", it is meant to be such an argumentation that each agent can have its own knowledge base, based on its own epistemology, and participate in argumentation with it. More specifically, each agent can attend the argumentation in which arguments are represented in EALP and annotated with its own truth-values which are assumed to represent modes of truth or epistemic states of propositions [2]. The syncretic argumentation is a new framework that allows agents to argue about issues of mutual interest even when they have their own annotations, for example, agent A has two values $\mathcal{TWO} = \{f, t\}$ as annotation and agent B has 4-values $\mathcal{FOUR} = \{\bot, \mathbf{t}, \mathbf{f}, \top\}$ as annotation. This reflects an attitude against unilateralism, so that one agent world may not be forced to assimilate to another unilaterally. We realize the goal by means of the lattice homomorphism since the mathematical structure of annotations is a complete lattice and the homomorphism is a natural way to syncretize the difference of epistemic states of propositions.

The syncretic argumentation is obviously a radical departure from the past argumentation frameworks [3][4] in the sense that they are basically frameworks using two-valued knowledge base, or simply a fixed multi-valued one [5]. Here we should emphasize that our approach to the syncretic argumentation is not only technically new but also has a profound philosophy that underlies our syncretic argumentation. They are,

- Golden Rule in the ethics of reciprocity: "Treat others (only) as you consent to being treated in the same situation." [6]
- Confucius' Golden Rule: "Never impose on others what you would not choose for yourself". or "Treat others as if their hearts were your own. " [7]

and may be said to be ethical in contrast with Dung's background idea on acceptability.

The paper is organized as follows. After outlining the underlying argumentation framework EALP/LMA in the next section, we describe the syncretic argumentation framework by introducing the lattice homomorphism that captures those Golden Rules, and the new definitions of arguments justified under syncretized knowledge base in Section 3. In Section 4, we illustrate the basic ideas and advantages of the syncretic argumentation through an argument example. In the final section, we argue about its implications and future directions to further work.

2   Outline of EALP and LMA

In this section, we outline the Logic of Multiple-valued Argumentation(LMA) [2] as an underlying preliminary to syncretic argumentation. EALP (Extended Annotated Logic Programming) is an expressive logic programming language we extended for argumentation by incorporating default negation in Generalized Annotated Logic Programming by Kifer and Subrahmanian [8]. EALP has two kinds of explicit negation: Epistemic Explicit Negation '¬' and Ontological Explicit Negation '∼', and the default negation 'not'. They are supposed to yield a momentum or driving force for argumentation or dialogue in LMA below. The basic language constituents are literals with truth-values or epistemic states of agents explicitly annotated. The structure of truth-values is required to be a complete lattice so that the paraconsistency of an agent's knowledge base is guaranteed under the ideals-based semantics [2]. LMA is A Logic of Multiple-valued Argumentation constructed on top of EALP. LMA allows agents to construct arguments under uncertain knowledge in EALP and to argue with other agents on uncertain issues in the open networked heterogeneous environment. As we can specify truth values every application domain that has its own proper uncertainty in EALP, such diversity of truth values brings us an extensive applicability of LMA. In what follows, we will illustrate how uncertain arguments proceed in LMA using a simple argument with a somewhat deviant use of truth values, without involving in lengthy definitions.

Example 1 (Job schedule management). Let us consider an argumentation about the monthly job schedule management. Here we use an unconventional complete lattice of truth values which is the power set $\mathcal{P}(\{1,\ldots,31\})$ of the set of the monthly dates, with the order of set inclusion. Then an annotated atom $work(a):\{5,6\}$, for example, reads "Agent a works on the 5th and the 6th". It asserts that the proposition $work(a)$ is true only in a certain time interval. $\sim work(a):\{5,6\}$ reads "Agent a does not work on the 5th and the 6th". We define the epistemic explicit negation so as to be $\neg A:\mu = A:\neg\mu$ and $\neg\mu = \{1,\ldots,31\} - \mu$ as like in GAP [8], and thus $\neg work(a):\{5,6\}$ reads "Agent a works on every day except the 5th and the 6th". The difference and significance between the ontological and epistemic explicit negations is obvious. Under this complete lattice of truth values, we consider $MAS = \{KB_m, KB_a, KB_b, KB_o\}$, where the knowledge base KB of each agent is, in EALP,

$KB_m = \{\ finish(project):\{6\} \leftarrow work(a):\{3,4,5\}\ \&\ arrive(component):\{5\},$
$work(a):\{3,4,5\} \leftarrow,\quad arrive(component):\{5\} \leftarrow,\quad pay(upcharge):\{8\} \leftarrow\ \},$

$KB_a = \{ \sim work(a) : \{5\} \leftarrow \textbf{not}\ work(b) : \{5\} \& holiday : \{5\},$
$\sim work(a) : \{12\} \leftarrow \textbf{not}\ work(b) : \{12\} \& holiday : \{12\},\ holiday : \{5, 6, 12, 13\} \leftarrow \ \},$
$KB_b = \{\neg work(b) : \{12, 19, 26\} \leftarrow,\ holiday : \{5, 6, 12, 13\} \leftarrow \ \},$
$KB_o = \{\sim arrive(component) : \{5\} \leftarrow \textbf{not}\ pay(upcharge) : \phi \ \}.$

KB_m, KB_a, KB_b and KB_o stand for knowledge bases of a manager agent m, employee agents a, b and a subcontractor agent o respectively. Agent m's argument which has the conclusion $finish(project) : \{6\}$ (the project should finish on the 6th) is justified by the dialectical proof theory as shown in Figure 1.

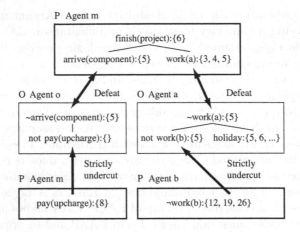

Fig. 1. The winning dialogue tree in Example 1

In the winning dialogue tree, initially Agent m (P: Proponent) says "if a component will arrive on the 5th, and Agent a works on the 3th, the 4th and the 5th, then the project will finish on the 6th", whose formal argument is constructed from its knowledge base KB_m as

$[finish(project) : \{6\} \leftarrow work(a) : \{3, 4, 5\} \& arrive(component) : \{5\},\ work(a) : \{3, 4, 5\} \leftarrow, arrive(component) : \{5\} \leftarrow].$

Then there are two places that can be attacked by the other party (O: opponent). In the left branch of the dialogue tree, Agent o defeats it as follows "I will be not able to bring a component on the 5th if the additional charge is not paid". But Agent m strictly undercuts o's argument by saying "I will pay it to you on the 8th". In the right branch of the dialogue tree, for the first argument of Agent m, Agent a (O: Opponent) also defeats by saying "the 5th is a holiday, and if the coworker b does not work, I do not want to work on the 5th", whose formal argument is constructed from its knowledge base KB_a as

$[\sim work(a) : \{5\} \leftarrow \textbf{not}\ work(b) : \{5\} \& holiday : \{5\},\ holiday : \{5, 6, 12, 13\} \leftarrow].$

This is a semantically correct argument since $holiday : \{5\}$ can be resolved upon $holiday : \{5, 6, 12, 13\}$ with the condition $\{5\} \leq \{5, 6, 12, 13\}$ in GAP and EALP. Agent a can put forward such a counter-argument since the conclusion of Agent a's argument $\sim work(a) : \{5\}$ conflicts with the second rule of Agent m, $work(a) : \{3, 4, 5\} \leftarrow$. This is due to the defeat (rebut) relation that $A : \mu$ conflicts with $A : \rho$ each other provided that $\mu \geq \rho$ or $\rho \geq \mu$ in LMA. In fact, Agent a claims that I do not want to work on the 5th, but Agent m asserts that it works on $\{3, 4, 5\}$ which is a superset of $\{5\}$.

However Agent b (P: Proponent) strictly undercuts this Agent a's argument by saying "I will work on days except the 12th, 19th and the 26th", whose formal argument is constructed from its knowledge base KB_b as

$[\neg work(b) : \{12, 19, 26\} \leftarrow]$.

This is equivalent to $\neg work(b) : D \leftarrow$, where $D = \{1, ..., 31\} - \{12, 19, 26\}$ and hence can undercut the first rule of Agent a's counter-argument above. This is due to the strict undercut relation that $A : \mu$ can attack **not** $A : \rho$ in one way provided that $\mu \geq \rho$ in LMA. In fact, Agent b claims that it works on the dates D including $\{5\}$, but Agent a asserts that it does not work on the date 5th.

There is not any further arguments at this stage of the argumentative dialogue, and it finishes at the proponent's move. Consequently, the first argument of Agent m becomes justified.

3 Syncretic Argumentation by Lattice Homomorphism

In this section, we propose a novel technique that allows agents to participate in argumentation even if they have knowledge bases with their own annotations as truth-values that reflect agents' epistemic states of propositions. As we have seen in the previous section, the annotation is a complete lattice. Naturally, we introduce the mathematical notion of a homomorphism between lattices. Such a homomorphism enjoys the order-preserving property, so that it guarantees agents to retain agents' epistemic structure when embedding one lattice to the other. We also consider the bidirectional homomorphism on lattices since it allows for a fair, unbiased and pluralistic argumentation, prohibiting unilateral one.

Then, we describe the new definitions to characterize the set of justified arguments, under the knowledge base reconstructed by the homomorphism on lattices.

3.1 Homomorphisms on Complete Lattices

Definition 1 (Homomorphism [9]). *Let* $< L, \vee_L, \wedge_L, \leq_L >$ *and* $< K, \vee_K, \wedge_K, \leq_K >$ *be complete lattices. A map* $h : L \to K$ *is said to be a homomorphism if* h *satisfies the following conditions: for all* $a, b \in L$,

- $h(a \vee_L b) = h(a) \vee_K h(b)$
- $h(a \wedge_L b) = h(a) \wedge_K h(b)$
- $h(0_L) = 0_K$ *for the least element*
- $h(1_L) = 1_K$ *for the greatest element*

For simplicity, we omit the suffix denoting a lattice from here on if no confusion arises in the context.

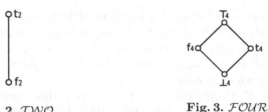

Fig. 2. $\mathcal{TWO}$ Fig. 3. $\mathcal{FOUR}$

Fig. 4. Homomorphism 1   **Fig. 5.** Homomorphism 2

Example 2. Let us consider two typical lattices: the two-valued complete lattice $\mathcal{TWO}$ and the four-valued one $\mathcal{FOUR}$. The former is typical in the West, and the latter in the early philosophical literature and text of Buddhism [10]. $\mathcal{TWO} =<$ $\{f,t\}, \vee, \wedge, \leq>,$ *where* $f \leq t$ in Fig. 2, and $\mathcal{FOUR} =< \{\bot, \mathbf{t}, \mathbf{f}, \top\}, \vee, \wedge, \leq>,$ where $\forall x, y \in \{\bot, \mathbf{t}, \mathbf{f}, \top\}$ $x \leq y \Leftrightarrow x = y \vee x = \bot \vee y = \top$ in Fig. 3. Note that we associate the suffix with annotations to avoid ambiguity of the same annotation names, that is, t_2 represents the annotation t in $\mathcal{TWO}$ and t_4 represents the annotation t in $\mathcal{FOUR}$, for example. For these lattices, there can be two possible homomorphisms as shown in Fig. 4 and 5. Naturally, homomorphism 1 is a reasonable choice in this case, from the original meanings of the annotations t and f. The selection, however, usually depends on various factors such as argument purposes, argument domains and so on.

Given two lattices, there can be many lattice homomorphisms in general, and also there can be no lattice homomorphism. In the latter case, it turns out that agents can not syncretize their knowledge bases as they are, resulting in no argumentation among them. In order to resolve this situation, we have to turn to alternative lattice operations such as lattice product, sum [9], or fusion. But we will consider them in our future paper.

3.2 Syncretically Justified Arguments

With the lattice homomorphism above, we will illustrate how agents who have their own epistemology can reach an agreement and accept arguments through the grounded semantics or the dialectical proof theory of LMA [2].

Example 3. Suppose two agents A and B have the following knowledge bases respectively.

$$K_A = \{ \ a : t_2 \leftarrow, \ \sim b : t_2 \leftarrow, \ c : t_2 \leftarrow, \ \sim d : t_2 \leftarrow \ \}$$
$$K_B = \{ \ \sim a : t_4 \leftarrow, \ b : t_4 \leftarrow, \ \sim c : \top_4 \leftarrow, \ d : \bot_4 \leftarrow, \ e : t_4 \leftarrow g : f_4, \ g : t_4 \leftarrow \ \}$$

Then the agents A and B can make the following set of arguments $Args_{K_A}$ and $Args_{K_B}$ from their knowledge bases respectively. (See [2] for the precise definition of arguments in LMA.)

$$Args_{K_A} = \{ \ [a:t_2 \leftarrow], \quad [\sim b:t_2 \leftarrow], \quad [c:t_2 \leftarrow], \quad [\sim d:t_2 \leftarrow] \ \}$$
$$Args_{K_B} = \{ \ [\sim a:t_4 \leftarrow], \quad [b:t_4 \leftarrow], \quad [\sim c:\mathsf{T}_4 \leftarrow], \quad [d:\perp_4 \leftarrow], \quad [g:t_4 \leftarrow] \ \}$$

The agents first assimilate their knowledge bases above to each other by the lattice homomorphism 1 in Fig. 4, and compute justified arguments from them using the grounded semantics or the dialectical proof theory [2], in each direction of the homomorphism as follows.

[1] Lattice homomorphism $h1$: $\mathcal{TWO} \to \mathcal{FOUR}$ (simply written as $\mathcal{T} \to \mathcal{F}$)
$h1(K_A) = \{ \ a:\mathsf{T}_4 \leftarrow, \ \sim b:\mathsf{T}_4 \leftarrow, \ c:\mathsf{T}_4 \leftarrow, \ \sim d:\mathsf{T}_4 \leftarrow \ \}$
$K_B = \{ \ \sim a:t_4 \leftarrow, \ b:t_4 \leftarrow, \ \sim c:\mathsf{T}_4 \leftarrow, \ d:\perp_4 \leftarrow, \ e:t_4 \leftarrow g:f_4, \ g:t_4 \leftarrow \ \}$
$Args_{h1(K_A)} = \{ \ [a:\mathsf{T}_4 \leftarrow], \ [\sim b:\mathsf{T}_4 \leftarrow], \ [c:\mathsf{T}_4 \leftarrow], \ [\sim d:\mathsf{T}_4 \leftarrow] \ \}$
$Args_{K_B} = \{ \ [\sim a:t_4 \leftarrow], \ [b:t_4 \leftarrow], \ [\sim c:\mathsf{T}_4 \leftarrow], \ [d:\perp_4 \leftarrow], \ [g:t_4 \leftarrow] \}$
Note that $Args_{h1(K_A)} = h1(Args_{K_A})$ since the homomorphism preserves the lattice ordering. From these argument sets, the agents can have the following set of justified arguments.
$Justified\_Args_{\mathcal{T} \to \mathcal{F}} = \{ \ [\sim b:\mathsf{T}_4 \leftarrow], \ [\sim d:\mathsf{T}_4 \leftarrow], \ [b:t_4 \leftarrow], \ [d:\perp_4 \leftarrow],$
$[g:t_4 \leftarrow] \ \}$

[2] Lattice homomorphism $h2$: $\mathcal{FOUR} \to \mathcal{TWO}$ (simply written as $\mathcal{F} \to \mathcal{T}$)
$K_A = \{ \ a:t_2 \leftarrow, \ \sim b:t_2 \leftarrow, \ c:t_2 \leftarrow, \ \sim d:t_2 \leftarrow \ \}$
$h2(K_B) = \{ \ \sim a:t_2 \leftarrow, \ b:t_2 \leftarrow, \ \sim c:t_2 \leftarrow, \ d:f_2 \leftarrow, \ e:t_2 \leftarrow g:f_2,$
$g:t_2 \leftarrow \ \}$
$Args_{K_A} = \{ \ [a:t_2 \leftarrow], \ [\sim b:t_2 \leftarrow], \ [c:t_2 \leftarrow], \ [\sim d:t_2 \leftarrow] \ \}$
$Args_{h2(K_B)} = \{ \ [\sim a:t_2 \leftarrow], \ [b:t_2 \leftarrow], \ [\sim c:t_2 \leftarrow], \ [d:f_2 \leftarrow], \ [g:t_2 \leftarrow],$
$[e:t_2 \leftarrow g:f_2, \ g:t_2 \leftarrow] \}$
Note that $Args_{h2(K_B)} \neq h2(Args_{K_B})$ in case of the homomorphism $h2$ since $[e:t_2 \leftarrow g:f_2, \ g:t_2 \leftarrow]$ has been qualified as an argument by $h2$ although its original form $[e:t_4 \leftarrow g:f_4, \ g:t_4 \leftarrow]$ in K_B is not an argument. From these argument sets, the agents can have the following set of justified arguments.
$Justified\_Args_{\mathcal{F} \to \mathcal{T}} = \{ \ [\sim d:t_2 \leftarrow], \ [d:f_2 \leftarrow], \ [g:t_2 \leftarrow], \ [e:t_2 \leftarrow g:f_2,$
$g:t_2 \leftarrow] \ \}$

Through the two-way homomorphism, we had two different sets of justified arguments: $Justified\_Args_{\mathcal{T} \to \mathcal{F}}$ and $Justified\_Args_{\mathcal{F} \to \mathcal{T}}$. Next, we are interested in defining a set of justified arguments as a "common good" that is acceptable for both agents. In what follows, we present three kinds of agent attitudes or criteria to chose it from among two different sets of justified arguments.

Definition 2 (Skeptically justified arguments).

- An argument a in $Args_{K_A}$ is skeptically justified iff
  $a \in Justified\_Args_{\mathcal{F} \to \mathcal{T}}$ and $h1(a) \in Justified\_Args_{\mathcal{T} \to \mathcal{F}}$.
- An argument a in $Args_{K_B}$ is skeptically justified iff
  $a \in Justified\_Args_{\mathcal{T} \to \mathcal{F}}$ and $h2(a) \in Justified\_Args_{\mathcal{F} \to \mathcal{T}}$.

This is a fair and unbiased notion of justified arguments in the sense that the both sides can attain a perfect consensus by the two-way homomorphism. Morally, it reflects such a compassionate attitude that agents look from the other agents' viewpoint, or place themselves in the other agents' position.

Example 4 (Example 3 cont.). The skeptically justified arguments in Example 3 are:

$$Skeptically\_Justified\_Args = \{ \ [\sim d : t_2 \leftarrow], \quad [d : \bot_4 \leftarrow], \quad [g : t_4 \leftarrow] \ \}$$

A weaker version of skeptically justified arguments is the following. This criterion is not uninteresting since it gives a useful information on arguments which are not rejected completely.

Definition 3 (Credulously justified arguments).

– *An argument a in $Args_{K_A}$ is credulously justified iff either $a \in Justified\_Args_{\mathcal{F} \rightarrow \mathcal{T}}$ or $h1(a) \in Justified\_Args_{\mathcal{T} \rightarrow \mathcal{F}}$.*
– *An argument a in $Args_{K_B}$ is credulously justified iff either $a \in Justified\_Args_{\mathcal{T} \rightarrow \mathcal{F}}$ or $h2(a) \in Justified\_Args_{\mathcal{F} \rightarrow \mathcal{T}}$.*

Example 5 (Example 3 cont.). The credulously justified arguments are:

$$Credulous\_Justified\_Args = \{ \ [\sim b : t_2 \leftarrow], \quad [\sim d : t_2 \leftarrow], \quad [b : t_4 \leftarrow], \quad [d : \bot_4 \leftarrow], \quad [g : t_4 \leftarrow]\}$$

The third criterion is somewhat deviant reflecting a unilateral attitude, but it can be seen in our daily life often.

Definition 4 (Self-centeredly justified arguments).

– *An argument a in $Args_{K_A}$ is self-centeredly justified iff $a \in Justified\_Args_{\mathcal{F} \rightarrow \mathcal{T}}$.*
– *An argument a in $Args_{K_B}$ is self-centeredly justified iff $a \in Justified\_Args_{\mathcal{T} \rightarrow \mathcal{F}}$.*

Example 6 (Example 3 cont.). The self-centeredly justified arguments are:

$$Self-centeredly\_Justified\_Args = \{ \ [\sim d : t_2 \leftarrow], \quad [b : t_4 \leftarrow], \quad [d : \bot_4 \leftarrow], \quad [g : t_4 \leftarrow] \ \}$$

Which criteria are the most suitable to argument-based agent computing depend on agent purposes, agent attitudes, and so on. Here we just mention only a relationship of those criteria as follows. The proof is straightforward from the definitions.

Proposition 1. *$Skeptically\_Justified\_Args \subseteq Self-centeredly\_Justified\_Args \subseteq Credulously\_Justified\_Args$.*

3.3   Creative Arguments

In the example 3, the argument $[e : t_2 \leftarrow g : f_2, g : t_2 \leftarrow]$ is included in $Justified\_Args_{\mathcal{F} \rightarrow \mathcal{T}}$, but not in $Args_{K_B}$ since t_4 and f_4 are non-comparable. We single out for special treatment such arguments to distinguish from original arguments.

Definition 5 (Creative justified arguments).

- *An argument a is said to be a creative justified argument if a ∉ Args$_{K_B}$ and a ∈ Justified_Args$_{\mathcal{F}\to\mathcal{T}}$.*
- *An argument a is said to be a creative justified argument iff a ∉ Args$_{K_A}$ and a ∈ Justified_Args$_{\mathcal{T}\to\mathcal{F}}$.*

Example 7 (Example 3 cont.). The creative justified arguments are:

$$Creative\_Justified\_Args = \{\ [e : t_2 \leftarrow g : f_2, g : t_2 \leftarrow]\ \}$$

Specifying "Creative justified arguments" is not trivial since they reveal indiscernible arguments in ourselves by standing on each other's positions and ways of thinking. We also sometimes change our thinking or notice new ideas by standing on the opposite side of an argumentation in our daily life. It, however, leads to expanding the range of argumentation.

Creative justified arguments turn to have only the property of the credulously justified arguments.

Proposition 2.

- *If an argument a ∈ Justified_Args$_{\mathcal{F}\to\mathcal{T}}$ is a creative justified argument, h1(a) ∉ Justified_Args$_{\mathcal{T}\to\mathcal{F}}$.*
- *If an argument a ∈ Justified_Args$_{\mathcal{T}\to\mathcal{F}}$ is a creative justified argument, h2(a) ∉ Justified_Args$_{\mathcal{F}\to\mathcal{T}}$.*

So far, we have given those definitions in a way specialized to the lattices $\mathcal{TWO}$ and $\mathcal{FOUR}$ for brevity of explanation. They can be carried on to any two lattices in a similar manner.

4 Worked Examples

In this section, we illustrate the basic ideas and advantages of the syncretic argumentation through two simple argument examples in natural language.

In the first example, let us take up an argumentation between "Copernican system [11]" and "Ptolemaic system [12]" in the 16th century here. Ptolemaic system was common in ancient Greece. It was embraced by both Aristotle and Ptolemy, and most Ancient Greek philosophers assumed that the Sun, Moon, stars, and naked-eye planets circle the Earth. However, from the late 16th century onward it was gradually replaced by the Copernican system of Copernicus, Galileo and Kepler.

We assume the following knowledge bases of each positions of the argumentation. The knowledge base's annotations are given by $\mathcal{FOUR}$ for Copernican system and $\mathcal{TWO}$ for Ptolemaic system. We will first represent each knowledge base in natural language as follows, where we write KB_p for the knowledge base on the side of Ptolemaic system and KB_c for the one on the side of Copernican system

$KB_p = \{$ *Ptolemaic system is correct if the stars, sun, and planets appear to revolve around the Earth each day.*

The stars, sun, and planets appear to revolve around the Earth each day.

Stellar parallax is not observed accurately if the observational consequences are not accurate and complete.

The observational consequences are not accurate and complete. $\}$

$KB_c = \{$ *Copernican system is correct if stellar parallax is observed.*

Stellar parallax is observed.

Ptolemaic system is not correct if there exists phases of Venus.

There exists phases of Venus.

It's not sure that the observational consequences are accurate and complete. $\}$

These knowledge bases are represented in EALP as follows.

$KB_p = \{$ $is\_correct(ptolemaic\_system) : t_2 \leftarrow revolve\_around\_the\_Earth$
$(the\_stars, sun, planets) : t_2,$
$revolve\_around\_the\_Earth(the\_stars, sun, planets) : t_2 \leftarrow,$
$\sim is\_observed(stellar\_parallax) : t_2 \leftarrow \sim are\_accurate\_and\_complete$
$(observational\_consequences) : t_2,$
$\sim are\_accurate\_and\_complete(observational\_consequences) : t_2 \leftarrow$ $\}$

$KB_c = \{$ $is\_correct(copernican\_system) : t_4 \leftarrow is\_observed(stellar\_parallax) : t_4,$
$is\_observed(stellar\_parallax) : t_4 \leftarrow,$
$\sim is\_correct(ptolemaic\_system) : t_4 \leftarrow exists(phases\_of\_Venus) : t_4,$
$exists(phases\_of\_Venus) : t_4 \leftarrow,$
$are\_accurate\_and\_complete(observational\_consequences) : \perp_4 \leftarrow$ $\}$

Then, according to our definitions we have four sets of the justified arguments calculated through the lattice homomorphisms as follows.

$Skeptically\_Justified\_Args = \{$
  $[revolve\_around\_the\_Earth(the\_stars, sun, planets) : t_2 \leftarrow],$
  $[\sim are\_accurate\_and\_complete(observational\_consequences) : t_2 \leftarrow],$
  $[exists(phases\_of\_Venus) : t_4 \leftarrow],$
  $[are\_accurate\_and\_complete(observational\_consequences) : \perp_4 \leftarrow]$ $\}$

$Credulously\_Justified\_Args = \{$
  $[revolve\_around\_the\_Earth(the\_stars, sun, planets) : t_2 \leftarrow],$
  $[\sim is\_observed(stellar\_parallax) : t_2 \leftarrow \sim are\_accurate\_and\_complete$
  $(observational\_consequences) : t_2,$
  $\sim are\_accurate\_and\_complete(observational\_consequences) : t_2 \leftarrow],$
  $[\sim are\_accurate\_and\_complete(observational\_consequences) : t_2 \leftarrow],$
  $[is\_correct(copernican\_system) : t_4 \leftarrow is\_observed(stellar\_parallax) : t_4,$
  $is\_observed(stellar\_parallax) : t_4 \leftarrow],$
  $[is\_observed(stellar\_parallax) : t_4 \leftarrow],$
  $[exists(phases\_of\_Venus) : t_4 \leftarrow],$
  $[are\_accurate\_and\_complete(observational\_consequences) : \perp_4 \leftarrow]$ $\}$

$Self-centeredly\_Justified\_Args = \{$
    $[revolve\_around\_the\_Earth(the\_stars, sun, planets) : t_2 \leftarrow],$
    $[\sim are\_accurate\_and\_complete(observational\_consequences) : t_2 \leftarrow],$
    $[is\_correct(copernican\_system) : t_4 \leftarrow is\_observed(stellar\_parallax) : t_4,$
    $is\_observed(stellar\_parallax) : t_4 \leftarrow],$
    $[is\_observed(stellar\_parallax) : t_4 \leftarrow],$
    $[exists(phases\_of\_Venus) : t_4 \leftarrow],$
    $[are\_accurate\_and\_complete(observational\_consequences) : \perp_4 \leftarrow]   \}$

$Creative\_Justified\_Args = \phi$

We show two dialogue trees for an issue : $[is\_correct(copernican\_system)]$ as an example in Fig. 6 of $\mathcal{F} \rightarrow \mathcal{T}$ and Fig. 7 of $\mathcal{T} \rightarrow \mathcal{F}$. According to the rules of EALP, arg 1 is defeated by arg 2 which is not defeated by any arguments in Fig. 6, but arg 4 is not by arg 5 in Fig. 7. Therefore, the issue is credulously justified.

Let us consider semantically the rationality of this argumentation for each arguments.

First, the arguments $[\sim are\_accurate\_and\_complete(observational\_consequences) : t_2 \leftarrow]$ and $[are\_accurate\_and\_complete(observational\_consequences) :$

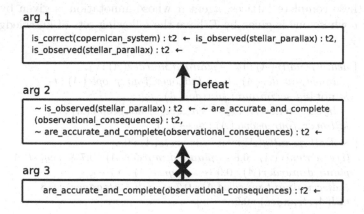

Fig. 6. The dialog tree $(\mathcal{F} \rightarrow \mathcal{T})$

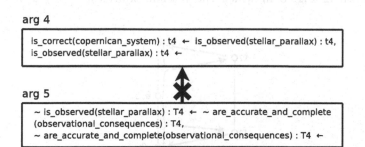

Fig. 7. The dialog tree $(\mathcal{T} \rightarrow \mathcal{F})$

$\perp_4 \leftarrow$] are both skeptically justified arguments since the latter argument just says that "It's not sure that the observational consequences are accurate and complete" which is a weak assertion. Therefore these arguments should not be conflict in any position and they fulfill the requirement.

Secondly, note that the assertion $[is\_correct(copernican\_system) : t_4]$ is credulously justified but $[is\_correct(ptolemaic\_system) : t_2]$ is not. As we consider this point, we have to associate the significance of each truth value. t_2 is upper than f_2 in $\mathcal{TWO}$. It logically means the condition t_2 includes the condition f_2. Specifically t_2 in $\mathcal{TWO}$ is close to $\top_4$ more than t_4 in $\mathcal{FOUR}$. In light of this point, the fact that the assertion $[is\_correct(copernican\_system) : t_4]$ defeats the assertion $[is\_correct(ptolemaic\_system) : t_2]$ but the assertion $[\sim is\_observed(stellar\_parallax) : t_2]$ does not defeat the assertion $[is\_observed (stellar\_parallax) : t_4]$ in the position of $\mathcal{FOUR}$ is a suitable consequence.

In the second example, we describe an argumentation about the sentence of a murderer A. Assume that the complete lattices of truth values of two agents' knowledge bases are $\mathcal{TWO}$ and $\mathcal{R} = \Re[0, 1]$, a unit interval of reals. $\mathcal{R}$ is often used to represent uncertain information in many traditional AI theories such as fuzzy logic, Bayesian theory, etc. as well as in possibility logic or probability theory.

Under these complete lattices, agent a whose annotation is given by $\mathcal{TWO}$ and agent b whose one is given by $\mathcal{R}$ have the following sets of knowledge bases respectively.

$KB_a = \{\ death\_penalty(A) : t_2 \leftarrow planned\_murder(A) : t_2,$
$\quad\quad planned\_murder(A) : t_2 \leftarrow kill\_over\_four\_people(A) : t_2$
$\quad\quad \&\ \mathbf{not}\ indiscriminant\_murder(A) : t_2,$
$\quad\quad \sim life\_sentence(A) : t_2 \leftarrow kill\_over\_four\_people(A) : t_2,$
$\quad\quad kill\_over\_four\_people(A) : t_2 \leftarrow \quad\ \}$
$KB_b = \{\ \sim death\_penalty(A) : 0.9 \leftarrow regrets(A) : 0.6,$
$\quad\quad life\_sentence(A) : 0.8 \leftarrow planned\_murder(A) : 0.7\ \&\ regret(A) : 0.4,$
$\quad\quad planned\_murder(A) : 0.9 \leftarrow,\ \ regret(A) : 0.7 \leftarrow,$
$\quad\quad indiscriminant\_murder(A) : 0.7 \leftarrow kill(A, stranger) : 0.8$
$\quad\quad kill(A, stranger) : 0.6 \leftarrow \quad\ \}$

The possible bi-directional homomorphisms between the lattices $\mathcal{TWO}$ and $\mathcal{R}$ are shown in Fig. 8 in which the interval $\Re[0, 0.5)(\subseteq \mathcal{R}))$ is mapped to

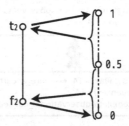

Fig. 8. Homomorphisms between $\mathcal{TWO}$ and $\mathcal{R}$

$f_2(\in \mathcal{TWO})$ and $\Re[0.5, 1](\subseteq \mathcal{R}))$ is mapped to $t_2(\in \mathcal{TWO})$. Between these lattices, there are infinite possible bi-directional homomorphisms since $\Re[0, 1]$ is an infinite set. Which homomorphism we should adopt depends on the issue, the property of knowledge bases, the relation between agents and so on.

Then, the four sets of the justified arguments are calculated through the lattice homomorphisms in Fig. 8 as follows.

$Skeptical\_Justified\_Args = \{$
  $[kill\_over\_four\_people(A) : t_2 \leftarrow], \quad [planned\_murder(A) : 0.9 \leftarrow],$
  $[regret(A) : 0.7 \leftarrow], \quad [kill(A, stranger) : 0.6 \leftarrow] \quad \}$

$Credulous\_Justified\_Args = \{$
  $[planned\_murder(A) : t_2 \leftarrow kill\_over\_four\_people(A) : t_2$
  $\& \, \mathbf{not}\, indiscriminant\_murder(A) : t_2, \, kills\_over\_four\_people(A) : t_2 \leftarrow],$
  $[\sim life\_sentence(A) : t_2 \leftarrow kill\_over\_four\_people(A) : t_2,$
  $kill\_over\_four\_people(A) : t_2 \leftarrow], \quad [kill\_over\_four\_people(A) : t_2 \leftarrow],$
  $[life\_sentence(A) : 0.8 \leftarrow planned\_murder(A) : 0.7 \& regret(A) : 0.4,$
  $planned\_murder(A) : 0.9 \leftarrow, regret(A) : 0.7 \leftarrow],$
  $[planned\_murder(A) : 0.9 \leftarrow], \quad [regret(A) : 0.7 \leftarrow],$
  $[kill(A, stranger) : 0.6 \leftarrow] \quad \}$

$Self - centerd\_Justified\_Args = \{$
  $[kill\_over\_four\_people(A) : t_2 \leftarrow],$
  $[life\_sentence(A) : 0.8 \leftarrow planned\_murder(A) : 0.7 \& regret(A) : 0.4,$
  $planned\_murder(A) : 0.9 \leftarrow, regret(A) : 0.7 \leftarrow],$
  $[planned\_murder(A) : 0.9 \leftarrow], \quad [regret(A) : 0.7 \leftarrow],$
  $[kill(A, stranger) : 0.6 \leftarrow] \quad \}$

$Creative\_Justified\_Args = \{$
  $[indiscriminant\_murder(A) : t_2 \leftarrow kill(A, stranger) : t_2,$
  $kill(A, stranger) : t_2 \leftarrow] \quad \}$

Fig. 9 and 10 show every possible argument and every possible attack relation among them. Fig. 9 represents arguments based on the homomorphism $h1 :$ $\mathcal{TWO} \rightarrow \mathcal{R}$ and Fig. 10 represents arguments based on the homomorphism $h2 : \mathcal{R} \rightarrow \mathcal{TWO}$ respectively, and the arguments which is enclosed by a heavy line are justified arguments.

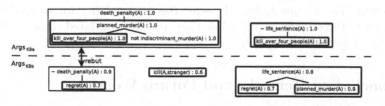

Fig. 9. Relation among arguments in case of the homomorphism $h1 : \mathcal{TWO} \rightarrow \mathcal{R}$

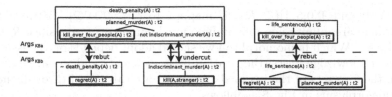

Fig. 10. Relation among arguments in case of the homomorphism $h2 : \mathcal{R} \to \mathcal{TWO}$

From the result of argumentation, we can know that the issue $death\_penalty(A)$: t_2 is not justified in both epistemology, however the issue $life\_sentence(A)$: 0.8 is justified in one side, so that it is credulously justified. Furthermore, the set of knowledges $[indiscriminant\_murder(A) : 0.7 \leftarrow kill(A, stranger) : 0.8, kill(A, stranger) : 0.6 \leftarrow]$ is not an argument, but in the epistemology of $\mathcal{TWO}$, it comes to an argument. It would be said that the argument has been created or uncovered by accepting another's sense of value than one's own.

As we have done above, we can syncretize argumentation with felicity by adopting the lattice homomorphisms which preserve the partial order relation.

5   Related Work

There seems to be only one work related to ours as far as we know although its goal and approach are based on extremely different awareness of the issue, and have been pursued independently. Coste-Marquis et al. proposed a general framework for merging argumentation systems based on Dung's theory of argumentation [13]. The purpose is to solve the problem of deriving sensible information from a collection of argumentation systems coming from different agents.

In comparison with their work [13], our approach focuses on the arguments whose constituents get involved in the lattices of truth values of literals, from a microscopic point of view on arguments. Coste-Marquis et al., on the other hand, see the issue of merging argumentation systems from a macroscopic point of view on AFs. And their knowledge base is homogeneous in that agents have a common knowledge representation language, while ours is heterogeneous.

Nevertheless, we share the the same final goal to characterize a set of arguments acceptable among multi-agents even if our motivation and starting place are different. To cite one technical point, the acceptability for merged AFs is classified into three kinds in [13], while they are closely related to three kinds of justified arguments of this paper.

6   Concluding Remarks and Future Work

Agents have to live in the multi-cultural computer-networked virtual society as well as humans living in the multi-cultural society. This implies that agents also get involved in arguing about issues of mutual interest on the basis of their own belief and knowledge. But, if they insisted only on their epistemology, we would lose chances to interact or communicate with each other. The enterprise in this paper is an attempt to avoid such a cul-de-sac appearing even in argument-based problem solving.

There has been no work on argumentation frameworks in which each agent has its own knowledge representation language, its own epistemology, and its own argumentation framework. They were all common to agents who participate in argumentation. Our work goes to the polar opposite direction from the perspective of the past works.

The Golden Rule has its roots in a wide range of world cultures: ancient Greece, ancient Egypt, ancient China, etc. and almost all religion and philosophy such as Buddhism, Christianity, Islam, Judaism, Confucianism, etc. The human history accepts it as a universal standard with which we resolve conflicts among different civilization and culture. Although the Golden Rule has had its critics on the one hand, the key element of it is that a person attempting to live by this rule should treat all people, not just members of his or her in-group, with consideration and compassion. Therefore it is reasonable for us to employ it and formalize the syncretic argumentation under the Golden Rule as the rationale of our attempt. Our bi-directional homomorphism (operation) between different annotations realizes the key and may be said to the Golden Rule itself in the syncretic argumentation. We hope that the syncretic argumentation could lead to overcome and bridge the gulf of incommensurability among different cultural agents, and result in fair and equal argumentation without unilateral imposition.

In the near future, we will undertake mainly three major works:

(i) introducing other types of lattice operations such as the product, sum, and fusion of lattices to produce more versatile and well-rounded arguments,
(ii) extending the syncretic argumentation to the case of more than two agents, taking into account the ordering of lattice homomorphism, and
(iii) implementing the syncretic argumentation on top of IAE, Integrated Argumentation Environment [14] that is an implementation of LMA. It is expected that the incorporation of the syncretism into LMA as well as the past argumentation systems could allow to expand application domains extensively.

References

1. Dung, P.: On the acceptability of arguments and its fundamental role in nonmonotonic reasoning, logics programming and n-person games. Artificial Intelligence 77, 321–357 (1995)
2. Takahashi, T., Sawamura, H.: A logic of multiple-valued argumentation. In: Proceedings of the third international joint conference on Autonomous Agents and Multi Agent Systems (AAMAS 2004), pp. 800–807. ACM, New York (2004)
3. Chesñevar, C.I., Maguitman, G., Loui, R.P.: Logical models of argument. ACM Computing Surveys 32, 337–383 (2000)

4. Prakken, H., Vreeswijk, G.: Logical systems for defeasible argumentation. In: Gabbay, D., Guenther, F. (eds.) Handbook of Philosophical Logic, pp. 219–318. Kluwer, Dordrecht (2002)
5. Chesñevar, C.I., Simari, G., Alsinet, T., Godo, L.: A logic programming framework for possibilistic argumentation with vague knowledge. In: Proc. of the Intl. Conference on Uncertainty in Artificial Intelligence, UAI 2004 (2004)
6. Gensler, H.J.: Formal Ethics. Routledge, New York (1996)
7. Confucius: The Analects, translated by D. Hinton. Counterpoint (1998)
8. Kifer, M., Subrahmanian, V.S.: Theory of generalized annotated logic programming and its applications. J. of Logic Programming 12, 335–397 (1992)
9. Davey, B.A., Priestley, H.A.: Introduction to Lattices and Order. Cambridge (2002)
10. Sawamura, H., Mares, E.: How agents should exploit tetralemma with an eastern mind in argumentation. In: Barley, M., Kasabov, N. (eds.) PRIMA 2004. LNCS (LNAI), vol. 3371, pp. 259–278. Springer, Heidelberg (2004)
11. Wikipedia: [heliocentrism], http://en.wikipedia.org/wiki/Heliocentrism
12. Wikipedia: [geocentric model],
    http://en.wikipedia.org/wiki/Geocentric_model
13. Coste-Marquis, S., Devred, C., Konieczny, S., Lagasquie-Schiex, M.C., Marquis, P.: On the merging of dung's argumentation systems. Artificial Intelligence 171, 730–753 (2007)
14. Fukumoto, T., Kuribara, S., Sawamura, H.: An integrated argumentation environment for arguing agents. In: Nguyen, N.T., Jo, G.-S., Howlett, R.J., Jain, L.C. (eds.) KES-AMSTA 2008. LNCS (LNAI), vol. 4953, pp. 351–360. Springer, Heidelberg (2008)

Adaptive Adjustment of Starting Price for Agents in Continuous Double Auctions

Huiye Ma and Harry Timmermans

Eindhoven University of Technology, Eindhoven, The Netherlands

Abstract. Software agents can act flexibly in a variety of electronic marketplaces. Continuous Double Auction (CDA) is an efficient and common form of these marketplaces. There are several bidding strategies proposed in the literature for agents to adopt to compute their asks or bids in CDAs. For all of these bidding strategies, starting price has not been taken into account. However, in online auction marketplaces, the starting price is an important parameter for sellers to set and has been discussed many a time in the literature. Given the importance of starting price, the main objective of our work is to explore the effect of starting price on agents using various bidding strategies and how to adjust it adaptively within a dynamic CDA market. Experimental results confirm that when agents set their starting prices at varying values in different market situations, their profit changes significantly no matter which strategy they adopt. In order to guide agents to adjust their starting prices in dynamic and unknown markets, an adaptive mechanism is proposed. Experimental results show that agents adopting the adaptive mechanism generally outperform the corresponding agents without. Furthermore, another set of experiments are carried out to let all the agents use the adaptive mechanism and compete together in one market. Not surprisingly, the profit of agents is observed to drop down a lot in this situation.

1 Introduction

Electronic commerce is playing an increasingly important role in many organizations [1]. It offers opportunities to improve the interactions among the customers and the suppliers. There are many successful applications of auctions in electronic commerce: such as 3G mobile-phone license [2], commodity trading, and electricity markets [3]. Auctions of various kinds are efficient mechanisms to allocate resources. Compared with other styles of auctions, continuous double auctions (CDAs) are complicated and normally generate competitive outcomes more quickly [4]. In CDAs, both buyers and sellers can submit their asks or bids at any time during a trading period.

Software agents are programs which are personalized, autonomous, interactive, and long term running [5]. Therefore agents can act on behalf of their owners who may be buyers or sellers or the auctioneer to achieve some goals in auctions [6]. An agent in CDAs can be viewed as a delegate of his user to achieve a good performance which usually means a good profit. There are several bidding strategies in the literature which can be adopted by agents to compute asks or

J.-J. Yang et al. (Eds.): PRIMA 2009, LNAI 5925, pp. 175–190, 2009.

bids. When an ask or a bid comes to a transaction, the agent who has submitted the ask or bid can make profit.

Starting price[1] is the price determined by the seller who owns the English auction in online marketplaces. Once the starting price is given, only bids higher than this price are acceptable for the seller. It has been well observed in online auctions that sellers have difficulties in deciding the exact values of starting price in their individual auctions. There are a lot of work in the literature studying how to set this price in online auction markets [7,8,9].

The protocol of English auction is similar to that of CDA if we look on English auction as a special kind of CDA where only one seller is trading and no ask has been submitted yet. This reminds us that sellers in CDAs may also have the motivation to set a starting price and similarly have the same difficulty on how to determine the value of the starting price. Through a set of experiments, it has been illustrated that different values of starting price affect the profit of agents heavily.

In practical CDA markets, sellers or buyers may enter or leave the market freely. As a result, the composition of sellers or buyers may change all the time. Hence such CDA markets are dynamic. Suppose there is a human seller who wants to sell some units of good in a CDA market. If he finds that he can often sell all the units of good he desires to sell, then he is not willing to set his starting price low. On the contrary, if he finds that he cannot sell many units of good, then he will prefer to make compromise by decreasing his starting price. For human traders, the adjustment is adaptive conditioning on the market context. Generally speaking, such adaptivity can increase transaction opportunities and consequently profits. Therefore agents should take into account such adaptive starting prices.

In order to guide agents to adjust starting prices in a dynamic CDA market, an adaptive mechanism is proposed. Further experimental results show that the performance of agents with the adaptive mechanism is superior compared with that of agents without adopting the adaptive mechanism.

If we enable all the agents to utilize the adaptive mechanism, another question comes, which is how about the current profit of these agents. Since there lacks similar research in the literature, we give the first try to examine the market full of agents utilizing different bidding strategies but with the same adaptive mechanism. It is not a surprise to see that the performance of agents is not as good as that of agents trading in the market where only part of them uses the adaptive mechanism.

The main contributions of this paper are the following:

- A novel adaptive mechanism algorithm to enable agents to adjust their starting prices dynamically.
- The analysis of the effect of various starting prices to agents in different market situations.
- The experimental results to explore the effect when part of and then all the agents adopt the same adaptive mechanism.

---

[1] Here is the definition of starting price on eBay
http://pages.ebay.com/help/sell/starting_price.html.

This paper is organized as follows. In the next section, we formalize a CDA market mechanism and introduce related work. Starting price for sellers and buyers are defined in section 3. Analysis and experimental results are also given to show the effect of various starting prices. Section 4 proposes the adaptive mechanism for agents utilizing different bidding strategies to trade in unknown CDA markets. Section 5 presents experimental results of agents utilizing classical bidding strategies with the adaptive mechanism. Section 6 concludes this paper and points out the future work.

2 Preliminaries

2.1 Continuous Double Auction

A continuous double auction (CDA) is a market institution where there are many buyers submitting bids and many sellers submitting asks. At any time, a seller is free to accept the highest bid offered by buyers (called the outstanding bid, denoted as ob), and a buyer is free to accept the lowest ask of sellers (called the outstanding ask, denoted as oa). We assume that for each agent (buyer or seller), there are a highest price for the market, denoted as P_{ul}, and a lowest price for the market, denoted as P_{ll}, which the agent can obtain from his own experiment and the market trading history.[2]

For each unit of good that a seller wants to sell, there is a reservation price which is only known by himself. If the seller sells the unit below the reservation price, he will lose money. Consequently, a rational seller will not sell the unit below the reservation price. Similarly, for each unit of good that a buyer desires to buy, there is a reservation price, above which a rational buyer will not buy the unit.

A bid which is lower than or equal to ob, is an invalid bid and will be ignored by the market. Similarly, an ask which is higher than or equal to oa, is an invalid ask and will be ignored by the market. When oa is lower than or equal to ob, a transaction occurs. The transaction price is the earlier one of oa and ob. If there is a transaction, or there is no update of oa or ob in a pre-specified time period, a round is terminated. In each transaction, one unit of good is traded. When either all the sellers or all the buyers have traded all the units of good they want to trade, a run ends. In general, a run is composed of many rounds. The supply of the market is the total number of units to be sold by all the sellers. The demand of the market is the total number of units to be bought by all the buyers. For example, if the supply is 30 and the demand is 38, then there will have 30 rounds in a run.

2.2 Related Work

The research into the design of bidding strategies for agents in CDAs originated from early experimental economics work. Smith [11] conducted experimental

---

[2] For example, Gode and Sunder [10] also assume that there is an entire feasible range of trading prices for the market, which is similar to the range of $[P_{ll}, P_{ul}]$.

double auctions with a small number of human traders and demonstrated a rapid convergence of transaction prices to the supply and demand competitive equilibrium.

Later, Gode and Sunder [10] substituted "zero-intelligence" (ZI) software agents for the human traders. They proposed two kinds of agents. One was ZI with Constraint (ZI-C) agent. ZI-C buyers submitted bids which were randomly generated between the lowest price of the market and the reservation price. Similarly, asks submitted by ZI-C sellers are random values between the reservation price and the highest price of the market. Another was ZI Unconstrained (ZI-U) agent which submitted a random ask or bid between the lowest price and the highest price of the market. Cliff and Bruten [12] further designed "zero-intelligence-plus" (ZIP) agents by employing an elementary form of machine learning and a set of heuristic rules. Preist and Tol [13] employed different heuristics to determine target profit margins in ZIP strategy, which is called CP strategy in this paper.

Gjerstad and Dickhaut [14] proposed a different bidding strategy, referred to as GD in this paper. They provided two belief functions for sellers and buyers. With the belief function, each agent estimated the probability for a possible bid or ask to be accepted based on recent market trading history, and then submitted the bid or ask corresponding to the maximum expected payoff. Tesauro and Bredin [15] developed a sequential bidding strategy utilizing dynamic programming in CDAs, dubbed GDX. They used a belief function together with a forecast of the changes of the beliefs over time. However, the belief function resembled that of GD strategy except for slight modifications.

In [16], FL-strategy was designed which introduced soft bids and fuzzy reasoning into the heuristic rules for traders. The authors also input adaptivity to FL-strategy which is referred to as A-FL strategy in this paper. If a seller or buyer waited too long to conduct a transaction, he should be more risk-averse in the ext round. On the contrary, he should become more risk-seeking.

In our previous work [17], adaptive attitude (AA) strategy was proposed to enable agents to have the feeling of being eager for more transaction or for more profit in different dynamic market situations. Agents adjusted their asks or bids along with the fluctuating eagerness and hence improved their profits in the end.

Recently Vytelingum et al. [18] introduced a strategy called "adaptive aggressiveness" which uses a learning rule to adapt to market conditions and gradually adjusts expected margins, much like ZIP, based on market activity. Through experiments, the strategy was shown to outperform ZIP and GDX in both static and dynamic scenarios.

A characteristic that is common to almost all the previously proposed strategies in CDAs is that the agent considers all the factors as required by the strategy in use, such as the transaction price, the trading history, the outstanding ask, the outstanding bid, the reservation price, the risk attitude, the price range of the market, etc. There lacks the discussion on whether to set the starting price and how to determine the price adaptively. In the next sections, the definition of starting price in CDAs is given and experiments are carried out by using ZI-C, ZIP, and GD strategies which are the most widely adopted ones in the literature.

3 Starting Price

3.1 Motivation

It has been widely observed from the online auction marketplaces that sellers need to set the price from which buyers start to bid and hence called starting price or reserve price.[3] The starting price is not the reservation price as we have defined in Section 2.1. The main difference is that for any seller, the reservation price is the value below which the seller will lose money while the starting price should be no less than the reservation price and requires all the valid bids to be higher than or equal to it so that there will be at least some profit left for the seller.

According to the definition of the starting price and the discussion in the literature [7,8,9], if the seller sets the value to be very large, then it will prevent buyers from bidding; otherwise, it will keep very few profit to the seller.

The same difficulty stands for sellers in CDAs. Assume a human seller who wants to sell a unit of good in a CDA market and the reservation price for the unit of good is $90. Considering a number of factors, he determines that he should submit all his asks at least $100 which is the so called starting price. This means that he can keep at least $10 as profit for himself if he achieve a transaction in the end. Of course, the seller will face a risk of selling the good or not, which depends on how much willingness buyers want to buy at a higher price. This relies a lot on the supply and demand relationship in the auction market and moreover the seller's feeling of that relationship. Thus the decision on which starting price to set varies for different persons.

Of course, if the seller feels that the buyers are not competing ferociously like before, then he might be willing to set the starting price to $91 in order to achieve more transactions. Therefore, the decisions on which starting price to set is not only different on persons, but also adaptive depending on the current market environment, for example, whether it is difficult or easy for the trader to have transactions in the market, and so on. We call such decision, adaptive starting price determination. These decisions often increase transaction opportunities of the trader at good, though not 'ideal' prices, and have positive effects on the amount of total profit the trader gains in general.

We believe that when agents utilize the bidding strategy which integrates adaptive starting price determination, their performance can be enhanced in general. The effect of adaptive starting price determination to agents utilizing different kinds of bidding strategies is investigated in this paper.

3.2 Definitions

For a seller i, suppose the ask determined by seller i is denoted as $[\delta_s, ask]$, which means that if the value of the ask is lower than δ_s, this ask is not acceptable

---

[3] For example, the starting price on eBay is
http://pages.ebay.com/help/sell/starting_price.html.

from the seller's point of view and will be replaced with δ_s. Otherwise, the seller will submit ask to the market. δ_s is called **starting price** for seller.

Definition 1. *For a seller,* **starting price,** *denoted as δ_s, is a price which satisfies*

- *if $oa \leq \delta_s$ then the seller will not submit his asks;*
- *the value of δ_s must be higher than or equal to the reservation price of the current good.*
- *if $ask < \delta_s$ then the seller will adjust the value of ask to be equal to δ_s.*

Similarly, the starting price for buyer can be defined below.

Definition 2. *For a buyer,* **starting price,** *denoted as δ_b, is a price which satisfies*

- *if $ob \geq \delta_b$ then the buyer will not submit his bids;*
- *the value of δ_b must be lower than or equal to the reservation price of the current good;*
- *if $bid > \delta_s$ then the buyer will adjust the value of bid to be equal to δ_b.*

3.3   Experimental Results and Analysis

Based on the definition of starting price, the key questions are when the adoption of starting price can enhance profits and which value of starting price should be adopted under different situations. The answer in conjecture is as follows. For a seller/buyer, if the current market favors the agent, it is easy for him to have transactions and he should set the starting price to be high/low. If the current market goes against the agent, it is difficult for him to make transactions and he should adjust the starting price to be low/high. The experimental results below have demonstrated the relationship between values of the starting price and the situation whether it is easy or difficult for the agent to buy or sell the units of good.

Three groups of experiments are conducted corresponding to ZI-C sellers, ZIP sellers, and GD sellers separately. For each kind of seller agents, there are experiments trading with a random combination of ZI-C, ZIP, and GD buyers. In each experiment, four sessions are provided in which the demand changes from 10, 25, 50, to 100 while the supply is 50. For the seller agents, the value of δ_s is changed from 1.0, 1.5, 2.0, and 2.5 under each supply and demand pair. All the buyers utilize randomly generated starting prices. The distribution of reservation prices for all the sellers and buyers are randomly drawn from [1.0, 3.0].

The profit of ZI-C seller agents utilizing δ_s are shown in Figure 1. According to the figure, the best starting price for ZI-C sellers when the supply is 50 and demand is 10 is 1.5, then 2.0, 2.0, 2.5. Due to space limit, we give Figure 2 which directly shows the best starting prices for ZI-C, ZIP, and GD sellers under different market situations.

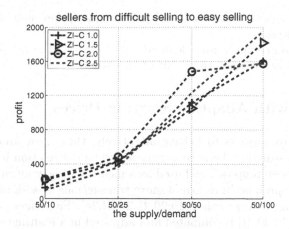

Fig. 1. The profit of ZI-C sellers when they use different fixed starting prices 1.0, 1.5, 2.0, and 2.5 under various market situations while a random combination of ZI-C, ZIP, and GD buyers use random starting prices

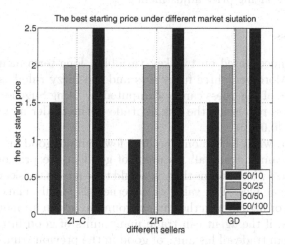

Fig. 2. The best staring price for different sellers under varying market situations

3.4 Summary

These experiments clearly show the following results. Similarly, buyer agents can reach the same conclusion.

- when a seller agent can trade all the units of his good very easily, he should adjust the starting price to be high. This can be observed in Figure 1. The reason is that when supply is smaller than or equal to demand, all the buyer agents have to compete for the units of good that they desire to buy. Therefore buyers are willing to pay a higher price which increases the profit of the seller per transaction. Hence the seller agents with higher starting prices generally outperform those with lower starting prices.

- when seller agents cannot trade all units of good, they should decrease their starting prices.
- under different supply and demand relationships, the adoption of proper starting prices increases the profit of the agents.

4 Agents with Adaptive Starting Prices

In order to enable agents to behave adaptively, they must know what is the current market situation, i.e., the supply and demand relation in their opinion. Eagerness has been proposed and used as a measure of how much willingness for an agent to compromise in return of more transactions or seek more profit with the risk of losing a transaction [19,20,21,22,23,24]. Eagerness proposed in our previous work [19,20,21] is computed and adjusted in a realtime manner according to the dynamic market situation. Therefore it can be used as an indicator of the current supply and demand relationship from the agent's point of view. Based on eagerness, we are able to provide an adaptive mechanism for agents to utilize adaptive starting price adjustment.

4.1 Eagerness

Eagerness is defined based on two key variables, long-term attitude and shot-term attitude. Moreover, three fuzzy sets and the fuzzy rule base are provided so that the value of eagerness can be computed by using Sugeno controller. The value of eagerness represents the risk attitude of the trader in a series of CDAs and it is within [0.0, 1.0].

For any agent, when he can only trade a few units of good in the past several rounds and he cannot trade all his units of good in the previous run, he will become risk averse which means that he would take minimal risks with his actions and reject fair gambles. The value of eagerness is small. Thus the agent will submit low asks or high bids in the current round in return for more transactions. On the contrary, if the agent can trade many units of good in the past several rounds and he can trade all his units of good in the previous run, he will become risk seeking, which means that he prefers fair gambles to sure results. The value of eagerness is large. Therefore the agent will submit high asks or low bids in the current round in order to gain more profits. Otherwise, the agent is risk neutral which means that he is neither risk seeking nor risk averse.

4.2 Enhancing Bidding Strategies for Sellers and Buyers by Adaptive Starting Prices

The corresponding algorithms are designed for seller agents and buyer agents utilizing different bidding strategies to integrate the adaptive mechanism. X represents any bidding strategy without integrating the adaptive mechanism. X_{δ_s} (X_{δ_b}) denotes the enhanced bidding strategy for sellers (buyers) with the adaptive mechanism. $F_{eager}^{(i)}$ is the value of eagerness for agent i.

```
calculate F_{eager}^{(i)};
let P_{ul}^{(i)} be the highest price of the market;
let C_k^{(i)} be the reservation price of the current unit of good;
let δ_s^{(i)} represent the degree of softness of seller i;
δ_s^{(i)} = C_k^{(i)} + F_{eager}^{(i)} × (P_{ul}^{(i)} − C_k^{(i)});
if δ_s^{(i)} ≥ oa then
      there is no ask;
else
      calculate an ask utilizing strategy X;
      if ask < δ_s^{(i)} then
            ask = δ_s^{(i)};
      else
            submit the ask;
      end
end
```

Fig. 3. The pseudo code of the bidding strategy with the adaptive mechanism for sellers

```
calculate F_{eager}^{(j)};
let P_{ll}^{(j)} be the lowest price of the market;
let R_k^{(j)} be the reservation price of the current unit of good;
let δ_b^{(j)} the degree of softness of buyer j;
δ_b^{(j)} = R_k^{(j)} − F_{eager}^{(j)} × (R_k^{(j)} − P_{ll}^{(j)});
if ob ≥ δ^{(j)} then
      there is no bid;
else
      calculate a bid utilizing strategy X;
      if bid > δ_b^{(j)} then
            bid = δ_b^{(j)};
      else
            submit the bid;
      end
end
```

Fig. 4. The pseudo code of bidding strategy with the adaptive mechanism for buyers

The algorithm for sellers is given in Figure 3. The enhanced bidding strategy works in the following way. The seller first calculates eagerness which tells the seller how is the current supply and demand relationship based on his trading experience. Then the value of the starting price δ_s is calculated according to eagerness, the reservation price, and the highest price of the market. If ask is smaller than the value of δ_s, ask is set to equal δ_s. Otherwise, the seller will submit an ask which is equal to the ask calculated by X. For buyers, the enhanced bidding strategy is shown in Figure 4. Similarly, the buyer calculates the eagerness and δ_b accordingly. If *bid* is larger than δ_b, set *bid* equal to δ_b. Otherwise, the buyer will submit a bid which is equal to the bid calculated by X.

For example, consider a seller. The long term attitude $T_{p,i}$ is 0.9 and the short term attitude $T_{i,\text{normalized}}^r$ is 0.3.[4] Then the value of eagerness is 0.29. Suppose the value of $P_{ul}^{(i)}$ is 3.0 and the value of $C_k^{(i)}$ is 1.2. As a result, the value of the starting price δ_s is 1.722. It means that when the value of *ask* is smaller than 1.722, the seller will adjust it to be 1.722. This will be sure to help him keep some profit although not high. The result also conforms to the intuition of humans. When the seller cannot trade many units of his good (i.e., the value of eagerness is small), then he will be more eager to trade his good in the current round and at the same time keep a little profit. Thus the value of δ_s is quite low.

5   Experimental Evaluation

In order to examine the performance of the adaptive mechanism, we carry out two series of experiments. In the first one, the performance of seller agents with adaptive mechanism is checked while the total amount of the adaptive sellers is half of the amount of all the sellers. In the second series, all the sellers adopt the adaptive mechanism and the profit is again compared with that got in the first series. The motivation to take the second series of experiments is to explore the agents' performance when everyone is the same intelligent to adjust the starting price.

5.1   Experimental Setup

For each pair of supply and demand, there are 100 runs. In each run, all the sellers and buyers will have the chance to trade what they want. We assume that each seller or buyer just desires one unit of goods. Once they achieve what they desire, they will leave the current run.

In each round, a buyer/seller is endowed with one unit of goods whose reservation price is independently and uniformly drawn from $[1.0, 3.0]$. The thinking time that a buyer/seller is allowed to elapse before submitting a bid is specified as a randomly distributed variable with a range $[1, 200]$. The fixed deadline to terminate a round is 20000 time units.

In order to measure how well an agent performs in the auction, we evaluate the performance by the profit he or she gains. For a buyer i, the total profit on all t units bought in a run is $\sum_{k=1}^{t} (C_k^{(i)} - P_k^{(i)})$ where $C_k^{(i)}$ is the reservation price and $P_k^{(i)}$ is the value of the transaction price. Similarly, for a seller, the total profit on all s units bought in a run is $\sum_{k=1}^{s} (P_k^{(j)} - R_k^{(j)})$. An agent's profit is calculated as the sum of the total profits in 100 runs.

At the beginning of each run, 10, 25, 50, or 100 buyers and 50 sellers will join the market. The reservation prices of the units of the goods desired by the sellers and buyers are randomly generated.

---

[4] Because of the page limit, please refer to [19,20,21] for the definitions of the long term attitude and the short term attitude.

Two series of experiments are conducted as follows. The first series of experiments examine performance of sellers using adaptive mechanism compared with those sellers which do not use the mechanism. The sellers are randomly selected from ZI-C, ZIP, GD, and X_{δ_s} sellers. The buyers are random combination of ZI-C, ZIP, and GD buyers. Except X_{δ_s} sellers, the rest sellers and buyers employ random starting prices generated from [1.0, 3.0]. With the random selection, the amount of X and X_{δ_s} sellers are almost the same and can be fairly compared together.

In the second series of experiments, the setup is kept the same except that all the sellers are now using adaptive mechanism to adjust their starting prices. Eventually, the profit of X_{δ_s} is compared with that obtained in the first series of experiments.

5.2   Experimental Result When Part of Agents Utilize the Adaptive Mechanism

The profit of ZI-C sellers utilizing the adaptive mechanism and ZI-C sellers without are shown in Figure 5. It can be seen that the profit of ZI-C seller agents using the adaptive mechanism is much better than the profit of those ZI-C sellers without. The good profit comes from the adaptive adjustment of starting prices. On the one hand, the properly set starting price helps the seller to earn more benefit. On the other hand, the starting price prevents the seller to be trapped into poor transactions. Therefore, in general, the profit is increased a lot for ZI-C sellers, ZIP sellers shown in Figure 6, and GD sellers in Figure 7 as well.

From these three figures, another phenomena can be observed that the enhancement of the adaptive mechanism for ZI-C, ZIP, and GD sellers is different when the supply and demand relation is different. As an example, it can been

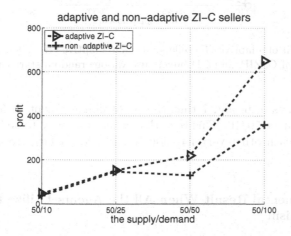

Fig. 5. The profit of adaptive ZI-C sellers and non-adaptive ZI-C sellers while a random combination of ZI-C, ZIP, and GD buyers use various random starting prices

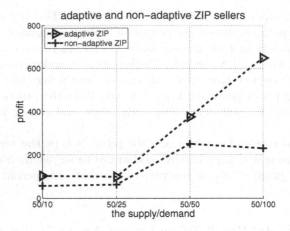

Fig. 6. The profit of adaptive ZIP sellers and non-adaptive ZIP sellers while a random combination of ZI-C, ZIP, and GD buyers use various random starting prices

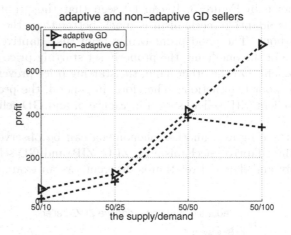

Fig. 7. The profit of adaptive GD sellers and non-adaptive GD sellers while a random combination of ZI-C, ZIP, and GD buyers use various random starting prices

seen from Figures 5, 6, and 7 that the profit enhancement at 50/100 is much larger than that at 50/10. This tells that when it is easy to sell goods, buyers compete with each other very ferociously and leave a large room of profit for sellers to take.

5.3 Experimental Result When All the Agents Utilize the Adaptive Mechanism

The following Figures 8, 9, and 10 illustrate the profit of these sellers in the current experiments where all the sellers utilize the adaptive mechanism, denoted as

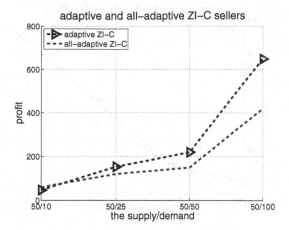

Fig. 8. The profit of adaptive ZI-C sellers when only half of sellers utilize the adaptive mechanism and when all the sellers use the adaptive mechanism while a random combination of ZI-C, ZIP, and GD buyers use random starting prices

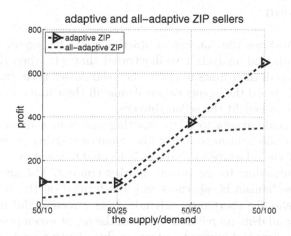

Fig. 9. The profit of adaptive ZIP sellers when only half of sellers utilize the adaptive mechanism and when all the sellers use the adaptive mechanism while a random combination of ZI-C, ZIP, and GD buyers use random starting prices

all-adaptive ZI-C/ZIP/GD, compared with that obtained in the previous experiments. After all the sellers utilize the adaptive mechanisms, the profit of ZI-C, ZIP, and GD sellers decreases dramatically in general. The possible explanation is when everyone is the same intelligent on adjusting their starting prices, no one can take advantage of others. Therefore, all the sellers' profit drops down.

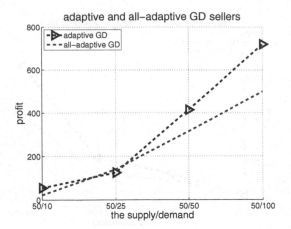

Fig. 10. The profit of adaptive GD sellers when only half of sellers utilize the adaptive mechanism and when all the sellers use the adaptive mechanism while a random combination of ZI-C, ZIP, and GD buyers use random starting prices

6   Conclusion

This paper introduces the concept of starting price for agents in CDAs. Experimental results and analysis have illustrated that: (1) when the seller/buyer agents can trade all their units of good, they should set their starting prices to be high/low; (2) when the agents cannot trade all their units of good, low/high starting prices can benefit the sellers/buyers.

In order to guide agents to adopt starting prices in a dynamic CDA market, an adaptive mechanism to adjust the value of starting prices is presented. The purpose of the adaptive mechanism is to enable agents to set an adaptive starting price according to the current market context. The key component of the adaptive mechanism is eagerness which is formed on the basis of the long term attitude and the short term attitude. It is a meaningful indicator of the current supply and demand relationship from the agent's own point of view. The algorithms for sellers and buyers to integrate the adaptive mechanism are given. Experiments to evaluate agents using ZI-C, ZIP, and GD with the adaptive mechanism are also implemented. Experimental results demonstrate that the adaptive mechanism can remarkably enhance the performance of agents using different bidding strategies in CDAs.

Nevertheless, this is not always the case. When all the seller agents use the adaptive mechanism, it is observed that the profit is decreased for all these agents in general. This observation tells agents to try to be the minority of the market and try to take advantage of this priority. In the future, we shall investigate more on the relation between the transaction price and the starting price, how to conjecture other agents' starting price, how to handle abrupt change of supply and demand, how to detect whether one agent is minority or majority, and so on.

References

1. He, M., Jennings, N.R., Leung, H.: On agent-mediated electronic commerce. IEEE Transactions on Knowledge and Data Engineering 15(4), 985–1003 (2003)
2. Klemperer, P.: Auctions: Theory and Practice. Princeton University Press, Princeton (2004)
3. Xiong, G., Hashiyama, T., Okuma, S.: An electricity supplier bidding strategy through q-learning. Power Engineering Society Summer Meeting 3, 1516–1521 (2002)
4. Li, L., Smith, S.F.: Speculation agents for dynamic multi-period continuous double auctions in b2b exchanges. In: Proceedings of the Proceedings of the 37th Annual Hawaii International Conference on System Sciences, pp. 1–9. IEEE Computer Society, Los Alamitos (2004)
5. Guttman, R.H., Moukas, A.G., Maes, P.: Agent-mediated electronic commerce: A survey. The Knowledge Engeering Review 13(2), 147–159 (1998)
6. Jennings, N.R.: An agent-based approach for building complex software systems. Communications of The ACM 44(4), 35–41 (2001)
7. Bapna, R., Jank, W., Shmueli, G.: Price formation and its dynamics in online auctions. Decis. Support Syst. 44(3), 641–656 (2008)
8. Ariely, D., Simonson, I.: Buying, bidding, playing, or competing? value assessment and decision dynamics in online auctions. Journal of Consumer Psychology 13, 113–123 (2003)
9. Lucking-Reiley, D., Bryan, D., Prasad, N., Reeves, D.: Pennies from ebay: The determinants of price in online auctions. Journal of Industrial Economics 55(2), 223–233 (2007)
10. Gode, D.K., Sunder, S.: Allocative efficiency of markets with zero-intelligence traders: Market as a partial substitute for individual rationality. Journal of Political Economy 101(1), 119–137 (1993)
11. Smith, V.: An experimental study of competitive market behavior. Journal of Political Economy 70(2), 111–137 (1962)
12. Cliff, D., Bruten, J.: Minimal-intelligence agents for bargaining behaviors in market-based environments. Technical Report HP–97–91, Bristol, UK (August 1997)
13. Preist, C., van Tol, M.: Adaptive agents in a persistent shout double auction. In: Proceedings of the 1st International Conference on Information and Computation Economies, pp. 11–18. ACM, New York (1998)
14. Gjerstad, S., Dickhaut, J.: Price formation in double auctions. Games and Economic Behavior 22, 1–29 (1998)
15. Tesauro, G., Bredin, J.L.: Strategic sequential bidding in auctions using dynamic programming. In: Proceedings of the 1st International Joint Conference on Autonomous Agents and Multiagent Systems, pp. 591–598. ACM, New York (2002)
16. He, M., Leung, H., Jennings, N.R.: A fuzzy-logic based bidding strategy for autonomous agents in continuous double auctions. IEEE Transactions on Knowledge and Data Engineering 15(6), 1345–1363 (2003)
17. Ma, H., Leung, H.: An adaptive attitude bidding strategy for agents in continuous double auctions. Electronic Commerce Research and Applications 6(4), 383–398 (2007)
18. Vytelingum, P., Cliff, D., Jennings, N.R.: Strategic bidding in continuous double auctions. Artif. Intell. 172(14), 1700–1729 (2008)

19. Ma, H., Leung, H.: Adaptive soft bid determination in bidding strategies for continuous double auctions. In: Proceedings of the 17th IEEE International Conference on Tools with Artificial Intelligence, Hong Kong, China (November 2005)
20. Ma, H., Leung, H.: Effect of time strategies on the profit of agents using adaptive bid softness determination in continuous double auctions with a fixed deadline. In: Proceedings of 2006 IEEE Joint Conference on E-Commerce Technology and Enterprise Computing, E-Commerce and E-Services, Washington, DC, USA, pp. 16–23. IEEE Computer Society, Los Alamitos (2006)
21. Ma, H., Leung, H.: Bidding Strategies in Agent-Based Continuous Double Auctions. Springer, Heidelberg (2008)
22. Ren, F., Zhang, M., Sim, K.M.: Adaptive conceding strategies for automated trading agents in dynamic, open markets. Decis. Support Syst. 46(3), 704–716 (2009)
23. Sim, K.: A market-driven model for designing negotiation agents. Computational Intelligence 18(4), 618–637 (2002)
24. Dumas, M., Aldred, L., Governatori, G., Hofstede, A.: Probabilistic automated bidding in multiple auctions. Electronic Commerce Research 5, 25–49 (2005)

SIM-MADARP: An Agent-Based Tool for Dial-a-Ride Simulation

Makarena Donoso, Daniel Sandoval, and Claudio Cubillos

Pontificia Universidad Católica de Valparaíso, Escuela de Ingeniería Informática,
Av. Brasil 2241, Valparaíso, Chile
makarena.donoso@gmail.com, daniel.sandoval.u@gmail.com,
claudio.cubillos@ucv.cl

Abstract. This work presents an agent based system devoted to the simulation of passenger transportation scenarios. The architecture is build over a system, called MADARP, devoted to the implementation of concrete passenger transportation planning Systems. The transportation type considered by the system is the demand-responsive one, that is, a flexible approach in which trips requests are tacked online and scheduled over a set of available vehicles. The simulator allows diverse scenarios by varying the geographical network, the requests, and the set of vehicles. By managing diverse eventualities, it gives dynamicity to the simulation, such as, delays of vehicles, clients' no-show and vehicles' breakdowns, among others. The general design is depicted using the PASSI methodology, together with its implementation over the Jade agent platform.

Keywords: Multiagent System, Agent simulation, Dynamic Dial a Ride Problem, Passenger Transportation.

1 Introduction

The present work proposes a simulator of passenger transportation scenarios and more precisely, the planning, scheduling, control and monitoring of passenger transportation requests. All above, by using the agent technology as design paradigm.

Our proposal extends a previous agent architecture called MADARP [3], devoted to the planning of trip requests under a Dial-a-Ride scenario. This architecture is the basis of our work, which is modified to achieve the dynamic functionalities of a complete and appropriate simulator for passenger transportation.

Under such dynamic simulation environment, the aim is to monitor the progress of the diverse vehicles and their schedules while servicing the passengers. Additionally, during this progression, diverse eventualities may happen such as customers modifying or canceling their requests for transport, delays of the vehicles, customers not reaching the point of collection and vehicles failing to continue due to mechanical problems (breakdown); all events involving the reprogramming of the travel and its management.

The following paper is structured around eight chapters. The second chapter is about a description of passenger transportation and the scheduling problem associated

J.-J. Yang et al. (Eds.): PRIMA 2009, LNAI 5925, pp. 191–199, 2009.

to it. The third chapter presents an overview of the MADARP architecture. Next, an explanation of the PASSI methodology comes. The chapter five shows in detail the new SIM-MADARP architecture, including models and explanations about the simulator, focus of this paper. The chapter six contains the results of the tests. Finally, chapter seven draws some conclusions and future work.

2 Passenger Transportation

The kind of transportation service considered regards Demand-Responsive Transportation (DRT), which is a form of advanced user-oriented public transportation characterized by the realization of flexible routes and scheduling of small vehicles / media operating in shared mode of travel according to the needs of Passengers, leveraging as a complement to the existing transport services.

From the standpoint of operations research, the problem is covered in literature as the Dial-A-Ride Problem (DARP), in which users formulate requests for transportation from a specific origin (collection point) to a specific destination (delivery point). The key problem is to design a set of vehicle routes of minimum cost to accommodate all requests for transportation made.

3 MADARP Architecture

MADARP is an agent architecture designed to plan and schedule orders for transportation in a dynamic environment within the context of passenger transport systems. The architecture provides a basis of agents that perform the basic interface, planning and support services to handle various types of requests for transport, using a heterogeneous fleet of vehicles.

There are four layers in the architecture which group the agents and structures according to the functionality provided. The following is a brief description of the functionality of each layer, based on [2] [4]:

- Interface Layer: Connects the system with the real world, providing agents capable of connecting the actors with the system (customers, operators of vehicles).
- Planning Layer: Contains agents dedicated to the processing and planning of travels in a distributed way.
- Service Layer: Supports the planning layer to provide various additional functionalities needed to manage an integrated transport service.
- Ontology Service: Provides a means of integration and cooperation of various actors and players in the top layers in a transparent and consistent way.

The routing and scheduling functionality provided by the system is based on the contract-net protocol (CNP) [10]. The process undertaken for the planning of a trip starts with a request from the client. An agent who manages the request through its process represents him. The request comes to the planner who acts as intermediary between customers and vehicles. On the vehicle side, there is an agent responsible for managing the schedule of the vehicle and processing the orders. For this last task, an heuristic that performs the insertion evaluations within a given vehicle schedule is used. Once a vehicle accepts a request, the user is informed with the service details.

This architecture allows the initial planning of trip requests coming from a set of clients and scheduling them on a given a set of vehicles. Such solution provides an agent architecture that allows the incorporation of dynamicity; however, such dynamics is not implemented. From that initial architecture, modifications were taken in order to manage the contingencies that may occur during the execution of a planned route (trip cancellations, delays, vehicles breakdowns) and the monitoring of the vehicles schedule.

4 The PASSI Methodology

This project will make use of PASSI (Process for Agent Societies Specification and Implementation) as development methodology, which uses UML as modeling language. This methodology accomplishes the specification of a multi-agent system with a bottom-up approach, and gives support for the verification and validation of its models and specifications. PASSI has a toolkit [6] for IBM Rational Rose to support this methodology, besides allows the user to follow and adequately implement the PASSI phases thanks to the automatic compilation of diagrams. For a detailed description of PASSI five models and its respective steps, please refer to [7].

In Figure 1 can be appreciated than in spite of the visible sequence, it is an iterative methodology across and within all the phases (except for the code and deployment steps)

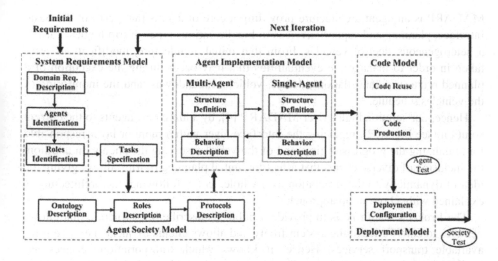

Fig. 1. The PASSI methodology

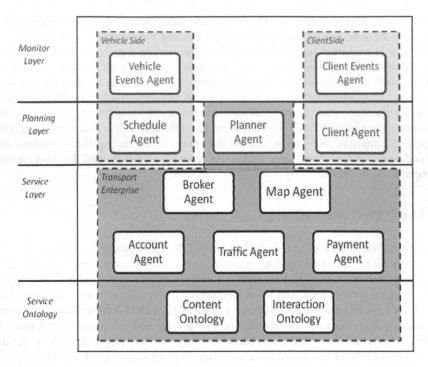

Fig. 2. The SIM-MADARP architecture

5   The SIM-MADARP Architecture

MADARP is an agent architecture providing a core of agents that perform the basic interface, planning and support services to handle various types of trip requests, using a heterogeneous fleet of vehicles. From that initial architecture, modifications were taken in order to manage the eventualities that may occur during the execution of a planned route (trip cancellations, delays, vehicles breakdowns) and the monitoring of the vehicles schedule.

Hence, our solution builds over MADARP [4], by adding new agents to the current solution (see Figure 2), replacing the interface layer with a monitor layer responsible for simulating the progress of time and of the vehicles serving the clients. In addition, the inclusion of diverse events that affect the initial planning of trips allows giving the idea of dynamicity to the simulation as a whole. In the following, the architecture is explained with a bottom-up approach.

The Broker's main role is to provide a publish/subscribe infrastructure that allows vehicles to enter or leave the system freely and allows clients to query the system for available transport services. Hence, it knows which transportation services are available and their characteristics. The Map is wrapping the underlying Geographical

Information System (GIS) providing the routes, distances and times between points within the zone under service coverage.

The Map agent models the actual geographical region under coverage and has the role of providing the rest of the agents with any information related to it. It also process traffic information relevant to the system that may cause a change on schedules.

Schedule agents manage the trip plans (work-schedule) of their corresponding vehicles. The main role of a Schedule agent is to manage the trip plan (work-schedule) of the vehicle. In practical terms, the agent will have to make proposals upon Planner request and in case of winning will have to include the trip into its actual plan. Upon changes (vehicle or client events) informed either by the Vehicle or Planner agents, the Schedule agent will update the plan and reschedule the remaining requests.

The Planner agent is the agent in charge of executing a mediation role in the layer. It processes all the client's requests coming through the Trip-request agents. For this, it uses the contract-net protocol (CNP) to contact all the Schedules (agents) of the available vehicles and ask them for trip proposals for a given client. It is also in charge of managing inbound and outbound events once an agreement has been reached.

The Client agent is responsible of having the client's request fulfilled and of communicating him about the result and possible changes in the original plan (e.g. delays, trip cancellations).

The monitor layer allows to observe how the system behaves upon changes and events from users and vehicles, considering the time variable and is achieved by bringing the entire transport process in real time.

To implement the simulation dynamics, the internal structures and agents of the planning layer were complemented, providing new methods that are capable of supporting new operations for tackling the re-planning and communication between actors and events agents. Below are detailed the new monitor layer and the entities that compose it:

The *Vehicle Events Agent*, is one for each vehicle and is responsible for generating and sending the events related to it. These events simulate the following:

- The routes to be undertaken by each vehicle showing the stops made, pickups/deliveries of passengers and departures/arrivals on depots. The monitoring indicates the events on a time basis, i.e. each event is associated with a time of occurrence, which then evaluates whether the time they occur is actually within the limits agreed in negotiations, from one pickup or delivery point to the next one, the vehicle may arrive on time, before or delayed; all situations handled by the system.
- "Breakdowns" of vehicles: events related to drops in the operation of vehicles, affecting all passengers being served and to be served by the vehicle, initiating a total replanning for each one.
- "Client no-show": Simulates the event of failure of a customer to appear at the place of pick-up, which implies the deletion from the actual vehicle schedule as is no longer necessary to go to the delivery place.

On the other hand, the MAS must generate events that simulate the behavior of real customers. In a similar way, each *Events Client Agent* manages the drivers eventualities that may generate a real client regarding his trip. These events consider:

- Any request for cancellation by the customer.
- Requests for changing the pick-up time from customers.

5.1 Sim-Madarp Agent Architecture

The Roles Identification Diagram is focused on the visible behavior of the agent rather than its structure, based on exploring all the possible routes involved in the inter-agent communication. This diagram describes a scenario in which agents are interacting with each other and working to achieve a behavior required by the system. Each of the agents can participate in different scenarios that are illustrated by means of sequence diagrams, in which objects are used to represent roles performed by agents.

In this sense, the Figure 3 describes the scenario in which an event is triggered by the vehicle, specifically a delay to a stop within the route, and after making the evaluation of the stops that follow, some of them become unfeasible in the same vehicle and a re-planning is needed.

This scenario is initiated by the Events Generator role of Vehicle Events agent. The agent generates a delay-to-the-arrival-point event. Such event is sent to the events communicator role in the same agent to be sent to the events viewer role.

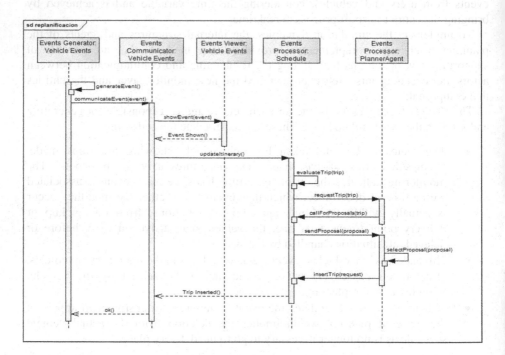

Fig. 3. Roles Identification Diagram

In turn, the events communicator role sends the event to Schedule agent (its event processor role) notifying the delay in order to update the schedule. The agent evaluates the changes in the trip requests it has. In case of any client trip resulting infeasible, a re-planning of that client must take place. For this, the event processor role of the schedule agent sends the trip to Planner agent (its event processing role) to perform a "Call for Proposals" to all the remaining vehicles. These vehicles, through their schedule agents, evaluate the request in order to verify its own feasibility of making the ride and make a proposal.

The Planner agent collects the proposals and selects the one that best meets the service conditions requested by the client. Hence, it informs the selected vehicle, through its schedule agent and notifies the other vehicles. Additionally, the planner acknowledges the vehicle that requested the re-planning of the trip about the success of the modification. Internally, the schedule agent notifies its own vehicle events agent about the success.

The routing algorithm used by vehicles (schedule agents) for finding the "optimal" sequence of pickups and deliveries is based on the ADARTW algorithm [9], a constructive greedy heuristic.

6 Tests

In order to check the proper working of the simulator, the system was tested with a scenario having the following settings:

- All the tests considered the same geographical net which models a small mountain community near Ivrea – Italy.
- 10 demand scenarios were generated, labeled from U1.txt to U10.txt, each considering 50 trip requests.
- The same utility function and scheduling algorithm have been used for all the vehicles.
- All the clients share the same utility function,
- The available fleet is of 30 identical vehicles with capacity 20
- One depot is used for all the vehicles
- In all cases the effectiveness measures (utility variables) were weighted with the same value.
- All event types for each of the parties (customers and vehicles) are randomly generated following a normal distribution.

The execution takes place in a real time environment from 6:00 am until 9:00 am, pretending to work one morning.

Regarding the considered distributed environment, the hosts were PCs with Intel Pentium 4 of 2 GHz. with 256 MB Ram, connected through a 10/100 Mb. Router.

The following Figure 4 summarizes the events messages shown by the simulator and their corresponding event type.

ID	Event	Answer	Event Type
Ev-01	18:03:41 - 06:11:39 Renew time required on bus $bus_30...		
	18:03:41 - 06:11:44 Client was removed	Client is removed from the vehicle and generates a new request	
	18:03:41 - 06:11:44 New time assigned...		
	18:03:41 - 06:11:44 Client U-U20 was sent to new scheduling...		
Ev-02	18:03:43 - 06:13:45 Renew time required on bus $bus_25...		Time Change Events
	18:03:43 - 06:13:46 Client was removed	Client is removed from the vehicle and generates a new request	
	18:03:43 - 06:13:46 New time assigned...		
	18:03:43 - 06:13:46 Client U-U17 was send to new scheduling...		
Ev-03	18:03:51 - 06:21:17 Vehicle is removing...	Client is removed from the vehicle and generates a new request	Vehicle Failure Events
	18:03:51 - 06:21:17 Client U-U15 was sent to new scheduling...		
Ev-04	18:04:19 - 06:50:07 Cancel required on bus $bus_4...		
Ev-05	18:04:21 - 06:51:44 Cancel required on bus $bus_18...		
Ev-04	18:04:41 - 07:11:39 Client was removed	Client is removed from the vehicle	Trip Cancel Events
Ev-05	18:04:47 - 07:17:15 Client was removed		
Ev-06	18:04:52 - 07:22:19 Vehicle is removing...		
	18:04:52 - 07:22:20 Client U-U13 was sent to new scheduling...		
	18:04:52 - 07:22:20 Client U-U19 was sent to new scheduling...		
Ev-07	18:05:33 - 08:03:47 Vehicle is removing...		
	18:05:33 - 08:03:48 Client U-U42 was send to new scheduling...		
Ev-08	18:05:40 - 08:10:51 Vehicle is removing...	Client is removed from the vehicle and generates a new request	Vehicle Failure Events
	18:05:40 - 08:10:51 Client U-U17 was sent to new scheduling...		
	18:05:40 - 08:10:51 Client U-U36 was sent to new scheduling...		
Ev-09	18:06:10 - 08:41:06 Renew time required on bus $bus_14...	Request not served	Time Change Events

Fig. 4. Simulation Results

7 Conclusions and Future Work

The proposed architecture allows simulating the planning and controlling under flexible passenger transportation settings. The use of the agent paradigm allowed building such a simulation tool by extending a prior agent architecture devoted to the initial planning of trip requests.

The simulator considers the use of diverse scenarios by varying the set of clients' requests, the fleet of available vehicles, the operation network and the statistical distribution of the diverse events considered by the system.

Future work considers incorporating to the simulator other probability distribution for the events, the use of other scheduling heuristics and objective functions. In addition, other important step is to develop a 3D graphical interface showing the vehicles moving around the map while servicing the passengers.

Acknowledgements

This work has been partially funded by CONICYT through Fondecyt Project No. 11080284 and the Pontifical Catholic University of Valparaíso (www.pucv.cl), through Nucleus Project No. 037.115 "Collaborative Systems".

References

1. Weiss, G.: Multiagent Systems: A Modern Approach to Distributed Artificial Intelligence. MIT Press, Massachusetts (1999)
2. Ambrosino, G., et al.: EBusiness Applications to Flexible Transport and Mobility Services (2001), http://citeseer.nj.nec.com/ambrosino01ebusiness.html
3. Cubillos, C., Crawford, B., Rodríguez, N.: MADARP: A Distributed Agent-based System for On-Line DARP. In: Stojmenovic, I., Thulasiram, R.K., Yang, L.T., Jia, W., Guo, M., de Mello, R.F. (eds.) ISPA 2007. LNCS, vol. 4742, pp. 160–169. Springer, Heidelberg (2007)
4. Cubillos, C., Gaete, S., Crawford, B.: Design of an Agent-Based System for Passenger Transportation using PASSI. In: Mira, J., Álvarez, J.R. (eds.) IWINAC 2007. LNCS, vol. 4528, pp. 531–540. Springer, Heidelberg (2007)
5. Wooldridge, M., Jennings, N.R.: Intelligent Agents: Theory and Practice. The Knowledge Engineering Review 10(2), 115–152 (1995)
6. PASSI Toolkit (PTK) disponible en, http://sourceforge.net/projects/ptk
7. Cossentino, M., Potts, C.: PASSI: a Process for Specifying and Implementing Multi-Agent Systems Using UML 2001 (2001)
8. Cordeau, J.-F.: A Branch-and-Cut Algorithm for the Dial-a-Ride Problem. Operations Research 54, 573–586; Canada Research Chair in Distribution Management, HEC Montréal 3000, Canada (2003)
9. Jaw, J., et al.: A heuristic algorithm for the multiple-vehicle advance request dial-a-ride problem with time windows. Transportation Research 20B(3), 243–257 (1986)
10. FIPA Contract Net Interaction Protocol Specification, http://www.fipa.org/specs/fipa00029/SC00029H.pdf

An Empirical Study of Agent Programs
A Dynamic Blocks World Case Study in GOAL

M. Birna van Riemsdijk and Koen V. Hindriks

EEMCS, Delft University of Technology, Delft, The Netherlands
{m.b.vanriemsdijk,k.v.hindriks}@tudelft.nl

Abstract. Agent-oriented programming has been motivated in part by
the conception that high-level programming constructs based on common
sense notions such as beliefs and goals provide appropriate abstraction
tools to develop autonomous software. Various agent programming languages and frameworks have been developed by now, but no systematic
study has been done as to how the language constructs in these languages may and are in fact used in practice. Performing a study of these
aspects may contribute to the design of best practices or programming
guidelines for agent programming, and clarify the use of common sense
notions in agent programs. In this paper, we analyze various agent programs for *dynamic blocks world*, written in the GOAL agent programming
language. We present several observations based on a quantitative and
qualitative analysis that provide insight into more practical aspects of
the development of agent programs. Finally, we identify important issues in three key areas related to agent-oriented programming that need
further investigation.

1 Introduction

The concept of a *goal* lies at the basis of our understanding of why we perform
actions. It is common sense to explain the things we do in terms of beliefs and
goals. The *reasons* for performing actions are derived from our motivations and
the notion of *rational behavior* is typically explained in terms of actions that are
produced in order to further our goals. For example, a researcher who has a goal
to have finished a paper but is going on a holiday instead is not considered to
behave rationally because holidays do not further the goal of writing a paper.

Shoham was one of the first who proposed to use such common sense notions to
build programs [14], coining a new programming paradigm called *agent-oriented
programming*. Inspired by Shoham, a variety of agent-oriented programming languages and frameworks have been proposed since then [3,4]. For several of them,
interpreters and Integrated Development Environments (IDEs) are being developed. Some of them have been designed mainly with a focus on building practical applications (e.g., JACK [17] and Jadex [13]), while for others the focus
has been also or mainly on the languages' theoretical underpinnings (e.g., GOAL
[10], 2APL [6], and Jason [5]).

J.-J. Yang et al. (Eds.): PRIMA 2009, LNAI 5925, pp. 200–215, 2009.

In this paper, we take the language GOAL as our object of study. GOAL is a high-level programming language to program rational agents that derive their choice of action from their beliefs and goals. Although the language's theoretical basis is important, it *is* designed by taking a definite *engineering stance* and aims at providing useful programming constructs to develop agent programs.

However, although it has been used for developing several small-size applications, no systematic study has been done as to *how the language constructs are used* in practice to program agents, and *how easy it is to read* the resulting programs. Also, if the language is going to be used for building real-world applications, *efficiency* and a programmer's knowledge of this becomes an important issue. We believe it is important to get a better understanding of these issues in order to identify which aspects need to be addressed with respect to them, and to be able to design a set of best practices or *programming guidelines* that support GOAL programmers. It is the purpose of this paper to contribute to this aim. We do this by analyzing three GOAL programs for the dynamic blocks world domain. To the best of our knowledge, this is the first time such comparative analysis of agent programs programmed in a dedicated agent programming language has been done. This kind of empirical software engineering is expected to form over time a body of knowledge leading to widely accepted and well-formed theories [2].

The dynamic blocks world domain is explained in Section 2 and in Section 3 we explain the GOAL language. We outline our approach in Section 4. In Section 5, we analyze the programs using various numeric measures on their code and execution. In Section 6, we look in more detail at how the programs were written and how the language constructs of GOAL were used. We conclude in Section 7.

2 The Dynamic Blocks World

The blocks world is a simple environment that consists of a finite number of blocks that are stacked into *towers* on a table of *unlimited* size. It is assumed that each block has a unique label or name $a, b, c, ...$ Blocks need to obey the following "laws" of the blocks world: (i) a block is either on top of another block or it is located somewhere on the table; (ii) a block can be directly on top of at most one other block; and, (iii) there is at most one block directly on top of any other block.

A *blocks world problem* is the problem of which actions to perform to transform an initial state or configuration of towers into a goal configuration, where the exact positioning of towers on the table is irrelevant. A blocks world problem thus defines an action selection problem. The action of moving a block is called *constructive* (see, e.g., [15]) if in the resulting state that block is in position, meaning that the block is on top of a block or on the table and this corresponds with the goal state, and all blocks (if any) below it are also in position. Observe that a constructive move always increases the number of blocks that are in position.

We have used a specific variant of the blocks world, which we call the *dynamic blocks world*. In the dynamic blocks world, a user can move blocks around while the agent is moving blocks to obtain a goal configuration. It was introduced in [11], and comes with an implemented environment[1]. In that environment, there is a gripper that can be used to move blocks and the user can move blocks around by dragging and dropping blocks in the environment's graphical user interface. The agent can steer the gripper by sending two kinds of actions to the environment: the action pickup(X) to tell it to pick up a block X, and the action putdown(X,Y) to tell it to put down the block X, which should be the block the gripper is currently holding, onto the block Y. The gripper can hold at most one block. The environment has a maximum of 13 blocks, and these can all be on the table at the same time (thereby realizing a table that is always "clear"). The user can move the blocks around on the table, put a block inside the gripper, or take away a block from the gripper. In contrast with the gripper, which can only pick up a block if there is no block on top of it and move it onto a block that is clear, the user can move any block in any way he likes.

The fact that a user can move around blocks can give rise to various kinds of possibly problematic situations. For example, the agent may be executing the action putdown(a,b), while the user moves some block on top of b. This means that a can no longer be put down onto b, since b is not clear anymore. It may also be the case that the agent is moving a block a from some other block onto the table, since a could not yet be moved in a constructive way. It may be the case that while the agent is doing that, the user moves blocks in such a way that now a *can* be moved into position, making the previous action superfluous. A comprehensive list of such cases where the agent has to deal with the dynamics of the environment, can be found in [16].

3   Explanation of GOAL

A GOAL agent decides which action to perform next based on its beliefs and goals. Such a decision typically depends on the current state of the agent's environment as well as general knowledge about this environment. The former type of knowledge is typically dynamic and changes over time, whereas the latter typically is static and does not change over time. In line with this distinction, two types of knowledge of an agent are distinguished: conceptual or domain knowledge stored in a *knowledge base* and beliefs about the current state of the environment stored in a *belief base*. In the implementation of GOAL, both knowledge base and belief base are Prolog programs. For example, the knowledge base may contain the definition of the predicate clear(X), and the belief base may contain information about which blocks are present and how they are stacked, represented using the predicate on(X,Y), as illustrated in Table 1.

A decision to act will usually also depend on the goals of the agent. Goals of an agent are stored in a *goal base*. The goal base consists of conjunctions of Prolog atoms. For example, the goal to build a tower where a is stacked on b can be represented as a conjunction of the corresponding on predicates (see Table 1).

---

[1]   http://www.robotics.stanford.edu/users/nilsson/trweb/TRTower/
TRTower_links.html

Table 1. Knowledge Base, Belief Base, Goal Base, Action Rules

```
 1    knowledge{
 2      clear(table).
 3      clear(X) :- block(X), not(on(Y,X)).
 4    }
 5    beliefs{
 6      block(a). block(b). block(c).
 7      on(a,table). on(c,b). on(b,table).
 8    }
 9    goals{
10      on(a,b), on(b,table).
11    }
12    program{
13      if bel(holding(X)), a-goal(on(X,table)) then putdown(X,table).
14    }
```

The goals of an agent may change over time, for example, when the agent adopts a new goal or drops one of its goals. As a rational agent should not pursue goals that it already believes to be achieved. GOAL provides a built-in mechanism for doing so based on a so-called *blind commitment strategy*. This strategy is implemented by removing conjunctions of atoms that represent goals from the goal base, as soon as they are believed to be achieved. These conjunctions will only be removed if they have been achieved *completely* in the current state. Together, the knowledge, beliefs and goals of an agent make up its *mental state*.

To select an action, a GOAL has so-called *action rules*. The action rules consist of a condition on the mental state of the agent, and an action that should be executed if the mental state condition holds. In essence, writing such conditions means specifying a *strategy* for action selection that will be used by the GOAL agent. A mental state condition can consist of conditions on the agent's beliefs and on the agent's goals. Informally, $\text{bel}(\varphi)$ can be read as "the agent believes that φ". $\text{bel}(\varphi)$ holds whenever φ can be derived from the belief base *in combination with the knowledge base*. In the example of Table 1, it follows that $\text{bel}(\text{clear}(a))$, which expresses that the agent believes that block a is clear.

Similarly, $\text{goal}(\varphi)$ can be read as "the agent has a goal that φ". $\text{goal}(\varphi)$ holds whenever φ can be derived from *a single goal* in the goal base *in combination with the knowledge base*. In the example of Table 1, it follows, e.g., that $\text{goal}(\text{on}(b,\text{table}))$. In order to represent achievement goals, i.e., goals that are not believed to be achieved yet, the keyword a-goal can be used. This is defined as follows:

$$\text{a-goal}(\varphi) \stackrel{df}{=} \text{goal}(\varphi), \text{not}(\text{bel}(\varphi))$$

In the example, $\text{a-goal}(\text{on}(a,b))$ holds, but $\text{a-goal}(\text{on}(b,\text{table}))$ does not. Similarly, $\text{goal-a}(\varphi)$ represents that φ can be derived from a goal in the goal base, but φ *is* already believed to be achieved. A mental state condition is a conjunction of these mental atoms, or their negation. Table 1 shows an example of an action rule that specifies the following: if the agent believes it is holding block X and has the achievement goal of having X on the table, then the corresponding putdown action should be selected. If the conditions of multiple action rules hold at the same time, an applicable rule is selected at random.

Actions that may be performed by a GOAL agent need to be specified by the programmer of that agent. GOAL does provide some special built-in actions but typically most actions that an agent may perform are derived from the environment that the agent acts in. Actions are specified by specifying the conditions when an action can be performed (preconditions) and the effects of performing the action (postconditions). Pre- and postconditions are conjunctions of literals. A precondition φ is evaluated by verifying whether (an instantiation of) φ can be derived from the belief base (as always, in combination with knowledge in the knowledge base). Any free variables in a precondition may be instantiated during this process just like executing a Prolog program returns instantiations of variables. In GOAL, the effect φ of an action is used to update the beliefs of the agent to ensure the agent believes φ after performing the action. The positive literals are added to the belief base, and negative literals are removed. In addition, actions that correspond to actions that can be executed in the agent's environment, are sent to that environment. In the dynamic blocks world, the `pickup` and `putdown` actions are specified as in [16]. They have a true postcondition, and therefore do not update the belief base.

In addition to the possibility of specifying user-defined actions, GOAL provides several built-in actions for changing the beliefs and goals of an agent, and for communicating with other agents. Here we only briefly discuss the two built-in actions `adopt`(φ) and `drop`(φ) which allow for modifying the goal base of an agent. The action `adopt`(φ) is an action to adopt a new goal φ. The precondition of this action is that the agent does not believe that φ is the case, i.e. in order to execute `adopt`(φ) we must have `not(bel(`φ`))`. The idea is that it would not be rational to adopt a goal that has already been achieved. The effect of the action is the addition of φ as a single, new goal to the goal base. The action `drop`(φ) is an action to drop goals from the goal base of the agent. The precondition of this action is always true and the action can always be performed. The effect of the action is that any goal in the goal base from which φ can be derived is removed from the goal base. For example, the action `drop(on(b,table))` would remove all goals in the goal base that entail `on(b,table)`; in the example agent of Table 1 the only goal present in the goal base would be removed by this action.

A final aspect of GOAL that we have to discuss, is sensing. Sensing is not represented as an explicit act of the agent but a perceptual interface is defined between the agent and the environment that specifies which percepts an agent will receive from the environment. Each time after a GOAL agent has performed an action, the agent processes any *percepts* it may have received through its perceptual interface. Incoming percepts are processed through percept rules. The percept rules for the dynamic blocks world are specified in [16]. Percept are of the form `block(X)`, representing that there is a block X in the environment, `holding(X)`, representing that the gripper is holding block X, and `on(X,Y)`, representing that block X is on Y. The percept rules specify that these atoms are added to the belief base as soon as they are perceived (indicated by the `percept` keyword), and they are removed from the belief base if they are not perceived.

4   Approach

In this section, we describe the research approach that we have followed. First, we have asked three programmers to program a GOAL agent for the dynamic blocks world. We refer to the resulting programs as A, B, and C. The code of the programs can be found in the corresponding appendices. The person who programmed A had the least experience with GOAL, while the programmer of C had the most. All programmers were somewhat familiar with the blocks world domain. As a starting point, they were given the action specification and percept rules of [16]. Another constraint was that the agent would only get one goal configuration to achieve. They were also given a set of test cases in order to test the functioning of their program. Some of these test cases are included in [16]. After the programs were handed in for analysis, they were not modified anymore.

We have performed three kinds of analyses on the programs. First, we have analyzed the code, both using quantitative metrics such as the number of action rules (Section 5.1), as well as performing a qualitative analysis, looking in more detail at the code itself (Section 6). Second, we have performed an experiment where we have asked six test subjects to look at the code of all three programs and comment on their readability (Section 6.2). The test subjects were somewhat familiar with the GOAL language, but did not have extensive experience in programming with it. All comments were removed from the programs before they were given to the test subjects, but white space was preserved. Third, we have performed limited testing of the programs to obtain quantitative metrics on the action sequences that were executed (Section 5.2).

5   Quantitative Analysis

In this section, we compare the three GOAL agent programs for the dynamic blocks world based on numeric measures of their code (Section 5.1) and of behavior shown during execution (Section 5.2). In this and the next section, we summarize our main findings by listing observations. It is important to note that these observations are based only on the three blocks world programs that we used for our analysis.

5.1   Code

We provide numeric measures for each of the sections of a GOAL program, except for the action specification and percept rules sections, since these formed the starting point for all three programs (see Section 4) and are the same (with a slight exception for A, see [16]). The results are summarized in Table 2.

Before we discuss the table, we provide some additional information on how to interpret our measures for action rules. The other measures speak for themselves. The total number of action rules is counted for each of the programs, and is also split into environment actions (`pickup` or `putdown`), and actions for adopting or dropping a goal. We also counted the number of belief and goal

Table 2. Numeric Measures of Code

Numeric measure	A	B	C
clauses knowledge base	16	4	8
defined Prolog predicates in knowledge base	11	2	3
clauses (initial) belief base	0	0	1
goals (initial) goal base	0	1	1
action rules [env. action/adopt/drop]	3 [3/0/0]	14 [5/6/3]	12 [3/3/6]
bel conditions in action rules (avr/min/max)	1.3/1/2	1.8/0/4	1.7/0/6
a-goal conditions in action rules (avr/min/max)	0	1.6/1/2	0.8/0/1
goal conditions in action rules (avr/min/max)	0	0	0.8/0/2
goal-a conditions in action rules (avr/min/max)	0	0	0.08/0/1

conditions in action rules. We provide the average (avr) number of conditions per rule, and the minimum (min) and maximum (max) number of conditions that have been used in one rule. The average number of conditions is obtained by dividing the total number of conditions by the total number of rules. The conditions have been counted such that each atom inside belief or goal keyword was counted as one condition. For example, a conjunctive belief condition with n conjuncts, bel(cond1, ..., condn)), is counted as n conditions, and similarly for a disjunctive belief condition. If the number of belief or goal conditions that are used is 0, we do not split this into avr/min/max, but simply write 0.

As can be seen in Table 2, the extent to which the knowledge base is used differs considerably across the three programs. Where A has 16 clauses and 11 defined predicates in the knowledge base, thereby making heavy use of Prolog, program B has only 4 clauses and 2 defined predicates. The belief base initially has very little information in all three programs, which suggests that it is used mostly through updates that are performed during execution by means of the percept rules. Both B and C initially have one goal in the goal base, which reflects the fact that in our setting we consider only one goal configuration of the blocks. Program A does not use the goal base for representing the goal configuration.

The number of action rules is very small for program A (only 3), while B and C use considerably more rules (14 and 12, respectively). Also, program A only uses action rules for selecting environment actions, while the majority of the rules of B and C (9 in each case) concern the adoption or dropping of goals. Moreover, A only uses a small number of belief conditions in the rules (maximum of 2), and does not make use of goal conditions. The latter corresponds with the fact that in A, no goals are inserted into the goal base (neither initially, nor through the use of action rules). The number of belief conditions in B and C are comparable, ranging from 0 to 4 or 6 conditions per rule, respectively. The number of conditions on goals in B and C is rather similar (1.6 on average), and is typically smaller than the number of belief conditions (maximum of 2). The use of conditions on goals differs for B and C in that B uses only a-goal conditions, while in C there is an equal number of a-goal and goal conditions, and one goal-a condition. Program C thus makes the most use of the various constructs offered by GOAL.

What we did not include in the table is that almost all rules in B and C have at least one positive, i.e., non-negated, condition on goals (only one exception in B). This corresponds with the idea that actions are selected because an agent wants to reach certain goals. None of the programs use the action rules to select actions for updating the belief base.

We summarize our findings through a number of main observations. The first concerns the relation between the experience that programmers have with the GOAL language, and how this relates to their use of the constructs.

Observation 1 (Experience with GOAL). *For our programs it is the case that the more experienced the programmer is with* GOAL, *the more of the language constructs offered by* GOAL *are used.*

This suggests that programmers have a tendency to stick to what they know best, rather than try out constructs they are less familiar with. This means that education and training is essential if programmers are to make full use of the features offered by GOAL. The observation is also in line with the following observation, which addresses the use of the knowledge base in comparison with the action rules.

Observation 2 (Focus on Knowledge Base or Action Rules). *Two ways in which the* GOAL *language can be used, are by focusing on the knowledge base and keeping the number of action rules small, or by focusing on the action rules and keeping the knowledge base small.*

A final observation of this section concerns the use of action rules for adopting and dropping goals, in comparison with rules for selecting environment actions.

Observation 3 (Many Action Rules for Adopt or Drop). *In both programs that use goals, the number of action rules for adopting or dropping goals is considerably larger than the number of rules for selecting environment actions.*

5.2   Execution

Besides looking at the code of the programs, we have also analyzed their behavior during execution. We have run the programs using four test cases (see [16]), of which two included dynamics (one block was moved by the user while the agent was executing). The number of blocks ranged from 3 to 13. We have recorded the number of actions (both environment actions as well as adopt and drop actions) that were executed by the agent in one run of each test case (see Table 3).[2] The number of executed actions to solve a certain problem can be taken as a measure for the *efficiency* of an agent program.

All three programs achieved the goal in all four test cases. The number of executed environment actions was comparable for all three programs throughout

---

[2] If the same action was sent to the environment multiple times in a row, this was counted as one action. Sending an action to the environment multiple times in a row can happen if the action rule for selecting that action keeps being applicable while the action is being executed.

Table 3. Executed Actions

Test Case	Action Type	A	B	C
1	adopt or drop	0	2	3
	env. action	4	4	4
2	adopt or drop	0	36	18
	env. action	28	36	30
3	adopt or drop	0	10	8
	env. action	11	12	10
4	adopt or drop	0	8	12
	env. action	8	9	8

the test cases, although program B always executed a little more than A and C (up to 20% more). Since A does not use adopt or drop actions in the program, the only actions executed by A were environment actions. By contrast, B and C execute a considerable amount of adopt and drop actions. The average portion of adopt or drop actions compared to the total number of actions was 0.44 and 0.46 across the four test cases for B and C, respectively. It ranged between 0.33 and 0.50 for B, and between 0.38 and 0.60 for C. We thus make the following observation, which seems in line with Observation 3.

Observation 4 (Number of Executed Adopt or Drop Actions). *In the programs that use goals, the adopt and drop actions form a considerable portion of the total number of executed actions.*

When taking the total number of executed actions as a measure for efficiency, it is clear that A is much more efficient than B and C. However, when looking only at environment actions, the programs' efficiency is comparable. Whether to take the number of executed environment actions as a measure for efficiency or whether to also take into account (internal) adopt and drop actions, depends on how much time it takes to execute them. Assuming that the selection and execution of adopt or drop actions takes comparably little time compared with the execution of environment actions, one can take only the executed environment actions as a measure for the efficiency of the program. However, if this is not the case then the selection of adopt and drop actions should be taken into account. In that case it should be carefully considered by the programmer whether the reasoning overhead is necessary and how it may be reduced. In our case study, however, environment actions took considerably more time than adopt or drop actions.

This data is based on one run per program per test case. However, we did do several more runs for some of the test cases. Those runs showed that there was non-determinism in the programs, since the execution traces were not identical in all cases. Non-determinism can, e.g., occur if the goal of the agent is to put block a on b on c on d on the table, and initially block a is on c and b is on d. In this case, the agent has no choice but to move both a and b onto the table. However, the order in which this is done may differ.

The fact that the programs show non-determinism, means that they *under-specify* the behavior of the agent. The programs are thus a high-level specification of agent behavior, in the sense that they do not specify the behavior to the full detail. This leaves room for *refinement* of the programs in several was (see, e.g., [8,1,9] for approaches that take advantage of this).

Observation 5 (Underspecification). GOAL *naturally induces the specification of non-deterministic agents, i.e., agents of which the behavior is underspecified.*

6 Analysis of Programming Aspects

In this section, we discuss the code of the GOAL programs in more detail. We describe their structure (Section 6.1), and discuss similarities and differences (Section 6.2). We do not discuss the process of programming GOAL agents. The reason is that we did not collect sufficient data on how the programmers went about programming the agents. Also, where usually one would start by thinking about percepts (and percept rules) and action specifications, these were given in our setting. Therefore, the focus was on programming the strategy of how to solve the dynamic blocks world problem.

6.1 Structure of Programs

Program A: The knowledge base is used to determine where blocks should be moved. This is done by defining a predicate goodMove(X,Y) on the basis of several other predicates. A distinction is made between a constructive move, which moves a block to construct a goal tower, and an unpile move, which moves a block to the table in order to clear blocks such that eventually a constructive move can be made. If possible, a constructive move is selected. The goal configuration of the blocks is specified in the knowledge base, rather than in the goal base. The predicate isgoal(tower(T)) is used for this, where T is a list of blocks specifying a goal tower. In order to derive which towers are currently built, the predicate tower(T) is defined, which specifies that the list T is a tower if the blocks in the list are stacked on top of each other, such that the head of the list is the top block and this top block is clear (defined using the predicate clear(X)).

Three action rules are defined. The first two specify that pickup(X) or putdown(X,Y) can be executed if goodMove(X,Y). The third rule specifies that if the agent is holding a block for which no good move can be derived, the block should be put onto the table. Most of the dynamics cases specified in [16] are handled by the knowledge base, and some are handled by one of the action rules (see [16]).

Program B: The knowledge base defines the predicates clear(X) and tower(T), where T is a list of blocks that are stacked on top of each other. In contrast with the definition of this predicate in A, here the top block of the tower does not have to be clear (i.e., a bottom part of a tower is also a tower). The belief base is empty. The goal base initially contains the goal configuration as a conjunction of on(X,Y) atoms. During execution, goals of the form clear(X) and holding(X) are adopted.

The action rules are divided into three parts: rules for clearing blocks, rules for moving blocks to construct towers, and rules for dealing with dynamics. In addition, there is one rule for selecting the pickup action, which can be used either for clearing blocks or for moving blocks to construct towers. The rules for clearing blocks mainly adopt goals: the goal to make a block clear, and on the basis of this goal the agent adopts the goal to hold a particular block and then to put the block on the table. The rules for dealing with dynamics mainly drop goals, or select the action of putting a block down onto the table. These rules explicitly address dynamics cases (2a), (2b), (2c), (2e), and (3a) (see [16]). Case (2d) is handled automatically by adopting a new goal of holding a block, and cases (3b-d) are not handled.

Program C: The knowledge base defines the predicates clear(X), tower(T) and above(X,Y). The definition of tower(T) is the same as in B, and above(X,Y) expresses that block X is somewhere above block Y, but not necessarily on Y. As in B, the goal base initially contains the goal configuration as a conjunction of on(X,Y) atoms. During execution, goals of the form do(move((X,Y)) are adopted, to express that block X should be moved onto Y. The belief base contains one clause for specifying when such a goal is reached (namely when on(X,Y) holds).

The action rules are divided into three parts: rules for adopting goals of the form do(move((X,Y)), rules for selecting pickup and putdown actions, and rules for dropping goals of the form do(move((X,Y)). The rules for adopting goals both adopt goals in order to construct towers, as well as to move blocks to the table in order to clear other blocks. For each of the actions pickup and putdown there is one regular rule, and in addition there is a rule for putdown for dealing with dynamics cases (2b) and (2e) (see [16]). The rules for dropping goals explicitly address dynamics cases (2a), (2c), and (3a-d). Case (2d) is handled automatically by adopting a new goal of moving a block.

6.2   Similarities and Differences in Structure

In this section, we discuss similarities and differences with respect to the structure of the GOAL programs, as can be found when looking in more detail at the code.

Similarities: Our first observation concerns the knowledge base.

Observation 6 (Basic Domain Predicates). *All programs define basic domain predicates in the knowledge base.*

In all three programs, the predicates clear(X) and tower(T) were defined in the knowledge base, although their definitions vary slightly. The definition of clear is needed, since this predicate is used in the action specifications. The tower predicate is needed in order to select constructive moves: a constructive move moves a block on top of a partial goal tower. One could view these two predicates as the most basic and essential for the domain, which explains why all programs define them.

An aspect where programs B and C are similar, is the use of dropping of goals.

Observation 7 (Dynamics of Environment). *In both programs that use goals, dropping of goals is used for dealing with the dynamics of the environment.*

If the user moves blocks around, it can be the case that a goal that was adopted in a certain situation, is no longer achievable or should no longer be achieved in the changed situation. This means that the goal should be dropped again. Since A does not adopt goals, it does not have to consider dropping them again if the environment is changed. Another more domain specific way in which the programs handle dynamics, is that they select the action putdown(X,table), e.g., if the agent is holding a block that it does not want to move in that situation.

Another aspect where B and C are similar, is the frequent use of negative goal conditions in the action rules for adopting goals, through which it is checked whether the goal that is to be adopted did not already have an instance in the goal base. In particular, in B there should not be more than one goal of the form holding(X) in the goal base, because this goal specifies which block the agent should pick up next. This is achieved by checking whether not(a-goal(holding(S))) is the case (where S is unbound), before adopting a goal holding(X). Similarly, in C there should not be more than one goal of the form do(move(X,Y)), and corresponding negative goal conditions are included in the action rules.

Observation 8 (Single Instance Goals). *In both programs that use goals, there are goals of which at most one instance can occur in the goal base at any one time. This is achieved through the use of negative goal conditions.*

Interestingly, in the Jadex framework the notion of cardinality is introduced [12] to restrict the number of instances of a goal that can be active at the same time. A similar feature may be added to GOAL in order to help the programmer specify these kinds of uses of goals.

Differences: One of the main differences between B and C are the goal predicates that are added during execution. B uses clear(X) and holding(X), while C uses do(move((X,Y)). The goals of B correspond to the most basic predicates of the domain. They do not allow to specify as part of the goal where a block that is or should be picked up, has to be moved. Instead, this is determined on the basis of the goal in the goal base that specifies the goal configuration of the blocks: if the block that an agent is holding can be moved onto a partially build tower, this should be done; otherwise, it should be moved onto the table. In C, a single goal do(move((X,Y)) represents that the agent should hold X if this is not yet the case, and move it onto Y if it holds X. Since predicates of the form do(move((X,Y)) are not added to the belief base through percepts, the programmer in this case has to define when such a goal is reached. This is done by adding a corresponding clause to the belief base. Moreover, since B uses action rules to derive the goal to clear blocks as an intermediate step for selecting a goal to hold a block, B uses more rules than C (6, where C uses 2) for specifying that blocks should be moved onto the table in order to clear blocks.

Observation 9 (Abstraction Levels of Goals). *Goals can be used on different abstraction levels. They can correspond to the most basic predicates of the domain, or higher-level goals can be defined. In the latter case, clauses can be added to the belief base in order to define when the higher-level goals are reached.*

In Section 5.2 we have shown that for programs B and C, the portion of adopt and drop actions compared to the total number of actions generated during execution is comparable. However, the number of adopt actions generated by B will most likely grow with the size and complexity of the initial configuration, since in that case many intermediate `clear` goals have to be generated, followed by the goal of holding a block. In C, by contrast, one `move` goal is created for each block that the agent choses to move.

Another difference between B and C is the way in which action rules are clustered. In B, they are clustered according to their function in the strategy (clearing blocks, making constructive moves, and dealing with dynamics), while in C they are clustered according to the type of their consequent (adopt, environment action, and drop). This points to a different style of programming, which may be related to the different levels of goals used in B and C. In C, there is only one type of goal that drives the selection of actions. It is then the job of the programmer to specify when this goal should be adopted, what should be done if the goal is adopted, and when it should be dropped. In B, by contrast, the goals for clearing blocks are selected as intermediate goals, on the basis of which the agent selects the goal of holding a block. Since the goals to clear blocks are thus closely related to the corresponding goal of holding a block, it seems more natural to cluster these rules. The way the rules are clustered in B may also be related to the fact that B was programmed in an incremental way. First a highly non-deterministic GOAL agent was programmed that solved the blocks world problem in a non-efficient way and that did not deal with the dynamics of the domain. Then, rules for dealing with dynamics were added and finally efficiency was addressed. The `tower` predicate was introduced in this last step, and was only used to modify the conditions of the rules for making constructive moves. B was thus developed through refinement (see also Observation 5) of a initial program, where refinement was done both through the addition of rules, as well as by modifying conditions of rules.

Observation 10 (Clustering of Action Rules). *Two ways in which action rules can be clustered are according to the type of their consequent, and according to their function in the action selection strategy.*

One of our motivations for doing this research is to find *code patterns* or typical ways in which the GOAL constructs are used, which can serve as guidelines for programming GOAL agents in various applications domains. Although no general conclusions can be drawn on the basis of our three blocks world programs, the observations that have been made so far in this section already suggest some possible code patterns or typical usages of the GOAL constructs.

A difference between A, compared to B and C, is that A does not use goals in the goal base. Instead, a predicate isgoal(tower(T)) is used in the knowledge base. Since goals are not explicitly adopted in A, they do not have to be dropped again in case the user moves blocks around. On the other hand, if the goal base is not used, it is the job of the programmer to check which parts of the goal configuration have already been reached, and which have not. If the a-goal operator is used in action rules, the semantics of GOAL takes care of this. Also, the GOAL IDE provides a means to inspect the agent's mental state while it is executing, but if goals are used only as part of the knowledge base, one cannot see them when running the agent. Being able to see the agent's goals while it is executing helps in debugging: one can see why the agent is executing a certain action.

A difference between B, compared to A and C, is that B does not deal with dynamics cases (3b-d). This corresponds to the results presented in Section 5.2, which show that B is slightly less efficient than A and C. More action rules would probably have to be added to deal with these cases.

Another difference between the programs concerns their readability. We have asked several subjects somewhat familiar with the GOAL language to comment on the readability of the programs. Program A was found to be the easiest to understand, while the readability of B and C varied across subjects. This seems to be related to Observation 1, which suggests that more of the GOAL constructs are used as more experience is gained. Since all subjects had relatively little experience with programming in GOAL, it seems natural that they find the program making the least use of GOAL constructs easiest to understand. This also suggests that sufficient training is necessary to familiarize programmers with the various GOAL— constructs. Another reason why action rules may be difficult to understand, as suggested by some of the subjects, is the relatively high number of belief and goal conditions that each have to be read and interpreted, in order to understand what the action rule is aimed at.

7 Conclusion and Future Work

In this paper, we have analyzed three GOAL programs for the dynamic blocks world. We have made several observations based on a quantitative and qualitative analysis. The observations concern the use of GOAL constructs, the behavior of GOAL programs during execution, and the readability of GOAL programs. Based on this analysis of three GOAL programs in a specific domain we cannot draw very general conclusions on how GOAL programs should be written. However, we do identify important issues in three key areas that need further investigation.

With respect to *use of the GOAL constructs*, we have identified several similarities and differences across the three programs. Concerning the similarities, it needs to be further investigated whether these can be used as guidelines for programming GOAL agents. Where we have identified different possible usages of GOAL, it needs to be investigated what the advantages and disadvantages of these approaches are, in order to be able to determine whether and if so, when, they can be used as guidelines. These investigations should lead to a *programming methodology* for GOAL.

Regarding *readability*, we have observed that the relatively high number of belief and goal conditions in action rules makes them difficult to understand. We believe it is essential to address this issue in order to make GOAL easier to use, and clear code is often argued to be less error-prone. We suggest that the use of macros and a notion of modules to structure action rules such as proposed in [7] may improve readability. In addition, we believe that proper training is essential to allow programmers to make full use of the features offered by GOAL.

A third area where more research is needed, is *efficiency*. We have observed that if goals are used, on average a little less than half of the executed actions were actions for adopting or dropping goals. The use of goals thus creates considerable overhead. In the blocks world domain, this is not problematic since the time it takes to execute environment actions is considerably larger than the time it takes to select and execute adopt and drop actions. However, in other domains this may not be the case. Then, it might be necessary to design the program such that a limited number of adopt and drop actions is executed.

In future work, we also aim at refining the approach that we have used for analyzing the programs. For example, it may be useful to obtain data on the level of familiarity of the test subjects with GOAL. One way to do this, is to give them a test program and let them suggest which actions the agent might execute next. Also, several subjects indicated that the assignment was quite hard to do. We may have to reconsider our decision to remove all comments from the programs before giving them to the test subjects. Moreover, in a future study we would also like to investigate the use of the debugging facilities of the GOAL IDE.

References

1. Astefanoaei, L., de Boer, F.S.: Model-checking agent refinement. In: AAMAS, pp. 705–712 (2008)
2. Basili, V.R., Briand, L.C. (eds.): Empirical Software Engineering: An International Journal. Springer, Heidelberg (2009),
   http://www.springer.com/computer/programming/journal/10664
3. Bordini, R.H., Dastani, M., Dix, J., El Fallah Seghrouchni, A.: Multi-Agent Programming: Languages, Platforms and Applications. Springer, Berlin (2005)
4. Bordini, R.H., Dastani, M., Dix, J., El Fallah Seghrouchni, A.: Multi-Agent Programming: Languages, Tools and Applications. Springer, Berlin (2009)
5. Bordini, R.H., Hübner, J.F., Wooldridge, M.: Programming Multi-agent Systems in AgentSpeak using Jason. Wiley, Chichester (2007)
6. Dastani, M.: 2APL: a practical agent programming language. Autonomous Agents and Multi-Agent Systems 16(3), 214–248 (2008)

7. Hindriks, K.V.: Modules as policy-based intentions: Modular agent programming in GOAL. In: Dastani, M.M., El Fallah Seghrouchni, A., Ricci, A., Winikoff, M. (eds.) ProMAS 2007. LNCS (LNAI), vol. 4908, pp. 156–171. Springer, Heidelberg (2008)

8. Hindriks, K., Jonker, C., Pasman, W.: Exploring heuristic action selection in agent programming. In: Hindriks, K.V., Pokahr, A., Sardina, S. (eds.) ProMAS 2008. LNCS (LNAI), vol. 5442, pp. 24–39. Springer, Heidelberg (2009)

9. Hindriks, K., van Riemsdijk, M.B.: Using temporal logic to integrate goals and qualitative preferences into agent programming. In: Baldoni, M., Son, T.C., van Riemsdijk, M.B., Winikoff, M. (eds.) DALT 2008. LNCS (LNAI), vol. 5397, pp. 215–232. Springer, Heidelberg (2009)

10. Hindriks, K.V.: Programming rational agents in GOAL. In: Bordini, R.H., Dastani, M., Dix, J., El Fallah Seghrouchni, A. (eds.) Multi-Agent Programming: Languages, Tools and Applications. Springer, Berlin (2009)

11. Nilsson, N.J.: Teleo-reactive programs and the triple-tower architecture. Electronic Transactions on Artificial Intelligence 5, 99–110 (2001)

12. Pokahr, A., Braubach, L., Lamersdorf, W.: A goal deliberation strategy for BDI agent systems. In: Eymann, T., Klügl, F., Lamersdorf, W., Klusch, M., Huhns, M.N. (eds.) MATES 2005. LNCS (LNAI), vol. 3550, pp. 82–93. Springer, Heidelberg (2005)

13. Pokahr, A., Braubach, L., Lamersdorf, W.: Jadex: a BDI reasoning engine. In: Bordini, R.H., Dastani, M., Dix, J., El Fallah Seghrouchni, A. (eds.) Multi- Agent Programming: Languages, Platforms and Applications. Springer, Berlin (2005)

14. Shoham, Y.: Agent-oriented programming. Artificial Intelligence 60, 51–92 (1993)

15. Slaney, J., Thiébaux, S.: Blocks World revisited. Artificial Intelligence 125, 119–153 (2001)

16. van Riemsdijk, M.B., Hindriks, K.: An empirical study of agent programs: A dynamic blocks world case study in goal, extended version (2009), http://mmi.tudelft.nl/~koen/prima09extended.pdf

17. Winikoff, M.: JACK[TM] intelligent agents: an industrial strength platform. In: Bordini, R.H., et al. (eds.) Multi-Agent Programming: Languages, Platforms and Applications. Springer, Berlin (2005)

A Multiagent Model for Provider-Centered Trust in Composite Web Services

Julien Bourdon[1], Laurent Vercouter[2], and Toru Ishida[1]

[1] Department of Social Informatics
Kyoto University
606-8501 Kyoto, Japan
julien.bourdon@ai.soc.i.kyoto-u.ac.jp,
ishida@i.kyoto-u.ac.jp
[2] Multi-Agent System department
Division for Industrial Engineering and Computer Sciences
École Nationale Supérieure des Mines de Saint-Étienne
158 cours Fauriel, 42023 Saint-Étienne cedex 02, France
Laurent.Vercouter@emse.fr

Abstract. Service-Oriented Architectures (SOA) provide infrastructures to make resources available to other participants in the network as independent services. However, service providers, not having the autonomy to decide who they collaborate with, might be reluctant to participate in such open systems, the client being the sole responsible of the selection of services for the composition. Multiagent systems research offer some solutions in term of trust and reputation mechanisms as well as in coalition formation theory. This paper presents a multiagent based negotiation model to enable provider autonomy in composite web services. QoS-based reputation is built from both feedbacks retrieved from execution and from subjective feedbacks given by the client. This model is illustrated by an example based on the Language Grid Project, an service infrastructure for language resources.

1 Introduction

Service-Oriented Architectures (SOA) aim to provide infrastructures for software providers to let a range of users access them in a distributed fashion without having to use a specific system or programming language. They are based on message exchanges, most of the time XML-based like SOAP[1] and thus do not rely on any specific programming language or do not force the user to know anything about the service internal implementation.

When coming up with a task, such as getting a word definition or translating a text, users can select the appropriate service since their interface are usually described in a machine-readable format such as WSDL. When a single service cannot answer to a user request, she can use several of them by specifying how

---

[1] http://www.w3.org/TR/soap/

J.-J. Yang et al. (Eds.): PRIMA 2009, LNAI 5925, pp. 216–228, 2009.

they should interact by describing a workflow in a language such as WS-BPEL[2] thus creating a composite service. The services being accessible to everyone, deciding who takes part in such a composition is the sole decision of the user. Not being to decide who to collaborate with, thus potentially working with untrustworthy partners, enabling trust and reputation mechanisms in SOAs should entice providers to participate in open SOAs to make more services available.

To make the parallel with the everyday world, where some tasks require the services of several providers, for example when building a house, you need a variety of providers such as a plumber, an electrician, a carpenter, an architect, material suppliers,... If we were in a SOA setting, the client would choose its providers one by one and then put them to work. In reality, the architect might refuse because she or he is not interested in the project, the plumber might not want to work with a specific electrician because they had some conflicts in the past in another construction site, and thus does not trust her or him anymore, or the carpenter might not want to get supply from a specific store since it is known to handle customer data in a unethical way. Being forced to work with untrusted would for sure repel many to take part in any collaboration.

Current research on web service selection [5,20,2,23] only focuses on the client and leaves no autonomy for the provider to choose his partners during a composition. As described in the previous example, we think that trust could be the primary criteria to choose a partner in a composition. In SOAs, trust and reputation have been closely related to quality of service (QoS) [20,21] as a better service is more likely to be trustworthy. Nevertheless, current research focuses on client trust towards services but not on inter-provider trust.

On the other hand, this problem is quite close to coalition formation [19,17] in multiagent systems. Agents, allowing a greater autonomy, are considered as a serious approach for SOAs [9,16]. In this paper, we propose a negotiation protocol inspired by multiagent trust management and coalition formation approaches to enable providers to choose their partners in a composition.

In Section 2, we will present some background on trust and reputation based mechanisms for web service selection, trust in multi agent systems and coalition formation. In Section 3, we will present our multiagent model and the negotiation protocol used to enable provider-centered trust. This model will be illustrated by a use case based on the Language Grid Project in Section 4. Finally, we conclude and present future research directions in Section 5.

2 Background

2.1 Trust and Reputation Based Selection

In order to go beyond the manual selection of services by the client willing to create a composition, some research focused on automated service selection, also known as matchmaking. It tries to match a client request with service

---

[2] http://www.oasis-open.org/committees/download.php/23964/wsbpel-v2.
0-primer.htm

specifications[3] [1]. More recently, research has focused on how to relate quality of service (QoS) [4], trust and reputation for selecting appropriate web services [21]. For example, [15] proposes to include QoS parameters defined according to an ontology to select the most suitable services. [13] proposes to distinguish objective quality parameters, such as response time or availability from subjective parameters, like usability or quality. Indeed, measuring objective quality allow automatic measures and does add a burden to the user and permit to reduce the effect of false ratings.

A last aspect of trust and reputation is that it should be time-dependent. Ideally, to allow redemption of past behaviour and to reward constant behaviour, more weight should be given to recent feedbacks. This can be done by adding time damping to the reputation aggregation functions [13].

[3] presents an argumentative approach to form communities of web services. Contrary to our work, coalition are not centered upon a composite web service but upon a community of functionally equivalent services. This work improves providers' autonomy by proposing an agent model but focuses on *starvation, non-competitiveness* and *unfairness* to give a chance to all services to be selected. It is interesting to note that trust and reputation mechanisms are mentioned as further work.

[16] proposes a multiagent system for dynamic web service selection. Trust is based on QoS parameters and the presented mechanism allows to match a client policy in terms of QoS with the providers' advertised QoS. Reputation values are time dampened and regularly updated through explorer agents that test the service.

As seen above, research on trust and reputation for web service selection mechanisms is an active research. However, these approaches focus on the selection of a service directly by a client and thus cannot resolve the problem of provider autonomy in composite services. Multiagent systems by their focus on autonomy are giving interesting insights in the aforementioned problem, especially in the trust and coalition formation domains.

2.2   Trust and Reputation in Multiagent Systems

The open and decentralised context of multiagent systems is interesting in terms of flexibility, adaptability and scalability, thus making it an ideal approach for SOAs. Nevertheless it also brings some risks and vulnerability. Agents, potentially developed by different people and acting in an autonomous way, can freely enter or leave the system, contribute to collective activities or transmit data to other agents. Agents, similarly to providers in SOAs, have their own goals and, being self-interested, may favour themselves above other or the system integrity. This kind of agent can harm the system if it does not know how to react against such an agent.

The problem raised by the possible presence of selfish agents lead to a trust management problem towards other agents. Grandison [6] defines trust management as *the activity of collecting, codifying, analysing and presenting evidence*

---

[3] Inputs, output and process flow.

relating to competence, honesty, security or dependability with the purpose of making assessments and decisions regarding trust relationships for Internet applications. Such a decision must be used in addition to classical security techniques which insure authentication, confidentiality of information,... but cannot garantee the behavior of transaction partners.

In multiagent systems, and generally speaking in many of the open web applications, trust management is often handled by reputation mechanisms. Some of those mechanisms work in a centralised way, for example, by using recommandations and opinions of the website users (cf. eBay[4] , Amazon[5] ,...). These advices can be presented as-is or interpreted by an aggregation function (e.g. Sporas [24]). Other mechanisms, inspired by the multiagent field, work in a decentralised manner (e.g. Repage [18]) by allowing each agent to evaluate locally its neighbour?s reputation such that the agent decides whether to trust or not. Nevertheless, reputation is a single element among others that can be used.

2.3 Coalition Formation

In our context, and since research on how providers can decide to collaborate together to meet a client's needs is absent, answers must be found in coalition formation as it is done in multi-agent systems. SOAs must be computationally efficient and thus cannot assume that agents' computing resource is unlimited. [19] leans in this direction and analyzes how self-interested agents can form coalitions to solve joint optimization problems.

In a more practical approach, [12] examines how job and team selection heuristics can be combined to form coalitions in large scale unpredictable dynamic environments of self-interested agents without enforceable contracts. An agent is randomly selected as a foreman agent to form a team to carry a task being rewarded proportionally to its length. Finally, [7] combines various trust metrics for task delegation in self-interested agents communities. This approach manages to grasp various facets of the trust and to weight them according to the specific agent's preferences.

By combining the previous approaches and applying them to SOAs, we aim to let providers form teams to meet the needs of users as explained in the next section.

3   Provider-Centered Selection Protocol

In order to give some autonomy to the service providers, we propose a negotiation protocol, taking place after the matchmaking step. This protocol must comply to several requirements:

Soundness: if the protocol returns at least one coalition, all the providers in it are willing to participate and trust each other.

Completeness: if there is any, the protocol will return all the possible coalitions where providers trust each other.

---

[4] http://www.ebay.com
[5] http://www.amazon.com

Low overhead: giving autonomy to providers not being the primary function of a SOA, coalition formation must be done with the lowest possible overhead, to not disturb the primary functions of the SOA.

3.1 Notations

In this section, we will give the notations we use to formally describe our approach.

Definition 1 (Service). *Let* $s(i, p) \in S$ *be a service implementation where* $i \in I$ *is the service interface, that* s *implements and* $p \in P$ *the provider making* s *available. We assume that* P *and* S *are finite sets.*

A service interface (abstract service) defines the type of data it needs as inputs and the type of data it gives as output.

Definition 2 (Coalition). *A coalition corresponds roughly to a composite service. Let* $c([s_1, ..., s_n]) \in C$ *be a coalition, consisting of a ordered sequence of services.*

For the sake of simplicity, branching and iterative constructs are no treated in this paper but this definition could be extended to add a element to specify the process structure.

Definition 3 (Coalition offer). *Let* $o([v_1, ..., v_n], p) \in O$ *be an coalition offer by provider* p *with* $v \in S \cup \Xi$, Ξ *being the set of* $\xi(i)$ *free slots for a coalition offer such as* $i \in I$.

For example, in a coalition involving three services, the provider p_1 might want to fill the first and last slot thus proposing $o_1(s_1, \xi(i_1), s_2)$, leaving the second slot for a service of interface i_1.

Definition 4 (Quality). *Let* $\theta \in \Theta$ *be the quality parameter of a service. For a specific service* s, $q_s(s, \theta)$ *is the value of* θ *for the service implementation* s. *For a specific coalition* c, $q_c(c, \theta)$ *is the value of* θ *for the coalition.* Θ *is divided in* Θ_{obj} *and* Θ_{subj} *such as* $\Theta_{obj} \cup \Theta_{subj} = \Theta$ *and* $\Theta_{obj} \cap \Theta_{subj} = \emptyset$. Θ_{obj} *and* Θ_{subj} *respectively contain the objective and subjective quality parameters of a service.*

The quality parameters could be defined thanks to an ontology as it is done in [15]. Objective quality parameters, such as speed or availability are directly measurable. Subjective quality parameters, such as usability or pertinence of the result depend on the user.

Definition 5 (Feedback). *Let* $feedback(source, trustee, \theta, t) \in F$ *be the feedback that source gives about trustee* $\in C \cup S$ *about quality* θ *at time* $t \in \mathbb{N}$.

In our system, two types of feedbacks are used. Objective feedback toward single services, retrieved from the execution, takes this form $feedback_{obj}(percept, s, \theta_{obj}, t)^6$ while user subjective feedback is $feedback_{subj}(u, c, \theta_{subj}, t)$.

---

[6] Since the feedback is objective, the source is not a specific user but actually a perception noted here as *percept*.

Definition 6 (Trust function). [7] *Let* $trust(p_i, p_j, F, t) \rightarrow] - 1, 1[$ *be the trust that provider* p_i *gives to* p_j. *trust is defined as:*

$$trust(p_i, p_j, F, t) \rightarrow aggregation(initialTrust((p_i, p_j), f_{damp}(t, F)) \quad (1)$$

where f_{damp} *is a time dampening function and aggregation combines the* apriori *trust* p_i *has in* p_j *with the set of feedbacks.*

The *aggregation* function is different for each provider. For example, despite any feedback value, p_1 might decide that he does not want to collaborate with p_2 in any case thus deciding that if $p = p_2$ then *aggregation* gets the a low value. It allows each provider to have a different trust model and thus to keep the control on who they collaborate with. f_{damp} is a time dampening function used to give more or less importance to latest feedbacks. It could be a constant function to give all feedbacks the same weight or a Gaussian distribution function as in [13].

3.2 Global Architecture

In order to enable the concepts described above and provider-centered trust, a multi-agent architecture is proposed in Fig. 1. The green circles correspond to agents, the orange ovals to active processes and the blue rectangles to mechanisms to share knowledge such as described in [10].

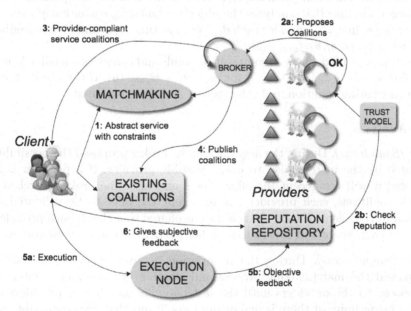

Fig. 1. Global agent architecture for provider-centered trust for composite web services

---

[7] The values -1 and 1 are excluded since we assume that full trust or distrust do not exist.

First of all, the client u, on the left, proposes an abstract service, a sequence of interfaces, with constraints (e.g. if she wants a specific implementation to be used for one the abstract services) to the matchmaker (1). Then the matchmaker searches for all the services satisfying these constraints. The matchmaking process is out of scope of this paper and the interested reader might refer to [1,2]. The set of acceptable services is then handed to the broker.

The broker then starts a negotiation (2) in two phases with the providers. First, and to reduce the overhead of the second phase, the broker asks each provider included in the results from the matchmaker if it is interested by the client workflow. Each provider then evaluates the proposition and decides to take part in the negotiation or not thus leading to a set $P_{nego} \subseteq P$. Each provider $p_i \in P_{nego}$ can then make a single offer o_i to the broker (2a). For example, it can decide to fill all the slots it can with its own services.

Then the broker, aggregates all the offers it received to build a set of possible coalitions. Each provider $p_i \in P_{nego}$ using its trust function, possibly using the reputation repository (cf. Equation 1), determines the value of the offer and decide to *accept* or to *refuse* it (2b). For instance, it can decide that to accept an offer, all the other providers trustworthiness must be above a specific threshold.

The set of provider-compliant coalitions is then returned to the client, who can choose one, noted $c_{chosen} \in C$, using client oriented selection processes [16] (3). In order to not repeat the negotiation process each time the client wants the same composition, the coalition is then stored in the existing coalitions repository (4). The client then requests the execution of the composition to the execution node (5a) that analyzes the objective quality parameters $q(s_i, \theta_j)$ for each service s_i in c_{chosen} and for each $\theta_j \in \Theta_{obj}$ at time t_{exec} and gives a feedback $feedback(percept, s_i, \theta_j, t_{exec})$ (5b).

u is then presented with the composition result and can gives a feedback of the form $feedback(u, c_{chosen}, \theta_k, t_{exec})$ for each $\theta_k \in \Theta_{subj}$ (6). If the client chooses to use an existing coalition, only the steps 5 and 6 are executed.

3.3   Analysis

Proof (Soundness). During the negotiation, the broker proposed the possibilities generated by the matchmaker to every possible provider. If a provider is not interested it will not accept the offer. Then, and after the broker searched for possible coalitions, each provider has to accept the offer to be validated and returned to the client. Hence, if a coalition is offered to a client, each provider is willing to participate and consider the other participants to be trustworthy.   □

Proof (Completeness). During the negotiation process, every single coalition that passed the matchmaking process and where every provider is interested is proposed to the providers until the last one. The number of providers and services being finite, if there is one or more coalitions that are compatible with the providers' trust models, they will be returned to the client.   □

As far as the overhead is concerned, reputation mechanisms require numerous interactions. If the same users use the same services overtime, the reputation stored by the system will give a more precise image of the actual trustworthiness of the participants. The number of interactions being high, and the negotiation protocol taking some computing power that should be reserved for the primary function of the system, i.e. providing services, negotiated coalitions are stored and can be reused if a user had the same requirements thus not disturbing the primary functions of the SOA.

In the current state, the model being quite simple, we are able to guarantee the soundness and completeness. When the model will be extended, other mechanisms should be adopted to guarantee these. Finding a coalition where providers communicate to find a trustworthy coalition can be viewed as a distributed constraint satisfaction problem [22]. Providers would have to find a service implementation for each component of the abstract service based on trust-related constraints. A similar approach using QoS parameters, user constraints and preferences have been presented in [8].

Now, our protocol is similar to a hyper-resolution algorithm, since the domain of possible solutions is pruned by the providers responses to the broker's offers. Even if such an algorithm guarantees completeness and soundness in a polynomial time, the number of offers generated by the broker can be unmanageably large.

4   Use Case

In order to anchor our research in reality, we present a use case based on the Language Grid Project [11]. The Language Grid Project aims to allow intercultural collaboration by providing a large range of language resources as services to identified users. Services must comply to one of the standard interfaces proposed by the system such as translator or dictionary. The interfaces constrain the type of inputs and outputs of the service as well as its parameters. For example, the *translator* interface imposes a source text, a source and target languages as inputs and a translation as output. Moreover, it must display the language pairs it supports and information about the provider[8].

In order to use the infrastructure, both clients and providers must sign an agreement guaranteeing only non-profit use of the resources, thus excluding rewards, and identify themselves. Contrary to most of the existing open service infrastructures, providers can monitor the use of their resources and set precise usage limits for each user or even prohibit the use of their resources. Composite services, like multi-hop machine translation[9], or customized translaton[10]. However, some providers of the system express their strict refusal to compose their services with other providers, or some others do not want their results to be modified, for example by a custom dictionary.

---

[8] Such as the provider homepage or copyright licence.

[9] When a a direct translation from a language to another is not available, a pivot language is used. For example, if machine translation from French to Japanese is not available, French to English and English to Japanese translators are used.

[10] Words from a specialized dictionary are used to override the translation result, thus allowing communities to accurately translate their specific vocabularies.

In our use case, as depicted in Fig. 2(a), a client u_1 wants to get the definition of a word in French as well as its relationship with other words, such as hypernyms or hyponyms[11]. Such a concept dictionary in French not being available on the Grid, she decides to go through a French to English translator to get the word in English and input it in the Concept Dictionary. Then, since her organization created a specific dictionary to overcome some translation errors, she wants to use it and finally get the information she got from the concept dictionary back in French.

After the matchmaking process, out of the scope of this paper, five providers p_1, p_2, p_3, p_4 and p_5 are estimated relevant for such a composition. p_1 provides two English-French translation services s_1^2 and s_1^3. p_2 provides a single one of those s_2^1. p_3 has been chosen by the client as a non-negotiable part of the selection process as it holds her organization dictionary s_3^1. Then p_4 offers 2 concept dictionaries s_4^2 and s_4^3 while p_5 proposes s_5^1. The resultant possibilities are displayed in Fig. 2(b).

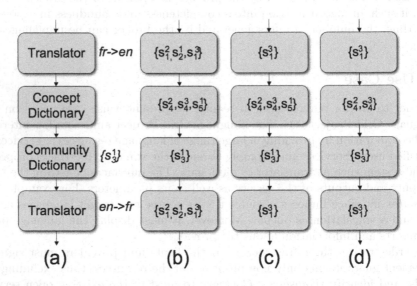

Fig. 2. Reduction of the solution space for workflow (a) after matchmaking (b) call for participation (c) and coalition formation (d)

Then, as depicted in Fig 3, the coalition formation process, lead by the broker agent, starts. First of all, the broker asks the owners of the compatible services if they are interested to take part in such a composition. p_1 replies with an offer b_1 such as $b_1 = (s_1^2, \xi(conceptDictionary), \xi(communityDictionary), s_1^2)$. p_3 replies with $b_3 = (\xi(translator), \xi(conceptDictionary), s_3^1, \xi(translator))$ and p_4 replies with $b_4 = (\xi(translator)i, s_4^2, s_4^3)$. Only p_2, for example because it does not want to be associated with community dictionaries, since it breaks its terms

---

[11] Such as what is done in WordNet http://wordnet.princeton.edu/

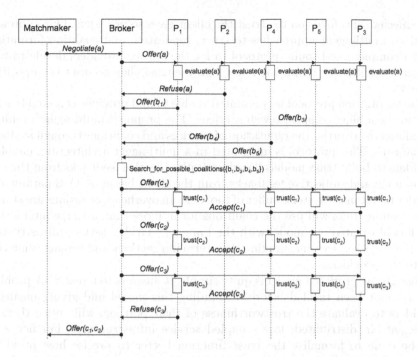

Fig. 3. Negotiation protocol execution after matchmaking

of utilization, decides it is not interested and sends a *refuse* to the broker. The remaining solutions before the coalition formation are depicted in Fig. 2(c).

The broker then computes all the possible coalitions and proposes them one by one to all the remaining candidate providers. $(c_1, c_2, c_3) \in C$ are defined by $c_1 = (s_1^3, s_4^2, s_3^1, s_1^3)$, $c_2 = (s_1^3, s_4^3, s_3^1, s_1^3)$ and $c_3 = (s_1^3, s_5^1, s_3^1, s_1^3)$. The providers then take a decision based on their trust model to accept or refuse the coalition proposition. Here, c_3 is refused by p_1. It could be because p_1 does not want to work with p_5 or because s_5^1, according to the execution node feedback, is highly unreliable or because a high number of coalitions containing this service were poorly evaluated by the clients, thus enticing p_1 to refuse the coalition to preserve its own credibility.

Finally, a set of provider compliant coalitions propositions as shown in Fig. 2(d) is sent back to the matchmaker, leaving the user make the final decision.

As far as the feedbacks mechanisms are concerned, the user then choose the coalition c_1 and request its execution. The execution node will leave 4 feedbacks for each step of the composition. For example, if the time cycle number of the system is 34 it could leave $(percept, s_1^3, speed, 34) = 14ms$. Then if the user is happy with the fluency of the result it could leave $(u_1, c_1, fluency, 34) = good$.

5   Conclusion

Integrating trust and reputation mechanisms in service-oriented architectures had been long planned as a way to improve selection mechanisms. However, these mechanisms focus on the trust the client gives to providers. Our approach, based on multi-agent approaches to trust, reputation and coalition formation, gives a complete and sound protocol to let the service providers decide to take part in a web service composition based on the trust they accord to composition partners.

The negotiation protocol we presented is able to find provider-centered trusted coalitions enabling composite web services. The proposed multi-agent architecture allows to advertise the reputation of services and coalitions through feedback mechanisms. This protocol is integrated in a multi-agent architecture, enabling providers to build trust models based on both objective feedbacks from the execution node and subjective feedbacks from the client based on QoS parameters. In order to not make systems suffer of too large an overhead, coalitions are stored, as we assume users will use the coalitions for in more than a single interaction. We then illustrated our model with the Language Grid, a service infrastructure with language services encouraging long-term interactions and leaving some control to the providers.

Though the proposed model is quite simple, it answers to a real SOA problem that has not been tackled before. Extending this model and giving means to providers to evaluate the trustworthiness of their partners will entice them to participate in distributed, loose-coupled service infrastructures. Further work will be done to formalize the trust function better to precise how providers take the decision to trust, and notably how they can aggregate the feedbacks from the user and providers to update their trust model. For this purpose, the model should be extended to include logic of trust and reputation [14]. Then, the protocol should be modified to update the coalitions, and giving the possibility for a provider to leave if the trust threshold was to fall under a certain value should be developed.

Acknowledgments

This work was supported by a Grant-in-Aid for Scientific Research (A) (21240014, 2009-2011) from Japan Society for the Promotion of Science (JSPS), and Kyoto University Global COE Program: Informatics Education and Research Center for Knowledge-Circulating Society.

References

1. Agarwal, S., Studer, R.: Automatic matchmaking of web services. In: International Conference on Web Services, ICWS 2006, September 2006, pp. 45–54 (2006)
2. Baldoni, M., Baroglio, C., Martelli, A., Patti, V.: Reasoning about interaction protocols for customizing web service selection and .... Journal of Logic and Algebraic Programming 70(1), 53–73 (2007)
3. Bentahar, J., Maamar, Z., Wan, W., Benslimane, D.: Agent-based communities of web services: an argumentation-driven approach. Service Oriented Computing and Applications 2(4), 219–238 (2008)

4. Diamadopoulou, V., Makris, C., Panagis, Y., Sakkopoulos, E.: Techniques to support web service selection and consumption with qos characteristics. Journal of Network and Computer Applications 31(2), 108–130 (2008)
5. Dustdar, S., Schreiner, W.: A survey on web services composition. International Journal of Web and Grid Services 1(1), 1–30 (2005)
6. Grandison, T., Sloman, M.: Trust management tools for internet applications. In: Nixon, P., Terzis, S. (eds.) iTrust 2003. LNCS, vol. 2692, pp. 91–107. Springer, Heidelberg (2003)
7. Griffiths, N.: Task delegation using experience-based multi-dimensional trust. In: Proceedings of the fourth international joint conference on Autonomous agents and multiagent systems, pp. 489–496 (2005)
8. Ben Hassine, A., Matsubara, S., Ishida, T.: Constraint-based approach for web service composition. In: Cruz, I., Decker, S., Allemang, D., Preist, C., Schwabe, D., Mika, P., Uschold, M., Aroyo, L.M. (eds.) ISWC 2006. LNCS, vol. 4273, pp. 130–143. Springer, Heidelberg (2006)
9. Hendler, J.: Agents and the semantic web. IEEE Intelligent Systems 16(2), 30–37 (2001)
10. Hübner, J.F., Vercouter, L., Boissier, O.: Instrumenting multi-agent organisations with artifacts to support reputation processes. In: Hubner, J.F., et al. (eds.) COIN 2008. LNCS (LNAI), vol. 5428, pp. 96–110. Springer, Heidelberg (2009)
11. Ishida, T.: Language grid: An infrastructure for intercultural collaboration. In: SAINT 2006: International Symposium on Applications and the Internet, pp. 96–100 (2006)
12. Jones, C.L.D., Barber, K.S.: Combining job and team selection heuristics. In: Hubner, J.F., et al. (eds.) COIN 2008. LNCS, vol. 5428, pp. 33–47. Springer, Heidelberg (2009)
13. Letia, I.A., Pop, O.: Web service selection based on trust. In: Proceedings of 9th International conference on Development and Application Systems (May 2008)
14. Lorini, E., Herzig, A., Hubner, J.F., Vercouter, L.: A logic of trust and reputation. Logic Journal of the IGPL (2009)
15. Michael Maximilien, E., Singh, M.P.: Toward autonomic web services trust and selection. In: Proceedings of the 2nd international conference on Service oriented computing, pp. 212–221 (2004)
16. Michael Maximilien, E., Singh, M.P.: Multiagent system for dynamic web services selection. In: Proceedings of 1st Workshop on Service-Oriented Computing and Agent-Based Engineering (SOCABE at AAMAS), January 2005, pp. 25–29 (2005)
17. Rathod, P., desJardins, M.: Stable team formation among self-interested agents. In: The Twentieth National Conference on Artificial Intelligence, AAAI 2005 (2005)
18. Sabater, J., Paolucci, M., Conte, R.: Repage: Reputation and image among limited autonomous partners. Journal of Artificial Societies and Social Simulation 9 (2006)
19. Sandholm, T.W., Lesser, V.R.: Coalition formation among bounded rational agents. In: International Joint Conference on Artificial Intelligence (1995)
20. Vu, L.-H., Hauswirth, M., Aberer, K.: Qos-based service selection and ranking with trust and reputation management. In: Meersman, R., Tari, Z. (eds.) OTM 2005. LNCS, vol. 3760, pp. 466–483. Springer, Heidelberg (2005)
21. Wang, Y., Vassileva, J.: A review on trust and reputation for web service selection. In: 27th International Conference on Distributed Computing Systems Workshops, ICDCSW 2007, June 2007, p. 25 (2007)

228   J. Bourdon, L. Vercouter, and T. Ishida

22. Yokoo, M., Hirayama, K.: Algorithms for distributed constraint satisfaction: A review. Autonomous Agents and Multi-Agent Systems 3(2), 185–207 (2000)
23. Yu, T., Zhang, Y., Lin, K.-J.: Efficient algorithms for web services selection with end-to-end qos constraints. ACM Transactions on the Web (TWEB) 1(1) (May 2007)
24. Zacharia, G., Moukas, A., Maes, P.: Collaborative reputation mechanisms for electronic marketplaces. Decision Support Systems 29(4), 371–388 (2000)

Memory Complexity of Automated Trust Negotiation Strategies

Indika H. Katugampala[1,*], Hirofumi Yamaki[2], and Yukiko Yamaguchi[2]

[1] Graduate School of Information Science, Nagoya University
indika@net.itc.nagoya-u.ac.jp
[2] Information Technology Center, Nagoya University
{yamaki,yamaguchi}@itc.nagoya-u.ac.jp

Abstract. Automated Trust Negotiation(ATN) has been proposed as a mechanism to establish mutual trust among strangers. Protocols and strategies to be used during ATN have also been studied. When considering the real world usage of ATN, there are many factors to be considered. One of the factors that has not been addressed by previous studies is the memory complexity of negotiation strategies. This paper analyses the memory complexities of previously proposed negotiation strategies and evaluates the average memory consumption through simulations using an ATN framework for web services. The experimental results revealed that memory complexity of Parsimonious strategy grows exponentially as the number of credentials increases, which is consistent with the theoretical analysis. As a solution, a method to reduce the memory consumption by exploiting the knowledge each entity has about the negotiation is presented. In addition, the paper presents a new criterion that enables the truncation of the negotiation to reduce the memory consumption in situations where the negotiation fails. Experiment results, which show the effectiveness of above methods in reducing the memory consumption, negotiation length are also presented.

1 Introduction

With the advancement of the Internet, the number of services users may use has dramatically increased. However, a major problem when using such services is to decide whether the service provider is trustworthy. On the other hand, service providers may also wish to restrict their services only to trustworthy users. As a solution to this issue, Automated Trust Negotiation(ATN) has been proposed to establish mutual trust among strangers [1,2,3,4,5].

Each entity participating in ATN has *digital credentials*, which certify attributes of the entity. For each credential, the entity has a *policy* which defines the prerequisites that must be fulfilled by the other entity. During the negotiation entities exchange credentials according to their policies. If the policy of service is satisfied during the negotiation, user will get access to the service.

---

* Student.

J.-J. Yang et al. (Eds.): PRIMA 2009, LNAI 5925, pp. 229–244, 2009.

Consider the following exemplary scenario. ABC Computers Inc., who manufactures personal computers and portable music players, is running a campaign which offers a discount to students who buy a personal computer and a music player at once. To qualify for this discount, one should prove that s/he is a current student at an educational institute by submitting the student's certificate. ABC Computers Inc. is a certified manufacturer with National Trade Commission and possesses a trade permission certificate. ABC Computers Inc. is ready to disclose trade permission certificate to anyone who wishes to buy their products.

Bob, who is a university student, has a student's certificate issued by his university, but does not wish to disclose it to untrusted parties. Bob considers anyone who can certify his/her identity by a credential issued by a government agency as a trusted party.

Suppose that Bob wants to be qualified for the discount. Under these circumstances one way to establish trust is as follows. When Bob asks for the discount, discount service requests him to submit his student's certificate. Since Bob discloses his student's certificate only to parties certified by a government agency, Bob asks for any credential issued to the service by such a institute. Since the service possesses a digital certificate issued by National Trade Commission and service's policy allows it to be disclosed without any prerequisites, service discloses that credential at this stage. After Bob verified the server's certificate, he discloses his student's certificate. Discount server verifies Bob's student's certificate and allows him to apply for a discount.

As shown in the above example, during the ATN process, entities participate in the negotiation exchange their policies and/or credentials, and establish mutual trust.

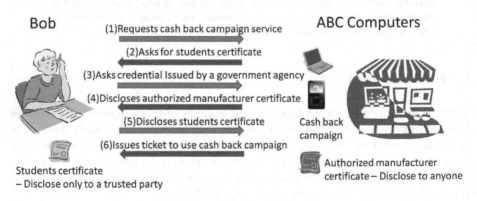

Fig. 1. Example of Trust Negotiation

This paper is organized as follows. Section 2 presents the formal definition of ATN and show that negotiation can be mapped to a distributed search on an AND/OR graph. Furthermore, we show how to represent policies of each entity using adjacency-list representation. In Sect. 2.4, we discuss the problems associated with ATN strategies and show the importance of reducing memory consumption. Through Sect. 3-6, we analyze the memory complexity of Eager strategy, Parsimonious strategy, PRUNES strategy and a strategy based on Dynamic programming approach. Section 7 summarizes the derived theoretical results. In Sect. 4 we describe how to implement Parsimonious strategy and propose a method to reduce the memory consumption using the knowledge each entity has about the negotiation. Section 8 describes results obtained by simulating strategies on WS-ATN – an ATN framework for web services. In particular, we present the effectiveness of the proposed method in reducing the memory consumption of Parsimonious strategy and a comparison of average memory consumption of different negotiation strategies. Finally, Sect. 9 concludes the paper.

2   Automated Trust Negotiation

2.1   Formal Definition

Throughout this paper, we use the same notation presented in [6]. We denote the user entity as *client*, the service entity as *server* and the target of the negotiation as *service*. We use the propositional symbols to denote the service, credentials of the server and credentials of the client. Accordingly, we denote the service by S, credentials of the client by $C_1, \ldots, C_{n_c}$, credentials of the server by $S_1, \ldots, S_{n_s}$. Where n_c is the number of credentials possessed by the client and n_s is the number of credentials possessed by the server. Policy for disclosing credential C is denoted by $C \leftarrow F_C(S_1, \ldots, S_k)$ where $F_C(S_1, \ldots, S_k)$ is an expression involving credentials $S_1, S_2, \ldots, S_k$ possessed by the other entity, boolean operators $\wedge, \vee$ and parentheses as needed. We say the policy of credential C is *satisfied*, if the logical expression $F_C(S_1, \ldots, S_k)$ evaluates to *true*, after substituting propositional symbols of already disclosed credentials by the other entity with *true* in the logical expression $F_C(S_1, \ldots, S_k)$. If the policy of credential C is satisfied, it can be disclosed to the other entity.

Since any logical expression can be converted to Disjunctive Normal Form (DNF), we can represent the policy of credential C as $C \leftarrow D_1 \vee \ldots \vee D_l$ where $D_i = S_{i1} \wedge \ldots \wedge S_{ik_i}$ and each S_{ij}, $1 \le i \le l$, $1 \le j \le k_i$, is a credential of the other entity. We say each D_i a *disjunct*. Similarly we say policy of the credential C is satisfied, when any of the disjuncts $D_1, \ldots, D_l$ evaluates to *true* after substituting propositional symbols of already disclosed credentials by the other entity with *true* in disjuncts $D_1, \ldots, D_l$.

If credential C can be disclosed without any credentials from the other entity, we denote that policy by $C \leftarrow true$, and we say credential C is an *unprotected credential*. On the other hand if credential C can not be disclosed under any circumstances, we denote such a policy by $C \leftarrow false$.

Even though the service is not a real credential, we may denote the access control policy of the service using the same notation mentioned above. As a result of the negotiation, if the policy of service is satisfied, the service will be available to the client, and we say the negotiation is a *successful negotiation*. Otherwise we say the negotiation is a *failed negotiation*.

2.2 ATN as a Distributed Search Problem

The dependencies among credentials possessed by both parties of a negotiation can be represented as an AND/OR graph. Instead of edges that connect two nodes in a normal graph, in an AND/OR graph there are *connectors* that connect one node to one or more nodes.

For example, dependencies among credentials in policies of Table 1 can be represented by an AND/OR graph as shown in Fig. 2. In the corresponding AND/OR graph credentials are represented by nodes. Hereafter the node corresponding to credential C is referred as *node C*. Policies are represented by connectors. When credential C's policy expressed in DNF is $C \leftarrow D_1 \vee \ldots \vee D_l$ and $D_i = S_{i1} \wedge \ldots \wedge S_{ik_i}$ then in the AND/OR graph there are l outgoing connectors from node C. The Connector which represents disjunct D_i connects node C to nodes $S_{i1}, \ldots, S_{ik_i}$. There is a special node, node *true*, which is used to represent policies of unprotected credentials. When C is an unprotected credential, i.e. $C \leftarrow true$, then in AND/OR graph there is a connector which connects node C to node *true*. Using this representation, trust negotiation can be interpreted as searching a path from node S – which represents the service – to node *true*. Since all the entities taking part in the negotiation do not have an insight into the entire AND/OR graph, searching is performed in a distributed manner by exchanging the knowledge that each entity has about the AND/OR graph.

Table 1. Example Policy Set

Server Policy	Client Policy
$S \leftarrow C_1 \vee (C_2 \wedge C_3)$	$C_1 \leftarrow S_1 \vee S_2$
$S_1 \leftarrow C_2 \vee C_4$	$C_2 \leftarrow S_5$
$S_2 \leftarrow C_2 \wedge C_3$	$C_3 \leftarrow S_3 \wedge S_4$
$S_3 \leftarrow true$	$C_4 \leftarrow S_3 \wedge S_4$
$S_4 \leftarrow true$	
$S_5 \leftarrow C_2$	

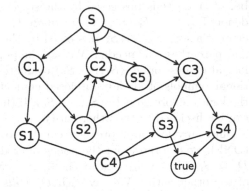

Fig. 2. AND/OR Graph Representation

2.3 Data Structure to Represent Policies

As mentioned already, none of the participating entities knows the whole AND/OR graph, but a part of it. The knowledge each entity has about whole AND/OR graph can be also represented by means of an AND/OR graph. Figure 3 shows how server's policy in Fig. 1 can be represented by an AND/OR graph. It uses two kinds of nodes: AND nodes (depicted in rectangles) to represent disjuncts, OR nodes (depicted in circles) to represent credentials. Policies in Fig. 3 can be represented using adjacency-list representation as shown in Fig. 4.

To compute the memory complexity of adjacency-list representation, assume that m_c, m_s correspond to number of distinct disjuncts in client policies, server policies respectively. Since the client side can have maximum of $n_c + n_s + 1 + m_c$ nodes, the size of adjacency array is $O(n_c + n_s + m_c)$. Furthermore, it can have at most $m_c(n_c + n_s)$ edges. Hence the total entries in adjacency lists is of order $O(m_c(n_c + n_s))$. It results in the memory complexity of adjacency-list representation of policies at the client side to be $O(m_c(n_c + n_s))$. Similarly, memory complexity at the server side is $O(m_s(n_c + n_s))$.

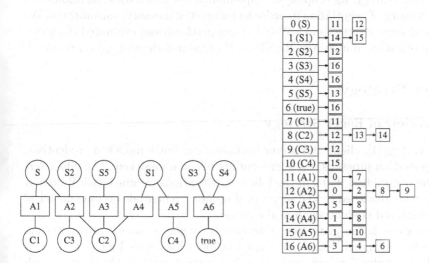

Fig. 3. Server Policy Graph   **Fig. 4.** Adjacency-list Representation of Server

2.4   Issues in ATN Strategies

Even though ATN is an ideal solution to establish trust among strangers, it has several issues to overcome if it is to be used in the real world situations. In particular, protection of sensitive policies, interoperability of strategies, communication cost and memory complexity are few such issues.

In previous studies, some of those problems had been addressed. Most of the negotiation strategies proposed in the past require that both entities use the same negotiation strategy. Since this restricts the applicability of ATN, it has been studied how to remove this restriction. Concept of *strategy family* has been proposed such that two strategies in the same strategy family can negotiate successfully and it is also possible to change the strategies during the negotiation given that both strategies are from the same strategy family. Interoperability of strategies is addressed in [7,8].

As mentioned in Sect. 2.2, since ATN is a distributed search process on AND/OR Graph, when implementing ATN strategies communication cost also should be considered. It is of paramount importance, specially when ATN is used to establish trust in ubiquitous environments, where minimization of number of messages exchange during the negotiation is desirable. In previous studies, communication cost of strategies has been addressed when those strategies were originally proposed.

An issue that has not been addressed so far is the memory complexity of negotiation strategies. Since ATN can be considered as a distributed search, as with the number of states in the search space increases, so does the number of information that should be kept in memory. In this paper, we concentrate on memory consumption of existing negotiation strategies. While giving a brief outline of proposed strategies, we analyze their worst case memory complexities. For Parsimonious strategy, we propose an implementation which uses the knowledge about the history of negotiation in order to reduce the memory consumption. We implemented some strategies in a Web services platform and evaluated the memory consumption by simulations. Results of these simulations are also presented.

3   Eager Strategy

3.1   Overview of Eager Strategy

In Eager strategy[1], client and server exchange currently unlocked credentials. As the negotiation proceeds, more credentials become unlocked. The client terminates the negotiation if any of the following situations occurs: either if no new credentials were disclosed by the server or if no new credentials become unlocked by newly disclosed credentials from the server.

Eager strategy is complete, and it terminates when a successful negotiation is impossible. Maximum length of a negotiation which uses Eager strategy is bounded by the value $2 \min (n_s, n_c)$. Also, Eager strategy finds the solution with optimal length. Since Eager strategy does not disclose access control policies of credentials explicitly, it may be suitable for situations where access control policies are sensitive. The weakness of Eager strategy is, it may disclose credentials which are not compulsory to gain access to the service. Also, it may disclose credentials when there is no successful negotiation.

3.2   Implementation of Eager Strategy

Implementation of Eager strategy is straight forward. Each entity has to keep records of credentials disclosed by itself and by the other entity. It can be achieved by augmenting one variable, to store the state of credential(disclosed or not), to each element in adjacency array. Based on this information, each entity can decide whether it is possible to disclose any credential that has not been disclosed yet.

3.3   Memory Complexity of Eager Strategy

Theorem 1. *Client side memory complexity of Eager strategy is* $O\left(m_c\left(n_c + n_s\right)\right)$. *Server side memory complexity of Eager strategy is* $O\left(m_s\left(n_c + n_s\right)\right)$.

Proof. First we analyze the memory complexity of client. Memory complexity of adjacency-list representation of policies is $O\left(m_c\left(n_c + n_s\right)\right)$. To store the disclosure status of credentials it needs $O\left(n_c + n_s\right)$ of memory. Therefore, client side memory complexity of Eager strategy is $O\left(m_c\left(n_c + n_s\right)\right)$. Similarly, memory complexity at the server side is $O\left(m_s\left(n_c + n_s\right)\right)$. □

4 Parsimonious Strategy

4.1 Overview of Parsimonious Strategy

In parsimonious strategy[1], first client requests the service and if the service is anonymous, service is granted. If not, server sends the access control policy of the service as reply. At the client side if that policy can not be satisfied, client generates a new counter policy, which must be satisfied by the server, for the client to satisfy the server's policy. This process proceeds until the policy requested by one entity can be satisfied by the other entity using that entity's unprotected credentials. When such situation occurs, the entity who can satisfy other entity's policy, starts to disclose credentials. With the disclosed credentials, it also sends the policy that it already requested in the previous step. Likewise the previously requested policies are replayed with the credentials that satisfy the policy requested by other entity, until the access is granted to the service eventually.

Parsimonious strategy is complete and maximum length of the negotiation, when a successful negotiation exists, is bounded by the value $4\min(n_c, n_s)$. In the case that there is no successful negotiation, it can be decided by the time that client has requested $n_c + 1$ requests, i.e. when total messages in negotiation is $2n_c + 2$. If no policy that can be satisfied with unprotected credentials appeared by the $2n_c + 2^{\text{th}}$ message, negotiation can be safely terminated by the client. The strength of Parsimonious strategy is, it does not disclose any unnecessary credentials. And in situations where no successful negotiation is possible, it does not disclose any credentials at all.

4.2 Implementation of Parsimonious Strategy

Although, the theoretical concepts of Parsimonious strategy were presented in [1], implementation method was not given. Specially topics such as how to derive counter requests from the policy requested by other entity, how to truncate negotiation early when a successful negotiation is impossible, to which extend the strategy is practical under the real world conditions were not addressed. Here we propose a method to implement Parsimonious strategy and show how we can truncate the negotiation early, when no successful negotiation exists.

In this implementation we keep the all policies in DNF format. When one entity is using the above implementation, it can easily use the information it has about the negotiation to make the negotiation efficient. How this can be achieved is described using the following concepts.

Consider two disjuncts t_1 and t_2. If $t_1 \vee t_2 = t_1$ then we say t_2 is *stricter* than t_1. If neither t_1 is stricter than t_2 nor t_2 is stricter than t_1, we say t_1 and t_2 are *independent* disjuncts. If t_1, t_2 are not independent disjuncts, we say t_1 and t_2 are *dependent* disjuncts.

When one entity is using the implementation mentioned above, it can improve the efficiency of the negotiation by using following facts.

1. While creating a counter request, if two disjuncts t_1, t_2 such that t_2 is stricter than t_1 appear, term t_2 can be neglected.
2. Assume the current counter request is $R_{current}$ and a previously requested counter request (if any) is $R_{previous}$. If there exists two disjuncts $t_1 \in R_{previous}$, $t_2 \in R_{current}$, such that t_2 is stricter than t_1, then t_2 can be neglected in the current counter request.

Utilizing above two facts, we can reduce the memory consumption of Parsimonious strategy. Consequently it reduces the communication cost. Besides above advantages, it also provides a method to truncate the negotiation when a successful negotiation does not exist. Since both items mentioned above reduce the number of terms in the generated counter request, sometimes it may result in a policy which has no disjuncts, meaning that it is impossible to have a successful negotiation and thus negotiation can be terminated.

4.3   Memory Complexity of Parsimonious Strategy

When analyzing the memory complexity of Parsimonious strategy, we use Lemma1, which states the maximum number of independent terms that can be created from fixed number of credentials. We omit the proof of Lemma1 due to space limitations.

Lemma 1. *Maximum number of independent disjuncts can be created from n literals is $\left(\begin{smallmatrix} n \\ \lfloor \frac{n}{2} \rfloor \end{smallmatrix} \right)$.*

Using the results from Lemma1 we can derive theorem 2.

Theorem 2. *Client side memory complexity of Parsimonious strategy is $O\left((n_c + n_s)\, 2^{n_s}\right)$. Server side memory complexity of Parsimonious strategy is $O\left((n_c + n_s)\, 2^{n_c}\right)$.*

Proof. Consider the client side first. Memory complexity of storing policies at client side is $O\left(m_c\left(n_c + n_s\right)\right)$. During the negotiation phase each entity stores the requested policies by itself. As shown in Sect. 4.2 it is not necessary to store two disjuncts which are dependent. According to Lemma1, number of such disjuncts is bounded by $\left(\begin{smallmatrix} n_s \\ \lfloor \frac{n_s}{2} \rfloor \end{smallmatrix} \right)$, and length of each disjuncts is at most n_s. Therefore, during the negotiation phase memory consumption of client is at most $n_s \left(\lfloor \frac{n_s}{2} \rfloor \right)$. During the credential exchange phase, credentials of the server get disclosed and client has to store them. Memory needs to store this information is bounded by n_s. So the total memory consumption is $(m_c (n_c + n_s)) + n_s \left(\lfloor \frac{n_s}{2} \rfloor \right) + n_s$. Using the facts that $m_c \leq \left(\lfloor \frac{n_s}{2} \rfloor \right)$ and $\left(\lfloor \frac{n_s}{2} \rfloor \right) < 2^{n_s}$, memory complexity of client is $O\left((n_s + n_c) 2^{n_s} \right)$. Similarly, it can be shown that memory complexity of server equals to $O\left((n_c + n_s) 2^{n_c} \right)$. $\qquad \square$

5   PRUNES Strategy

5.1   Overview of PRUNES Strategy

Main features of PRUNES[6] are it is complete and it does not disclose any credentials when negotiation fails, and does not disclose irrelevant credentials when negotiation succeeds. In the worst case communication complexity is $O(n^2)$ and the computational complexity is $O(nm)$, where n is the number of credentials and m is the size of the credential disclosure policies in disjunctive normal form.

Since PRUNES strategy is a refined version of complete brute-force back-tracking negotiation strategy, we start with its brief description. Brute-force backtracking strategy begins with a request for service S. During the brute-force backtracking strategy, when an entity receives a request for credential C, it behaves as follows. If C is an unprotected credential, C is *granted* immediately; at this juncture C is not disclosed, but the entity informs to the other entity that it can be disclosed. If credential C does not exist, a *deny* message is sent to the other entity, which means credential C can not be disclosed. Otherwise, assume the access control policy for C expressed in DNF is $C \leftarrow D_1 \vee \ldots D_l$, where $D_i = S_{i1} \vee \ldots S_{ik_i}$, and each $S_{ij} 1 \leq i \leq l$ and $1 \leq j \leq k_i$ is a credential to be disclosed by the other entity. In this case, entity attempts to solve the first disjunct D_1 of C's policy, starting from S_{11}. If S_{1i} has already been granted, then it moves to $S_{1(i+1)}$. If this entity has already requested S_{1i} during the negotiation, but has not yet been granted or denied by the other entity, it does not request S_{1i} again and S_{1i} fails to be granted. Otherwise, it requests S_{1i} from other entity. If all of the credentials of D_i are granted, it informs the other entity that C can be granted. If any of credentials in D_i can not be granted, it moves to next disjunct D_{i+1}. If no disjunct can be solved, it sends a deny message to the other entity informing that C can not be granted.

Eventually, if request for service S is denied, it means that no successful negotiation is possible and negotiation halts. Otherwise, two entities start to disclose credentials according to grant messages exchanged in the previous steps. Since this credential exchange phase is the same as that of PRUNES strategy, it will be addressed in detail later.

PRUNES improves the efficiency of the aforementioned brute-force backtracking strategy, by using the following fact: if request R_1 for credential C was requested at time t_1, but was denied by the other entity, then requesting the same credential at a later time also will be denied if no new credentials were granted after time t_1. To decide whether new credentials have been granted after credential C was requested, PRUNES associates a variable with each credential C, that stores the number of credentials granted by both parties at the time credential C is being requested, and a global variable to store the number of credentials granted by both parties at any given time.

If service S was granted, then two entities move to credential exchange phase. During the negotiation phase, when a credential is granted by an entity, it sends information about conditions in which it can be granted. Each entity stores this information and builds a directed graph according to these conditions. For example, the condition for credential C to be disclosed is the disclosure of credentials $S_1, \ldots, S_n$, then edges from vertices which represent credentials $S_1, \ldots, S_n$ to vertex which represents credential C are added. In the case of unprotected credentials, an edge from special node *true* to that corresponding credential is added. In the credential exchange phase, each entity executes the topological sort on this directed graph and exchanges credentials according to the result.

5.2   Implementation of PRUNES Strategy

Besides data structures needed to store policies, PRUNES strategy needs, one global variable – to store the value of total number of granted credentials – and one variable per each credential of opponent entity – to store the value of total number of granted credentials at the time that relevant credential is being requested. Granted information, which stores the dependency relationship among credentials, can be stored using adjacency-list implementation of a graph.

5.3   Memory Complexity of PRUNES Strategy

Theorem 3. *Client side memory complexity of PRUNES strategy is* $O\left(m_c\left(n_c + n_s\right) + n_c n_s\right)$. *Server side memory complexity of PRUNES strategy is* $O\left(m_s\left(n_c + n_s\right) + n_c n_s\right)$.

Proof. Consider client side first. As mentioned in 2.3, memory necessary to store policies using adjacency-list representation is $O\left(m_c\left(n_c + n_s\right)\right)$. Memory complexity of variables which stores number of granted credentials is $O\left(n_s\right)$. Dependency graph contains at most $n_c + n_s + 1$ vertices. Since this dependency graph is a bipartite graph, each client node can have at most n_s edges, each server node can have at most n_c edges and *true* node can have at most $n_c + n_s$ edges. So the total number of edges is at most $n_c n_s + n_s n_c + (n_c + n_s) = O\left(n_c n_s\right)$. Adding up memory complexities of representing policies and representing dependency graph, client side memory complexity of PRUNES strategy is $O\left(m_c\left(n_c + n_s\right) + n_c n_s\right)$. Similarly, it can be proved that server side memory complexity of PRUNES strategy is $O\left(m_s\left(n_c + n_s\right) + n_c n_s\right)$. $\square$

6 Dynamic Programming Approach

6.1 Overview of Dynamic Programming Approach

Negotiation strategies described so far assume that the user preferences of all credentials are equal. Which is not necessarily true when consider the real world scenarios. The negotiation strategy proposed in [9], takes in to account the user preferences of credentials and assigns a cost – which is a positive real number – to each credential. Furthermore, it assigns a cost to each policy. Larger cost of a credential/policy means the larger mental barrier to disclose that credential/policy. It assumes that negotiation parties are cooperative and try to find a solution that minimizes the total cost of both parties. By using dynamic programming, it calculates a solution with the minimum cost, that is the path whose sum of costs of policies and credentials contained in it is minimum. Since the solution is the path with minimum total cost, it assures that no unnecessary credentials or policies are disclosed. One major drawback in this strategy is that, it assumes that policies of two parties have no confluences, i.e. there are no policies such that $C_1 \leftarrow S_1 \wedge S_2$, $S_1 \leftarrow C_2$, $S_2 \leftarrow C_2$, where C_1, C_2 are credentials of one entity and S_1, S_2 are credentials of the other entity.

Algorithm described in [9] is as follows. To prevent the disclosure of unnecessary policies, it expresses the policies in a slightly different way than we mentioned in Sect. 2.1. Assume that the policy of credential C expressed in DNF is given by $C \leftarrow D_1 \vee \ldots \vee D_l$, where $D_1, \ldots, D_l$ are disjuncts. Instead of expressing C's policy using all l disjuncts at once, in this method C's policy is expressed as l distinct policies $C \leftarrow D_i$ $(1 \leq i \leq l)$. To reflect the user preferences, it assigns a cost to each credential and to each policy expressed in the above format. If the credential C's policy is denial policy, $C \leftarrow false$, then cost of C is set to $+\infty$. The total cost after disclosing some credentials/policies is defined as the sum of costs of each disclosed credential/policy. The weight of connectors of corresponding AND/OR tree is assigned in such a way that, if there is a policy $C \leftarrow S_1 \wedge \ldots \wedge S_k$ then the cost of the connector from node C to nodes $S_1, \ldots, S_k$ equals to the sum of cost of credential C and cost of policy $C \leftarrow S_1 \wedge \ldots \wedge S_k$. During the negotiation both entities maintain an *OPEN* set which contains credentials c such that the cost of partial tree which has credential c as root has determined.

In this strategy, negotiation starts by client after adding unprotected credentials to its OPEN set. In response, server adds its unprotected credentials to its OPEN set, and discloses the name and the cost of the credential which has minimum cost in its OPEN set. After that both entities behave as follows. If an entity gets the cost of a credential, using that value it calculates cost of any of its credentials and if the calculated value is less than the present value, it overwrites the cost with the new value. In case that this credential is not in OPEN set or previously disclosed value is higher than the new value, it is added to OPEN set. Then if the cost of credential disclosed by opponent is higher than the cost of credential which has the minimum cost in its OPEN set, this entity discloses that credential name and cost. Otherwise, it sends an empty message.

If an entity gets an empty message and its OPEN set is empty, that means no successful negotiation is possible and negotiation terminates. If cost of service S is determined, it means that successful negotiation is possible. In this case, two parties exchange credential names in the solution tree and determine the credential exchange order; then exchange credentials according to that order.

6.2 Implementation of Dynamic Programming Approach

Dynamic Programming Approach can be implemented by augmenting following data to adjacency list representation: variables to store *individual cost* of each credential/policy and *total cost* of the partial tree where that node is the root. To briefly describe how the values change during the algorithm, consider the client side. In the initialization process all the *total cost* values are set to $+\infty$, *individual cost* of each client node is set to the cost of relevant credential, *individual cost* of each AND node is set to the cost of relevant policy, and *individual cost* of server nodes are set to $+\infty$. Once the values of server credentials are informed to the client during the negotiation, *individual cost* and *total cost* of server nodes are set to that value. Using the latest values of server nodes, *total cost* of AND nodes and client nodes are updated accordingly.

6.3 Memory Complexity of Dynamic Programming Approach

Theorem 4. *Client side memory complexity of Dynamic Programming Approach is $O\left(m_c\left(n_c + n_s\right)\right)$. Server side memory complexity of Dynamic Programming Approach is $O\left(m_s\left(n_c + n_s\right)\right)$.*

Proof. Consider client side first. As described in 6.2, dynamic programming approach can be implemented by augmenting 2 variables to each node. Since it does not change the memory complexity of adjacency list representation of policies, memory required to store policies and cost values is $O\left(m_c\left(n_c + n_s\right)\right)$. At the end of the negotiation phase, two parties exchange information concerning the order in which to exchange credentials. This information takes at most $O(n_c)$ space at client side. Therefore, client side memory complexity of Dynamic Programming Approach equals to $O\left(m_c\left(n_c + n_s\right)\right)$. Similarly, it can be proved that server side memory complexity of Dynamic Programming Approach equals to $O\left(m_s\left(n_c + n_s\right)\right)$. $\square$

7 Summary of Analysis

Theoretical results we derived so far as well as some other factors that should be considered when choosing a strategy are summarized in Table 2.

From Table 2, it is clear that we have to consider trade-off between memory complexity, communication cost and optimality of solution length, when choosing a negotiation strategy for ATN. Parsimonious strategy, which finds a solution with optimal solution length and gives maximum flexibility of choosing

Table 2. Comparison of Negotiation Strategies

Criteria / Strategy	Client Memory Complexity	Total Communication Cost	Disclose Unnecessary Credentials	Optimal Solution Length
Eager	$O(m_c n)$	$O(n)$	Yes	Yes
Parsimonious	$O(n 2^{n_s})$	$O(n_c 2^{n_s} + n_s 2^{n_c})$	No	Yes
PRUNES	$O(m_c n + n_c n_s)$	$O(n^2)$	No	No
Dynamic Program.	$O(m_c n)$	$O(n_c m_c + n_s m_s)$	No	No

which credentials to disclose, has a main drawback: its memory complexity and communication complexity grows exponentially with the number of credentials. Other strategies, which have lower memory footprint than that of Parsimonious strategy have other drawbacks: Eager strategy discloses unnecessary credentials, PRUNES restricts the flexibility of choosing which credentials to disclose, Dynamic programming approach assumes the cooperativeness of two entities.

8   Evaluation of Memory Consumption by Simulation

In this section we present results obtained by simulations using WS-ATN [10] which is an ATN framework for web services platform. In Sect. 8.1 we present the method we used to generate random policy sets. Sect. 8.2 presents the improvements to Parsimonious strategy and in Sect. 8.3 we compare the memory consumption of several strategies.

8.1   Random Input Generation for Simulation

Inputs for simulation were generated using the Procedure 1,2. Procedure 1 generates policies for both parties, by calling Procedure 2 which generates a single policy. Procedure 1 receives the total number of credentials n as a parameter and values of n_s, n_c are determined using a pseudo random generator such that the conditions $1 \le n_s \le n-1$ and $1 \le n_c \le n-1$ are satisfied. These conditions assure that all generated policy sets have at least one credential for both entities. Then it generates policy for service S (line 9), and condition in line 8 makes sure that the policy of S is not empty, i.e. service is not anonymous. Then it calls Procedure 2 (line 13,16) to generate the remaining policies. Condition in line 11 makes sure there exists at least one unprotected credential, which is essential in order to have a successful negotiation.

Procedure 2 receives a set of credentials of opponent entity as the parameter. First it decides which opponent credentials to be included in the policy. Probability of being included is 0.5, independently to other credentials. Using the credentials selected, it creates disjuncts to be included in the policy. Whether a particular credential should be included in a disjunct is decided with probability 0.5 independently to other credentials. Although it is not explicitly stated in Procedure 2, after a new disjunct is added (line 16) procedure makes sure that existing terms are mutually independent by removing redundant terms if any.

Procedure 1. GenerateInputGraphs(n)

1: $n_s \leftarrow random()\%(n-1)+2$
2: $n_c \leftarrow n - n_s$
3: $S \leftarrow \emptyset$
4: $S_i \leftarrow \emptyset \, 1 \leq i \leq n_s$
5: $C_j \leftarrow \emptyset \, 1 \leq j \leq n_c$
6: $ClientCreds \leftarrow C_1 \cup \ldots \cup C_{n_c}$
7: $ServerCreds \leftarrow S_1 \cup \ldots \cup S_{n_s-1}$
8: **while** $S = \emptyset$ **do**
9:    $S \leftarrow$ CreatePolicy($ClientCreds$)
10: **end while**
11: **while** $S_i = \emptyset$ and $C_j = \emptyset$ **do**
12:    **for** $i = 1$ to n_s **do**
13:       $S_i \leftarrow$ CreatePolicy($ClientCreds$)
14:    **end for**
15:    **for** $j = 1$ to n_c **do**
16:       $C_j \leftarrow$ CreatePolicy($ServerCreds$)
17:    **end for**
18: **end while**

Procedure 2. CreatePolicy(L)

1: $Q \leftarrow \emptyset$
2: $S \leftarrow \emptyset$
3: **for all** $c \in L$ **do**
4:    **if** random()%2 = 0 **then**
5:       $S \leftarrow S \cup \{c\}$
6:    **end if**
7: **end for**
8: $size \leftarrow |S|$
9: **for** $i = 0$ to $size$ **do**
10:    $T \leftarrow \emptyset$
11:    **for all** $c \in S$ **do**
12:       **if** random()%2 = 0 **then**
13:          $T \leftarrow T \cup \{c\}$
14:       **end if**
15:    **end for**
16:    $Q \leftarrow Q \cup \{T\}$
17: **end for**
18: **return** Q

8.2   Improvements to Parsimonious Strategy

In this section we present the effectiveness of the method presented in Sect. 4.2 to reduce the memory consumption of Parsimonious strategy. Simulation was done by changing n – total number of credential of both parties – from 9 to 23 and number of total disjuncts stored in memory was observed. 1000 inputs were used for each value of n. Simulations were done using both previous implementation, which does not use the history of the negotiation at all, and the implementation presented in Sec.4.2, which uses the history of negotiation. Variation of average of total number of disjuncts stored in memory with the n for both implementations is shown in Fig. 5. As it is clear from Fig. 5, the method presented in Sec.4.2 is effective in reducing the memory consumption of Parsimonious strategy.

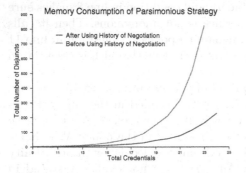

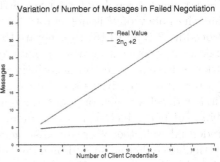

Fig. 5. Reduction of Memory Consumption   **Fig. 6.** Negotiation Length Variation

To figure out how effectively information about the history of negotiation can be used to truncate negotiation, we summarized the results of failed negotiations in Fig. 6. In Fig. 6 x axis denotes the number of client credentials and y axis denotes the number of exchanged messages. Values shown are averages of 139 samples for each n_s. The limit proposed in [1] is to terminate the negotiation if no satisfiable condition appears in first $2n_c + 2$ messages. But, it is clear from Fig. 6 that condition we proposed in Sect. 4.2 is effective in terminating negotiation when no successful negotiation exists.

8.3   Comparison of Memory Consumption of Negotiation Strategies

Comparison of memory consumptions of Eager strategy, Parsimonious strategy is shown in Fig. 7. In Fig. 7, x axis represents n and y axis represents the average memory consumption. For Eager strategy it is the total number of credentials stored in memory; for Parsimonious strategy it is the number of disjuncts stored in memory. Values shown in Fig. 7 are averages of 1000 inputs. As it is clear from Fig. 7, memory consumption of Parsimonious strategy increases exponentially compared to that of Eager strategy, in which the increase of memory consumption is very little, being consistent with the theoretical analysis.

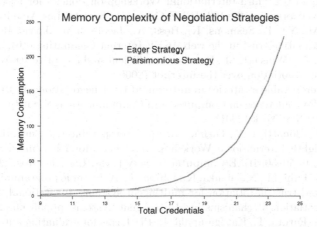

Fig. 7. Variation of Memory Consumption of Negotiation Strategies

9   Conclusion

In this paper, we focused on the memory complexity of ATN strategies. We analyzed the memory complexity of several negotiation strategies, and in Sect. 7 showed that we have to consider trade-off between memory complexity, communication cost and optimality of solution length, when choosing a strategy. Parsimonious strategy, which finds a solution with optimal solution length and gives maximum flexibility of choosing credentials to disclose, has the highest memory footprint. To overcome this, we proposed a method which exploits the history of negotiation to reduce the memory footprint and to terminate negotiation early when no successful negotiation is possible. Simulation results showed that the method we proposed is effective in reducing the memory consumption.

Even after those improvements, using Parsimonious strategy may be difficult in situations where there are high memory limitations, such as the ubiquitous environment. Achieving a lower memory and communication footprint than Parsimonious strategy, while keeping the optimality of solution length is difficult with already proposed strategies, and is the focus of future work.

References

1. Winsborough, W.H., Seamons, K.E., Jones, V.E.: Automated trust negotiation. In: DARPA Information Survivability Conference and Exposition, vol. I, pp. 88–102. IEEE Press, Los Alamitos (2000)
2. Winsborough, W.H., Jones, V.E.: Negotiating disclosure of sensitive credentials (1999)
3. Yu, T., Winslett, M., Seamons, K.E.: Supporting structured credentials and sensitive policies through interoperable strategies for automated trust negotiation. ACM Transactions on Information and System Security 6, 1–42 (2003)
4. Winsborough, W.H., Li, N.: Towards practical automated trust negotiation. In: Proceedings of the Third International Workshop on Policies for Distributed Systems and Networks, pp. 92–103. IEEE Computer Society, Los Alamitos (2002)
5. Winslett, M., Yu, T., Seamons, K., Hess, A., Jacobson, J., Jarvis, R., Smith, B., Yu, L.: Negotiating trust in the web. IEEE Internet Computing 6(6), 30–37 (2002)
6. Yu, T., Ma, X., Winslett, M.: Prunes: An efficient and complete strategy for automated trust negotiation over the internet (2000)
7. Yu, T.: Interoperable strategies in automated trust negotiation. In: Proceedings of the 8th ACM conference on Computer and Communications Security, pp. 146–155. ACM Press, New York (2001)
8. Baselice, S., Bonatti, P.A., Faella, M.: On interoperable trust negotiation strategies. In: Eighth International Workshop on Policies for Distributed Systems and Networks, pp. 39–50. IEEE Computer Society Press, Los Alamitos (2007)
9. Yamaki, H., Fujii, M., Nakatsuka, K., Ishida, T.: A dynamic programming approach to automated trust negotiation for multiagent systems. In: Rational, Robust, and Secure Negotiation Mechanisms in Multi-Agent Systems, pp. 55–66 (2005)
10. Yamaki, H., Furuta, T., Katugampala, I.: Platforms for evaluating automated trust negotiation protocols and strategies (2008)

Layered Distributed Constraint Optimization Problem for Resource Allocation Problem in Distributed Sensor Networks

Kazuhiro Ota, Toshihiro Matsui, and Hiroshi Matsuo

Nagoya Institute of Technology, Gokiso-cho, Showa-ku, Aichi, 466-8555 Japan
ohta@matlab.nitech.ac.jp, {matsui.t,matsuo}@nitech.ac.jp

Abstract. Distributed sensor network is an important research area of multi-agent systems. We focus on a type of distributed sensor network systems that cooperatively observe multiple targets with multiple autonomous sensors that can control their own view. The problem of allocating observation resource of the distributed sensor network can be formalized as distributed constraint optimization problems. However, in the previous works, the computation cost to solve the resource allocation problem highly increases with its scale/density. In this work, we divide the problem into two layers of problems, and two layered cooperative solvers are applied to those problems. The result of the experiment shows that our proposed method reduces the number of message cycles.

Keywords: Distributed Constraint Optimization Problem, Multi-agent, Distributed sensor network.

1 Introduction

Distributed Constraint Optimization Problem (DCOP) is an important research area of multi-agent systems[1][2][3][4]. In DCOPs, agent's state is represented by variables; and, relations between agents are represented by constraints and cost functions. Each agent decides/determines the values of its own variables by exchanging information with other agents. The goal is to assign global optimal values to the variables. DCOPs are an important model that represents cooperated resource scheduling problems in distributed systems. On the other hand, distributed sensor networks are studied as practical problems of multi-agent systems. In previous studies, resource allocation problems of the distributed sensor network are formalized as DCOPs[5][6]. There are various purposes of distributed sensor networks. An important purpose is to give information in a large observation area. Other purposes include cooperative navigation of robots using distributed sensor networks. In this paper, we focus on a type of observation system that cooperatively observes multiple targets with multiple autonomous sensors that can control own view. An important problem in the observation system can be formalized as an allocation problem of observation resources. In this paper, we considered the problem at a snapshot for an initial examination of the

J.-J. Yang et al. (Eds.): PRIMA 2009, LNAI 5925, pp. 245–260, 2009.
© Springer-Verlag Berlin Heidelberg 2009

proposed method. In the actual system, the environment changes dynamically in situations such as observation targets are moving. Therefore, it is necessary to allocate observation resources responding to the changing environment. That problem can be represented by repeatedly solving a consecutive set of snapshot problems. On the other hand, the time for a snapshot is limited. Therefore it is reasonable to apply stochastic methods that can find solution in comparatively short time. However, the problem including cooperation by agents and the resource allocations is complex. Then, in this paper, we propose a method that divides the problem into two layers: layer of leader election and the layer of observation resource allocation. It is expected that our proposed method reduces the complexity of the problem and efficiently solves the problem.

In section 2, DCOP and a search algorithm for the DCOP are shown. In section 3, we explain how to represent the resource allocation problem in the distributed sensor network. Then, some conventional formalizations of the problem are shown. A model based agency is also shown. In section 4, we propose the method that divides the problem into two layers. In section 5, our proposed method is evaluated. And we conclude in section 6.

2   Distributed Constraint Optimization Problem

DCOP consists of a set of agents. Each agent a_i has some variables $X_i = \{x_i^1, \cdots, x_i^k\}$. x_i^k takes a value from discrete finite domain D_i^k. a_i is the only agent that can decide the values of X_i. That is, the variable shows agent's state and decision. The relation between a set of variables is defined as a constraint c. A cost function f_c defines the cost for a set of variables. f_c is the cost function of c. A cost value represents the degree of violation on constraint c. There are constraints which cannot be relaxed and constraints which can be relaxed. The constraints which cannot be relaxed are defined as hard constraint. The constraints which can be relaxed are defined as soft constraint. A goal of the problem is to find optimal assignments of variables that minimize global cost value.

ADOPT[1] and DPOP[7] have been proposed as exact methods for DCOP. ADOPT performs as distributed version of branch and bound/A∗ search based on depth first search tree for constraint network. DPOP is based on dynamic programming. In these methods, search iterations or memory uses exponentially increase according to induced-width[7] of the depth first search tree. On the other hand, DSA[2] and DSTS[3] have been proposed as stochastic algorithms. The solution found by these methods may not be optimal. However, these stochastic methods find suboptimal solutions with less number of cycles than ones of exact algorithms. In this work, we apply DSTS to the resource allocation problem in the distributed sensor network.

DSTS is a distributed stochastic search algorithm based on DSA. DSTS employs a tabu search to get out from local optimal solution. In search processing, each agent exchanges the values of its variables. Then each agent a_i calculates costs for assignments. The costs are evaluated for assignments of a_i's variables

```
1   initialize own variables;
2   empty tabu_list;
3   send variables' values to agents related by constraints;
4   while not terminated do
5       receive variables' values from other agents rlated by constraints;
6       call maintainance;
7   end while
8   procedure maintainance
9   if all variables' values are in the tabu_list then
10      noting to do;
11  else if NA_VALUEs have been received from all agents related by constraints
        then
12      assign new values to variables;
13  else if Δ ≥ 0 then
14      assign new values to variables with p₁;
15  else if current cost > 0 then
16      assign new values to variables with p₂;
17  end if
18  if all values are in the tabu_list then
19      send NA_VALUE to agents related by constraints;
20  else if new valiables's value is assigned then
21      send own variable's value to agents related by constraints;
22      add new variable's value to the tabu_list;
23  end if
24  end procedure
```

Fig. 1. Pseudo code of DSTS

with values of other agent's variables that are related by constraints. According to the costs, the agent a_i stochastically changes its variable's value to value which obtains best cost with probability p_1. Moreover, each agent uses the tabu search to get out from local optimal solution. Each agent adds variable's value to tabu_list. It prevents the variable from changing its value for a certain term(i.e. tabu period). Improvement of the cost value Δ takes negative value because of tabu search. In that case, each agent changes the values of variables with probability p_2. A pseudo code of DSTS is shown in Fig. 1. In Fig. 1, NA_VALUE represents that all values of a_i's variables are in the tabu_list.

3   Resource Allocation Problems in Distributed Sensor Network

In this section, a model of resource allocation problem for the distributed sensor network is shown. Then we show some formalization for the resource allocation problem based on DCOPs. Another framework based on the concept of agency is also shown.

3.1   Grid Model

Grid model is a basic representation of allocation problem that allocates observation resource of a sensor to a target. In the grid model, sensors are arranged

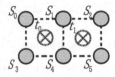

Fig. 2. Example of grid model

on the nodes of a uniform grid. Targets are located within the area enclosed by the grid. In related studies, models like this were used[6][5]. In this work, we focus on a type of observation system that consists of autonomous sensor nodes. That is, a sensor is an agent. In Fig. 2, s_i represents the sensor and t_j represent the target. We assume that only one target can exist in one area.

There is the limitation about the view of the sensor. This restriction cannot be compromised. The limitation about the view is modeled as a constraint such that the sensors can observe adjoining areas. Moreover, the sensors cannot observe multiple targets at a time. This limitation is modeled as a constraint such that the sensors can observe only one target at a time. On the other hand, it is preferable to observe one target with multiple sensors because more information about the target is obtained. This purpose is modeled as a constraint such that each target has to be observed by three sensors. However, this purpose can be relaxed because the targets can be observed by a smaller number of sensors.

3.2 Formalization Based on DCOP

In the following, two DCOP based formalizations for sensor resource allocation problem are shown. These are STAV[1] and TAV[5].

STAV (Sensor-Target As Variable): STAV is a model of formalization which defines a variable for a pair of a sensor and a target. An example of a sensor network shown in Fig. 2 is formalized as a STAV problem shown in Fig. 3. In Fig. 3, $x_{t_j}^{s_i}$ represents a variable of s_i for target t_j. For each sensor s_i, variables are defined for targets that can be observed by s_i. In this example, s_0, s_2, s_3, and s_5 have one variable because they can observe only one target. s_1 and s_4 have two variables because they can observe two targets. A value of $x_{t_j}^{s_i}$ represents which sensors are allocated to t_j. If a set of sensors that

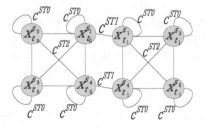

Fig. 3. Constraint network with STAV   **Fig. 4.** Constraint network with TAV

can observe t_j is $\{s_0, \cdots, s_n\}$, $x_{t_j}^{s_i}$ takes a combination of sensors as a value. $\{\phi, \{s_0\}, \cdots, \{s_n\}, \{s_0, s_1\}, \cdots, \{s_0, \cdots, s_n\}\}$ is the domain of $x_{t_j}^{s_i}$. With this formalization, three types of constraints are defined, and they are shown in Fig. 3 as c^{ST0}, c^{ST1} and c^{ST2}. Details of the constraints are as follows.

- $c^{ST0}(x_{t_j}^{s_i})$: Allocating sensors to observation target
  This constraint represents a requirement that three sensors are allocated to a target. If the number of sensors allocated to t_j is fewer than three, the constraint is not fully satisfied. In such case, this constraint can be relaxed. The cost function $f_{c^{ST0}}$ for c^{ST0} is defined as follows. $w^{c^{ST0}}$ is the weight parameter which represents degree of violation. In expression (1), a value of n_{t_j} represents the number of sensors allocated to t_j.

$$f_{c^{ST0}(x_{t_j}^{s_i})} = \begin{cases} w_0^{c^{ST0}} & n_{t_j} = 0 \\ w_1^{c^{ST0}} & n_{t_j} = 1 \\ w_2^{c^{ST0}} & n_{t_j} = 2 \\ 0 & otherwise \end{cases} \tag{1}$$

- $c^{ST1}(x_{t_j}^{s_i}, x_{t_{j'}}^{s_i})$: Restriction of observation resource
  This constraint represents a restriction about the number of targets where a sensor can be allocated. If a sensor is allocated to multiple targets, the constraint is violated. This constraint cannot be relaxed. The cost function $f_{c^{ST1}}$ for c^{ST1} is defined as follows. $w^{c^{ST1}}$ is the weight parameter.

$$f_{c^{ST1}(x_{t_j}^{s_i}, x_{t_{j'}}^{s_i})} = \begin{cases} w^{c^{ST1}} & x_{t_j}^{s_i} \cap x_{t_{j'}}^{s_i} \neq \phi \\ 0 & otherwise \end{cases} \tag{2}$$

- $c^{ST2}(x_{t_j}^{s_i}, x_{t_j}^{s_{i'}})$: Consistency of allocation of observation resource
  This constraint represents cooperation that sensors are allocated to targets without contradiction. If the variables' values for the same target are different between sensors, the constraint is violated. This constraint cannot be relaxed. The cost function $f_{c^{ST2}}$ for c^{ST2} is defined as follows. $w^{c^{ST2}}$ is the weight parameter.

$$f_{c^{ST2}(x_{t_j}^{s_i}, x_{t_j}^{s_{i'}})} = \begin{cases} w^{c^{ST2}} & x_{t_j}^{s_i} \neq x_{t_j}^{s_{i'}} \\ 0 & otherwise \end{cases} \tag{3}$$

The variable and the constraint increase because this model represents the explicit agreement between agents.

TAV (Target As Variable): TAV is a model of formalization which defines a variable for a target. An example of a sensor network shown in Fig. 2 is formalized as a TAV problem shown in Fig. 4. In Fig. 4, x_{t_j} represents a variable for target t_j. A value of x_{t_j} represents which sensors are allocated to t_j. If a set of sensors that can observe t_j is $\{s_0, \cdots, s_n\}$, x_{t_j} takes a combination of sensors as a value. $\{\phi, \{s_0\}, \cdots, \{s_n\}, \{s_0, s_1\}, \cdots, \{s_0, \cdots, s_n\}\}$ is the domain of x_{t_j}. With this formalization, two types of constraints are defined. They are shown in Fig. 4 as c^{T0} and c^{T1}. Details of the constraints are as follows.

– $c^{T0}(x_{t_j})$: Allocating sensors to observation target
This constraint represents a requirement that three sensors are allocated to a target. If the number of sensors allocated to t_j is fewer than three, the constraint is not fully satisfied. In such case, this constraint can be relaxed. The cost function $f_{c^{T0}}$ for c^{T0} is defined as follows. $w^{c^{T0}}$ is the weight parameter which represents the degree of violation. In expression (4), a value of n_{t_j} represents the number of sensors allocated to t_j.

$$f_{c^{T0}(x_{t_j})} = \begin{cases} w_0^{c^{T0}} & n_{t_j} = 0 \\ w_1^{c^{T0}} & n_{t_j} = 1 \\ w_2^{c^{T0}} & n_{t_j} = 2 \\ 0 & otherwise \end{cases} \quad (4)$$

– $c^{T1}(x_{t_j}, x_{t_{j'}})$: Restriction of observation resource
This constraint represents a restriction about the number of targets where a sensor is allocated. If a sensor is allocated to multiple targets, the constraint is violated. This constraint cannot be relaxed. The cost function $f_{c^{T1}}$ for c^{T1} is defined as follows. $w^{c^{T1}}$ is the weight parameter.

$$f_{c^{T1}(x_{t_j}, x_{t_{j'}})} = \begin{cases} w^{c^{T1}} & x_{t_j} \cap x_{t_{j'}} \neq \phi \\ 0 & otherwise \end{cases} \quad (5)$$

In TAV, variables are defined for targets. It seems that target has a variable. However, in the system assumed in this paper, targets are not agents. It is not clear what variables agents have. Therefore, TAV cannot be applied.

3.3   Cooperation Model with Agency

The observation system by distributed cooperative processing with the agency[8] has been proposed besides the frame of DCOP. An agency is a group of agents. Fig. 5 shows the concept of the agency based cooperative observation system. This system consists of camera agents which can control a view (AVA: Active Vision Agent) and there are some observation targets. Each AVA operates autonomously. The basic characteristic of autonomous camera agents is similar to

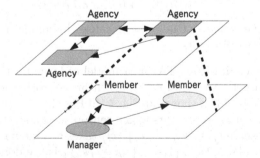

Fig. 5. Cooperation model based on agency[8]

that of sensors as it is assumed in this paper. The outline of this system is as follows.

- Each AVA is an observation resource which can be allocated to a target.
- When AVA detects a target, each AVA makes an agency.
- One of AVAs in a agency performs as a manager(AM:Agency Manager). Other AVAs follows the AM's decision.
- Each AM exchanges information, and decides the distribution of the observation resource.
- Observed information is gathered and managed by each AM.

The efficiency of this system was demonstrated by a small-scale experimental environment with real machines. Therefore, it is thought that use of layered structures for cooperation is more effective. However, in this system, the problem is not formalized as an optimization problem like DCOP, and optimization method in DCOP frameworks is not used.

4 Applying Layered Structure into Formalization by DCOP

In our proposed method, we apply a layered structure into formalization by DCOP. The original resource allocation problem in the distributed sensor network is divided into two problems that represent the leader election problem and the observation resource allocation problem. These two problems are rather easy compared to the original problem. It is thought that this formalization can integrate efficient cooperated operation by agency with flexible problem description with constraint network.

4.1 Layer1: Leader Election Problem

In this layer, some agents are elected as leader of a target. In the following, each sensor is identified with an agent. The leader can be considered as the manager of the agency based cooperation model[8]. In this work, we define a rule that each leader must be allocated to its relative target. An example of a sensor network shown in Fig. 2 is formalized as a leader election problem shown in Fig. 6. In

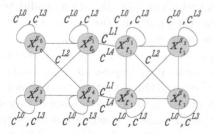

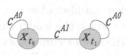

Fig. 6. Leader election problem layer   **Fig. 7.** Resource allocation problem layer

Fig. 6, $x_{t_j}^{s_i}$ represents a variable of s_i for t_j. For each sensor s_i, variables are defined for targets that can be observed by s_i. A value of $x_{t_j}^{s_i}$ represents which sensor is a leader of t_j. If a set of agents that can observe t_j is $\{s_0, \cdots, s_n\}$, the value of $x_{t_j}^{s_i}$ is selected from $\{\phi, s_0, \cdots, s_n\}$. With this formalization, five types of constraints are defined, and they are shown in Fig. 6 as c^{L0}, c^{L1}, c^{L2}, c^{L3} and c^{L4}. Details of the constraints are as follows.

- $c^{L0}(x_{t_j}^{s_i})$: Requirement of a leader for a target
  This constraint represents a requirement that a leader is selected for a target. If there is no leader of the target, the constraint is not fully satisfied. This constraint can be relaxed. The cost function $f_{c^{L0}}$ for c^{L0} is defined as follows. $w^{c^{L0}}$ is the weight parameter which represents the degree of violation.

$$f_{c^{L0}(x_{t_j}^{s_i})} = \begin{cases} w_0^{c^{L0}} & x_{t_j}^{s_i} = \phi \\ 0 & otherwise \end{cases} \quad (6)$$

- $c^{L1}(x_{t_j}^{s_i}, x_{t_{j'}}^{s_i})$: Restriction of a leader
  This constraint represents that each sensor is allocated to one target as its leader. If a sensor is the leader of multiple targets, the constraint is violated. This constraint cannot be relaxed. The cost function $f_{c^{L1}}$ for c^{L1} is defined as follows. $w^{c^{L1}}$ is the weight parameter.

$$f_{c^{L1}(x_{t_j}^{s_i}, x_{t_{j'}}^{s_i})} = \begin{cases} w^{c^{L1}} & x_{t_j}^{s_i} = x_{t_{j'}}^{s_i} \\ 0 & otherwise \end{cases} \quad (7)$$

- $c^{L2}(x_{t_j}^{s_i}, x_{t_j}^{s_{i'}})$: Consistency of allocation of leader
  This constraint represents cooperation that all leaders are elected without contradiction. If the variables' values for the same target are different between sensors, the constraint is violated. This constraint cannot be relaxed. The cost function $f_{c^{L2}}$ for c^{L2} is defined as follows. $w^{c^{L2}}$ is the weight parameter.

$$f_{c^{L2}(x_{t_j}^{s_i}, x_{t_j}^{s_{i'}})} = \begin{cases} w^{c^{L2}} & x_{t_j}^{s_i} \neq x_{t_j}^{s_{i'}} \\ 0 & otherwise \end{cases} \quad (8)$$

- $c^{L3}(x_{t_j}^{s_i})$: Ensuring allocation candidate 1
  This constraint represents a requirement which ensure allocation candidates. Because the leader has to observe the target where the leader has been allocated as mentioned above, the leader is excluded from the allocation candidate of other targets. That may prevent fair sensor resource allocation. For that reason, there are situations where it is impossible to allocate a sufficient number of sensors to a target. To avoid this situation, the number of targets which the leader can observe should be small. If the number of targets that the leader can observe is not minimum value in candidate sensors, the constraint is not fully satisfied. This constraint can be relaxed. The cost function $f_{c^{L3}}$ for c^{L3} is defined as follows. $w^{c^{L3}}$ is the weight parameter. In

expression (9), S_{t_j} represents that set of sensors which can observe t_j and v_i represents the number of targets which can be observed by s_i.

$$f_{c^{L3}(x_{t_j}^{s_i})} = \begin{cases} w^{c^{L3}} & \exists s \in S_{t_j}, v_s < v_{x_{t_j}^{s_i}} \\ 0 & otherwise \end{cases} \tag{9}$$

- $c^{L4}(x_{t_j}^{s_i}, x_{t_{j'}}^{s_i})$: Ensuring allocation candidate 2
   This constraint represents a requirement which ensure allocation candidates. This is a constrain for avoiding situations where areas that can be observed by leaders are overlapped. Especially, in the grid model, each sensor can observe its four adjoining areas. If two or more adjoining areas of a leader overlap with another leader's adjoining areas, the constraint is not fully satisfied. This constraint can be relaxed. The cost function $f_{c^{L4}}$ for c^{L4} is defined as follows. $w^{c^{L4}}$ is the weight parameter. In expression (10), R_{s_i} represents set of areas that can be observed by s_i.

$$f_{c^{L4}(x_{t_j}^{s_i}, x_{t_{j'}}^{s_i})} = \begin{cases} w^{c^{L4}} & |R_{x_{t_j}^{s_i}} \cap R_{x_{t_{j'}}^{s_i}}| > 1 \\ 0 & otherwise \end{cases} \tag{10}$$

The number of variables in the leader election problem is the same as STAV. However, in this problem, each variable's domain contains five values because there are four agents which can observe each target. In STAV, each variable's domain contains 16 values. Therefore, the leader election problem is easier than STAV. On the other hand, this model can be considered that agents decide which agents own variables in TAV.

4.2   Layer2: Observation Resource Allocation Problem

In this layer, the observation resource allocation problem is solved by leaders. The leaders exchange information and solve the problem. Agents which are not leader follow leaders' decisions. Because one leader is elected each target in the layer of leader election problem, an example of a sensor network shown Fig. 2 is formalized as an observation resource allocation problem shown in Fig. 7. In Fig. 7, x_{t_j} is a variable of leader of t_j. A value of x_{t_j} represents which sensors are allocated to t_j. If a set of sensors that can observe t_j is $\{s_0, \cdots, s_n\}$, x_{t_j} takes a combination of sensors as a value. $\{\phi, \{s_0\}, \cdots, \{s_n\}, \{s_0, s_1\}, \cdots, \{s_0, \cdots, s_n\}\}$ is the domain of x_{t_j}. With this formalization, two types of constraints are defined, and they are shown in Fig. 7 as c^{A0} and c^{A1}. Details of the constraints are as follows.

- $c^{A0}(x_{t_j})$: Allocating sensors to targets
   This constraint represents a requirement that three sensors are allocated to a target. If the number of sensors allocated to t_j is fewer than three, the constraint is not fully satisfied. In such case, this constraint can be relaxed. The cost function $f_{c^{A0}}$ for c^{A0} is defined as follows. $w^{c^{A0}}$ is the weight parameter which represents degree of violation. In expression (11), a value of n_{t_j} represents the number of sensors allocated to t_j.

$$f_{c^{A0}(x_{t_j})} = \begin{cases} w_0^{c^{A0}} & n_{t_j} = 0 \\ w_1^{c^{A0}} & n_{t_j} = 1 \\ w_2^{c^{A0}} & n_{t_j} = 2 \\ 0 & otherwise \end{cases} \tag{11}$$

– $c^{A1}(x_{t_j}, x_{t_{j'}})$: Restriction of observation resource
This constraint represents a restriction about the number of targets to which a sensor is allocated. If a sensor is allocated to multiple targets, the constraint is violated. This constraint cannot be relaxed. The cost function $f_{c^{A1}}$ for c^{A1} is defined as follows. $w^{c^{A1}}$ is the weight parameter.

$$f_{c^{A1}(x_{t_j}, x_{t_{j'}})} = \begin{cases} w^{c^{A1}} & x_{t_j} \cap x_{t_{j'}} \neq \phi \\ 0 & otherwise \end{cases} \tag{12}$$

Because the representation of the constraint network of this layer is similar to using TAV, the number of variables in this layer is fewer than the number of variables in using STAV. So the constraint network is sparser. Moreover, because the leader must observe at a target, the number of values that can be taken by variables is reduced. Therefore, it is thought that the problem in this layer is solved easily.

4.3   Synchronization between Two Layers

It is necessary to synchronize between two layers in the proposed method. On the other hand, each agent needs only information of agents which are related by constraints. In other words, each agent can solve own problem by receiving information from agents which relate by constraints. In the proposed method, each agent elected as a leader sends messages to agents which have the possibility of relating by constraint on a resource allocation problem. In this way, each agent can realize which agent is a leader and shift to solving the resource allocation problem. Conditions to judge that s_i has been selected as a leader are defined as follows.

– The agent is a leader for one of targets: if J is a set of targets which can be observed by s_i, this condition is defined as follows.

$$l_1 = \begin{cases} true & \exists t_j \in J, x_{t_j}^{s_i} = s_i \\ false & otherwise \end{cases} \tag{13}$$

– All of hard constraints of s_i in leader election problem are satisfied: if C is a set of hard constraints of s_i in leader election problem, this condition is defined as follows.

$$l_2 = \begin{cases} true & \forall c \in C, f_c = 0 \\ false & otherwise \end{cases} \tag{14}$$

If $l_1 \wedge l_2 = true$, the agent is a leader and sends messages to other agents. When the problem has not been globally solved, there is a possibility that $l_1 \wedge l_2$ become

```
1   initialize variables;
2   is_leader ← false;
3   empty leader_list;
4   while not terminated do
5       previous_status ← is_leader;
6       receive messageses from other agents related by constraints;
7       clear current_status;
8       if new leader has been elected then
9           add new leader to leader_list;
10          store the information of new leader into current_status;
11      end if
12      if elected leader came off then
13          remove old leader from leader_list;
14          store the information of removed leader into current_status;
15      end if
16      call maintenance of DSTS for solving leader election;
17      if previous_status = false then
18          if l₁ ∧ l₂ = true then
19              is_leader ← true;
20              store is_leader into current_status;
21      end if
22      if previous_status = true then
23          if l₁ ∧ l₂ = false then
24              is_leader ← false;
25              store is_leader into current_status;
26          end if
27      end if
28      if is_leader = true then
29          call maintenance of DSTS for resource allocation problem
30      end if
31      send current_status and variables' values to agents related by the constraints.
32  end while
```

Fig. 8. Pseudo code of the proposed method

$false$ again. At that time, the agent send message about $l_1 \wedge l_2 = false$ to the others. In proposed method, the agent send messages to other agents which are related by constraints, instead of sending to all agents. That reduces message passing cost. However, non-neighborhood agents on the grid can be related by constraints. Considering that case, each agent propagates the message. In the grid model, each agent has to propagate message only one hop. A pseudo code of the proposed method is shown in Fig. 8. In Fig. 8, is_leader represents whether the agent is a leader. leader_list represents list of leaders. Information about the election of leaders is stored in current_status. "maintenance" procedures in Fig. 1 are performed for each layer. As shown in the line 31 of Fig. 8, a couple of current_status and variables' values of two layers of problems are sent at a same time.

5   Experiments

We compared the proposed methods with previous method using STAV and evaluated the efficiency of dividing the problem into two problems which can be solved comparatively easily. The previous method is shown as STAV, and

Table 1. Parameters of DSTS

	p_1	p_2	tabu period
STAV	0.8	0.4	1 cycle
LYR			
Layer1	0.9	0.3	2 cycles
Layer2	0.7	0.2	1 cycle

Table 2. Weight parameters

STAV		LYR Layer1		Layer2	
c^{ST0}	$w_0^{c^{ST0}} = 15$ $w_1^{c^{ST0}} = 5$ $w_2^{c^{ST0}} = 1$	c^{L0}	$w^{c^{L0}} = 10$	c^{A0}	$w_0^{c^{A0}} = 15$ $w_1^{c^{A0}} = 5$ $w_2^{c^{A0}} = 1$
		c^{L1}	$w^{c^{L1}} = 200$		
		c^{L2}	$w^{c^{L2}} = 100$		
c^{ST1}	$w^{c^{ST1}} = 200$	c^{L3}	$w_0^{c^{L3}} = 1$	c^{A1}	$w^{c^{A1}} = 200$
c^{ST2}	$w^{c^{ST2}} = 100$	c^{L4}	$w^{c^{L4}} = 1$		

the proposed method is shown as LYR. While several algorithms are applied to similar problem[5]. We applied DSTS that is a extended version of DSA in both methods. In LYR, we applied DSTSs to two layers of problems shown in Fig. 8. Original DSTS does not have termination detection mechanism. Therefore we apply a simple rule to DSTS for termination. We define the suboptimal solution as a solution which satisfies all hard constraints. We also evaluated the cases that any soft constraints are not optimized. In other words, the weight parameters of soft constraints are 0. Moreover, in LYR, we evaluated the cases that the soft constraints are not optimized in resource allocation problem. The experiment aims to evaluate impact of optimality of leader election problem to global optimality. Those methods are shown as follows.

- STAV: Previous method that all constraints are considered in optimization.
- STAV-NoOpt: Previous method that any soft constraints are not optimized.
- LYR: Proposed method that all constraints are considered in optimization.
- LYR-NoOpt: Proposed method that any soft constraints are not optimized.
- LYR-NoOptInAllo: Proposed method that any soft constraints relaxed in resource allocation problem are not optimized.

The experiments are performed using simulation programs. The simulation iterates cycles of globally synchronized processing shown as follows.

(1) Each agent receives messages and processes the local part.
(2) Each agent sends messages to the other agents if necessary.

We evaluated the number of cycles when a solution is found, distance of cost of suboptimal solution and cost of optimal solution, the number of sensors allocated to a target, and the number of messages. The maximum number of cycles for a trial is limited to 1000. If a solution could not be found within the 1000 cycles, the number of cycles is considered as the upper limit value. In such case, the result of the trial is not included in other evaluations. We prepare four problem classes. There are ten instances in each class. The result of a class is the average of result of all instances in the class. For each instance 1000 trials are performed.

5.1   Parameters of DSTS and Weight Parameters of Constraints

Parameters of DSTS are shown in Table 1. The parameters are decided according to the best results of preliminary experiments. Weight parameters of DSTS are shown in Table 2. The total degrees of violations of soft constraints must be smaller than a weight parameter of a hard constraint. Moreover, the weight parameters of hard constraints are set according to the total number of constraints. If the type of hard constraints is mostly contained in problem instances, relatively small weight value is set for the constraint. That aims to keep a balance on total weight parameters. The balance is expected to reduce number of search iterations because it reduces cases of local optima. In leader election problem, in order to elect a leader in all targets as much as possible, w^{L0} is bigger than w^{L3} and w^{L4}.

5.2   Change Conditions of Variable's Value and Termination Rule

In addition to the above parameter settings, we modified change conditions of variable's value of DSTS. The modifications aim to obtain the best result for each method. And as shown above, we have applied termination rule to DSTS.

- Condition to take other values of variables
  In leader election problem of LYR, the variable's value is changed with probability p_1 if $\Delta > 0$. On the other hand, in STAV and resource allocation problem of LYR, the variable's value is changed with probability p_1 if $\Delta \geq 0$. This condition increases frequency to get out from local optimal because it increases neighborhood solutions that can be selected as the locally best solution.
- Condition to find the solution early
  Each agent changes the variable's value with p_2 if $\Delta < 0$ when the agent has a violation for hard constraints. This condition is applied to STAV and LYR. By this condition, each agent does not change the values if $\Delta < 0$ when the agent satisfied the all of the hard constraints. It aims to find suboptimal solution in fewer number of cycles.
- Termination rule to decide a suboptimal solution
  If each agent changes the variable's value when $\Delta \geq 0$, the agent cannot decide a solution because there is no rule to choose one solution from the set of solutions which have same degree of violation . Therefore, when the agent satisfied all of the hard constraints, the agent changes the variable's value with probability p_1 if $\Delta > 0$. This rule is applied to DSTS of STAV and LYR. By this rule, each agent does not change variable's value even if there are some solutions which have same degree of violation.

5.3   Problem Settings

We prepared four classes of problem. Each problem is generated according to t and n as parameters. t decides the number of targets. n decides the limitation number of targets which exist in each target's adjoining area. We used the parameters $t = 5, 10$ and $n = 2, 3$. Problems are generated as follows.

(1) The first target is placed on an area at random. (2) The next candidate areas to place a new target are the empty adjoining areas of target. (3) The area where

the number of adjacent targets is more than n is excluded from the candidates. (4) The new target is placed into an area that is randomly selected from the candidate areas. (5) Repeat 2 to 4 until the number of target becomes t.

5.4   Results

The number of cycles until finding suboptimal solution are shown as Fig. 9(a). The results show that LYR needs less number of cycles. Main reason of the result is that complexity of the problem is reduced by dividing the problem into two layers. In the results of STAV-NoOpt, less number of cycles is required, when compared to STAV. It is a reasonable result because optimization problem is more difficult than satisfaction problem.

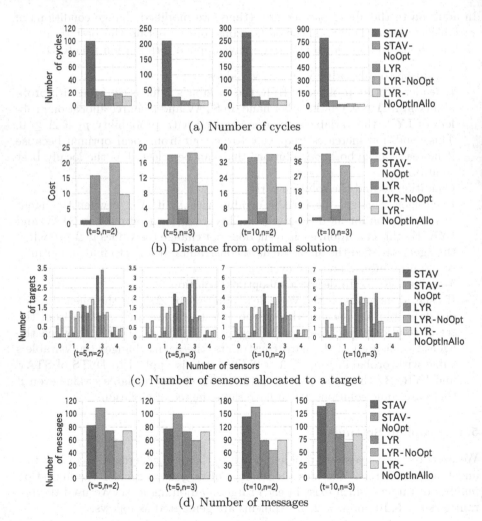

(a) Number of cycles

(b) Distance from optimal solution

(c) Number of sensors allocated to a target

(d) Number of messages

Fig. 9. Results

The difference of cost between suboptimal solution and optimal solution are shown as Fig. 9(b). The result shows that LYR's cost is larger than STAV's cost. A reason of this drawback is local optimal solution in leader election problem. Such local optimal solution causes a situation that some targets are ignored in sensor resource allocation by relaxing soft constraints. In addition, number of sensors which can be allocated for each target is often disproportional in sensor resource allocation layer. That is caused by a bias of greedy decision in leader election. There might be targets which can not be allocated enough number of sensors according to the leader's arrangement. Costs of STAV-NoOpt, LYR-NoOpt and LYR-NoOptInAllo are relatively large, because these methods do not optimize soft constraints as mentioned above.

The number of sensors allocated to a target are shown as Fig. 9(c). The number of targets with no sensors in LYR is more than in STAV. However, this difference is relatively small. In LYR, the number of sensors allocated to a target is disproportional due to the bias in leader election. In the case of STAV-NoOpt, LYR-NoOpt and LYR-NoOptInAllo, the number of sensors allocated to targets is relatively few.

The number of messages per cycle are shown as Fig. 9(d). Each agent sends messages to other agents which are related by constraints. However, each agent does not have to send messages if its variables' value are not changed. Therefore, in the leader election of LYR, each agent that has been found a local suboptimal solution does not send the message. Leaders have to send message of resource allocation problem. In resource allocation problem, the number of messages sent by leader is fewer than the number of messages in leader election. The reason of less number of messages is that only leader agents are related with constraints in the resource allocation problem. In addition, the messages for synchronization are not sent if it is not necessary. Therefore, the number of messages per cycle is reduced by LYR. On the other hand, in the later period of search, the number of agents that have been found local suboptimal solution is increased. That relatively decreases average number of messages in the methods that need much number of cycles. Therefore, in STAV and LYR-NoOpthe, the number of messages per cycle is comparatively few.

In LYR, although the number of cycles is significantly reduced, the number of sensors allocated to a target is disproportional. However, we think this type of trade off can be acceptable in some actual systems that need fast reasons. On the other hand, the number of sensors allocated to target by LYR is more than that by STAV-NoOPt, LYR-NoOPt and LYR-NoOptInAllo. Therefore LYR is more effective than those methods.

6   Conclusions

In this paper, we proposed a DCOP based cooperative resource allocation method for distributed sensor network systems. In the proposed method, the problem is divided into two layers of sub-problems: leader election and sensor resource allocation. Then a stochastic DCOP solvers is applied to each layer of problems. The solvers cooperate with partial synchronization. Experimental result shows that proposed method significantly reduces number of cycles in distributed search processing. It is efficient to divide the complex problem into two or more comparatively easy problems. On the other hand, the number of sensors allocated to a target is disproportional due to bias of leader election problems. More detailed analysis, applying other previous algorithms including DSA[2], improving design of constraints and search strategy, and applying to practical observation systems are included in future works.

References

1. Modi, P.J., Shen, W.M., Tambe, M., Yokoo, M.: ADOPT: Asynchronous Distributed Constraint Optimization with Quality Guarantees. Artifi. Intell. 161, 149–180 (2005)
2. Zhang, W., Wang, O., Wittenburg, L.: Distributed stochastic search for constraint satisfaction and optimization: Parallelism, phase transitions and performance. In: AAAI Workshop on Probabilistic Approaches in Search, pp. 53–59 (2002)
3. Iizuka, Y., Suzuki, H., Takeuchi, I.: Multi-agent tabu search method for distributed constraint satisfaction problems (in japan). The IEICE Transactions on Information and Systems J90-D(9), 2302–2313 (2007)
4. Farinelli, A., Rogers, A., Petcu, A., Jennings, N.R.: Decentralised Coordination of Low-Power Embedded Devices Using the Max-Sum Algorithm. In: AAMAS, pp. 639–646 (2008)
5. Bejar, R., Domshilak, C., Fernandez, C., Gomes, C., Krishnamachari, B., Selman, B., Valls, M.: Sensor networks and distributed csp. Artif. Intell. 161, 117–147 (2005)
6. Ali, S., Koenig, S., Tambe, M.: Preprocessing techniques for accelerating the DCOP algorithm ADOPT. In: AAMAS, July 2005, pp. 1041–1048 (2005)
7. Petcu, A., Faltings, B.: A scalable method for multiagent constraint optimization. In: IJCAI, August 2005, pp. 266–271 (2005)
8. Ukita, N.: Real-time Dense Communication among Agents for Active Tracking. In: AAMAS, July 2005, pp. 1335–1336 (2005)

NegoExplorer: A Region-Based Recursive Approach to Bilateral Multi-attribute Negotiation*

Miguel A. Lopez-Carmona, Ivan Marsa-Maestre, Enrique de la Hoz, and Juan R. Velasco

Computer Engineering Department, Universidad de Alcala
Escuela Politecnica, 28871, Alcala de Henares (Madrid), Spain
{miguelangel.lopez,ivan.marsa,enrique.delahoz,juanramon.velasco}@uah.es

Abstract. Most real-world negotiations involve multiple, interdependent issues or attributes. These negotiation scenarios are specially challenging because agents' preferences on the attributes may be non-monotonic. The existing works in the area of non-monotonic preference scenarios are mainly restricted to mediated approaches and to very specific agents' preference models. In this research we propose NegoExplorer, a generic framework for non-mediated automated bilateral multi-attribute negotiations. NegoExplorer is based on a region-based recursive bargaining mechanism. The mechanism is named recursive because agents negotiate on regions and not on specific contracts in the negotiation space, and because an agreement on a region implies a new bargaining which is constrained to that region. Agents may reach an agreement on a contract by iteratively applying this recursive mechanism. In order to evaluate the effectiveness of our proposal we have compared it with a classical similarity based negotiation protocol. The preliminary results are promising, showing better results in terms of utility and negotiation time for the case of non-monotonic and non-differentiable utility spaces, and similar results for monotonic spaces. We believe that the ideas presented in this paper may be the starting point of a new family of negotiation mechanisms.

1 Introduction

Automated multi-attribute negotiation is an important research area in agent and multi-agent systems [1,2]. It provides an important mechanism for distributed decision makers to reach agreements on multiple issues or attributes. Similarity based protocols [3,4], where an agent chooses the offer with the shortest distance (or more similar) to the best offer made by the opponent in the previous period from her current indifference curve/surface, evolutionary algorithms [5], or mediated negotiation protocols [6,7,8,9], have been successfully

---

* This work has been partially developed in the framework of the European ITEA-2 project 2008005, "Do-it-Yourself Smart Experiences", and partially supported by the Spanish Ministry of Education and Science grant TIN2008-06739-C04-04.

J.-J. Yang et al. (Eds.): PRIMA 2009, LNAI 5925, pp. 261–275, 2009.

used in multi-attribute negotiation. However, most of these approaches have been focused on negotiations where agents' preferences on the different issues are independent, while most real-world negotiations involve multiple, interdependent issues. These scenarios are specially challenging, since issue interdependencies may yield non-monotonic and even non-differentiable utility functions for the agents, and thus the mentioned mechanisms cannot be applied.

The literature shows great achievements from researchers in complex negotiation scenarios where agents' preferences are non-monotonic. Klein et al. [10], Ito et al. [11] and Marsa et al. [12,13] propose and evaluate a set of mediated mechanisms which operate in highly non-monotonic scenarios. The proposals overcome the difficulty of multiparty negotiations and non-monotonic preferences with the aid of a mediator. In [10] the agents' preferences are defined as binary issues, while in [11,12,13] the preference model is restricted to constraint-based nonlinear utility spaces. Hindriks et al. [14] propose to approximate the utility functions by means of linear regression techniques or average weighting methods, which is only applicable for smooth utility functions. Lopez-Carmona et al. [15,16] suggest the use of expressive negotiation protocols, which use gradient information and relax requirements to bias the search for solutions in non-mediated negotiations.

Though these works have reached great achievements, there is still need of research in generic negotiation models which operate under complex preference structures. In this paper we propose a novel generic framework for non-mediated bilateral multi-attribute negotiation which is able to operate under non-monotonic and non-differentiable utility spaces. The negotiation mechanisms proposed are based on the exchange of regions of the negotiation space. The joint exploration of the solution space is recursive, which means that when agents agree on an offer (a region proposed by an agent), then a new negotiation on regions of a lower size is performed within the previously agreed region. If a new agreement is not possible, agents may return to upper level regions to perform new searches. The framework proposed will be compared with a classical similarity based approach, and evaluated under monotonic and non-monotonic scenarios. Based on these ideas, our research work opens the door to a new family a negotiation mechanisms which could be extended to mediated and multiparty scenarios. The rest of the paper is organized as follows. In Section 2 we present our negotiation framework. In Section 3 we evaluate the negotiation framework and compare it with a classical similarity based approach. The last section summarizes our conclusions and sheds light on some future research.

2   A Framework for Region-Based Recursive Bilateral Multi-attribute Negotiation

We consider a bargaining protocol performed concurrently and synchronously by two agents. The only restriction for the description of agents' preferences is that the issues under negotiation must define an euclidean space, where issues can take values from the real or integer domain. Without loss of generality, in this paper we will assume both quasi-concave utility functions and non-monotonic utility functions, and a real domain for the issues under negotiation. However, the framework proposed could be used for instance with any fuzzy, weighted or probabilistic constraint-based utility function [17].

2.1 The Preference Structure

We define the issues under negotiation as a finite set of variables $X = \{x_i|i = 1, \ldots, n\}$, where each issue x_i can be normalized to a continuous range $d_i = [0, 100]$. Thus, the negotiation domain can be denoted by $D = [0, 100]^n$. A contract is a vector $s = \{x_i^s|i = 1, \ldots, n\}$ defined by the issues' values. Each agent $A_{i \in \{b,s\}}$ embeds an utility function $U_i : D \rightarrow \mathbb{R}$ that gives the payoff the agent assigns to a given contract. The preferences on the issues of each agent are rational, and can be non-monotonic and non-differentiable. The NegoExplorer framework relies on the concept of *region*. The basic idea is to iteratively and recursively perform a joint search for regions of the utility space where efficient agreements can be found.

Definition 1. *A region of the n-dimensional negotiation space of agent A_i is formed by the set of contracts lying within the hypersphere defined as a 2-tuple $R = <c, r>$, where $c \in D$ and $r \in \mathbb{R}$ define the hypersphere center and radius. We name the region $R = <c, r>$ as a region of size r.*

An agent can estimate the *overall satisfaction degree (osd)* of a region in terms of the utility of the contracts which fall within the region. In order to compute the osd estimate, an agent uniformly samples the negotiation space within the region and evaluates the utility of each sampled contract.

Definition 2. *The overall satisfaction degree (osd) of a region R for an agent A_i, is an estimate of the overall utility of the region for that agent. Let $S_{nsc}^R = \{s_k \in D|k = 1, \ldots, nsc\}$ be a set of nsc uniformly distributed contracts in R, u_{th} the utility threshold or reservation value for any contract, and $S_{nsc_{u_{th}}}^R$ the subset of l acceptable contracts in S_{nsc}^R which satisfy $U_i(s_k) \geq u_{th}$. An agent A_i computes the osd of a region R by means of the following formula:*

$$osd(A_i, R) = \gamma \cdot \frac{l}{nsc} + (1 - \gamma) \cdot \frac{\sum_{s_k \in S_{nsc_{u_{th}}}^R} (U_i(s_k) - u_{th})}{l \cdot (1 - u_{th})}.$$

The parameter γ weights the ratio of the number of contracts above the utility threshold, and the normalized overall utility surplus for contracts above the utility threshold. In an extreme, for $\gamma = 1$, the osd computation depends only on the number of contracts with an utility value above the utility threshold. For $\gamma = 0$, only the utility values from the filtered contracts are considered. The idea behind this definition of osd is that an agent can consider separately both the probability that a random contract in R falls above u_{th}, and the utility of the acceptable contracts.

2.2   The Negotiation Protocol

We adopt a simultaneous-offer game protocol. Agents make their offers (proposals) available at the same time. Also, the responses to the offers are made available simultaneously. This can be made using secret keys to encript offers and responses. In a given period of the negotiation process, an agent reveals the secret key only when it has received the encripted offer or response from the opponent.

An offer of agent A_i in period $t \in \mathbb{N}^+$ can be defined as a single-region R_i^t. Based on the simultaneous-offer game concept defined above, and the notion of region, our negotiation protocol is formalized as a set of sequential *bargaining threads*.

Definition 3. *A negotiation dialogue* $\mathcal{N}_d = \{b_{r_{i1}}^{t_0} \rightarrow b_{r_{i2}}^{t_1} \rightarrow \ldots\}$ *is a sequence of bargaining threads, where each thread starts in a period* t_n. *Each* bargaining thread $b_{r_{im}}^{t_n} = \{(R_b, R_s)_{r_{im}}^{t_n} \rightarrow (res_b, res_s)_{r_{im}}^{t_n+1} \rightarrow (R_b, R_s)_{r_{im}}^{t_n+2} \rightarrow \ldots \rightarrow (R_b, R_s)_{r_{im}}^{t_{n+1}-2} \rightarrow (res_b, res_s)_{r_{im}}^{t_{n+1}-1}\}$ *is a sequential exchange of offers (regions) and responses to the offers, where* $(R_b, R_s)_{r_{im}}^{t_n+a}$ *represents the simultaneous exchange of offers of size* r_{im} *in period* $t_n + a$, *and* $(res_b, res_s)_{r_{im}}^{t_n+a+1}$ *the responses to the offers made in period* $t_n + a$. *There are three types of responses: Accept, Reject, and Suggest. Each bargaining thread is restricted to the exchange of offers of size* r_{im}. *We denote a thread exchanging offers of size* r_{im} *as a bargaing thread of size* r_{im}. *Before the beginning of a negotiation dialogue, it is assumed that agents agree on a finite set of region sizes* $Rs = \{r_i | i = 1, \ldots, m; \forall l < k, r_l > r_k\}$, *being* r_m *the lowest region size and* r_1 *the highest size.*

The main goal of the agents is to reach an agreement on a region of size r_m (i.e. the lowest one). A negotiation starts with a bargaining thread of size r_1. Every time an offer is accepted by the opponent, the current bargaining thread ends, and negotiation moves towards a new thread of lower size. This search is restricted by the domain of the agreement reached in the previous thread. This process can be seen as a search tree which is structured by the set Rs. An agreement on a region of the lowest size means the end of the negotiation. Now, we provide a detailed description of the transition rules which refine how the negotiation progresses through the different bargaining threads:

1. Every negotiation begins with the thread $b_{r_1}^{t_0}$, where the domain of the offers is restricted by the global domain D.
2. For any transition between two threads $b_{r_l}^{t_n} \rightarrow b_{r_k}^{t_{n+1}}$, r_l and r_k must satisfy that $|l - k| = 1$.
3. A descending transition $b_{r_{im}}^{t_n} \rightarrow b_{r_{im+1}}^{t_{n+1}}$ is fired when, in any given period in $b_{r_{im}}^{t_n}$, $R_b^{t_{n+1}-2}$ or $R_s^{t_{n+1}-2}$ or both $R_b^{t_{n+1}-2}$ and $R_s^{t_{n+1}-2}$ are respectively *accepted* as a solution by A_s or A_b or both A_s and A_b. Once a region in $b_{r_{im}}^{t_n}$ has been accepted by the opponent, we can say that $b_{r_{im}}^{t_n}$ is the child of the most recent region accepted in $b_{r_{im-1}}^{t_n-a}$. If two regions are simultaneously accepted, only one region is selected. In order to balance the negotiation power, each agent alternatively selects the preferred region.

4. An ascending transition $b^{tn}_{r_{im}} \rightarrow b^{tn+1}_{r_{im-1}}$ is fired when in any given period in $b^{tn}_{r_{im}}$, A_b or A_s or both A_b and A_s consider that it is *unfeasible* to find an agreement on regions of size r_{im} for the current thread. The unfeasibility condition of a thread is considered below in the negotiation strategy description.

5. The exchange of offers in any given thread $b^{tn}_{r_{im}}$, is confined to the negotiation space defined by the accepted offer in the most recent thread of size r_{im-1} (i.e. $b^{tn-a}_{r_{im-1}}$). This rule enforces the recursive search in the negotiation space. For $b^{tn}_{r_1}$, the search is confined to the global domain of the negotiation space.

6. A negotiation ends when an agreement is reached on a thread $b^{tn}_{r_m}$ (i.e. on a region with the lowest size), or when being the current thread $b^{tn}_{r_1}$, the thread is considered unfeasible and then rule 4 is fired. The negotiation ends without an agreement when, being the current thread $b^{t0}_{r_1}$, the thread is considered unfeasible (i.e. no region of any size has been accepted).

7. Being $b^{tn}_{r_{im}}$ the current thread, in addition to the agreements in the most recent threads from r_{im-1} to r_1, the agents save the most recent and lowest agreement in the negotiation process if any. This rule ensures a solution if the negotiation ends without an agreement on a a region of size r_m.

8. In order to ensure the completion of a negotiation, agents agree on an upper bound $lnbt_{r_{im}}$ for the number of child threads derived from a thread $b^{tn}_{r_{im-1}}$. For $b^{tn}_{r_1}$, an unique virtual father thread is considered. For $b^{tn}_{r_{m-1}}$ the protocol itself enforces that the number of children is limited to one because once $b^{tn}_{r_m}$ comes to an agreement the negotiation ends (see rule 6). It means that the value of $lnbt_{r_m}$ is always 1.

Figure 1 shows an example of a negotiation search tree for $Rs = \{r_1, r_2, r_3\}$ and $Lnbt = \{lnbt_{r_1} = 2, lnbt_{r_2} = 3, lnbt_{r_3} = 1\}$. Each node represents a type of bargaining thread of size r_{im} (i.e. a bargaining thread where agents try to find an agreement on a region of size r_{im}). The general rule that governs the movement through the negotiation search tree is that each node can be visited once only. In the example, the number of different threads where agents can exchange regions

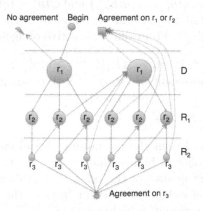

Fig. 1. Example of negotiation search tree

of size r_2 is limited to 6. The threads of a given type (size) are grouped together between two horizontal lines. D, R_1 and R_2 specify the domain of the negotiation space where a bargaining thread works. For example, the two possible instances of bargaining threads of size r_1 in the upper level are confined to the domain D (i.e. the global domain). The solid lines show descending transitions (i.e. a region has been accepted), and the dashed lines ascending transitions (i.e. the current thread is unfeasible). The dotted lines represent ascending transitions for the special case in which the limit of threads in the upper levels has been reached. Though these transitions traverse two or more levels (sizes), in order to satisfy rule 2, we can think of these transitions as a set of partial transitions through adjacent levels, such that an unfeasible virtual bargaining thread automatically fires the different partial transitions.

The transition rules described above determine the joint exploration strategy in the negotiation space. The acceptability of a region, and the unfeasibility of agreements in a bargaining thread govern the transitions between the different threads. The analysis of these elements within the scope of a bargaining thread is covered in the next section. Specifically, we will define how an agent generates an offer, when an offer is accepted or rejected, and how a received offer is valued in order to suggest a new derived offer.

2.3   The Negotiation Strategy

We divide the negotiation strategy of an agent into two components: *responding* and *proposing*. The responding strategy determines whether an agent should *accept, reject* or *suggest the movement* of an offer (region) proposed by the opponent. The proposing strategy determines which offers should be *proposed* to the opponent.

The Responding Strategy: The responding strategy depends on two *osd* thresholds, the *acceptance osd threshold* $(ath_{r_{im}})$, and the *quality osd threshold* $(qth_{r_{im}})$. Each agent defines acceptance and quality thresholds for each region size: $Ath^i = \{ath^i_{r_1}, ath^i_{r_2}, \ldots, ath^i_{r_m}\}$ and $Qth^i = \{qth^i_{r_1}, qth^i_{r_2}, \ldots, qth^i_{r_m}\}$. Thus, let us assume that the current exchange of offers within the bargaining thread $b^{t_n}_{r_{im}}$ is $(R_b, R_s)^{t_n+a}_{r_{im}}$. From the perspective of agent A_b:

1. A_b *accepts* $(R_s)^{t_n+a}_{r_{im}}$, if $osd(A_b, (R_s)^{t_n+a}_{r_{im}}) \geq ath^b_{r_{im}}$;
2. A_b *suggests* the movement of $(R_s)^{t_n+a}_{r_{im}}$ if it is not accepted and $ath^b_{r_{im}} > osd(A_b, (R_s)^{t_n+a}_{r_{im}*fr_{im}} - (R_s)^{t_n+a}_{r_{im}}) \geq qth^b_{r_{im}}$;
3. Otherwise, A_b *rejects* $(R_s)^{t_n+a}_{r_{im}}$.

An offer is accepted and then the bargaining thread ends if the overall satisfaction degree of the offer is higher than $ath_{r_{im}}$. If an offer is not accepted, the agent evaluates the quality of the offer. The evaluation of quality implies the computation of the osd in the surroundings of the offer. Our proposal is to define a concentric region of a higher size $(R_s)^{t_n+a}_{r_{im}*fr_{im}}$ where $fr_{im} > 1$ and $Fr = \{fr_1, fr_2, \ldots, fr_m\}$, and to evaluate the osd of the space between both regions. If the osd is higher than $qth_{r_{im}}$ then the agent responds with a message which includes an offer movement suggestion, and optionally, the computed quality level of the offer; otherwise, the agent rejects the offer. The suggestion of movement is a vector $\vec{vq}_{(R_s)^{tn+a}_{r_{im}}}$ which indicates the preferred direction for the movement of $(R_s)^{tn+a}_{r_{im}}$. In order to obtain $\vec{vq}$, we use the mass center of the filtered samples (those above the reservation value u_{th}) taken in the computation of the osd for the surroundings of the offer. Then, the vector proposed by A_b is characterized by:

$$\vec{vq}_{(R_s)^{tn+a}_{r_{im}}} = norm(\frac{\sum_{s_k \in S^{R_s}_{mu_{th}}} (U_b(s_k) \cdot s_k)}{\sum_{s_k \in S^{R_s}_{mu_{th}}} U_b(s_k)} - c^{tn+a}_s),$$

where the first term is the center of mass, and the second term c^{tn+a}_s is the center of the opponent's offer $(R_s)^{tn+a}_{r_{im}}$. The *norm* function converts the difference into an unit vector.

Figure 2 shows an example of the responding strategy. For simplicity, only the proposals of agent A_b are shown. In Figure 2 (a) A_s rejects R^{tn+1}_b. All the contracts within R^{tn+1}_b give agent A_s a payoff below the threshold $u_{th} = 0.45$, and obviously, $osd(A_s, R^{tn+1}_b)$ will be below the acceptance threshold ath. For

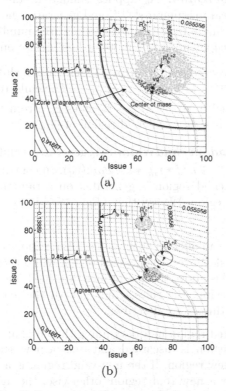

(a)

(b)

Fig. 2. Example of the responding strategy

simplicity in the presentation we assume that the evaluation of quality falls below the threshold qth. In period $t_n + 2$ agent A_b offers $R_b^{t_n+2}$ which also falls below ath. Then agent A_s computes the osd for the region between the two concentric circunferences in order to evaluate the quality of the offer. In this case we have several sample contracts which give A_s an utility above 0.45. If we assume that the osd computed is higher than qth, then the offer is considered to be of a good quality and the vector vq is obtained and sent to agent A_b. In Figure 2 (b) agent A_b attends the suggestion of movement submitted by agent A_s, and proposes $R_b^{t_n+3}$ which is finally accepted by agent A_s.

The Proposing Strategy: The agents generate new offers (proposals) when the previous offers in the thread have not been accepted. In order to generate a new offer an agent evaluates the response of the opponent, a suggest or a reject message, and the history of her past offers. The proposing strategy is based on three basic mechanisms which generate regions, and a set of rules which govern the generation of offers. In the proposing strategy we distinguish between region and offer. A region is a candidate to be an offer, and an offer is a region that has been or is going to be proposed as a solution to the opponent. Let $b_{r_{im}}^{t_n}$ be the current thread, and let us assume the proposing strategy from the perspective of agent A_b. We describe below the mentioned mechanisms and rules.

Generation of a *root region*: A_b applies simulated annealing to her utility function to find a local maximum s^{t_n+a}, and generates the region $(R_b)_{r_{im}}^{t_n+a} =< s^{t_n+a}, r_{im} >$. Depending on the temperature and the number of iterations used by the optimizer, each agent can be more or less precise on the search.

Generation of a *directed child region*: A_b generates a child region $(R_b)_{r_{im}}^{t_n+a+2}$, where $s^{t_n+a+2} = s^{t_n+a} + krf * r_{im} * \bar{vq}_{(R_b)_{r_{im}}^{t_n+a}}$. The child region is generated on the direction proposed in $\bar{vq}$, at $krf \in \mathbb{R}$ times r_{im} from the center s^{t_n+a}. We say that $(R_b)_{r_{im}}^{t_n+a+2}$ is a directed child region of $(R_b)_{r_{im}}^{t_n+a}$.

Generation of a *random child region*: A_b generates a child region $(R_b)_{r_{im}}^{t_n+a+2}$, where $s^{t_n+a+2} = s^{t_n+a} + krf * r_{im} * random(\bar{vq})$. In contrast to a directed child region, the random child region is generated on a random direction from the center of the father region. We say that $(R_b)_{r_{im}}^{t_n+a+2}$ is a random child region of $(R_b)_{r_{im}}^{t_n+a}$.

In order to prepare an offer an agent generates a region by means of any of the mechanisms described above. A generated region will be considered a valid proposal (offer) if its osd is above the acceptance threshold (i.e. $osd(A_b, (R_b)_{r_{im}}^{t_n+a}) \geq ath_{r_{im}}$). In the following, the rules which govern the generation of proposals within a bargaining thread are described.

1. The first generated region in a bargaining thread is always a root region.
2. Any non-valid region is discarded and then a new search is performed in order to find a new region. If the non-valid region is a root region then the agent searchs for a new root region; otherwise, the agent generates a new random child region. The parameter $lnfc$ limits the number of non-valid

child regions of an offer $(R_b)^{t_n+a}_{r_{im}}$. If this limit is reached, the offer $(R_b)^{t_n+a}_{r_{im}}$ is discarded and the agent moves upwards to the discarded offer's father in order to find the new region.

3. The parameter $lnsro$ limits the number of trials when searching for a root offer in a thread. The parameter $lnro$ limits the number of generated root offers during a thread. The thread is considered unfeasible when any of these limits is reached.

4. The rejection by the opponent of an offer implies that the agent moves to the rejected offer's father, and then searchs for a new random child region. If the rejected offer is a root offer then the agent searches for a new root region in order to prepare a new root offer. The parameter $lnrco$ limits the number of rejected children of each offer. If this limit is reached, the offer is discarded and the agent moves upwards to the discarded offer's father in order to prepare a new offer.

5. When an agent receives a suggestion of movement of an offer, she evaluates the expressed quality by the opponent about the offer. If the expressed quality falls below the quality of the offer's father, the agent chooses with a predefined probability to consider the offer as a non-valid or as valid offer. In the first case the agent acts as in rule 4. In the second case the agent tries to generate a directed child region.

6. The parameter $lndro$ limits the number of generated descendants (i.e. offers) for a root offer. If this limit is reached, then the agent generates a new root region.

7. The parameter $lnco$ limits the number of child offers of a given offer. If this limit is reached, then the agent moves one step upwards. It the offer's father is a root offer, then the agent generates a new root region.

It is worth noting that the process for A_s is identical, and that both processes work in paralell. For example, at a given point in the negotiation process, agent A_b may have received a suggestion of movement of her prior proposal, while A_s may have received a reject to her previous offer. It means that under NegoExplorer, negotiation within a bargaining thread is decomposed into two symmetric and decoupled dialogues, one where A_b submits offers and receives accept, suggest or reject messages from A_s, and another one where A_s submits offers and receives responses from A_b.

2.4   The Negotiation Profile

In this section we define the negotiation profile (i.e. we define the parameters which configurate a negotiation scenario). We divide the negotiation profile into two components: the common negotiation profile and the individual negotiation profile. It is assumed that the common negotiation profile is agreed and known by both agents prior to the negotiation dialogue. For the individual negotiation profile we assume an incomplete information setting, which means that an agent does not know the individual negotiation profile of the opponent.

Common negotiation profile: Both agents agree on the issues under negotiation X and on the negotiation space D. In addition, agents agree on a set of bargaining thread sizes $Rs = \{r_1, r_2, \ldots, r_m\}$ and limits $Lnbt = \{lnbt_{r_1}, lnbt_{r_2}, \ldots lnbt_{r_m}\}$.

Individual negotiation profile: All the parameters in the individual profile of an agent are assumed to be private. Each agent A_i owns an utility function U_i, and defines an utility threshold for a contract u_{th}^i. In order to compute de osd of a region, in addition to the utility function and the utility threshold, the agent defines the parameter γ^i and the number nsc of sample contracts per region. The set $Fr^i = \{fr_1^i, fr_2^i, \ldots, fr_m^i\}$ modulates for each region size, the size of the concentric region in order to compute the quality of an offer.

The acceptance and quality thresholds are defined individually for each region size: $Ath^i = \{ath_{r_1}^i, ath_{r_2}^i, \ldots, ath_{r_m}^i\}$ and $Qth^i = \{qth_{r_1}^i, qth_{r_2}^i, \ldots, qth_{r_m}^i\}$.

Finally, the set $Ln^i = \{lnsro^i, lnro^i, lnrco^i, lnco^i, lnfc^i, lndro^i\}$ defines the limits for the proposing strategy of the agent.

3   Experimental Evaluation

For ease of representation we considered two agents bargaining on two issues $X = \{x_1, x_2\}$. We evaluated the proposal for two different scenarios. In the first scenario agents have monotonic preferences on the issues. We use an instance of the utility functions usually adopted in the Cournot game [8] (for other instances the results have been similar):

$$U_b(x_1, x_2) = x_1 \cdot (100 - x_1 - x_2)$$
$$U_s(x_1, x_2) = x_2 \cdot (100 - x_1 - x_2).$$

In the second scenario agents have non-monotonic preferences on the issues. In this case the utility functions are defined as an aggregation of Bell functions. The Bell functions are usually used in the definition of landscapes for the performance evaluation of evolutionary optimizers. Each bell function is defined by its center $c = (c_1, c_2)$, height h, and radius r. Being $d = \sqrt{(x_1 - c_1)^2 + (x_2 - c_2)^2}$ the distance from the center to a point, then the bell function is defined as:

$$fbell(x_1, x_2, c, h, r) = \begin{cases} h - 2h\frac{d}{r^2} & if\, d < r/2, \\ \frac{2h}{r^2}(d - r) & if\, r > d \geq r/2; \end{cases}$$

and the utility function as:

$$U_{b,s}(x_1, x_2) = \sum_{}^{nb} fbell(x_1, x_2, [0, 100]^n, [h_{min}, h_{max}], [r_{min}, r_{max}]) \, .$$

For both scenarios we compare the results to those obtained when applying a non-mediated similarity based approach. For the similarity based approach both agents adopt the time-dependent strategy [18] which is charaterized by:

$$U_i^{obj}(t) = 1 - (1 - u_{th}^i)(\frac{t}{T})^{\frac{1}{\beta_i}} \, ,$$

where $U_i^{obj}(t)$ is the objective utility of agent i in period t (i.e., the opponent's offer in this period needs to provide at least this utility level); T is the negotiation deadline (in periods) for the agent; u_{th}^i is the reservation utility (utility threshold) of agent i for this negotiation (i.e., the lowest utility level that is willing to accept); and $\beta_i > 0$ represents the strategy parameter of agent i. In order to generate an offer, an agent updates her objective utility, and then applies an optimizer to obtain a contract with the updated objective utility and which is close to the opponent last offer. An opponent's offer is accepted if its utility is higher than the current objective utility. In the generation of offers two different optimizers have been used. In the monotonic scenario the utility functions are differentiable, and so, a gradient based optimizer is used. In the non-monotonic scenario gradient based optimizers are not applicable, and then, a direct search optimizer has been applied.

3.1   Experimental Settings

We evaluate the performances of the different approaches measuring the distances of an outcome from the Pareto frontier, and the negotiation time. For each pair of agents' utility functions we compute the Pareto frontier. The Pareto frontier is computed analytically for the Cournot functions, and using an genetic optimizer for the Bell functions. In each experiment, we ran 100 negotiations between agents.

Monotonic scenario

- Utility functions: $U_b(x_1, x_2) = x_1 \cdot (100 - x_1 - x_2)$; $U_s(x_1, x_2) = x_2 \cdot (100 - x_1 - x_2)$.
- Negotiation profile for the Similarity based approach: $T = 50$; $\beta_{b,s}$ in the range $[0.2\,1.5]$; and $u_{th}^{b,s}$ in the range $[0.3\,0.7]$ for the objective utility of the agents. Agents use a gradient based optimizer to generate offers. The optimizer minimizes the euclidean distance to the opponent last offer, constrained to the contracts lying in the isocurve defined by her current objective utility.
- Negotiation profile for the NegoExplorer approach:

$$A_{b,s}$$
$$[r_1 = 20, r_{\{1,2,5,10,15\}} = 0.1](equally\ spaced), Lnbt = \{3, 3, \ldots 1\}$$
$$u_{th}^{b,s} = [0.3\,0.7], \gamma^{b,s} = 0.15, nsc = 64, Fr^{b,s} = \{2 \cdot r_1, r_1, r_2, \ldots, r_{m-1}\}$$
$$ath_{r1\ldots m}^{b,s} = 0.15, qth_{r1\ldots m}^{b,s} = 0.05$$
$$Ln^{b,s} = \{lndro = 50, ln\{sro, ro, rco, co, fc\} = 2\}$$

Non-monotonic scenario

- Utility functions: $U_{b,s}(x_1, x_2) = \sum^{200} fbell(x_1, x_2, [0, 100]^n, [0.1, 1], [2, 10])$.
- Negotiation profile for the Similarity based approach: $T = 10$; $\beta_{b,s}$ in the range $[0.2\,1.5]$; and $u_{th}^{b,s}$ in the range $[0.1\,0.2]$ for the objective utility of the

agents. Agents use a direct search optimizer to generate offers. The optimizer minimizes the euclidean distance to the opponent last offer, constrained to the contracts lying in the isocurve defined by her current objective utility. The optimizer is restricted to 5 seconds in each optimization process.

– Negotiation profile for the NegoExplorer approach:

$$A_{b,s}$$

$$[r_1 = 10, r_{15} = 0.1](equally \ spaced), Lnbt = \{3, 3, \dots 1\}$$

$$u_{th}^{b,s} = [0.1 \ 0.2], \gamma^{b,s} = 0.15, nsc = 512, Fr^{b,s} = \{2 \cdot r_1, r_1, r_2, \dots, r_{m-1}\}$$

$$ath_{r1\dots15}^{b,s} = 0.2, qth_{r1\dots15}^{b,s} = 0.15$$

$$Ln^{b,s} = \{lndro = 50, ln\{sro, ro, rco, co, fc\} = 2\}$$

3.2   Experimental Results

Figures 3 and 4 show the results of the experiments respectively for the monotonic and non-monotonic scenarios. The graphics on the left are for the similarity based approach, and the graphics on the right for the NegoExplorer approach.

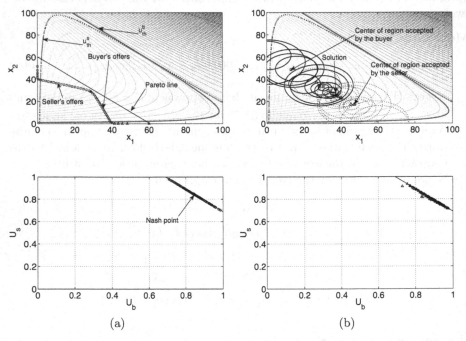

(a)   (b)

Fig. 3. (a) Example of negotiation ($u_{th}^{b,s} = 0.7; \beta_{b,s} = 0.8; T = 50$) and the results for 100 negotiations under the monotonic scenario settings for the similarity based approach. (b) Example of negotiation and the results for 100 negotiations under the monotonic scenario settings for NegoExplorer.

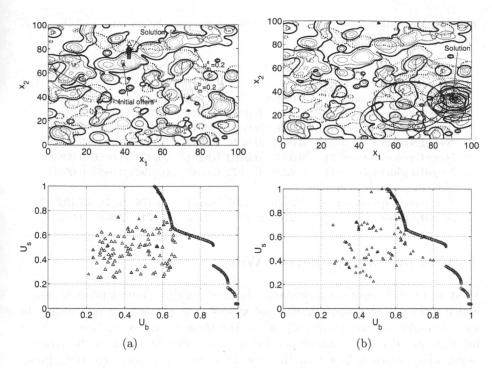

Fig. 4. Example of negotiation and the results for 100 negotiations under the non-monotonic scenario for (a) similarity based approach ($u_{th}^{b,s} = 0.2; \beta_{b,s} = 1; T - 10$), and (b) NegoExplorer

The graphics at the bottom report the utilities achieved by the agents for 100 negotiations. The upper graphics show an example of negotiation in the solution plane.

In Table 1 we report the numerical results of the experiments. In order to analyze the effectiveness of the recursive element in the proposed negotiation protocol, for the NegoExplorer approach in the monotonic scenario we have tested different values for the length of the set Rs.

For the monotonic scenario the Similarity and NegoExplorer approaches perform similar. The Similarity approach performs better in terms of distance to the pareto frontier, but it is slower than NegoExplorer. The experiments with the different values for the m parameter confirm the effectiveness of the recursive approach. For $m = 1$ ($r_1 = 0.1$) the distance to the pareto frontier is 10 times higher than for $m = 15$. In the non-monotonic scenario NegoExplorer performs better in time and distance. The most significant improvement has been achieved in the negotiation time, where NegoExplorer is 15 times faster. It must be noted that for the similarity approach we have limited the optimizers to 5 seconds per execution. We have conducted experiments without explicit time limits, but the results does not improve those reached with the 5 seconds limit.

Table 1. Mean distance to the Pareto-frontier, mean negotiation time, and the corresponding 95% confidence intervals

	Distance	Negotiation Time
Monotonic scenario		
Similarity approach	0.00064 [0.0006 0.0007]	1.5133 [1.4069 1.6197]
NegoExplorer ($m = 15$)	0.0027 [0.0017 0.0037]	0.7529 [0.7399 0.7659]
NegoExplorer ($m = 10$)	0.0037 [0.0027 0.0047]	0.4724 [0.4710 0.4738]
NegoExplorer ($m = 5$)	0.0071 [0.0046 0.0097]	0.2480 [0.2439 0.2520]
NegoExplorer ($m = 2$)	0.0208 [0.0163 0.0254]	0.0973 [0.0956 0.0989]
NegoExplorer ($m = 1$)	0.0228 [0.0172 0.0285]	0.0496 [0.0487 0.0505]
Non-monotonic scenario		
Similarity approach	0.2746 [0.2567 0.3125]	48.476 [34.76 62.192]
NegoExplorer	0.2161 [0.1847 0.2475]	3.7741 [2.8682 4.68]

4   Conclusions and Future Work

Most real-world negotiation scenarios involve multiple, interdependent issues which yield non-monotonic preference spaces. The problem of negotiating in such scenarios is computationally hard. For these scenarios, in this paper we have presented a novel framework for non-mediated bilateral multi-attribute negotiation, which is based on the idea of region-based recursive bargaining. We have compared the proposal with a classical similarity based negotiation protocol. The preliminary results are promising, showing better results in terms of utility and negotiation time than the similarity based approach for the case of non-monotonic utility spaces, and similar results for monotonic spaces.

The presented framework exhibits a high number of configurable parameters that should be evaluated in depth. For instance, we have used in the experiments a flat configuration for the acceptance and quality thresholds. However, other configuration should be explored and analyzed. In addition to a more detailed analysis of the negotiation profiles, the negotiation framework could be extended to mediated and multiparty negotiation scenarios.

References

1. Lai, G., Li, C., Sycara, K., Giampapa, J.: Literature review on multiattribute negotiations. Technical Report CMU-RI-TR-04-66, Robotics Institute, Carnegie Mellon University, Pittsburgh, USA (December 2004)
2. Fatima, S., Wooldridge, M.J., Jennings, N.R.: An agenda based framework for multi-issues negotiation. Artificial Intelligent Journal 152(1), 1–45 (2004)
3. Faratin, P., Sierra, C., Jennings, N.R.: Using similarity criteria to make issue trade-offs in automated negotiations. Artificial Intelligence 142(2), 205–237 (2002)
4. Lai, G., Sycara, K.: A generic framework for automated multi-attribute negotiation. Group Decision and Negotiation 18, 169–187 (2009)

5. Lau, R.Y., Tang, M., Wong, O.: Towards genetically optimised responsive negotiation agents. In: Society, I.C. (ed.) Proceedings of the IEEE/WIC/ACM International Conference on Intelligent Agent Technology (IAT 2004), Beijing, China, September 20-24, pp. 295–301. IEEE Computer Society, Los Alamitos (2004)
6. Ehtamo, H., Hamalainen, R.P., Heiskanen, P., Teich, J., Verkama, M., Zionts, S.: Generating pareto solutions in a two-party setting: constraint proposal methods. Management Science 45(12), 1697–1709 (1999)
7. Heiskanen, P., Ehtamo, H., Hamalainen, R.P.: Constraint proposal method for computing pareto solutions in multi-party negotiations. European Journal of Operational Research 133(1), 44–61 (2001)
8. Gatti, N., Amigoni, F.: An approximate pareto optimal cooperative negotiation model for multiple continuous dependent issues. In: Society, I.C. (ed.) Proceedings of the 2005 IEEE/WIC/ACM Int. Conference on Web Intelligence and Intelligent Agent Technology, pp. 1–8 (2005)
9. Li, M., Vo, Q.B., Kowalczyk, R.: Searching for fair joint gains in agent-based negotiation. In: Decker, S., Sierra, C. (eds.) Proc. of 8th Int. Conf. on Autonomous Agents and Multiagent Systems (AAMAS 2009), Budapest, Hungary, May 10-15, pp. 1049–1056 (2009)
10. Klein, M., Faratin, P., Sayama, H., Bar-Yam, Y.: Protocols for negotiating complex contracts. IEEE Intelligent Systems 18(6), 32–38 (2003)
11. Ito, T., Klein, M., Hattori, H.: A multi-issue negotiation protocol among agents with nonlinear utility functions. Journal of Multiagent and Grid Systems 4(1), 67–83 (2008)
12. Marsa-Maestre, I., Lopez-Carmona, M.A., Velasco, J.R., de la Hoz, E.: Effective bidding and deal identification for negotiations in highly nonlinear scenarios. In: Decker, S., Sierra, C. (eds.) Proc. of 8th Int. Conf. on Autonomous Agents and Multiagent Systems (AAMAS 2009), Budapest, Hungary, May, 10-15, pp. 1057–1064 (2009)
13. Marsa-Maestre, I., Lopez-Carmona, M.A., Velasco, J.R., Ito, T., Klein, M., Fujita, K.: Balancing utility and deal probability for auction-based negotiations in highly nonlinear utility spaces. In: 21st International Joint Conference on Artificial Intelligence (IJCAI 2009), Pasadena, California, USA, July 2009, pp. 214–219 (2009)
14. Hindriks, K., Jonker, C., Tykhonov, D.: Eliminating interdependencies between issues for multi-issue negotiation. In: Klusch, M., Rovatsos, M., Payne, T.R. (eds.) CIA 2006. LNCS (LNAI), vol. 4149, pp. 301–316. Springer, Heidelberg (2006)
15. Lopez-Carmona, M.A., Velasco, J.R.: An expressive approach to fuzzy constraint based agent purchase negotiation. In: Proceedings of the International Joint Conference on Autonomous Agents and Multi-agent Systems (AAMAS 2006), Hakodate, Japan, pp. 429–431 (2006)
16. Lopez-Carmona, M.A., Velasco, J.R., Marsa-Maestre, I.: The agents' attitudes in fuzzy constraint based automated purchase negotiations. In: Burkhard, H.-D., Lindemann, G., Verbrugge, R., Varga, L.Z. (eds.) CEEMAS 2007. LNCS (LNAI), vol. 4696, pp. 246–255. Springer, Heidelberg (2007)
17. Zhang, J., Pu, P.: Survey on solving multi-attribute decision problems. Technical report, EPFL (2004)
18. Faratin, P., Sierra, C., Jennings, N.R.: Negotiation decision functions for autonomous agents. Robotics and Autonomous Systems 24(3-4), 159–182 (1998)

Applying User Feedback and Query Learning Methods to Multiple Communities

Tsunenori Mine[1,2] and Hirotake Kobayashi[2]

[1] Faculty of ISEE, Kyushu University,
744 Motooka, Nishi-ku, Fukuoka 819-0395, Japan
[2] Graduate School of ISEE, Kyushu University,
744 Motooka, Nishi-ku, Fukuoka 819-0395, Japan
{mine,koba}@al.is.kyushu-u.ac.jp

Abstract. This paper proposes a novel Peer-to-Peer Information Retrieval (P2PIR) method using user feedback and query-learning. The method actively utilizes negative feedback information so that other agents can filter it out when retrieving it. The proposed method effectively increases retrieval accuracy and decreases communication loads required for document retrieval in communities.

The experiments were carried out on multiple communities constructed with multi-agent framework Kodama [1]. The experimental results illustrated the validity of our proposed method.

1 Introduction

The growth of the Internet brings users a lot of beneficial information and convenient services. In particular, search engines increasingly become services of importance and indispensable for helping users to access various kinds of information the users want. Since almost conventional search engines are constructed as centralized server-type systems which give their services to client systems, they are often forced to be decentralized with paying a lot of costs for their decentralization, maintenance and management, to deal with the increase of their clients.

On the other hand, Peer-to-Peer (P2P) network systems are excellent at fault-tolerance and scalability by imposing each node of the network on partial charge of the services, and a lot of studies on the P2P network have been conducted so far. The P2P network can be divided into two types: unstructured and structured. The unstructured P2P network model (e.g. [2],[3]) provides flexible lookup services, but often requires huge communication loads to search for the results from all over the network. On the other hand, the structured P2P network model provides efficient lookup services using distributed hash tables (DHTs) (e.g. [4], [5]), but the services are often restricted to exact match of words, such as titles or names of music, movies, books and so forth. Consequently, the unstructured P2P network model has been employed by previous work for document retrieval that uses a mechanism ranking retrieved results based on the relevancy between a query and retrieval documents (e.g. [6],[7],[8], [9]). The previous work has well studied methods for looking up documents relevant to a query with high accuracy, or for finding destinations to issue the query. However, since the similarity

J.-J. Yang et al. (Eds.): PRIMA 2009, LNAI 5925, pp. 276–291, 2009.
© Springer-Verlag Berlin Heidelberg 2009

calculation employed by the methods does not well consider the meaning of the query and retrieval documents, all the documents retrieved with higher score of the similarity are not always relevant to the query, and some documents with lower score might be relevant to it. Moreover, their retrieval performance is not usually superior to that of centralized server-type IR systems either, due to the difference of their computing architectures.

Although the Agent-Community-based Peer-to-Peer information retrieval (ACP2P) method[10] also employs the unstructured P2P network model, unlike the previous work, it considers the way to construct relationships between users by introducing agent communities that can reflect the structures of human groups or societies. An agent residing the communities is allowed to manage its user's information and to judge if the information can be given to other agents, according to its user's instruction. This concept is completely different from the other P2PIR systems that only focus attention on the characteristics of the P2P network such as the scalability and fault-tolerance of the systems or the efficiency of looking up information on the network. The concept is also different from a centralized server-type IR system that gathers all information in advance to make indices of the information and that gives the information to any client systems of the server. Unfortunately, the ACP2P method also suffers from the low retrieval performance as well as the other P2PIR systems due to its similarity calculation method without considering the meaning of the query. In addition, query-multicasting method employed by the ACP2P does not consider the reuse of the results retrieved by queries issued in the past in a community and repeatedly multicast the queries.

In order to deal with the problems, we proposed a new formula to calculate a document score to a query[11]. The formula uses user feedback, that can be positive or negative judgement for a document to a query. Considering the user feedback to calculate the document score, a highly evaluated document will get a higher score and be ranked at a higher rank. In addition, we discussed a query-learning method employed by a middle agent called a Portal Agent (PA). The method predicts IR agents having a lot of documents relevant to a query by using a history of query-responder agent relationships learned by the PA. Since the PA can determine the IR agents to be issued a query, it reduces the number of query-multicasting in the community.

However our previous work did not much consider negative feedback as a filter of irrelevant information. In addition, the query-learning method was only applied to a single community. Therefore in this paper, we propose a method that actively uses negative feedback as well as positive feedback. The method is useful for filtering out irrelevant document information that has been evaluated by some agents. In addition, we discuss a way to apply the query-learning method to multiple communities.

We conduct several experiments in multiple community environments with NTCIR test collections. The experimental results illustrate the validity of the proposed method.

In what follows, section 2 describes the overview of the ACP2P method and presents a new formula to calculate a document score with user feedback; section 3 describes our proposed query-multicasting method; section 4 discusses the validity of the proposed method considering experimental results; section 5 discusses related work; finally we conclude and discuss the future work.

2   ACP2P Method

2.1   Overview of ACP2P

The ACP2P method[10] assigns an Information Retrieval (IR) agent to each user. In order to search for information relevant to a query issued by a user, the user's IR agent communicates with other IR agents mainly in the same community as it belongs to and also asks IR agents in other communities. The communication between IR agents belonging to different communities is firstly done via PAs in the communities. A PA has a role of a manager or a router in the community, keeps the addresses of all the member IR agents in its community, and helps to multicast a query to the IR agents in the community. The PA is a representative of a community and also a member IR agent of the upper community. This mechanism can comprise a hierarchical community structure.

Fig. 1 shows actions of an IR agent when the IR agent searches for information its user wants. The procedure is as follows: when receiving a query, an IR agent looks for target query-receiver IR agents (target agents for short), by using Content files, Query-Retrieved-Document-History (Q/RDH), and Query-Sender-Agent-History (Q/SAH). Where Content files consist of document files created by their owner user or ones returned by other IR agents. The Q/RDH holds queries issued by the user and their retrieved results. The Q/SAH holds

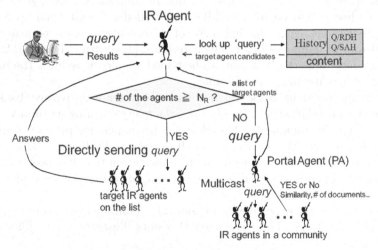

Fig. 1. Actions for retrieving information

Table 1. The Structures of Content File and Two Histories: Q/RDH and Q/SAH

	id	document id
	title	document title
Content file	*body*	content of document@
	original	the address of the IR agent whose user created the document
	range	the range allowed to be distributed (ALL, Community, Agent)
	query	issued query
Q/RDH	*from*	the address of IR agent which has replied to the query in the query field
	content	the content of a retrieved document followed by the format of the content above
	reputation	evaluation to the content
	query	received query
Q/SAH	*from*	the address of IR agent that issued the query
	attribute	format of received query

queries issued by other IR agents and their addresses. These three files are shown in Table 1.

If an IR agent can search for a sufficient number, say N_R, of target agents, the IR agent directly issues a query to them. Otherwise, the IR agent asks a PA to make up for the short by multicasting the query to all the IR agents in its community. When having received the query issued by the PA, the target agent returns a three-tuples <YES, Maximum Document Score, # of relevant documents> if it holds relevant information, or returns just <NO>, otherwise. The PA gathers the answers and makes a list of N_R target agents in descending order of the Maximum Document Score of the answers. The query-sender IR agent issues the query to all the target agents in the list. When receiving a query directly issued by a query-sender IR agent, the target agent directly returns retrieved results to the query-sender IR agent. The relevancy judgement of the information that an IR agent holds is done according to the method described in Section 2.2.

2.2   Relevancy Judgement and Evaluation

The score of a document D to a query Q is calculated by a formula (1) based on BM25[12].

$$Sim_d(Q, D) = \sum_{T \in Q} w \frac{(k_1 + 1)tf}{K + tf} \tag{1}$$

Where $K = k_1((1-b)+b\frac{dl}{avdl})$, k_1 and b are empirically determined by a document set to be used. According to preliminary experiments we conducted, we set $k_1 = 2.5$ and $b = 0.85$. dl is the number of words in D, $avdl$ is the average number of words in documents each IR agent has. So, $avdl$ is varied according to a set of documents each IR agent has. T is a word in Q. tf is the number of occurrences of T in D. w is a weight of T and defined by the following equation.

$$w = \log \frac{N - n + 0.5}{n + 0.5} \qquad (2)$$

Where N is the total number of documents each IR agent has. n is the number of documents including T in N documents. As the same as $avdl$, N and n are also varied according to a set of documents each IR agent has.

2.3   Determination of Target Agent

The score of target agents will be calculated by equation (3), where $Score(Q, agent_j)$ $(j = 1 \cdots n)$ is a score of an IR agent $agent_j$ to a query Q and n is the number of IR agents in history Q_{RDH} and Q_{SAH}.

$$Score(Q, agent_j) = \sum_{i=1}^{k} \cos(\vec{Q}, \overrightarrow{Q_{RDHi}})$$

$$+ \sum_{i=1}^{l} (\cos(\vec{Q}, \overrightarrow{Q_{SAHi}}) + \varphi(i))$$

$$+ \max_{1 \le i \le m} Sim_d(Q, doc_i) \qquad (3)$$

$$\varphi(i) = \begin{cases} \delta \text{ a query in } Q_{SAHi} \text{ is issued directly by other IR agents} \\ 0 \text{ otherwise (a query is issued via PA)} \end{cases}$$

The first term presents the total scores of query Q and k queries in Q_{RDH}, which were issued to $agent_j$, where $cos(\vec{Q}, \overrightarrow{Q_{RDHi}})$ calculates the cosine of word vectors of Q and Q_{RDHi}. The second term is the total scores of query Q and l queries in Q_{SAH}, which were issued by $agent_j$. $\varphi(i)$ is a weight to a query in Q_{SAHi}. The value of $\varphi(i)$ is set to $\delta = 0.1$ according to [10]. The 3rd term is the maximum similarity to Q of m documents in whose *original* field $agent_j$ is registered. $Sim_d(Q, doc_i)$ is a score of document doc_i to query Q and calculated by equation (1). Where N is the number of documents a query-sender agent has. N_R $agent_j$ will be selected as target agents in descending order of the score $Score(Q, agent_j)$.

2.4   User Feedback

Introducing User Feedback. We assume that a user will evaluate results retrieved by the user's IR agent and give a grade to them. Then, the user's IR agent will store the results with grades into the Q/RDH as shown in Fig. 2.[1]

---

[1] Since this grade assignment burdens the user, we should use implicit- or pseudo-user-feedback. However, in this paper, we aim to make clear the ideal case that every assignment is correctly and completely given by the user.

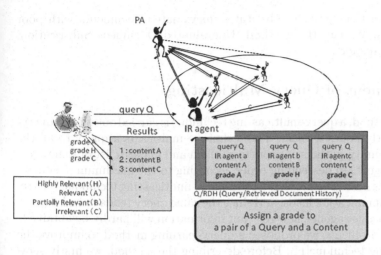

Fig. 2. Grade assignment to a pair of a query and a retrieval document by User Feedback

Similarity Calculation with User Feedback. When searching for a relevant document, we calculate the similarity between a query and a document by equation (4), considering user feedback stored in the reputation field of Q/RDH. In this equation (4), D is a document retrieved by a query Q, and E is a value of relevancy judgement given by a user. Due to the restriction of our test collections, we assume in this paper that this value is uniquely determined according to a pair of a query and a document.

$$Sim_f(Q, D) = Sim_d(Q, D) * r_{Q,D}(E) \tag{4}$$

Where $Sim_d(Q, D)$ is calculated by equation (1) and $r_{Q,D}(E)$ is a function returning a value determined by a grade E that was given to a document D retrieved by a query Q. In our experiments in Section 4, $r_{Q,D}(E)$ returns 4, 3, 0.5, 0.5, and 1 when E is highly relevant, relevant, partially relevant, irrelevant, and unevaluated, respectively.

Hereafter, when calculating $Score(Q, agent_j)$ in equation (3), we use Sim_f in equation (4) instead of Sim_d in equation (3).

2.5   Unevaluated Document Substitution Method

According to Sim_f, documents rated as 'highly relevant' or 'relevant' to a query will tend to be returned to users who issued the query. On the other hand, poor grade documents that were negatively evaluated as 'partially relevant' or 'irrelevant' will hardly be returned to the users, although the poor grade documents are useful to filter them out for other users who will issue the same query. It is true that unevaluated documents may be relevant, but that is less likely from our empirical experiments. Therefore, if the IR agent has poor grade documents, it should return them instead of unevaluated documents. Based on this idea, we propose a method that actively substitutes unevaluated documents with poor grade documents. We call this method 'Unevaluated Document Substitution' method or UDS in short.

3   Improvement of Query-Multicasting

In the ACP2P method, a query-multicasting technique is carried out when a query-sender agent firstly issues a query. The technique multicasts a query to all the agents in a community, gathers answers from them and makes a list of some specified number of agents in descending order according to the maximum document score returned by them. The problem of the query-multicasting technique is to require a lot of communication loads, and since the same query tends to be issued to almost the same target agents, new relevant information will hardly be obtained.

To solve these problems, we proposed a query learning method to improve the query-multicasting technique[11]. Before describing the method, we firstly show a Query/Multicast-Request-History (Q/MRH) file.

3.1   Query/Multicast-Request-History (Q/MRH)

The Q/MRH consists of four types of fields: *query*, *from*, *ra-list*, and *ta-list*, which are an issued query, the address of a query-sender IR agent, a list of responder agents to the query, and a list of target agents, respectively. Using Q/MRH, the PA can know which IR agent obtains the documents relevant to a query Q from which IR agents. In addition, the PA does not have to re-multicast the query already issued in the community. Consequently communication loads in the community are drastically reduced. Furthermore, without loosing top-ranked relevant documents, the PA can gather other relevant documents with the Q/MRH. In this way, the retrieval accuracy in the community will be improved. Table 2 shows an example of Q/MRH such that the number of target query-receiver IR agents, N_R, is 3.

3.2   The Query-Learning Method

The method first makes a list *ra-list* of IR agents responding to a query by making the PA multicast the query in a community, and makes a list *ta-list* by selecting some specified number of IR agents from *ra-list* in order. From next

Table 2. The Structure of Q/MRH – an Example

Query-Multicast-Request-History (Q/MRH)			
query	*from*	*ra-list*	*ta-list*
a query issued by an IR agent	the address of the IR agent that issued the query	a list of addresses of IR agents responding to the query	a list of addresses of target IR agents to be issued the query
Q_A	A	B, C, D, E, F, G, H, I, J	B, C, D

Table 3. An Example of a List of IR Agents created by the PA, where $N_R = 3$

query	Q	Query-Sender IR agent (*from*)	List of Query-Receiver IR agents (*ta-list*)
from	A	A	B, C, D
ra-list	B, C, D, E, F, G, H, I, J	K	A, E, F
		L	K, G, H

time, *ta-list* is made just by selecting IR agents from *ra-list* in order. At that time, the method always adds the latest query-sender IR agent in *from* field into *ta-list* so as to accumulate the previous retrieval results.

For example, we assume that *ra-list* for query Q is created as shown in Table 3. Hereafter, when receiving query Q again, the PA selects $N_R - 1$ IR agents from *ra-list* in order and makes a list *ta-list* of N_R IR agents including the latest query-sender IR agent in *from* field. When reaching the bottom of the list, the IR agent selection comes back to the top of *ra-list*. The query-multicasting for each query will accordingly be carried out only once.

This method drastically reduces communication loads since the number of target IR agents receiving a query is limited except the first multicasting time for each query. In addition, since the variety of target agents will be selected in order, the redundancy of retrieved documents will be decreased and greater number of relevant documents will be obtained, consequently.

However, there is a concern that the PA may become a single point failure in a community. Our solution for this is to replicate PAs by assigning the role of PA to member agents[13]. This method is worth not only maintaining a community, but also load balancing in the community. Since this is out of the scope in this paper, we will discuss the method elsewhere.

3.3 Query Multicasting in Multiple Communities

When getting shortage of target agents of a query, a PA can ask an upper PA to multicast the query to other PAs in the upper PA's community. The PAs that received a query-multicasting request from the upper PA, carry out the query-multicasting in their communities. In this way, the query-multicasting-requester PA to the upper PA can receive documents returned by IR agents in the other PA's communities. However this method does not consider if the IR agents in the communities can answer relevant documents. More than anything, it easily causes query flooding as shown in Fig. 3.

To solve the problem, we apply the Query-Learning method applied to multiple communities as follows. When receiving a query-multicasting request from the upper PA, a PA will, instead of performing query-multicasting, return to the upper PA the IR agent in the *from* field of the query recorded in its Q/MRH, and do nothing if the query has not been recorded in the Q/MRH. The PA that asked a query-multicasting to the upper PA selects $N_R - 1$ target agents from those returned by the upper PA. If some numbers of target agents are short, the PA covers them by selecting target agents from the *ra-list* of its Q/MRH.

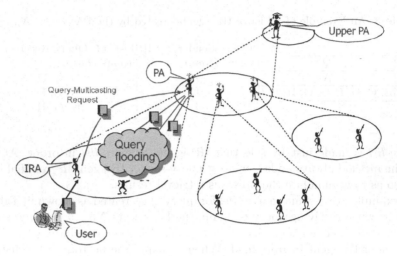

Fig. 3. Query Multicasting in Multiple Communities

4   Experiments

4.1   Preliminary

We conduct several experiments to evaluate the validity of our proposed method. The evaluation points are the followings: how much the precision ratio of the methods will approach to that of a centralized server-type IR system and how much the communication loads will be reduced for obtaining a list of target agents from a PA.

We use NTCIR3 WEB and NTCIR4 WEB[14] test collections for the experiments. The document set of the collections consist of about 11 million Web documents. The 150 thousand documents among them are given five-level rating: highly relevant, relevant, partially relevant, and irrelevant. Only the documents evaluated highly relevant or relevant to a query are dealt with as documents relevant to the query in the experiments. The number of retrieval assignments given by NTCIR3 is 47 and that by NTCIR4 is 80. We use both assignments. So, the total number of the assignments is 127.

We use three-layered hierarchical communities, which are composed of the first-layer (topmost) community, one second-layer community and 5 third-layer communities. The topmost community has one IR agent which has a role of PA of the second-layer community. 5 IR agents reside in the second-layer community. Each IR agent in the second-layer community has a role of PA of a third-layer community where 100 IR agents without a role of PA reside. So the total number of IR agents without the role of PA is 500. Each IR agent without the role of PA is hereafter just called an IR agent and an IR agent with the role of PA, a PA. The PA in the topmost community is called the upper PA from the point of view of a PA in the second-layer community.

To assign 3000 documents to each IR agent, we evenly divide into 500 IR agents 1500 thousand documents that include both the 150 thousand rated documents and 1350 thousand unrated documents selected randomly from a set of unrated documents of the collections. The IR agent is also given to 20 assignments selected randomly among 127 ones. Each IR agent extracts keywords in the $CONCEPT$ field of each given assignment and uses the keywords of the assignment as its query. The keywords include concept words related to the assignment and the synonym, hypernym and hyponym of the concept word. In this way, 10,000 queries are totally issued. This means each query is averagely issued 16 times in each third-layer community. The number of target agents, N_R, is set to 10. Each target agent returns at most 10 documents to the query-sender IR agent in descending order according to their score.

4.2   Evaluation Measure

We use the Average Precision measure to evaluate the proposed methods. The average precision is defined as follows:

$$\text{Average Precision} = \frac{\sum_{r=1}^{L} I(r)P(r)}{R}$$

Where R is the total number of relevant documents; L is the number of results retrieved by a system. In this experiment, we set L to 10; $I(r)$ is 1 if the r-th ranked document is relevant, and 0 otherwise; $P(r)$ is $\frac{count(r)}{r}$; $count(r)$ is the number of relevant documents among r documents returned by the system.

4.3   Query Learning on Multiple Communities

To evaluate the effect of the Query-Learning (QL) method described in Section 3.3, we had every IR agent carry out query-multicasting every time to select target agents and compared the following three methods: (a) QM-UF-woQL (Query-Multicasting using User Feedback, but not using Query Learning Method), (b) QM-UF-wQL (Query-Multicasting using User Feedback and Query Learning Method), and (c) CS-UF (Centralized Server-type IR method using User Feedback). The experimental results are shown in Fig. 4.

The results show the big difference between QM-UF-woQL and QM-UF-wQL. We assume that the reasons would be divided into the following two factors:

- An IR agent that issued a query tend to be a target agent of other IR agents that will issue the query.
- Regardless of the number of communities, QM-UF-woQL in multiple communities obtains the same result as the QM-UF-woQL performed in a single community that all the communities are merged into.

The first one says that target agents will be determined by a query and consequently retrieval results obtained by the query will also be fixed. Therefore the value of Average Precision for the query will not be increased.

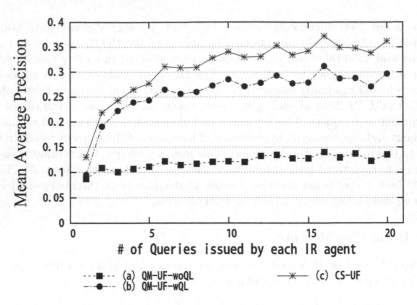

Fig. 4. Comparison of the Query Multicasting Methods Applied to Multiple Communities

Fig. 5 depicts the average number of non-overlap documents received by an IR agent when we perform QM-UF-woQL and QM-UF-wQL. The results illustrate the validity of the above assumptions.

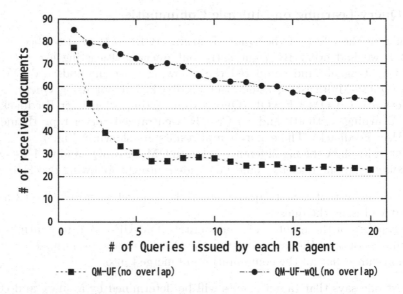

Fig. 5. Comparison of the number of non-overlap documents retrieved by Query Multicasting Methods with/without Query-Learning Method in Multiple Communities

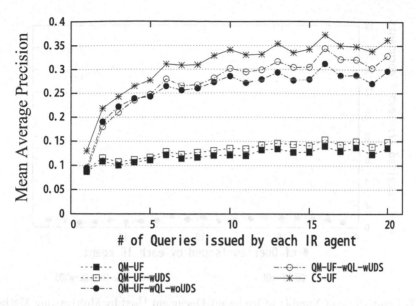

Fig. 6. Comparison of Query Multicasting Methods with/without Unevaluated Document Substitution Method on Multiple Communities

4.4   Evaluation of Unevaluated Document Substitution Method on Multiple Communities

Fig. 6 depicts the effect of the UDS method by comparing with query-multicasting methods with or without the UDS. The query multicasting method using both QL and UDS is mostly approaching the CS-UF and the difference is very small on the number of relevant documents returned by them, which is only one.

Fig. 7 shows that query multicasting method with the UDS tends to the greater number of irrelevant document information than the other query-multicasting methods without the UDS.

4.5   Comparison of Communication Loads

We here define the communication load of a method as the number of messages exchanged by IR agents for document retrieval of a query. We set the number of target IR agents to N_R, the number of communities to N_{com}, and the number of IR agents in a community to N_{agent}. We compare the communication loads of two query multicasting methods: the method with or without using Query Learning.

Query Multicasting Method without using Query Learning. When an IR agent carries out document retrieval, the number of messages required to each procedure is shown in the brackets [ ] as follows:

1. Asking its PA to multicast a query .. [1]
2. Query-multicasting by the PA and its response .. [$2(N_{agent}-1)$]
3. Asking the upper PA by the PA to multicast a query .. [1]

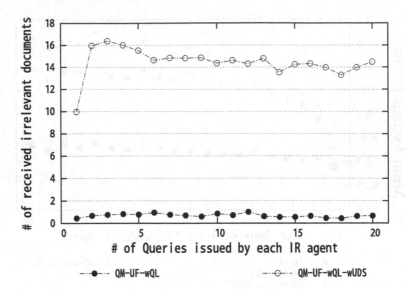

Fig. 7. Comparison of Number of Irrelevant Document Used by Multicasting Methods in Multiple Communities

4. Query-multicasting by the upper PA .. $[N_{com}-1]$
5. Query-multicasting in each community and its response .. $[2N_{agent} \times (N_{com}-1)]$
6. Response to the upper PA .. $[N_{com}-1]$
7. Receiving a list of IR agents from the upper PA .. $[1]$
8. Receiving a list of IR agents from the PA .. $[1]$
9. Query-issuing to IR agents in the list and receiving their response .. $[2N_R]$

The total number of messages is consequently $2(N_{com} \times (N_{agent} + 1) + N_R)$.

Query Multicasting using Query Learning. When a query is first issued in a community, the total number of required messages is $2(N_{agent}+N_{com}+N_R)$ because query-multicasting in each community of step 5 in the previous section will not be occurred.

Moreover, if a query has been issued in a community, query-multicasting by the PA of step 2 in the previous section will not be occurred either. Then, at this time, the total number of required messages is only $2(1+N_{com}+N_R)$.

Compared with the query-multicasting method without using query-learning, this method saves $2(N_{com} \times N_{agent} -1)$ messages after the query was once issued in the community.

Consequently the proposed query learning method can drastically reduce the communication loads.

5   Related Work

A lot of previous work (e.g. [6],[7],[8], [9]) show that using content information in P2P networks for query routing can greatly reduce average number of query messages per query, and get higher precision[6],[8] and higher recall[9]. Their methods first collect resource descriptions from all peers and classify them into some decided number of clusters, then, make hubs or super-peers learn their neighbors' resource descriptions for query routing. Since each peer does not redistribute any documents obtained from other peers, the database volume of each peer does not change. On the other hand, the ACP2P method considers the situation of changing the volume of each peer's database. Zhang et. al's work [15] is also a kind of content-based P2P IR method, and adopts a reinforcement learning approach on an unstructured peer-to-peer network. On the other hand, this paper shows the effects of query learning and user feedback given to a pair of a query and a document.

Routing Indices (RIs)[16] are local routing indices so that they can forward queries to neighbors that are more likely to have answers. The RI stores information concerning which neighbors have what topics of documents, and thus gives a "direction" towards the document, rather than its actual location[16]. On the other hand, the ACP2P method uses contents of documents and query histories instead of their topics, then does not need to cluster the documents into a set of topics and has no restriction that forces to use topic keywords. Furthermore the ACP2P directly searches for target agents with relevant information, using retrieved documents and two histories. In particular, Q/SAH provides similar effects to link analysis like the PageRank[17] or HITs algorithm[18], and can be expected to make a natural collaborative filtering effect emerge because users want to send a query again to the peers that can return results which satisfy them, and vice versa. However, query forwarding like RIs would be able to help the ACP2P search for more relevant information, and the query learning methods proposed in this paper actually have similar effects to the RIs.

I-Gaia[19] is an application layer for information processing in the DIET architecture, which is a Multi-Agent System development platform. It provides information-push (information filtering) and pull (information retrieval) functions. In addition it uses a mediator agent called "t-infocyte" which learns the relationships between a query issued and documents provided by agents. On the other hand, this paper discusses the query learning method that learns relationships between a query and responder-agents, not documents.

6   Conclusion and Future Work

This paper discussed the effects of the query learning method and user feedback method with the Unevaluated Document Substitution (UDS) method. Experimental results showed the query learning method was effective both for reducing communication loads and increasing retrieval accuracy, and the UDS method worked for increasing retrieval accuracy. Compared with several query multicasting methods, the method using both the query learning and the unevaluated document substitution methods achieved the best retrieval accuracy. Nevertheless, from the point of view of retrieval accuracy, the method did not reached the centralized server-type IR method. This is due to the difference in their total number of accumulated user feedback information, in particular, negative feedback information, i.e., irrelevant document information. In order to solve this problem, we will first improve the query learning method so that it can accumulate greater number of negative feedback information. Next, we will introduce several user models that give implicit user feedback instead of explicit user feedback touched on in this paper. We will also try to combine relevance feedback methods (e.g. [20]) with our proposed method.

Our future work is to make experiments under dynamic environments such that the number of documents kept by an IR agent in a community will be increased and decreased, the volume of a document set in a community will also be changed, and IR agents will frequently join and leave the community.

Acknowledgements

We used NTCIR3 and NTCIR4 WEB Test Collections under permission from National Institute of Informatics.

References

1. Zhong, G., Amamiya, S., Takahashi, K., Mine, T., Amamiya, M.: The design and application of kodama system. IEICE Transactions INF.& SYST E85-8, 637–646 (2002)
2. Clarke, I., Sandberg, O., Wiley, B., Hong, T.W.: Freenet: A distributed anonymous information storage and retrieval system. In: International Workshop on Design Issues in Anonymity and Unobservability:Designing Privacy Enhancing Technologies, http://www.doc.ic.ac.uk/~twh1/academic/ (2001)
3. Gnutella: Gnutella protocol development v6.0, http://rfc-gnutella.sourceforge.net/ (2003)
4. Stoica, I., Morris, R., Karger, D., Kaashoek, M.F., Balakrishnan, H.: Chord: A scalable peer-to-peer lookup service for internet applications. In: Proceedings of the 2001 conference on applications, technologies, architectures, and protocols for computer communications, pp. 149–160 (2001)
5. Ratnasamy, S., Francis, P., Handley, M., Karp, R., Shenker, S.: A scalable content-addressable network. In: SIGCOMM, pp. 161–172 (2001)
6. Lu, J., Callan, J.: Content-based retrieval in hybrid peer-to-peer networks. In: Proceedings of the twelfth international conference on Information and knowledge management (CIKM 2003), pp. 199–206 (2003)
7. Renda, M.E., Callan, J.: The robustness of content-based search in hierarchical peer to peer networks. In: Proceedings of the thirteenth ACM conference on Information and knowledge management, pp. 562–570 (2004)
8. Lu, J., Callan, J.: Federated search of text-based digital libraries in hierarchical peer-to-peer networks. In: Losada, D.E., Fernández-Luna, J.M. (eds.) ECIR 2005. LNCS, vol. 3408, pp. 52–66. Springer, Heidelberg (2005)
9. Bawa, M., Manku, G.S., Raghavan, P.: Sets: search enhanced by topic segmentation. In: Proceedings of the 26th annual international ACM SIGIR conference on Research and development in informaion retrieval, pp. 306–313 (2003)

10. Mine, T., Matsuno, D., Kogo, A., Amamiya, M.: Design and implementation of agent community based peer-to-peer information retrieval method. In: Klusch, M., Ossowski, S., Kashyap, V., Unland, R. (eds.) CIA 2004. LNCS (LNAI), vol. 3191, pp. 31–46. Springer, Heidelberg (2004)
11. Mine, T., Kogo, A., Amamiya, S., Amamiya, M.: Refinement of the acp2p by sharing user-feedbacks and learning query-responder-agent-relationships. In: The 8th International Conference on Autonomous Agents and MultiAgent Systems, pp. 1341–1342 (2009)
12. Robertson, S.E., Walker, S., Jones, S., Hancock-Beaulieu, M.M., Gatford, M.: Okapi/keenbow at trec-8. In: NIST Special Publication 500-246: The Eighth Text REtrieval Conference (TREC-8), pp. 151–162 (1999)
13. Kimura, K., Mine, T., Amamiya, S., Amamiya, M.: Construction method for robust and secure agent-community network (in japanese). In: Joint Agent Workshops and Symposium (2008)
14. NTCIR3-4: The 3rd and 4th ntcir workshop data, http://research.nii.ac.jp/ntcir/ntcir-ws3/work-en.html#data (2002), http://research.nii.ac.jp/ntcir/ntcir-ws3/work-en.html#data (2003) (2002-2003)
15. Zhang, H., Lesser, V.: A reinforcement learning based distributed search algorithm for hierarchical peer-to-peer information retrieval systems. In: AAMAS 2007, pp. 231–238 (2007)
16. Crespo, A., Garcia-Molina, H.: Routing indices for peer-to-peer systems. In: The 28th International Conference on Distributed Computing Systems (2002)
17. Brin, S., Page, L.: The Anatomy of a Large-Scale Hypertextual Web Search Engine. In: Proc. of 7th International World Wide Web Conference: WWW7 Conference (1998)
18. Kleinberg, J.M.: Authoritative sources in a hyperlinked environment. Journal of the ACM 46, 604–632 (1999)
19. Gallardo-Antolin, A., Navia-Vasquez, A., Molina-Bulla, H.Y., Rodriguez-Gonzalez, A.B., Valverde-Albacete, F.J., Cid-Sueiro, J., Figuieras-Vidal, A., Koutris, T., Xiruhaki, C., Koubarakis, M.: I-Gaia: an Information Processing Layer for the DIET Platform. In: The first international joint conference on Autonomous Agents and Multi Agent Systems (AAMAS), pp. 1272–1279 (2002)
20. Robertson, S.E.: On term selection for query expansion. Journal of Documentation 46, 359–364 (1990)

An Adaptive Human-Aware Software Agent Supporting Attention-Demanding Tasks

Tibor Bosse[1], Zulfiqar A. Memon[1,2], Jan Treur[1], and Muhammad Umair[1,3]

[1] VU University Amsterdam, Department of Artificial Intelligence
De Boelelaan 1081, 1081 HV Amsterdam
{tbosse,zamemon,treur,mumair}@few.vu.nl
http://www.few.vu.nl/~{tbosse,zamemon,treur,mumair}
[2] Sukkur Institute of Business Administration (Sukkur IBA)
Air Port Road Sukkur, Sindh, Pakistan
[3] COMSATS Institute of Information Technology,
Department of Computer Science,
Lahore, Pakistan

Abstract. This paper presents a human-aware software agent to support a human performing a task that demands substantial amounts of attention. The agent obtains human awareness in an adaptive manner by use of a dynamical model of human attention which is parameterised for specific characteristics of the human. The agent uses a built-in adaptation model to adapt on the fly the values of these parameters to the personal characteristics of the human. The software agent has been implemented in a component-based manner within the Adobe® Flex® environment.

Keywords: software agent, human-aware, adaptive, attention.

1 Introduction

The area of Ambient Intelligence envisions a world in which humans are surrounded by intelligent software agents that are unobtrusively embedded in their direct environment, and support them in various tasks (e.g., [1], [2], [3]). Such ambient agents can provide more dedicated support when they have a certain level of human-awareness. This may require awareness not only of personal characteristics such as preferences, but also of (dynamically changing) states of the human. Examples of such states are emotion and stress, fatigue and exhaustion, goals and intentions, and attention states. Acquiring awareness of such states is a nontrivial challenge. Sensors may be used by the agent to get information about the human's current state, such as face readers, eye-trackers or heart rate sensors, but sensor information can rarely be directly related in a one-to-one manner to the human's states that are of concern.

A more general situation is that such sensor information can be used in a more indirect manner in dynamical models that express temporal relationships between a number of variables including these human's states and the sensor information; e.g., [17]. As humans may show substantial individual differences in characteristics in

J.-J. Yang et al. (Eds.): PRIMA 2009, LNAI 5925, pp. 292–307, 2009.
© Springer-Verlag Berlin Heidelberg 2009

cognitive functioning, such a dynamical model usually includes a number of parameters for a number of specific characteristics of the human. Therefore they only can be used in a dedicated manner when sufficiently accurate estimations can be made for the values of these parameters as representations for the characteristics of the human considered. For applications in software agents this implies that such an agent does not only need a dynamical model of the human's processes, but also an adaptation model describing how the parameter values of the former model can be adapted over time to the characteristics of the human.

This paper presents a software agent that makes use of such a parameterised dynamical model of the human, and in addition possesses an adaptation model that on the fly tunes the parameter values to the human characteristics. A case study was undertaken to test it for a human's attention states. The human-attention-awareness for this case study uses three ingredients: (1) sensor information on the human's gaze, (2) information on features of objects in the environment, and (3) a dynamical (differential equations) model of the dynamics of attention levels over time integrating the instantaneous information from (1) and (2), and using partial persistency of attention over time.

The agent's adaptation model was designed and implemented in a generic manner, but for the case study was applied to the dynamical model for attention, thereby addressing, among others, parameters for weights of different features of objects, the effect of distance between an object and gaze, and an attention persistency factor.

The software agent and the further ambient support software environment has been implemented within the Adobe® Flex® development environment according to a component-based design. For the gaze sensing it integrates the Tobii® eye-tracker.

In this paper Section 2 presents the assessment of the human's attention state for the case study and the parameters involved in this model, depending on personal characteristics of the human. Section 3 presents the background ideas of the parameter adaptation approach developed, and in Section 4 the overall adaptation model is described. In Section 5 some more details of the developed software and some results for the case study are discussed. In Section 6 a verification of the model is presented. Section 7 is a discussion.

2   The Dynamical Model for the Human's Attentional State

In this section the dynamical model for attentional states related to a number of objects used is briefly described, it was adopted from [7]. As a first step for each object its potential for attracting attention is determined. The *attention-attracting potential* of an object O is expressed by a weighted sum $\Sigma_i w_i * V_i$ where V_i is the value of object feature i, and the *object feature weight factors* w_i (normalised so that their sum is 1) are parameters that may depend on the human. Examples of features are: brightness, colour, and size. The values for these variables are expressed by numbers in the interval $[0, 1]$, with 0 no attraction potential and 1 highest attraction potential. To take gaze into account the potential of the object for attraction human's attention is divided by a function depending on the human's gaze location:

$$V(O) = (\Sigma_i w_i * V_i) / (1 + \alpha * d(O, G)^2)$$

Here $d(O, G)$ is the Euclidean distance between the location of the object O and the human's gaze G. The parameter α (represented by a real number ≥ 0) is a *gaze distance effect rate*; it affects how fast an object loses the human's attention as the gaze moves further away from the object. The higher α is, the lower the attention for objects distant from the human's focus.

It is assumed that a person can have a fixed total amount of attention A distributed over all available objects; for convenience the attention scale is set in such a way that $A = 1$. The *attention level* $AV(O)$ of an object O expresses the amount of the human's attention directed at the object O as a fraction of the human's total attention. If there are n objects in total and the attention value $V(O_j)$ of the object O_j is indicated by V_j ($1 \leq j \leq n$), then the attention level $AV(O_i)$ of the object O_i (in the context of the other objects) is determined in a normalised form as

$$AV(O_i) = V(O_i) / \Sigma_j V(O_j)$$

Note that due to the normalisation $AV(O_i)$ also depends on the other objects. It is assumed that attention for a certain object persists over shorter time periods. To model this the attention values for object O can be modelled as a *persistent attention value* $PAV(O)$ using the following difference equation:

$$PAV(O)(t+\Delta t) = PAV(O)(t) + \beta *(AV(O)(t) - PAV(O)(t))\Delta t$$

Here β is an *attention flexibility rate* with a positive value between 0 and 1, and time step Δt with $0 \leq \Delta t \leq 1$; a high value of β results in fast changes and a low value in a high persistence of the old value. Written in a more concise differential equation format the dynamical model is as follows:

$$dPAV(O) / dt = \beta *(AV(O) - PAV(O))$$

This represents a system of n differential equations for all of the n objects involved, which via $AV(O)$ integrates the gaze information and information about the object features over time.

For the case study also for objects that need attention, a model was used to estimate the level of urgency of objects. This is done based on a number of *urgency-indication factors* by a weighted sum

$$UV(O) = \Sigma_i r_i * UV_i$$

Here UV_i is the value of the i-th urgency aspect and r_i the *urgency aspect weight factor* for this aspect (with total sum 1). The values for these variables are expressed by numbers in the interval $[0, 1]$, with 0 no urgency and 1 highest urgency. As for attention values, also for these urgency values a certain extent of persistence is applied, thus obtaining $PUV(O)$:

$$PUV(O)(t+\Delta t) = PUV(O)(t) + \beta' *(UV(O)(t) - PUV(O)(t))\Delta t$$

or

$$dPUV(O) / dt = \beta' *(UV(O) - PUV(O))$$

Here β' is the *urgency flexibility rate*, which determines how fast the PUV values are changing upon new input.

To determine whether there is enough attention for objects that demand attention some comparison has to be made. The attention levels that are estimated are considered as offered attention utilisation, and the urgencies can be considered as demands. However, in principle these quantities are not expressed according to a measure such that they are comparable. Therefore some rescaling has been made in the comparison, in the following discrepancy assessment:

$$D(O) = s_1 * PUV(O) - s_2 * PAV(O)$$

with s_i *comparison weight factors*. The interpretation is that $D(O) = 0$ represents sufficient attention for the object, $D(O) < 0$ more than sufficient, and $D(O) > 0$ insufficient attention. The resulting discrepancy assessments can be used as input to determine appropriate intervention actions; how this can be done will not be discussed in this paper; however, see [14].

As shown, the overall dynamical model involves a number of parameters some of which relate to characteristics of the human and some others to characteristics of the environment, or to a combination. As a summary an overview is given in Table 1.

Table 1. Overview of the parameters in the dynamical model

characteristics	parameter	symbol	range
human characteristics	object feature weight factors	w_i	$0 \leq w_i \leq 1$ & $\Sigma w_i = 1$
	gaze distance effect rate	α	$0 \leq \alpha$
	attention flexibility rate	β	$0 < \beta \leq 1$
environmental characteristics	urgency aspect weight factors	r_i	$0 \leq r_i \leq 1$ & $\Sigma r_i = 1$
combined characteristics	comparison weight factors	s_i	$0 \leq s_i \leq 1$

3   The Adaptation Approach

When using a dynamical model to assess a human's states in the context of a task and environment, the software agent has to maintain beliefs about characteristics of the human, used as parameters in the model. As often it is not possible to determine accurate values at forehand, this section describes a method by which the agent adapts its beliefs concerning human characteristics to the real characteristics. The main idea is as follows. The agent initially receives rough estimations of the values for these human characteristics, and maintains them as beliefs. Using the dynamical model with parameter values as represented by these initial beliefs, the agent predicts the human state, up to a certain time point. When at that time point, for example by observation, information is obtained that can be related to the real value of one or more state variables of the model, this can be used as input for the adaptation process. The agent then tries to minimize the difference between predicted and real value by adjusting the beliefs on the human characteristics (i.e., the parameter values which were initially assumed). This process of adaptation is kept going on until the difference is low enough, i.e., until the agent has a sufficiently accurate set of beliefs about the human's characteristics. To be able to make reasonable adjustments it is needed to obtain information on how a change in a parameter value affects the difference between predicted and real value of the variable that is considered; this is called the sensitivity of the variable value for the parameter value. In more detail the adaptation process is described as follows.

3.1 Sensitivities: How They Are Determined

Within this adaptation process sensitivities of state variables for changes in parameter values for human characteristics play an important role. The *sensitivity* S of variable X for parameter P is the number such that a change ΔP in the value of P of parameter P will lead to a change ΔX in X which is (approximately) proportional to ΔP with proportion factor S:

$$\Delta X = S \, \Delta P$$

This is an approximation which is more accurate when the Δ's are taken small; in fact the sensitivity is the partial derivative $\partial X/\partial P$. To determine a sensitivity S (so determining the partial derivative $\partial X/\partial P$) in principle both analytical and experimental/heuristic methods or a combination of them can be used. As systems of differential equations encountered usually cannot be solved analytically, a purely analytical approach to determine sensitivities is often not feasible. As an approximation method the following can be done. A small change ΔP in the parameter is tried to make an additional prediction for X, and based on the resulting change ΔX found in the two predicted values for X, by

$$S_{X,P} = \Delta X / \Delta P$$

the sensitivity S can be estimated. The idea is that this is done for each of the parameters, one by one.

3.2 Sensitivities: How They Are Used

Given that a sensitivity $S_{X,P}$ of variable X for parameter P is known it can be used in the following manner. First it can be noticed that sensitivities for some parameters P can be 0 or almost 0. Apparently, such parameters do not have any serious effect on the outcome of the value of variable X. Therefore, changing them based on available values for X does not make much sense: a deviation in value of X cannot be attributed to them, due to their low influence. Based on the estimation of a sensitivity which has distance at least τ_S to 0 (where τ_S is a small threshold value), in principle a better guess for the value of P can be determined by taking

$$\Delta P = -\lambda * \Delta X / S_{X,P}$$

where ΔX is the deviation found between observed and predicted value of X; so, for example, when $\Delta X = 0.25$ and $\lambda = 0.3$, then for $S_{X,P} = 0.75$ this obtains $\Delta P = -0.3*0.25 /0.75 = -0.1$. However, when the sensitivity $S_{X,P}$ is a bit smaller, it could be possible that the adjustment of the value of P based on the formula above would exceed the maximum or minimum value of its range. For example, when $\Delta X = 0.25$, $\lambda = 0.3$, and $S_{X,P} = 0.025$ it results in $\Delta P = -0.3*0.25 /0.025 = -3$. To avoid such problems, a kind of threshold function can be applied that maps, for example for a parameter with values in the interval $[0, 1]$, the proposed adjustment on a $[0, 1]$ interval (which can still be multiplied by a factor for other intervals):

$$\Delta P = \quad \lambda * th(\sigma, \tau, \Delta X / S_{X,P}) * (1-W) \qquad \text{when } \Delta X / S_{X,P} \geq 0$$
$$\Delta P = -\lambda * th(\sigma, \tau, -\Delta X / S_{X,P}) * W \qquad \text{when } \Delta X / S_{X,P} < 0$$

Here the threshold function with steepness σ and threshold value τ is defined by

$$th(\sigma, \tau, V) = 1/(1+e^{-\sigma(V-\tau)})$$

or, to allow for lower steepness values by

$$th(\sigma, \tau, V) = [\ 1/(1+e^{-\sigma(V-\tau)}) - 1/(1+e^{\sigma\tau})\ ] / [\ 1 - 1/(1+e^{\sigma\tau})\ ]$$
$$= [\ 1/(1+e^{-\sigma(V-\tau)}) - 1/(1+e^{\sigma\tau})\ ] / [\ e^{\sigma\tau}/(1+e^{\sigma\tau})\ ]$$
$$= [\ 1/(1+e^{-\sigma(V-\tau)}) - 1/(1+e^{\sigma\tau})\ ] * [1+e^{-\sigma\tau}]$$

When for more than one variable X information about its real value is obtained, the adjustment ΔP for parameter P is taken as the average of all calculated adjustments based on the different variables X such that the sensitivity $S_{X,P}$ is not close to 0.

4 The Overall Adaptation Process

Based on the adaptation approach explained in Section 3 above, the overall adaptation process was modelled as follows:

Initialisation

1. Take VF the *focus set of variables* X for which information about its real value can be obtained and take a time point t for which information about the real value of all X in F is to be obtained.
2. Take G the subset of parameters P for which adaptation is desired; the other parameters are kept constant.
3. Assume initial values for all of the parameters P.
4. Choose a value for adaptation speed λ.

Sensitivity Determination

5. By simulation determine predicted values V_X at time point t for each X in VF, using the assumed values of the parameters.
6. For each parameter P in G, by simulation determine predicted values CV_X at time point t for each X in VF, using only for P a value changed by some chosen ΔP and the unchanged assumed values for the other parameters.
7. For each parameter P in G and each variable X in VF, determine the sensitivity $S_{X,P}$ of X for P at time point t by dividing the difference between values for X found in 5. and 6. by ΔP:

$$S_{X,P} = (CV_X - V_X) / \Delta P$$

8. Take $VF(P)$ the *focus set of variables X for P* of those variable X for which the sensitivity $S_{X,P}$ has distance to 0 of at least the sensitivity threshold τ_S:

$$VF(P) = \{ \ X \in VF \ | \ |S_{X,P}| \geq \tau_S \ \}$$

9. Take PF the *focus set of parameters* for which the sensitivity for at least one $X \in VF$ has distance to 0 of at least the sensitivity threshold τ_S:

$$PF = \{ \ P \in G \ | \ \exists X \in VF \ |S_{X,P}| \geq \tau_S \ \} = \{ \ P \in G \ | \ VF(P) \neq \varnothing \}$$

Adjustment Determination

10. For each variable $X \in VF$ determine the deviation ΔX of the predicted value of X at t from information that is obtained about the real value of X at t.

11. For each parameter $P \in PF$ determine the change ΔP as

$$\Delta P = \lambda * th(\sigma, \tau, (\Sigma_{X \in VF(P)} \ \Delta X / S_{X,P}) / \#(VF(P))) * (1-W)$$
$$\text{when } (\Sigma_{X \in VF(P)} \ \Delta X / S_{X,P}) \geq 0$$
$$\Delta P = - \lambda * th(\sigma, \tau, -(\Sigma_{X \in VF(P)} \ \Delta X / S_{X,P}) / \#(VF(P))) * W$$
$$\text{when } (\Sigma_{X \in VF(P)} \ \Delta X / S_{X,P}) < 0$$

12. For each parameter $P \in PF$ adjust its value by ΔP.

By repeating this process a number of times both for each time point considered and for different time points, over time an approximation is obtained.

5   Further Details of the Implementation

In this section some details of the ambient support environment for attention-demanding tasks are described. The software environment has been implemented within the Adobe® Flex® development environment. The software was implemented according to a component-based design. Between the different components event-driven interaction takes place, implemented using ActionScript. Moreover, for the gaze sensing a specific sensing component was included that connects the Tobii® eye-tracker used.

To address the possibilities for human-aware ambient support of attention-demanding tasks a (simplified) simulated environment to perform such a type of task has been developed; for more details, see [14]. A person has to (1) inspect visually displayed moving objects in the environment, and identify whether such an object is dangerous (enemy) or not (ally), and (2) for each of such objects, depending on the identification perform some actions. The player's task consists in classifying each object as ally or enemy, and shooting down the enemies while letting allies land safely. Identification of an object is a cognitive task, in a simplified form represented by an arithmetical calculation. The player uses a cannon at the bottom of the screen to shoot down (hostile) objects.

The main idea for an ambient agent supporting this task is that it has awareness about whether or not the human pays enough attention to urgent situations. Urgency is determined as a weighted sum of a number of factors, which is multiplied by an identification factor which is 0 for friends and 1 for enemies; so for friends the urgency will always be 0. Examples of factors used are speed, direction and time and distance to the ground. Using this urgency model the agent can determine how urgent the situations concerning certain objects are, and compare this to the amount of attention, thus obtaining the discrepancies for each of the objects (according to the model described in Section 2). These discrepancies play the role of the variables indicated by X in Section 4.

For the adaptation model a crucial aspect is the way in which a deviation between the discrepancy value estimated by the agent and in reality can be determined. In this case, as an approximation the mouse clicks of the person have been used as an indication of discrepancy; see Table 2.

Table 2. Determination of deviations

enemy/ friend	mouse click	indicated discrepancy	current discrepancy	deviation based on current minus indicated discrepancy
enemy	+	negative	positive	current discrepancy + 0.2
enemy	+	negative	negative	0
enemy	-	positive	positive	0
enemy	-	positive	negative	current discrepancy - 0.2
friend	+	negative	positive	current discrepancy + 0.2
friend	+	negative	negative	0
friend	-	negative	positive	current discrepancy + 0.2
friend	-	negative	negative	0

For example, if at some time point a mouse click occurs at a certain position of an enemy, it is assumed that this indicates sufficient attention for that position at that point in time which implies an indication that the discrepancy should be negative. Similarly, when for a certain duration no mouse click occurs at a friendly position, this is considered a sign for negative discrepancy. If the current discrepancy is positive and the indicated negative, the deviation is determined as the current discrepancy estimation plus 0.2.

Fig. 1 shows for the example scenario how the three objects move compared to gaze positions. Object 1 (upper graphs), representing an enemy, moves almost vertically, and almost all the time the gaze position has some distance to this object, except maybe around time points 800 and 950, here the gaze is a bit closer. In contrast, the positions of the friendly object 2, depicted in the second row of graphs, often coincide with the gaze positions. The lowest part shows that the positions of object 3 coincide with gaze positions only around time points 250 and 950. Tables 3 and 4 describe information about the settings in the example scenario. Note that the person considered performs far from perfect as the gaze is often at (friendly) object 2 and not at object 1 which is the enemy. Therefore an appropriate estimation of discrepancy between urgency and attention would show a rather positive value for object 1 and a rather negative value for object 2.

Table 3. Some of the object features

	Brightness	Size	Identification
Object 1	0.9	0.2	enemy
Object 2	0.1	0.9	friend
Object 3	0.25	0.3	friend

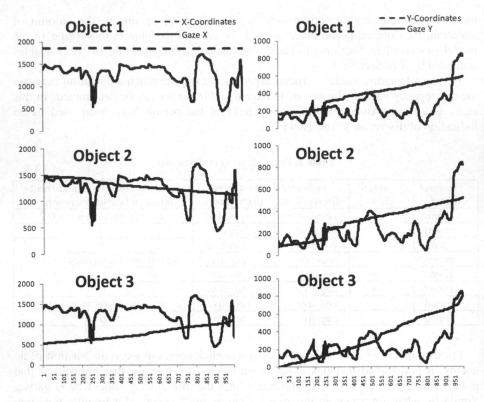

Fig. 1. Positions of three objects over time compared to gaze positions in the example scenario: left hand sides show x-coordinates, right hand sides y-coordinates. It shows that from time point 0 to 200 the gaze is near object 2, around 250 near object 3, from 300 to 500 near object 2 again, around 800 most close to object 1, and after 900 near object 3 again.

Table 4. Parameter values

α	β	Identification weight	Urgency weight	Attention weight	λ	Urgency flexibility
1	0.2	1	0.3	0.9	0.02	0.02

In Fig. 2 it is shown how the discrepancies develop over time for each of the objects. It shows that initially the discrepancies are not estimated well. For example, for object 1 discrepancy starts negative. This incorrect estimation of the discrepancy can be explained by the parameter setting for weight factors for brightness and size: the brightness weight factor is initially *0.9*, and object 1 happens to have a high brightness. The more or less converse situation is shown for object 2, which has a low brightness and high value for size. However, for the estimation of discrepancy the high size is not counted much as initially the weight factor parameter for size is only *0.2*.

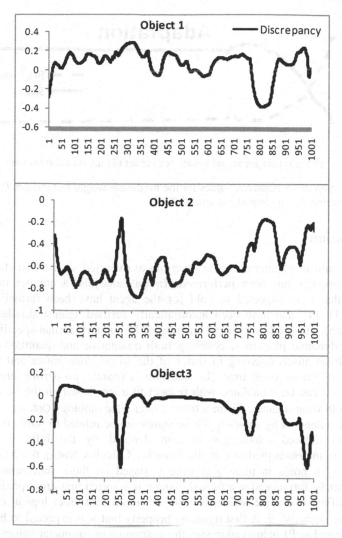

Fig. 2. Estimated discrepancies between urgency and attention for the three objects

Due to these apparently inadequate parameter settings, the ambient software agent initially has a false awareness of the person's attention; for the agent it is as if the person pays enough attention to the enemy object but this is not the case in reality. By the adaptation process the initially inadequate parameter values for the brightness and size weight factors are changing to more appropriate values: from *0.2* vs *0.9* to around *0.8* vs *0.2*, as shown in Fig. 3. As a result of this adaptation, the discrepancies shown in Fig. 2 show a more faithful representation of the situation after, say time point 100 or 150: the discrepancy for object 1 is estimated as rather high positive, and for object 2 strongly negative. This gives the ambient software agent an appropriate awareness of the attention of this person who is almost all the time looking at the wrong (friendly) object, and does not seem to notice the enemy object.

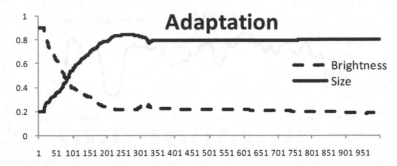

Fig. 3. Adaptation of the parameter values for the brightness weight factor (from *0.9* to around *0.2*) and size weight factor (from *0.2* to around *0.8*)

6 Evaluation

In order to evaluate whether the agent functions as expected, an automated analysis of dynamic properties has been performed. In this analysis, a number of dynamic statements that were expected to hold for the agent have been formalised in the language TTL [4], and have been automatically verified against simulation traces (using Matlab). The predicate logical language TTL supports formal specification and analysis of dynamic properties, covering both qualitative and quantitative aspects. TTL is built on atoms referring to *states* of the world, *time points* and *traces*, i.e. trajectories of states over time. In addition, *dynamic properties* are temporal statements that can be formulated with respect to traces based on the state ontology Ont in the following manner. Given a trace γ over state ontology Ont, the state in γ at time point t is denoted by state(γ, t). These states can be related to state properties via the formally defined satisfaction relation denoted by the infix predicate |=, comparable to the Holds-predicate in the Situation Calculus: state(γ, t) |= p denotes that state property p holds in trace γ at time t. Based on these statements, dynamic properties can be formulated in a formal manner in a sorted first-order predicate logic, using quantifiers over time and traces and the usual first-order logical connectives such as $\neg$, $\wedge$, $\vee$, $\Rightarrow$, $\forall$, $\exists$. A first dynamic property that was expected to hold for the agent (expressed as P1 below) addresses the adaptation of parameter values:

P1 - Smaller range of adaptation over time
For all traces γ, and all parameters p
the difference between the highest and the lowest value of p is larger in the first part of γ than in the second part.

    P1 $\equiv$ $\forall\gamma$:TRACE $\forall$p:PARAMETER $\forall$x1,x2,y1,y2:REAL
    max(x1, p, γ, 0, end_time/2) & min(x2, p, γ, 0, end_time/2) &
    max(y1, p, γ, end_time/2, end_time) & min(y2, p, γ, end_time/2, end_time)
    $\Rightarrow$ x1 - x2 > y1 - y2

Here, end_time denotes the last time point of the simulation trace, and max and min are defined as follows:

    max(x:REAL, p:PARAMETER, γ:TRACE, tb:TIME, te:TIME) $\equiv$
    $\exists$t:TIME

state(γ, t) |= has_value(p, x) & tb ≤ t ≤ te &
¬ [∃t':TIME ∃x':REAL   state(γ, t') |= has_value(p, x') & tb ≤ t' ≤ te & x' > x]

min(x:REAL, p:PARAMETER, γ:TRACE, tb:TIME, te:TIME) ≡
∃t:TIME
state(γ, t) |= has_value(p, x) & tb ≤ t ≤ te &
¬ [∃t':TIME ∃x':REAL   state(γ, t') |= has_value(p, x') & tb ≤ t' ≤ te & x' < x]

Automated checks pointed out that this property indeed holds for all generated traces. For example, for the first half of the trace shown in Figure 3, it turns out that the parameter 'brightness' varies between *0.18* and *0.90* (a difference of *0.72*), whereas for the second half of the trace it only varies between *0.20* and *0.17* (a difference of *0.03*). Similarly, the parameter 'size' varies between *0.20* and *0.84* in the first half of that trace (a difference of *0.64*), and between *0.79* and *0.80* in the second half (a difference of *0.01*). In addition to checking whether the parameter adaptation is performed correctly, it is interesting to check whether the accuracy of the model improves over time due to these parameter adaptations. To this end, one basically needs to check whether the estimated attention corresponds more to the actual attention over time. Since no information about the actual attention is available, the estimated attention is compared to the mouse clicks of the participant. In particular, the amount of *hits*, *misses*, *false alarms*, and *correct rejections* are counted, similar to signal detection approaches [13]. For the current purposes, these notions are defined as follows:

hit - The model estimates a *high* attention level for contact c at time point t, and indeed the participant *does click* on this contact within d time points

miss - The model estimates a *low* attention level for contact c at time point t, whilst the participant *does click* on this contact within d time points

false alarm - The model estimates a *high* attention level for contact c at time point t, whilst the participant *does not click* on this contact within d time points

correct rejection - The model estimates a *low* attention level for contact c at time point t, and indeed the participant *does not click* on this contact within d time points

These cases have been summed over all time points and all contacts. Within TTL, the following properties have been formalised to count the above cases (where th is a threshold to estimate high attention, and D is a constant to represent response time, which was taken 500 msec):

hit   hit(γ:TRACE, t:TIME, x:CONTACT) ≡
            ∃t':TIME ∃i:real
                state(γ,t) |= belief(has_value(av_for(x), i)) & i > th &
                state(γ,t') |= belief(clicked_on(x)) & t < t' ≤ t+D

miss   miss(γ:TRACE, t:TIME, x:CONTACT) ≡
            ∃t':TIME ∃i:real   state(γ,t) |= belief(has_value(av_for(x), i)) & i ≤ th &
                state(γ,t') |= belief(clicked_on(x)) & t < t' ≤ t+D

false alarm   false_alarm(γ:TRACE, t:TIME, x:CONTACT) ≡
            ∃i:real   state(γ,t) |= belief(has_value(av_for(x), i)) & i > th &
                ¬∃t':TIME [state(γ,t') |= belief(clicked_on(x)) & t < t' ≤ t+D]

correct rejection   correct_rejection(γ:TRACE, t:TIME, x:CONTACT) ≡
            ∃i:real   state(γ,t) |= belief(has_value(av_for(x), i)) & i ≤ th &
                ¬∃t':TIME [state(γ,t') |= belief(clicked_on(x)) & t < t' ≤ t+D]

By counting these occurrences, one can calculate the sensitivity and specificity of the model as follows:

sensitivity = hits/(hits+misses)
specificity = correctrejections/(correctrejections+falsealarms)

In principle, an accurate model has a high sensitivity and a high specificity. However, these values also depend on the choice of the threshold th. An extremely low threshold (of *0*) always results in a sensitivity of *1* and a specificity of *0*, whereas an extremely high threshold (of *1*) always results in a sensitivity of *0* and a specificity of *1*. Therefore, the accuracy should be determined with the threshold as a variable. To this end, an ROC (Relative Operative Characteristic) analysis has been performed [10].

The results of this analysis are shown in Figure 4. This figure shows the ROC curves for an example situation in which our agent was applied. The blue curve indicates the start of the scenario, in which the parameters were not yet tuned (in particular, the first 12000 entries of the log file), whereas the red curve indicates the end of the scenario, in which the parameters were tuned (the last 12000 entries). The green curve indicates the results of a baseline agent which makes random estimations with respect to attention. Each curve contains 11 data points (representing 11 different values for th) As shown in Figure 4, the model produces much better after parameter adaptation results than before.

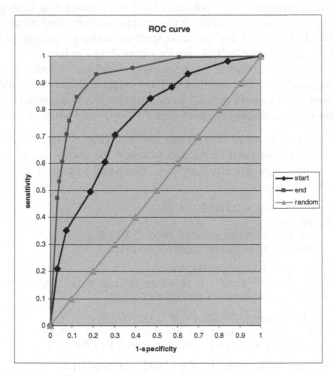

Fig. 4. ROC curves for the model in two different stages, and a random estimation

7 Discussion

In order to function in a knowledgeable manner, intelligent support agents need awareness of the characteristics and states of the human(s) they are supporting. In fact to acquire such human-awareness they need to perform some form of mindreading (e.g., [9], [11], [12]). In order to obtain the capability of mindreading the presented agent was assumed to be equipped with a dynamical model of the human (cf. [7], [15], [17]). In addition to the variables for which values are calculated over time, typically such a dynamical model involves a number of parameters that represent characteristics of the human and the environment. As often individual differences between humans exist, a major challenge here is how the agent can acquire appropriate beliefs on values for parameters representing human characteristics that indeed reflect the specific person involved. Sometimes personal characteristics of a human can be determined at forehand by means of questionnaires and/or interviews. However, such methods do not guarantee appropriate outcomes, as what a person says he or she does is not always the same as what a person actually does. Therefore the option to estimate such parameters (e.g., [16], [18]) may be a better direction to explore. If such parameter estimation is performed by the agent at runtime, this results in an adaptive agent that over times gets more accurate beliefs on the characteristics of the human.

The adaptive software agent presented here possesses a parameter adaptation model that enables it to perform mindreading in particular concerning a human's attention states (e.g., [7], [15]). This attention-reading capability is based on information acquired by sensoring of the gaze, features of the relevant objects in the environment, and a dynamical model in the form of a system of differential equations integrating all this information. For the latter the dynamical model described in [7] was adopted. As a case study for the parameter adaptation model it was applied to the parameters in this attention-reading model. By a formal verification process it was shown for this case study that the adaptive software agent satisfies a number of expected properties.

Despite this encouraging result, care should be taken not to over-generalise the results. Although the verification of dynamic properties pointed out that the model performed better than a model making random estimations, one should keep in mind that these results were obtained in an experiment that involved only one participant in one specific scenario. In future research, more extensive experiments involving more participants will be conducted.

The software environment was implemented according to a component-based design within the Adobe® Flex® development environment, which makes it easy to adapt. Interaction between components was implemented using ActionScript, in an event-driven manner. A sensoring component was included for the gaze sensoring which connects to the Tobii® eye-tracker. Initially, a prototype implementation of the simulation was also carried out in Microsoft Excel®

The software agent with a capability to adapt to personal human characteristics as presented here may be the basis for applications in Ambient Intelligence or Pervasive Computing (e.g., [1], [2], [3]), where it is assumed that computing takes place in the background without addressing the human by an explicit interaction. When such agents can perform some forms of mindreading based on observations and dynamical models they possess, they can indeed act in the background without directly addressing the human. Some steps in this direction for the case of attention-reading were explored in [5] and [6]; however these approaches are not adaptive: parameter values need to be given initially. Another approach, not on attention-reading but on emotion-reading can be found in [8]. Although there parameter adaptation takes place, this is only for a simple case where only two parameters are adapted and where an analytical approach for parameter adjustment was used as the differential equation could be solved analytically to obtain an explicit formula for the sensitivity. As far as the authors know, no other approaches in the literature present attention-reading models that are integrated with mechanisms for parameter adaptation.

References

1. Aarts, E., Collier, R.W., van Loenen, E., de Ruyter, B. (eds.): EUSAI 2003. LNCS, vol. 2875, p. 432. Springer, Heidelberg (2003)
2. Aarts, E., Harwig, R., Schuurmans, M.: Ambient Intelligence. In: Denning, P. (ed.) The Invisible Future, pp. 235–250. McGraw Hill, New York (2001)
3. Bosse, T., Hoogendoorn, M., Klein, M., Treur, J.: A Component-Based Ambient Agent Model for Assessment of Driving Behaviour. In: Sandnes, F.E., Zhang, Y., Rong, C., Yang, L.T., Ma, J. (eds.) UIC 2008. LNCS, vol. 5061, pp. 229–243. Springer, Heidelberg (2008)
4. Bosse, T., Jonker, C.M., van der Meij, L., Sharpanskykh, A., Treur, J.: Specification and Verification of Dynamics in Cognitive Agent Models. International Journal of Cooperative Information Systems 18, 167–193 (2009)
5. Bosse, T., van Lambalgen, R., van Maanen, P.P., Treur, J.: Attention Manipulation for Naval Tactical Picture Compilation. In: Baeza-Yates, R., Lang, J., Mitra, S., Parsons, S., Pasi, G. (eds.) Proc. of the 9th IEEE/WIC/ACM International Conference on Intelligent Agent Technology, IAT 2009, pp. 450–457. IEEE Computer Society Press, Los Alamitos (2007)
6. Bosse, T., van Lambalgen, R., van Maanen, P.-P., Treur, J.: Automated Visual Attention Manipulation. In: Paletta, L., Tsotsos, J.K. (eds.) WAPCV 2008. LNCS (LNAI), vol. 5395, pp. 257–272. Springer, Heidelberg (2009)
7. Bosse, T., Maanen, P.-P., van, T.J.: Simulation and Formal Analysis of Visual Attention. Web Intelligence and Agent Systems Journal 7, 89–105 (2009)
8. Bosse, T., Memon, Z.A., Treur, J.: Adaptive Estimation of Emotion Generation for an Ambient Agent Model. In: Aarts, E., Crowley, J.L., Ruyter, B., de, G.H., Pflaum, A., Schmidt, J., Wichert, R. (eds.) AmI 2008. LNCS, vol. 5355, pp. 141–156. Springer, Heidelberg (2008)
9. Bosse, T., Memon, Z.A., Treur, J.: A Two-Level BDI-Agent Model for Theory of Mind and its Use in Social Manipulation. In: Proceedings of the AISB 2007 Workshop on Mindful Environments, pp. 335–342 (2007)
10. Fawcett, T.: An introduction to ROC analysis. Pattern Recognition Letters 27, 861–874 (2006)
11. Gärdenfors, P.: How Homo Became Sapiens: On The Evolution Of Thinking. Oxford University Press, Oxford (2003)
12. Goldman, A.I.: Simulating Minds: the Philosophy, Psychology and Neuroscience of Mindreading. Oxford University Press, Oxford (2006)

13. Green, D.M., Swets, J.A.: Signal Detection Theory and Psychophysics. Wiley, NY (1966)
14. Memon, Z.A., Oorburg, R., Treur, J., Umair, M., de Vos, M.: A Software Environment for Human-Aware Ambient Support of Attention-Demanding Tasks. Technical Report, VU University, Department of AI
15. Itti, L., Koch, C.: Computational Modeling of Visual Attention. Nature Reviews Neuroscience 2(3), 194–203 (2001)
16. Pearson, C.E.: Numerical Methods in Engineering and Science. CRC Press, Boca Raton (1986)
17. Port, R.F., Gelder, T.: Mind as Motion: Explorations in the Dynamics of Cognition. MIT Press, Cambridge (1995)
18. Sorenson, H.W.: Parameter estimation: principles and problems. Marcel Dekker, Inc., New York (1980)

Designing a Two-Sided Matching Protocol under Asymmetric Information

Masanori Hatanaka* and Shigeo Matsubara

Department of Social Informatics, Kyoto University,
Yoshida-honmachi, Sakyo-ku, Kyoto, Japan
hatanaka@ai.soc.i.kyoto-u.ac.jp, matsubara@i.kyoto-u.ac.jp

Abstract. We have developed a new two-sided matching protocol including job applicants and employers in the condition that applicants have conditional preferences and well informed applicants exist. In past research, two-sided matching has covered some assignment problems such as residency matching. However, in the case of matching on the information network, different applicants are differently informed and well informed applicants hide its information to obtain more desirable matching. That is, asymmetric information possessed by applicants causes unstable matching. To overcome this difficulty, we design a new two-sided matching protocol in which applicants are allowed to report their conditional preferences and well informed applicants generally have an incentive to share information among applicants by allowing applicants to report their conditional preferences and deciding the matching on the basis of the preferences of applicants who share information (informers). We experimentally evaluated our protocol through simulation and found that the protocol can attain more satisfactory matching.

1 Introduction

An aim of research in designing two-sided matching protocols is to formulate matchings of two distinct sets of agents such as employers and job-applicants in the labor market. It has been actively studied and applied to the real-world problems such as the National Residency Matching Program in the USA.

The beginning of this research was the seminal work by Gale and Shapley and they proposed the deferred-acceptance algorithm [1]. They defined a stable matching as one in which there are no blocking pairs, that is, each matching pair has no preferred partners in the matching, and they showed that a matching with no blocking pairs can be obtained using the deferred-acceptance algorithm if each job-applicant has a complete order of preference for employers, and vice versa. In the past research, some extensions of the problem, e.g., allowing preferences with ties or incomplete preferences, have been discussed, and efficient algorithms for solving these problems have been proposed [10].

---

* Masanori Hatanaka is a student of Department of Social Informatics, Kyoto University.

J.-J. Yang et al. (Eds.): PRIMA 2009, LNAI 5925, pp. 308–321, 2009.
© Springer-Verlag Berlin Heidelberg 2009

If we consider the scenarios of matchings in the network environment, we find new problems in formulating stable matching. Getting enough information about employers through the network may be difficult for applicants. If getting information about employers is expensive for some applicants, they must decide their order of preference based on limited information. Furthermore, an investigation about employers may still leave applicants uncertain about the employers. In this case, applicants may be able to infer additional information from the actions of others, leading them to revise their evaluations and, possibly their own actions. They, however, cannot reflect their change of preference in the ordering if they get additional information after the matching has been determined, which causes the matching to be unstable. Thus, uncertainty over one's own preferences brings a problem to two-sided matchings. Multiagent researches have been tried to deal with uncertainty in mechanism design, so they are promising to solve this problem.

It may happen that some applicants know an employer well, e.g., they have an experience working with the employer. The above problem can be mitigated if well-informed applicants disclose their information voluntarily, and we achieve more stable matching. However, this is difficult to achieve because each applicant behaves selfishly. For instance, an applicant who has favorable information about an employer may think that disclosing it will increase the number of applicants competing for jobs with that employer, so he/she will not disclose the information voluntarily. These problems, which we call problems of asymmetric information among applicants, have been considered in research on auctions, but they have not been discussed sufficiently in the area of two-sided matching.

To address these problems, we propose a new matching protocol. We assume that applicants have preferences conditioned on the information from other applicants, and we design protocols that can attain the information sharing among the applicants by inducing them to disclose there information. The matching agent decides a unique matching based on the applicants preferences and the disclosed information. In the proposed protocol, the applicants generally have an incentive to disclose their information.

Chakraborty et. al. discussed two-sided matching with interdependent values and showed that a stable matching mechanism does not generally exist [8]. On the other hand, this paper tries to find a stable matching mechanism by limiting the problem class, although keeping the problem setting realistic.

Our main contribution is the introduction of a two-sided matching model in which asymmetric information among applicants exists and the proposition of the protocol to deal with such a situation. This model enables applicants to share information voluntarily and to reveal definitive preferences under the shared information.

2 Preliminaries

2.1 Model

Consider a many-to-one matching market between applicants and employers. The set of job-applicants is denoted by $A = \{a_1, ..., a_n\}$ with typical element a and the set of employers is denoted by $E = \{e_1, ..., e_n\}$ with typical element e. We introduce a generic term $x \in X$ which collectively means all applicants and all employers. The number of the job openings of e is denoted by n_e, such that the number of applicants who are matched to the employer e does not exceed n_e.

A two-sided many-to-one matching μ is a function from $A \cup E$ to itself such that:

1. $\forall a \in A, \mu(a) \in (E \cup \{a\})$
2. $\forall e \in E, \mu(e) \subseteq (A \cup \{e\}), |\mu(e)| \le n_e$
3. $\forall e_i, e_j \in E, \mu(e_i) \cap \mu(e_j) = \Phi$
4. $\forall a \in A, a \in \mu(\mu(a))$

In other words, the set of applicants and employers is broken into applicant-employer pairs (a, e) for whom $\mu(a) = e$ and $a \in \mu(e)$ and unmatched agents a' for whom $\mu(a') = a'$. Let M be the set of all feasible matchings.

Each employer e is characterized by an unobserved quality $q_e \in Q$, where Q is a finite set. Applicant a may receive a private signal $s_{a,e} \in S$, where S is a finite set. This paper assumes each applicant receives at most one private signal but more than one applicants may receive the same signal about employer e, i.e., $s_{i,e} = s_{j,e}$. Signals and qualities are positively correlated. Thus, applicants can obtain more accurate preferences by learning signals. The set of signals about e is denoted by $S_e = \{s_{i,e} | i = 1, ..., n\}$. Each employer e has preference $p_e = \{a_i, a_j, ...\}$ over their matches, which means e prefers a_i to a_j and so on. Similarly, each applicant a also has preference $p_a = \{e_i, e_j, ...\}$. The notation $p_e = \{..., e, a_k, ...\}$ means that the employer e does not accept matching with the applicant a_k and vice versa. We introduce a decision rules about applicant a_k fs preference $d_k(s_{a,e} \cup \{y\})$ which returns the preference over employers, where $\{y\}$ denotes the information obtained from other applicants. If other applicants publicly announce their private signals, all the applicants can share the information $\{y\}$.

The preferences of applicants in the initial stage $(t = 0)$ are determined by only their private information $p_k^{(0)} \leftarrow d_k(s_{a,e})$. After hearing other applicantsf announcements, the preferences of applicants are revised to those given by their decision rules based on their private information and information obtained from other applicants. When applicant a obtains information $\{y\}$ from other applicants, his/her preference is updated to be $p_k^{(t)} \leftarrow d_k(s_{a,e} \cup \{y\})$.

2.2   Metrics

For discussions about the evaluation of the matching results in the later section, we define two metrics of the matching stability.

At first, agent x's matching rank is denoted by $r_x(\mu(x))$, which means preference order of $\mu(x)$. We deal with the asymmetric information among applicants, so the first one is the sum of applicants' utilities. We assume that the utility of applicant a_k is determined by $r_{a_k}(\mu(a_k)) = r_k^a(e, d_k)$, that is, the rank of the matching partner e on a_k's decision rule d_k.

Definition 1. *We define the sum of applicants' utility $U(\mu)$ as follows:*

$$U(\mu) = \sum_{a_k \in A} \{|E| + 1 - r_k^a(\mu(a_k), d_k(S_{\mu(a_k)}))\}$$

The pair (a, e) satisfying $e \succ_a \mu(a)$ and $\forall a' \in \mu(e), a \succ_e a'$ is called a blocking pair. The classic concept of stability is defined as that no blocking pair exists in the matching. In contrast, under asymmetric information, a particular matching may be stable after one mechanism and unstable after another. Therefore, we introduce quantitative evaluations about the matchings obtained by our mechanisms on the basis of blocking pairs.

At first, we define the blocking partner $b(\mu : x)$ as follows: If x's blocking pairs exist in matching μ, then $b(\mu : x)$ is the top-ranked partner among x's blocking pairs, else $b(\mu : x)$ is the matching partner. The larger the difference between $r_x(\mu(x))$ and $r_x(b(\mu : x))$ become, the more agent x is unpleased with the matching.

Definition 2. *We define the stability of matching $S(\mu)$ as follows:*

$$S(\mu) = - \sum_{x \in A \cup E} \{r_x(\mu(x)) - r_x(b(\mu : x))\}$$

$S(\mu)$ can have a zero or negative values. In fact, $S(\mu) = 0$ if μ is stable in the classic concept of stability.

2.3 Gale-Shapley Algorithm

The preferences of applicants and employers are given in Table 1. For example, the first choice of applicant 1 is A, the second choice is B, and so on.

Each agents report their preference orders to the matching designer and the matching designer execute the deferred-acceptace algorithm (which we call GS algorithm). The GS algorithm proceeds as follows.

1. The first applicant is temporarily assigned to the employer of his/her first choice.
2. The kth applicant selects the employer of his/her first choice.

Table 1. Preferences of applicants and employers

Applicants	Employers
1: A B C D E	A: 3 2 5 1 4
2: A C B E D	B: 4 5 2 1 3
3: B A C D E	C: 3 2 1 5 4
4: B C A D E	D: 4 2 3 1 5
5: A D C E B	E: 2 3 1 4 5

3. When applicant a selects e,
   (a) if e has a remaining job opening, a is temporarily assigned to e.
   (b) if e has already been assigned with someone, e chooses higher-ranked applicant a', and matches with a'. Then, the rejected applicant relabeled as a chooses his/her preferred employer from employers that a has not yet selected, and selects the employer.
4. Process 3 is repeated until all applicants have been assigned to an employer or have been rejected by all employers.
5. $k \leftarrow k + 1$ and back to process 2 until all applicants have selected.

Table 2 shows the results for applying the GS algorithm to Table 1.

Table 2. The matching result obtained by GS algorithm

Applicants	Employers
1: A B C <u>D</u> E	A: <u>3</u> 2 5 1 4
2: A <u>C</u> B E D	B: <u>4</u> 5 2 1 3
3: B <u>A</u> C D E	C: 3 <u>2</u> 1 5 4
4: <u>B</u> C A D E	D: 4 2 3 <u>1</u> 5
5: A D C <u>E</u> B	E: 2 3 1 4 <u>5</u>

In this paper, we try to extend GS Algorithm to address problems of asymmetric information.

We formalize the concept of a "matching protocol." We define it as a centralized direct revelation protocol, in which applicants and employers report their information to the matching designer and the designer proposes who should be matched with whom. More formally, a *direct revelation matching protocol* is a function Γ from the set S of reported signals of agents to the set M of all matchings. Let μ_I be a matching generated by a direct revelation matching protocol under shared information I in which GS algorithm is applied.

3   Information Hiding Problem

Applicants who have positive information about an employer seldom disclose it on the assumption that the competition for that employer would become more severe. So the positive information is not shared, and applicants cannot get enough information to report their own preference orders. Thus, the matching results might be unstable.

Consider the case where applicants $\{a_1, a_2, a_3\}$ and employers $\{e_1, e_2, e_3\}$ exist, $p_{e_1} = \{a_2, a_3, a_1\}$, $p_{e_2} = \{a_1, a_3, a_2\}$, $p_{e_3} = \{a_3, a_2, a_1\}$ and $p_{a_1} = \{e_3, e_1, e_2\}$. Applicant a_1 has an beneficial information i_{a_1} about e_1 but a_2 and a_3 does not know the information. At the beginning, $p_{a_2} = \{e_3, e_2, e_1\}$ and $p_{a_3} = \{e_2, e_3, e_1\}$, but they might change preference if they knew this information.

- Case 1. $p_{a_2}(\{i_{a_i}\}) = \{e_1, e_3, e_2\}$
  In this case, a_2's true preference is $\{e_1, e_3, e_2\}$, but he/she reports $\{e_3, e_2, e_1\}$ to the matching designer if he/she doesn't know a_1's information. If a_1 hides

the information, a_3 reports $\{e_3, e_2, e_1\}$ as his/her preference. As a result, the matching pairs are $< (a_1, e_1), (a_2, e_3), (a_3, e_2) >$, but (a_2, e_1) is a blocking pair when the matching is evaluated based on a_2's true preference. Thus, we can not obtain stable matchings. If a_1 provides the information, the matching pairs are $< (a_1, e_3), (a_2, e_1), (a_3, e_2) >$, so we can obtain stable matchings without decreasing the utility of a_1.

- Case 2. $p_{a_3}(\{i_{a_i}\}) = \{e_1, e_2, e_3\}$

  Similarly, the matching pairs are $< (a_1, e_1), (a_2, e_3), (a_3, e_2) >$ when a_1 hides the information and $< (a_1, e_2), (a_2, e_3), (a_3, e_1) >$ when a_1 provides the information. In this situation, the utility of informer a_1 decreases by declosing his/her information.

Applicant a_1 does not know about other's preferences, so he does not disclose the information for fear of the losing (Case 2). Consequently, the stable matching like Case 1 may not be achieved.

4   Protocol Design

To address the problem shown in the previous section, we need to design new protocols in which applicants who have information have incentives to disclose it. Even if the protocol satisfies the incentive requirement, it remains possible that some applicants might declare false information. However, we cannot externally inspect the existence or nonexistence of information hiding, while it is likely that declarations of false information turn out to be false.

We propose the informers as coodinators protocol (IACP) as a two-sided matching protocol under asymmetric information in which the matching designer determines the matching based on the agents' utilities who report information as true (we call them "informers").

IACP proceeds as follows:

1. The matching designer orders applicant at random.
2. Each applicant evaluates some desired employers on the basis of information obtained over the network, and drafts his/her conditional preference list. This list consists of several pairs of conditions and a preference order for the case where the conditions are true. First, each applicant creates his/her conditional preference list based on only the private information, and reports it to the matching designer.
3. Applicants can report the matching designer whether some conditions are true. The matching designer later determines the matching based on reported true information and reporters' preferences. we call the reporting applicants "informers").
4. The matching designer transmits information about conditions, which includes all of the conditions on reported conditional preference lists and all true information. However, applicants do not know which information are truth.

5. All applicants update their conditional preference lists based on the reported conditions by the matching designer, and they report the updated preference lists to the matching designer again. They can ignore some conditions that do not alter their preference order.
6. All true information is denoted by I. The matching designer obtains matching results by GS Algorithm under for all the subsets of I in advance.
7. The matching designer divides all matching results into 2^n cases according to whether or not an informer provides his/her true information, and finds a subgame perfect equilibrium.
8. The matching designer notifies all applicants and employers of the matching result determined as above and also reveals all true information with the reporters' names as meta-information.

Consider the case where employers A and B both currently have offices on only the east coast. If an applicant has a preference such as if an employer had an office on the west coast, then he/she would want to get a job with the employer. His/her conditional preference list is given by Table 4. If there is no shared information, his/her preference is (C, B, A). If employer A moves office to the west coast, the applicant's preference order becomes (A, C, B).

This applicant is happy if offices are moved to the west coast, but other applicants may not be happy. In general, the directions of changes in preference differ from one applicant to another.

We also investigate how to find a desirable matching if we already have utilities of agents over matches. Each informer's strategy is whether he/she discloses the information or not. The simplest method is to select a Nash equilibrium based on the utility of informers. However, Nash equilibrium is not always available.

The matching results of all the subsets of true information $\{i_1, i_2\}$ expressed by a strategic game are given in Table 4. Each cell represents the utilities of a_2 and a_1. In this case, there are no Nash equilibria, so the matching designer cannot make a unique generation of the matching.

To find a unique solution, we incorporate the order of the provided information to be evaluated. The matching designer orders applicants at random and finds a subgame perfect equilibrium [6]. We describe ordered applicants as $a_1, a_2, \cdots, a_n$, where i_{a_k} denotes the true information reported by applicant a_k. The matching designer sequentially classifies all matching results as to whether each item of true information exists or not according to the ordering of applicants. The classification result is expressed as a n-layer binary tree, and each leaf corresponds to a matching.

Table 3. A conditional preference list of an applicant

Conditions	1	2	3
Both employers A and B move office to the west coast.	A	B	C
Only employer A moves office to the west coast.	A	C	B
Only employer B moves office to the west coast.	B	C	A
Default	C	B	A

Table 4. A strategic game

	i_1	Φ
i_2	(3, 4)	(2, 3)
Φ	(4, 1)	(1, 3)

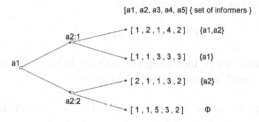

Fig. 1. An Instance in the case where two informers exist

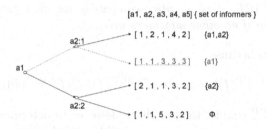

Fig. 2. Matching determination process by backward induction

A binary tree of the instance where ordered applicants $\{ a_1, a_2, a_3, a_4, a_5 \}$ exist, and $\{a_1, a_2\}$ are informers is shown in Fig.4. Each vector at a leaf represents the match ranks of applicants based on their true preferences. If both a_1 and a_2 report true information, for example, then applicants a_1 and a_5 match their first choices, a_2 and a_5 match their second choices, and a_4 matches his/her fourth choice.

The determination process is represented in Fig.4. Here, $\mu_I(a)$ denotes the matching partner of a determined by the GS algorithm over the shared information I. At node of $a_2 : 1$, the matching $\mu_{\{i_{a_1}\}}$ is left because a_2 prefers $\mu_{\{i_{a_1}\}}(a_2)$ to $\mu_{\{i_{a_1}, i_{a_2}\}}(a_2)$. At node of $a_2 : 2$, $\mu_{\{i_{a_2}\}}(a_2)$ and $\mu_{\Phi}(a_2)$ are the same for applicant a_2. In this situation, the matching that includes true information reported by a_2 must be left. Thus, matching $\mu_{\{i_{a_2}\}}$ is left. In the same manner, informer a_1 prefers $\mu_{\{i_{a_1}\}}(a_1)$ to $\mu_{\{i_{a_2}\}}(a_1)$, so the matching designer determines $\mu_{\{i_{a_1}\}}$ as the final result.

5   Game Theoretical Analysis

At first, we define some notations for analysis. All disclosed true information are denoted by $I = \{i_k\}$ and let μ_I be a matching generated by a direct revelation matching protocol under shared information I in which GS algorithm is applied. Our protocol is a direct revelation matching protocol, so IACP is denoted by Γ^{IACP} which is a function from the set I and the set of conditional preferences of agents to $M = \{\mu_S\}$ where $S \subseteq I$. The utility of informer who discloses the information i is denoted by $U_i(\mu_S) = |E| + 1 - r_i(\mu_S(i))$ where $\Gamma^{IACP}(I) = \mu_S$.

Remark 1. Let S be the set of all subset of I.

$$\Gamma^{IACP}(I) = \mu_s, s \in S$$

It means that the number of matching candidates is limited, and is at most $2^{|I|}$ in IACP when disclosed information set I is given.

Definition 3. *A direct revelation matching protocol Γ is incentive-compatible iff:*

$$U_i(\Gamma(I - i)) \leq U_i(\Gamma(I)), \forall i \in I$$

Theorem 1. *In IACP, it is incentive-compatible for an informer to disclose his/her information if no other informers exist.*

Proof. It is obvious because

$$U(\Gamma^{IACP}(I)) = \max(U(\Gamma^{IACP}(I)), U(\Gamma^{IACP}(\Phi))).$$

The protocol Γ^{IACP} enables the matching designer to determine the matching uniquely, though it is not incentive-compatible for all informers. An example is shown in Fig.5 that is not incentive-compatible for informers when a simple subgame perfect equilibrium is used.

The matching is $\mu_{\{i_{a_1}\}}$ when both a_1 and a_2 provide true information, but if only a_1 does, the matching is μ_Φ in which the utilities of both a_1 and a_2 increases.

Theorem 2. *In IACP, it might be not incentive-compatible for an informer to disclose his/her information.*

Proof. We can easily induce the following condition:

$$U_i(\Gamma^{IACP}(S - i)) \leq U_i(\Gamma^{IACP}(S)), \forall S \subseteq I, S \ni i$$

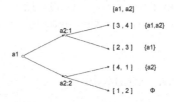

Fig. 3. An Example in the case where incentive-compatible is not satisfied

Table 5. The strategic game in the case of two informers

	1	Φ
2	$(U_1(\Gamma(I)), U_2(\Gamma(I)))$	$(U_1(\Gamma(\{2\})), U_2(\Gamma(\{2\})))$
Φ	$(U_1(\Gamma(\{1\})), U_2(\Gamma(\{1\})))$	$(U_1(\Gamma(\Phi)), U_2(\Gamma(\Phi)))$

It means that, for all subset S which does include i, the utility of i informer when S are shared must be equal or higher than the utility of i informer when $S - \{i\}$ are shared. However, the matching generation $\Gamma^{IACP}(S - \{i\})$ must be indifferent from the utility of i informer because the protocol must be applicable if the all information set was $S - \{i\}$.

The example when two informers exist is expressed by the game of strategic form is shown by Table 5. It is without loss of generalty to assume the situation that:

$$U_1(\mu_2) > U_1(\mu_S), S \in \{\Phi, \{1\}, \{1, 2\}\} \tag{1}$$
$$U_2(\mu_1) > U_2(\mu_{S'}), S' \in \{\Phi, \{2\}, \{1, 2\}\} \tag{2}$$
$$U_1(\mu_1) \geq U_1(\mu_\Phi) \tag{3}$$
$$U_2(\mu_2) \geq U_2(\mu_\Phi) \tag{4}$$

In this situation, $\Gamma^{IACP}(\{1\}) = \mu_{\{1\}}$ and $\Gamma^{IACP}(\{2\}) = \mu_{\{2\}}$.

1. Suppose $\Gamma^{IACP}(I) = \mu_{\{1,2\}}$. It is not incentive-compatible for informer 1 and informer 2 according to the conditions (1)(2). It is similary when $\Gamma^{IACP}(\{1, 2\}) = \mu_\Phi$.
2. Suppose $\Gamma^{IACP}(I) = \mu_{\{1\}}$. It is not incentive-compatible for informer 1 because $U_1(\Gamma^{IACP}(I)) < U_1(\Gamma^{IACP}(\{2\})) = U_1(\mu_{\{2\}})$.
3. Similarily, It is not incentive-compatible for informer 2 when $\Gamma^{IACP}(\{1, 2\}) = \mu_{\{1\}}$.

There are no other matching candidates in $\Gamma^{IACP}(I)$ because of the property shown by Remark 1. Therefore, it is not incentive-compatible for both informer 1 and informer 2 in IACP.

6 Evaluations

6.1 Rationality of Agents

Theoretically, IACP cannot satisfy incentive compatibility of disclosing information. However, we investigated how many such cases actually occur through simulations. Table. 6 shows how the utility of the informer who disclose information varies when another informer disclose information in one-to-one matching situations. The number of applicants is 8, and two of them are informers. As a result, we figured out that the informer seldom move down the match rank, even if the information is positive about an employer. Therefore, in most cases, it is Nash equilibrium for informers to disclose information.

Table 6. The relation between informers and match rank

information types	rank up	even	rank down
only negative	22240	77721	39
at random	12500	87425	75
only positive	1544	98400	56

6.2 Quality of Matching

The more applicants are affected by the sharing of true information, the worse the matching result is likely to be if no information is shared. However, the directions of preference changes are not homogeneous, so not sharing information may bring a better matching result. Therefore, we should check the influence that the ratio of affected applicants has on the matching result. Through simple simulations, we evaluated the utilities of applicants and the matching stability when the ratio of affected applicants was changed.

First, we explain the simulation settings. We set the number of applicants as 32, the number of employers as 8, the number of job openings as 8 for all employers, and the number of informers as 2. We suppose that informers have information about their first choice's employers.

In general, the larger the number of applicants submitting true information, the more the ratio of affected applicants increases. However, we suppose that the preference changes do not depend on the number of informers, but depends on the shared information itself. And in this simulation, we presumed that each condition depends on one employer, so the order of preference except for employer e does not vary according to the true information about employer e.

We simulated more than 10000 incidents and compared the results for IACP with those obtained by the Gale-Shapley protocol with shared information ("All Shared") and without shared information ("Simple GS").

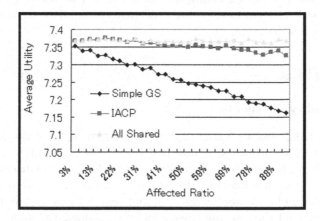

Fig. 4. Average utilities of applicants

The graph in Fig. 4 shows the average utilities of applicants who are not informers organized by the ratio of affected applicants.

It indicates that the larger the number of affected applicants, the worse their average utilities tended to be. The introduction of IACP prevented the utilities of non-informers from decreasing and kept them as high as in the Gale-Shapley protocol with shared true information. Fig. 5 shows the case that disclosed information is positive. In that case, applicants who accept the information about an employer may raise its rank, so we can easily predict that informer's match rank is likely to decline. However, the graph indicates that the proposing protocol is effective even if informers have positive information.

The average number of agents who have blocking pairs organized by the ratio of affected applicants is shown in Fig. 6. The figure indicates that the stability became worse as the ratio of affected applicants increased in "Simple GS". It is natural that the number of blocking pairs is always 0 in the case of "All Shared" because the matchings were obtained by the GS algorithm. Fig. 6 shows that

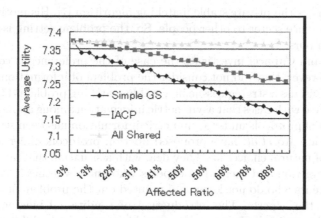

Fig. 5. Average utilities of applicants when disclosed information is positive

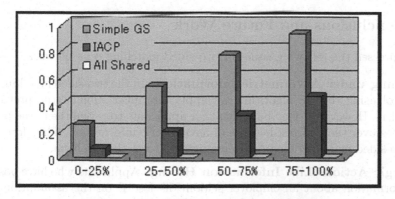

Fig. 6. The stability of the matching

the average stabilities were improved in IACP. We checked the rate of incidents in which the number of agents who have blocking pairs was 0 and it turned out that the matching was stable in more than 90% of incidents.

7 Related Work

Roth [4] has analyzed residence matching in the USA and pointed out the problem if some couples of applicants exist. A couple of applicants may prefer each first choice of hospitals to hospitals that are close geographically. He has designed protocols that enable couples to submit the preference of the pair. The preference of a pair consists of the ordering of pairs of hospitals. Their research is similar to ours in dealing with a situation that an applicant behavior affect another applicant preference.. However, the preferences of couples are not affected by the preferences of other single applicants. Thus, the problem of information revelation does not occur. Therefore, Roth's technique cannot solve the problems treated here.

Golle discusses the private stable matching algorithm [7], His motivation is to keep the preference secret to other people. So, the problem setting is completely different from ours.

Caldarelli and Capocci investigate the case of the preference is correlated to others [9]. However, they did not consider the problem of information revelation.

Teo, et.al. discuss a strategic issue in a stable matching problem [11]. However, they did not deal with cases that asymmetric information among applicants exists.

The design of protocols under asymmetric information has been studied in the area of auctions. Ito et.al. have proposed auction protocols under asymmetric information of natural choices [5]. They deal with a situation that an antique pot is put up for auction and there exist experts who know whether it is genuine or not and amateurs who do not know and pointed out the problem of information revelation by the experts. The introduction of conditional bids enables these problems to be avoided. However, the matching protocol is different from the auction protocols in that no monetary transfer occurs in our problem setting.

8 Conclusions and Future Work

We addressed the following issues in two-sided matching on a network.

Matching under Asymmetric Information. In the two-sided matching protocol using the GS algorithm, all applicants must submit true preference orders. However, it may be difficult for applicants to reveal their true preferences over the network because of asymmetric information. Therefore, new two-sided matching models are required to treat this problem.

Strategic Actions Like Information Hiding. Applicants who have positive information about an employer seldom disclose it on the assumption that the competition for that employer would become more severe. As a result of strategic actions like this, other applicants cannot get useful information.

To solve the issues above, we studied IACP on the basis of conditional preferences and information sharing as a matching model under asymmetric information. We analyzed the disclosure strategies of applicants who have information by means of game theories and designed a protocol in which information holders generally have an incentive to provide information over the network via the matching designer. We considered asymmetric information only on the applicant side in this paper, so the study of asymmetric information on both sides remains for future work. In addition, our approach in this paper needs a lot of calculation. We will study protocols that have low computational costs, considering the relationship between information and preference changes.

This research was partially supported by a Grant-in-Aid for Scientific Research (B) (19300054, 2007-2009) from Japan Society for the Promotion of Science (JSPS).

References

1. Gale, D., Shapley, L.S.: College Admissions and the Stability of Marriage. The American Mathematical Monthly 69(1), 9–15 (1962)
2. Roth, A.E.: Misrepresentation and Stability in the Marriage Problem. Journal of Economic Theory 34(2), 383–387 (1984)
3. Roth, A.E.: Conflict and Coincidence of Interest in Job Matching: Some New Results and Open Questions. Mathematics of Operations Research 10(3), 379–389 (1985)
4. Roth, A.E., Peranson, E.: The Redesign of the Matching Market for American Physicians: Some Engineering Aspects of Economic Design. National Bureau of Economic Research Cambridge, Mass., USA (1999)
5. Ito, T., Yokoo, M., Matsubara, S.: Designing an Auction Protocol under Asymmetric Information on Nature's Selection. In: Proceedings of the First International joint Conference on Autonomous Agents and Multiagent Systems, AAMAS-2002 (2002)
6. Kreps, D.M.: A Course in Microeconomic Theory. Princeton University Press, Princeton (1990)
7. Golle, P.: A private stable matching algorithm. In: Di Crescenzo, G., Rubin, A. (eds.) FC 2006. LNCS, vol. 4107, pp. 65–80. Springer, Heidelberg (2006)
8. Chakraborty, A., Citanna, A., Ostrovsky, M.: Two-Sided Matching with Interdependent Values (2007)
9. Caldarelli, G., Capocci, A.: Beauty and distance in the stable marriage problem. Physica A: Statistical Mechanics and its Applications 300(1-2), 325–331 (2001)
10. Iwama, K., Manlove, D., Miyazaki, S., Morita, Y.: Stable marriage with incomplete lists and ties. In: Wiedermann, J., Van Emde Boas, P., Nielsen, M. (eds.) ICALP 1999. LNCS, vol. 1644, pp. 443–452. Springer, Heidelberg (1999)
11. Teo, C.P., Sethuraman, J., Tan, W.P.: Gale-Shapley Stable Marriage Problem Revisited: Strategic Issues and Applications. Management Science 47(9), 1252–1267 (2001)
12. Ackermann, H., Goldberg, P.W., Mirrokni, V.S., Roglin, H., Vocking, B.: Uncoordinated two-sided markets. In: Proceedings of the 8th ACM Conference on Electronic Commerce (EC), pp. 256–263 (2008)

Emotion Detection from Body Motion of Human Form Robot Based on Laban Movement Analysis

Megumi Masuda, Shohei Kato, and Hidenori Itoh

Dept. of Computer Science and Engineering, Graduate School of Engineering,
Nagoya Institute of Technology,
Gokiso-cho Showa-ku Nagoya, 466-8555 Japan
{masuda,shohey,itoh}@juno.ics.nitech.ac.jp

Abstract. A set of physical feature values, called a Laban's feature set, is proposed to explain an observer's impression of bodily expression. The design concept of our Laban's feature value set is based on Laban Movement Analysis, which is a well known theory in body movement psychology. For practical application to human-agent interaction (HAI), use a human-form robot (HFR) as a motioning object. A correlation between our Laban's feature set and the HFR's emotions (*Pleasure, Anger, Sadness* and *Relaxed*), which subjects estimated, was examined. In reference to Russell's circumplex model of affect, we discuss the correlation using two axial ("pleasure-displeasure" and "degree of arousal") characteristics. Finally, we present four estimation equations with accuracy rates of more than 85%.

1 Introduction

Expression of emotions is studied with keen interest as a requisite of robot-human communication. The reason is that robot technology and the study of human-agent interaction (HAI) have advanced. There are two methods for a robot to express an emotion state. One uses verbal information (e.g., [1], [2]) and the other uses nonverbal information (e.g., [3], [4]). Each has advantages and disadvantages. In this paper, bodily expression as nonverbal information is examined as an expression of emotion. (e.g., [5], [6], [7]). To express emotion using its body parts is advantageous, that is, this does not require additional devices (e.g., an indication device, a speaker, facial expression). Moreover, body movements are important to understanding verbal interaction (e.g., [8]). Nonverbal information is indispensable for social interaction [9].

There are three important factors for robot's mental-like interaction using bodily expression, 1) a robot needs to be able to recognize an observer's impression of its whole-body movements, 2) it needs to automatically move its entire body, and 3) it needs to express the appropriate emotion.

Our aim is to examine the correlation between a robot's whole-body movements and its emotions, which an observer can estimate. Also, emotion estimation equations are presented.

J.-J. Yang et al. (Eds.): PRIMA 2009, LNAI 5925, pp. 322–334, 2009.

First, we propose a set of motion feature values, called the Laban's feature value set. This set distills features of a human-form robot's (HFR's) whole-body movement. Next, a correlation between the Laban's feature value set and an HFR's emotions, which subjects determine, is examined. Emotion estimations equations are also presented, and multiple linear regression analysis is used to generate them. Finally, there equations are examined to confirm their accuracy. As a result, the accuracy rates were more than 85%.

2 Laban's Feature Value Set

In this section, we discuss our set of motion feature values, called the Laban's feature value set, which is based on Laban Movement Analysis.

2.1 Laban Movement Analysis

Laban Movement Analysis [10] is a well known theory in dance. The correlation between an agent's body movements and psychological condition is analyzed. Laban Movement Analysis was developed by German expressionism dance creators mainly Rudolf von Laban. It has succeeded Darwin's theory [11], which focuses on structure of an animal's bodily expression. Laban's theory suits science and engineering, because it is mathematical and specific.

2.2 Using Human Form Robots

We used our Laban's feature value set on an HFR. HFRs have human-like degrees-of-freedom and extremities. The reasons an HFR was selected are as follows;

- It reduces human's fear and discomfort of robots.
- It allows humans to easily understand emotions expressed by a robot's whole-body movements.
- It allows humans to empathize with robots.

The position vectors of extremity points, and the direction vector of the face and angle data of each joint are used to distill features of HFR's entire body movement (see Fig. 1). We use the right-hand rule and origin of the coordinate system is set on the center of HFR's chest. That is, positive direction of x is forward, y is left, and z is upward. The information of HFR's whole-body movement does not depend on the degrees-of-freedom. Therefore, the Laban's feature value set is distilled from all HFRs in the same way.

2.3 Extraction of Laban's Feature Value Set

Space, Time, Weight, Inclination, Height, and Area are distilled from the HFR's whole-body movements. They are the six main features of Laban Movement Analysis. Table 1 lists the features of whole-body movement in Laban Movement Analysis and how to distill them. The Laban's feature values at timepoint t are defined as follows;

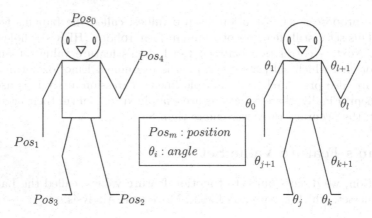

Fig. 1. Link structure of HFR and observed information

Table 1. Laban's Feature Set

Laban's feature	Feature	Extraction of feature
Space	bias of whole-body movement	weighted sum of inner product between unit movement vectors of each extremity point and direction unit vector of face
Time	speed of whole-body movement	weighted sum of angular velocity of each joint
Weight	powerfulness of whole-body movement	weighted sum of each joint's torque
$Inclination_x$	bias of posture against front	difference between position of center of gravity and center position of support foot against front
$Inclination_y$	bias of posture against right and left	difference between position of center of gravity and center position of support foot against right and left
Height	height of posture	difference between position of center of gravity and that of erection against ups and downs
Area	extent of body against plane	area of quadrangle made by extremity points

Space represents the bias of whole-body movements, and is defined by the following equation:

$$Space(t) = \sum_{m=0}^{3} \sum_{n=m+1}^{4} a_m a_n (\vec{r_m}(t) \cdot \vec{r_n}(t)), \qquad (1)$$

where m and n is the distinction number of the face and the extremity points. $\vec{r_m}$ is the unit movement vectors of extremity's point ($m=1,2,3,4$) or the unit direction vector of the face ($m=0$), and a_n is the weight coefficient of n. It was heuristically determined depending upon its appearance.

Time represents the speed of whole-body movement and is defined by the following equation:

$$Time(t) = \sum_i b_i \dot{\theta}_i(t), \tag{2}$$

where i is the joint number and $\dot{\theta}_i$ is the angle velocity of joint i, and b_i is the weight coefficient of i. It was heuristically determined depending upon its appearance.

Weight represents the powerfulness of whole-body movement, and is defined by the following equation:

$$Weight(t) = \sum_i c_i \tau_i(t), \tag{3}$$

where τ_i is the torque of joint i, and c_i is the weight coefficient of i. It was heuristically determined depending upon its appearance.

Inclination represents the bias of posture, and is defined by the following equation:

$$Inclination(t) = cog(t) - col(t), \tag{4}$$

where cog is the center position of the gravity of HFR and col is the center position of the support foot. $Inclination_x$ is $Inclination$ of forward and backward. $Inclination_y$ is $Inclination$ of right and left. The positive direction of x is forward and y is left.

Height represents the height of posture, and is defined by the following equation:

$$Height(t) = cog(t) - cog_0, \tag{5}$$

where cog_0 is the center position of gravity of the HFR when standing straight.

Area represents the extent of the HFR's body, and defined by the following equation:

$$Area(t) = \sum_{m=1}^{3} \sum_{n=m+1}^{4} \frac{1}{2} |x_m(t)y_n(t) + y_m(t)x_n(t)|, \tag{6}$$

where x_m is the x coordinate of the extremity point of m, and y_m is y coordinate of the extremity point of m.

A sequence of Laban's feature values is defined as a normalization of the above equations. For example, $Space$ is follows:

$$Space = \frac{1}{N} \int Space^*(t)dt, \tag{7}$$

where N is the operating time and $Space^*(t)$ is the normalization of $Space(t)$. The others of Laban's feature values set are likewise normalized.

3   Pilot Experiment

We conducted an impression experiment as a pilot experiment. Fifteen subjects between the ages of 20 and 40 observed an HFR's whole-body movements and estimated its emotions. The HFR made 40 whole-body movements each lasting 8 seconds. The HFR, KHR-2HV (Degree-of-freedom = 17, height = 353 mm), was used as the agent. Fig. 2 is a photograph of the KHR-2HV.

3.1   The Whole-Body Movement

Ten motions for four emotions (*Pleasure*, *Anger*, *Sadness*, and *Relaxed*) were made similar to positions used in clay animation, and then, each motion was modified four variations that are designed for the four emotions. Examples of motions are shown in Fig. 4.

3.2   Method

The questionnaire used for the experiment is shown in Fig. 3. The pilot experiment was conducted follows.

The subjects estimated and marked the strength of each emotion expressed through the motions of the agent. They marked on the segment in the questionnaire as answer. The strength of each emotion was rated on a scale from 0 to 1, put, 0 being weakest and 1 being strongest. If mark was checked at left end of the segment, the whole-body movement was estimated as expressing no emotion. Homogeneous transformation following the mark was done to quantify the estimation. The quantified estimations are called "values of estimated emotion".

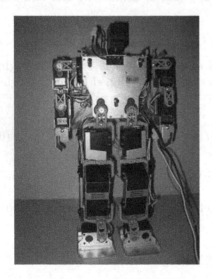

Fig. 2. KHR-2HV

Fig. 3. Questionnaire

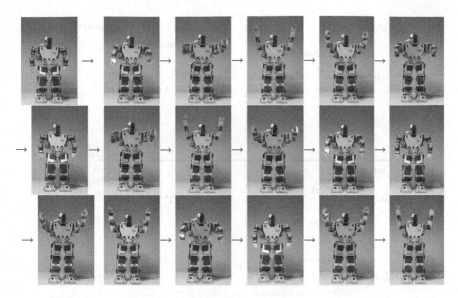

Fig. 4. An example of a motion

The averages of each value of estimated emotion are called "average of subject estimations".

4 Correlation between Value of Emotion Estimation and our Set of Laban's Feature Values

The correlation between the values of estimated emotion and our set of Laban's feature values was examined. In this experiment, $Inclination_y$ was removed, because there was no confirmation of it having correlation with $Space$, $Inclination_x$, $Height$, or $Area$.

The correlation coefficients between the values of emotion estimation and our set of Laban's feature values are listed in Table 2. Light gray represent positive correlation (significance level is over 1%), and dark gray represent negative correlation (significance level is over 1%). The correlation between the values of emotion estimation and proposed our set of Laban's feature values was demonstrated from Table 2.

Table 2. Correlation Coefficient between Values of Emotion Estimation and Set of Laban's Feature Values

	Spa	Tim	Wei	Inc$_x$	Hei	Are
Pleasure	-0.04	0.45	0.46	-0.27	0.33	0.36
Anger	-0.21	0.30	0.33	0.01	-0.02	0.20
Sadness	0.03	-0.38	-0.42	0.47	-0.51	-0.39
Relaxed	0.16	-0.15	-0.12	-0.37	0.36	0.01

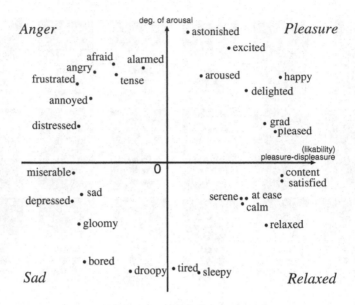

Fig. 5. Russell's circumplex model of affect

Below, the correlation between the values of emotion estimation and our set of Laban's feature values was examined.

We used Russell's the circumplex model of affect[12]. In this model, emotions are placed in a circle in a two-dimensional (pleasure-displeasure and degree-of-arousal) space. This model is applied to *Pleasure*, *Anger*, *Sadness*, and *Relaxed* (Fig. 5). That is, *Pleasure* and *Relaxed* are classified in the pleasure group, and *Anger* and *Sadness* are classified in the displeasure group. Alike *Pleasure* and *Anger* are classified in the arousal group, and *Sadness* and *Relaxed* are classified in the sleep group.

4.1 Pleasure-Displeasure and Our Set of Laban's Feature Values

The four emotions were divided into pleasure and displeasure groups (see Table 3). From this, the correlations regarding about $Inclination_x$ and $Height$ are reversed. In other words, a posture such that it has a bias to the backward and its c.o.g. is high effectively expresses emotions that are classified into *Pleasure* or *Relaxed*. On the contrary, a posture such that it has a bias to the forward and its c.o.g. is low effectively expresses emotions that are classified into *Anger* or *Sadness*.

4.2 Degree-of-Arousal and Our Set of Laban's Feature Values

The four emotions were divided into arousal and sleep groups (see Table 4). From this, the correlations regarding $Time$ and $Weight$ are reversed. In other words, a quick and powerful movement effectively expresses emotions that are

Table 3. Pleasure and Displeasure Groups

		Spa	Tim	Wei	Inc_x	Hei	Are
pleasure	Pleasure	-0.04	0.45	0.46	-0.27	0.33	0.36
	Relaxed	0.16	-0.15	-0.12	-0.37	0.36	0.01
	Anger	-0.21	0.30	0.33	0.01	-0.02	0.20
displeasure	Sadness	0.03	-0.38	-0.42	0.47	-0.51	-0.39

Table 4. Arousal and Sleep Groups

		Spa	Tim	Wei	Inc_x	Hei	Are
arousal	Pleasure	-0.04	0.45	0.46	-0.27	0.33	0.36
	Anger	-0.21	0.30	0.33	0.01	-0.02	0.20
	Sadness	0.03	-0.38	-0.42	0.47	-0.51	-0.39
sleepy	Relaxed	0.16	-0.15	-0.12	-0.37	0.36	0.01

in a state of arousal. On the contrary, a slow and weak movement effectively expresses emotions that are in a state of sleepiness.

5 Emotion's Estimation Equations

In the previous section, the correlation between expressed emotions and our Laban's feature value set was observed. In this section, we present emotion estimation equations by using multiple linear regression analysis. In the analysis, Laban's feature value set calculated in Section 2 and values of estimated emotion, that is expressed emotion value, examined in Section 3 are used. In each of the equations, expressed emotion value is response variable and our Laban's feature value set is a set of explanatory variables. The response variable are valued between 0 and 100.

5.1 Generating Emotion Estimation Equations

First, explanation variables must be determined. Before generating the emotion's estimation equations, standard partial regression coefficients of each Laban's feature value were calculated. The features whose standard partial regression coefficients were meaningful (significance level over 10% except for sudness; 15% for sadness) were determined as explanation variables. Each elected features is listed in Table 5. By using these as explanation variables, each emotion's estimation equations was generated by multiple linear regression analysis.

The emotion estimation equations are as follows;
Pleasure

$$E_{Pleasure} = 26.5 + 15.9 Time + 9.6 Height, \qquad (8)$$

Anger

$$E_{Anger} = 19.1 - 19.6 Time + 24.4 Weight$$
$$- 8.7 Inclination_x - 17.6 Height$$
$$- 17.6 Area, \qquad (9)$$

Table 5. Standard Partial Regression Coefficients

		Laban's feature					
		Spa	Tim	Wei	Inc_x	Hei	Are
Emotions	Pleasure	0.08	$0.65^{\dagger\dagger}$	0.05	0.07	0.67^*	-0.25
	Anger	-0.18	-1.00^*	1.20^{**}	$-0.50^{\dagger\dagger}$	-0.92^*	0.65^*
	Sadness	-0.02	-0.03	$-0.38^\dagger$	0.39^*	$-0.31^\dagger$	-0.12
	Relaxed	0.04	0.50	-0.71^*	-0.07	0.99^{**}	$-0.46^{\dagger\dagger}$

† : significance level over 15% †† : significance level over 10%
* : significance level over 5% ** : significance level over 1%

Sadness

$$E_{Sadness} = 22.7 - 11.7 Weight$$
$$+ 7.7 Inclination_x - 9.8 Height, \tag{10}$$

Relaxed

$$E_{Relaxed} = 21.5 - 8.1 Weight + 13.5 Height. \tag{11}$$

The emotion estimation values of whole-body movements were calculated using these equations. The Laban feature values distilled from the bodily movements substituted variables for calculating. Notice that when the result was below 0 or more than 100, the emotion estimation value was, respectively, 0 or 100.

6   Emotion's Estimation Exam

A four-fold cross-validation was done to confirm the equations' accuracy. We used the 40 bodily movements discussed in Section 3.

6.1   Criterion for Evaluation

The differences between averages of subject estimations and emotion estimation values were used to confirm the equations' accuracy. We assumed that values of emotion estimation follow a normal distribution. The correct emotion estimations are defined as the difference between average subject estimations and values of emotion's estimations are less than standard deviation of subjects' emotion distribution. We thus considered only the cases that distribution of value of emotion estimation follow a normal distribution. Because the values are used for a corrigendum decision. The Jarque-Bera statistical value was used for decision of normal distribution. The Jarque-Bera statistical values of each emotion estimations were calculated and the item whose distribution follows a normal distribution (significance level over 5%) was determined. Others were excluded from decision target.

For example, a set of Laban's feature values, which is listed in Table 4, was distilled from the 40 motions (see Fig. 4).

Table 6. Laban's Feature Values of Fig. 4

	Spa	Tim	Wei	Inc_x	Hei	Are
Feature Value	0.05	1.34	1.17	-0.25	-0.32	0.09

Table 7. Average of Estimations of Subjects and Emotion Estimation Values of Fig. 4

Emotion	Pleasure	Anger	Sadness	Relaxed
Emotion estimation values	45.18	27.86	9.80	-
Average of Estimations of Subjects	41.67	20.50	4.17	-
Difference	3.52	7.36	5.64	-
Standard deviation	32.12	29.31	5.95	-
Decision				-

For example, the *Pleasure* estimation values of the motions shown in Fig. 4 were calculated as follows:

$$E_{Pleasure} = 26.5 + 15.9 \times 1.34 + 9.6 \times (-0.32) = 45.18. \qquad (12)$$

Likewise, the *Anger* (E_{Anger}=27.86) and *Sadness* estimation values ($E_{Sadness}$ =9.80) were calculated. The motions' (shown in Fig. 4) averages of subject estimations are as follows; *Pleasure*: 41.62, *Anger*: 20.50, *Sadness*: 4.17. Each averages of estimations of subjects' standard deviation of the motion are as follows; *Pleasure*: 42.12, *Anger*: 29.31, *Sadness*: 5.95 (see Table 7). Therefore, emotion estimations of these motions were accurate. *Relaxed* was not evaluated because the distribution value of *Relaxed*'s averages of subject estimations standard deviation did not follow the normal distribution.

6.2   Accuracy Rate of Emotion Estimations

The rates of accurate emotion estimations are listed in Table 8. From this table, each emotion estimation has high accuracy rate of over 85%. It should be noticed that "All emotions" means the rate of movement for which all emotion estimations were accurate. Compared to the accuracy rate estimated at random (21% $= 0.68^4 \times 100$), "All emotions" had a sufficient high accuracy rate. Therefore, the emotion estimation equations presented in this paper can be used to sufficiently estimate each emotion.

The differences between average subject estimations and values of emotion estimations are listed in Tables 9-12. For example, in Table 9, at 48.7%, the differences between average subject estimations of *Pleasure* and values of *Pleasure*'s estimation were from 0 to 5. From these results, it is seen that the emotion estimation equations were estimated nearer to the average estimation than to the value of emotion that subjects estimated.

Therefore the accuracy of the emotion estimation equations was confirmed.

Table 8. Correct Answer Rate

	Pleasure	Anger	Sadness	Relaxed	All emotions
rate	89.2%	87.5%	90.0%	97.2%	69.7%

Table 9. Distributions of Difference from Average Estimation (*Pleasure*)

estimation by	-10-5	-50	0 5	510	Sum
equation	8.1%	8.1%	48.7%	10.8%	75.7%
subject	7.3%	24.7%	6.7%	3.6%	42.3%

Table 10. Distributions of Difference from Average Estimation (*Anger*)

estimation by	-10-5	-50	0 5	510	Sum
equation	5.0%	22.5%	12.5%	25.0%	65.0%
subject	22.0%	9.7%	6.5%	6.0%	44.2%

Table 11. Distributions of Difference from Average Estimation (*Sadness*)

estimation by	-10-5	-50	0 5	510	Sum
equation	15.0%	20.0%	20.0%	17.5%	72.5%
subject	16.0%	14.3%	5.5%	5.5%	41.3%

Table 12. Distributions of Difference from Average Estimation (*Relaxed*)

estimation by	-10-5	-50	0 5	510	Sum
equation	16.7%	13.9%	16.7%	25.0%	72.3%
subject	20.7%	10.3%	8.2%	3.3%	42.5%

7 Related Works

The robot used by Nakata et al.[13] has 3 joint degrees-of-freedom and moves on wheels. In contrast, we generated emotion estimation equations for which the whose target robot is an HFR with joint degrees-of-freedom. An HFR is a robot best adapted to mental-like interaction; therefore, HFRs are expected to interact with humans in various situations in the future.

Maeda et al. [5] also studied emotion detection from body movement. They used the images of humans and robots. Their Laban's feature values have a weakness due to lack of information retrieved from the images. Therefore, we proposed our Laban's feature value set as being sensitive to whole-body movements. Moreover, we considered body movements by a real robot. This is supported by studies (e.g., [14], [15], [16]), which reports that a robot agent can create more positive impressions than a virtual agent.

8   Conclusion

A Laban's feature value set was proposed to distill features HFR's whole-body movements. An impression experiment was conducted, and the correlation between our set of Laban's feature values and HFR's emotions, which subjects estimated, was examined. In addition, emotion estimation equations using our set of Laban's feature values were generated. Cross-validation was done to confirm the emotion estimation equations' accuracy. From an experiment using the HFR, it was showed that there is a sufficient correlation between our Laban's feature value set and HFR's expression of emotions that subjects estimated, and the accuracy of emotion estimation equations was confirmed. Those emotion estimation equations will be able to use for checking the emotion of created motion. To express emotion using its body parts is advantageous, that is, this does not require additional devices.

Our Laban's feature value set was distilled from an HFR. Our Laban's feature value set is applicable to robots except HFR if minor modifications are done. If the center bottom is considered as the center of the support foot, then it can be distilled from robot that moves on wheels, or has more than three arms. The experiment was pilot study. In the future work, we will dedicate to the experiments with much more subjects and much more motions.

Though our Laban's feature value set was distilled from motion information, we could like to distill this information from video as well. This will allow us to easily analyze a human's whole-body movements in dance and drama. Moreover, analysis of a human's whole-body movements will be useful for studying human-robot interaction. We would like to distill our Laban's feature value set from long movement. We will also study an HFR's whole body movements for expressing accurate emotions.

Acknowledgment

This work was supported in part by the Tatematsu Foundation, and by a Ministry of Education, Science, Sports and Culture, Grant–in–Aid for Scientific Research under grant #20700199 and #21500187.

References

1. Hara, I., Asano, F., Asoh, H., Ogata, J., Ichimura, N., Kawai, Y., Kanehiro, F., Hirukawa, H., Yamamoto, K.: Robust Speech Interface Based on Audio and Video Information Fusion for Humanoid HRP-2. In: IEEE/RSJ International Conference on Intelligent Robots and Systems (IROS 2004), pp. 2404–2410 (2004)
2. Yamamoto, S., Nakadai, K., Nakano, M., Tsujino, H., Valin, J.M., Komatani, K., Ogata, T., Okuno, H.G.: Real-Time Robot Audition System That Recognizes Simultaneous Speech in the Real World. In: IEEE/RSJ International Conference on Intelligent Robots and Systems (IROS 2006), pp. 5333–5338 (2006)
3. Brooks, A.G., Arkin, R.C.: Behavioral overlays for non-verbal communication expression on a humanoid robot. Autonomous Robots 22, 55–74 (2007)

4. Itoh, C., Kato, S., Itoh, H.: A Characterization of Sensitivity Communication Robots Based on Mood Transition. In: Ho, T.-B., Zhou, Z.-H. (eds.) PRICAI 2008. LNCS (LNAI), vol. 5351, pp. 959–964. Springer, Heidelberg (2008)
5. Maeda, Y.: Emotional Generation Model for Autonomous Mobile Robot. KANSEI Engineering International 1, 59–66 (1999)
6. Hattori, M., Nakabo, Y., Tadokoro, S., Takamori, T., Yamada, K.: An analysis of the Bunraku puppet's motions based on the phase correspondence of the puppet's motions axis-for the generation of humanoid robots motions with fertile emotions. In: IEEE International Conference on Systems, Man, and Cybernetics., pp. 1041–1046 (1999)
7. Mizoguchi, H., Sato, T., Takagi, K., Nakao, M., Hatamura, Y.: Realization of Expressive Mobile Robot. In: IEEE International Conference on Robotics and Automation (ICRA 1997), pp. 581–586 (1997)
8. Rogers, W.T.: The Contribution of Kinetic Illustrators towards the Comprehension of Verbal Behavior within Utterances. Human Communication Research 5, 54–62 (2006)
9. Fong, T., Nourbakhsh, I., Dautenhahn, K.: A survey of socially interactive robots. Robotics and Autonomous Systems 42, 143–166 (2003)
10. Laban, R.V.: Mastery of Movement. Princeton Book Co. Pub, Princeton (1988)
11. Darwin, C.: On the Expression of the Emotions in Man and Animals. John Murray, London (1872)
12. Russell, J.A.: A circumplex model of affect. Journal of Personality and Social Psychology, 1161–1178 (1980)
13. Nakata, T., Mori, T., Sato, T.: Analysis of Impression of Robot Bodily Expression. Journal of Robotics and Mechatronics 14, 27–36 (2002)
14. Wainer, J., Feil-Seifer, D.J., Shell, D.A., Mataric, M.J.: Embodiment and Human-Robot Interaction. In: 16th IEEE International Conference on Robot & Human Interactive Communication, pp. 872–877 (2007)
15. Powers, A., Kiesler, S., Fussell, S., Torrey, C.: Comparing a computer agent with a humanoid robot. In: 2nd ACM/IEEE International Conference on Human-Robot Interaction (HRI 2007), pp. 145–152 (2007)
16. Kidd, C.D., Breazeal, C.: Effect of a Robot on User Perceptions. In: IEEE/RSJ International Conference on Intelligent Robots and Systems (IROS 2004), pp. 3559–3564 (2004)

HoneySpam 2.0: Profiling Web Spambot Behaviour

Pedram Hayati[*], Kevin Chai, Vidyasagar Potdar, and Alex Talevski

Digital Ecosystem and Business Intelligence Institute, Curtin University,
Perth, Western Australia
{Pedram.Hayati,Kevin.Chai}@postgrad.curtin.edu.au
{v.potdar,a.talevski}@curtin.edu.au

Abstract. Internet bots have been widely used for various beneficial and malicious activities on the web. In this paper we provide new insights into a new kind of bot termed as *web spambot* which is primarily used for spreading spam content on the web. To gain insights into web spambots, we developed a tool (HoneySpam 2.0) to track their behaviour. This paper presents two main contributions, firstly it describes the design of HoneySpam 2.0 and secondly we outline the experimental results that characterise web spambot behaviour. By profiling web spambots, we provide the foundation for identifying such bots and preventing and filtering web spam content.

Keywords: honeyspam, web spambot, web robot detection, spam detection, web usage mining.

1 Introduction

Web content which provides false or unsolicited web information is defined as Web Spam [1]. Spam content is prolific on the web due to the development and widespread adoption of Web 2.0 as spammers no longer need to purchase, host and promote their own domains. Spammers can now use legitimate websites to host spam content such as fake eye-catching profiles in social networking websites, fake promotional reviews, responses to threads in online forums with unsolicited content and manipulated wiki pages etc. This spamming technique which is different from previous Web spamming techniques is referred to as *Web 2.0 Spam* or *Spam 2.0* [2]. Figure 1 illustrates Spam 2.0 and its relation to other spamming campaigns.

Little is known about the amount of Spam 2.0 on the Internet. At the time of writing this paper, *Live Spam Zeitgeist* has shown over a 50% increase in the amount of spam messages (e.g. spam comments in blogging tools) since 2008 [3]. This report showed a dramatic increase in the amount of successful Spam 2.0 attacks and the inadequacy of existing countermeasure tools [2].

In this paper, we conduct an effective study on Spam 2.0 and the behaviour of web spambots. Web spambots are a new kind of Internet robot which is primarily used for spreading spam content on the web. To gain insights into this kind of bot we have developed a tool (HoneySpam 2.0) to track their behaviour.

---

[*] Pedram Hayati is PhD student at Curtin University.

J.-J. Yang et al. (Eds.): PRIMA 2009, LNAI 5925, pp. 335–344, 2009.
© Springer-Verlag Berlin Heidelberg 2009

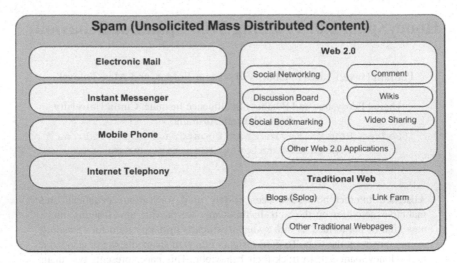

Fig. 1. Spam 2.0 among other spamming campaigns

HoneySpam 2.0 draws on the idea of honeypots (a technique for tracking cyber attackers). It implicitly tracks web usage data which includes detailed monitoring of click streams, pages navigation, forms, mouse movements, keyboard actions and page scrolling. Our results illustrate that HoneySpam 2.0 is effective in profiling web spambots. HoneySpam 2.0 is a tracking solution that can be integrated in any web application ranging from blogging tools to social networking applications. To the best of our knowledge, there is no existing literature that studies web spambots from a web usage perspective. We believe that this work is the first step in finding the attributes of web spambots and is a roadmap for future research.

This paper is organised as follows; in Section 2, we provide taxonomy on Spam 2.0 and web spambots, Section 3 explains the HoneySpam 2.0 architecture. Next, Section 4 discusses our experimental results. Section 5 explains previous work. This is followed by conclusions and future works in Section 6.

2   Taxonomy of Spam 2.0 and Web Spambots

Along with its web applications, Web 2.0 provides a collaboration platform for flexible web content management. Spam 2.0 has existed since web 2.0 concepts have appeared online. Spammers misuse/use this functionality to distribute spam content. The act of spamming can be done through two channels: manual and automated. The former refers to using human operations such as hiring cheap labour to manually distribute spam content [4] (e.g. A sample job advertisement for spam content publishing can be found in [5]). The latter is achieved by exploiting software or scripts which can be in the form of client-side software or web robots. Web or Internet robots are programming scripts or automated agents that are designed for specific tasks such as crawling webpages and parsing URLs without human interaction [6].

Unfortunately, web robots can be exploited for malicious activities such as checking web servers for vulnerabilities, harvesting email addresses from webpages as well as performing Denial-of-Service attacks (DoS) [7]. Recently, some web robots have been used for distributing spam content on web applications through posting promotional comments, placing ads in online forums, submitting links through trackbacks etc. [2]. We call this type of web robots as *web spambots*. Web spambots can be designed to be *application specific* which target specific web applications like Wordpress blogging tools, phpBB, Mediawiki or *website specific* infecting websites like Amazon, MySpace, Facebook etc.

It should be noted that web spambots are different from spambots. According to [7] spambots are Internet robots that crawl webpages to harvest email addresses in order to send spam emails. However web spambots act completely differently from spambots. Web spambots can crawl the web or discover new victims via search engines, register new user accounts and submit spam content in Web 2.0 applications. Their main task is to distribute spam content on to the web. They can reside on different machines (e.g. infected user computers, free or commercial web hosting sites). Web spambots can be programmed once and used many times. The motivations behind such spamming activities are [2]:

- Deceiving search engines to rank spam and junk content higher. For instance, the more spam content added to different websites linking back to the spammer's websites, will increase their website's ranking.
- Misleading users to view unsolicited contents such as webpages, link-farms, ad-hosted website, phishing websites, etc.

By employing automated web spambots, spammers are able to get more traffic on their campaigns. This highlights the importance of web spambot detection as a possible way to eliminate spam 2.0. In the next section we discuss current techniques to discover web spambots along with our proposed solution.

2.1 Web Spambot Countermeasure Techniques

One of the most popular countermeasures to differentiate web robots (include web spambots) from humans is *Completely Automated Public Turing test to tell Computers and Human Apart* (CAPTCHA) [8]. It is a type of challenge-response test usually in the form of a distorted image of numbers and letters, which humans have to infer and type in to a web form. However, CAPTCHA is inconvenient for users as it wastes their time, causes distraction, is unpleasant and at times scary. A number of recent works have reported approaches to defeat CAPTCHAs automatically by using computer programs [9-11]. CAPTCHA's drawbacks includes the following:

1. Decrease user convenience and increase complexity of human computer interaction.
2. As programs become better at deciphering CAPTCHA, the image may become difficult for humans to decipher.
3. As computers get more powerful, they will be able to decipher CAPTCHA better than humans.

Therefore, CAPTCHA is only a short term solution that is about to expire. Web spambots armed with anti-CAPTCHA tools are able to bypass this restriction and spread spam content easily while the futile user inconvenience remains.

Other countermeasures for combating automated request are by using *Hashcash*, *Nonce* and *Form variation* [12, 13]. The idea behind *Hashcash* is that the sender has to calculate a stamp for the submitted content [13]. The calculation of the stamp is difficult and time-consuming for sender but comparatively cheap and fast for receiver to verify. Although *Hashcash* cannot stop automated spamming, it can slow down the spamming process. On the other hand, using *nonce* and *Form variation* techniques can only guarantee that users use their submission forms rather than posting directly.

However, we believe that one effective way to detect web spambot is by looking at web spambot behaviour through its page navigations, click-streams, mouse interactions, keyboard actions and form filling. We put forward the notion that their web usage behaviour is intrinsically different from humans. The focus of this work is on profiling web spambot behaviour. We proposed HoneySpam 2.0 to detect, track and monitor web spambots. In following section we explain our proposed method.

3   HoneySpam 2.0 Architecture

HoneySpam 2.0 is a stand-alone tool that is designed to be integrated with any web application with the aim to track and analyse web spambot behaviour. HoneySpam 2.0 is based upon the idea of a honeypot where a vulnerable server is deployed to attract cyber attackers in order to study their behaviour. HoneySpam 2.0 is designed to study the web spambots which are considered to be attackers in the spamming scenario.

HoneySpam 2.0 consists of two main components: Navigation Tracking Component (NTC) & Form Tracking Component (FTC). Figure 2 illustrates the detailed Model-View-Control (MVC) architecture of HoneySpam 2.0 inside a web application.

3.1   Navigation Tracking Component

This component is designed to track page navigation patterns and header information of incoming traffic. The following information is captured by this component: the time of request, the IP address, the browser identity and the referrer URL.

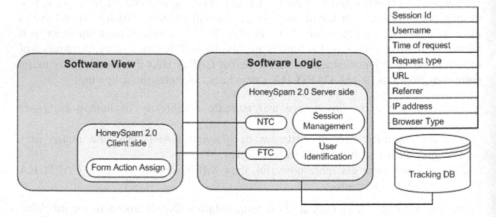

Fig. 2. HoneySpam 2.0 Architecture

NTC is also designed to automatically differentiate individual visit sessions. Session information is captured to identify user's web usage behaviour during each visit. NTC stores the captured data along with session identity (session id) into the tracking database, which is used during an analysis and profiling stage.

3.2 Form Tracking Component

Other than the NTC, we felt the need to develop additional functionality that could provide us insights into how web spambots use web forms. It is a common belief that web spambots do not interact with web forms, however, our study aims to test this here. We developed a form tracking component to specifically study form input behaviour. This component captures and stores the following form related actions such as:

⇒ Mouse clicks and movements
⇒ Keyboard actions
⇒ Form field focus and un-focus
⇒ Form load and submission
⇒ Page navigation

For each of the above mentioned actions we also captured header information e.g. IP address, browser identity, referrer link session id etc. We decided to store header information since we wanted to ensure that form action events are originating from the same session with the same header information.

Additionally, both components check whether requests are initiated from registered users or visitors. If it was initiated from a registered user then it stores the username along with other web usage information for that request. This was done to differentiate registered web users usage data and visitor usage data, which can be used for further analysis. Visitors are termed as guests in our database. Also, most web applications require the registration of a valid username before further interaction with the system.

3.3 Deploying HoneySpam 2.0

Deploying HoneySpam 2.0 involves implementing both client side and server side code. The client side code, assigns FTC actions to web forms so once a user triggers an action it would be captured, transmitted to FTC server side code and would be recorded in the database. On the server side, NTC tracks the users navigation behaviour based on incoming traffic requests. In the next section, we explain our experimental setting by outlining where we integrated HoneySpam 2.0 and discuss our results and key observations.

4   Experimental Results

The HoneySpam 2.0 tool was employed onto 1 commercial and 5 free web hosting servers. The web applications provided on these servers include online discussion forums and social bookmarking. We did not add any initial content to any of these applications and placed a message (in the form of an image) to notify human users not to use these applications. Additionally, as described in Section 4.4 our FTC component did not capture any form activity records which ensures that there were no human activities inside our hosted campaigns.All of the content added to our web applications is added by web spambots. The data presented in this paper has been collected for a period of 60 days[1] and is summarised in Table 1.

Table 1. Summary of Data for Honeyspam 2.0 showing the total number of bots, total number of posts, average posts per day etc

Summary of Data for Honey Spam	#
No. of tracking records	11481
No. of web spambots' tracking records	6794
Total No. of registered bots	643
Total No. of unique used IP addresses	314
Total No. of posts	617
Average Posts per day	8.27
Average Registered web spambots per day	7.91
Average online web spambot per day	2.72

In terms of content, 60% of spam content was adult-related, 13% consisted of an assorted category of content (e.g. free software, keyword spam) and 9% of content was related to drug (pharmaceutical) and movies (Fig 3a). Demographically, 51% of observed web spambots originated from the United Kingdom followed by the United States of America at 22% (Fig 3b). However, it is quite possible for web spambots to be used by spammers on hijacked machines so these figures do not reveal the true origin of the spammers.

Web browsers commonly used by the web spambots were Internet Explorer and Opera (Fig 3c). Surprisingly, two relatively unknown browsers which were OffByOne and BrowseX were also used. Additionally, Firefox was only used by 2 web spambots and Safari was not used at all. It should be mentioned that this header information can be modified and is not a true indication of browser usage or the use of an actual browser at all. A number of specific observations were discovered from examining the behaviour of web spambots and are now discussed.

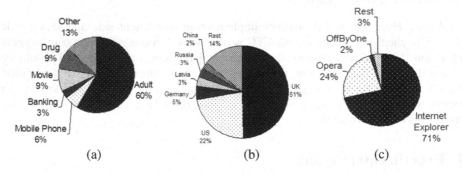

(a)   (b)   (c)

Fig. 3. Percentage of top content categories, countries and internet browsers

---

[1] The HoneySpam 2.0 tool has tracked spambot behaviour from the 25th of May 2009 to the 9th of August 2009. However, only 60 days of data is collected due to server downtime periods caused by maintenance and issues.

4.1 Use of Search Engines to Find Target Websites

Of the 6 monitored web hosts, the commercial server received the most attention from web spambots. This highlights the possibility that web spambots are using search engine intelligence (e.g. Google PageRank scores) to identify and focus on higher ranked websites that potentially yield more visitor traffic.

The initial 15 days of hosting and tracking did not yield much activity but a number of web spambots began registering and posting content after this period (Fig. 4a). The reason behind this could be related to search engine indexing, which also suggests that some web spambots find their targets through search engine results.

4.2 Create Numerous User Accounts

It was identified from our experiment that web spambots would create a number of new accounts to post their content rather than using their existing accounts. This is shown in Table 1, where the total number of web spambots accounts is 643 but only 314 unique IP addresses are used between these accounts. On average 7.91 new accounts were created per day within our dataset.

It is possible that web spambots adopt this behaviour for additional robustness in delaying account banning (e.g. one user account is associated with numerous spam content items is easier to detect and manage) and/or to handle the event in which their previous accounts are banned.

4.3 Low Website Webpage Hits and Revisit Rates

The observed web spambots adopt similar surfing patterns to one another and commonly visit a number of specific web pages. As illustrated in Fig. 4b most web spambots perform less than 20 page hits in total during their account lifetime.

Fig. 5b supports the claim that web spambots do not revisit many times as 554 web spambots only revisit the websites once and 75 bots revisit less than 5 times. It is likely that these bots revert to creating new user accounts to continue their spamming activities as discussed in section 4.2.

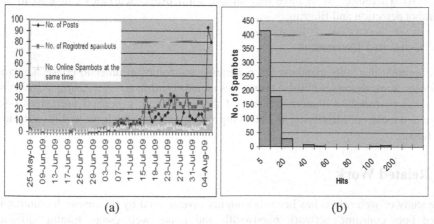

(a)   (b)

Fig. 4. Number of posts, registered, and online web spambots, frequency of Spambots visits on each Webpages

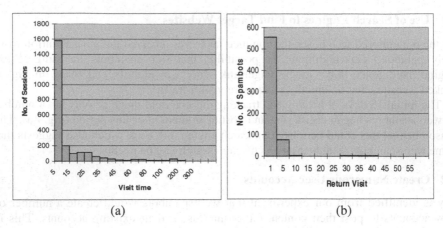

Fig. 5. Frequency of Web Spambots' spending time (sec) on each session, frequency of revisiting by Web Spambots (1 means they just visit once)

4.4 Distribute Spam Content in a Short Period of Time

The amount of time most web spambots spend on each visit (session) is less than 5 seconds. This indicates that web spambots are distributing spam content in a short amount of time possibly to move on to other websites to distribute more spam content (Fig. 5a). Additionally their online activitiy time was an average of 2.71 second.

4.5 No Web Form Interaction

While not shown in the figures, the form-tracking component of the HoneySpam 2.0 tool was unable to track form usage behaviour of web spambots. These bots adopt a conventional method of directly posting through their own forms / interface to submit content. We suspect they have not been designed to be intelligent enough to mimic the behaviour of a human in submitting a web form because of a lack of a requirement to do so. Therefore, we believe that simple form usage heuristics can lead to web spambot detection and filtering.

4.6 Generated Usernames

It is apparent that web spambots are generating usernames in order to create numerous accounts. Some examples of these usernames include *Oxidylozaxygixoc*, *Ufigowigelyniwyl* and *Ynutaznazabalekil*. Pattern analysis of these randomly generated usernames could serve as a means of identifying and blocking web spambots, which we will investigate in the future.

5   Related Work

The study of web robots has been thoroughly investigated by the research community since bots consume network bandwidth and make web usage mining difficult. Conventional methods to detect web robots are based on identifying IP addresses and user agents [14]. However, unknown and camouflaged web robots can not be detected by these techniques.

In the web usage mining, Tan and Kumar [6] proposed a model to discover web robots. They use navigational pattern on click-stream data approach to detect web robots. They show that the features such as the request method, the length of the session, the depth and width of webpage coverage of web robots are different from humans. They did not explicitly focus on web spambots as the aim of their work was to detect web robot such as search engine crawlers, offline browsers, link checkers and email collectors. In our proposed work, we concentrate on profiling web spambots which are different to other types of web robots not covered by Tan and Kumar.

By looking at the existence of HTTP requests for CSS and JavaScript files along with mouse movement activities on the Web pages, Park et al. (2006) proposed a technique to detect malicious web robots [7]. The focus of their work was on camouflaged web robots that are normally used for security attacks, harvesting email addresses etc. Similar to previous work, their focus was not on identifying web spambots.

In the area of spam detection, Webb et al. (2008) proposed a social honeypot for detection of spammers in social networking websites [15]. They hosted 51 social honeypots in one of the famous social networking websites. The result of their work shows that temporal and geographic patterns of social spam have unique characteristics.

Andreolini et al. (2005) proposed a method to slow down email harvesting process and poison spamming email databases [16]. Additionally they proposed the creation of fake open proxies to increase the probability of email spam detection.

6 Conclusion and Future Work

In this paper we detailed the design and implementation of HoneySpam 2.0 for detecting, monitoring and analysing web spambots. HoneySpam 2.0 is based upon the idea of honeypots to monitor and characterize web spambots which are a type of web robot that are programmed to surf through the web and distribute the spam content. We integrated Honeyspam 2.0 in popular open source web applications for period of 60 days to monitor web spambot behaviour.

Through our experiments, we discovered that web spambots use search engines to find target websites, create numerous user accounts, distribute spam content in a short amount of time, do not revisit the website, do not interact with forms on the website, and register with randomly generated usernames. By profiling web spambots, we provide the foundation for identifying such bots and filter and removing their spam content.

While this paper focussed on analysing web spambots as a way to combat spam in the future we will focus on adopting clustering algorithms to detect web spambots on the fly. Additionally, artificial neural networks and analytical techniques can be used to gain a better understanding of the data collected from web spambots.

References

[1] Gyongyi, Z., Garcia-Molina, H.: Web spam taxonomy. In: Proceedings of the 1st International Workshop on Adversarial Information Retrieval on the Web, Chiba, Japan (2005)
[2] Hayati, P., Potdar, V.: Toward Spam 2.0: An Evaluation of Web 2.0 Anti-Spam Methods. In: 7th IEEE International Conference on Industrial Informatics Cardiff, Wales (2009)

[3] Zeitgeist, L.S.: Comment Spam. In: Akismet, ed. (2009),
    http://akismet.com/stats/
[4] Cobb, S.: The Economics of Spam. EPrivacyGroup (2003),
    http://www.eprivacygroup.com
[5] Workathome, Work from home online ad placing work pay per posting (2009),
    http://www.workathomeforum.in/online-adplacing-homejob.htm,
    http://www.workathomeforum.in/online-adplacing-homejob.htm
[6] Tan, P.-N., Kumar, V.: Discovery of Web Robot Sessions Based on their Navigational
    Patterns. Data Mining and Knowledge Discovery 6, 9–35 (2002)
[7] Park, K., Pai, V.S., Lee, K.-W., Calo, S.: Securing Web Service by Automatic Robot
    Detection. In: USENIX 2006 Annual Technical Conference Refereed Paper (2006)
[8] Chellapilla, K., Simard, P.: Using Machine Learning to Break Visual Human Interaction
    Proofs (HIPs). In: NIPS (2004)
[9] Abram, H., Michael, W.G., Richard, C.H.: Reverse Engineering CAPTCHAs. In:
    Proceedings of the 2008 15th Working Conference on Reverse Engineering. IEEE
    Computer Society, Los Alamitos (2008)
[10] Mori, G., Malik, J.: Recognizing objects in adversarial clutter: breaking a visual
    CAPTCHA. In: Proceedings. 2003 IEEE Computer Society Conference on Computer
    Vision and Pattern Recognition, vol. 1, p I-134-I-141 (2003)
[11] Baird, H.S., Bentley, J.L.: Implicit CAPTCHAs. In: Proceedings SPIE/IS&T Conference
    on Document Recognition and Retrieval XII (DR&R2005), San Jose, CA (2005)
[12] Ogbuji, U.: Real Web 2.0: Battling Web spam (2008),
    http://www.ibm.com/developerworks/web/library/wa-realweb10/
[13] Mertz, D.: Charming Python: Beat spam using hashcash (2004),
    http://www.ibm.com/developerworks/linux/library/
    l-hashcash.html
[14] Cooley, R., Mobasher, B., Srivastava, J.: Web mining: information and pattern discovery
    on the World Wide Web. In: Proceedings of Ninth IEEE International Conference on
    Tools with Artificial Intelligence 1997, pp. 558–567 (1997)
[15] Webb, S., Caverlee, J., Pu, C.: Social Honeypots: Making Friends with a Spammer Near
    You. In: Proceedings of the Fifth Conference on Email and Anti-Spam (CEAS 2008),
    Mountain View, CA (2008)
[16] Andreolini, M., Bulgarelli, A., Colajanni, M., Mazzoni, F.: HoneySpam: honeypots
    fighting spam at the source. In: Proceedings of the Steps to Reducing Unwanted Traffic
    on the Internet on Steps to Reducing Unwanted Traffic on the Internet Workshop (2005),
    Cambridge, MA, p. 11 (2005)

A Modeling Tool for Service-Oriented Open Multiagent Systems

Emilia Garcia*, Estefania Argente, and Adriana Giret

Departamento de Sistemas Informaticos y Computacion,
Universidad Politecnica de Valencia, Camino de Vera S/N, Valencia, Spain
{mgarcia,eargente,agiret}@dsic.upv.es

Abstract. Service-oriented Open technology is becoming more and more the enabler tool for today open enterprise ISs. In this field, it seems interesting to work with the Multi-Agent System research focusing on open distributed, complex and dynamic systems, in which information and resources are distributed among several agents, which interact by means of services. In this paper, an engineering tool for Service-oriented Open Multi-Agent Systems is presented. This tool is based on a platform independent unified meta-model. In this way, a Model Driven Architecture mechanism is applied, thus defining a Service-Oriented Multi-agent System meta-model based on Virtual Organizations and employing the Eclipse technology to develop the IDE tool.

Keywords: Services, Agents, Meta-models, CASE tools.

1 Introduction

Nowadays service-oriented computing has become the enabler technology for today open IS for enterprises. In todays bergaining scenarios, the e-Business approach is becoming more and more a "must-have" tool. The service oriented research field has experienced a lot of work developments. But the emphasis has mainly been on the execution of individual services and not on the more important problems of how services are selected and how they can collaborate to provide higher levels of functionality. However, research in Multi-Agent Systems (MAS) has focused on covering open distributed, complex and dynamic systems, in which information and resources are distributed among several agents [16], which can interact by means of services.

In our research work, we deal with the problem of engineering Service-oriented open MAS. To this end, we work on models and a tool for engineering large-scale open systems in which the constituent entities interact among them by means of services. The solution domain for IS that we propose is built upon Virtual Organizations (VOs), which represent a set of individuals and institutions

---

* This work is partially supported by the PAID-06-07/3191, TIN2006-14630-C03-01 projects and CONSOLIDER-INGENIO 2010 under grant CSD2007-00022. The first author is a student.

J.-J. Yang et al. (Eds.): PRIMA 2009, LNAI 5925, pp. 345–360, 2009.

that need to coordinate resources and services across institutional boundaries
[8]. They are open systems, in the sense that they are inhabited by heterogeneous agents whose behaviours are unknown to the system designer. VOs allow
modeling systems at a high level of abstraction. They include the integration
of organizational and individual perspectives and also the dynamic adaptation
of models to organizational and environmental changes by forming groups with
visibility boundaries.

In this work, we apply a Model Driven Architecture (MDA) [19] mechanism
to define a Service-Oriented Open MAS (SOMAS) meta-model that enhances
the Virtual Organization Model [8]. Moreover, we present a prototype of an
engineering tool for SOMAS that employ Eclipse technology to implement the
proposed meta-model.

2 Background

In order to introduce the context of this work, we present here the background
of Service-oriented Open MAS, describing their main features and modeling
requirements. We also briefly describe the state of the art for modeling organizations for complex and large-scale open MAS, mainly focusing on detailing the
Virtual Organization Model concepts [8], which is the basis of our proposal.

2.1 Service-Oriented Open MAS

A Service-oriented Open Multi-Agent System (SOMAS) is a multi-agent system
in which the computing model is based on well-defined, open, loosely-coupled
service interfaces, such as Web services. Such services could support several applications, including: heterogeneous information management; scientific computing
with large, dynamically reconfigurable resources; mobile computing; pervasive
computing, etc. Instead of passively waiting for discovery, services could proactively contribute to an application, thereby behaving like agents in a MAS [15].

The development of large-scale SOMAS calls for new engineering methods. Such
systems must be self-organizing and support runtime reconfiguration and design.
As services become increasingly "alive" and their interactions become increasingly
dynamic, they will begin to do more than just manage information in explicitly
programmed ways. In particular, MASs or services acting in concert can function
as computational mechanisms in their own right, thus significantly enhancing our
ability to model, design, build and manage complex software systems.

SOMAS is a new approach for constructing complex applications wherein
developers concentrate on high-level abstractions, such as overall behavior and
key conceptual structures (the active entities, their objectives, and their interactions), without having to go further into individual details or interactions. This
vision becomes more compelling as the target environments become more pop-
ulated, distributed and dynamic. Interactions should be given primacy in terms
of representation and reasoning.

Societal representations of large-scale systems, such as Virtual Organization
Model described in next section, facilitate the exploration and understanding of
relationships between elements of the real life problem domain [3,11].

2.2 Modeling Virtual Organizations

The Virtual Organization (VO) concept represents a collection of entities that interact and produce some form of output [6]. Virtual Organizations comprise the integration of organizational and individual perspectives, and the dynamic adaptation of models to organizational and environmental changes [11]. Organizational models have been recently used in agent theory to model coordination in open systems and to ensure social order in MAS. An organization meta-model describes the entities and relationships that comprise an organization and its environment.

There have been several organization models proposed, many of them giving support to multiagent methodologies. Relevant examples are: the Gaia model [20], which considers the organization in terms of agents, groups and roles, which have responsibilities, permissions, activities and protocols; the AGR model [13] whose basic concepts of agents, groups and roles have been lately applied in other organization models in a similar way; MOISE+ [14], which improved the notion of an organization model, considering three aspects: structural, functional and deontic; the OperA model [10], based on the ISLANDER framework [12], allows heterogeneous agents to enter the organization with their own goals, beliefs and capabilities, without assuming cooperative agents; the Tropos model [5], which mainly improves the requirement analysis using actors, softgoals, plans and dependencies; the PASSI model [7], which goes from more abstract concepts (problem aspects) to more practical ones (solution domain aspects); the MenSA model [2] that integrates Tropos, Gaia, PASSI and SODA [17] models; the O-MaSE model [9] that provides suitable mechanisms for allowing the system to reorganize at runtime in order to adapt to its environment and changing capabilities; the INGENIAS model [18] that focuses on component description (organizations, agents, roles), functionality (goals and tasks), environment, interactions and agent internal features (autonomy, mental state processing); and the Virtual Organization Model (VOM) [8], aimed at modeling open societies in which heterogeneous and autonomous agents work together, focused on the integration of both Web Services and MAS technologies. Despite the number of research work in the field, concepts such as: support for the integration of services and agents in a transparent way; dynamicity features for on-the-fly creation, modification and deletion of organizational structures, norms, services, etc.; specific CASE tools for SOMAS; among others, are still open issues.

In this work we deal with the previous requirements building our approach on top of VOM [8]. VOM takes into account the main aspects of a Virtual Organization: (i) *Structural dimension*, describing the components of the system and their relationships; (ii) *Functional dimension*, detailing the specific functionality of the system, based on services, tasks and goals, as well as system interactions, activated by means of goals or service usage; (iii) *Environmental dimension*, describing the environment in terms of its resources and how agents can perceive and act on them; and (iv) *Normative dimension*, defining the organizational norms and normative goals that agents must follow, including sanctions and rewards.

In VOM, organizations are structured by means of Organizational Units (OU) [4], which represent a set of agents that carry out some specific and differentiated activities or tasks, following a predefined pattern of cooperation and communication. An OU is formed by different entities along its life cycle which can be both single agents or other organizational units, viewed as a single entity. System entities are capable of offering and/or requesting services and their behavior is motivated by their pursued goals. Services represent the functionality that agents offer to other entities, independently of the concrete agent that makes use of it. Moreover, an organizational unit can also publish its requirements of services, so then external agents can decide whether participate inside, providing these services.

In this work we enhance VOM with support for integration of services and agents, dynamic features for organization modeling, and a specific CASE tool for SOMAS. Next section details our approach.

3   EMFGormas Proposal

This section details our approach to model Service-oriented Open MAS using the MDA Eclipse technology. As explained before, this technology requires defining a platform independent unified meta-model that describes the modeling language in a formal way, establishing the primitives and syntactic-semantic properties of organizations and multiagent systems. The unified meta-model that we define, named *EmfGormas*, is based on VOM [8] and it can be consulted in *http://www.dsic.upv.es/users/ia/sma/tools/EMFgormas*.

3.1   EMFGormas Modeling Process

The proposed unified meta-model can be analyzed from different points of view, i.e. different diagrams, that simplifies the modeling task. Figure 1 summarizes our proposed modeling process.

Firstly, the analysis of the system requirements is carried out, defining the global goals of the organization, the stakeholders and the functionality that the organization provides and requires from these stakeholders. All this is depicted in the **Organization external view** diagram.

Secondly, the analysis of the goals of the organization is carried out in which the global goal of the organization is refined into more goals, which represent both functional and non-functional requirements that must or should be accomplished by the organizational units of the system. All this is defined in the **Objectives view** diagram.

Next, the components of the organization are defined, i.e. the Organizational Units (OU), which represent groups of members of the organization; the roles defined inside each OU that will be related to the system functionality; their social relationships; the products available by the OUs that can be accessible for their members; and the norms that control the global behavior of the OU members. These concepts are described in the **Structural view** diagram.

Moreover, the products of the environment are analysed, divided into applications (functional interfaces) or resources (with consumable features). The

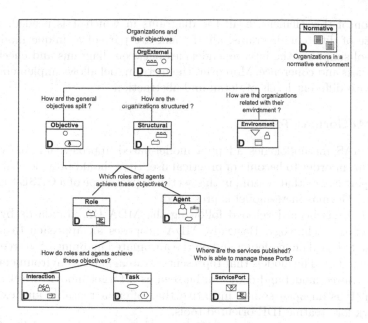

Fig. 1. Unified meta-model for SOMAS

permissions for accessing these elements of the enviroment are also defined. All them are depicted in the **Environment View** diagram.

Thirdly, the internal functionality of the OUs is defined, by means of the Role and Agent Views. In the **Role View** (Figure 6), the roles are related with their responsibilities (tasks), capabilities (services) and objectives. The **Agent View** (Figure 8) describes the concrete responsibilities of agents (tasks), the roles that they can play inside an OU, the services that offer to other entities, their mental states (believes, events and facts) and the goals that they pursue.

The way in which the roles and agents achieve their goals is defined by means of the Interaction and Task Views. In the **Interaction View**, the participants of the interaction are identifed, as well as the sequence of activities (task and services) and performatives that are employed through the interaction. In the **Task View** (Figure 10), the specific functionality of the services and tasks is detailed, more specifically, the service description (*ServiceProfile*); its specific implementation, by means of service or task composition; as well as the sequence of tasks that is needed.

Finally, the **Service Port View** defines the way in which the services must be published so as to be discovered by any agent. Thus, the service publication points (service port) are identified, as well as the entities that control each port and give permissions for registring or accessing services.

Throught the whole process, whenever a restriction on the behavior of the system entities is identified, it should be described in the **Normative View** diagram.

As explained before, this is not a linear process but an iterative one, in which the identification of a new element of functionality of the system implies the integration of this element in all the diagrams in which it is needed. Despite of the use of different diagrams, all of them are part of a unique model. The CASE tool simplifies the interdependencies between diagrams and checks their completeness and coherence. Moreover, the meta-model allows implementing the system with different levels of detail and abstraction.

3.2 EMFGormas Tool

Current MAS methodologies adopt a model-based approach for analysis and design, but, in order to become of practical use, they should provide CASE tools that support it. For that reason, in this section a prototype of a CASE tool based on the EmfGormas meta-model is presented.

This tool has been developed following the MDA [19] standards by means of the Eclipse technology. Basically, MDA proposes an approach to software development based on modeling and on the automated mapping of source models to target models. The models that represent a system and its environment can be seen as a source model and code can be seen as a target model as well. Eclipse Platform [1] is an open source initiative that offers a reusable and extensible framework for creating IDE oriented tools.

EmfGormas tool consists of several Eclipse plugins that allow modeling Service-oriented Open MAS using the modeling language defined in Section 3. The tool offers several graphical editors, one for each view of the model, that restricts the modeling task to the elements and relationships defined in the meta-model. The entire information detailed in the different diagrams is saved in a unique ecore model. Therefore, all the diagrams of the same model are connected and designers can navigate from one view to another clicking into the main entity of the diagram. In this way, a system modeled with the EMFGormas tool consists of a unique ecore model and several diagrams that have been developed with different graphical environments.

Figure 2 shows a snapshot of the EMFGormas tool in which the organization external view of a case study is developed. This figures shows that the EMF-Gormas tool offers a traditional interface of CASE tools. This fact reduces the learning time and makes its usage more intuitive. The *Eclipse Project navigator* shows the hierarchy of project files. The file *default.gormas* contains the information of all the diagrams in the ecore format. The file *mWater.gormas_diagram* represents the graphical editor of different views of the system. Users can navigate from this file to the other diagrams. The *Organization External Palette* allows selecting the entities and relationships that can be modeled in the Organization External view of the meta-model. Finally, the *Properties view* shows and allows modifying the attributes of each entity and relationship.

3.3 Using EMFGormas

In order to illustrate the usage of the proposed meta-model and tool we have modeled a case study based on a water market, which is called mWater. Let's suppose there is a water market that is an institutional, decentralized framework

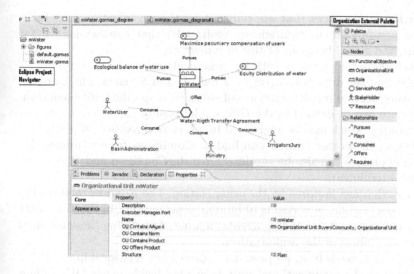

Fig. 2. mWater Organization External diagram

where users with water rights (right-holders) are allowed to voluntarily trade their water rights with other users, in exchange of some compensation, economic or not but always fulfilling some pre-established rules. It represents a virtual market base system, in which water right transfer agreements are executed by autonomous entities that may be humans or software programs acting on their behalf. They will be able to negotiate the terms and conditions of the transfer agreement following normative laws. Due to space limitations, only some views of the case study will be presented.

In order to develop the case study we follow the development process of Figure 1. Firstly, the global goals of the organizations and the functionality that organizations provide and require from their environment is defined in the **Organization External view**. The part of the unified meta-model related with this view is presented in Figure 3. More specifically, this view defines:

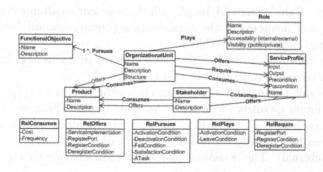

Fig. 3. Organization External view

- the *Functional objectives* that are pursued by the organization, i.e., functional or non-functional requirements (softgoals) that can be defined for describing the global behavior of this organization.
- the *Stakeholders* that interact with the organization.
- the results that the organization offers (*Products* and *Services*, which are described using service profiles). In case of services, a specific implementation of the service can be defined in the *Offers* relationship (*ServiceImplementation* attribute), which may be registered in a service directory (*RegisterPort* attribute), so then other entities can find it. Conditions for controlling this registration process can also be specified (*RegisterCondition* and *DeregisterCondition* attributes).
- the services that are *Required* by the organization. The *Requires* relationship is similar to a job offer advertising of human organizations, in the sense that it represents a necessity of finding agents capable of providing these required services as members of the organization.
- the organization needs from its providers (*Consumes* relationship).
- the *Roles* that the organizational unit may play inside other OUs (*Plays* relationship), when considered as a unique entity. *ActivationCondition* and *LeaveCondition* attributes of this relationship indicate in which situation an OU acquires or leaves a role.

Figure 2 shows the external view of the *mWater organization*. The mWater market is modeled as a virtual organization that pursues 3 main goals (*Ecological balance of water use, Maximize pecuniary compensation of users, Equity distribution of water*). *mWater* offers a general service that is called *Water-Right transfer agreement*. This service is used by several stakeholders that interact with the mWater organization.

In the second step of the process of Figure 1, the designer defines the objectives decomposition and dependencies using the EmfGormas **Objectives view**. Furthermore, the **environment** elements (resources and applications) related with the organization are specified(see EMFGormas url[1]).

Following the sequence of Figure 1, the static components of the organization, i.e. all elements that are independent of the final executing entities are defined using the **Structural view**. More specifically, this view defines:

- the entities of the system (*AAgent*), which represent an atomic entity (*Agent*) or a group of members of the organization (*Organizational Unit*), are seen as a unique entity from outside.
- the *Organizational Units* (OUs) of the system, that can also include other OUs in a recursive way, as well as single agents.
- the *Roles* defined inside the OUs. In the *contains* relationship, a minimum and maximum quantity of entities that can acquire this role can be specified. For each role, the *Accessibility* attribute indicates whether a role can be adopted by an entity on demand (external) or it is always predefined by design (internal). The *Visibility* attribute indicates whether other entities

---

[1] http://www.dsic.upv.es/users/ia/sma/tools/EMFgormas

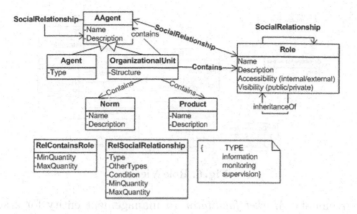

Fig. 4. Structural View

can obtain information from this role on demand, from outside the organizational unit (public role) or from inside, once they are already members of this OU (i.e. private role). A hierarchy of roles can also be defined with the *InheritanceOf* relationship.

– the organization *social relationships*. The type of a social relationship between two entities is related with their position in the structure of the organization (i.e. information, monitoring, supervision), but other types are also possible. Moreover, a condition on when this social relationship is active can also be established.
– the *products* available by an OU.
– the *norms* that control the global behavior of the members of the OU.

In the specific case of mWater (Figure 5), several types of roles are defined: *Water User* (a water right-holder of the basin); *Buyer* (a Water User that wants to transfer its rights and/or buy a transportation resource); *Seller* (a Water User that wants to purchase rights and/or sell a transportation resource); *Basin regulating authority* (the Basin Administration representative that can authorize a water-right transfer agreement); *Third party* (a Water User that can be affected by a water-right transfer agreement); *Jury* (the referee entity in problems among the contracting parties and possibly third parties of a water-right

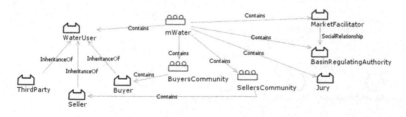

Fig. 5. mWater structural diagram

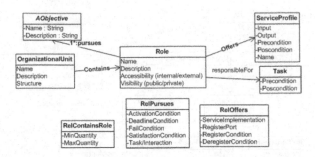

Fig. 6. Role View

transfer agreement); *Market facilitator* (a management entity for assuring the execution of the different activities in the market scenario). Moreover, several buyers or sellers are allowed to form temporal groups in order to buy or sell water rights as a unique entity. Between the role *MarketFacilitator* and the role *Basin regulating authority* there is a social relationship because the first one is a subordinate of the second one. The type of social relationships can be consulted in the properties view of the relationship.

The **Role view** (Figure 6) allows defining the internal functionality of the organizational units and MAS systems, associating the roles with responsibilities, capabilities, objectives and the services that agents playing each role should offer. More specifically:

- the *goals* (*AObjective*) pursued by a role, which can be *functional objectives* (i.e. softgoals or non-functional requirements) or operational goals (i.e. hardgoals or *objectives*). In the *pursues* relationship, activation and deadline conditions can be defined to stablish a temporal timeline in which the objective is followed. In case of an operational goal (*objective*), a satisfaction or fail condition can be defined in order to stablish when this objective has been fulfilled.
- the services (*ServiceProfile*) related to the role, i.e., the services that the role is enabled to offer or provide to other entities.
- the *tasks* that the role is responsible for, i.e. the specific functionality that the role is expected to be able to carry out.

In order to exemplify this view, Figure 7 shows the description of the *Market-Facilitator* role. Its main goal is assuring the execution of trade in the market

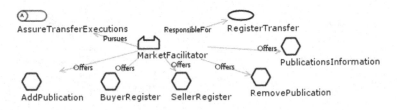

Fig. 7. mWater Role diagram

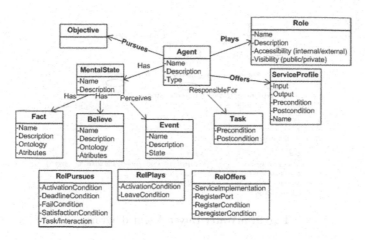

Fig. 8. Agent View

system, therefore this role pursues a global objective called *Assure Transfer Executions*. *MarketFacilitator* is responsible of registering each transaction (Task *RegisterTransfer*). It also provides several services to register at the market as a buyer or seller and to manage the publications of offers and demands.

In the next step of the process of Figure 1, the **Agent view** (Figure 8) describes concrete responsibilities of agents and their internal functions, i.e., the agent goals, roles and tasks. The sociability features of agents are represented by means of services, which are implemented through tasks. Thus, an agent is not only capable of executing some tasks, but also of providing a specific functionality (services) to other agents. More specifically:

- the *objectives* pursued by agents. Activation and deadline conditions can be defined to stablish a temporal timeline in which the objective is followed. Moreover, a satisfaction or fail condition can be defined in order to stablish when this objective has been fulfilled.
- the *roles* played by the agent. Conditions for acquiring and/or leaving the role can be defined. *ActivationCondition* and *LeaveCondition* attributes of this *play* relationship indicate in which situation an agent can acquire or leave a role.
- the services (*ServiceProfile*) related to the agent, i.e., the services that the agent might offer to other entities. When adopting a role as a member of an organization, the concrete set of services that the agent will be allowed to provide is determined by its own set of offered services and those ones related to the adopted role.
- the *tasks* that the agent is responsible for, i.e. the set of tasks that the agent is capable of carrying out.
- the *Mental States* of the agent, using believes, events and facts.

An example of this type of diagram is the mWater *Buyer* agent definition (Figure 9). This agent pursues the objective *BuyWaterRight* and it executes the task

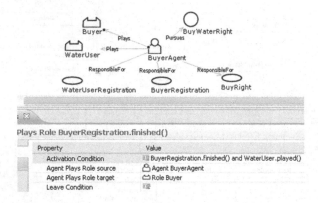

Fig. 9. mWater Buyer Agent diagram

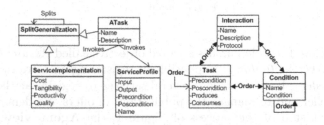

Fig. 10. Task View

BuyRight in order to achieve it. This agent can play two different roles: *WaterUser* and *Buyer*. As shown in Figure 9, the condition to play the Buyer role is to have executed the task *BuyerRegistration* and being playing the *WaterUser* role.

The **Tasks view** (Figure 10) allows defining the functionality of the services and tasks. More specifically:

- The *ATask* component describes the service functionality and represents both concrete tasks, task-flows or service composition (*Invokes* relationship). This *ATask* component can be split into other ATasks, thus allowing service refinement or task composition.
- A *Task* represents a basic functionality, that consumes and produces changes in the agent's Mental States.
- The *order* relationship between tasks, in which ordering conditions can be defined, as well as interactions. The entity *Condition* allows defining the sequence of tasks depending on a condition.
- The service interface (*ServiceProfile*), which indicates activation conditions of the service (preconditions), its input and output parameters and its effects over the environment (postconditions). It can be lately used in an OWL-S service description.
- The service specific functionality (*ServiceImplementation*), which describes a concrete implementation of a service profile.
- The service composition, by means of *invokations* between services.

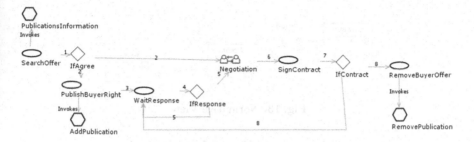

Fig. 11. mWater BuyRight Task diagram

Figure 11 defines the task *BuyRight*. It represents the protocol that follows the *BuyerAgent* in order to try to buy a specific water right. Firstly, the agent invokes the service *PublicationsInformation* in order to analyze if there are any offer that fulfills its requirements. If there is no appropriate offer, the buyer will publish its demand and will wait until a response. If there is an appropriate offer or someone answers its publication, then the negotiation begins. If they reach an agreement the buyer removes its publication and the process finishes. Otherwise, the buyer continues waiting for any response.

The negotiation process is defined as sequence of interactions, therefore it can be specified in the **Interaction View** of the process in Figure 1.

Furthermore, EMFGormas allows defining where are the services published and who is able to manage its ports. This information is specified in the **Services Port View** (Figure 12). More specifically, it details:

- A *service port*, which is considered as a service publication point that offers the possibility of registering and searching services by their profile.
- The entities (*Executer*) (roles, agents or organizations) that control the service port (*Manages* relationship), so they can define the usage permissions over this port.
- The entities (*Executer*) that are *allowed to* use the port, for registering new services or accessing existing ones.

Finally, the **Normative view** of Figure 1 describes normative restrictions over the behavior of the system entities. More specifically, it defines:

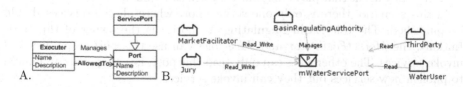

Fig. 12. A)*ServicePort View* B)mWater Service Port diagram

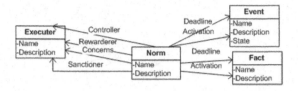

Fig. 13. Normative View

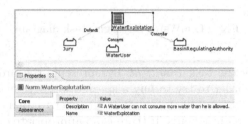

Fig. 14. mWater Normative diagram

- the *Norm* concept, which represents a specific regulation. The properties of the norm detail all facts and events of the environment that provoke the activation or deactivation of the norm. The description attribute can be used to specify the norm with a formal or informal language.
- The entity (*Executer*) to whom the norm is applied (*Concerns* relationship).
- The *Executer* that is in charge of monitoring the norm satisfaction (*Controller* relationship).
- The *Executer* that is responsible of punishments (*Defender* relationship).
- The *Executer* that is responsible of rewards (*Rewarderer* relationship).
- The *ATask* attribute of all these relationships indicates which task or service will be invoked when monitoring this norm and when punishing or rewarding agents.

The *mWater* is a normative environment so it defines many norms that concerns agents, roles and even the whole organization. Figure 14 shows the definition of a norm that controls the correct use of water. The *Basin Regulating Authority* role controls that no *WaterUser* uses more water than it is allowed. If someone violates the norm, any agent that plays the role *Jury* will sanction him.

In this scenario, there is only one service port where all the services should be published. The role Basin Regulating Authority is the owner of this port. Initially, the *MarketFacilitator* and *Jury* roles can use this port to publish and invoke services. The other roles can only read this port, i.e., they are not allowed to publish new services but they can invoke services.

As explained before, the *mWater* case study is not presented completely. It has been simplified here due to space limitations, although it can be consulted completely in the EMFGormas url where the tool also can be downloaded.

4 Conclusions

In this paper we have dealt with the problem of enginering Service-oriented open MAS. To this end, we have proposed a unified meta-model for engineering large-scale open systems in which the constituent entities interact among them by means of services. Moreover, it supports dynamic features for creation, modification and deletion of organizational structures, norms, services, etc. A prototype of a CASE tool based on the proposed meta-model has been developed. It simplifies the modeling task and check the interdependencies between the models and their coherence with the metamodel. The use of the ecore standard improves the interoperability with other tools and other Eclipse plugins. For example, using the Mofscript plugin is possible to translate between ecore models and any target code in a semi-automatically way. Therefore, we plan to improve the verification module of the CASE tool and add a new module to automatically generate code from the ecore model. Finally, the usage of this tool has been presented by means of a case study.

References

1. Eclipse - an open development platform (2008)
2. Ali, R., Bryl, V., Cabri, G., Cossentino, M., Dalpiaz, F., Giorgini, P., Molesini, A., Omicini, A., Puviani, M., Seidita, V.: MEnSA Project - Methodologies for the Engineering of complex Software systms: Agent-based approach. Technical Report 1.2, UniTn (2008)
3. Argente, E., Julian, V., Botti, V.: Multi-agent system development based on organizations. Electronic Notes in Theoretical Computer Science 150, 55–71 (2006)
4. Argente, E., Julian, V., Botti, V.: Mas modelling based on organizations. In: Proc. AOSE 2008, pp. 1–12 (2008)
5. Bresciani, P., Perini, A., Giorgini, P., Giunchiglia, F., Mylopoulos, J.: Tropos: An agent-oriented software development methodology. Autonomous Agents and Multi-Agent Systems 8(3), 203–236 (2004)
6. Chang, M., Harrington, J.: Agent-Based Models of Organizations, vol. 1, pp. 1–60 (2005)
7. Cossentino, M.: From requirements to code with the passi methodology. Agent Oriented Methodologies IV, 79–106 (2005)
8. Criado, N., Argente, E., Julian, V., Botti, V.: Designing Virtual Organizations. In: Proc. PAAMS 2009. Advances in Soft Computing, vol. 55, pp. 440–449 (2009)
9. DeLoach, S.: Multi-Agent Systems: Semantics and Dynamics of Organizational Models. In: chapter Organizational Model for Adaptive Complex Systems, pp. 1–26. IGI Global (2009)
10. Dignum, V.: A model for organizational interaction:based on agents, founded in logic. PhD thesis, Utrecht University (2003)
11. Dignum, V., Dignum, F.: A landscape of agent systems for the real world. Technical report 44-cs-2006-061, Institute of Information and Computing Sciences, Utrecht University (2006)
12. Esteva, M., Rodriguez-Aguilar, J., Sierra, C., Arcos, J., Garcia, P.: On the Formal Specification of Electronic Institutions. In: Sierra, C., Dignum, F.P.M. (eds.) AgentLink 2000. Lecture Notes in Computer Science(LNCS), vol. 1991, pp. 126–147. Springer, Heidelberg (2001)

13. Ferber, J., Gutknecht, O., Michel, F.: From Agents to Organizations: an Organizational View of Multi-Agent Systems. In: Giorgini, P., Müller, J.P., Odell, J.J. (eds.) AOSE 2003. LNCS, vol. 2935, pp. 214–230. Springer, Heidelberg (2004)
14. Hubner, J., Sichman, J., Boissier, O.: A model for the structural, functional, and deontic specification of organizations in mulitagent systems. In: Bittencourt, G., Ramalho, G.L. (eds.) SBIA 2002. LNCS, vol. 2507, pp. 118–128. Springer, Heidelberg (2002)
15. Huhns, M., Singh, M., Burstein, M., Decker, K., Durfee, E., Finin, T., Gasser, L., Goradia, H., Jennings, N.R., Lakartaju, K., Nakashima, H., Parunak, V., Rosenschein, J., Ruvinsky, A., Sukthankar, G., Swarup, S., Sycara, K., Tambe, M., Wagner, T., Zavala, L.: Research directions for service-oriented multiagent systems. IEEE Internet Computing 9(6), 52–58 (2005)
16. Luck, M., McBurney, P., Gonzalez-Palacios, J.: Agent-based computing and programming of agent systems. In: Bordini, R.H., Dastani, M.M., Dix, J., El Fallah Seghrouchni, A. (eds.) PROMAS 2005. LNCS, vol. 3862, pp. 23–37. Springer, Heidelberg (2006)
17. Molesini, A., Omicini, A., Denti, E., Ricci, A.: SODA: A roadmap to artefacts. In: Dikenelli, O., Gleizes, M.-P., Ricci, A. (eds.) ESAW 2005. LNCS, vol. 3963, pp. 49–62. Springer, Heidelberg (2006)
18. Pavon, J., Gomez-Sanz, J., Fuentes, R.: The INGENIAS Methodology and Tools, pp. 236–276. Idea Group Publishing, USA (2005)
19. Soley, R.: The OMG Staff Strategy Group. Model driven architecture. Object Management Group White Paper Draft 3.2 (2005)
20. Zambonelli, F., Jennings, N.R., Wooldridge, M.: Developing multiagent systems: The gaia methodology. ACM Trans. Softw. Eng. Methodol. 12(3), 317–370 (2003)

Analysis, Comparison and Selection of MAS Software Engineering Processes and Tools

Emilia Garcia*, Adriana Giret, and Vicente Botti

Departamento de Sistemas Informaticos y Computacion,
Universidad Politecnica de Valencia, Camino de Vera S/N, Valencia, Spain
{mgarcia,agiret,vbotti}@dsic.upv.es

Abstract. The evaluation of multiagent system software engineering techniques is an open research topic. Nowadays, on the market there are a great number of methods and frameworks to develop multiagent systems. It makes difficult the selection between one and another. In this paper, an evaluation framework for analyzing, comparing and selecting methods and tools for developing multiagent systems is presented.

Keywords: Multiagent systems development tools, methodologies, software engineering.

1 Introduction

Recently, a great number of methods and frameworks for developing multiagent systems have appeared [3,17]. Each proposal has focused in different aspects, offers different functionality and some approaches only offer tools that cover a part of the development process. Furthermore, some approaches do not offer tools to model or implement multiagent systems, they only provide theoretical descriptions and guides to develop this kind of systems.

This situation makes the selection of one or another multiagent development tool, a very hard task. In the last few years the evaluation of multiagent systems (MAS) software engineering techniques has gained the research community attention, deriving in standardization efforts. Despite this, there is no complete and systematic way to evaluate MAS development methods and tools.

In this work we try to contribute a framework that deals with some open issues in the field of software engineering MAS evaluation. Masev[1] (MAs Software engineering EValuation framework) is an online application that allows analyzing and comparing methods, techniques and environments for developing MAS. Moreover, Masev allows the evaluation of how these methods and tools support the development of Organizational MAS and Service-oriented MAS.

The rest of the paper is organized as follows. Section 2 overviews the state of the art of the evaluation of multiagent system engineering techniques. Section 3

---

* This work is partially supported by the PAID-06-07/3191, TIN2006-14630-C03-01 projects and CONSOLIDER-INGENIO 2010 under grant CSD2007-00022. The first author is a student.
[1] http://masev.gti-ia.dsic.upv.es/

J.-J. Yang et al. (Eds.): PRIMA 2009, LNAI 5925, pp. 361–375, 2009.
© Springer-Verlag Berlin Heidelberg 2009

introduces Masev, our proposed evaluation framework. Firstly, the evaluation process followed to define Masev is presented (Section 3.1). Secondly, Section 3.2 summarizes the selected evaluation criteria. Thirdly, Section 3.3 explains the metric used by Masev for offering numerical comparison. Section 4 describes Masev functionalities and shows some snapshots of the application. At the end of this section, some lacks and advantages of Masev are analyzed. Finally, Section 5 presents some conclusions and future work.

2   Related Work

Following, some of the most relevant studies on the evaluation of MAS engineering techniques are presented.

Some works, like [5,19,17] focus their efforts on the analysis of methodologies, but do not analyze the tools that provide support for these methodologies. Nevertheless, this is a very important feature because a well-defined methodology loses a great part of its functionality if there is no sound and complete tool to apply it easily. Furthermore, these works do not analyze economical aspects (like the availability of documentation and examples of the studied methodologies) and the offered support for MAS issues such as ontologies, organizational MAS and so on.

Eiter and Mascardi [8] analyze environments for developing software agents. They provide a methodology and general guidelines for selecting a MASDK (MAS Development Kit). Bitting and Carter [2] use the criteria established by Eiter and Mascardi to analyze and compare five MASDKs. In order to obtain objective results from the evaluation Bitting and Carter add a quantitative evaluation. This work does not analyze the gap between modeling and platform implementation which is studied by Sudeikat and Braunch in [20].

Braubach and Pokahr [4] propose universal criteria catalog for evaluation of heterogeneous agent development artifacts. This work presents a good software engineering evaluation criteria mainly based on ISO 9126-1 [16] and ISO 9241, but it does not analyze specific features of MAS methodologies and development tools.

Works like [6,21] not only provide a list of concepts to analyze but they facilitate the evaluation task providing a questionnaire. The use of questionnaires makes the answers be more concrete and easy to compare. Also it reduces the evaluation time and simplifies the evaluation process.

The main lack of [6,21] is that they only evaluate methodologies and do not take into account the other tools and techniques needed in the MAS development process. Furthermore, they do not take into account the gap between what is proposed by the methods and the final models and implementation code.

Currently, there is no tool that implements and simplifies the evaluation process and the comparison task. The works related with this topic only provide theoretical guidelines and some comparison of a few methods and tools in a specific moment. If any of these methods or tools improves or adds new functionality, the evaluation results will be outdated. Furthermore, there is no comparative repository of the current methods and techniques to develop MAS.

In this paper we try to solve some detected drawbacks of this topic implementing a framework that analyzes the whole development process, that offers comparison and recommendations depending on the application requirements, that could have continuity over time (the criteria and the analysis could be easily updated) and that offers a comparative repository of current methods and techniques.

Moreover, we have taken into account two approaches that are getting more and more importance as powerful paradigms for developing complex systems: Organizational MAS and Service-oriented MAS. Both approaches require new techniques and specific features to be developed. For this reason, studies of the state of the art in these paradigms and about which new requirements arise in their development process have been done. The results of these studies can be consulted in [9,12].

3   Masev

Masev is an online application that allows analyzing and comparing methods, techniques and environments for developing MAS. Moreover, Masev allows the evaluation of how these methods and tools support the development of Organizational MAS and Service-oriented MAS. Finally, Masev provides a quantitative comparison based on a simple metric whose parameters can be modified by the users.

The main objective of Masev is to facilitate and simplify the evaluation and comparison task. For that reason, the criteria summarized in Section 3.2, including the special criteria to analyze Organizational MAS and Service-oriented MAS, are presented as a set of questionnaires. The use of questionnaires makes the answers be more concrete and easy to compare. Also it reduces the evaluation time and simplifies the evaluation process.

Other objectives of Masev are to achieve the greatest possible number of evaluations and to keep these evaluations constantly updated. For that reason, Masev is implemented as an online application that can be accessed anywhere and anytime. Moreover, the evaluation process has been simplified and the time needed to evaluate a tool has been reduced as much as possible.

3.1   Masev Evaluation Process

The evaluation process should follow a standard procedure in order to be as objective and reproducible as possible. To this end the standard ISO 14598 [15] was published. It introduces four phases that the evaluation process should follow: (1) Establish evaluation requirements; (2) Specification of the evaluation; (3) Design of the evaluation process; (4) Execution of the evaluation.

The evaluation process followed by Masev is based on the standard ISO 14598 and some critical reviews of it [18]. Firstly, the purpose of the evaluation and which types of tools to evaluate were identified based on different studies of the state of the art. Secondly, the evaluation framework was defined specifying the evaluation criteria (Section 3.2) and a metric that allows obtaining quantitative results (Section 3.3). Thirdly, Masev was implemented and some case studies were executed in order to get some empirical evaluations of the tool.

The process defined in Figure 1 shows that the updating phase is accessible from any stage of the evaluation process. It allows updating the selected evaluation criteria, the metric and Masev implementation when the knowledge of each area is growing, and also allows updating Masev to new requirements and techniques.

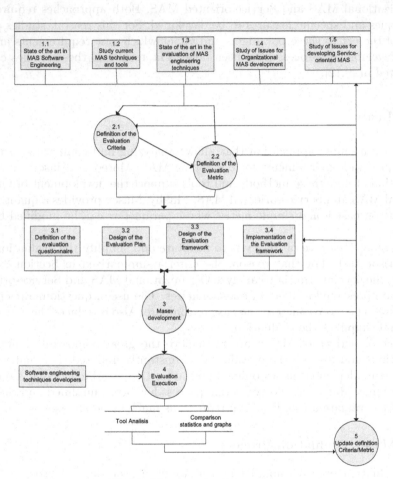

Fig. 1. Masev evaluation process

3.2   Evaluation Criteria

Because of the different perspectives, the identification of a set of independent, orthogonal features which completely characterize the MAS development process is a difficult task. The selected criteria for this evaluation framework are derived from the studies related in Section 2 and previous works like [10,11,13]. These

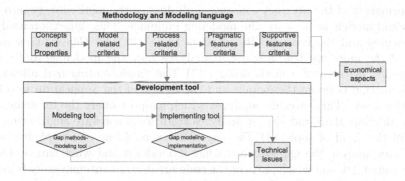

Fig. 2. Criteria classification

criteria takes into account traditional software engineering features and MAS specific characteristics. It tries to cover the whole development process, from the extraction of requirements to the implementation stage.

Due to space limitations, this section does not explain in detail each criterion and only a brief overview of each evaluated dimension is presented. For further information see [13] and Masev website (*http://masev.gti-ia.dsic.upv.es/*).

In order to cover all the necessary method characteristics and tools features from the requirements extraction stage to the final implementation code, the evaluation criteria are structured in two main dimensions: (1) Methodology and Modeling language; (2) Development tools that involves the Modeling tool and the Implementation tool (See Figure 2).

The **Methodology and modeling language** dimensions defines a process for evaluating methodologies and modeling languages, comparing their strengths, their weaknesses and identifying ways to improve on a particular methodological feature. These criteria include 71 criteria and analyze methodologies from five different points of view: (1) *Concepts and properties criteria* that evaluate whether or not a methodology adheres to the features of agent and MAS; (2) *Model related criteria* that deal with various aspects of a methodology's models and notational components, including the concepts represented by the models, and their expressiveness and other software engineering issues; (3) *Process related criteria* that analyze the development process and which guidelines offer the methodology for each development stage; (4) *Pragmatic features criteria* that assess software engineering features that evaluate the techniques provided by the methodology for the execution of its process steps and for the development of its models; (5) *Supportive feature criteria* that include high-level and complementary features of MAS and the offered support to the integration with other techniques and technologies. This classification is based on [17].

The methodology provides guidelines to help developers during the development process, but methodologies are only theoretical specifications and **Development tools** are needed to create the models and the final implementation. The analysis of the development tools includes 65 criteria and, as shown in Figure 2, it is divided into five dimensions: (1) the *Modeling tool*; allows the transformation of the abstract concepts and ideas of the methodology into diagrams and models using a specific modeling language. This dimension analyzes the features and the functionality of these tools. (2) The *Gap between methods and the modeling tool dimension* analyzes how the modeling tool covers the specific features of a methodology. (3) The *Implementing tool* allows the transformation between the models and the design of the application into final execution code. This category analyzes which support offers the implementing tool to develop MAS and also, it analyzes traditional software engineering features of this kind of tools. (4) *The gap between modeling and implementation dimension* analyze the gap between what is modeled and what can be finally implemented [20] and which parts of the code are derived automatically from the models.(5) *Technical issues dimension* analyzes traditional software engineering features that are related with the requirements of a tool to be installed, executed and used. These criteria should be applied to evaluate both for the modeling and the implementing tool.

Finally, *Economical aspects* have to be evaluated both for the methodologies and for the development tools. These criteria do not only include the cost of the application, also features like the vendor organization and the documentation offered are analyzed.

Masev also tries to analyze the new requirements for developing MAS in open-systems, with an organizational structure [9] and when MAS are integrated with web services [12].

In order to analyze which support is offered to develop **organizational MAS**, a set of 51 criteria is defined. These criteria are structured using the main classification presented in Figure 2. The methodology and modeling language dimension analyzes how the methodology and its models support the model of organizational MAS and which social guidelines are offered. Moreover, specific organizational concepts are analyzed based on five dimensions [1]: (1) Structural dimension; (2) Dynamic dimension; (3) Functional dimension; (4) Normative dimension; and (5) Environment dimension. The Development tools dimension analyzes how the Modeling tool and Implementing tool support the model and implementation of organizational concepts. These criteria analyzes which facilities are offered and how organizations are materialized in the models and in the final implementation.

In order to analyze which support is offered to develop service-oriented MAS, a set of 44 criteria is defined. These criteria are structured using the main classification presented in Figure 2. The Methodology and modeling language dimension analyzes the way in which the relationship between agents and services is considered. Furthermore, these criteria analyze in which development stages is considered this integration and which guidelines are offered. The Development tools dimension considers the Modeling tool and the Implementing tool. These criteria analyze the facilities offered to model and implement this kind of systems and, their communication and definition standards. Moreover, these criteria analyze how this integration is implemented and which tools are offered to translate between service and agent standards and viceversa.

3.3   Metric

A quantitative evaluation offers a fast and general evaluation overview which allows to compare and evaluate methods and tools easily. For that reason, in this section a method to obtain numerical results of the evaluation is presented. This metric is based on previous works like [2,7].

Each established criterion is associated with a weight that represents the importance of this criterion (**W**).

max(P) represents the best possible answer for each criterion.

R represents the evaluator answer for each criterion. Each possible answer is associated with a weight.

$$result = \frac{\sum(W \cdot R)}{\sum(W \cdot max(P))} \cdot 100 \tag{1}$$

When the answer can have multiple values, i.e., when the evaluator checks which features of a list support its approach, the second formula is used.

$$result = \frac{\sum(W \cdot \sum(R))}{\sum(W \cdot max(\sum(P)))} \cdot 100 \tag{2}$$

$\sum(R)$ represents the summation of the checked answers weight.

$max(\sum(P))$ represents the summation of all the answers that could be checked.

Finally, the numerical evaluation is the result of the dot product between the weight vector and the evaluation vector. This formula will be applied to each dimension and a global vision of the development state and the completeness of each method or tool in this category is obtained. These values are useful to compare different approaches rapidly because they give a fast overview that can be completed with the qualitative evaluation.

4   Masev Functionalities

The main functionalities of Masev are the analysis and the qualitative and quantitative comparison of methodologies, modeling and implementing tools for developing MAS. Masev offers a personal site where users can define their own evaluations of tools and their own metric parameters.

4.1   Analysis of Methods and Tools

The evaluation process consists of completing a sequence of forms about the method or tool to evaluate. Firstly, the user has to specify what he is going to analyze (Figure 3). It can be a methodology, a modeling tool, an implementing tool or a toolkit, i.e, a group of related methods and tools. For example a toolkit can a methodology that has its own modeling tool associated.

Masev shows only the questionnaires related to the type of tool to evaluate. Moreover, it only shows the questionnaires related to organizations and services whether the evaluated tool offers some support to them. These forms

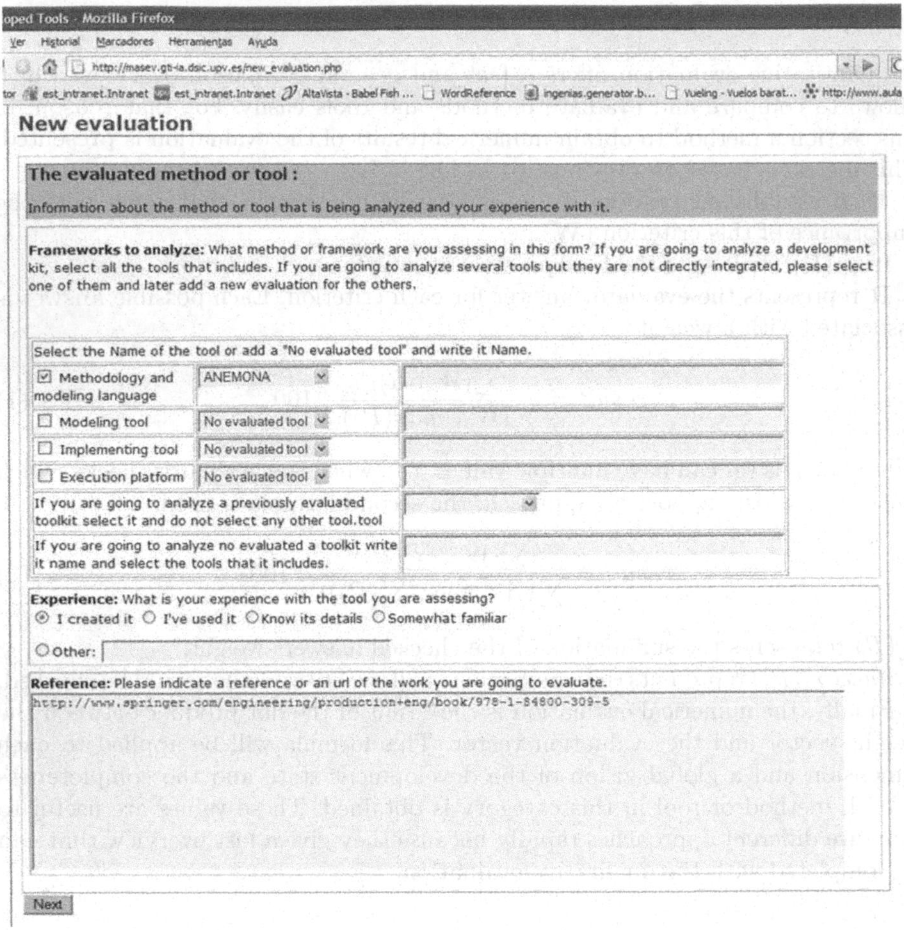

Fig. 3. Masev new evaluation

consist of several questions based on the selected evaluated criteria summarized in Section 3.2. Figure 4 shows an snapshot of the evaluation of the methodology ANEMONA [14]. This questionnaire analyzes how ANEMONA support the basic concepts and properties of multiagent systems.

Finally, users can view and modify their previous evaluated methods and tools and update them at any time.This functionality allows users to update their evaluations if a feature is improved or when adding a new feature.

4.2   Comparison of Methods and Tools

Users can compare different evaluations of a specific method or tool or compare some methods or tools of the same type (Figure 5).

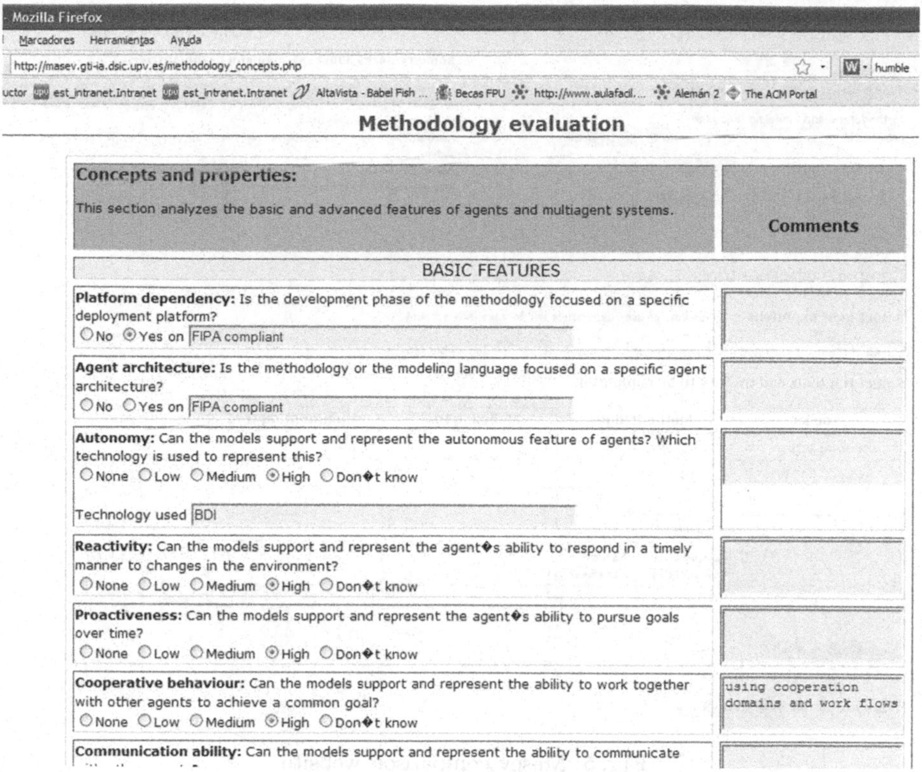

Fig. 4. Masev questionnaire

The results of the qualitative comparison are presented as summarized tables like Figure 6. These tables allows comparing the engineering tool taking into account the selected evaluation criteria.

Masev also implements the metric proposed in Section 3.3 and allows obtaining quantitative comparison of the evaluated tools.

The default weight of each criteria and the value of each answer has been defined taking into account the study of the state of art and the experience of Masev authors and collaborators. Despite this, users can define their own vector of weights (Figure 7). This fact simplifies the selection task between one engineering tool or another. Users can adapt the metric parameters to the specific requirements of their application, so they would obtain a ranking of the most appropriate methods and tools to develop a specific application.

Figure 8 shows how users can filter the data of the comparison selecting the experience of the evaluators and selecting the default metric values or their personal metric values.

Numerical comparisons offer a fast overview of the analyzed methods and tools in each category of the evaluation criteria. Figure 9 shows the numerical comparison of four methodologies obtained using the metric presented in Section 3.3

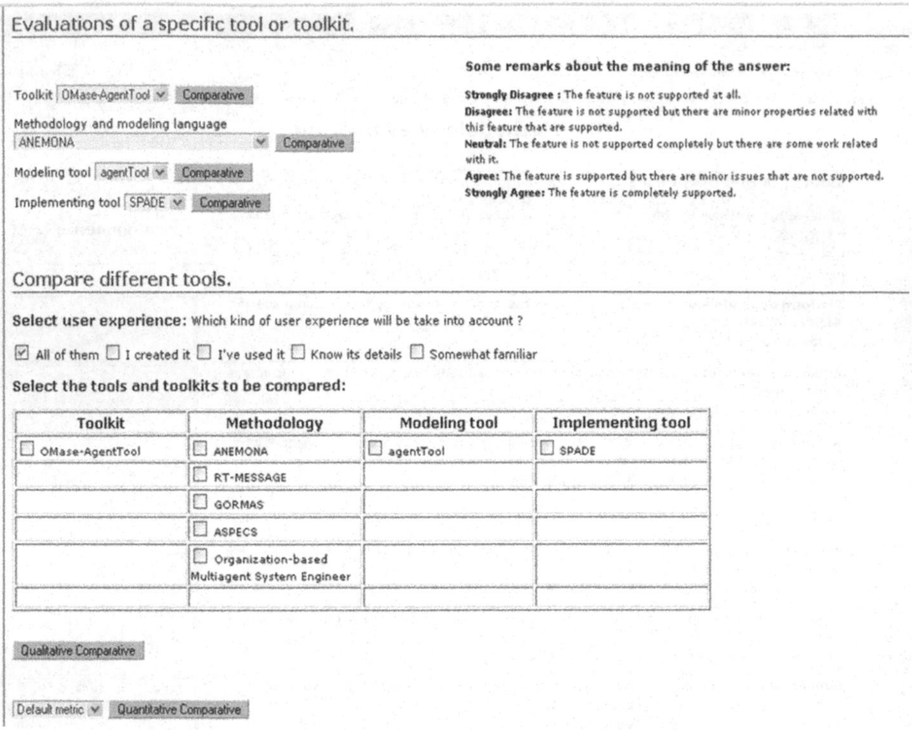

Fig. 5. Masev comparison website

and Masev default criteria weights. These results allow an overview comparison of these methodologies. For example, the results of the Concepts and Model dimension show that there are no significant differences between them in this area. The good results obtained in the Economical dimension show that they are free and offer good documentation. Obviously, none can based the decision of selecting one or another tool only in the numerical results. It is only a general idea that can be more specific by the use of personal metric values.

4.3 Masev Disadvantages and Advantages

Masev has been initially tested anlyzing some methods and tools.

Despite the fact that no evaluator knew Masev befor, each evaluation process lasted about 15 minutes and facilitated the necessary information to analyze and compare these methodologies and tools. Therefore, one can conclude that Masev simplifies the evaluation process. It produces a large volume of information in a very short time. No evaluator had problems during the evaluation process and the information was easily structured through Masev.

The comparatives provided by Masev have been very useful to analyze the tools and to detect their weakness. Masev structures the information in tabular

Methodology evaluation

TOOLS:	ANEMONA	RT-MESSAGE	GORMAS	INGENIAS
Concepts and properties:				
BASIC FEATURES				
Platform dependency:	Yes on FIPA compliant	Yes on ARTIS	No	No
Agent architecture:		Yes on ARTIS	No	No
Autonomy:	High	High	Medium	Medium
Reactivity:	High	High	High	None
Proactiveness:	High	Medium	High	Medium
Cooperative behaviour:	High	Medium	High	High
Communication ability:	High	High	High	High
Communication language:	Speech acts	Speech acts	Speech acts	Speech acts
Non-cooperative agents:	Agree	Agree	Strongly Agree	Agree
Mental attitudes:	High	Medium	Medium	High
Adaptability:				

Fig. 6. Masev comparison of 4 methodologies

form so it is very easy to find similarities and differences between the evaluated tools. Finally, the numerical results obtained allow an overview of the evaluated methodologies and a quick comparison of them.

The experiences from the case studies reveal that the informal evaluation makes the results totally dependent on the opinion of the evaluator. This fact introduces too much subjectivity in the process. Thus, Masev was prepared to support multiple evaluations of the same tool or methodology and to calculate the average value at the time of showing the comparative. Furthermore, Masev allows the user to select which types of evaluators will be considered, for example, a user can use only the information provided by the creators of the tool.

The experiences of some users have highlighted that there are few terms that are not clearly defined in the literature and this fact can produce ambiguity in the answers. In order to solve this problem we are adding extra information of these terms and splitting some of them into several questions that clarify the meaning.

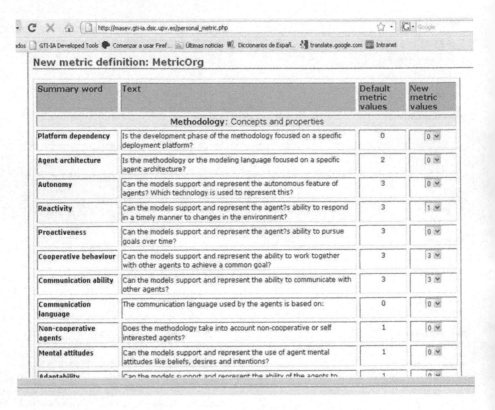

Fig. 7. New metric values definition

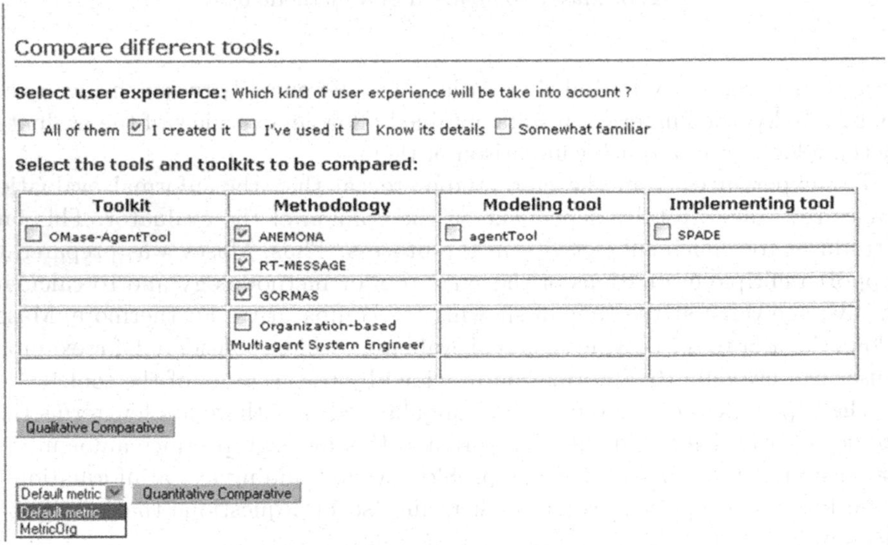

Fig. 8. Masev quantitative comparative

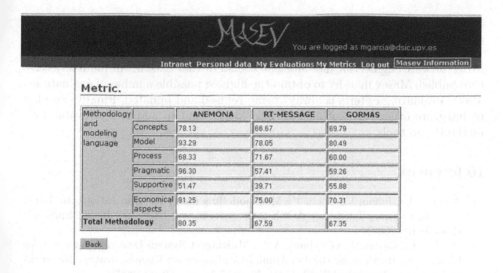

You are logged as mgarcia@dsic.upv.es

Intranet Personal data My Evaluations My Metrics Log out Masev Information

Metric.

Methodology and modeling language		ANEMONA	RT-MESSAGE	GORMAS
	Concepts	78.13	66.67	69.79
	Model	93.29	78.05	80.49
	Process	68.33	71.67	60.00
	Pragmatic	96.30	57.41	59.26
	Supportive	51.47	39.71	55.88
	Economical aspects	81.25	75.00	70.31
Total Methodology		80.35	67.59	67.35

Back

Fig. 9. Quantitative comparison of 4 methodologies

5 Conclusions and Future Work

This paper presents an evaluation framework for multiagent systems software engineering. It is an online evaluation framework that allows analyzing and comparing methods, techniques and environments for developing multiagent systems.

Masev analyzes methods and tools through a set of criteria selected by studying the state of the art. These criteria are related to both system engineering dimensions and multiagent system features. They analyze the MAS development process from the requirement stage to the implementation of the final code taking into account the most important features and tools involved in the process. The gap between what can be defined by the methodology and what can be modeled with the modeling tool is also analyzed. Moreover, the gap between what is modeled and what can be directly translated into code is also analyzed. Finally, the support for developing organizational and service-oriented MAS is studied.

The comparison module simplifies the comparison task and could help developers to select the most appropriate MAS method and tools for developing a specific system. Developers can obtain qualitative and numerical comparisons of MAS engineering tools. The metric used in the quantitative comparison can be modified by the users by means of the definition of personal criteria weights. These parameters can be adapted taking into account the requirements of the system to be developed. With this information, Masev shows a ranking of the most appropriate methods and tools.

Masev questionnaires summarizes the most important issues for developing MAS, organizational MAS and service-oriented MAS, so it could be used for MAS software engineering developers to detect and improve lacks in their methods and tools. Also, developers of new tools can understand this application as a way to publish their tools and demonstrate which is their contribution to the state of the art.

Currently, we are working in order to provide a repository of the most used MAS software engineering methods and tools.For that reason, our main objective is to publish Masev in order to obtain the highest possible number of evaluations. Masev evaluating criteria is always being revised and updated. Finally, we plan to integrate other types of metrics into Masev and to add formal evaluations methods and tools.

References

1. Argente, E., Julian, V., Botti, V.: Mas modelling based on organizations. In: Luck, M., Gomez-Sanz, J.J. (eds.) AOSE 2008. LNCS, vol. 5386, pp. 16–30. Springer, Heidelberg (2009)
2. Bitting, E., Carter, J., Ghorbani, A.A.: Multiagent System Development Kits: An Evaluation. In: Proc. of the 1st Annual Conference on Communication Networks and Services Research (CNSR 2003), May 15-16, pp. 80–92 (2003)
3. Bordini, R.H., Dastani, M., Winikoff, M.: Current issues in multi-agent systems development (invited paper). In: Proc. Workshop on Engineering Societies in the Agents World, pp. 38–61 (2007)
4. Braubach, L., Pokahr, A., Lamersdorf, W.: A universal criteria catalog for evaluation of heterogeneous agent development artifacts. In: Sixth International Workshop From Agent Theory to Agent Implementation, AT2AI-6 (2008)
5. Cernuzzi, L., Rossi, G.: On the evaluation of agent oriented modeling methods. In: Proceedings of Agent Oriented Methodology Workshop (2002)
6. Dam, K.H.: Evaluating and Comparing Agent-Oriented Software Engineering Methodologies. Master's thesis, Master of Applied Science in Information Technology - RMIT University, Australia (2003)
7. Dubielewicz, I., Hnatkowska, B., Huzar, Z., Tuzinkiewicz, L.: An Approach to Software Quality Specification and Evaluation (SPoQE). In: IFIP International Federation for Information Processing, vol. 227, pp. 155–166. Springer, Boston (2007)
8. Eiter, T., Mascardi, V.: Comparing environments for developing software agents. AI Commun. 15(4), 169–197 (2002)
9. Garcia, E., Argente, E., Giret, A., Botti, V.: Issues for organizational multiagent systems development. In: Sixth International Workshop From Agent Theory to Agent Implementation (AT2AI-6), pp. 59–65 (2008)
10. Garcia, E., Giret, A., Botti, V.: Evaluating mas engineering tools. In: International Conference on Evaluation of Novel Approaches to Software Engineering, pp. 181–1874 (2008)
11. Garcia, E., Giret, A., Botti, V.: On the evaluation of mas development tools. In: International Conference on Artificial Intelligence in Theory and Practice (IFIP AI 2008), vol. 276/2008, pp. 35–44. Springer, Boston (2008)
12. Garcia, E., Giret, A., Botti, V.: Software engineering for Service-oriented MAS. In: Klusch, M., Pěchouček, M., Polleres, A. (eds.) CIA 2008. LNCS, vol. 5180, pp. 86–100. Springer, Heidelberg (2008)
13. Garcia, E., Giret, A., Botti, V.: Towards an evaluation framework for MAS software engineering. In: Bui, T.D., Ho, T.V., Ha, Q.T. (eds.) PRIMA 2008. LNCS, vol. 5357, pp. 197–205. Springer, Heidelberg (2008)

14. Giret, A., Botti, V.: Engineering holonic manufacturing systems. Computers in Industry 60, 428–440 (2009)
15. ISO. Information technology - software product evaluation part 6: Documentation of evaluation modules. ISO 14598-1:1999 (1999)
16. ISO. Software engineering - product quality - part 1: Quality model. *ISO IEC 9126-1:2001 edition*, 2001.
17. Lin, C.-E., Kavi, K.M., Sheldon, F.T., Daley, K.M., Abercrombie, R.K.: A methodology to evaluate agent oriented software engineering techniques. In: HICSS 2007: Proceedings of the 40th Annual Hawaii International Conference on System Sciences, p. 60. IEEE Computer Society, Los Alamitos (2007)
18. Punter, T., Kusters, R., Trienekens, J., Bemelmans, T., Brombacher, A.: The w-process for software product evaluation: A method for goal-oriented implementation of the iso 14598 standard. Software Quality Control 12(2), 137–158 (2004)
19. Sturm, A., Shehory, O.: A framework for evaluating agent-oriented methodologies. In: Giorgini, P., Henderson-Sellers, B., Winikoff, M. (eds.) AOIS 2003. LNCS, vol. 3030, pp. 94–109. Springer, Heidelberg (2004)
20. Sudeikat, J., Braubach, L., Pokahr, A., Lamersdorf, W.: Evaluation of agent-oriented software methodologies examination of the gap between modeling and platform. In: Odell, J.J., Giorgini, P., Müller, J.P., et al. (eds.) AOSE 2004. LNCS, vol. 3382, pp. 126–141. Springer, Heidelberg (2005)
21. Tran, Q.-N., Low, G.: Comparison of ten agent-oriented methodologies, pp. 341–367 (2005)

A Synchronous Model of Mental Rhythm Using Paralanguage for Communication Robots

Takanori Hayashi, Shohei Kato, and Hidenori Itoh

Dept. of Computer Science and Engineering, Graduate School of Engineering,
Nagoya Institute of Technology,
Gokiso-cho Showa-ku Nagoya, 466-8555 Japan
{hayashi,shohey,itoh}@juno.ics.nitech.ac.jp

Abstract. We aimed to achieve smooth human-robot communication by using a communication model based on synchronization between human and robot paralanguages. We also described a robot's mental rhythm that controls its own paralanguage and entrains its mental rhythm into a human paralanguage rhythm for human-robot communication. We built three robots to evaluate our proposed model: the first used our communication model and the other two used extreme models that either completely imitated human paralanguage or did not imitate it at all. We prepared several conversations between subjects and each of the three robots. The experimental results revealed that synchronized conversation using human and robot paralanguages gave humans a positive impression of the robots. This paper also reports the results from analyzing the correlation between human and robot paralanguages.

1 Introduction

Research and development on robots designed for communication with humans has recently been actively pursued in the research field of advanced robotics ([1], [2], [3]). The most important communication is conversation that helps humans and robots to understand one another. Communication robots are aimed at accomplishing smooth communications with humans. Robots in conversation should therefore not only understand word meanings but also demonstrate a variety of nonverbal communication called paralanguage (e.g., speech speed, switching pause, intonation, accent, and sound pressure level). Paralanguage has an inclination to be entrained into the paralanguage of the speaker's counterpart. It is known that one speaker's paralanguage and his/her counterpart's (called a dialogist's) paralanguage synchronize with each other [4].

We have focused on paralanguage and described a method of robot conversation using a synchronous model of mental rhythm where the robot's paralanguage is synchronized with human paralanguage. This paper reports the results from a human-robot conversation test and our analysis of the synchronous inclination between humans and robots.

J.-J. Yang et al. (Eds.): PRIMA 2009, LNAI 5925, pp. 376–388, 2009.

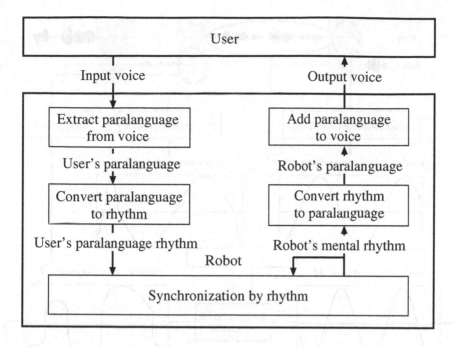

Fig. 1. Paralanguage control model

2 Synchronous Model

Fig. 1 is a flowchart overviewing our model of paralanguage control using synchronization. This model, where humans and robots speak alternately, controls the robot's paralanguage according to human paralanguage. We used the concept of a mental tempo for this model. The mental tempo is a proper tempo that influences conversation, walking, and work. We use a **mental rhythm** that mathematically models the concept of the mental tempo. A robot has a mental rhythm and this is entrained into human paralanguage. Human rhythm is extracted from human paralanguage. Rhythms between a robot's mental rhythm and a human-paralanguage rhythm are synchronized. The robot's mental rhythm, which is synchronized with the human rhythm, controls the robot's paralanguage.

We used a switching pause as the robot's paralanguage. The switching pause is the time from the end of one speaker's speech to the beginning of the other speaker's speech. In other words, it is the time for speaker's to alternate speech. Nagaoka et al. found the switching pauses synchronize between speakers in an experiment [5]. They considered that this was because the speaker could feel the change in the length of the dialogist's switching pause and adjust his own switching pause. Moreover, as a speaker begins to speak, he/she should distinguish pauses in speech from pauses due to speaker alternation, and he/she needs to be conscious of his/her own speech speed. Consequently, one's switching pause is considered to be influenced by the other's speech speed. This was observed by Ohishi and Oda in an experiment [6]. In summary, one's switching pause

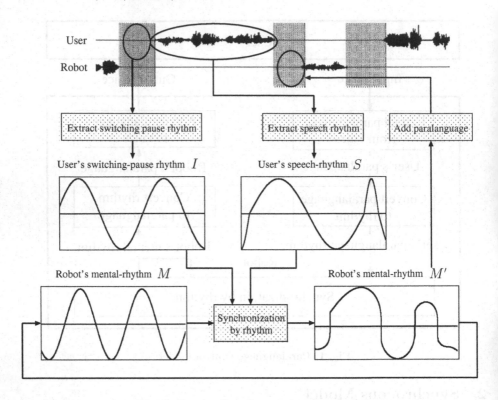

Fig. 2. Process flow for synchronous model

is influenced by the time structure of the other's speech: the switching pause and speech speed. We used the human **switching-pause rhythm** and **speech rhythm** in human paralanguage in this paper as the factors that influence a robot's switching pauses.

Fig. 2 shows the process flow for our synchronous model. The top of the figure shows speech waves and switching pauses during human-robot conversation. The human switching-pause rhythm was extracted from the human switching pause just before the robot's utterance started. Similarly, the human's speech rhythm was extracted from the human voice wave just before the robot's utterance started. As the robot's mental rhythm was entrained into these human rhythms, the robot's mental rhythm seemed to adjust to that of the human. The robot's switching pause was controlled by this robot's mental rhythm. In the following, we describe our used rhythms that are the robot's mental rhythm M, human switching-pause rhythm I, and human-speech rhythm S.

The mathematical model of our robot's mental rhythm was based on the van der Pol equation, which is a nonlinear wave transducer that has self-excited oscillation and characteristics of entrainment. Displacement $m(t)$ of the robot's mental rhythm, M, at time t is calculated as:

$$\ddot{m}(t) = -\omega_0^2 m(t) + \epsilon(1 - m(t)^2)\dot{m}(t) + \alpha i(t) + \beta s(t), \qquad (1)$$

where ω_0^2 is the energy conservation coefficient, and ϵ is the viscous coefficient. These coefficients are used to determine robot's mental rhythm, M. The $i(t)$ and $s(t)$ are human paralanguage rhythms that influence the robot's mental rhythm. The $i(t)$ is the displacement of human switching-pause rhythm I at time t on the rhythm, and $s(t)$ is the displacement of human speech rhythm S at time t on the rhythm. The $\alpha(0 \leq \alpha \leq 1)$ and $\beta(0 \leq \beta \leq 1)$ are entrainment coefficients, which are used for controlling the intensity of synchronization with human paralanguage. Finally, the robot's switching pause is controlled by the time cycle of the robot's mental rhythm adjusted to the human.

Displacement $i(t)$ of the human switching-pause rhythm I at time t is defined as:

$$i(t) = \sin(\frac{2\pi t}{kp}),\qquad(2)$$

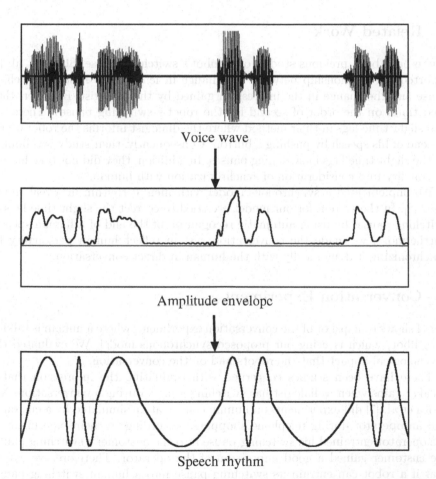

Voice wave

Amplitude envelope

Speech rhythm

Fig. 3. Example of calculating human speech rhythm corresponding to human utterance "ki-no-u-se-tsu-me-i"

where p is the length of the human switching pause observed during conversation, and k is constant. Switching-pause I can be explained as a sine wave that has a cycle of constancy k multiplied by the length p of the human switching pause. If the switching pause is long, a slow switching-pause rhythm is generated. However, if the switching pause is short, a quick switching-pause rhythm is generated.

Human speech rhythm S is defined as a wave that consists of two half cycles: the time per mora and the silent time when a wave is extracted from the human voice. Fig. 3 has an example of the calculation of a human speech rhythm corresponding to the human utterance "ki-no-u-se-tsu-me-i". In detail, the amplitude envelope is calculated by passing the human-voice wave through a low-pass filter. The cutoff frequency of this low-pass filter is 80 [Hz]. Then, human speech-rhythm S is calculated by forming a sine wave from the shape of the amplitude envelope.

3   Related Work

There have been previous studies of a robot's switching pause. Shiwa et al. [7] reported the relationship between the change in length of a robot's switching pause and the change in the impression gained by the dialogist. However, they used times on the order of second for the robot's switching pauses. There are also slight time lags in their method where the dialogist informs the robot about the end of his speech by pushing a button. Consequently, their study was limited by the slight time lags in switching pauses. In addition, they did not take human personality into consideration of synchronization with human.

We implemented a synchronous model with mental rhythm in a real robot, ifbot [8]. In the system for our model, we tried to correct the slight time lags in switching pauses by using automatic recognition of the end of a human speech. Furthermore, we made the conversation system reflect human personality by synchronizing it dynamically with the human in direct conversation.

4   Conversation Experiment

Fig. 4 shows a snapshot of the conversation experiment, where a human is talking with ifbot, which is using our proposed synchronous model. We evaluated the psychological impact that the robots had on the conversation.

There have been studies concerned with evaluating the impression that a speaker gains when a dialogist has switching pauses during a conversation. Nagaoka et al. [5] did experiments on human conversation simulated by a customer and an operator during telephone shopping. According to their experiment, if the operator entrained his switching pause into the customer's switching pause, the customer gained a good impression of the operator. Therefore, we expect that if a robot can entrain its switching pause into a human switching pause, humans can gain a good impression of the robot. However, Giles and Philip [9] reported that a speaker does not always gain a good impression of the dialogist,

Fig. 4. Snapshot of dialog

if he/she imitates all the speaker's paralanguage. However, they found in their experiment that synchronous behavior was the best in that the speaker gained a better impression if he adjusted his paralanguage to a part of the dialogist's paralanguage rather than to all of it.

We built three robots to evaluate our proposed model, and prepared conversations between a human and each of the three robots. The three robots were:

(a) **a synchronous model:** robot that used our proposed synchronous model of mental rhythm,
(b) **an imitative model:** robot that used completely imitated human paralanguage, and
(c) **a fixed model:** robot that retained its paralanguage without being influenced by that of humans.

The imitative- and fixed-model robots, which we used as targets for comparison, made it possible to change the entrainment coefficients of our proposed synchronous model. The imitative-model robot completely imitated human paralanguage with entrainment coefficients of $\alpha = 1$ and $\beta = 0$. Similarly, the fixed-model robot that did not imitate human paralanguage at all used entrainment coefficients of $\alpha = 0$ and $\beta = 0$.

The conversation we used for the experiment was on a specific scenario (Table 1). As we considered paralanguage to be without word meaning in our

Table 1. The Conversation Scenario We Used for the Experiment*

Robot : Let's talk to me.
User   : Are you thirsty?
Robot : Yes, I want to drink orange juice.
User   : I don't have any.
Robot : Really?
User   : How about apple juice, instead?
Robot : Apple? Is apple red and round?
User   : That's right.
Robot : I don't like it. Let's talk about something different.
User   : Then, do you like dog?
Robot : Dog? Does dog have four legs, a long neck and a yellow body?
User   : I think you are talking about giraffe.
Robot : Oh, I was wrong. So, does dog have four legs and two long ears, and hop?
User   : I think you are talking about rabbit.
Robot : It's wrong again. So, what is dog like?
User   : Dog is the one that barks "bowwow".
Robot : Really? So, I like dog very much. Have you ever kept dog?
User   : Yes, I have.
Robot : Oh, is it hard to keep it?
User   : Yes, it is.
Robot : Really? Did you hate doing it?
User   : Occasionally.
Robot : Oh, did you throw it away?
User   : No, I didn't.
Robot : Oh, good. I thought what if you throw me away.
User   : Let's talk about another topic.
Robot : Then, can chick fly?
User   : No, chick can't fly.
Robot : I thought so, and that's why I've never seen that chick is flying. Then, is chick swan's baby?
User   : I think so.
Robot : Really? But swan is white. Does chick become white?
User   : Yes.
Robot : But, human never changes its skin color as he grows up. Chick becomes white, really?
User   : Yes, chick becomes white.
Robot : I see. I will get chick and grow it to be swan. Good bye.

* We experimented on Japanese version though this scenario was described in English.

research, we prepared a scenario that prevented conversation from a unique context to conversation as thinking time. We experimented on conversations between three robots and 16 subjects who were university students.

We used the semantic differential (SD) [10] in these experiments to evaluate impressions. The 10 pairs of adjectives that we used for SD, were:

- human – mechanical
- natural – artificial
- complicated – simple
- intelligent – unintelligent
- sociable – unsociable
- soft – hard
- interesting – uninteresting
- likable – unlikable
- familiar – unfamiliar
- warm – cold

5   Analysis of Tendency to Synchronize

We carried out Pearson correlation analysis to investigate the relation in conversation between our proposed robot's paralanguage rhythm (switching-pause rhythm) and human paralanguage rhythms (switching-pause and speech rhythms). The switching-pause rhythm in this analysis was replaced by the length of the switching pause. Similarly, the speech rhythm was replaced by the speech speed per mora. To conduct analysis at the time line, the conversation was divided into three groups: the first, middle, and last parts, and we calculated the correlation coefficients. Table 2 lists the results of analysis.

From the table, we discovered that the correlation coefficient between the robot's switching pause and that of the humans increased with time, and there was a significant correlation in the last part of the conversation ($r = 0.272$ and $p < 0.01$). However, although the correlation coefficient between the human switching pause and human speech speed was significant in the first and middle parts, it was not significant in the last. We also discovered that there was no significant correlation between the robot's switching pause and the human speech speed. As a result of the robot-human conversation, we found that the relation between the robot's switching pause and the human switching pause drew closer as the conversation progressed, while the relation between the human switching pause and the human speech speed grew further apart as the conversation

Table 2. Correlation Coefficient between Robot's Paralanguage and User's Paralanguage

	First	Middle	Last
Robot's switching pause & user's switching pause	0.118	0.193	0.272(**)
Robot's switching pause & user's speech speed	0.184	0.050	0.140
User's switching pause & user's speech speed	-0.202(*)	-0.226(*)	-0.082

** Significance level: 0.01
* Significance level: 0.05

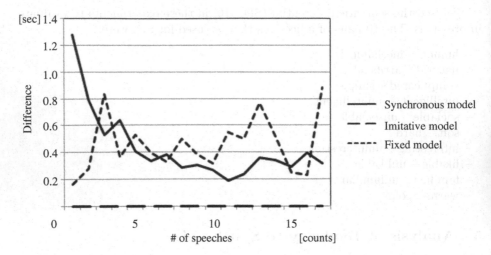

Fig. 5. Difference between user's switching pause and robots' switching pause

progressed. As the conversation progressed, the human switching-pause rhythm deviated from his/her own speech rhythm; simultaneously, this approached the robot's switching-pause rhythm. That is, the human switching-pause rhythm in human-paralanguage rhythm, which the robots were synchronized with, changed by being entrained into the robots.

The time series in Fig. 5 plots, the average difference between the human switching pause and the switching pauses of the three robots with our proposed synchronous model and the targets we used for comparison, i.e., the imitative and fixed models. There is no difference between the human switching pause and the imitative-model's switching pause, because this model has the switching pause as a human. The difference between the human switching pause and the fixed-model's switching pause is about 0.5 [sec] from the beginning to the last part of the conversation. The difference between the human switching pause and the synchronous-model's switching pause decreases as the conversation progresses; as a result, this difference is smaller than that for the fixed model.

These results suggest that there is no difference between the human switching pause and the robot's switching pause during conversation with the imitative model; therefore, humans feel that the conversation is monotonous. The difference between the human switching pause and the robot's switching pause changes with the fixed model, but the difference is insignificant; therefore, it is difficult for humans to obtain a good impression of the robot. However, the difference between the human switching pause and the robot's switching pause decreases with our proposed synchronous model, because, the robot entrains its switching pause into the human switching pause as the conversation progresses. Consequently, humans feel as though they are on intimate terms with the robot, and obtain a good impression of it.

Table 3. Transition in Robot's Switching Pause and User's Switching Pause

	First	Middle	Last
User A Length of robot's switching pause	1.757	0.876	0.849
Length of user's switching pause	0.660	0.757	0.840
User B Length of robot's switching pause	1.883	0.897	0.560
Length of user's switching pause	0.440	0.543	0.360

We then analyzed the results from evaluations where subjects in the experiments responded to how impressed they were with the robots during conversations. As a result, we found that our proposed synchronous model gave the subjects the best impressions of the three robots we tested. This is the same result as the guess from Fig. 5 that indicates the difference between the human switching pause and the robots' switching pauses. Further, details on the evaluations of impressions can be found in [11].

We next selected two subjects based on the evaluation results, and focused on their switching pauses and those of the synchronous-model robot in detail. Fig. 6 plots the transition in switching pauses of this robot and human A who gained a positive impression of it. Similarly, Fig. 7 plots the transition in switching pauses of our synchronous-model robot and human B who gained a negative impression of it. Table 3 lists the average switching pauses of the human subject and robot in the first, middle, and the last parts of a conversation. human A's switching pause gradually approaches the robot's switching pause, while human B's switching pause does not get close to the robot's switching pause. These results indicate that human A, who tends to be entrained, lets his own switching

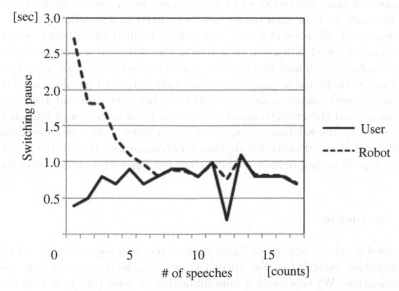

Fig. 6. Transition in switching pause for User A (gained positive impression of robot)

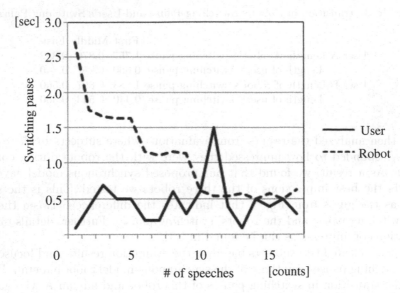

Fig. 7. Transition in switching pause for User B (gained negative impression of robot)

pause be entrained into the robot's switching pause, synchronizes his with the robot's, and gains a positive impression of the robot. However, human B, who does not tend to be entrained, retains his own switching pause without being influenced by that of the robot, does not synchronize his with the robot's, and gains a negative impression of the robot. In brief, both subjects had various evaluations of their impressions of our proposed synchronous-model robot and were influenced by their own tendencies to be entrained into dialogists.

Nagaoka et al. [5] called this tendency to be entrained into others a social skill. They defined a social skill as an indicator of the ability to smoothly accomplish a social task. They found through experiments that a speaker who has high level of social skills has a synchronous inclination toward paralanguage during conversation, and evaluates this inclination highly. The different tendencies to be entrained and the evaluations of impression by human A and human B can be explained by the existence of social skills. In other words, because human A has high level of social skills, his rhythm is entrained into that of the robot, and he gains a positive impression of their conversation with our new synchronous model.

6   Conclusion

We focused on the synchronous inclination of paralanguage, which is nonverbal communication included in the speech voice, to achieve smooth human-robot communication. We described a communication model based on synchronization between human and robot paralanguages. We also described a robot's mental rhythm that controls its own paralanguage and entrains its mental rhythm into a human paralanguage rhythm for human-robot communication. We built a robot that used our proposed synchronous model. We conducted experiments with conversations to analyze the synchronous inclination between robots and humans,

We only built three robots that had different degrees of synchronization with humans to conduct the conversation experiments. Therefore, the degree of synchronization was insufficient to assess changes in impressions while talking to the robots. Consequently, we intend to study the degree of robot synchronization changes with humans more closely, and explain the relation between the degree of robot synchronization and impressions of the robots. We confirmed that the synchronous model we proposed, which only entrains its switching pauses into those of humans, left a positive impression on humans. In the future, we intend to let robots be entrained not only into switching pauses but also voice volume, voice pitch, and speech speed to study whether these paralanguage characteristics can effectively smooth human-robot communications.

Acknowledgment

Ifbot was developed as part of an industry-university joint research project among the Business Design Laboratory Co,. Ltd., Brother Industries, Ltd., A.G.I. Inc, ROBOS Co., and the Nagoya Institute of Technology. We are grateful to all of them for their input. This work was supported in part by the Tatematsu Foundation, and by a Ministry of Education, Science, Sports and Culture, Grant–in–Aid for Scientific Research under grant #20700199 and #21500187.

References

1. Breazeal, C.: Kismet,
   http://www.ai.mit.edu/projects/humanoid-robotics-group/kismet/
   kismet.html
2. Fujita, Y.: Childcare Robot PaPeRo. Journal of Robotics Society of Japan 24, 162–163 (2006) (in Japanese)
3. Kato, S., Ohshiro, S., Itoh, H., Kimura, K.: Development of a communication robot ifbot. In: IEEE International Conference on Robotics and Automation (ICRA 2004), pp. 697–702 (2004)
4. Kimura, M., Daibo, I.: Interactional synchrony in conversations about emotional episodes: A measurement by the between-participants pseudosynchrony experimental paradigm. Journal of Nonverbal Behavior 30, 115–126 (2006)
5. Nagaoka, C., Komori, M., Yoshikawa, S.: Synchrony Tendency: Interactional Synchrony and Congruence of Nonverbal Behavior in Social Interaction. In: Proc. of the 2005 International Conference on Active Media Technology, pp. 529–534 (2005)
6. Ohishi, S., Oda, M.: The Personal Tempo's Effect on Dialogue Smoothness: from an index of switching pause. Technical report of IEICE. HIP 105, 31–36 (2006) (in Japanese)
7. Shiwa, T., Kanda, T., Imai, M., Ishiguro, H., Higata, N.: How quickly should a communication robot respond. International Journal of Social Robotics 1, 141–155 (2009)

8. Business Design Laboratory Co. Ltd.: The Extremely Expressive Communication Robot, Ifbot, http://www.business-design.co.jp/en/product/001/index.html
9. Giles, H., Philip, S.: Accommodation theory: Optimal levels of convergence. Language and Social Psychology, 45–65 (1979)
10. Osgood, C.E., Suci, G.J., Tannenbaum, P.H.: The measurement of meaning.University of Illinois Press, Urbana (1967)
11. Hayashi, T., Kato, S., Itoh, H.: A Mental Rhythm Synchronous Model Using Paralanguage for Communication Robot. In: The 23rd Annual Conference of The Japanese Society for Artificial Intelligence, pp. 1H2–04 (2009) (in Japanese)

Generating Association-Based Motion through Human-Robot Interaction

Satona Motomura, Shohei Kato, and Hidenori Itoh

Dept. of Computer Science and Engineering, Graduate School of Engineering,
Nagoya Institute of Technology,
Gokiso-cho Showa-ku Nagoya, 466-8555 Japan
{motomura,shohey,itoh}@juno.ics.nitech.ac.jp

Abstract. A method of generating new motions associatively from novel trajectories that the robot receives is described. The associative motion generation system is composed of two neural networks: nonlinear principal component analysis (NLPCA) and Jordan recurrent neural network (JRNN). First, these networks learn the relationship between a trajectory and a motion using training data. Second, *associative values* are extracted for associating a new corresponding motion from a new trajectory using NLPCA. Finally, a new motion is generated through calculation by JRNN using the *associative values*. Experimental results demonstrated that our method enabled a humanoid robot, KHR-2HV, to associatively generate the new motions corresponding to trajectories that the robot had not learned.

1 Introduction

Humanoid robots are expected to cooperatively work with humans in environments designed for human use. There are many unpredictable situations for robots in such environments. It is inconvenient for a user to provide the robot with the actions that the robot may need to deal with unforeseen situations. As an approach to this problem, autonomous generation of the robot's actions considering interaction with the environment and humans, has attracted much attention [1]. For example, imitation learning has been researched as a technique for the robot to acquire its motion by mimicking a human's action [2] [3]. This technique is useful for the motion generation of a humanoid robot because it has a similar body structure to a human.

Another approach develops the robot's cognitive action system. In this approach, the robot learns the relationships between motors controlling its movement and sensors receiving information from the environment. Aoyama et al. [4] proposed a cognitive action system based on a self-organizing map with hidden Markov models (HMM-SOM), which enabled a robot to follow an observed ball's movement with its arms. However, the robot could imitate only previously experienced motions. The ability to generate an appropriate reaction to sensor-acquired information that the robot has not previously experienced is very important for operation in a real environment.

J.-J. Yang et al. (Eds.): PRIMA 2009, LNAI 5925, pp. 389–402, 2009.

A robot needs a key to associate and generate a motion as the appropriate reaction. Nishide et al. [5] presented a technique for the robot to generate object manipulation motions based on the consistency of object dynamics. The robot trained an object's rolling movement by its pushing motion and acquired an object dynamics prediction model. Subsequently, the robot generated pushing motions to roll untrained objects consistently based on its training experience. Lee et al. [6] designed a tool-use motion model for humanoid robots that contains tool manipulation and body motion, for instance, a tennis stroke with a racket. The model was composed of hidden Markov models (HMMs). Their robot acquired two HMMs as knowledge for each motion: tool manipulation knowledge that contained the trajectory of the tool and grasping hand, and body motion knowledge that contained motion information of a full body including grasping hand. Since the knowledge linked with information for using its hands, the robot was able to select the appropriate knowledge and generate its whole body motion by observation of a specific tool motion by a human that it had not learned. This related work utilized the shape of the object that the robot manipulated in order to generate the robot's motion, and an HMM was often used for recognition of observed time-series information. In contrast, we utilize the trajectories given by a human teacher, and neural networks to compose a system using the generalization property of neural networks.

We describe a method that enables a robot to generate a motion corresponding to a trajectory given by a teacher. The robot learns the correspondence relationship between a trajectory and its own motion. Therefore, when faced with a novel indication, the robot generates a new motion based on that indication's similarity with learned indications.

2   Method of Associative Motion Generation

In this work, the robot generates a motion corresponding to an indication given by an indicator. We define this motion as a *corresponding motion*. An indication is time-series data that the robot acquires through a sensor. A robot cannot generate a motion that corresponds with an indication that the robot has not learned. In this paper, a novel indication that is given to a robot is called an *unfamiliar indication*. To generate a corresponding motion appropriately, requires the ability to:

- relate an indication to the joint angles of the robot's posture (*motion association*), and
- generate a motion that is a time-series of postures (*motion generation*).

In our method, we use the five-layer sandglass neural network for motion association. It performs a principal component analysis with non-linear bases, the so called nonlinear principal component analysis (NLPCA) [7] [8]. A value that expresses a feature of an indication is extracted using NLPCA. We define this value as the *associative value*. The value relates an indication to a robot's motion in our method.

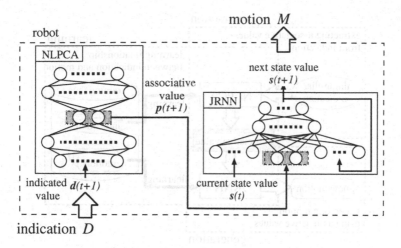

Fig. 1. Composition of associative motion generation system

In addition, we use the Jordan recurrent neural network (JRNN) [9] for motion generation. JRNN has feedback from the output layer to the input layer and a property in which the current output value influences the next output value. Therefore, consecutive postures are obtained as output vectors when the joint angle in each step is used as input and output. This sequence of postures is a motion for the robot.

Thus, the system can generate corresponding motion that is specific to each indication by connecting NLPCA and JRNN using an associative value. Furthermore, a new corresponding motion can be associated with a previous indication and generated by extracting the associative value from the given unfamiliar indication. The associative motion generation system in which NLPCA and JRNN are connected is shown in Figure 1.

3   Motion Generation Process

There are three phases in our method: learning, extraction, and generation (Figure 2). In the learning phase, the robot learns indications and their corresponding motions using training data, and the connection weights of each network are updated. After the learning, the indicator gives a new indication that the robot has not experienced. In the extraction phase, the robot inputs the new indication to NLPCA and extracts the associative values. In the generation phase, the motion corresponding to the unfamiliar indication is associated and newly generated by inputting the associative value to JRNN.

3.1   Learning the Relationship between an Indication and a Motion

NLPCA and JRNN learn the relationship between an indication as input and a motion as output using training data. Training data are pairs of an indication and

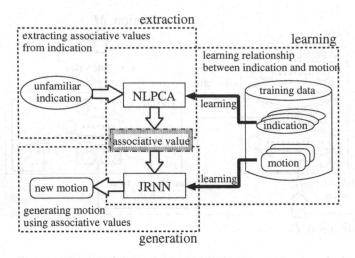

Fig. 2. Overview of motion generation

its corresponding motion. The connection weights of each network are updated using the backpropagation algorithm [10].

Formulation of Associative Space. The learning by NLPCA is shown in Figure 3(a). NLPCA learns an identity mapping that output $\hat{d}(t)$ is approximated to input $d(t)$ when the indicator gives an indication $D = [d(1), \cdots, d(T)]$ to the robot. The squared error $e(t) = ||\hat{d}(t) - d(t)||^2$ is minimized by learning. NLPCA acquires a function to extract the value representing a feature of the input from the input layer to the middle layer because units of the middle layer are less than those of the input layer. In this work, we define the middle layer of NLPCA as an *association layer* and its output at t as *associative value* $p(t) = (p_1(t), \ldots, p_n(t))^{\mathrm{T}}$. Moreover, n-dimensional space in which associative values are plotted is defined as *associative space*. The associative values are calculated as follows:

$$p(t) = sig(w_2 sig(w_1 d(t))), \tag{1}$$

where w_1 and w_2 are weight matrices between two layers from the input layer to association layer and sig is the sigmoidal function. If two arbitrary indication values $d(i)$ and $d(j)$ are close to each other, two associative values $p(i)$ and $p(j)$ will also be close by sigmoidal continuity in Equation 1. That is, topological relationships of input values are maintained in the associative values. This continuity is an effective property for recognizing the similarity of indications in the associative space. After the learning by NLPCA, associative values $P = [p(1), \cdots, p(T)]$ are extracted from each indication D based on Equation 1.

Construction of the Motion Generator The inputs to JRNN are the associative values and joint angles of the robot in a corresponding motion. JRNN

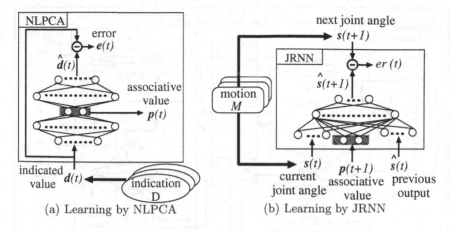

Fig. 3. Learning phase

has feedback that inputs the previous output as partial units of the input layer. The robot acquires the joint angles retaining sequential information because its next output posture depends on the previous posture through the feedback. Consequently, JRNN learns to predict the next joint angles $s(t+1)$ on the basis of the input current joint angles $s(t)$ and the next associative value $p(t+1)$. The squared error $er(t) = ||\hat{s}(t+1) - s(t+1)||^2$ is minimized by learning. The predictive learning of JRNN is shown in Figure 3(b). By this predictive learning, JRNN becomes an associative motion generator. The units to which the associative value is input are called the *association layer*.

If an unfamiliar indication is given to the robot, the robot generates a corresponding motion through two phases: extracting the associative value using NLPCA and generating the associative motion using JRNN.

3.2 Extraction of Associative Value

The left of Figure 4 presents the extraction of associative values P^{unf} from an unfamiliar indication D^{unf}. When the unfamiliar indication $D^{unf} = [d^{unf}(1), \cdots, d^{unf}(T)]$ is given to the robot, its series of associative values $P^{unf} = [p^{unf}(1), \cdots, p^{unf}(T)]$ is extracted based on Equation 1. The similarity between the unfamiliar indication and a learned one can be replaced by degrees of similarity with learned associative values in the associative space of P^{unf}. In this work, the robot generates the motion corresponding to a given unfamiliar indication D^{unf} by this property.

3.3 Associative Generation of Motion

The right of Figure 4 presents the generation of the new motion M^{unf} corresponding to the unfamiliar indication D^{unf}. The corresponding motion to the unfamiliar indication is generated by repeating forward calculation of JRNN

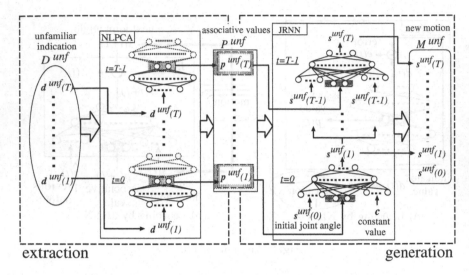

Fig. 4. Extraction phase (left) and generation phase (right)

using the series of associative values P^{unf} as input to the associative layer in JRNN. Joint angles of the next posture $s^{unf}(t+1)$ are obtained as output of JRNN by inputting the current joint angles $s^{unf}(t)$ and the associative value $p^{unf}(t+1)$ to produce the next posture. The joint angles of the initial posture are given at $t = 0$. The following calculation is repeated from 0 to $T - 1$.

$$s^{unf}(t+1) = \begin{cases} f(s^{unf}(t),\ p^{unf}(t+1),\ c) & \text{if}\ t = 0 \\ f(s^{unf}(t),\ p^{unf}(t+1),\ s^{unf}(t)) & \text{if}\ 1 \le t \le T - 1, \end{cases} \quad (2)$$

where f is the map function that JRNN acquired by learning, and its arguments are input to the input layer, association layer, and context layer that receives feedback from the output. c is a vector value constant at $t = 0$. The series of joint angles $M^{unf} = [s^{unf}(0), \cdots, s^{unf}(T)]$ is acquired by this calculation. The corresponding motion to the unfamiliar indication is this M^{unf}.

4   Experiments

We conducted motion generation experiments to test the effectiveness of our method. In experiments, we used the humanoid robot KHR-2HV [11], which has three degrees of freedom in each arm (Figure 5). Both its arms were used for the motions. We prepared a time series of three-dimensional coordinates to imitate the trajectories of the indicator's hand ($T = 100$) for indications. A motion of the robot was the movement of its arms to draw a given trajectory using each hand ($T = 100$). The motion sampling interval is 20 msec and the length of each motion pattern is 2.0 second. The coordinate system complied with the right-hand rule based on the robot.

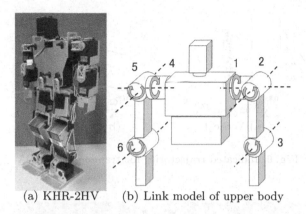

(a) KHR-2HV   (b) Link model of upper body

Fig. 5. Humanoid robot KHR-2HV (left) and its link model (right)

First, the indicator gave two pairs of an indication and its corresponding motion to the robot as training data for learning by NLPCA and JRNN. After learning, the indicator gave the robot unfamiliar indications that were different from the training data. Then, the robot generated corresponding motions by extracting the associative values of the indications.

4.1   Experimental Setup

NLPCA has 3 units in its input/output layer, 2 units in its association layer, and 9 units in its hidden layer. Input values to NLPCA are the coordinates of time-series in the internal three-dimensional trajectory [0,1].

JRNN has 6 units in its input/output/context layer, 2 units in its association layer, and 20 units in its middle layer. Input values to JRNN are the normalized joint angles of the robot's arms [0,1]. The outputs of the association layer of NLPCA are input to that of JRNN.

NLPCA was trained with indications 400,000 times. The indications of the training data were 'Vertical' and 'Horizontal', which were the parallel trajectories to the Z-axis and Y-axis, respectively. Three-dimensional coordinate points as the indications of the training data are shown in Figure 6. The shape of a trajectory was represented on the Y-Z plane. The solid lines shown in Figure 6 were projected trajectories on the Y-Z plane. The X-coordinate values of a trajectory were random.

JRNN was trained with corresponding motions 200,000 times. The corresponding motions of the training data were 'Vertical motion' and 'Horizontal motion', where the robot moved its arms up and down, and from side to side, respectively. The two motions as corresponding motions of the training data are shown in Figure 7. In these figures, the white circles and rhombuses represent positions of the robot's left hand and right hand, respectively. These motions were very simple movements of the robot's arms.

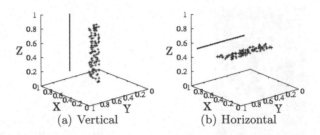

Fig. 6. Indicated trajectories for training of NLPCA

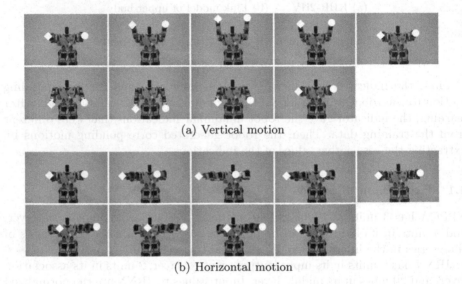

(a) Vertical motion

(b) Horizontal motion

Fig. 7. Motions for training of JRNN

4.2 Generating New Motion from an Unfamiliar Indication

We carried out this experiment to confirm whether the robot can generate motions corresponding to unfamiliar indications. The indicator gave the following three trajectories as unfamiliar indications to the robot, and the robot associatively generated new motions corresponding to the indications.

- Diagonal: a trajectory located in the middle of 'Vertical' and 'Horizontal'.
- Circle: a circular trajectory.
- Figure eight: a trajectory of a figure eight rotated 90 degrees around the center point.

The center point in all the trajectories was the point at which the indication 'Vertical' intersected with 'Horizontal'. The trajectories given to the robot are shown in Figure 8.

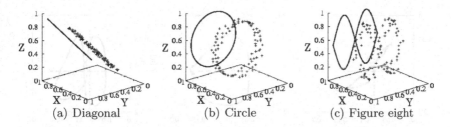

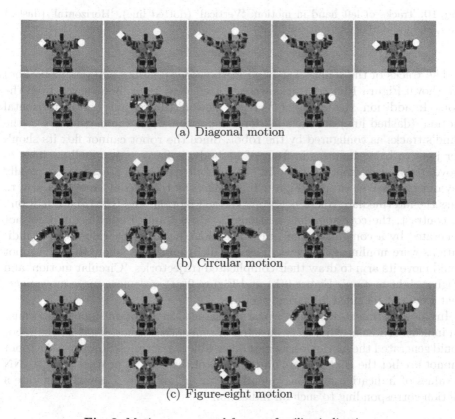

(a) Diagonal   (b) Circle   (c) Figure eight

Fig. 8. Unfamiliar indications

(a) Diagonal motion

(b) Circular motion

(c) Figure-eight motion

Fig. 9. Motions generated from unfamiliar indications

Results. The corresponding motions generated associatively from these indications are shown in Figure 9. Two white marks represent the same hand positions as previously described. In 'Diagonal motion' (Figure 9(a)), the positions of the robot's hands shift to the right and left. Thus, the robot drew the trajectory of 'Diagonal' well with its arm movements. We speculate that 'Diagonal motion' was generated by combining 'Vertical motion' and 'Horizontal motion' because 'Diagonal' was the composite trajectory of 'Vertical' and 'Horizontal'.

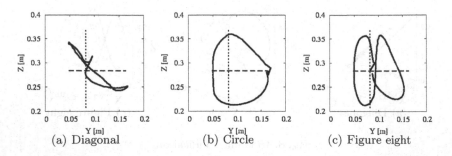

(a) Diagonal   (b) Circle   (c) Figure eight

Fig. 10. Tracks of left hand in motion: 'Vertical' (dotted line), 'Horizontal' (dashed line), and unfamiliar motion (solid line)

The tracks of the robot's left hand in the corresponding motions (solid line) are shown Figure 10. The tracks were plotted with the robot viewed from the front. In addition, the tracks of 'Vertical motion' (dotted line) and 'Horizontal motion' (dashed line) are included for comparison. Note the asymmetry of the hand's tracks as configured by the robot. Since the robot cannot flex its shoulder joint to bring its arms in front of its body, it flexes only its elbow joint to move its hand in front of its body. As a result, the hand tracks are Y-axially asymmetrical. We see from Figure 10(a) that the robot could move its arm to pass the intermediate tracks between 'Vertical motion' and 'Horizontal motion'. In contrast, the corresponding motions to 'Circle' and 'Figure eight' were not generated by a combination of learned motions because the values of the indications were nonlinear. However, Figures 10(b) and 10(c) show that the robot could move its arm to draw their complicated trajectories. 'Circular motion' and 'Figure-eight motion' (Figure 9(b) and Figure 9(c)) were new curve movements that were not included in learned motions.

In this experiment, the robot's posture changed in a motion smoothly because an indication was a trajectory consisted of sequential values. That is, the robot could generated the motions drawing traversable trajectories. However, the robot cannot predict the next posture on the basis of the current posture using JRNN if values of indication are nonsequential. Our future issue is how to generate a motion corresponding to such an indication.

4.3   Evaluation of Corresponding Motion

We conducted another experiment to verify whether differences in indications were correctly reflected in the generated motions. The corresponding motions we evaluated were generated from the following indications.

- Ellipse A: an elliptical trajectory whose minor axis was 0.5 times the diameter of 'Circle'.
- Ellipse B: an elliptical trajectory whose minor axis was 0.8 times the diameter of 'Circle'.

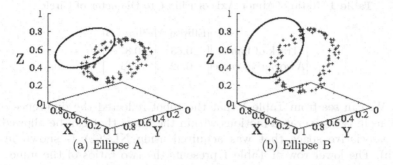

(a) Ellipse A   (b) Ellipse B

Fig. 11. Unfamiliar indications

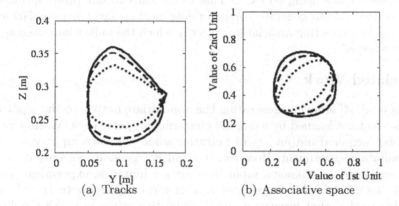

(a) Tracks   (b) Associative space

Fig. 12. Trajectories of left hand in motion and the associative space: 'Ellipse A' (dotted line), 'Ellipse B' (dashed line), and 'Circle' (solid line)

The centers of both indications were the same point as 'Circle' and their major axes were the same length as the diameter of 'Circle'. Their trajectories are shown in Figure 11.

Results. The tracks of the robot's left hand in generated corresponding motions are shown in Figure 12(a). The tracks were plotted in the same way as previously described, and the track of 'Circular motion' is included for comparison. The solid line represents 'Circle', the dotted line represents 'Ellipse A', and the dashed line represents 'Ellipse B'. As can be seen from Figure 12(a), the movement of the robot's arm became smaller in the order of 'Circular motion', 'Ellipse B motion' and 'Ellipse A motion'. The minor axis of indications 'Ellipse A' and 'Ellipse B' corresponded to the up-and-down movement of the robot's arm. Therefore, there were appropriate changes in the generated motions. The upper row of Table 1 presents the two ratios of the minor axes of 'Ellipse A' and 'Ellipse B' to the Z-axial diameter of 'Circle' in Figure 12(a). The ratios of the indications of 'Ellipse A' and 'Ellipse B' to 'Circle' were 0.5 and 0.8, respectively. Accordingly, we expected that the ratios in the generated corresponding motions would be

Table 1. Ratio of Minor Axis of Ellipse to Diameter of Circle

	Ellipse A	Ellipse B
Track of hands	0.63	0.87
Associative value	0.52	0.81

similar. We can see from Table 1 that the robot reflected the difference of the indications in two generated motions within the range that can be allowed.

The associative space that was acquired using NLPCA is shown in Figure 12(b). The lower row of Table 1 presents the two ratios of the minor axes of 'Ellipse A' and 'Ellipse B' to the Z-axial diameter of 'Circle' in Figure 12(b). We can see from this result that similar ratios to the indications were extracted in associative space using NLPCA. This result leads to our presumption that the robot was able to generate corresponding motions involving similarities of indications by extracting associative values in which the indications were appropriately reflected.

5   Related Work

Aoyama et al. [4] aimed at generating the appropriate output to the input that the robot had not learned by using the clustering property of SOM. As a result, their robot acquired output voices imitating some unknown input voices in a vocal imitation experiment. However, it could not generate an output motion corresponding to an unknown input in a motion imitation experiment. In our method, the robot is able to generate a motion corresponding to an indication unfamiliar to the robot because we used associative values in which topological relationships of input values are maintained for motion generation. Moreover, it generated the motions that were not represented as a combination of learned motions by calculation using the nonlinear function.

Lee et al. [6] proposed a method to associate whole body motion of tool-usage from the trajectory of a tool that a human was grasping by partial observation [12] using HMM. In this method, when their robot observed an unknown tool trajectory, it selected the most similar body motion knowledge from a database of learned motion depending likelihood of HMM. However, generation of a new motion was not considered when an observed tool trajectory was not similar to learned trajectories. In our method, when the robot is given an unfamiliar indication, it generates a new motion corresponding to the indication by a motion generator that was constructed during a learning phase. The unfamiliar indication is quite different from learned indications. The foregoing experimental results showed that the generated motion from the indication was very different from learned motions.

6   Conclusion

We described a motion generation method for a robot to associate the motion corresponding to a given indication. The method consists of three phases using

NLPCA and JRNN for generating the new motion from the indication. In the learning phase, the robot learns relationships between indications and their corresponding motions using NLPCA and JRNN. In the extraction phase, the associative values are extracted from a given indication using NLPCA. In the generation phase, the robot generates the new motion by inputting the associative values to JRNN.

We performed two experiments to test the effectiveness of our method. The first demonstrated that the robot was able to generate new motions corresponding to indications that it had not previously experienced. The second demonstrated that our method reflected the similarity of indications appropriately in generated motions.

In this work, five new motions were generated associatively by learning two pairs of an indication and corresponding motion. Our future work will be to conduct experiments using more indications and motions and to evaluate the range of motion that can be associated.

Acknowledgment

This work was supported in part by the Tatematsu Foundation, and by a Ministry of Education, Science, Sports and Culture, Grant–in–Aid for Scientific Research under grant #20700199 and #21500187.

References

1. Asada, M., MacDorman, K.F., Ishiguro, H., Kuniyoshi, Y.: Cognitive Developmental Robotics As a New Paradigm for the Design of Humanoid Robots. Robotics and Autonomous System 37, 185–193 (2001)
2. Kuniyoshi, Y., Inaba, M., Inoue, H.: Learning by Watching: Extracting Reusable Task Knowledge from Visual Observation of Human Performance. IEEE Transactions on Robotics and Automation 10(6), 799–822 (1994)
3. Schaal, S.: Is Imitation Learning the Route to Humanoid Robots. Trends in Cognitive Sciences 3, 233–242 (1999)
4. Aoyama, K., Minamino, K., Shimomura, H.: Learning of Cognitive Action Based on Self-Organizing Maps with HMMs. Transactions of the Japanese Society for Artificial Intelligence 22(4), 375–388 (2007) (in Japanese)
5. Nishide, S., Ogata, T., Yokoya, R., Tani, J., Komatani, K., Okuno, H.G.: Object Dynamics Prediction and Motion Generation Based on Reliable Predictability. In: Proceedings of IEEE-RAS International Conference on Robotics and Automation (ICRA-2008), pp. 1608–1614 (2008)
6. Lee, D., Kunori, H., Nakamura, Y.: Association of Whole Body Motion from Tool Knowledge for Humanoid Robots. In: IEEE/RSJ International Conference on Intelligent Robots and Systems (2008)
7. Kramer, M.A.: Nonlinear Principal Component Analysis Using Autoassociative Neural Networks. AIChE Journal 37, 233–243 (1991)

8. DeMers, D., Cottrell, G.: Non-Linear Dimensionality Reduction. Proceedings of Neural Information Processing Systems 5, 580–587 (1993)
9. Jordan, M.I.: Attractor Dynamics and Parallelism in a Connectionist Sequential Machine. In: Proceedings of the Eighth Annual Conference of the Cognitive Science Society, Erlbaum, Hillsdale, NJ, pp. 531–546 (1986)
10. Rumelhart, D., Hinton, G., Williams, R.: Learning Internal Representation by Error Propagation. Parallel Distributed Processing 1, 318–362 (1986)
11. Kondo Kagaku co. ltd. KHR-2HV.,
    http://www.kondo-robot.com/EN/product/khr-2hv.html
12. Lee, D., Nakamura, Y.: Mimesis from Partial Observations. In: IEEE/RSJ International Conference on Intelligent Robots and Systems (IROS 2005), pp. 1911–1916 (2005)

SmartContractor: A Distributed Task Assignment System Based on the Simple Contract Net Protocol

Bipin Khanal[1,2], Hideyuki Sugiura[1,2], Takayuki Ito[1,2], Masashi Iwasaki[1,2], Katsuhide Fujita[1,2], and Masao Kobayashi[1,2]

[1] Nagoya Institute of Technology,
Gokiso, Showa-ku, Nagoya 466-8555, Japan
{bipin,sugiura,ito,iwakami,fujita,kobayashi}@itolab.mta.nitech.ac.jp
[2] Makoto Lab., Inc. Nagoya, Japan

Abstract. In this paper, we present and demonstrate *SmartContractor*: a distributed task assignment system based on the simple ContractNet protocol. In Japan, housewives doing side work in their free time at home is common practice which helps those that have children and the ability to do work. Recently, a franchised sideline business has grown. They started by establishing a systematic business process for sideline work shops, then franchising and networking those shops .In such franchised sideline businesses, it is of utmost necessity to allocate or delegate tasks among the shops by using a web-based network system. This business process of task allocation/delegation is very similar to the famous ContractNet protocol. Thus, a ContractNet approach is a smart and straightforward for us. The initial *SmartContractor* system has been delivered, and is improved with an Agile-based development process. The system will be implemented from September 2009.

1 Introduction

In Japan, housewives doing side work in their free time at home is common practice.This helps those that have children and enough ability to do work. They can work in the daytime at home when their children are at school.A sideline business is not a new concept. Small companies that have many of jobs are approaching to accomplish their jobs by the coordination with clients (customer companies) and side workers.

Recently, a franchised sideline business company has grown. They established a systematic business process for sideline work shops, franchised and networked shops. Franchising shops have large effect on reducing the cost for using IT systems and increasing the efficiency of the distribution of tasks. For example, some shops can collaboratively complete a large number of tasks even if each shop cannot complete those tasks alone.

In such a franchised sideline business, it is of utmost importance to allocate or delegate tasks among the shops. When a shop gets an order for tasks, the

J.-J. Yang et al. (Eds.): PRIMA 2009, LNAI 5925, pp. 403–415, 2009.

shop must decide whether those tasks can be completed by its own workers, or delegate some or all tasks to nearby shops. Because this allocation management has been done manually with a huge number of hand-written e-mails, we found web-based network system to be of utmost necessity.

This business process of task allocation and delegation is very similar to the famous ContractNet protocol, which has been a promising distributed protocol in the last few decades. Thus, a ContractNet approach is smart and straightforward for us. *SmartContractor* is a web-based system which has been implemented in PHP. It enables shop managers to make decisions for distribution and delegation of ordered tasks.

The initial *SmartContractor* system has been delivered, and improved with an iterative style of software development. The system will be implemented starting in September 2009.

The rest of this paper is organized in the following 5 sections. In section 2, we explain our targeted business domain. In section 3, we show the traditional ContractNet protocol, and how it was applied for a practical business. In section 4, we explain the details of the system architecture, and present a demonstration of *SmartContractor* in section 5. Finally, we summarize our contributions in section 6.

2   Distributed Task Allocation among Franchise Shops

2.1   Domain Description

The target franchise network consists of one headquarters and 80 or more franchise shops in the entire area of Japan. Some franchise shops are managed by a single company. Shops can get orders from customers in their area. An order is composed of several elementary tasks. For example, creating 10,000 table calendars, making 20,000 direct mails, putting 10,000 name cards into 10,000 envelopes, etc.

A single shop has its own workers, basically housewives and senior people who bring the tasks to their home, do the tasks, and bring them back to the shop. The shop can also allocate some of the entire tasks to nearby shops if the shop manager judges the shop unable to complete the entire volume of tasks. In this case, the shop manager needs to consider the delivery cost, the labor cost, etc. Basically, shops are cooperative.

2.2   Contract Net Protocol

The Contract Net protocol was first introduced in the seminal paper[1] as a market-based protocol for distributed problem solvers. It facilitates distributed control of cooperative task execution (task-sharing[2]) with efficient internode communication. Now, some developed contract net protocols have appeared[3].

In the classical contract net protocol, the collection of nodes is referred to as a contract net and the execution of a task is dealt with as a contract between two nodes. Each node in the net takes on one of two roles related to the execution of an individual task; manager or contractor. A manager is responsible for monitoring the execution of a task and processing the results of its execution. A contractor is responsible for the actual execution of the task.

Firstly, managers generate a task and advertise existence of that task to the other nodes with a task announcement message (**Task Announcements**). Secondly, available contractors evaluate task announcements made by several managers(**Task Announcement Processing**). Thirdly, contractors submit bids on those for which they are suited (**Bidding**). Forth, the managers evaluate

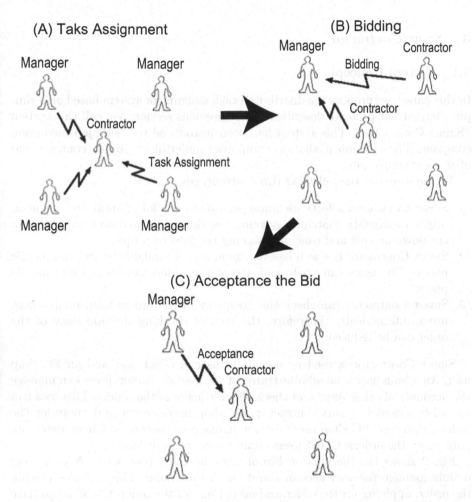

Fig. 1. Contract Net Protocol

the bids and award contracts to the nodes they determine to be most appropriate(**Bidding Processing**). Finally, a contractor may further partition a task and award contracts to other nodes(**Contract Processing**). The most important feature of the ContractNet protocol is *mutual selection*, which both of managers and contracts have rights to select their partners based on their contract condition which was indicated in the announcements or bids. As Fig. 1 shows, a Contract Net Protocol can allocate the task using a task announcement, bidding and acceptance of the bid.

A contract net protocol is an easy way to employ distributed task assignment in real life. This is because that contract net protocol is similar to a real life contract. Our proposed system is a good example for implementation of the contract net protocol.

3   *SmartContractor*

3.1   System Concept

In this paper, we propose the distributed task assignment system based on a simple contract net protocol described in the previous section. We call this system "Smart Contractor". This system has been introduced to a side job mediation company. The side job mediation companies undertake a simple contract and offer some simple jobs.

This system has the following three advantages,

1. Smart Contractor selects adequate persons from a lot of applicants using an original automatic matching system. The side job mediation companies can cut down on cost and time of assigning the jobs to people.
2. Smart Contractor is a web based system and is available by PC and mobile phone. The users can apply and accept the orders anywhere using mobile phone.
3. Smart Contractor can check the adequacy of the orders from many client users automatically. Therefore, the cost of checking the adequacy of the order can be reduced.

Smart Contractor is used by an admin user, a client user and an FC shop user. An admin user is an administrator of the system. Admin users can manage the accounts of other users and check the adequacy of the orders. This user can use all functions in smart contractor. FC shop users accept and apply for the orders. However, FC shop users cannot manage the accounts. Client users can only apply the orders. Client users cannot accept the orders.

Fig. 2 shows the the relationship of users in smart contractor. Admin users mainly manage the user accounts and check the trades. This includes placing the order, applying for the order and acceptance of the order. Client shops have some works such as generating 500 name cards, and placing an order for work. Client users send the announcement to all FC shops in a contract net protocol. After that, some FC shops apply for orders. In a contract net protocol, some FC

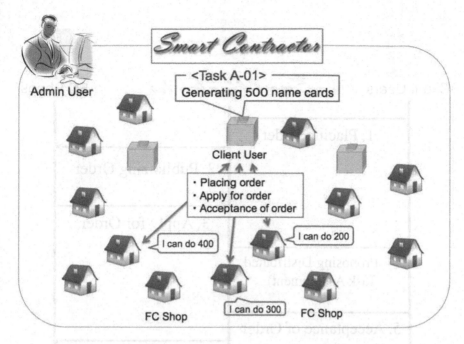

Fig. 2. The relationship between users in smart contractor

shops bid for the announcement. Finally, client users accept the orders based on their cost and eagerness. In a contract net protocol, client users give the awards to the FC shops. Smart contractor supports the deals between managers and contractors in real life.

3.2 Functional Specification

Smart Contractor has several functions for coordinating between client users and FC shops. The following items are major functions in Smart Contractor.

- User registration and edition (only for Admin user)
- Placing of orders
- Acceptance of orders

In addition to these items, confirmation mail function, maintaining a log of users and orders and the like. Fig. 3 shows the details flow of a deal between client users and FC shops occurs . Firstly, client users place the order by registering the work and then send the information to smart contractor. Secondly, smart contractor publicizes the order to all FC shops if there are no problems. Thirdly, FC shops search the work and apply for the order if they want to handle the work. Forth, Smart contractor propose the optimal distributed task assignment based on the FC shops information (e.g. cost, eagerness). Fifth, client user decides the FC shops placing orders officially, and registering to the smart contractor. Finally, smart contractor sends the acceptance notification to the FC shops.

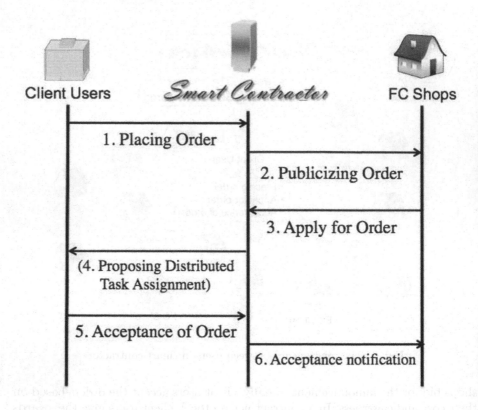

Fig. 3. The flow of a deal between client user and FC shop

3.3   System Architecture

Fig.4 shows the system architecture for Smart Contractor. Smart contractor has Work DB, Application DB and User DB. In Work DB, the information for the work (e.g. works ID, subject of work, start date, deadline etc.) is stored. In Application DB, the information for applying for the order (e.g. status of applying, work name, quantity of applying etc.)is stored . In User DB, the information for user data (e.g. use name, address, e-mail address, user type etc.) is stored. There are many correlations between Application DB and Work DB. Additionally, Smart Contractor has 6 functions. The order processing function stores work information to a Work DB. When a client user places an order, this function checks entry items for any formatting mistakes. The order publicizing function stores the publicizing information and sends mail to FC shop and Admin users. Usually, all FC shops receive this mail order. However, if a client predesignates an FC shop in placing it, this mail is send directory to this FC shop. The order applying function stores the information for the order application in the application DB. The function for proposing the distributed task assignment proposes the task allocation to a client user based on Work DB, User DB and Application DB. The order acceptance function changes the status

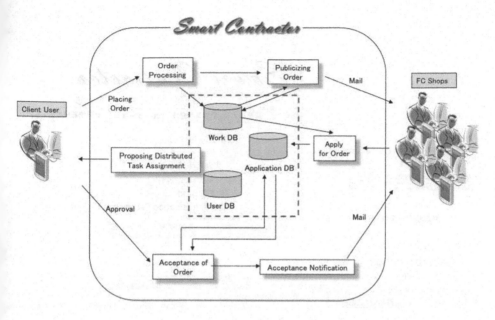

Fig. 4. System architecture

of applying information in application DB. Finally, the acceptance notification function sends the e-mail using the e-mail server.

3.4 Development

The entire codes are written in PHP and JavaScript. PHP has high affinity fro MySQL.

We have been adopting an Agile development process, in which we have had close discussion (once a week) with our customers. The Agile development process is a type of iterative and incremental development. This software development method is a development process that was developed to overcome the weaknesses of a classic water fall model.

10 man-month have been invested in system development so far. The system development period is relatively short compared with similar volume software development projects because we do not follow the traditional waterfall development process. In addition, it was a huge impact on the labor costs and the clarity of the customer's needs.

4   Demonstration

4.1 Web-Based Interface

Fig. 5 shows the main page of an admin user. A table in Fig. 5 shows the names of each part and the accompanying descriptions. Admin users are empowered to

Fig. 5. Main menu page of Admin users

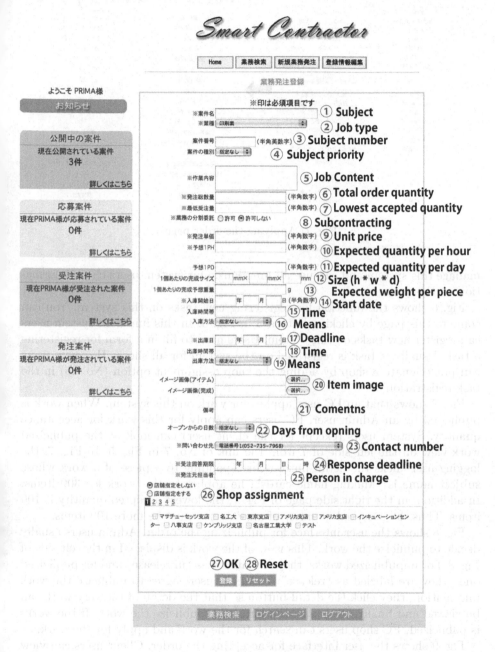

Fig. 6. Placing the order page

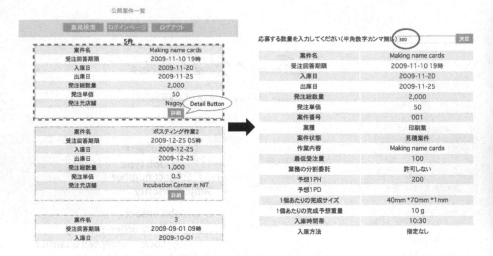

Fig. 7. Applying the order page

manage this system and can use all functions. Our system users check information on this page.

Fig. 6 shows the function for registering new tasks on this system. You can come to this page by clicking button 3 in Fig. 5. In this function, system users can register new tasks on this system. Users need to fill in a form for registering a task. Usually, a task is registered on the system for all shops. However, users can predesignate a shop by adding the shop assignment option (No. 26) in the task registration.

Fig. 7 shows that an FC user applies for work on this system. When work is publicized by an Admin user, FC users can apply for this work for acceptance quantity. System users (except for the client user) can look at the publicized work view on the left side of 7 from the link of No. 7 in Fig. 5. In Fig. 7, the logging user clicks the detail button corresponding to a piece of a work whose subject name is "Making name cards", he applies to this work for 300 items. In addition, in the right side page of Fig. 7, the lowest accepted quantity is 100 items. Thus,the accepted quantity of an FC user must be more 100 items.

Fig. 8 shows the user interface for publicizing the order. Admin users usually decide to publicize the work. This view of the work is displayed in the left side of Fig. 8. For unpublicized works, they are labeled as "unrelease" and for publicized ones, they are labeled as "release". If Admin users agree to publicize the work information, they click the detail button so that the detail of the very work can be viewed and finally, they push the button to publicize the work. If the works is publicized, FC shop users can search for the work and apply for the work.

Fig. 9 shows the user interface for accepting the order. Client users can view the list of placed work orders. If they want to confirm the FC user who has

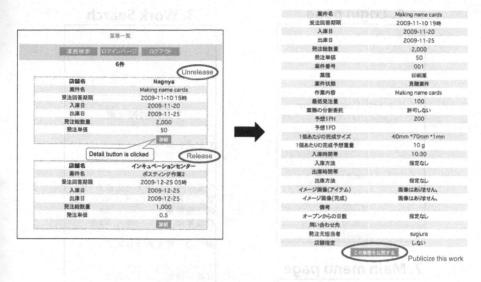

Fig. 8. Publicizing the order page

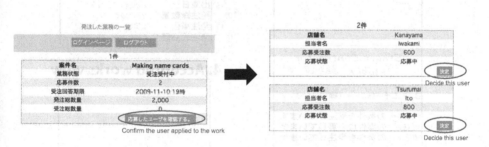

Fig. 9. Accepting the order page

applied for this work, they click the button and after clicking the button, the confirmation of the FC user is complete. If client users accept the FC user's application, they click the decide button. Client users can choose many FC users to finish the work efficiently.

4.2 Mobile

Fig. 10 shows a part of a mobile interface for Smart Contractor. Table 1 shows functions in the mobile interface. Our system is available in mobile too. System users can login with ID and pass on 1. Login page in Fig. 10. For example, when FC user, Tsurumai logs into the system, a main menu page is displayed like 2. of Fig. 10. System users can register new orders or check work as well in the PC version. In work search, 3. of Fig. 10, users can search work and sort by some items: No. 9, 10 and 11 in the table 1.

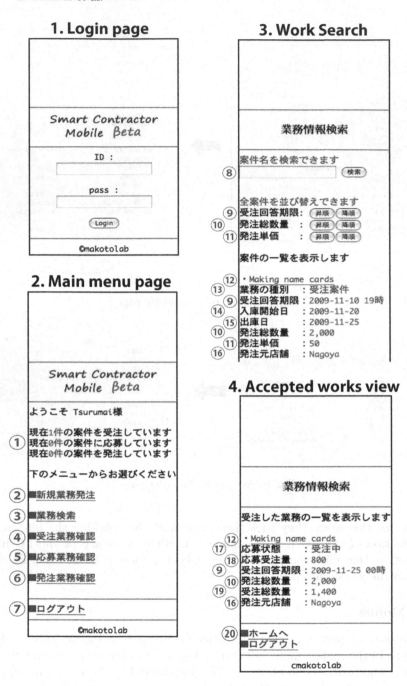

Fig. 10. Mobile Interface

Table 1. Mobile functions

No.	Name	Description
1	User Information	Detail data on works
2	New Work Order	Go to the function of registering new work
3	Work Search	Go to the function of works search
4	Accepted works view	Show the accepted works
5	Applied works	Show the applied works
6	Placed works	Show the placed works
7	Logout	Logout and go to login page
8	Search Form	Search with subject
9	Response Deadline	This work can be accepted until the date
10	Total Order Quantity	All work quantity of this work
11	Unit Price	Unit price of one order
12	Subject	the name of this work
13	Subject Priority	Admin user checks this value for publicizing
14	Start Date	Date when this work actually starts
15	Deadline	Expected date when this work ends
16	Orderer Shop	the name of orderer
17	Application State	Progress of this work
18	Application order quantity	Quantity that this user apply to this work for
19	Total Accepted Quantity	A total of quantity of order for this work
20	Home	Go to home page

5   Conclusion and Future Work

SmartContractor will be in implementation from September 2009. We developed this system with a Contract Net approach in order to solve the problem of franchised sideline business in Japan. This system is a web-based system which has been implemented in PHP. It enables shop managers to make decisions for distribution and delegation of ordered tasks.

In the future, our system needs automatic intelligent support for users. The initial Smart Contractor system has several functions for clients and FC shops. However, for example,if there are a lot of application to an order, the ordered client can't decide the optimum combination of FC shops. Therefore, we should add a function of detailed match-making among workers and tasks to the user system with user and order information.

References

1. Smith, R.G.: The Contract Net Protocol: High-Level Communication and Control in a Distributed Problem Solver. IEEE Transactions on Computer C-29, 1104–1113 (1980)
2. Smith, R.G., Davis, R.: Cooperation in distributed problem solving. In: Proc.of 1979 International Conference on Cyber net Society, pp. 366–371 (1979)
3. Goos, G., Hartmanis, J., van Leeuwen, J.: The Evolution of the Contract Net Protocol. In: Wang, X.S., Yu, G., Lu, H. (eds.) WAIM 2001, vol. 2118, pp. 257–264. Springer, Heidelberg (2001)

Participatory Simulation Environment gumonji/Q: A Network Game Empowered by Agents

Shohei Yamane[1], Shoichi Sawada[1], Hiromitsu Hattori[1], Marika Odagaki[2], Kengo Nakajima[2], and Toru Ishida[1]

[1] Department of Social Informatics, Kyoto University
Yoshida-Honmachi, Sakyo-ku, Kyoto, 606-8501, Japan
{yamane,sawada}@ai.soc.i.kyoto-u.ac.jp, {hatto,ishida}@i.kyoto-u.ac.jp
[2] Community Engine Inc., 4-31-8 Yoyogi Shibuya-ku Tokyo 151-0053 Japan

Abstract. Network games are attracting attention as simulation platforms for social experiments because of their rich visualization performance and scalability. Our objective in this study is to develop a participatory simulation platform on a network game. Unlike non player characters (NPCs) in network games, agents in a participatory multiagent-based simulation (PMAS) should behave as real-world humans according to behavior models. We developed a novel networked participatory simulation platform called gumonji/Q by integrating scenario description language Q with the network game gumonji. This paper details the implementation of gumonji/Q. In order to connect Q and gumonji, we implement communication sub-components that realize TCP/IP communication between them, and a scenario translator to convert a request from Q into a sequence of operators. This makes it possible for the gumonji simulator to deal with human-controlled avatars and Q-controlled agents in a unified way.

Keywords: Multiagent Simulation, Simulation Platform, Participatory Simulation, Gaming, Networked Simulator.

1 Introduction

Network games are attracting attention as simulation platforms for social experiments. Virtual worlds can be made available on the network, and many humans can participate in them. Network games can be used as simulation environments since they enable us to observe the social phenomena caused by the interactions among multiple actors. In addition, many network games have rich 3D visualization performance. This helps users to observe the simulation environment and other users' activities. These features of network games can be great advantage if we can use them as platforms for participatory multiagent-based simulation (PMAS) in which some humans participate by controlling agents. PMAS enables us to observe how humans behave in the simulation and is used as a platform for participatory modeling[1,2,3,4].

J.-J. Yang et al. (Eds.): PRIMA 2009, LNAI 5925, pp. 416–427, 2009.

Our objective in this study is to develop a new participatory simulation platform based on a network game. We address the following two issues; 1) Since we
do not target a specific simulation environment, extensibility is a key requirement. The platform should have extensibility to support the customization of
the environment and agents' actions; 2) When a PMAS is used for designing
socially embedded systems, definitions of agent behavior are given by the PMAS
conductor and are changed repeatedly according to the simulation process.

Against this background, we have developed gumonji/Q, a novel networked
participatory simulation platform, by integrating the scenario description language Q and the network game gumonji[1]. Q is a scenario description language
that enables us to describe complex social interactions among agents and their
surrounding world (humans, other agents, simulation environment)[5]. gumonji
is a network game that offers visually rich playing fields for virtual life. Users can
engage in a large variety of activities via characters on that field as though they
are in the real-world. "gumonji" also has extensibility for the cusomization of the
environment by plugins. gumonji/Q is thus able to realize a participatory simulation environment where "human-agent" and "human(agent)-environment" relationships are well reproduce; it allows us to understand a large variety of social
phenomena.

The remainder of the paper is organized as follows. First, we show the background of our research; related works and the two primary software programs
(Q and gumonji). Second, we present the new participatory simulation platform
gumonji/Q. We then detail the implementation of gumonji/Q and show an example of participatory modeling on gumonji/Q. Concluding remarks are given
in the final section.

2 Background

2.1 Related Works

FreeWalk is a platform for constructing virtual collaborative events in which
agents and humans can socially interact with each other in a virtual space[6].
An agent is controlled through the platform's API. A human participant enters
the virtual space as an avatar, which he/she controls through the UI devices
connected to the platform. The primary objective of FreeWalk is to realize a
virtual space for communication and collaboration between humans and agents.
However, while humans and agents can engage in diverse social interactions in
FreeWalk, it does not simulate the environment in detail, which means humans
cannot alter their surrounding environment and receive feedback. To provide
better real-world experience, we need an interactive simulation environment.

CORMAS can be used to build simulation models of coordination modes between individuals and groups who jointly exploit the resources[7]. In CORMAS,
users can define the diffusion of environmental changes, and agent's behaviors
governed by the surrounding environment. The computational model behind

---

[1] "gumonji" is a product of Community Engine Inc. (http://www.gumonji.net/)

CORMAS simulations is a cellular automaton. A natural environment is modeled as a two dimensional mesh, and the diffusion between neighboring cells is calculated at each unit time. CORMAS is useful to describe interactions between a natural environment and humans. However, while FreeWalk emphasizes graphics functions, CORMAS just shows abstract graphics; its low level visual information makes it is hard for humans to behave as they would in the real-world.

2.2 Scenario Description Language Q

Q is a scenario description language for multiagent systems that allows us to define how agents are expected to interact with their environment including humans and other agents[5]. Q is suitable for describing complex social interactions[8,9]. Q scenarios foster the emergence of dialogs between agent designers (computing professionals) and application designers (scenario writers)[10]. The computational model behind Q scenarios is an extended finite state automaton, which is commonly used for describing communication protocols. By using Q, users can directly create scenario descriptions from extended finite state automata. Q's language functionality is summarized as follows:

- **Cues and Actions**
  An event that triggers interaction is called a cue. Cues are used to request agents to observe their environment. Cues keep waiting for the event specified until observation is completed successfully. Comparable to cues, actions are used to request agents to change their environment.
- **Scenarios**
  Guarded commands are introduced for the situation wherein we need to observe multiple cues simultaneously. A guarded command combines cues and actions. After one of the cues becomes true, the corresponding action is performed. A scenario is used for describing protocols in the form of an extended finite state machine, where each state is defined as a guarded command. Scenarios can be called from other scenarios.
- **Agents and Avatars**
  Agents, avatars and a crowd of agents can be defined. An agent is defined by a scenario that specifies what the agent is to do. Even if a crowd of agents executes the same scenario, the agents exhibit different actions as they interact with their local environment (including other agents and humans). Avatars controlled by humans do not require any scenario. However, avatars can have scenarios if it is necessary to constrain their behavior.

2.3 Network Game gumonji

gumonji is a network game developed and released by Community Engine Inc. that offers environmental simulations. Figure 1 shows a snapshot of the virtual space of gumonji. In gumonji, animals and plants exist in a virtual space, and the atmosphere and water circulate according to realistic physical laws. Users participate in the simulation environment by operating characters (avatars[2])

---

[2] In this paper, we call a human-controlled character "avatar" in order to distinguish human-controlled character(agent) and Q-controlled agent

Fig. 1. A Screenshot of gumonji

in the virtual space, and can manipulate living things through the actions of their characters. The changes made to a living thing persist over time, and the change in the environment is reflected in the 3D virtual space. Many users can participate in the same environment, and communicate with other users through the actions and dialogs of the characters.

In gumonji, all users have own simulation environment on individual computers and participate in other users' simulation environment through P2P network. By using a P2P network, users can move freely across multiple simulation environments and participate anytime and anywhere.

Since gumonji is a network game where many users participate and communicate with each other, the actors in the environment are the characters operated by users. Therefore, gumonji has no function to construct or run autonomous agents. To realize participatory simulations, it is necessary to add a function that can ascribe diverse interaction patterns to different agents.

3   Participatory Simulation Platform gumonji/Q

Our approach has the following advantages.

- **Network games have interfaces that enable humans to act in the virtual space.**
  Humans observe the virtual space and operate avatars visually in network games, so humans can act naturally in the virtual space.

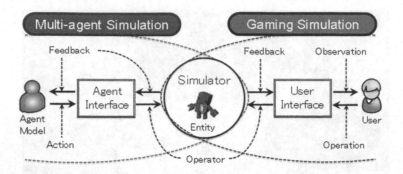

Fig. 2. Participatory simulation with network game and multiagent system

- **Many humans can interact with each other in the virtual environment.**
  Network games provide virtual environments wherein many humans can participate. Humans can participate in the environment freely and interact with each other in the virtual space.
- **Humans can participate from everywhere at anytime via the Internet.**
  Due to the Internet, human participation is not restricted to specific geographical areas.
- **The virtual environment exhibits persistence.**
  The virtual environment exists continuously regardless of the participation of humans. Though the number of participants fluctuates, the virtual environment progresses continuously and keeps changing.

We extended a network game by integrating into it a multi-agent system. Figure 2 shows how this was done. Right side of the figure shows the network game part and the left side shows the multi-agent system part. This integration realizes a platform where humans and agents can jointly participate in simulations.

Humans participate through the user interface provided by the game. The user interface conveys the operations by humans to the simulator, and an output function, which conveys the latest virtual environment to the humans. The input devices include the mouse and keyboard. Input operations are converted into commands that control avatar actions. The actions in and changes to the simulation environment are converted into graphics and sounds, and conveyed to humans through displays and speakers.

An agent interface is newly added to allow agents to participate in the simulation. Its input function conveys requests by agents to the simulator and its output function conveys the latest virtual environment to the agents. Based on given scenarios, agents decide actions according to the surrounding circumstances and send requests for actions. Requests are converted into the operators that trigger the actions of avatars. The results of all actions and changes to the

simulation environment are converted into the data that can be processed by
the agents.

Our platform for participatory simulation consists of the server part, which is
responsible for the simulation environment, and the client part, which is the user
interface for human participation. We used the gumonji client as it is, and established a new server-based simulator responsible for the simulation environment
in which both humans and agents can participate.

4   Implementation of gumonji/Q

Any truly useful participatory simulator must support two types of interaction:
interaction between entities (humans, agents, etc.) and interaction between entities and the environment. As we mentioned in the previous section, to control
the interaction between entities, the scenario description language Q is useful,
and we can utilize gumonji to establish the interactive simulation environment.
This section shows how we integrated these two components in constructing the
simulation platform gumonji/Q.

4.1   Overview

Figure 3 shows architecture of gumonji/Q. Colored boxes are newly implemented
sub-components. As shown in this figure, gumonji/Q consists of gumonji's primary components, gumonji Zone Server and gumonji Client, and a Q processor. Zone Server has an environment simulator (just written as "simulator" in

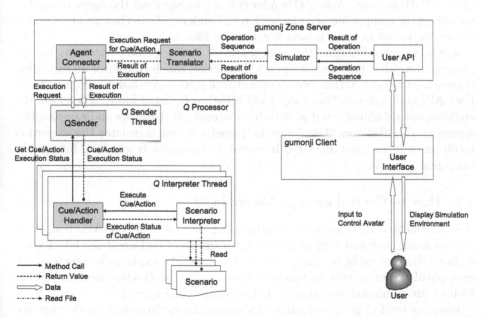

Fig. 3. An overview of gumonji/Q

the figure) as its sub-component which simulates the natural environment and maintains all objects, such as human-controlled avatars, plants, animals, in the environment. A user can access the Zone Server from a gumonji Client on each computer, and control an avatar in the environment. To put it concretely, user's input data is converted to a sequence of operators that control an avatar based on gumonji's User API. The Q interpreter, which transforms a gumonji character into an autonomous agent, is connected to the Zone Server. In order to achieve a connection between gumonji's Zone Server and Q processor, we implemented two sub-components, "Agent Connector" and "Q Sender", within the Zone Server and Q processor, respectively. These components communicate via TCP/IP. A Q-controlled gumonji character can act as an autonomous agent. A crucial point is that the environment simulator in Zone Server deals with human-controlled avatars and Q-controlled agents in a unified way.

Cue/Action execution requests are sent to Zone Server via Q Sender and Cue/Action Handler. Cues and actions are defined as functions in Cue/Action Handler. These functions first call a function for sending execution request messages in Q Sender, and then keep checking cue/action execution status to determine if execution is finished or not. One Q interpreter thread is run for each scenario and agent pair. When one scenario description is assigned to two agents, two Q interpreter threads are created.

Q Sender Thread, on which the Q Sender process runs, is created only once in each Q processor. Q Sender manages the cue/action execution list. When the cue/action handler starts a certain cue/action, Q Sender adds its execution status to the execution list, and sends an execution request to the agent connector as a TCP/IP message. When Q Sender gets a message from the agent connector indicating the completion of a cue/action, Q Sender updates the execution status of the cue/action in the cue/action execution list.

gumonji cannot interpret the requests issued by the Q processor. Thus, we implemented a sub-component, Scenario Translator, which translates an execution request for Cue and Action into an operator sequence. As shown in Figure 3, the User API and Scenario Translator yield identical forms of input. Therefore, the environment simulator can deal with human-controlled avatars and Q-controlled agents in a unified way. The Scenario Translator first translates the execution result into a format suitable for Q Interpreter. The result is sent to Q Interpreter via Agent Connector.

4.2   How to Control gumonji Avatar by Q

We implemented the functions for processing cues and actions. Agents operate avatars using cues and actions according to the described agent models. Figure 4 shows the process of handling cues and actions. We explain the process with example of executing cues and actions. Please note that Q sender and cue/action handler are combined and named "Q Connector" in Figure 4.

Cues are used to get information of surrounding environment for the purpose of observing the events used to trigger interactions. Agents set cues according to

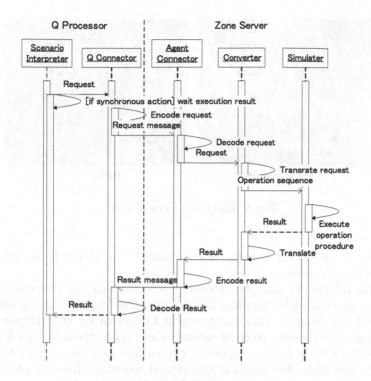

Fig. 4. Process of executing cues and actions

the agent models described in scenarios. Each cue specifies the originating agent and the desired trigger. Requests for cues are sent from Q Processor to gumonji Zone Server. When gumonji Zone Server receives a cue request, it executes observations according to the specified condition. When the specified event is observed, the observation's results are returned to Q Processor. When the agent receives the results of the cue, it begins to perform the actions specified by the scenario.

We implemented seven observation functions for executing cues, such as "hear" and "see". We implemented general-purpose functions for cues in order for agents to observe events which gumonji users can observe via GUI. Agent abilities such as the range of observations can be constrained by the scenario. Scenario writers can constrain the observation abilities of agents freely according to the purpose of the simulation and the situations of agents.

We explain the process of cue execution using the example of the cue "hear". Figure 5 shows the situation wherein the cue "(?hear-message :message "Hello!" :id $id)" is executed. This cue means that the agent observes whether the word "Hello!" is said, and gets the ID of the speaker when this expression is spoken. If agent Jiro, who is a yellow colored avatar, said the word "Hello!" as shown in the right figure, the cue is observed and the ID of Jiro is acquired. On the other

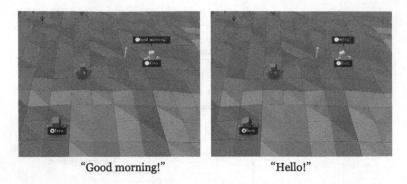

"Good morning!"   "Hello!"

Fig. 5. Executing a cue "?hear"

hand, if agent Jiro said the word "Good morning!", as shown in the left figure, the cue is not observed.

Scenario Interpreter interprets scenarios and requests cue execution according to the agent models described in scenarios. Cue requests are encoded into strings and sent from Q Connector to Agent Connector by TCP/IP messaging. Agent Connector decodes received messages and sends them to Cue & Action Converter. In Cue & Action Converter, cue requests are converted into operators which establish observation of the virtual space. In this example, the cue request "(?hear-message :message "Hello!" :id $id)" is converted into operators that search for the word "Hello!" and get the ID of speaker once the word is captured. The ID of the speaker is returned as the result of cue execution. The results are sent to Cue & Action Converter and converted into a format appropriate for Q Interpreter. The acquired ID of speaker is added to the result message at the same time. The result message is encoded as a string and sent from Agent Connector to Q Connector via TCP/IP. When Q Connector receives the result message, it is decoded and the results are sent to Scenario Interpreter. Through these processes, agents receive the results of cue execution such as ID of Speaker. Acquired information is used in subsequent actions.

We replicated 45 actions that are reasonable for humans to execute via the user interface. The actions include "walk", "speak", "pickup"···. We gave agents the ability to operate avatars to the same extent as humans. In other words, agents can operate avatars to the same extent as humans.

5   Sample of Participatory Simulation

We used gumonji/Q to conduct a participatory simulation based on five farmers and 16 farms. Each farmer owns some of the 16 farms. Each farmer is controlled by human participant or Q scenario. The aim of each farmer is to maximize his/her earnings by cultivating, selling, buying, lending and renting the farms. Each step of the simulation consists of following phases.

Negotiation phase. A farmer negotiates with other farmers to sell, buy, lend or hire one or more farms. If the farmer rents a certain farm, he/she has to pay the agreed rent to the owner though he/she can get the harvest from the farm.

Cultivation phase. For each farm, the farmer decides whether to cultivate the it or not. If he/she thinks the farm is not worth cultivating, he/she can abandon it.

Simulation phase. Farmers cultivate the farms, cast seeds and gather the harvest. The growth of crop plants and the condition of the earth are calculated based on realistic models.

Settlement phase. Settlement; income and expenditure are displayed for each farmer.

A typical scenario is shown in Figure 6. This scenario describes the behavior model of the generic farmer in the negotiation phase. Based on such scenarios, the agents interact with other agents and participants.

Figure 7 is a screen shot of this simulation. Agents are cultivating the earth and casting seeds. Seeds and plants are drawn using the same color as their owner. The participants can visually see the condition of the farms (how plants grow) and agents' activities. The participants use this visualized information in the negotiation phase. For example, if plants do not grow well in the farm currently being cultivated, the farmer may stop cultivating the farm or lend or sell the farm. If the other farmers can discover the low output of the farm, they may refuse to buy it or set a low price on it. The agents' scenarios can be improved based on the analysis of such participants' behavior.

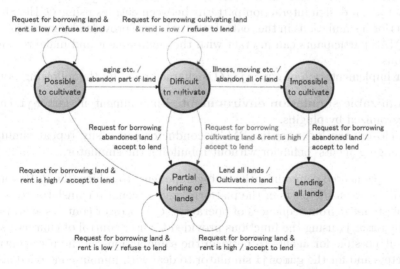

Fig. 6. Behavior Model of a Generic Farmer

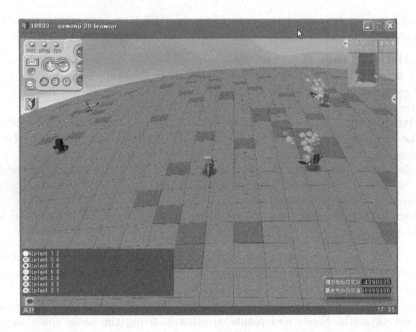

Fig. 7. Executing example scenario

6   Conclusion

In this paper, we detailed our implementation of the participatory simulation environment gumonji/Q, which is a platform that integrates the scenario description language Q and the network game gumonji. By gumonji/Q, A PMAS conductor can design interaction patterns between entities using Q. He/She can also perform simulations in the realistic virtual space provided by gumonji where the PMAS participants can interact with the environment and make reasonable decisions.

Our implementation of gumonji/Q is characterized by the following points.

Customizable simulation environment. Environment in gumonji can be customized by plugins.

Scenario-controlled agents. PMAS conductor can easily repeat simulation changing agents' behavior without rebuilding the simulator.

We implemented communication sub-components to achieve TCP/IP communication between the parts of the platform, and a scenario translator to convert Q requests into/ from sequences of operators. Q Processor controls avatars that exist in gumonji using the functions provided for user control of characters, this makes it possible for agents to perform the same actions as the user-controlled characters and for the gumonji simulator to deal with human-controlled avatars and Q-controlled agents in a unified way.

By using gumonji/Q as a simulation platform, we can expect that users will become more interested in participating in simulations given the excellent graphics provided by gumonji. The network capabilities of gumonji allow users to participate in simulations via the Internet.

References

1. Gilbert, N., Maltby, S., Asakawa, T.: Participatory simulations for developing scenarios in environmental resource management. In: Third workshop on agent-based simulation, pp. 67–72 (2002)
2. Torii, D., Ishida, T., Bousquet, F.: Modeling agents and interactions in agricultural economics. In: Proceedings of the 5th International Joint Conference on Autonomous Agents and Multiagent Systems (AAMAS 2006), pp. 81–88 (2006)
3. Colella, V., Borovoy, R., Resnick, M.: Participatory simulations: using computational objects to learn about dynamic systems. In: CHI 1998: CHI 98 conference summary on Human factors in computing systems, pp. 9–10 (1998)
4. Murakami, Y., Sugimoto, Y., Ishida, T.: Modeling human behavior for virtual training systems. In: Proceedings of the 20th National Conference on Artificial Intelligence (AAAI 2005), pp. 127–132 (2005)
5. Ishida, T.: Q: A scenario description language for interactive agents. Computer 35(11), 42–47 (2002)
6. Nakanishi, H., Ishida, T.: Freewalk/q: social interaction platform in virtual space. In: VRST 2004: Proceedings of the ACM symposium on Virtual reality software and technology, pp. 97–104 (2004)
7. Bousquet, F., Bakam, I., Proton, H., Page, C.L.: Cormas: Common-pool resources and multi-agent systems. In: Mira, J., Moonis, A., de Pobil, A.P. (eds.) IEA/AIE 1998. LNCS, vol. 1416, pp. 826–837. Springer, Heidelberg (1998)
8. Murakami, Y., Ishida, T., Kawasoe, T., Hishiyama, R.: Scenario description for multi-agent simulation. In: AAMAS 2003: Proceedings of the second international joint conference on Autonomous agents and multiagent systems, pp. 369–376 (2003)
9. Nakanishi, H., Nakazawa, S., Ishida, T., Takanashi, K., Isbister, K.: Can software agents influence human relations?: balance theory in agent-mediated communities. In: AAMAS 2003: Proceedings of the second international joint conference on Autonomous agents and multiagent systems, pp. 717–724 (2003)
10. Ishida, T.: Society-Centered Design for Socially Embedded Multiagent Systems. Lecture notes in computer science, pp. 16–29 (2004)

A Multi-Agent System Based Approach to Intelligent Process Automation Systems

Vu Van Tan and Myeong-Jae Yi*

School of Computer Engineering and Information Technology
University of Ulsan, San-29, Moogu-2 dong, Namgu, Ulsan 680-749, South Korea
{vvtan,ymj}@mail.ulsan.ac.kr

Abstract. A more promising technology to integrate existing software systems and their functionalities and to add assistant systems for the shop floors is to be found in software agents. Concerning with the applications of agent technology to intelligent process automation systems, a flexible and extensible approach based on multi-agent system (MAS) and distributed planning technique to reach for increased flexibility and fault-tolerance in process monitoring and control operations is proposed. The monitoring operations are aimed at combining information from different sources depending on the monitoring tasks. The control operations are supervisory control tasks performing either in both sequential and iterative forms. The agent layer is used for monitoring the operations of the lower-level automation systems and reconfiguring its control logic. It operates as a distributed planning and plan execution system to increase the operational flexibility of the whole process automation systems. The software architecture and its functionalities and components for the implementation of the proposed approach are also presented. The design strategy and the discussion on the proposed approach are provided.

Keywords: Agent, Automation system, Control operation, Monitoring operation, Software agent.

1 Introduction

Agent technology is currently an active research field and is widely accepted in research laboratories in over the world. However, research on this field in order for applying to process automation systems where the problem domain is truly distributed and heterogenous is still challenging due to the complexity of the related decision tasks and information systems [13].

As a promising technology to integrate existing software systems and their functionalities and to add assistant systems for the shop floors, software agents allow for the implementation of distributed planning and control algorithms. The agents are able to act autonomously, but their communication abilities ensure a cooperative behavior and the fulfillment of global system goals [9,19].

---

* Corresponding author.

J.-J. Yang et al. (Eds.): PRIMA 2009, LNAI 5925, pp. 428–442, 2009.

More recently, it seems that the improvement of operational processes creates the best opportunity to realize the necessary cost reductions in intelligent process automation systems. Therefore, the development of efficient planning and control strategies is highly desirable. However, it is hard to integrate more advanced production control strategies in real-world situations because of the widely used legacy software systems. The research effort should try to reach for several factors: (i) the gradually increasing functional requirement of a process automation system, (ii) the progress of agent technology, and (iii) the easier implementation of the multi-agent system (MAS) for a specific application. In addition to combine monitoring and control operations in a intelligent process automation system based on the MAS mechanism, the proposed approach improves the limitation of existing approaches that focused only on control operations, but they have limited in attention to the monitoring operations [17,21]. Monitoring tasks are assumed to be composites which refer to several process observations and their logical relations. Thereby, combination of symbolic data with numerical monitoring data is to provide better information for the operator about the state of the monitored processes.

The aim of this paper is to propose an approach based on the MAS and distributed planning schemes to intelligent process automation systems. A suitable combination of planning and reactive operations is needed for extended functionalities because agents with purely reactive operation scheme are only capable to a limited set of process automation operations [20]. By this way the proposed approach increases flexibility and fault tolerance in process monitoring and control operations and enhances the maintenance of these systems.

This paper is organized as follows: The next section deals with agent technology, process automation systems, and their applications in real-world situations. In Section 3, a flexible and extensible approach to intelligent process automation systems based on the MAS and planning techniques is presented. The distributed planning and its execution processes are described in Section 4. The design strategy and discussion on the proposed approach are provided in Section 5. Finally, Section 6 concludes some remarks and future works.

2   Agent Technology and Process Automation Systems

The applications of agents can be divided into two main groups such as *distributed systems* and *personal software assistants* as pointed by Wooldridge [31] and Weiss [29] and Sycara [23]. A multi-agent system (MAS) consists of multiple agents by some cooperation mechanism. Each agent can implement tasks independently. Thereby, through cooperation and interaction among agents, MASs can accomplish complex tasks and their optimization.

Frameworks used for developing MAS applications are widely accepted and provide support for easy and fast development. The widely used frameworks such as JADE [8] or FIPA-OS [6] have been assessed with respect to the capabilities to easily adapt the agent model and the underlying system to a specific field of interest, specially to the process automation domain. Four keys that are crucial for agent systems in process control are (i) representation of agent hierarchies, (ii) representation of decision rules, (iii) modeling of process restrictions, and (iv) support for discrete event simulation.

In recent years research on MAS applications to process automation agents has been used for several different purposes. Agents were proposed to use as modules of an automation system [28,18,22], an integration mechanism [19,3], and a new type of intelligent controller [27]. They have also used for planning of higher-level control operations via negotiations. MAS-based controllers have been applied to continuous, sequential, and batch control [27,26]. Furthermore, agent-based planning techniques are used as approaches for run-time specifications of control sequences [26,12]. These approaches were based on planning with centralized coordination scheme.

Distributed planning is a research topic in distributed artificial intelligence. Some methods for planning in different situations with varying degree of distribution have been developed. Many of them rely on a centralized coordinator. The role of centralized coordinator is to tackle conflicts between other planners. In addition, intelligent supervisory control has been studied in process automation systems for a long time. It extends process controllers with reasoning capabilities of artificial intelligence. The intelligence is in a supervisory controller that guides the operation of an ordinary primary controller [27].

Process automation can be classified into three types on the basis of the control architectures: *centralized control*, *hierarchical control*, and *decentralized control*. However, centralized control is unreliable and inflexible because only one supervision unit is used. Control frameworks can alternatively be classified into *hierarchical*, *heterarchical*, and *hybrid* control frameworks [7]. The hierarchical approach assumes that there is a hierarchy and a master-slave relationship between higher and lower levels of controls. The hierarchy is introduced to handle the complexity of a system [11]. The heterarchical approach focuses on interactions between unit controllers to allow system flexibility, while the relationship between higher- and lower-level controllers is ignored. The hybrid approach has features of both hierarchical and heterarchical approaches. It allows direct interactions among the lower-level controllers as well as between higher and lower levels [15]. Monitoring and control tasks from process automation are still challenging because of the complexity of the related decision tasks and information systems [2]. In addition, research on applications of the MAS in process automation has been less extensive than in discrete manufacturing [22,1].

In terms of software engineering for developing agent systems, the design of MASs using object-oriented design patterns proposed by Kendall and Malkoun [10]. This addresses agent concurrency, virtual migration, collaboration, and reasoning based on the role of design patterns. On the other hand, Xue et al. [32] proposed a customized methodology to develop MAS applications in order to realize an engineering change in agent-oriented software engineering. This method can cover the whole development life-cycle from agent-oriented analysis to software implementation. Developers then use it to combine different meta models originated from various methods for forming the best suited development process to particular application domain. However, it seems to be hard to enrich these design patterns or the mentioned methodology for developing multiple agents-based process automation systems.

It seems that intelligent agent systems can cope with complex requirements for managing distributed information because agents integrate information dynamically as a normal part of their operations. This feature will improve the limitation of existing approaches. Monitoring the production processes is one of the the main tasks of process operators together with pre-planned operations and disturbance control. The requirements of this work have become harder in recent years due to ever increasing demands of cost reductions [17,30]. These problems need to be considered and solved.

3 Software System Architecture

3.1 Infrastructure Issues and Technical Details

Agent technology is used for integrating existing software systems and their functionalities and for adding assistant systems for the shop floor staff. The integration on an agent platform is illustrated in Fig. 1. Agent platforms usually offer a standard way of communication among the agents hosted on the platform. Using ontologies for different subsystems assures the uniqueness of concepts to be exchanged [16]. The use of agent technology for integration of new and existing systems takes two advantages: (i) currently available IT-systems can be integrated and (ii) seamless use of information and functions. Furthermore, FIPA [5] established the need for agent technology to link with the physical world and now has working groups involved in the manufacturing production and scheduling areas for solving the real-time control interface problem.

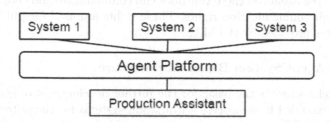

Fig. 1. Integration of new and existing systems via an agent platform

The Agent Runtime Environment provides the infrastructure for agent execution and allows the agents a concurrent execution on the some host. An agent directory, a message transport system, an agent communication language (ACL), and a service directory are specified in the FIPA Abstract Architecture as shown in Fig. 2. In the case for the development of MAS applications, Microsoft .NET might be chosen as a middleware for the implementation of the Agent Runtime Environment or JADE may be selected. The .NET Remoting Framework provided by Microsoft .NET is a powerful and scalable technology for implementing a message transport system.

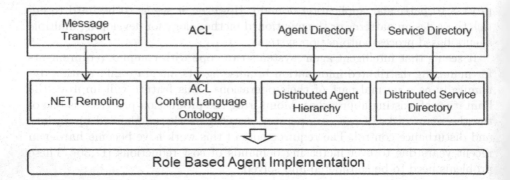

Fig. 2. FIPA abstract architecture and its usage for the implementation

3.2   Communicational Issue

Communication among agents is a key issue of the MASs to enable cooperation and coordination features. For systems using some kind of peer-to-peer services instead of the FIPA suggested global Directory Facilitator, communication rights to form a relation among the agents should be used [13,5]. This relation is symmetric, i.e., when agent α has the right to communicate with agent β, the agent β can also communicate with agent α. However, the relation is not transitive due to the hierarchical structures of the control systems.

The Directory Service agent is responsible for establishing connection between different remote runtimes. It manages the hierarchical as well as the local organization of the agents within an agent system. In the case the runtimes are known to each other, the agents on these runtimes can communicate and cooperate with respect to their communication rights. These rights are used for publishing the agent's services provided by the MAS.

3.3   Multi-Agent System Based Architecture

The agent architecture is the basic for the further development of generic MAS applications extended from process automation systems for the automation domain. Therefore, different organizational types of automation systems, i.e., production control, job shops, flexible job shops, and flow shops with several types of production control paradigms should be guaranteed. Combining the single agent with the MAS architecture, the well-known hybrid architecture (InteRRaP) developed by Müller [14] utilizes three layers within each single agent. The first layer is a behavior-based layer incorporating reactivity and procedural knowledge for routine tasks. The second layer is a planning layer that provides the facilities for means-ends reasoning for the achievement of local tasks and to procedure goal-directed behavior. The last one is a cooperative layer for agent interactions. The proposed architecture based on the MAS and distributed planning techniques is shown in Fig. 3, which is extended from general process automation systems. The agent layer is used for monitoring the lower-level automation, for

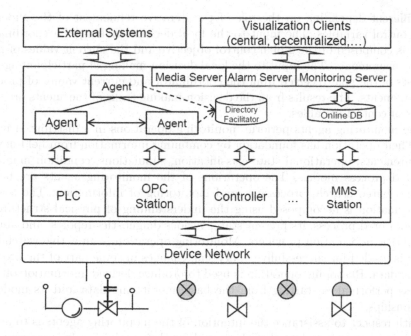

Fig. 3. The MAS-based architecture for intelligent process automation

delivering enhanced information on its operations to users, and for reconfiguring the operation logic of the automation system.

Due to the monitoring and control operations used in process automation, the proposed architecture is composed of two types of agents: (i) monitoring agents and (ii) control agents. Control agents form a hierarchy based on authority relations. The leaf agents supervise some part of the controlled process and its related information. Monitoring agents cooperate with control agents to perform advanced monitoring tasks. They operate as an extension to existing automation and information systems at a process plant. The operations of the monitoring agents include (i) conversation with human users, (ii) composition of the monitoring tasks from the lower-level monitoring services, and (iii) cooperation with other agents.

3.4 Monitoring and Control Operations

The multi-agent based process automation system, i.e., a process control and monitoring system, consists of two types of the agent: (i) process agents and (ii) monitoring agents [24]. The process agents perform supervisory control operations either in a sequential or iterative fashion. They relate to process state change or batch control operations and the later to tuning of continuous control. The task of the agent is first to plan a shared sequence of control actions and then to execute this sequence. It is to calculate optimal values for the supervisory control variables. Therefore, the decision-making processes of the agents are different depending on the role of the iterative refinement of the supervisory control variables. The input to the local decision-making of a coordinator agent is composed of the global control objective and the current values of process measurements. The input to the local decision-making of participant agents consists of the goal received from the coordinator and current values of process measurements. The results from the decision-making tasks of the agents are new values of control variables.

The monitoring agents perform monitoring operations in a distributed manner. Their operation has foundation by combining information from field-device measurements, operational state classification, simulations, condition monitoring, and process models. The operations of the monitoring agents are based on distributed search, processing, and monitoring of information. The search of information is decomposed using the understanding of physical structure of the monitored process, its present state, various diagnostics reports, and ability of different information providers. Monitoring operation is an active watchdog, which is needed for successfully supervising changes in some part of the process related data. Reasoning operation is used to produce derived information on the process performance starting from the basic monitoring data and its modeled relationships.

With respect to assistance the intention of the monitoring agents is to assist operators in accessing data that they need for their activities. It is expected to reduce the information overload that some users are facing. The functions of the monitoring agents include planning of information access and interpreting intermediate results, e.g., communication of process events to operators and flexible definition of alarm conditions. Information access and its combination are used for collecting data from separate external data sources and for transforming them into a suitable symbolic form for the monitoring tasks of monitoring agents. In the case of data sources that naturally produce symbolic events, e.g., maintenance database, there is still need to convert data into unite syntax and semantics. Therefore, ontologies are used for representing the structure, events, and behavior of the monitored process [16].

3.5   Agent Model for Monitoring and Control Operations

Definition 1. *An agent is defined as an autonomous entity that can carry out some actions on behalf of another agent or a user.*

The agent can also perceive information from its environment and tries to achieve a set of explicit or implicit goals. An agent has communication capabilities for message exchanges with the underlying automation system and other agents. It also has data models of process instruments and other agents.

The agent model of an automation agent[1] specifies the internal modules of an agent and its operations. However, automation agents need to conform to the agent models of some FIPA-compliant generic agent platform. In general, an agent consists mainly of a set of behaviors and actions that define the agent's

---

[1] This term is used to indicate either a process agent or a monitoring agent.

reaction to different circumstances such as incoming messages or events [13]. The agent's behaviors, which form the basis for reactivity and pro-activity, are used to implement agent interactions. An automation agent will use its actions to fulfill its goals. The automation agent is composed of modules that can be classified into operational and modeling modules and runtime data structures. This is illustrated in Fig. 4.

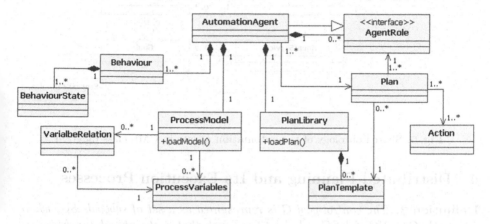

Fig. 4. A UML class diagram for the automation agent

The process model describes the knowledge of an automation agent on the controlled process. Automation agents can have knowledge about the existence of process variables, measured values, and relation between variables. A control variable may be controlled by one agent only, whereas the measurements can be shared among several agents. The plan library contains plans that an automation agent can use when creating runtime plans. Each automation agent is configured during agent application development with a set of plans that it needs to be able to plan its control operations. The runtime data structure of an automation agent includes goals, runtime plans, and contracts. The role of data structures is to store information on which the agent's goal is currently trying to fulfill.

Ontology for Automation Agents: On the one hand, the automation agents share a common ontology that indicates the concepts for the need of agents in communication. These concepts are used when accessing information about agent services registered to the Directory Facilitator. On the other hand, the automation agents also share another ontology that specifies the concepts for their need when cooperatively performing automation operations. The main concepts of this ontology includes relation, goal, contract, and process variable [22]. Relations are used for expressing the organizational supervisor in contrast to subordinate relations between the agents. Information about goals and contracts is exchanged between the agents during the cooperative planning and the execution of the automation operations. Goals may refer to process variables that are shared knowledge among the agents. Fig. 5 shows a shared ontology of automation agents representing in the UML class diagram.

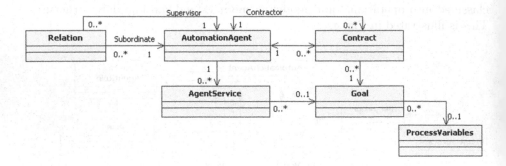

Fig. 5. Shared ontology of the automation agents in UML class diagram

4   Distributed Planning and Its Execution Processes

Definition 2. *The control goal G is represented as a set of subgoals SG, where $SG \in G$, $G = SG_1 \cup SG_2 \cup ... \cup SG_n$, such that each subgoal can be solved completely.*

For example, the `startup` of the tank is subgoal of the whole process goal. For the models of the controlled processes and the agent society, an agent will hold data on its activities including communication with other agents and its planning process. The activities of an agent are modeled as concurrently executing tasks and its communication with other agents as conversations.

The automation agents do create control plans during runtime to solve given goals from control operations or status of the process. The planning process can be characterized as distributed and cooperative planning. Each agent creates locally its part of the overall plan and adapts it to other agents' plans via a negotiation process. The negotiation process is carried out via two axes with different purposes. There are two cases for agents' interaction in a multi-agent based process automation system: (i) supervisory agents assign control goals to their subordinates as subgoals of a whole goal, and (ii) peer agents request goals from their peers in order to handle interrelations between their plans.

The cooperative planning process can appear in different forms depending on the controlled process and the requested planning tasks. The need for coordination is caused by the interrelations of the controlled variables in the target process. In principle, the planning process can start from any agents and it ends when originating agent observes if its goals can be fulfilled or not. By the use of decision-making and staff agents [13] as a starting point for further adaptation to specific control problems, the proposed approach is considered as a hybrid layered architecture offering a separate planning layer by the staff agents and a reactive and proactive layer by the decision-making agents.

In cooperation planning of parallel control sequences, the cooperation among the subprocess agents has a form of distributed path-finding process. The search starts from a given goal state of a subprocess. It is intended to find a set of possibly parallel control actions that will bring the controlled process from the current state to the goal state. The search path is formed by decisions of the agents to decompose goals into subgoals or control actions. The search process is controlled by the plans configured into the subprocess agents. As an illustrative example [22], a plan in distributed planning of control sequences can be described as follows:

```
Plan:{
        Name: "Startup Tank Subprocess"
        Goal: ACHIEVE startup;
        Body:
            ACHIEVE Tank_Filled "yes";
            EXECUTE Plan_Control_Action "evsp"  "1650";
            EXECUTE Negotiate "Temperature_Control_On"
                "upper_level" "non-blocking";
            EXECUTE Negotiate "Temperature_Control_On"
                "lower_level" "startup";
    }
```

Agents in the execution process execute those plans in which they have to commit during the planning process. Each agent has local plans including a number of process control and communication actions. Control actions are executed locally while communication actions are used for coordinating and scheduling actions between agents. A supervisory agent or a peer agent may request another agent to perform a plan in order to achieve a certain state related to goal. Control actions are executed on the underlying automation systems via an OPC station [25] and/or a PLC, etc.

5 Design Strategy and Discussion

In this section, the design strategy in order to design and develop MAS applications for process automation and the discussion on the proposed approach for deploying to real process automation applications are presented, respectively.

5.1 Design Strategy

The design strategy process is executed in three phases that may interleave each other (see Fig. 6). The design of the agent society by identifying necessary agents and their interactions via an agent platform is performed in the first phase. The interactions for agent exchange are specified mainly as goals. The second phase is the design of external connections of various agents. On the basic of developing MAS applications, these connections are based on FIPA standards for the communication. They can include I/O to the process devices and connections to external data sources. The last phase is the design of the internal logic of agents. It is to be defined with plans that describe how agents are going to fulfill their goals. Therefore, a hierarchical architecture is a powerful way to map the organizational structure of process automation systems to an agent-based system. A chain of responsibility can be built through the whole hierarchy to decompose a production control problem into different subproblems.

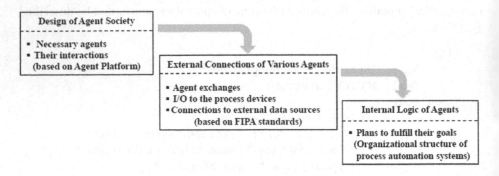

Fig. 6. The design strategy process in three phases

5.2   Discussion

Application research based on the MAS and planning techniques for both control and monitoring operations is subject to be designed in a flexible and extensible way within the same agents. The proposed approach is extended from automation architecture that separates agent platform for process automation for real applications in industry. The automation agents are used for both control and monitoring applications. Nevertheless, monitoring agents are subject to monitoring applications from the real-world, e.g., applying to several functions such as communication of process events to operators and flexible definition of alarm conditions, etc. The plan execution is performed by goals, which represent the monitoring objectives configured to the monitoring tasks by the operator (or staff). The goal-oriented operation scheme is expected to focus on the monitoring tasks according the intention of the operator. Consequently, information access and combination of the monitoring tasks to collect data from separate external data sources and to transform them into a suitable form for the monitoring tasks should be fulfilled [17].

In addition to the integration of automation systems, a MAS today has been considered as a system development method for intelligent process automation. Using modularization and versatile communication mechanisms, other aspects of MASs have expected to be useful in the development of automation systems because MAS societies with organizational structures have been proposed for organizing these systems. Furthermore, the coordination mechanisms of MASs are used for building a sort of self-configuration in automation systems. Thereby, the capability of the automation system adapts to a new situation via reconfiguring parts of itself, e.g., its application logic.

The proposed approach demonstrates the capabilities of MAS-based problem-solving methods that are expected to enhance the flexibility and responsiveness properties of process automation systems. It is designed as a distributed planning of control sequences and a distributed iterative search of values for supervisory control variables. The distributed planning process in turn is able to create new sequences as a combination of the sequences wrapped in the plans. Besides, the distributed iterative search process can be used to find new values for a set of control variables [26].

An example dealing with the monitoring and control of a district heating system [30,4] can be solved by the proposed approach. The basic idea behind district heating is to use cheap local heat production plants to produce hot water. This water is then distributed through pipes to the customers who use it as a source of heated tap water and/or to heat the building. At the customer side, substations are used to exchange heat from the primary flow of the distribution pipes to the secondary flow of the building. The main problem encountered by the control engineer is to decide the correct amount of heat to produce at each point in time. Another problem is that if there is a shortage of heat in the system, the control engineer needs to make sure that consumers receive appropriate amounts of heat according to the circumstances. To resolve these problems the proposed architecture has two functions: (i) serves as a decision support system for the control engineer by providing information on the current state and predictions of future states and (ii) has a fully automated control mechanism for dealing with heat shortages. Heat prediction is based on the average consumption during the corresponding time period. It continuously monitors the heat consumption and sends a report to the redistribution agent.

6   Concluding Remarks and Future Works

An approach based on the MAS and distributed planning techniques to intelligent process automation systems was proposed. By combining information access and control operations in a process automation system with the agent technology, the proposed approach has tried to solve existing problems in automation and information systems, e.g., monitoring operations, increasing flexibility and fault tolerance in process monitoring and control operations, etc. It provides a flexible reference model to efficiently distribute knowledge and information. There have been significant contributions for a specification of a generic MAS platform for process automation in industry, which will be implemented for several different kinds of cooperative and intelligent supervisory applications.

The agents plan and run supervisory control sequences via distributed planning and execution processes for intelligent process automation with using distributed planning techniques. The distributed planning process is able to create new sequences as a combination of the sequences wrapped in the plans. If operational change situations can be handled these new sequences the proposed system can facilitate flexibility and responsiveness. By the utilization of decision-making agents and staff agents, the proposed approach is developed as a hybrid layered architecture offering a separate planning layer and a reactive and proactive layer. Moreover, the distributed search process as a problem-solving method is used to find new values for a set of control variables. However, this method makes us difficult to design a decision logic which would guarantee acceptable performance of the distributed search process in more and more complicated test cases for process automation and information systems.

As a promising technology being applicable on the industrial applications, the agent technology has a long tradition in the academic field but its use in production and real-time applications has been very limited to date. In the future, extending process monitoring systems with information access handling semantic data need to be studied more thorough. The usage of ontologies should be in a rather generic stage. The applicability of the approach to more useful information access scenarios in process automation should be validated. In addition, trying to implement the proposed approach as a flexible and extensible solution used for intelligent process automation systems is a major task.

Acknowledgements. This work was supported in part by the Korean Ministry of Knowledge Economy and Ulsan Metropolitan City through the Network-based Automation Research Center (NARC) at the University of Ulsan and by the Korea Research Foundation Grant funded by the Korean Government (KRF-2009-0076248). The authors would like to thank the anonymous referees for their valuable comments and suggestions that helped us to improve this work.

References

1. Bussmann, S., Jennings, N.R., Wooldridge, M.: On the Identification of Agents in the Design of Production Control Systems. In: Ciancarini, P., Wooldridge, M.J. (eds.) AOSE 2000. LNCS, vol. 1957, pp. 141–162. Springer, Heidelberg (2001)
2. Choinski, D., Nocon, W., Metzger, M.: Multi-Agent System for Hierarchical Control with Self-organising Database. In: Nguyen, N.T., Grzech, A., Howlett, R.J., Jain, L.C. (eds.) KES-AMSTA 2007. LNCS, vol. 4496, pp. 655–664. Springer, Heidelberg (2007)
3. Cockburn, D., Jennings, N.R.: ARCHON: A Distributed Artificial Intelligence System for Industrial Applications. In: O'Hare, G.M.P., Jennings, N.R. (eds.) Foundations of Distributed Artificial Intelligence, pp. 319–344. Wiley & Sons, Chichester (1996)
4. Davidsson, P., Wernstedt, F.: A Multi-Agent System Architecture for Coordination of Just-in-time Production and Distribution. In: Proceedings of the 2002 ACM Symposium on Applied Computing, pp. 294–299 (2002)
5. FIPA – The Foundation for Intelligent Physical Agents (2009), http://www.fipa.org/
6. FIPA-OS Agent Toolkit (2009), http://sourceforge.net/projects/fipa-os/
7. Heragu, S.S., Graves, R.J., Kim, B.I., Onge, A.S.: Intelligent Agent Based Framework for Manufacturing Systems Control. IEEE Transactions on Systems, Man, and Cybernetics - Part A 32(5), 560–573 (2002)
8. JADF – Java Agent Development Framework (July 24, 2009), http://jade.tilab.com/

 9. Jennings, N.R.: An Agent-Based Approach for Building Complex Software Systems. Communication of the ACM 44(4), 35–41 (2001)
10. Kendall, E.A., Malkoun, M.T.: Design Patterns for the Development of Multiagent Systems. In: Dickson, L., Zhang, C. (eds.) DAI 1996. LNCS (LNAI), vol. 1286, pp. 17–31. Springer, Heidelberg (1997)
11. Leduc, R.J., Lawford, M., Dai, P.: Hierarchical Interface-Based Supervisory Control of a Flexible Manufacturing System. IEEE Transactions on Control Systems Technology 14(4), 654–668 (2006)
12. Maturana, F.P., Tichy, P., Staron, R., Slechta, P.: Using Dynamically Created Decision-Making Organizations (Holarchies) to Plan, Commit and Execute Control Tasks in a Chilled Water System. In: Proceedings of the 13th International Workshop on Database and Expert Systems Applications, pp. 613–622. IEEE CS Press, Los Alamitos (2000)
13. Mönch, L., Stehli., M.: ManufAg: A Multi-agent-System Framework for Production Control of Complex Manufacturing Systems. Information Systems and e-Business Management 4(2), 159–185 (2006)
14. Müller, J.P.: The Design of Intelligent Agents - A Layered Approach. In: Carbonell, J.G., Siekmann, J. (eds.) The Design of Intelligent Agents. LNCS (LNAI), vol. 1177, pp. 1–197. Springer, Heidelberg (1996)
15. Nahm, Y.E., Ishikawa, H.: A Hybrid Multi-Agent System Architecture for Enterprise Integration using Computer Networks. Robotics and Computer-Integrated Manufacturing 21(3), 217–234 (2005)
16. Obitko, M., Mařík, V.: Adding OWL Semantics to Ontologies Used in Multi-agent Systems for Manufacturing. In: Mařík, V., McFarlane, D.C., Valckenaers, P. (eds.) HoloMAS 2003. LNCS, vol. 2744, pp. 189–200. Springer, Heidelberg (2003)
17. Pirttioja, T., Seilonen, I., Pakonen, A., Halme, A., Koskinen, K.: Information Agents Handling Semantic Data as an Extension to Process Monitoring Systems. In: Mařík, V., Vyatkin, V., Colombo, A.W. (eds.) HoloMAS 2007. LNCS, vol. 4659, pp. 411–420. Springer, Heidelberg (2007)
18. Sanz, R.: Agents for Complex Control Systems. In: Samad, T., Weyrauch, J. (eds.) Automation, Control, and Complexity, pp. 171–190. Wiley & Sons, Chichester (2000)
19. Sauer, O., Sutschet, G.: A Step towards Real time. Manufacturing Engineer 85(3), 32–37 (2006)
20. Seilonen, I., Pirttioja, T., Pakonen, A., Appelqvist, P., Halme, A., Koskinen, K.: Distributed Planning Agents for Intelligent Prcess Automation. In: Proceedings of the 2003 IEEE International Symposium on Computational Intelligence in Robotics and Automation, pp. 614–619. IEEE Press, Los Alamitos (2003)
21. Seilonen, I., Pirttioja, T., Pakonen, A., Appelqvist, P., Halme, A., Koskinen, K.: Information Access and Control Operations in Multi-agent System Based Process Automation. In: Mařík, V., William Brennan, R., Pěchouček, M. (eds.) HoloMAS 2005. LNCS, vol. 3593, pp. 144–153. Springer, Heidelberg (2005)
22. Seilonen, I.: An Extended Process Automation System: An Approach based on a Multi-Agent System. Doctoral Thesis, Helsinki University of Technology, Finland (2006)
23. Sycara, K.P.: Multiagent Systems. Magazine of American Association for Artificial Intelligence 19(2), 79–92 (1998)
24. Tan, V.V., Yoo, D.-S., Yi, M.-J.: A Multiagent-System Framework for Hierarchical Control and Monitoring of Complex Process Control Systems. In: Bui, T.D., Ho, T.V., Ha, Q.T. (eds.) PRIMA 2008. LNCS (LNAI), vol. 5357, pp. 381–388. Springer, Heidelberg (2008)

25. The OPC Foundation, http://www.opcfoundation.org/
26. Tichý, P., Šlechta, P., Maturana, F., Balasubramanian, S.: Industrial MAS for Planning and Control. In: Mařík, V., Štěpánková, O., Krautwurmová, H., Luck, M. (eds.) ACAI 2001, EASSS 2001, AEMAS 2001, and HoloMAS 2001. LNCS (LNAI), vol. 2322, pp. 280–295. Springer, Heidelberg (2002)
27. van Breemen, A., de Vries, T.: An Agent-Based Framework for Designing Multi-Controller Systems. In: Proceedings of the 5th International Conference on the Practical Applications of Intelligent Agents and Multi-Agent Technology, pp. 219–235 (2000)
28. Wang, H., Wang, C.: Intelligent Agents in the Nuclear Industry. IEEE Computer 30(11), 28–34 (1997)
29. Weiss, G. (ed.): Multiagent Systems. MIT Press, Cambridge (1999)
30. Wernstedt, F., Davidsson, P.: An Agent-Based Approach to Monitoring and Control of District Heating Systems. In: Hendtlass, T., Ali, M. (eds.) IEA/AIE 2002. LNCS, vol. 2358, pp. 801–811. Springer, Heidelberg (2002)
31. Wooldridge, M.J.: An Introduction to Multiagent Systems. Wiley & Sons, Chichester (2002)
32. Xue, X., Liu, X., Li, R.: Towards a Customized Methodology to Develop Multiagent Systems. In: Shi, Z.-Z., Sadananda, R. (eds.) PRIMA 2006. LNCS(LNAI), vol. 4088, pp. 105–116. Springer, Heidelberg (2006)

Non-equity Joints among Small and Medium Enterprises and Innovation Management: An Empirical Analysis Based on Simulation

Marco Remondino, Marco Pironti, and Roberto Schiesari

University of Turin, e-business L@B
Cso Svizzera 185, Turin, Italy
{remond,pironti}di.unito.it

Abstract. In this work a simulation model is described and implemented, with the purpose of analyzing the non-equity collaborations among small and medium enterprises (SMEs) and the effects of innovation management strategies on enterprise networks. Non-equity links are usually stable, but not strong. In this context the strong links are joint-ventures and participation exchanges, while non-equity collaboration (as a consortium) are stable, but leaving each enterprise as an autonomous entity. In particular, the governance of SMEs remains independent, but in the long term we observe a co-evolution of strategies among the enterprises which take part in the collaborative network. An enterprise can decide to exploit innovative processes it owns, thus potentially gaining competitive advantage, but risking, in turn, that other players could reach the same technological levels. Or it could decide to share it, in exchange for other competencies or money. These strategies could be the basis for a network formation and/or impact the topology of an existing network. The model presented in the paper aims at exploring how a process innovation and the strategies to manage it can facilitate network formation, affect its topology, induce new players to enter the market and spread onto the network by being shared or developed by new players.

Keywords: Process Innovation, Enterprise Management, Network Topology, Business Process, Agent Based Simulation.

1 Introduction

The features of Socio-Economical environment in which the enterprise acts considerably affect its productive choices, the decisional models, internal organization and the relations with other enterprises. The key point of every Economical activity should be an aptitude to second and favor market changes. Today, enterprises operate in dynamic markets where acquisition problems of productive factors constantly change along with the new technologies, customers' needs, peculiar features of demand in different sectors, internal situation of the enterprise (financial, economical and organizational), social conditions of the country, and so on.

J.-J. Yang et al. (Eds.): PRIMA 2009, LNAI 5925, pp. 443–458, 2009.
© Springer-Verlag Berlin Heidelberg 2009

Unlike product innovation, which is targeted towards product engineering, development and commercialization activities, process innovation relates to improving organizational processes. Our understandings of business process innovation come from the growing researches on organizational learning and knowledge management. The transfer and sharing of process innovation is not easy to attain, but information sharing/knowledge transfer (both within and across the boundary of the organization) is seen as an essential element for innovation. The network promote not only the transfer of knowledge (and the possible transfer of process) but also the creation of new knowledge as well, through synergies or competition. Within an organization, cross-unit knowledge transfer can produce "creative abrasion" [3], generate "improvisational sparks" [4] and create new information patterns by rearranging information already in use and incorporating information previously neglected. Enterprises also actively look for external knowledge, for example by expanding their networks to learn new practices and technologies [5]. The process innovation could impact on the network not only by improving the knowledge of the involved enterprises, but also by changing the number of actors (exit and entry), and changing the numbers and patterns of link information [2]. The network can expand, churn, strengthen or shrink. At the level of a single enterprise, if it is the only one (or among the few) possessing an innovative process, it could become the focal point in a network, attracting others, wishing to link with it. Each network change is brought about by specific combination of changes in tie creation, tie deletion, and by changes in an actor's portfolio size (number of link) and portfolio range (numbers of partners) [2]. While [2] presents four types of network changes, they find that only an expanding network and a churning network are a reflection of a structural change, because new alliances are formed with new partners. An expanding network is brought about by an increase of new alliances without a deletion of old ones (meaning a large average of portfolio), together with an increasing portfolio range (more difference in partners). A churning network reflects the formation of new alliances and the deletion of existing alliances. While the average portfolio remains stable in term of the number of partners, there is a rotation of partners.

In order to empirically study how process innovation can affect an enterprise network, an agent based model is used. Agent based simulation is an effective paradigm for studying complex systems. It allows the creation of virtual societies, in which each agent can interact with others basing on certain rules. In this way, a social system can be observed as if it were a laboratory study, by repeating the experiments all the needed times, and changing just some parameters, by leaving all the others still (*ceteris paribus* analysis), something that would be impossible in the real system. The agents are basic entities, endowed with the capacity of performing certain actions, and with certain variables defining their state. In the model presented here, the agents are reactive, meaning that they simply react to the stimuli coming from the environment and from other agents, without cognitively elaborating their own strategies. An agent based model consists of a multitude of software agents (both homogeneous or heterogeneous), each type being endowed with particular local properties and rules, put together within an environment, formally described as a set of parameters and rules. When the model is formally built and implemented, emergent results can be observed, thus inferring cause-effect relations by simulating different core scenarios.

In the present work, social network theory is briefly analyzed and a definition of process innovation is given. Then, the comprehensive agent based model used is formally introduced, and it is discussed how it can be employed to study how a process innovation affects an enterprise network. Last, some empirical results coming from the model are given and the future work in this direction is discussed.

2 Social Networks

A social network is a social structure made of nodes (which are generally individuals or organizations) that are tied by one or more specific types of interdependency, such as values, visions, ideas, financial exchange, friendship. Social network analysis views social relationships in terms of nodes and ties. Nodes are the individual actors within the networks, and ties are the relationships between the actors. These concepts are often displayed in a social network diagram, where nodes are the points and ties are the lines.

The idea of drawing a picture (called "*sociogram*") of who is connected to whom for a specific set of people is credited to [6], an early social psychologist who envisioned mapping the entire population of New York City. Cultural anthropologists independently invented the notion of social networks to provide a new way to think about social structure and the concepts of role and position, an approach that culminated in rigorous algebraic treatments of kinship systems. At the same time, in mathematics, the nascent field of graph theory [7] began to grow rapidly, providing the underpinnings for the analytical techniques of modern social network analysis. The strategic network perspective avers that the *embeddedness* of enterprises in networks of external relationships with other organizations holds significant implications for enterprise performance [10].

Specifically, since resources and capabilities such as access to diverse knowledge [11], pooled resources and cooperation, are often acquired through networks of inter-firm ties, and since access to such resources and capabilities influences enterprise performance, it is important from a strategy perspective to examine the effect of network structure on enterprise performance [9]. Relationships between enterprises and their partners affect enterprises' alliance-building, behavior and performance. There is evidence that enterprises' network positions have an impact on their survival, innovativeness, market share [12], and financial returns [18]. However, evidence remains mixed on which particular patterns of inter-organizational relationships are advantageous for enterprises. One of the key ideas currently dominating the literature is [11]) open network perspective, according to which an enterprise can obtain important performance advantages when exploiting relationships to partners that do not maintain direct ties among one another. The absence of direct ties among a firm's partners (the presence of structural holes) indicates that these partners are located in different parts of an industry network, that they are connected to heterogeneous sources of information, and that their invitations to jointly exploit business prospects present the focal enterprise with access to diverse deal-making opportunities [1]. Several studies have shown that enterprises improve their performance as a result of maintaining relationships, whereas other studies have shown negative performance effects of firms' maintaining positions in open networks.

3 Process Innovation

A business process is a set of logically related tasks performed to achieve a defined business outcome [19], e.g.: sequencing of work routines, information flow and so on.

Process innovation is defined as "the introduction of a new method of production, that is, one yet tested by experience in the branch of manufacture concerned a new way of handling a commodity commercially" [16]. Edquist [20] defines process innovation like the result in a decrease in the cost of production. The drives of process innovation are primarily reduction in delivery lead time, lowering of operational costs, and increase in flexibility: process innovations are a firm's new way of design or manufacturing existing or new products. While newness on product innovation is defined at a macro level (market, industry), newness of process innovations is often defined at a micro level (enterprise and business unit).

Meeus and Euist divide process innovations into two categories: technological and organizational innovations: technological process innovations change the way products are produced by introducing change in technology (physical equipment, techniques, system); organizational innovations are innovations in an organization's structure, strategy and administrative processes [16].

Process innovation can and should happen at various levels within the organization as no organization can depend solely upon innovation occurring at one level only. Successful organizations have an innovation process working its way through all levels of the organization..

4 Impact on the Network

Process innovation is a key factor for both competing in a market and creating links with other players. An enterprise owning a proprietary process would in fact exploit it, by gaining a competitive factor over those who do not possess it. On the other hand, it could decide to share it with other enterprises in exchange for money or, even better, in exchange for other competencies it does not know. This is the most important factor behind the creation of what we here define "network for competences exchange", i.e.: a social network of enterprises, where the ties semantically represent a synergy among players exchanging process innovations or, to a more general extent, competences.

Philippen and Riccaboni [13] in their work on "radical innovation and network evolution" focus on the importance of local link formation and the process of distant link formation. Regarding the formation of new linkages [8] finds that the process of new tie creation is heavily embedded in an actor's existing network. This means that new ties are often formed with prior partners or with partners of prior partners, indicating network growth to be a local process. Particularly when considering inter-firm alliances, new link formation is considered "risky business" and actors prefer alliances that are embedded in a dense clique were norms are more likely to be enforceable and opportunistic behavior to be punished ([10]; [2]). Distant link formation implies that new linkages are created with partners whom are not known to the existing partners of an actor. At the level of the enterprise, [11] shows that distant linkage that serve as bridge between dense local clique of enterprises, can provide access to new source of information and favorable strategic negotiation position, which improves the firms' position in the network and industry.

In order to examine and study how a process innovation can spread and affect the network for competences exchange, an agent based model is used. The model is a comprehensive one, showing the network dynamics for enterprises, and is described in detail in the next paragraph.

5   The E³ Agent Based Model

The model has been developed at the e-Business L@B, University of Turin. It is built in pure Java, thus following the Object Oriented paradigm. This is particularly suitable for agent based modeling, since the individual agents can be seen as objects coming from a prototypal class, interacting among them basing on the internal rules (methods). While the reactive nature of the agents may seem a limitation, it's indeed a way to keep track of the aggregate behavior of a large number of entities acting in the same system at the same time. All the numerical parameters can be decided at the beginning of each simulation (e.g.: number of enterprises, and so on).

Everything in the model is seen as an agent; thus we have three kinds of agents: Environment, Enterprises and Emissaries (E³). This is done since each of them, even the environment, is endowed with some actions to perform.

5.1   Heat Metaphor

In order to represent the advantage of an enterprise in owning different competences, the "heat" metaphor is introduced. In agent based models for Economics, the metaphor based approach [14] is an established way of representing real phenomena through computational and physical metaphors. In this case, a quantum of heat is assigned for each competence at each simulation turn. If the competence is internal (i.e.: developed by the enterprise) this value is higher. If the competence is external (i.e.: borrowed from another enterprise) this value is lower. This is realistic, since in the model we don't have any form of variable cost for competencies, and thus an internal competence is rewarded more. Heat is thus a metaphor not only for the profit that an enterprise can derive from owning many competences, but also for the managing and synergic part (e.g.: economy of scale).

Heat is also expendable in the process of creating new internal competences (internal exploration) and of looking for partner with whom to share them in exchange of external competences (external exploration). At each time-step, a part of the heat is scattered (this can be regarded as a set of costs for the enterprise). If the individual heat gets under a threshold, the enterprise ceases its activity and disappears from the environment. At an aggregate level, average environmental heat is a good and synthetic measure to monitor the state of the system.

5.2   Environment

The environment is regarded as a meta-agent, representing the world in which the proper agents act. It's considered an agent itself, since it can perform some actions on the others and on the heat. If features the following properties: a grid (X,Y), i.e.: a lattice in the form of a matrix, containing cells; a dispersion value, i.e.: a real number used to calculate the dissipated heat at each step; the heat threshold under which an enterprise ceases; a value defining the infrastructure level and quality; a threshold over which new enterprises are introduced; a function polling the average heat (of the whole grid).

The environment affects the heat dispersion over the grid and, based on the parameter described above, allows new enterprises to join the world.

5.3 Enterprise Agents

This is the most important and central type of agent in the model. Its behavior is based on the reactive paradigm, i.e.: stimulus-reaction. The goal for these agents is that of surviving in the environment (i.e.: never go under the minimum allowed heat threshold). They are endowed with a heat level (energy) that will be consumed when performing actions. They feature a unique ID, a coordinate system (to track their position on the lattice), and a real number identifying the heat they own. The most important feature of the enterprise agent is a matrix identifying which competences (processes) it can dispose of. In the first row, each position of the vector identifies a specific competence, and is equal to 1, if disposed of, or to 0 if lacking. A second row is used to identify internal competences or outsourced ones (in that case, the ID of the lender is memorized). A third row is used to store a value to identify the owned competences developed after a phase of internal exploration, to distinguish them from those possessed from the beginning. Besides, an enterprise can be "settled", or "not settled", meaning that it joined the world, but is still looking for the best position on the territory through its emissary. The enterprise features a wired original behavior: internally or externally explorative. This is the default behavior, the one with which an enterprise is born, but it can be changed under certain circumstances. This means that an enterprise can be naturally oriented to internal explorative strategy (preferring to develop new processes internally), but can act the opposite way, if it considers it can be more convenient. Of course, the externally explorative enterprises have a different bias from internally explorative ones, when deciding what strategy to actually take.

Finally, the enterprise keeps track of its collaborators (i.e.: the list of enterprise with whom it is exchanging competencies and making synergies) and has a parameters defining the minimum number of competencies it expects to find, in order to form a joint. The main goal for each enterprise is that of acquiring competences, both through internal (e.g.: research and development) and external exploration (e.g.: forming new links with other enterprises). The enterprises are rewarded with heat based on the number of competences they possess (different, parameterized weights for internal or external ones), that is spread in the surrounding territory, thus slowly evaporating, and is used for internal and external exploration tasks.

5.4 Emissary Agents

These are agents that strictly belong to the enterprises, and are to be seen as probes able to move on the territory and detect information about it. They are used in two different situation: 1) if the enterprise is not settled yet (just appeared on the territory) it's sent out to find the best place where to settle. 2) If the enterprise is already settled and chooses to explore externally, an emissary is sent out to find the best possible partners. In both cases, the emissary, that has a field of vision limited to the surrounding 8 cells, probes the territory for heat and moves following the hottest cells. When it finds an enterprise in a cell, it probes its competencies and compares them to those possessed by its chief enterprise verifying if these are a good complement (according to the parameter described in the previous section). In the first case, the enterprise is settled in a cell which is near the best enterprise found during the movement. In the second case, the enterprise asks the best found for collaboration). While moving, the emissary consumes a quantum of heat, that is directly dependant on the quality of infrastructures of the environment.

5.5 Main Iterations

The main iterations for the simulation model are described in this section. At step 0, a lattice is created *(X, Y)*. A number n of enterprises are created, *k* of them internally explorative and *n-k* of them externally explorative. X, Y, n, and k are set by the user, before the simulation starts. At step 1, the environment checks if some enterprise reached the minimum heat threshold; if so, removes it from the world. After that, each enterprise, if idle (not doing anything) decides what behavior to follow. At step 2, all the enterprises that selected to be EE move their emissary by one cell. All the IE ones work on the R&D cycle (one step at a time). At step 3, the EE enterprises check if the emissary finished its energy and, in that case, ask the best found enterprise for collaboration (they can receive a positive or negative reply, based on the needs of the other enterprise). The IE enterprises check if R&D process is finished and, in that case, get a competence in a random position (that can be already occupied by an owned competences, thus wasting the work done). At step 4, the environment scatters the heat according to its parameters. Loop from step 1.

5.6 Parameters in the Model

At the beginning of a simulation, the user can change the core parameters, in order to create a particular scenario to study.

Some of the parameters are constituted by a scalar value, others are in percentage, others are used to define stochastic (normal) distributions, given their mean value and their variance. Here follows a synthetic explanation for the individual parameters:

Maximum number of steps: is the number of iterations in the model. 0 sets the unbounded mode

Initial number of enterprises: is the number of enterprise agents present at start-up (0 is random)

Initial heat for enterprise: a normal distribution setting the initial energy for each enterprise, given the mean and the variance

Number of competences: the length of the vector, equal for all the enterprises (metaphorically representing the complexity of the sector in which they operate)

Competences possessed at start-up: a normal distribution referring to how many processes an enterprise owns internally, given the mean and the variance

Threshold for new enterprise to enter the market: a delta in the average heat of the world, after which a new enterprise is attracted in the market

Infrastructure quality: affects the cost of external exploration

Minimum heat threshold: level under which an enterprise cease

Minimum percentage of competences to share for link creation: when asked for a competences exchange, the other enterprise looks at this value to decide whether to create a link or not

Emissary step cost: percentage of the heat possessed by the enterprise spent for each step of its emissary, during external exploration task

Internal exploration duration: quantity of steps for internally developing a new competence

Internal exploration cost: percentage of the heat possessed by the enterprise spent for each step of internal exploration

Environment control cycles: quantity of steps for sampling the average heat of the environment

Heat dispersion index: percentage of heat evaporated at each step

Lattice dimension: the dimension of the grid hosting the enterprise (i.e.: the whole environment)

Internal Exploration cost: "una tantum" cost for setting up an emissary for external exploration

Propensity to External Exploration for new enterprises: when a new enterprise enters the market, it looks at the average number of links in the network. If more than this value, it behaves as externally explorative, otherwise internally explorative

Number of initial enterprises doing external exploration: variable to divide the initial behavior

Value of internal/external competence: reward (heat) given for each internal/external competence possessed

6   Qualitative Results

While the main object of this paper is to present the model itself as a tool for studying the effects of process innovation on enterprise networks, in the present paragraph some insights will be given about preliminary results obtained from the model itself. The presented ones will be mainly qualitative results, although the model can give many quantitative individual and aggregate results. In particular, a *"computational only"* mode is present in the model, allowing it to perform a *multi-run* batch execution. This is done according to the theory presented in [15]: the model is executed a defined number of times (chosen by the user) and the different outputs are sampled and collected at every *n* steps (again, n decidable by the user) with the same parameters (in order to overcome sampling effects that could be caused by stochastic distributions) or by changing one parameter at a time by a discrete step, in order to carry on a *ceteris paribus* analysis on the model.

While this kind of analysis will be discussed in detail in future works, here some qualitative and semi-quantitative outputs will be discussed, obtained from the model. The model can give the following different kinds of outputs, when running in *"normal"* mode: 1) a real-time graph, depicting the social network, in which the nodes are the enterprises, whose color represent the behavior they are following at a given step, and the links are the ties indicating two or more enterprises mutually exchanging one or more competences. 2) A set of charts, showing in real time some core parameters, namely: *average heat in the environment, number of links (in the network), number of links (average), number of enterprises doing internal exploration, number of ceased enterprises since the beginning, number of born enterprises since the beginning, number of available competences (overall), total number of skills possessed at the beginning, obtained by external exploration, obtained by internal exploration.*

In figures 1, 2 and 3, the output graph is depicted at times 0 (no links), 100 and 500. These pictures belong to the same simulation, so the parameters are the same for all of them, with the only variation of time, giving a hint about the development of the enterprise network. In figure 1 the initial state of the network is shown, where no ties have been created, yet. A total of 20 enterprises is on the territory, 10 of which have an internally explorative behavior and the other 10 have an externally explorative mood. Internal competences are rewarded 10% more than external ones, but internal exploration strategy (e.g.: research & development) is 30% more expensive.

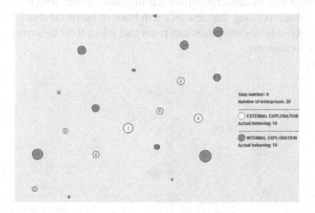

Fig. 1. The network at time 0

After 100 steps (figure 2) some new players have entered the market (an average of 1 new enterprise each 10 steps), meaning that the average heat of the system increased significantly; this can be thought as a starting network, attracting new players thanks to a good overall balance. Some ties have formed and many new competences (the dimension of enterprises) have been internally produced. After the initial steps in which 50% of the enterprise was doing internal exploration, now at the 100th step, only one third (i.e.: 33%) is doing that, since almost all the smaller players are trying to outsource them from the bigger ones, in order to gain some energy.

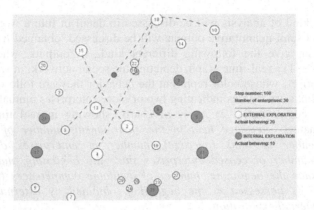

Fig. 2. The network at time 100

Unfortunately, many of these small enterprises have no competence to give to the bigger one in exchange for theirs. They will eventually die (ceased enterprises) or try to change strategy, by starting an internal exploration. That's why at time 500 (figure 3) the total number of players increased again, but at a lower rate (1 every 15 steps, as an average) and now, in percentage, most of the survived enterprises are doing external exploration (62% circa) and have become quite big (many internal competences possessed). Notice that in this experiment the threshold under which an enterprise must cease is a low value, meaning that few of them have to leave the market. This was done intentionally to show how enterprises can react and adapt their behavior even if they are modeled as reactive agents.

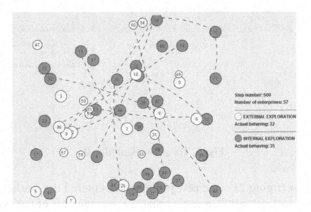

Fig. 3. The network at time 500

6.1 Introduction of Process Innovation

The impact of innovation diffusion on the network depends on the collaboration degree of the system. If the network is collaborative the diffusion of innovation strengthens the ties and increases the number of the links among organizations. The firms are more inclined to exchange competences than to create them inside the organization: they favor an externally explorative behavior that obviously strengthens the network. A feature referred to as "*shock mode*" is used in this section, allowing the user to stop the model at a given step, and change some inner parameter. For example, it is possible to add a specific competence to one enterprise only, so that it's the only one in all the network possessing it. In that way it becomes possible to study how and based on which dynamics this specific competence spreads on the network and which kind of competitive advantage it gives, in terms of central position in the network and bargaining power to obtain other competences not possessed internally.

In particular, here this is used to introduce a process innovation, in the form of a totally new competence; all the enterprises can achieve it, but only one of them possesses it at a starting point.

As shown in figure 4 and figure 5, where some other output graphs obtained from the E³ simulation model are depicted, a collaborative network (A1) is defined by the existence of a large number of strong ties (compared to the number of enterprises). In our example, there are 10 strong ties among the enterprises. In a network structured in this way, the introduction and consequent diffusion of an innovation strengthens the collaborations through:

- An higher number of ties
- Ties that get even stronger (A2). In particular, the existing links get stronger and new ties are created ex novo.

In this case, the "shock effect" defined as the introduction of a process innovation brings effects in the networks that affect the decree of collaboration of the network itself. The introduction of an innovation in the network strengthens the links among the enterprises and the collaboration efficiency increases.

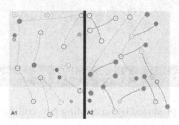

Fig. 4. Collaborative network before (A1) and after (A2) the introduction of an innovation

On the other side, in the case of a network with low propensity to collaboration the strong links do not exist or are a few when compared to the number of enterprises. The introduction of innovation in a network structured in this way can affect the degree of collaboration of the enterprises, according to industry complexity. In this situation (B1), it's possible to notice two different scenarios.

If industry complexity is not too high (e.g.: the textile industry), as represented in B2, the number of ties is low and the firms prefer to create innovation inside the

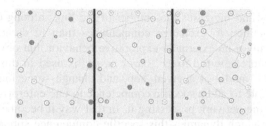

Fig. 5. Non-collaborative network before (B1) the introduction of an innovation. After (B2) in case of non complex industry, and after (B3) in case of complex industry.

organization than receiving it from other organizations: in this case the firms favor internal exploration. So, when the complexity is low, the propensity to collaboration does not change and the enterprises are still loosely connected. The number of links could even increase, but much more slowly compared to the case of a collaborative network (B2 vs A2). If industry complexity is high (B3), the diffusion of innovation increases the number of ties (but less than in a collaborative network) but the structure of ties is weak: in this case, again, the firms prefer an externally explorative behavior. So, in this case, the propensity to collaborate gets higher than before after the introduction of an innovation, but the links are always weaker when compared to the case of a collaborative network (B3 vs A2).

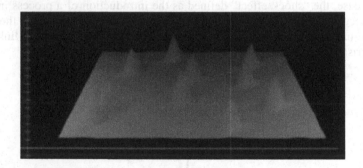

Fig. 6. "Heat" produced by an existing non-collaborative network

This qualitative analysis carried on through an agent based model allow to study "in the lab" a social system, like an enterprise network, and to study the effects of an innovation on collaborative and non-collaborative networks. While the purpose of this work is the description of the model itself, the qualitative results in this section show that the innovation diffusion in a network can create new ties among the enterprises (and thus it can be regarded as a driver for links creation in a network). Though, only in a collaborative network, or in a non-collaborative network acting in a complex industry, the number of the links increases significantly, while in non-collaborative networks acting in an industry which is not too complex, the number of links among the enterprises stays more or less the same, even after the introduction of the innovation (the enterprises being more focused on internal explorative behavior).

Another kind of view is given in figures 6 and 7; this 3D graph shows how the environmental heat (see paragraph III.A) is scattered, according to and after the evolution of the network.

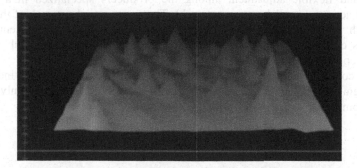

Fig. 7. The same network with new players and new joints

It's quite evident that the 3D plain in figure 7 is at an higher global level, when compared to that in figure 6, thanks to the new links increasing the global value of the system. Besides, new peaks appeared (the new players that entered the market).

6.2 An Empirical Evidence

In order to propose an empirical validation of the obtained results two real world scenarios have been considered: Silicon Valley and Route 128. While the former succeeded in adapting to the transformations of the environment, the latter seems to be losing its competitive strength. Despite the similar origins, these regions developed different industrial systems: their different response to the crises happened during the 80s made clear the differences of productive organization whose significance had been underestimated during the quick economic growth of the first decade. During the 70s both Silicon Valley, in Northern California, and Route 128, near Boston, were highly praised by the World for being the leading edges in technological advances in Electronics. Both were honored for their technical vitality, entrepreneurship, and incredible economic growth. The two realities had a similar beginning: university research and post-war financing.

At the beginning of the 80s, the enchant rapidly vanished; the chip producers, located in the Silicon Valley, lost their market to the Japanese competitors, while the producers of mini-computers, located in the Route 128 area, saw the passage of their customers to workstations and personal computers. Notwithstanding the two economies took very different roads; in the Silicon Valley a new generation of enterprises rose, producing semi-conductors and computers, joining the big players already settled. The success of realities like Sun Microsystems, Conner Peripherals and Cypress Semiconductor, along with the dynamism of companies like Intel and Hewlett-Packard proved that Silicon Valley had recovered its previous vitality. On the contrary, Route 128 showed few signs of recovery and, by the end of the decade, most of the producers located there had given away their crown to those settled in Silicon Valley, that became the headquarter of more than one third of the technology societies created after 1965. The market value of these companies increased of 25 billions, when compared to 1 billion of those located in the Route 128 area.

Silicon Valley region features has an industrial system which promotes collective learning and flexible adjustment among the producers specialized in a series of connected activities (collaborative network). The dense social network of this region, along with the open labor market, encourage research and entrepreneurship; the companies compete among them, but at the same time learn from each other and exchange competences to face the market.

On the contrary, the enterprises in the Route 128 region are fewer and independent among them (non-collaborative network), whose industrial system is mainly based on internal competences, not shared with others (figure 8).

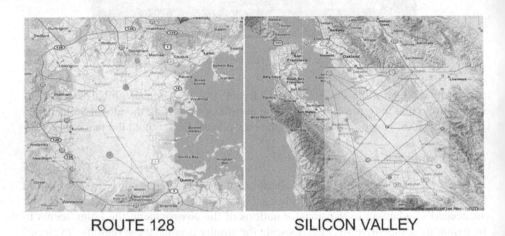

ROUTE 128   SILICON VALLEY

Fig. 8. A "collage" of geographical maps and the output from the model

The two scenarios look alike those exemplified in the previous paragraph; while Silicon Valley resembles the example shown in A1-A2, Route 128 is similar to the one seen in B1-B3. Even if in a simplistic way, this real world case constitutes an empirical evidence supporting the qualitative results coming from the E^3 model, and clarifies what kind of analyses can be carried on through this simulation tool.

7 Conclusion and Outlook

Process innovation is characterized by two important aspects: one critical and typical aspect is the ability to gather, develop and transform information and knowledge in a potential competitive advantage. The second aspect regards spending resources like time and money: the development of process innovation is usually time and resource consuming and is difficult to attain, especially when referring to radical cases.

Though, process innovation is a key factor for building a network for competences exchange and a very important variable when considering the strategies performed by an enterprise; once possessed, the advantage can be exploited or shared. In the first case, the enterprise can gain customers and money, by being the only one (or among the few ones) possessing it. But it risks to lose its advantage as soon as other players can develop it. Another strategy is that of sharing the process innovation, in exchange for other competencies and/or money.

An agent based model is introduced in this work, aiming at capturing the dynamics behind the creation and the following modifications of an enterprise network for competences exchange, i.e.: a network in which enterprises can internally develop and/or share processes with other players. This is, by the way, one of the focal points behind the creation of industrial districts, enterprise clusters and so on. A well established network of this kind can attract new players, that will probably bring new knowledge and competences in it.

The model is formally discussed in detail, and so the agents composing it and its iterations. While studying quantitative results is beyond the purpose of this work, a qualitative analysis is described, and the network graph, one of the graphical outputs supplied by the model, is analyzed: in order to show how network dynamics emerge from the model and its parameters, settable by the user.

At the beginning, when the enterprises have few competences and high perception of how can be difficult develop and innovation process, they try to link with the enterprises that have already developed innovative processes. That's why, in an initial phase, the number of enterprises doing external exploration tends to increase. After some steps, the number of enterprises choosing external exploration is lower and lower and limited to the smallest players, or the newly arrived ones. The reason is that at the beginning, the enterprise's capability are low and the perception of the effort for developing a process innovation is high. The enterprise at this phase typically try to share and exchange competences with others that have already developed the innovative process, not having to face the risk of inside developing, even if this can be more gainful in the long run. As time passes by, the enterprises start to become bigger and be more conscious about their capabilities and knowledge, thus reducing the perception of the effort to develop innovative processes internally.

Another qualitative example is given, to show the difference among collaborative and non-collaborative networks, depicted by means of simulation, at the introduction of a process innovation; while in the former process innovation proves to be a driver for new link creation, in the latter the impact is quite smaller and almost irrelevant, especially if the sector is not a complex one.

To empirically validate these qualitative results, and in order to connect them to the real world, two cases are quickly analyzed, resembling those depicted in the computational examples: Silicon Valley and Route 128.

The model is comprehensive and its scope is wide. In future works other features will be described in detail, and also quantitative analysis will be carried on in order to study real-world cases (e.g.: existing industrial districts and so on) and the underlying dynamics that lead to their creations. In particular, computational only mode will be used to study the iterative behavior of networks, in ceteris paribus conditions (i.e.: by changing a single parameter at a time).

References

1. Zaheer, A., Bell, G.G.: Benefiting from network position: firm capabilities, structural holes, and performance. Strategic Management Journal (2005)
2. Koka, B.R., Prescott, J.E.: Designing alliance networks: the influence of network position, environmental change, and strategy on firm performance. Strategic Management Journal (2008)
3. Leonard-Barton, D.: Wellsprings of knowledge. Harvard Business School Press, Boston (1995)
4. Brown, J.S., Duguid, P.: Organizational Learning and Communities of Practice: Toward a Unified View of Working, Learning and Innovation. Organization Science 2, 40–57 (1991)
5. Kogut, B.: Joint ventures: theorical and empirical perspectives. Strategic Management journal (1988)
6. Moreno, J.L., with foreword by White, W.A.: Who shall survive? A new approach to the problem of human interrelations. Nervous and Mental Disease Publishing Co., Washington; Psych. Abs. 8, 5153 (revised edition published by Beacon House in 1953. Psych. Abs. 28, 4178)
7. Harary, F.: Mathematical aspect of electrical network analysis (1969)
8. Gulati, R., Gargiulo, M.: Where do interorganizational networks come from? American Journal of Sociology 104(5), 1439–1493 (1999)
9. Gulati, R., Nohria, N., Zaheer, A.: Strategic networks. Strategic Management Journal 21(3), 203–215 (2000)
10. Gulati, R.: Alliances and networks. Strategic Management Journal, Special Issue 19(4), 293–317 (1998)
11. Burt, R.S.: Structural Holes. Harvard University Press, Cambridge (1982)
12. Nohria, N.: The Differentiated Network: Organizing Multinational Corporations for Value Creation (1997)
13. Phlippen, S., Riccaboni, M.: Radical Innovation and Network Evolution (2007)
14. Remondino, M.: Agent Based Process Simulation and Metaphors Based Approach for Enterprise and Social Modeling. In: ABS 4 Proceedings, pp. 93–97. SCS Europ. Publish. House (2003) ISBN 3-936-150-25-7
15. Remondino, M., Correndo, G.: MABS Validation Through Repeated Execution and Data Mining Analisys. International Journal of SIMULATION: Systems, Science & Technology (IJS3T) 7 (September 2006), ISSN: 1473-8031
16. Sherer: Innovation and Growth: Schumpeterian Perspectives (2007)
17. Srivardhana, T., Pawlowskiv, S.D.: ERP systems as an enabler of sustained business process innovation: A knowledge-based view. Science Direct (2007)
18. Rowley, T., Behrens, D., Krackhardt, D.: Redundant goverance structures: An analysis of structural and relational embeddedness in the steel and semiconductor industries. Strategic Management Journal 21, 369–386 (2000)
19. Davenport, T.H., Short, J.E.: The New Industrial Engineering: Information Technology and Business Process Redesign. Sloan Management Review, 11–27 (Summer 1990)
20. Edquist, C.: The Systems of Innovation Approach and Innovation Policy: An account of the state of the art. Paper presented at DRUID Conference, Aalborg, June 12-15 (2001)

Wide-Area Traffic Simulation Based on Driving Behavior Model

Yuu Nakajima, Yoshiyuki Nakai, Hattori Hiromitsu, and Toru Ishida

Department of Social Informatics, Kyoto University
Yoshida-Honmachi, Sakyo-ku, Kyoto, 606-8501, Japan
{nkjm,hatto,ishida}@i.kyoto-u.ac.jp,
nakai@ai.soc.i.kyoto-u.ac.jp

Abstract. Multiagent-based simulations are a key part of several research fields. Multiagent-based simulations yield multiagent societies that well reproduce human societies, and so are seen as an excellent tool for analyzing the real world. A multiagent-based simulation allows crowd behavior to emerge through interactions among agents where each agent is affected by the emerging crowd behavior. The interaction between microscopic and macroscopic behaviors has long been considered an important issue, termed the "micro-macro problem", in the field of sociology, but research on the issue is still premature in the engineering domain. We are focusing on citywide traffic as a target problem and are attempting to realize mega-scale multiagent-based traffic simulations. While macro-level simulations are popular in the traffic domain, it has been recognized that micro-level analysis is also beneficial. However, there is no software platform that can realize analyses based on both micro and macro viewpoints due to implementation difficulties. In this paper, we propose a traffic simulation platform that can execute citywide traffic simulations that include driving behavior models. Our simulation platform enables the introduction of individual behavior models while still retaining scalability.

1 Introduction

Simulation methodologies fall into two main categories; macro simulation and micro simulation. In macro simulations, the subjects are modeled from the macroscopic viewpoint and expressed using governing equations. The macro simulation methodology is suitable for the analysis of physical phenomena because there are obvious and uniform rules/mechanisms that well explain the subjects behaviors, *i.e.* physical laws. On the other hand, it is inadequate to replicate the social phenomena that emerge from human-human interactions because a human's decision-making mechanism is imprecise and diverse. For such phenomena, micro simulations are to be preferred. Micro simulations allow each entity to be distinctly represented so we can replicate societies consisting of humans in a natural way.

Multiagent-based simulation, one version of micro simulation, has been applied in various research fields [1,2,3]. Multiagent-based simulation yields

J.-J. Yang et al. (Eds.): PRIMA 2009, LNAI 5925, pp. 459–470, 2009.

multiagent societies that well reproduce human societies, and so are seen as an excellent tool for analyzing the real world. In a multiagent-based simulation, crowd behavior can emerge though interactions among agents while each agent can be impacted by the emerging behavior. The relation between individual behavior and crowd behavior is known to be an important problem, the "micro-macro problem", in the sociology domain. Current platforms, however, are not powerful enough to resolve this problem.

This paper has citywide traffic as its target problem. To understand citywide traffic, the analysis must combine two different viewpoints. The micro-level analysis (e.g. driving behavior) is achieved by considering the individual's viewpoint, while the macro-level analysis (e.g. congestion analysis) requires a consideration of the crowd viewpoint. No existing simulation platform can provide the power and sophistication needed. Additionally, almost all previous works on multiagent traffic simulations, which can represent a human driver as an agent, assumed that each agent has the same driving style [4,5,6]. For example, in [4], each agent chooses a driving route based on his/her own preferences. Unfortunately, there is no diversity in route choice mechanisms among the agents.

In this paper, we propose a traffic simulation platform that can execute citywide traffic simulations with individual driving behavior models. Our simulation platform realizes both scalability and the introduction of individual behavior models. Our platform can execute both micro and macro analyses and we can analyze the effect of micro-level behaviors on the macro-level traffic.

The remainder of this paper is as follows. Section 2 describes our approach to traffic analysis through multiagent-based simulations. We propose a simulation platform architecture and implementation in Sections 3 and 4 and demonstrate an application example in Section 5.

2 Overview of Mega-Scale Traffic Simulations with Diverse Behavior Models

Figure 1 shows an overview of the challenges faced when trying to realize mega-scale multiagent-based traffic simulations with intimate driving behavior models. Following our participatory modeling perspectives [7], we have already developed a driver modeling methodology [8,9] as explained in the next section. The next technical issue is how to run large-scale simulations with driving behavior models obtained from human subjects. We elaborate the design and implement the first prototype of the simulator.

2.1 Extracting Driver Model

The key factor in constructing multiagent-based simulations is agent modeling. This is because collective phenomena emerge from the local behaviors of many agents; that is, the simulation result depends on each agent's micro-level behavior. Most existing studies, however, use simple or abstract agent models [6,10,11].

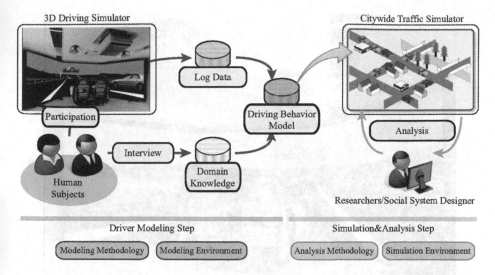

Fig. 1. Overview of analysis process of city traffic with multiagent based simulation

For handling the diverse characteristics of drivers, we extract a driver model from each human subject. The process of this approach, called participatory driver modeling, is shown in the left part of Fig. 1.

During participatory driver modeling, we construct driving behavior models from human driving data by collaborating with the human subjects. Using the participatory modeling technique allows us to construct behavior models from not only our (modeler's) knowledge, but the actual behavior of the human subjects. The modeling process consists of the following five steps.

1. Use a 3D virtual driving simulator to collect realistic driving log data from human subjects. The 3D virtual driving simulator has a lifelike cockpit and a wide screen for displaying the virtual environment (see Figure 2).
2. Together with domain experts, identify individual driving behaviors by investigating collected log data. Figure 3 is one example of a chart made from log data. This example shows the transition in speed (the graph on the top), acceleration (graph second from the top), and the usage of accelerator/brake (graphs on the bottom) for a virtual road that includes curves and slopes. Because of the joint work with traffic engineers, we could access the extensive log data that they had accumulated.
3. Collect prior knowledge constituting a driving behavior model by interviewing the subjects of the driving simulation. We interview some subjects to collect driving rules, which contain domain knowledge. We used screen shots of the 3D simulator and charts showing speed, acceleration, and the usage of accelerator/brake in order to make it easy for the subjects to remember his/her behavior in the simulation. We then construct unique driving models, which can explain each driver's behavior, by the application of hypothetical reasoning.

462   Y. Nakajima et al.

Fig. 2. A 3D virtual driving simulator used for collecting driving log data

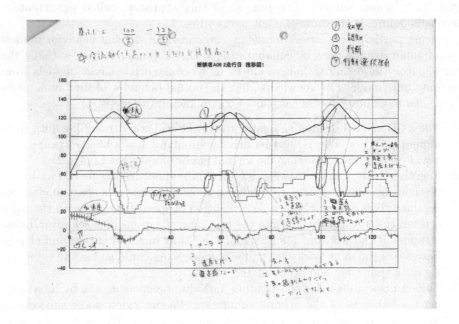

Fig. 3. An example of a chart made from driving log data. Circles on the graph represent the subject's specific behaviors identified by traffic engineers.

4. Select meaningful prior knowledge and represent it in formal expressions.
5. Construct a driving behavior model that can explain the human subject's actions based on hypothetical reasoning [12]. The precise algorithm used is described in [13].

2.2 Execute Multiagent-Based Simulations with Intricate Driver Agents

Multiagent simulations are a promising tool with which to analyze the effects of local driving behavior on the entire traffic pattern. We built a multiagent-based simulation platform that can execute citywide traffic simulations with intricate driver agent models (see the right part of Fig. 1).

Previous traffic simulation research consists of either local driving behavior on single roads or route selection on a road network. Research on local driving behavior has considered observations and actions about road geometry, signals, and surrounding cars. Research on route selection has lead to the modeling of decision processes and route utility functions.

We assume that there is some interaction between local driving behavior and route selection. What we need is to analyze how local driving behavior affects citywide traffic patterns. Therefore, the simulation platform must be able to incorporate both driving behavior models and route selection models.

For example, we want to analyze the traffic environment created by aged drivers because driver behavior changes with age and the number of aged drivers is increasing in Japan. We extract driver models for several age groups and execute large-scale multiagent-based simulations for estimating the traffic patterns yielded by large numbers of aged people.

It is difficult to execute driving behavior simulation in the whole traffic environment because the calculation cost becomes enormous. Therefore, the driving simulations in this paper examine only a major road; other simulations consider a simple road network.

3 Architecture

Our proposed platform can deal with intricate driving behavior when analyzing the relation between personal driving behavior and crowd behavior. The architecture of our platform is shown in Fig. 4. This platform has three layers.

- **Mental layer**
  Mental layer receives road network data and OD (Origin-Destination) data. Road network data describes road status and OD data consists of tuples of starting point and destination point of agents. In the mental layer, an agent is regarded as the entity performing route selection. The agent sets the route that has minimum cost considering map information and previous simulation results. A route plan consists of paths, mode choice, daily activity and so on.

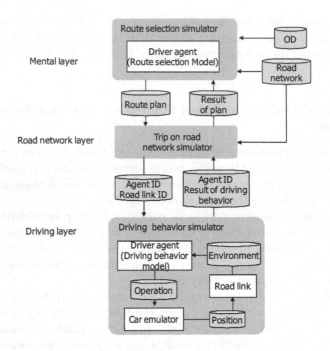

Fig. 4. Platform Achitecture

– **Road network layer**

Road network layer receives a route plan from each driver agent on the mental layer. In the road network layer, the agent is regarded as the plan executor. A road network is abstracted as a network consists of nodes and links. The agent acquires location information on node and link basis. The agent moves along road network so as not to violate road network constraints. Road network layer sends agent ID and road ID to driving layer, when the agent enters the road that the social system designer is focused on.

– **Driving layer**

Driving layer receives agent ID and road ID from road network layer. In the driving layer, the agent is regarded as a virtual driver and vehicle. They move over a 2D space rather than an abstract road network.

If the simulator was forced to calculate the driving behavior on all roads, the computational cost would be too high. Therefore, in our architecture, driving behaviors are only simulated on certain roads which an social system designer pays attention to, for example, which are applied the new rule of traffic law.

The execution process is summarized as follows. When an agent enters the area of interest, the wide area traffic simulator invokes the driving behavior simulator and sends agent ID to it. The driving behavior simulator orders the corresponding driver agent to initiate the decision making cycle. Driver agent decides the operation commands for acceleration/braking/steering based on his/her driving model and road condition. Driver agent sends its decisions to the vehicle module. Vehicle module transforms acceleration/brake/steering operations into an acceleration vector according to the vehicle's specification.

4   Implementation

We implement a platform using the proposed architecture. We combined the traffic simulation tool kit MATSim[1], which is a large-scale multiagent-based traffic simulation platform, with our driving behavior simulator. MATSim has been applied to estimate the traffic of real cities such as Zurich [4] and Berlin [14].

MATSim manages mental layer and road network layer. We combined driving layer to MATSim. These three layers are described precisely in following section.

4.1   Route Selection Simulator

The route selection simulator calculates the average trip time of each road based on the traffic information of the previous day. The agents decide the best route considering the trip time and their activity plan.

The route selection simulator receives road network and the execution result of previous plan from the road network simulator.

4.2   Road Network Simulator

We use QueueSimulation in MATSim as the road network simulator. In QueueSimulation, the road network consists of road links and road nodes. Each road link is associated with a running queue and a waiting queue. Road link parameters imply the physical form of the road.

Figure 5 describes the execution process of road link and road node.

- **Process of road link**
  Road link put driver agents who enter the road into the running queue. Road link assumes that the driver agents can drive at any speed up to some limit which is decided by the road's physical form and speed limits. When the driver agent arrives at the end of the road link, it is popped from the running and pushed into the waiting queue.
- **Process of road node**
  Road node pops a driver agent from the waiting queue and pushes it onto the running queue of the next road link, if the running queue on the next road link has enough space.

The road network simulator abstracts the driver agents as homogeneous grains on abstracted road networks, not two dimensional spaces.

---

[1] http://www.matsim.org/

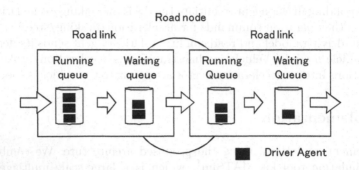

Fig. 5. Road link and road node

4.3 Driving Behavior Simulator

The driving behavior simulator calculates vehicle behavior with each driver model. On the driving behavior simulator, the driver agents are assumed as heterogeneous grains. The driver agents are mapped on two dimensional spaces.

Figure 6 shows the architecture that combines the driving layer with the road network layer. The main components of the driving layer are driver agent and vehicle module. The driver agents decide their operations through the following steps.

1. **Ovservation**
   Driver agent observes surrounding environment. He observes state of own car, surrounding cars, and the roads in the immediate vicinity.
2. **Recognision**
   Drivers may not be able to recognize all observed information. This step filters the observed information based on the driver's characteristic. For example, an aged driver is unable to mentally map the surrounding traffic situation as quickly as a young driver.
3. **Decision**
   Driver agents decide their acceleration/brake/steering operations according to the recognized information.
4. **Execution**
   The driver agents execute the acceleration/brake/steering operations. This involves not only setting the accelerator/brake/steering values directly but also execute sequential acts such as changing lane.

Each vehicle module holds car specifications, such as size, maximum speed, fuel consumption, car type, type of fuel, etc. Vehicle module and driver agent are separated. Vehicle module converts the operations set by the driver agent into acceleration/deceleration.

When a driver agent enters the especial road, the driver agents send agent ID to the driving layer, and then the driving layer calculates driving behavior of

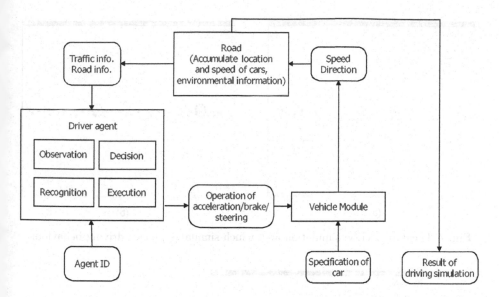

Fig. 6. Construction of driving layer

the corresponding driver agent. Driver agents observe the simulated road environment, recognize the observed information, decide car operation, and execute the operation.

5 Application Example

Street parking in urban areas is a major cause of traffic jams. If many cars try to use a road link with a lot of parked cars, the capacity of the link becomes small. Drivers do not like links with small capacity, and will thus change their routes.

To see the micro-macro link effect in the case of street parking, two sample scenarios were run on Kyoto City's road network using our simulator. The wide-area simulation is queue based, and only the street indicated by arrow in Fig. 8 was simulated about driving behavior in detail.

– **First scenario**
There are 500 driver agents. All agents leave Kyoto Station at 6:30 and their goal is Yasaka Shrine. Boxes are cars and there are no parked cars in the street as shown in Fig. 7 (a). This street is indicated by arrow in Fig. 8 (a).
– **Second scenario**
There are 500 driver agents. All agents leave Kyoto Station at 6:30 and their goal is Yasaka Shrine. Circled boxes are parked cars and there are parked cars in the street as shown in Fig. 7 (b). This street is indicated by arrow in Fig. 8 (b).

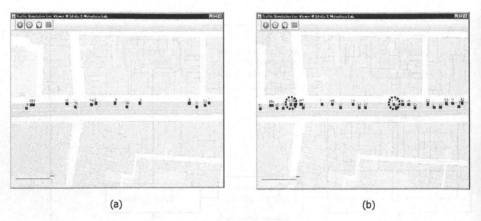

(a)   (b)

Fig. 7. Local area view: simulation area which simulates precice driving behaviour

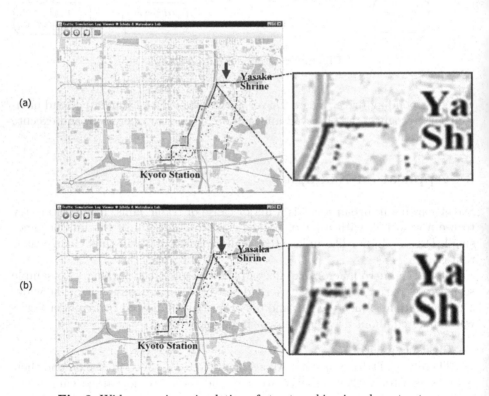

Fig. 8. Wide area view: simulation of street parking in urban streets

Fig. 7 (a) shows the first scenario at the micro level: with no parked cars, the driver agents proceeded smoothly. Fig. 7 (b) shows the second scenario: the same street with some parked cars, the driver agents tried to move around stopped cars and the traffic flow became jam.

Figure 8 (a) shows the first scenario at the macro level: driver agents found several routes and chose one as they like, and (b) shows the second scenario: a few agents changed their routes to the north street or the south street to avoid the jam caused by the parked cars.

6 Conclusion

Multiagent-based simulations yield multiagent societies that well reproduce human societies, and so are seen as an excellent tool for analyzing the real world. In a multiagent-based simulation, agents interact with each other and generate crowd behavior. Moreover, crowd behavior can influence agents. The relation between personal behavior and crowd behavior is taken to be an important problem in the domain of sociology, unlike the domain of engineering.

The platform proposed in this paper enables us to analyze how micro driving behavior affects to large area traffic patterns in a city. We demonstrate the effect of street parking in urban streets as an example.

In future work, we will extract driver models of several age groups and execute large-scale multiagent-based simulations for estimating the traffic patterns created by many aged people.

Acknowledgment

We would like to thank Mr. Satoshi Yokota, Mr. Masahiro Okada and Mr. Atsushi Yamada at ASTEM (Advanced Scientific Technology & Management Research Institute of KYOTO) for their various help in the implementation process. This work was supported by Panasonic Corp. - Kyoto University Joint Research: Crowd Navigation for Region EMS Considering Individual Behaviors and Preferences and Kyoto University Global COE Program: Informatics Education and Research Center for Knowledge-Circulating Society.

References

1. Jacyno, M., Bullock, S., Luck, M., Payne, T.: Emergent service provisioning and demand estimation through self-organizing agent communities. In: Proceedings of the 8th International Joint Conference on Autonomous Agents and Multiagent Systems (AAMAS 2009), pp. 481–488 (2009)
2. Tesfatsion, L.S.: Introduction to the special issue on agent-based computational economics. Journal of Economic Dynamics & Control 25(3-4), 281–293 (2001)
3. Vasirani, M., Ossowski, S.: A market-inspired approach to reservation-based urban road traffic management. In: Proceedings of the 8th International Joint Conference on Autonomous Agents and Multiagent Systems (AAMAS 2009), pp. 617–624 (2009)
4. Balmer, M., Cetin, N., Nagel, K., Raney, B.: Towards truly agent-based traffic and mobility simulations. In: 3rd International Joint Conference on Autonomous Agents and Multiagent Systems, AAMAS 2004, pp. 60–67 (2004)

5. Halle, S., Chaib-draa, B.: A collaborative driving system based on multiagent modelling and simulations. Journal of Transportation Research Part C 13, 320–345 (2005)
6. Panait, L.: A pheromone-based utility model for collaborative foraging. In: Proceedings of the 3rd International Joint Conference on Autonomous Agents and Multiagent Systems (AAMAS 2004), pp. 36–43 (2004)
7. Ishida, T., Nakajima, Y., Murakami, Y., Nakanishi, H.: Augmented experiment: Participatory design with multiagent simulation. In: International Joint Conference on Artificial Intelligence (IJCAI 2007), pp. 1341–1346 (2007)
8. Tanaka, Y., Nakajima, Y., Hattori, H., Ishida, T.: A driver modeling methodology using hypothetical reasoning for multiagent traffic simulation. In: Ghose, A., Governatori, G., Sadananda, R. (eds.) PRIMA 2007. LNCS (LNAI), vol. 5044, pp. 278–287. Springer, Heidelberg (2009)
9. Hattori, H., Nakajima, Y., Ishida, T.: Agent modeling with individual human behaviors. In: Proceedings of the 8th International Conference on Autonomous Agents and Multiagent Systems (AAMAS 2009), pp. 1369–1370 (2009)
10. Moyaux, T., Chaib-draa, B., D'Amours, S.: Multi-agent simulation of collaborative strategies in a supply chain. In: 3rd International Joint Conference on Autonomous Agents and Multiagent Systems, AAMAS 2004, pp. 52–59 (2004)
11. Yamashita, T., Izumi, K., Kurumatani, K., Nakashima, H.: Smooth traffic flow with a cooperative car navigation system. In: AAMAS 2005, pp. 478–485. ACM Press, New York (2005)
12. Poole, D.: Theorist: A logical reasoning system for defaults and diagnosis. In: The Knowledge Frontier. Springer, Heidelberg (1987)
13. Murakami, Y., Sugimoto, Y., Ishida, T.: Modeling human behavior for virtual training systems. In: AAAI 2005, pp. 127–132 (2005)
14. Illenberger, J., Flotterod, G., Nagel, K.: Enhancing matsim with capabilities of within-day re-planning. In: Intelligent Transportation Systems Conference (ITSC 2007), pp. 94–99 (2007)

An Agent-Based Framework for Healthcare Support System

Hideyuki Takahashi[1], Satoru Izumi[1,2], Takuo Suganuma[1,2],
Tetsuo Kinoshita[2,3], and Norio Shiratori[1,2]

[1] Research Institute of Electrical Communication, Tohoku University
[2] Graduate School of Information Sciences, Tohoku University
[3] Cyberscience Center, Tohoku University,
2-1-1 Katahira, Aoba-ku, Sendai 980-8577, Japan
{hideyuki,izumi,suganuma,norio}@shiratori.riec.tohoku.ac.jp,
kino@riec.tohoku.ac.jp

Abstract. There is a steady increase of number of people who are suffering from lifestyle-related diseases. Although much work has been done on healthcare support system, these existing systems are limited in ability of healthcare support service. This paper proposes an agent-based framework for advanced healthcare support system. In order to provide useful information for healthcare of an object person, not only to him/herself but also to the related people of that person, the system needs to acquire variety of information, knowledge, data, etc. and store/manage them in a systematic manner. This paper mainly focuses on the concept and design of the system, and also we describe the implementation details of several functions for the healthcare.

1 Introduction

Recently the personal health maintenance to prevent lifestyle-related diseases such as obesity, hypertension, and diabetes has been an issue of social concern. With the Information Technologies (IT) development, people have expected IT to give practical solutions to this issue and some research groups have been investigating the solutions from engineering viewpoints [1,2,3]. Ubiquitous computing is a promising technology because it contributes to expand the scope of system support to users' daily lives. Hand-held terminals, wearable vital sensors, wireless communications, etc. are playing important roles in this healthcare application domain [5,6,7,8,9,10,11].

Although much work has been done on healthcare support system, these existing systems are designed by using some specific vital sensors and electronic devices. Therefore they are limited in ability of healthcare support in spite of its wide range of the service domain. To provide useful advice and information for healthcare of an object person, not only to him/herself but also to related people of the object person, the system needs to acquire variety of information, knowledge, data, etc. from real space and store/manage them in a systematic manner. Thus we have to tackle a new design methodology for such large-scale

J.-J. Yang et al. (Eds.): PRIMA 2009, LNAI 5925, pp. 471–486, 2009.

and complex systems which can cope with many kinds and amount of information on the unstable computation environment such as ubiquitous computing environment.

We have been developing an advanced healthcare support system in ubiquitous computing environment [12]. The system provides useful information regarding health condition effectively and in user-oriented manner by utilizing knowledge about healthcare and various kinds of information obtained from real space. This paper describes the concept and design of an agent-based framework for user-oriented healthcare support system. The comprehensive design of our healthcare system is based on symbiotic computing [13], a concept of post-ubiquitous computing with the co-existence of real space and digital space. This paper mainly focuses on the concept, design, and implementation of several functions of our system with our proposed agent-based framework that matches to this kind of complex systems. Employment of such properties as autonomy, cooperativeness, and adaptability of agents, can address the issues. We also show the effectiveness of our prototype system with results of initial experiments.

2   Backgraound

2.1   Existing Healthcare Support System

There are many attempts to assist healthcare support based on IT. We describe existing healthcare support system and summarize their problems.

Various kinds of information about healthcare are provided by administrative organizations on the Web [1]. Several companies have developed a medical device and provide a healthcare service utilizing the device [2].

There are some research groups which developed support systems. The systems can recognize health condition of a user by monitoring user's vital signs using compact sensors, hand-held PCs, and wireless network in ubiquitous computing environment [5,6,7,8]. These existing systems can infer user's behavior, activity, and emergency situation according to the vital signs and location information of the user's by using wearable sensors. There is a method that can automatically recognize what type of exercise the user is doing and how many repetitions he/she has done so far [9]. This method incorporated a three-axis accelerometer into a workout glove to track hand movements and put another accelerometer on the user's waist to track body posture.

One research group which aims to develop a prototype system based on next generation network [3], have studied to offer the high quality healthcare service with sufficient security and protection of user's privacy. They have also developed a health advice derivation system according to the object person's health condition and knowledge [4].

2.2   Problems

In spite of numerous efforts to provide idea healthcare support system, there are some technical problems in existing system as follows.

- **Effective acquisition of various and amount of information for multiple object persons:** The existing studies determine the health condition based on vital sign by specific sensing devices in real-time. The information has limitations for obtaining an accurate estimation of the health condition because the information is obtained by the vital sign limited piece of information on only a certain individual. It would be possible to perceive the health conditions of multiple object persons with greater accuracy using physical location of the persons, environmental information such as ambient temperature and room brightness, and video information of the persons, as well as the vital sign. Because there are the limitation of computational resources and network resources in the ubiquitous computing environment, it is difficult to acquire all the information in real space for multiple object persons. As a result, we have to tackle the effective way of information acquisition from real space.
- **Effective inference mechanism using various kinds of information of real space:** After acquisition of various kinds of information from real space, effective information and real-time service provisioning using the information would be a challenge. The information and data including vital sign, location information, environmental information, multimedia data, specialized knowledge, etc. contain significant diverse aspects in both qualitative and quantitative. We can not cope with these kinds of information and knowledge in real-time by using existing inference mechanism. For actively-provisioning in real-time, we need to consider an effective inference mechanism.
- **Infrastructure of system construction:** There are specialized systems in each area of healthcare. The systems have been developed in an ad-hoc manner. There does not have an infrastructure of system construction to facilitate implementation of systems for various healthcare areas. The infrastructure requires system extendibility to introduce new sensor device, wireless network technology, diagnosis algorithm for analyzing condition of health, DB system etc. in easy ways. We need to consider common software infrastructure containing platform and components dedicated to healthcare support to enhance extendibility and flexibility of system implementation.

3 Concept of Agent-Based Healthcare Support System

3.1 Overview of User-Oriented Healthcare Support System

The concept of our proposed system is shown in Fig. 1. We propose an agent-based framework for user-oriented healthcare support system to solve the problems mentioned in Section 2.2.

Our system aims to assist the object persons and healthcare community members related healthcare support services. The healthcare community members mean the relations of the object person such as family member, sports gym instructor, doctor, etc. to circulate healthcare related information and knowledge effectively. The system obtains information on the object person such as profiles, preferences, medical records, history of exercise, human relation, etc. from

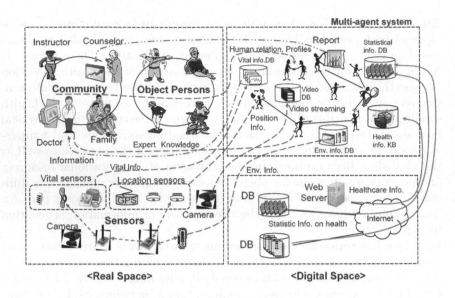

Fig. 1. Concept of agent-based healthcare support system

the community members. The system actively observes the current status of the object person and his/her surrounding environment such as physical location, temperature, body warmth, HR, BP, etc. by using various types of sensors. These are the information flows from real space to this system.

Meanwhile the system accesses to databases (DBs) and the Web site via the network to obtain useful healthcare information. These are the information flows from digital space to this system. The system accumulated the information, data, and knowledge in adequate forms. These are used to analyze the object person's situation in detail as necessary. The information is sometimes provided to the person and the community members by proper timing and forms while considering privacy concerns and resource limitations of the devices.

Our healthcare support system facilitates information circulation in order to promote the healthcare tasks from the perspective of symbiosis between real space and digital space. However, it is very difficult to handle huge amount and functional diversity of the information including the privacy concerns.

3.2 Multi-agent for Large-Scale and Complex Healthcare Support System

We apply a multi-agent framework for our healthcare support system that matches to large-scale and complex systems by employing properties of agents such as autonomy, cooperativeness, and adaptability. We wrap various types of system component as agents, called "agentification"; then the multiple agents can dynamically configure organization to process some intended tasks.

We can consider the situation where a sensor device acquires some vital data or location information and transmits the information to a DB via the network, and the DB stores the information. Each agent individually resides in various sensor devices and DBs. The agent monitors and controls corresponding hardware; the DB agent stores and transmits the acquired data. The agents control quality of information and frequency of the acquired data depending on network status, operational condition of the sensor device, and load of the DB. The agents including sensor agent, DB agent, and network agent can effectively control the data flows based on the situation and the object person's health condition in a coordinated manner.

Since the stored information is basically raw data, the system needs to convert into more user-friendly forms such as tables and graphs. To create advice or knowledge with high-level expression, the system analyzes some data which is related to the object person's situation with data mining algorithm, some algorithm, etc. The agents transform the system behaviors based on the results of analyses. For example, when the object person is in bad health condition, the sensor agent that manages the object person's vital data would try to obtain the data in shorter time intervals to recognize more detailed information. Each agent has basic inference mechanism based on the rule-base system to realize these kinds of intelligent analysis. To carry out more special knowledge processing, some kinds of powerful tools, such as ontology-base, data mining algorithms, software for statistics, etc. are required to cooperate with each other. To elicit the various health conditions and assist the object person, these tools need to be collaborated and cooperated by wrapped agents.

Because of the agentification of various devices, database, knowledge, algorithm for analysis, software components, etc., we can reuse the agents as reusable modules and develop a complex system by the dynamic configuration of the agents. When new component is introduced, it is possible to build the component into the existing system at lower cost. Therefore the agent-based infrastructure matches to the reduction of system development cost.

In particular, a vital sensor agent obtains an object person's vital data as stream data and sends the data to a DB agent. The data stream mining agent analyses the stream data including vital data using data stream mining technology in cooperation with the DB agent. When the data stream mining agent detects the each person's health condition, the sensor agents control the quality and frequency of data acquisition based on the health condition. Therefore the agents obtain the object person's vital data in a coordinated manner; the agents store and extract the data in the database according to the person's condition; the agents can effectively provide a useful information and advice in real-time according to the person's location, available devices, combining vital data, environment data, and knowledge (ontology) on health, etc.

3.3   AMUSE: Agent-Based Framework

To provide healthcare support service in ubiquitous computing environments, we employ a multi-agent-based framework based on concept of symbiotic computing

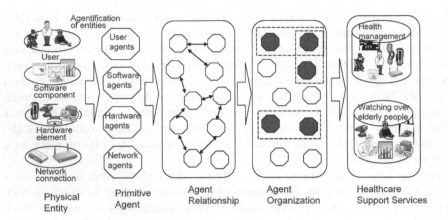

Fig. 2. Framework of AMUSE

[13], called AMUSE (Agent-based Middleware for Ubiquitous Service Environment) [14], as a software platform. The fundamental framework of AMUSE is shown in Fig. 2. All the entities in the ubiquitous computing environments are wrapped as agents based on AMUSE framework. The agents which are wrapped by "agentification" based on our framework have some characteristics as follows:

- Recognition of statuses of each entity: Each agent can autonomously manage target entity's situation based on the domain knowledge of the entity such as devices and users.
- Coordination of multiple contexts: Agents can effectively exchange context information of entities with each other. When an agent informs another agent about own context, Inter-Agent Relationship (IAR) is efficiently constructed to reduce unnecessary communication between agents.
- Service composition: Agents can make contract to configure organization of entities in order to dynamically build healthcare support services based on IAR.

When the agents construct agent organization and inform the context information, the agents consider not only user mobility and sensor information, but also resource condition, etc. based on IAR. IAR consists of three kinds of relationships: Tight-Relationship (TR), Group-Relationship (GR), and Competing-Relationship (CR) like shown in Fig.3.

(a) Tight-Relationship(TR)

TR is created among agents that provide some services by constructing organization of the agents. By using this relationship, it is possible for the agent to have past cases of successes and failures in cooperation.

(b) Group-Relationship(GR)

GR is given to the group of agents that have some potential dependencies. For instance, there is GR among hardware entities such as sensor node and sink node, desktop PC, speaker and PC displays, etc. By using GR, it is possible that agent informs changes in their states frequently to the agents within the group.

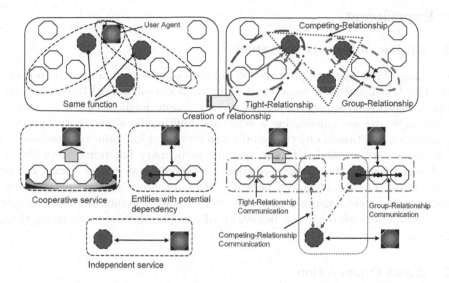

Fig. 3. Creation of Inter-Agent Relationship

(c) Competing-Relationship(CR)

CR is formed among agents that have same function. The reason behind using this relationship is these agents would compete when task announcement of the function is issued. By using CR, the competing agents routinely inform their status to each other, and they can create good organization effectively when Contract Net Protocol(CNP)[15]-based negotiation runs.

4   Implementation

At present, we are designing and developing some functions of our healthcare support system. In this paper we present the behavior of prototype system based on developed functions.

We implemented agents based on AMUSE framework. We also used DASH [16] and IDEA [18] for implementation of agents. DASH is an agent-based programming environment based on ADIPS [17]; IDEA is an integrated development tool for the DASH. We employed IDEA for the development and simulation of the agents.

As for current hardware configurations for sensing the location information of our framework, we use two sensor types to sense the location information of users in the room: an ultrasonic-based sensor (Zone Positioning System (ZPS)) [19] and an active-type RFID system [20]. We also used MOTE (MTS310) [21] as the environmental sensor node. This sensor can sense acceleration, temperature, and illuminance etc.

5   Experiments

5.1   Outline of Prototype System

We suppose healthcare support system consists of various functions to support daily life. Our framework based on the functions organizes health management service, multimedia supervisory service, and remote medical care service, etc. For example, we are considering a real-time multimedia supervisory function, visualization function of object person's situation, and functions of coordination with various sensors and database systems as primary functions. Actually we developed three functions: the real-time multimedia supervisory function, the visualization function of object person's situation, and the functions of coordination with environmental sensor. We evaluate adaptability and extensibility of our framework through the behaviors of our prototype system using these functions.

5.2   Agent Organization

Each agent individually manages context information which is obtained from the state of device or the data of sensor device. The agent informs the context information to another agent based on IAR. The main roles of each agent which are used in our prototype system are as follows.

User Ag: This agent maintains user's information such as requirement, location information, etc., and notifies other agents of the information.
ZPS Ag: This agent maintains location of tags that are held by users using ultrasonic. It provides location information of the target users to other agents. This agent can control the frequency of update of information based on the request of other agent.
RFID Ag: This agent maintains location of RFID tags that are held by users using radio frequency.
EnvSensor Ag: This agent manages environmental sensors. This agent obtains information about sense acceleration, temperature, and illuminance etc., and informs other agents.
Manager Ag: This agent manages all the agents related to the corresponding PC. This plays a role to propagate information from *User Ag* to the related agents, and controls the organizational behaviors of the agents such as activation, termination, and re-configure of agents.
JMFSend Ag and JMFRecv Ag: These agents provide video communication by controlling JMF (Java Media Framework) Software. It has many encoding format and parameters, thus it can adapt to diverse type of networks.
DVTSSend Ag and DVTSRecv Ag: These agents provide video communication in very high quality by controlling DVTS Software.
DB Ag: This agent manages and controls database system (MySQL). This agent stores data which is sent by other agents and provides information based on other agent's requirement.

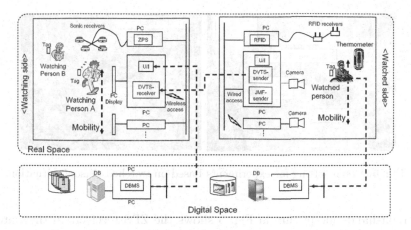

Fig. 4. An example of real-time multimedia supervisory system for healthcare support

EmailSend Ag: This agent sends e-mail to address specified by user or agents. This agent can also send an attachment file such as picture file.

JMFSnap Ag: This agent takes a picture by controlling JMF Software. This agent performs it based on the requirement of *Manager Ag*.

Map Ag: This agent replaces the location information of *ZPS Ag* with the position information and displays the position information on a map. This agent can change the position color by the request from *Manager Ag*.

Graph Ag: This agent provides the distance between the ZPS receiver and ZPS tag using graph.

5.3   Experimental Results

(1) Real-time multimedia supervisory function
The multimedia supervisory systems are widespread as care-support systems that enable supervision of elderly people from remote sites. The real-time multimedia supervisory system delivers live video streaming captured with cameras at the watched person's site, with a PC or a hand-held device at the distant supervisor site as shown in Fig. 4. In this experiment, a watching person (son) watches over an elderly watched person (his father) in remote sites.

Our system displays a live video with suitable quality on one of the displays considering the watching person's requirement for the watching over and the status of devices. The agents cooperatively work to accomplish QoS that meets to user's requirements on a watching task and device situations. Therefore, our system makes the construction of agent organization by considering the most appropriate camera, the PC with reasonable network connection, and the display devices based on multiple contexts.

In the watched person's room (Fig. 5), we set a DV camera and a USB camera for delivering a live video as shown in the left-hand side picture in Fig. 5. The watched person has ZPS tag for sensing tag height and location information.

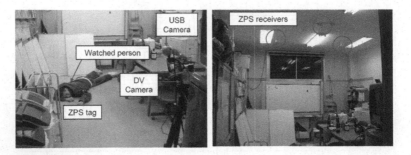

Fig. 5. Room setting for experiments based on watched person's situation

The right-hand side picture in Fig. 5 shows the ZPS receivers in the watched person's room. We observed our system behavior based on the watched person's situation.

[Case-1: normal situation]
The watching person always brings the user terminal as shown in Fig. 6. Here, the watched person is in normal situation such as watching TV in the dining room. In this case, *JMFRecv Ag* in the nearest user terminal from watching person displays the watched person's image from *JMFSend Ag* with reasonable quality as shown in the left-hand side picture in Fig. 6. On the other hand, when the watching person approaches the plasma television as shown in the right-hand side picture in Fig. 6, the live video also stays the user terminal. It means agents selected the user terminal, *JMFRecv Ag*, and *JMFSend Ag* using USB camera with respect to their personal relationship with the watched person and the watched person's situation (normal situation).

[Case-2: emergency situation]
This case shows emergency situation of the watched person. Our rule-based inference mechanism can understand emergency situations using the period of time (he has not moved), the location information, and tag's height. For example, the

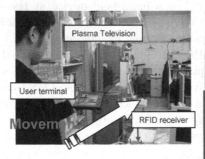
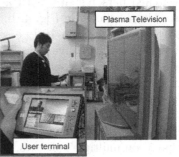

Fig. 6. The case of normal situation

watched person lying in the dinning room is unusual and it is an emergency situation. We compare our framework with a location-based service configuration. The left-hand side picture in Fig. 7(a) shows the behavior of our proposal-based scheme when the watching person moves closer to the plasma television. The video streaming was migrated to the high definition television from the user terminal to show the situation more clearly by *DVTSSend Ag* and *DVTSRecv Ag* when the watched person lay down. Then, the most adequate display devices around the watching person, and finally the most suitable display, video streaming software (DVTS) and network connection were selected and configured to deliver the live video. In the case of a location-based scheme as shown in Fig. 7(b), the video service stayed in the user terminal by the *JMFRecv Ag* and the *JMFSend Ag* because it was judged as the nearest display.

As the individual agent could decide own action by considering the situations of the watching person and watched person, we confirmed our real-time multimedia supervisory function based on our framework could provide the supervisory service and adapt to change of the situations.

(2) Visualization function of object person's situation

To assist analysis and observation of the object person's health condition, we are trying to visualize the sensor data such as vital information, location information, and environmental information. We suppose DB systems cooperate with various agents depending on the situation. We carry out experiments in the coordination with a *DB Ag* which is managing the object person's location information and his tag's height as part of multimedia supervisory system.

The bottom image in Fig. 8 shows agent organization of the visualization function. The top-left image in Fig. 8 shows the behavior of a *Map Ag* which displays the watched person's position information in his house. The watched person walks around with a ZPS tag. A *ZPS Ag* sends the watched person's location information as the raw data to *DB Ag*. The *DB Ag* processes the information and sends the information to *Map Ag* in the user terminal. The *Map Ag* shows the watched person's position information based on the information of *DB Ag*.

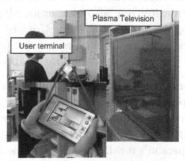

(a) Our proposal-based service configuration   (b) Location-based service configuration

Fig. 7. The case of emergency situation

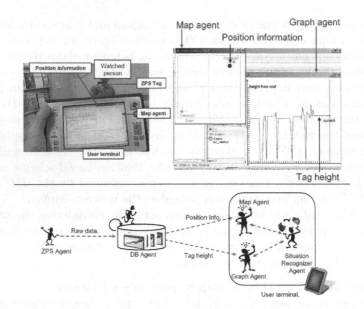

Fig. 8. An example of visualization function

The behaviors of cooperation with a *Graph Ag*, the *Map Ag*, and a situation recognizer agent are shown in top-right image in Fig. 8. The *Graph Ag* displays the watched person's tag height. The tag's height is used to judge the watched person's emergency condition such as the falling down etc. by the situation recognizer agent. The *Map Ag* alerts the watching person to the watched person's situation in emergency by the flashing point; The *Map Ag* also changes the color of position information from blue to red. When the system can not deliver the video streaming and the system derives the great deal of the watched person's privacy, this function will be helpful for the watching person and the watched person.

We confirmed the visualization function could perform not only the display of information but also the action depending on object person's situation by the cooperation with *DB Ag*, *Map Ag*, and *Graph Ag*. Because the agent works independently, this function can also provide information using multiple display devices depending on computational resources and network resources.

(3) Function of coordination with environmental sensor

We applied our framework to assistive system using function of coordination with environmental sensor for diet such as aiming eating-pattern changes and avoiding late-evening snacks. This system stores and extracts the image of the object person's meal. For example, the image is sent to object person's counselor, doctor, and family members by *EmailSend Ag*; the images in the database system are accessed and used for analyzing his eating-pattern or providing advice to avoid late-evening snacks by his counselor's. In this experiment, *JMFSnap Ag* takes a picture of food which he tries to eat or had eaten based on the detection

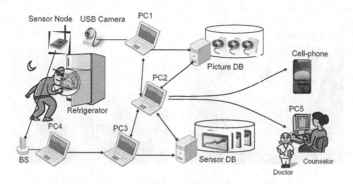

Fig. 9. System structure for coordination with environmental sensor

of a *EnvSensor Ag*. *EmailSend Ag* sends the picture to his family's cell-phone or his counselor's PC when object person looks for something to have for a midnight snack in his refrigerator.

The system structure for this experiment is shown in Fig. 9. We located the USB camera and environmental sensor on top of the refrigerator. The PC3 analyzes data from the *EnvSensor Ag* in PC4 and informs *DB Ag* in the sensor DB. The data that is stored in the sensor DB is used for data-mining about object person's situation. We used the acceleration data for detecting the refrigerator's door if it is opened or closed. When the *EnvSensor Ag* in the PC4 recognizes a change of the refrigerator's door, the *Manager Ag* requests the *JMFSnap Ag* in the PC1 connected the USB camera to take a picture. The *JMFSnap Ag* in the PC1 stores the image in the Picture DB. Then the *EmailSend Ag* in the PC2 sends the image file depending on the request of the object person's counselor, doctor, and family members, and the situations of the object person.

An *EnvSensor Ag* in the PC4 detects the state of the refrigerator's door (open or close) by measuring the acceleration of sensor. The *DB Ag* in the Picture DB can extract the latest image file in the Picture DB through time. The algorithm for flexibly extracting the image file depending on the situation or a certain period for supporting the doctor and counselor is considered as a future work.

Fig. 10 shows the experimental environment. The left-hand side picture in Fig. 10 shows the refrigerator, sensor node, and USB camera. The right-hand side picture in Fig. 10 shows an object person. When the object person opened the refrigerator's door and got food or something, the *JMFSnap Ag* took a picture by the coordination with *EnvSensor Ag* and *Manger Ag*.

Fig. 11 shows the behavior of our system. The left-hand side picture in Fig. 11 shows the situation of the cell-phone received the image file from *EmailSend Ag*. This snap shot shows the object person got a piece of pizza. The right-hand side picture in Fig. 11 also shows the snap shot of e-mail software of the PC received from *EmailSend Ag* based on user requirement. This snap shot shows the object person got a yogurt. We confirmed the cooperation of agents depending on the situation and user request from this experiment. We also confirmed that our framework can adapt various sensors and DB. Additionally our framework can

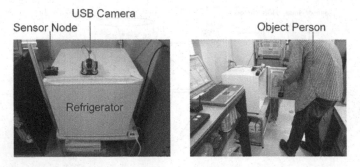

Fig. 10. Experimental environment

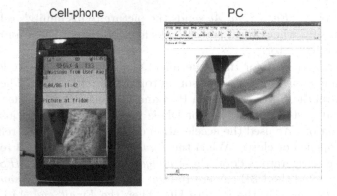

Fig. 11. Screenshot of system behavior

change the function depending on the object person's situation. For example, when his situation is in emergency, *JMFSend Ag* can deliver his situation using USB camera.

We think this system is useful for inhibiting late-evening snacks and diet modifications through the doctor and counselor. We will investigate the revulsion for the object person and privacy concerns for our future work.

5.4   Discussion

We discuss the adaptability and extensibility of our framework through the experiments as follows:

Adaptability: Our proposal-based construction scheme for healthcare support services could select and organize multiple agents to provide service that matches person's requirement, coping with not only the user location information, but also the device status around the users. In the experiment of multimedia supervisory function, we especially confirmed heterogeneous entities like display devices, capture devices, PCs, networks, different kinds of sensors, software components, etc., were efficiently integrated. We also confirmed our system could control the privacy level depending on human-relationship and watched person's situation. Therefore our framework can provide healthcare support services in adapting to various situations in ubiquitous computing environment.

Extensibility: We confirmed the cooperation of various entities was successful through three experiments. Our system is aiming to provide useful advice and information related healthcare to the object persons and community members. Therefore our framework needs to acquire and manage various types and huge amount of information. Through the experiments of visualization function of object person's situation and function of coordination with environmental sensor, agents could obtain, manage, and provide various information by the organization of agents though limited information. Additionally we confirmed modularity and autonomy of agent through these experiments. Our framework can be easily adapted to the diversity of entities; the system development and extension can be easily accomplished by our framework.

6 Conclusion

This paper presented the concept and design of an agent-based framework for healthcare support system in ubiquitous computing environment. We are aiming to develop the system which provides useful advice and information regarding object person's health condition effectively. We also showed the implementation of several functions.

As future work, we would like to perform the quantitative evaluation of our framework and our system. We are tackling the detailed design the data actuation mechanism. We are trying to extend the current visualization function using vital sensors.

Acknowledgement

This work was partially supported by Sendai Intelligent Knowledge Cluster and the Ministry of Education, Culture, Sports, Science and Technology, Grants-in-Aid for Scientific Research, 19200005.

References

1. http://www.mhlw.go.jp/bunya/kenkou/seikatsu/index.html
2. http://www.ch-kentatsu.jp/
3. http://air.silpheed.jp/users/sfais/0.php
4. Izumi, S., Kato, Y., Takahashi, K., Suganuma, T., Shiratori, N.: Proposal of an Ontology-based Health Support System and Its Evaluation. IPSJ Journal 49(2), 822–837 (2008)
5. Brown, B., Chetty, M., Grimes, A., Harmon, E.: Reflecting on Health: A System for students to monitor diet and exercise. In: Conference on Human Factors in Computing Systems (CHI 2006), pp. 1807–1812 (2006)

6. Gockley, R., Marotta, M., Rogoff, C., Tang, A.: AVIVA: A Health and Fitness Monitor for Young Women. In: Conference on Human Factors in Computing Systems (CHI 2006), pp. 1819–1824 (2006)

7. Cruz, D., Barros, E.: Vital Signs Remote Management System for PDAs. In: 8th Euromicro Conference on Digital System Design, pp. 170–173 (2005)

8. Dröes, R.-M., et al.: Healthcare Systems and Other Applications. IEEE Pervasive Computing 6(1), 59–63 (2007)

9. Chang, K., Chen, M.Y., Canny, J.: Tracking Free-Weight Exercises. In: Krumm, J., Abowd, G.D., Seneviratne, A., Strang, T. (eds.) UbiComp 2007. LNCS, vol. 4717, pp. 19–37. Springer, Heidelberg (2007)

10. Ouchi, K., Suzuki, T., Doi, M.: LifeMinder: A Wearable Healthcare Support System with Timely Instruction Based on the User's Context. IEICE Transaction on Information and Systems E87-D(6), 1361–1369 (2004)

11. Ali-Hasan, N., Gavales, D., Peterson, A., Raw, M.: Fitster: social fitness information visualizer. In: Conference on Human Factors in Computing Systems (CHI 2006), pp. 1795–1800 (2006)

12. Takahashi, H., Izumi, S., Suganuma, T., Kinoshita, T., Shiratori, N.: An Agent-based Healthcare Support System in Ubiquitous Computing Environments. In: Mokhtari, M., et al. (eds.) ICOST 2009. LNCS, vol. 5597, pp. 237–240. Springer, Heidelberg (2009)

13. Suganuma, T., Uchiya, T., Konno, S., Kitagata, G., Hara, H., Fujita, S., Kinoshita, T., Sugawara, K., Shiratori, N.: Bridging the E-Gaps: Towards Post-Ubiquitous Computing. In: 1st International Symposium on Frontiers in Networking with Applications (FINA 2006), pp. 480–484 (2006)

14. Takahashi, H., Suganuma, T., Shiratori, N.: AMUSE: An Agent-based Middleware for Context-aware Ubiquitous Services. In: International Conference on Parallel and Distributed Systems (ICPADS 2005), pp. 743–749 (2005)

15. Smith, R.G.: The Contract net protocol: High-level communication and control in a distributed Problem solver. IEEE Trans. Comput. 29(12), 1104–1113 (1980)

16. Sugawara, K., Hara, H., Kinoshita, T., Uchiya, T.: Flexible Distributed Agent System programmed by a Rule-based Language. In: 6th IASTED International Conference of Artificial Intelligence and Soft Computing, pp. 7–12 (2002)

17. Fujita, S., Hara, H., Sugawara, K., Kinoshita, T., Shiratori, N.: Agent-based design model of adaptive distributed systems. Applied Intelligence 9, 57–70 (1998)

18. Uchiya, T., Maemura, T., Hara, H., Sugawara, K., Kinoshita, T.: Interactive Design Method of Agent System for Symbiotic Computing. International Journal of Cognitive Informatics and Natural Intelligence 3(1), 57–74 (2009)

19. http://www.furukawakk.jp/products/

20. http://jp.fujitsu.com/group/fst/services/ubiquitous/rfid/

21. http://www.xbow.jp/motemica.html

Interpolation System of Traffic Condition by Estimation/Learning Agents

Tetsuo Morita, Junji Yano, and Kouji Kagawa

Sumitomo Electric Industries, Ltd.,
Information & Communication Laboratories,
1-1-3, Shimaya, Konohana-ku, Osaka, 554-0024 Japan
{morita-tetsuo,yano-junji,kagawa-kouji}@sei.co.jp

Abstract. Interpolation system of traffic condition is proposed, which consists of estimation and learning agents. To evaluate the interpolation accuracy, coefficient of determination (CD) and mean square error (MSE) are used. The interpolation accuracy can be improved by the alternate use of estimation and learning agents, and the iterative uses of the same probe data. The standard deviation of the normalized velocity can be improved to 0.1353, and that of the velocity is 6.77 km/h in the mid velocity region. Furthermore, the CD and MSE could be improved by the additional repetition of estimation and learning.

Keywords: Probe car, Multivariate analysis, Coefficient of determination, Mean square error.

1 Introduction

To drive a car along the crowded road without knowing the traffic congestion causes the social problems, such as the increase of the consumption of fossil fuels and carbon dioxide. Traffic information service is the effective method to decrease the traffic congestion. Traffic information classify into two types, such as time and space domain. The time information denotes the forecast technology, and the spatial information corresponds to the traffic congestion map. There is no effective way to forecast future traffic congestions. Our target is to develop the interpolation system to estimate the traffic congestion by a small amount of information.

Vehicle Information and Communication System (VICS) is the well-known system for the traffic information service. The VICS system gathers the traffic information from roadside sensors, and provides it to drivers. The VICS system is very useful to provide the traffic information, but the huge capital investment for roadside sensors is essential. The probe car system is the effective method to reduce the capital investment. Probe cars measure the traveling-time of road links by the Global Positioning System (GPS) sensor etc. The probe car system is unnecessary to put sensors at the roadside. However the number of the probe cars is very few, it is difficult to estimate the traffic congestion from only the probe data.

The commonly used method to interpolate traffic conditions is statistic analysis. In this method, statistics data are the time-sliced average of the past probe data from

J.-J. Yang et al. (Eds.): PRIMA 2009, LNAI 5925, pp. 487–499, 2009.

road links. In present, the number of the probe cars with the same time and conditions is very few, and the sampling errors are very large.

The pheromone model [1] is used to make up the deficit of the probe data, and the deposit, propagation, and evaporation are the pheromone parameters. While the pheromone model is the forecast technology, it can be used for the interpolation system. The intensity of pheromone depends on the velocity of cars, and is changed by the propagation and evaporation mechanism. By the intensity of pheromone, the traffic congestion can be estimated. But the pheromone parameters are determined by the human experience, and it is difficult to determine it objectively.

The Feature Space Projection (FSP) method [2][3] is proposed to interpolate the traffic condition, and the feature is obtained by the Principal Component Analysis (PCA) with missing data. The PCA method without data missing is commonly used for multivariate analysis. But in this case, the probability to get the simultaneous probe data from the two road links is very small, therefore the method of the PCA with missing data is essential for this calculation. The size of this model [2] depends on the product of the number of day factors and time resolution, and it is beyond the capacity of ordinary PCs.

In this paper, we propose a new method to solve these problems. Learning agents calculate the weight value corresponding to the pheromone parameters, and estimation agents make up the deficit of the probe data. In other words, the interpolation accuracy can be improved by collaboration of estimation and learning agents, and this system is some kind of artificial intelligent. To evaluate the progress of learning, coefficient of determination (CD) and mean square error (MSE) are used.

2 Interpolation System of Traffic Condition

Fig. 1 shows the configuration of the interpolation system of traffic condition. This system consists of two agents, such as estimation and learning agents, which are allocated to all the road links. Estimation agents renew the velocity of each road link, and learning agents renew the weight values for estimation. The estimated velocities

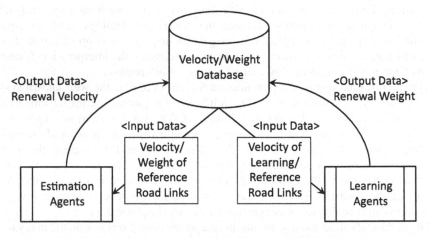

Fig. 1. Configuration of Interpolation System of Traffic Condition

and the weight values are stored into the velocity/weight database. Estimation and learning agents alternately calculate the results to improve the interpolation accuracy.

The normalized velocity (NV) is used in this system, and Fig. 2 shows the definition of it. This chart consists of the 3 lines, such as (1) $y = 1 - x/1000$, (2) $y = 1.2 - x/50$, (3) $y = 0.1 - x/1000$. The estimated NVs and the weight values are stored in the database shown in Fig. 1. The slope of the middle velocity region is steeper than that of the high and low velocity regions. In the mid velocity region, the interpolation accuracy is supposed to be better than that of the other regions.

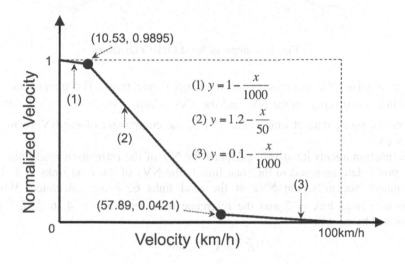

Fig. 2. Definition of Normalize Velocity

2.1 Estimation Agents

Estimation agents calculate the NV of the estimation road link with the NVs of the reference road links and the weight values at time t, and the reference road links are adjacent to the estimation road link. The initial NV of each road link is 0, and the initial weights are $w_0^{(i)} = 0$, $w_1^{(i)}, \cdots, w_n^{(i)} = 1/n$.

$V^{(i)}$ denotes the NV vector of the reference road links for the road link i, and ${}^t w^{(i)}$ the weight vector of the i-th road link at time t. $V^{(i)}$ consists of the n-NV of the reference road links and constant value 1. Equation (1) shows the definition of the estimated NV ${}^{t+1}\tilde{E}^{(i)}$ of the road link i at time $t+1$. In other words, the estimated NV is the inner product of the NV vector and the weight vector. Occasionally, the weight value ${}^t w_0^{(i)}$ is called threshold.

$$ {}^{t+1}\tilde{E}^{(i)} = V^{(i)} \cdot {}^t w^{(i)} \tag{1} $$

$$ V^{(i)} = \begin{pmatrix} 1 & V_1^{(i)} & \cdots & V_n^{(i)} \end{pmatrix} \tag{2} $$

$$ {}^t w^{(i)} = \begin{pmatrix} {}^t w_0^{(i)} & {}^t w_1^{(i)} & \cdots & {}^t w_n^{(i)} \end{pmatrix}^T \tag{3} $$

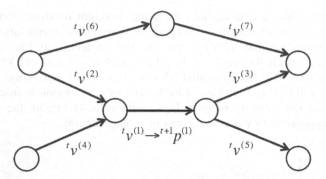

Fig. 3. Example of Road Link Connections

Fig. 3 shows the example of the road link connections. The travel-time of each road link is converted to the NV, and the NVs at time t are $^{t}v^{(1)}, \cdots, ^{t}v^{(7)}$. When the NV of the probe data at time $t+1$ is $^{t+1}p^{(1)}$, the component of the NV vector $V^{(i)}$ is renewed.

Estimation agents iteratively calculate the NV of the estimation road links. Firstly new probe data assigned to the road link 1, the NVs of the road links 2, 3, 4, 5 are calculated. Secondly, the NVs of the road links 6, 7 are calculated. When the estimation road link is 2 and the reference road links are 1, 4, 6, $^{t+1}\tilde{E}^{(2)}$ can be calculated by eq. (4).

$$^{t+1}\tilde{E}^{(2)} = V^{(2)} \cdot {}^{t}w^{(2)} \tag{4}$$

$$V^{(2)} = \begin{pmatrix} 1 & ^{t+1}p^{(1)} & ^{t}v^{(4)} & ^{t}v^{(6)} \end{pmatrix} \tag{5}$$

$$^{t}w^{(2)} = \begin{pmatrix} ^{t}w_0^{(2)} & ^{t}w_1^{(2)} & ^{t}w_2^{(2)} & ^{t}w_3^{(2)} \end{pmatrix}^{T} \tag{6}$$

By the same method, $^{t+1}\tilde{E}^{(4)}$ can be calculated by eq. (7).

$$^{t+1}\tilde{E}^{(4)} = V^{(4)} \cdot {}^{t}w^{(4)} \tag{7}$$

$$V^{(4)} = \begin{pmatrix} 1 & ^{t+1}p^{(1)} & ^{t+1}\tilde{E}^{(2)} \end{pmatrix} \tag{8}$$

$$^{t}w^{(4)} = \begin{pmatrix} ^{t}w_0^{(4)} & ^{t}w_1^{(4)} & ^{t}w_2^{(4)} \end{pmatrix}^{T} \tag{9}$$

Therefore, when the new probe datum is assigned to the road link, the NVs of the adjacent road link are calculated, and finally the NVs of all the road links can be calculated. We should pay attention that the NV vector $V^{(i)}$ includes both of the NV components at time t and $t+1$.

2.2 Learning Agents

Learning agents calculate the weight vector $w^{(i)}$ of the learning road link i referred to the probe NVs of the road link i and the NVs of the reference road links. The time suffix is omitted from the notation. $P^{(i)}$ denotes the probe vector of the road link i with the m-NV, $V^{(i)}_{m\times(n+1)}$ denotes the matrix, which consists of the m-NV vectors of the n reference road links and m constant values 1. Equation (10) is the m simultaneous equation with the $n+1$ unknowns.

$$P^{(i)} = V^{(i)}_{m\times(n+1)} \cdot w^{(i)} \tag{10}$$

$$P^{(i)} = \begin{pmatrix} P_1^{(i)} & P_2^{(i)} & \cdots & P_m^{(i)} \end{pmatrix}^T \tag{11}$$

$$V^{(i)}_{m\times(n+1)} = \begin{pmatrix} 1 & V_{1,1}^{(i)} & \cdots & V_{1,n}^{(i)} \\ \vdots & \vdots & \ddots & \vdots \\ 1 & V_{m,1}^{(i)} & \cdots & V_{m,n}^{(i)} \end{pmatrix} \tag{12}$$

When $n+1$ is less than m, the answers of simultaneous equation eq. (10) are not fixed. When $n+1$ is not less than m, and the rank of $V^{(i)}_{m\times(n+1)}$ is $n+1$, eq. (10) can be solved. The number of independent equation is greater than $n+1$, eq. (10) cannot be solved. In this case, the method to minimize MSE is used, such as the least squares method. $E^{(i)}$ denotes the estimated NV vector of the road link i with m-NV, which is the product of the NV matrix $V^{(i)}_{m\times(n+1)}$ and the weight vector $w^{(i)}$.

$$E^{(i)} = V^{(i)}_{m\times(n+1)} \cdot w^{(i)} \tag{13}$$

$$E^{(i)} = \begin{pmatrix} E_1^{(i)} & E_2^{(i)} & \cdots & E_m^{(i)} \end{pmatrix}^T \tag{14}$$

$\varepsilon_k^{(i)}$ denotes the residuals of the k-th component of $P^{(i)}$ and $E^{(i)}$. The sum of square errors $Q^{(i)}$ is given by eq. (15).

$$Q^{(i)} = \sum_{k=1}^{m} (\varepsilon_k^{(i)})^2 = \sum_{k=1}^{m} \left(P_k^{(i)} - E_k^{(i)} \right)^2 = \sum_{k=1}^{m} \left(P_k^{(i)} - w_0^{(i)} - \sum_{j=1}^{n} V_{k,j}^{(i)} \cdot w_j^{(i)} \right)^2 \tag{15}$$

The MSE of the road link i have the minimum value, when the partial differential equations of (16)(17) equals 0.

$$\frac{\partial Q^{(i)}}{\partial w_0^{(i)}} = 0 \tag{16}$$

$$\frac{\partial Q^{(i)}}{\partial w_u^{(i)}} = 0 \quad (u = 1, \cdots, n) \tag{17}$$

As eqs. (17) are linear, multiple regression analysis can be used for this case. The dependent variables are the probe NVs, and the independent variables are the NVs of the reference road links. Equation (18) is the transformed equation of (17). Equation (18) can be solved by Gaussian elimination method, and the regression coefficients, such as $w_1^{(i)}, \cdots, w_n^{(i)}$, can be calculated.

$$
\begin{pmatrix}
s_{1,1}^{(i)} & s_{1,2}^{(i)} & \cdots & s_{1,n}^{(i)} \\
s_{2,1}^{(i)} & s_{2,2}^{(i)} & \cdots & s_{2,n}^{(i)} \\
\vdots & \vdots & \ddots & \vdots \\
s_{n,1}^{(i)} & s_{n,2}^{(i)} & \cdots & s_{n,n}^{(i)}
\end{pmatrix}
\begin{pmatrix}
w_1^{(i)} \\
\vdots \\
\vdots \\
w_n^{(i)}
\end{pmatrix}
=
\begin{pmatrix}
p_1^{(i)} \\
\vdots \\
\vdots \\
p_n^{(i)}
\end{pmatrix}
\tag{18}
$$

$$
s_{q,r}^{(i)} = \sum_{j=1}^{m} \frac{\left(V_{j,q}^{(i)} - \overline{V}_q^{(i)}\right)\left(V_{j,r}^{(i)} - \overline{V}_r^{(i)}\right)}{m-1}
\tag{19}
$$

$$
p_q^{(i)} = \sum_{j=1}^{m} \frac{\left(P_j^{(i)} - \overline{P}^{(i)}\right)\left(V_{j,q}^{(i)} - \overline{V}_q^{(i)}\right)}{m-1}
\tag{20}
$$

$$
\overline{V}_q^{(i)} = \frac{\sum_{j=1}^{m} V_{j,q}^{(i)}}{m}
\tag{21}
$$

$$
\overline{P}^{(i)} = \frac{\sum_{j=1}^{m} P_j^{(i)}}{m}
\tag{22}
$$

The weight value $w_0^{(i)}$ can be also calculated form eq. (23), which is transformed from eq. (16).

$$
w_0^{(i)} = \overline{P}^{(i)} - \sum_{j=1}^{n} w_j^{(i)} \cdot \overline{V}_j^{(i)}
\tag{23}
$$

3   Evaluation

The probe data of Nagoya taxis are used in this evaluation, and the evaluation area for this system is Nagoya district including Nagoya station, and the size of this area is approximately 10km square. The longitude is from 136° 52' 30" to 137° 00' 00", and the latitude from 35° 10' 00" to 35° 15' 00". The number of taxis is approximately 1200, and the total number of the road links is 1128. The probe data can be obtained every 15 minutes. It is possible to use the VICS data, but the constant VICS data are assigned to some road links. Therefore, only the probe data are used in this evaluation. The evaluation period is 4 months, such as from 2007/11/01 to 2008/2/29.

Firstly, the existences of the probe data at the 1128 road links are checked (see Fig. 4). For the first ten days, more than 80% of the road links (946 road links) obtain the probe data. At the end of evaluation (2008/2/29), the number of the road links with the probe data is 1062 at most. The rest of the 66 road links has no probe data. The number of the road links with the probe data abruptly increases at the New Year's Day and the mid of February. At these periods, Nagoya taxis choose the different route from normal days. We should pay attention that the number of the probe data must be greater than that of the unknowns to begin learning.

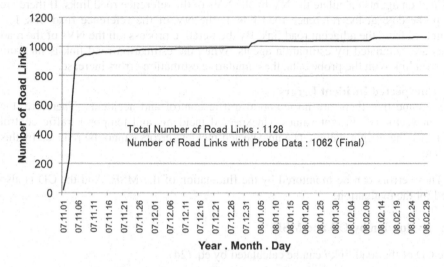

Fig. 4. Number of Road Links with Probe Data

3.1 Errors of the Interpolation System

The target of interpolation system is to calculate the average velocity in the same condition. We classify the errors of the interpolation system into the five categories, such as (A) fundamental errors, (B) sampling errors, (C) approximation errors, (D) cumulative estimation errors, and (E) unexpected incident errors.

(A) Fundamental Errors
The input data include the fundamental errors, such that the probe data originally include the measurement errors on the GPS system. Even if the traffic condition is same, the driver's characteristics and technique influence the probe data. In addition, the influence of traffic signals is the major factor of the fundamental errors, such that the link traveling-time increases by the traffic signals. These errors cause the variance of the input data, which cannot be reduced by the interpolation system.

(B) Sampling Errors
In this system, the average velocity is calculated from the probe data. At present, the number of the probe cars is a few, therefore the average of the probe (sampling) data differs from that of population. As the number of the probe data increases, the average of the sampling data approaches to that of population. Therefore the sampling errors decreases to zero, when the number of the probe data increases to infinity.

(C) Approximation Errors

Learning agents minimize the MSE shown in eqs. (16)(17). The MSE is the square distance from the hyper-plane of the linear regression model. As the order of the hyper-plane increases, the approximation errors decrease.

(D) Cumulative Estimation Errors

Estimation agents calculate the NV by the NVs of the reference road links. If there are no probe data at the reference road link 1, the NV of the reference road link 1 is estimated from the adjacent road link. By the iterative process, all the NVs of the road links are calculated by estimation agents. When the estimation road link is far from the road link with the probe data, the cumulative estimation errors increase.

(E) Unexpected Incident Errors

We assume that there are no temporal traffic control and accidents. Therefore, the weight vector is constant values. Unexpected incidents and temporal traffic control influence the weight values. The unexpected incident errors cannot be reduced by this system.

These errors can be monitored by the fluctuation of the MSE. And the CD is also used for the evaluation.

3.2 Evaluation by CD and MSE

The CD of the road link i can be calculated by eq. (24).

$$R^{(i)} = \frac{e^{(i)}}{p^{(i)}} \tag{24}$$

$$p^{(i)} = \sum_{j=1}^{m} \frac{\left(P_j^{(i)} - \overline{P}^{(i)}\right)^2}{m-1} \tag{25}$$

$$e^{(i)} = \sum_{j=1}^{m} \frac{\left(E_j^{(i)} - \overline{E}^{(i)}\right)^2}{m-1} \tag{26}$$

$$\overline{E}^{(i)} = \frac{\sum_{j=1}^{m} E_j^{(i)}}{m} \tag{27}$$

Fig. 5(a) shows the fluctuation of the CD of the several road links in the evaluation area. X-axis denotes the number of the probe data, and y-axis the CD. The fifth-digit of the road link number (ex. 30281) denotes as follows;

1 : Inter-city Expressways,
2 : Inner-city Expressways,
3 : Local roads

The rest digits denote the number assigned to the road link. Therefore the road link in Fig. 5(a) denotes local roads.

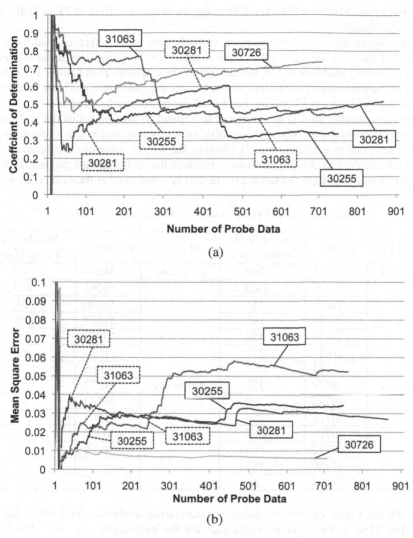

(a)

(b)

Fig. 5. Fluctuation of Coefficient of Determination

When the number of the probe data is less than that of the unknowns ($m < n +1$), the CD is assigned 0. When eq. (10) can be solved, the CD becomes 1. As the number of probe data additionally increases, the CD abruptly decreases, and then increases gradually. The minimum value of the CD of the road link 30726 is approximately 0.45 after learning, and its value gradually increases to 0.75. The CDs of the road links 30281 and 30255 abruptly decreases when the number of the probe data is approximately 450, and increases gradually. The reason, that the CD abruptly changes, is considered that the weight value of the road links abruptly changes. The reason, that CD increases gradually, is considered that the probe data are concentrated at the hyper-plane of the linear regression model. When the number of the probe data at the road link 31063 is 250, the CD abruptly decreases from 0.75 to 0.45, and increases gradually.

To investigate the reasons, the numbers of probe data at the reference road links are measured. Table 1 shows the results of the numbers of the probe data at the reference road links. For the road link 30726, the number of the reference road links is 13, and the number of the probe data greater than 100 is 12. For the road link 31063, the number of the reference road links is 11, and the number of the probe data less than 50 is 8.

From these results, the CD is considered to depend on the number of the probe data at the reference road link. When the number of the probe data at the reference road links is a few, one probe datum greatly changes the weight value of the reference road link. Therefore the CD abruptly decreases, because the probe data are plotted far from the hyper-plane. The slight fluctuation of the CD is considered as the same reason.

Table 1. Number of Probe Data at the Reference Road Links

Road Link Number		Number of Probe Data	Road Link Number		Number of Probe Data
Learning	30726	709	Learning	31063	762
Reference	30720	1328	Reference	31062	417
	30724	213		31076	24
	30729	195		31082	25
	30733	459		30907	14
	31047	222		31070	17
	31121	754		31065	37
	30721	220		31077	2
	30725	198		31083	12
	30728	203		31064	517
	30727	767		30906	347
	30732	166		31069	32
	31050	497			
	31124	28			

The weight values can be calculated by multivariate analysis, which minimize the MSE. The MSE is the essential parameter for the evaluation. Fig. 5(b) shows the fluctuation of the MSE. X-axis denotes the number of the probe data, and y-axis the MSE. When no probe data exist at the road link, the MSE is assigned 1. When eq. (10) can be solved, the MSE becomes 0. As the number of probe data additionally increases, the MSE abruptly increases, and then decreases gradually. The tendency of MSE is the opposite of the CD. When the learning is finished (2008/02/29), the MSE of the road link 30726 has the minimum value, and that of the road link 31063 has the maximum value. From these results, the MSE is also supposed to depend on the number of the probe data at the reference road links shown in Table 1.

When the learning is in progress, the weight values are renewed. Even if the learning road link obtains the same probe data, estimation agents calculate the NVs at the reference road links with the different weight values. Learning agents use the different NVs for the multivariate analysis. As the same probe data are used twice, the number of the probe data increases substantially. When the number of the probe data is m, and the same data are used twice, the actual number of probe data becomes $2m$. The estimation errors at the first run are very large, therefore the iterative use of the same data is preferable.

Fig. 6(a) shows the fluctuation of the CD, when the same probe data are used twice. X-axis denotes the lapse of days, and y-axis the CD. Fig. 6(a) indicates that the CD increases by the same probe data. The CD abruptly increases at the several road links on the second run, the reason is considered that the number of the probe data exceeds the upper limit. When the number of the probe data exceeds 1000, the oldest probe datum is deleted from the database. As the old probe data, which is far from the hyper-plane, are deleted, the CD can be improved. From these results, the CD can be effectively increased, when the probe data is more than 1000.

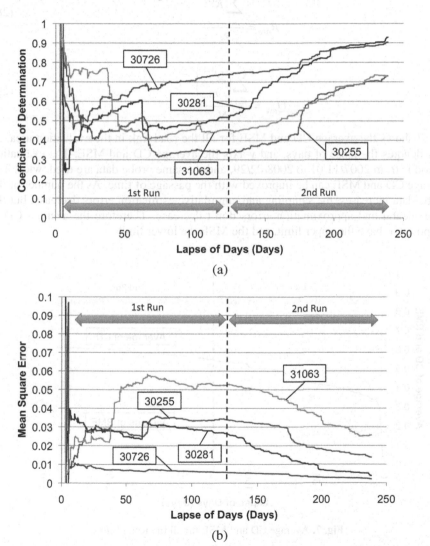

Fig. 6. (a) Fluctuation of Coefficient of Determination. (b) Fluctuation of Mean Square Error.

Fig. 6(b) shows the fluctuation of the MSE, when the same probe data are used. X-axis denotes the lapse of days, and y-axis the MSE. Fig. 6(b) indicates that the MSE has the same kind of tendency that of the CD. The MSE of the road link 30762 at the end of the evaluation is 0.002139, and the standard deviation is 0.046249. The standard deviation of the velocity is 2.31 km/h in the mid velocity region shown in Fig. 2, because the slope in the mid velocity region is 1/50.

R_{ave} is the average CD of all the road links in the evaluation area, and eq. (28) shows the definition. N denotes the number of the road links in the evaluation area. The average MSE Q_{ave} is given by eq. (29).

$$R_{ave} = \frac{\sum_{i=1}^{N} R^{(i)}}{N} \tag{28}$$

$$Q_{ave} = \frac{\sum_{i=1}^{N} \left(\frac{Q^{(i)}}{m} \right)}{N} \tag{29}$$

Fig. 7 shows the average CD and MSE for all the road link in the evaluation area. X-axis denotes the lapse of days, and y-axis the average CD and MSE. The evaluation period is from 2007/11/01 to 2008/02/29, and the same probe data are used twice. The average CD and MSE can be improved with the passage of time. As the number of the probe data increases, the sampling and cumulative estimation errors decrease, but the fundamental and approximation errors don't decrease. Therefore the average CD is supposed to have the upper limit, and the MSE the lower limit.

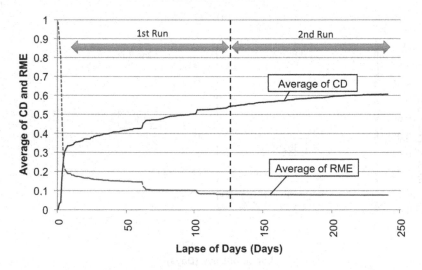

Fig. 7. Average CD and MSE for all the Road Links

The final value of the average MSE is 0.076818, and this value includes the road links without the probe data. As the MSE of the road links without the probe data is 1, it is suitable to subtract this value. The number of the road links without the probe data is 66, and the total number of links N is 1128. Therefore, the actual average MSE at this area is 0.018307 (=0.076818-66/1128), and the standard deviation of the NVs is 0.1353, and that of the velocity is 6.77 km/h in the mid velocity region shown in Fig. 2, because the slope in the mid velocity region is 1/50. The standard deviation of the high and low velocity regions is 135.3 km/h. Therefore, this type of the NV can be suitable for the mid velocity region only, not for the expressway. However, the average CD and MSE can be improved by the repetition of estimation/learning.

4 Conclusion

We propose the interpolation system by estimation and learning agents. The interpolation accuracy is improved by the collaboration of estimation/learning agents. To evaluate the progress of learning, the CD and MSE are used. The CD and MSE can be improved by the repetition of estimation/learning. The fluctuation of CD and MSE depends on the number of the probe data at the reference road links. In addition, the effective ways to improve the CD and MSE are as follows; (1) Iterative use of the same probe data, (2) Adequate removal of the old probe data. The average standard deviation of the velocity in the evaluation area can be decreased to 6.77 km/h in the mid velocity region. Furthermore, the CD and MSE could be improved by the additional repetition of estimation/learning.

References

1. Ando, Y., Fukazawa, Y., Masutani, O., Iwasaki, H., Honiden, S.: Performance of Pheromone Model for Predicting Traffic Congestion. In: Proc. of the fifth international joint conference on Autonomous agents and multiagent systems, pp. 73–80 (2006)
2. Kumagai, M., Fushiki, T., Kimita, K., Yokota, T.: Long-range Traffic Condition Forecast using Feature Space Projection Method. In: Proc. of 11th World Congress of ITS, Nagoya, CD-ROM (October 2004)
3. Kumagai, M., Fushiki, T., Kimita, K., Yokota, T.: Spatial Interpolation of Real-time Floating Car Data Based on Multiple Link Correlation in Feature Space. In: Proc. of 13th World Congress of ITS, London, CD-ROM (October 2006)

A Fuzzy Rule-Based System for Ontology Mapping

Susel Fernández[*], Juan R. Velasco, and Miguel A. López-Carmona

Department of Automatic, University of Alcala. Edificio Politécnico,
CTRA N-II. Km 31, 600 28871. Alcalá de Henares. Madrid, Spain
{susel,juanra,miguellop}@aut.uah.es

Abstract. Ontologies are a crucial tool for formally specifying the vocabulary and the concepts of agent platforms, so, to share information, agents that use different vocabularies must be able to translate data from one ontological framework to another. The treatment of uncertainty plays a key role in the ontology mapping, as the degree of overlapping between concepts can not be represented logically. This paper aims to provide mechanisms to support experts in the first steps of the ontology mapping process using fuzzy logic techniques to determine the similarity between concepts from different ontologies. For each pair of concepts, two types of similarity are calculated: the first using the Jaccard coefficient, based on relevant documents taken from the web, and the second based on the linguistic relationship of concepts. Finally, the similarity is calculated through a fuzzy rule-based system. The ideas presented in this work are validated using two real-world ontologies.

Keywords: Ontology mapping, fuzzy rule-based system, similarity, concepts.

1 Introduction and Related Works

Research on semantic web services promises a great interoperability among software agents and web services, utilizing shared ontologies published on the semantic web. However, services produced by different developers may use different or partially overlapping sets of ontologies. The ontology mapping process is needed for the exchange of information and services within an agent platform, finding correspondences between the concepts of different ontologies.

There are some previous works aimed at ontology mapping, which have made interesting contributions. Noy and Musen have developed SMART [14], PROMPT [15] and PROMPTDIFF [16] tools, using linguistic similarity matches between concepts, and a set of heuristics for identifying further matches between the ontologies. Doan et al. developed the GLUE system [6], which employs machine learning techniques to find mappings. Ron Pang et al. developed a probabilistic framework for automatic ontology mapping based on Bayesian Networks (BNs) [17]. This approach only takes into account the probability of occurrence of concepts in the web; it fails if two very similar concepts have not the same level of popularity.

---

[*] Student. University of Alcala. Spain.

J.-J. Yang et al. (Eds.): PRIMA 2009, LNAI 5925, pp. 500–507, 2009.
© Springer-Verlag Berlin Heidelberg 2009

Our proposal focuses on the initial phase of ontology mapping. We first calculate a similarity between concepts using the Jaccard coefficient, based on relevant documents taken from the web in a similar way to [17]. Then we calculate the linguistic similarity, and finally obtain the total similarity using a fuzzy rule-based system. The organization of work is as follows: section 2 describes the use of the Jaccard coefficient and the method used to obtain the linguistic similarity. In Section 3 shows the fuzzy rule-based system and Section 4 shows results of applying our method on two real-world ontologies. Finally in section 5 presents conclusions and lines of future work.

2 Similarities between Concepts

In this section we present the Jaccard similarity and the linguistic similarity. These measures are used as input variables to the fuzzy rule-based system to calculate the total similarity between concepts in ontologies.

2.1 Jaccard Coefficient

The Jaccard coefficient [20] is one of the binary indices of similarity best known and most used. This coefficient is defined as the size of the intersection divided by the size of the union given two sets of data and its value is in [0, 1]. For two observations i and j, the Jaccard coefficient is calculated using the following formula:

$$S_{ij} = \frac{a}{a+b+c} \tag{1}$$

Where a is the number of times that both observations have the value 1, b is the number of times observation i has value 1 and observation j has value 0, and c is the number of times observation i has value 0 and observation j has value 1.

In this work we have applied the Jaccard coefficient to calculate the similarity between two concepts from different ontologies. The values involved in this formula were obtained through successive searches of relevant documents from the web. In a similar way to [17], to ensure that the search on the web only return those documents that are relevant to the concept, the search query is formed by combining all the terms on the path from root to the current node in the taxonomy. Supposes the set A^+ that containing exemplars that support A, and the set A^- containing the exemplars that support the negation of A. Exemplars in A^+ are obtained by searching in the web for pages that contain A and all A's ancestors, while exemplars of A^- would be those where A's ancestors are present but not A. For each pair of concepts A and B, are counted (a) documents which appear the two concepts, (b) documents which appear A and B does not appear, and (c) documents which appear B and not A. Once these values are obtained for each pair of concepts of origin and destination ontologies respectively, their similarity is calculated by formula (1).

2.2 Linguistic Similarity

The linguistic similarity is the strongest indicator of similarity between two concepts, because usually the ontology developers within the same domain use linguistically related terms to express equivalent concepts.

Given the concepts A and B from two different ontologies, the first step of our proposal to calculate the linguistic similarity is to obtain their synonyms lists using WordNet [21]. Subsequently, we applied the Porter stemming algorithm [18] to each of the words from the lists of synonyms, which is simply the process of removing the morphological ends of English words. If we call L_A and L_B to the lists of roots of the synonyms of each concept obtained in this way, we may calculate the linguistic similarity between the concepts as follows:

$$S = \min\left[\frac{c_A}{T_A}, \frac{c_B}{T_B}\right] \tag{2}$$

Where c_A is the number of words in the list L_A that are on L_B, T_A is the total number of words in the list L_A, c_B is the number of words in the list L_B that are in L_A, and T_B is the total number of words in the list L_B.

3 Fuzzy Rule-Based System

In this work we are using the XFuzzy 3.0 development environment [22], which integrates several tools that cover different stages of fuzzy systems design.

3.1 Variables

The system has two input variables and one output. For each of them we associate linguistic terms set whose semantics are defined by means of triangular-shaped fuzzy membership functions. These variables are:

Sim_Jaccard: It is an input variable and represents the value of the similarity calculated by Jaccard coefficient. This variable has associated the following linguistic terms set: $D_{jacc} = \{Low, Regular, Medium, High, Very\ high\}$. Membership functions are shown graphically in Figure 1a). In the definition of the membership functions we decided to use the quartiles of all similarities to narrow membership triangles as follows: *Low*: (-0.00224168, 0, 0.00224168), *Regular*: (0, 0.00224168, 0.03031929), *Medium*: (0.00224168, 0.03031929, 0.10712543), *High*: (0.03031929, 0.10712543, 1), *Very high*: (0.10712543, 1, 1.10712543).

Sim_Ling: It is an input variable that represents the value of linguistic similarity. This variable has associated the following linguistic terms set: $D_{ling} = \{Low, Regular, Medium, High, Very\ high\}$. The membership functions are shown in Figure 1b).

Similarity: Represents the output of the fuzzy system. This variable has associated the following linguistic terms set: $D_{Similarity} = \{Very\ low, Low, Medium\ low, Regular, Medium\ high, High, Very\ high\}$. The membership functions are shown in Figure 1c).

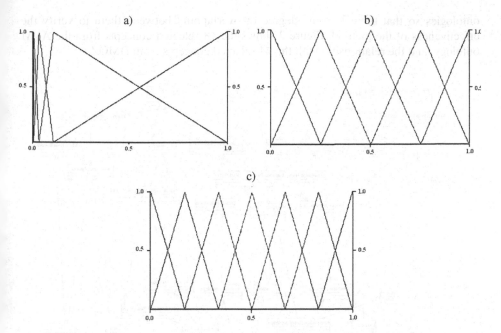

Fig. 1. Fuzzy triangular-shaped membership functions for: a) *Sim_Jaccard* variable, b) *Sim_Ling* variable, c) *Similarity* variable

3.2 Rule Base

The rule base defined in the fuzzy system has been formed by the heuristics of experts and shown in Table 1.

Table 1. Rule Base

Sim_Jaccard	Sim_Ling				
	Low	**Regular**	**Medium**	**High**	**Very high**
Low	Very low	Low	Medium low	Regular	Medium high
Regular	Low	Medium low	Regular	Medium high	High
Medium	Low	Medium low	Regular	Medium high	High
High	Medium low	Regular	Medium high	High	Regular
Very high	Regular	Medium high	High	High	Very high

4 Experiments

We have performed an experiment using two real-world ontologies. These are the ACM topic taxonomy [1], and DMOZ hierarchy [5]. Our objective was to demonstrate the effectiveness of this proposal for obtaining a valid index of similarity between concepts, to assist the ontology mapping process. We have selected the *Artificial Intelligence* sub-domain as in [17], and pruned some concepts in both ontologies so that there is some degree of overlapping between them to verify the effectiveness of the method. Figure 2 shows the 18 selected concepts from the ACM ontology, and the relationship with the 24 selected concepts from DMOZ.

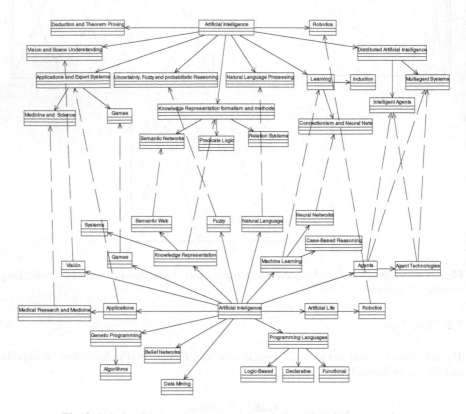

Fig. 2. Relationship between concepts in ACM and DMOZ taxonomies

For each pair of concepts A and B, from the ontologies ACM and DMOZ respectively, we first calculated the Jaccard similarity, using the relevant documents sets retrieved from the web, then the linguistic similarity, as described in previous sections are calculated and then we apply the fuzzy rule-based system to obtain the final similarity. If we consider n as the number of concepts in the first ontology and m the number of concepts in the second, the process would be completed in $n \times m$ iterations. Table 2 shows the concepts for which we have obtained higher similarity Table 3 shows the concepts for which the similarity has been found to be higher than they should.

In the work in [17], using similar fragments of ontologies ACM and DMOZ, argue that their method provides a similarity index of 0.61 for the concepts *connectionism and neural nets* and *Neural Networks*, because it only takes into account the probability of occurrence of both concepts in the web, and the term *connectionism* is not very popular. As shown in Table 2, in our case these two concepts provide a higher degree of similarity, because of their linguistic relationship.

Table 2. Concepts with highest values of similarity

Concepts ACM	Concepts DMOZ	Similarity
Robotics	Robotics	0.99
Games	Games	0.99
Multiagent Systems	Agent Technologies	0.90
Multiagent Systems	Systems	0.88
Natural Language Processing	Natural Language	0.88
Learning	Machine learning	0.87
Knowledge Representation Formalisms and Methods	Knowledge Representation	0.85
Intelligent Agents	Agents	0.75
Vision and Scene Understanding	Vision	0.74
Uncertainty, fuzzy and probabilistic reasoning	Fuzzy	0.74
Connectionism and neural nets	Neural Networks	0.72
Semantic Networks	Semantic Web	0.72
Multiagent Systems	Agents	0.71
Applications and Expert Systems	Applications	0.58
Multiagent Systems	Semantic Web	0.58
Medicine and Science	Medical Research and Medicine	0.58
Intelligent Agents	Agent Technologies	0.58
Semantic Networks	Neural Networks	0.57
Intelligent Agents	Logic-Based	0.57
Multiagent Systems	Logic-Based	0.57

Table 3. Concepts for which the similarity has been found to be higher than they should

Concepts ACM	Concepts DMOZ	Similarity
Multiagent Systems	Systems	0.88
Multiagent Systems	Semantic Web	0.58
Semantic Networks	Neural Networks	0.57
Intelligent Agents	Logic-Based	0.57
Multiagent Systems	Logic-Based	0.57

Finally, we performed a χ^2 statistical test to see if the results match those expected for these two ontologies. To do this we raised the hypothesis H_0 that is assumed that there is no difference between these values. Table 4 shows the values of contingency for the experiment.

Table 4. Contingency table for χ^2 prove

	Low	High	Total
Expected	412	15	432
Observed	417	20	432

Calculating the value with 1 degree of freedom, we found that the hypothesis H0 is true with 95% confidence, so we accept the assumption that there is no difference between the values of observed and expected similarity and demonstrates the effectiveness of the proposed method.

5   Conclusions and Future Work

This paper describes our work to provide a method to assist experts in the initial phase of ontology mapping. Our proposal consists of a fuzzy system for similarities between concepts in different ontologies. The system uses as input the values obtained using the Jaccard coefficient of documents retrieved from the web, and a linguistic similarity of concepts, which is the most important factor for the calculation of the total similarity. Currently this is done for each pair of concepts of two ontologies, and we are working to reduce the number of iterations, making the system takes into account other factors such as the similarities between brother concepts in the taxonomy of ontologies. Another of our goals is to refine the calculation of the linguistic similarity including other linguistic relationships between concepts. Also as future work, we proposed to include the properties of the concepts in the mapping process and the scalability of the application.

Acknowledgments. This work is part of the T2C2 Project. It has been supported by the Spanish Ministerio de Educación y Ciencia, TIN2008-06739-C04-04, and the EU ITEA-2 Project No 2008005, "Do-it-Yourself Smart Experiences", founded by the Spanish Ministerio de Industria, Turismo y Comercio -Avanza- TSI-020400-2009-124.

References

1. ACM Topic, http://www.acm.org/about/class/1998/
2. Barwise, J., Seligman, J.: Information Flow: The Logic of Distributed Systems. Cambridge University Press, Cambridge (1997)
3. Calvanese, D., Giacomo, G., Lenzerini, M.: Ontology of integration and integration of ontologies. In: Description Logic Workshop (DL 2001), pp. 10–19 (2001)
4. Cordón, O., Herrera, F., Hoffman, F., Magdalena, L.: Genetic Fuzzy Systems. In: Evolutionary Tuning and Learning of Fuzzy Knowledge Bases. World Scientific, Singapore (2001)
5. DMOZ hierarchie, http://www.dmoz.org/
6. Doan, A., Madhavan, J., Domingos, P., Halevy, A.: Ontology Matching: A Machine Learning Approach. In: Staab, S., Studer, R. (eds.) Handbook on Ontologies in Information Systems, invited paper, pp. 397–416. Springer, Heidelberg (2004)
7. Fernández-Breis, J., Martínez-Béjar, R.: A cooperative framework for integrating ontologies. International Journal of Human-Computer Studies 56, 665–720 (2002)
8. Gruber, T., Olsen, G.: An ontology for engineering mathematics. In: Doyle, J., Torasso, P., Sandewall, E. (eds.) Fourth International Conference on Principles of Knowledge Representation and Reasoning, San Mateo, CA, USA, pp. 258–269 (1994)
9. Grüninger, M.: Ontologies for translation: Notes for refugees from Babel. EIL Technical Report, Enterprise Integration Laboratory (EIL), University of Toronto, Canada (November 1997)

10. Jannink, J., Pichai, S., Verheijen, D., Wiederhold, G.: Encapsulation and Composition of Ontologies. In: AAAI 1998 Workshop on Information Integration, Madison, WI, USA (July 1998)
11. Kalfoglou, Y., Schorlemmer, M.: Ontology mapping: the state of the art. The Knowledge Engineering Review 18(1), 1–31 (2003)
12. McGuinness, D., Fikes, R., Rice, J., Wilder, S.: An Environment for Merging and Testing Large Ontologies. In: 17th International Conference on Principles of Knowledge Representation and Reasoning (KR 2000), Colorado, USA (April 2000)
13. Mitra, P., Noy, N.F., Jaiswal, A.R.: OMEN: A Probabilistic Ontology Mapping Tool. In: Workshop on Meaning Coordination and Negotiation at the Third International Conference on the Semantic Web (ISWC 2004), Hiroshima, Japan (2004)
14. Noy, N.F., Musen, M.A.: SMART: Automated Support for Ontology Merging and Alignment. In: 12th Workshop on Knowledge Acquisition, Modelling and Management (KAW 1999), Banff, Canada (October 1999)
15. Noy, N.F., Musen, M.A.: The PROMPT suite: Interactive tools for ontology merging and mapping. International Journal of Human-Computer Studies 59(6), 983–1024 (2003)
16. Noy, N.F., Musen, M.A.: PROMPTDIFF: A Fixed-Point Algorithm for Comparing Ontology Versions. In: 18th National Conference on Artificial Intelligence (AAAI 2002), Edmonton, Alberta, Canada (August 2002)
17. Pan, R., Ding, Z., Yu, Y., Peng, Y.: A Bayesian Network Approach to Ontology Mapping. In: Gil, Y., Motta, E., Benjamins, V.R., Musen, M.A. (eds.) ISWC 2005. LNCS, vol. 3729, pp. 563–577. Springer, Heidelberg (2005)
18. Porter Stemming algorithm, http://tartarus.org/~martin/PorterStemmer/
19. Quesada, V., Isidoro, A., López, L.: Curso y Ejercicios de Estadística. Alhambra Longman, Madrid (1994)
20. van Rijsbergen, C.J.: Information Retrieval, 2nd edn. Butterworths, London (1979)
21. Wordnet, http://wordnet.princeton.edu/
22. XFuzzy 3.0, http://www.imse.cnm.es/Xfuzzy/Xfuzzy_3.0/tools/xfuzzy_sp.html

Where Are All the Agents? On the Gap between Theory and Practice of Agent-Based Referral Networks

An Inter-agent Communication Perspective

Nicola Dragoni

Department of Informatics and Mathematical Modelling
Technical University of Denmark, 2800 Kongens Lyngby, Denmark
ndra@imm.dtu.dk

Abstract. The intrinsic openness and dynamism of the Service-Oriented Computing (SOC) vision makes it crucial to locate useful services and recognize them as trustworthy. To address this challenge, referral networks have recently been proposed as a decentralized approach based on software agents technology. Although in theory this idea might look promising for enabling the SOC vision, real-world referral systems are still missing. In this paper we study this gap between theory and practice from the point of view of agent communication, since it represents a key feature of agent-based distributed systems. To do this, we firstly highlight the main agent communication requirements needed to cope with real-life agent-based referral networks. Secondly, we discuss why the standard language for agent communication (FIPA ACL) is not suitable for supporting these requirements. Finally, we briefly illustrate how they can be easily satisfied by an advanced agent communication language, namely FT-ACL.

1 Introduction

Consensus is growing that the Service-Oriented Computing (SOC) "revolution" will not eventuate until we resolve trust related issues [1]. For instance, lack of consumer trust still represents a critical impediment to the success of e-marketplaces based on software agents and Web services ([2,3]). In particular, the key challenge to be addressed concerns the problem of Web service selection: the intrinsic openness of the SOC vision makes it crucial to locate useful services and *recognize them as trustworthy* [4].

Several approaches have been proposed in the last decade to address this problem. The vast majority of them ([5,6,7]) are based on a centralized Trusted Third Party (TTP) that manages ratings of services and provides them on request of software agents. The agents will take their decision (whether or not to trust a service) according to the results provided by the TTP. Depending on how the TTP computes and provides the assessments, we can find two main TTP systems: reputation and recommendation systems.

A common weakness that makes TTP based approaches not suitable for the SOC vision lies in their being conceptually and implementationally centralized: a single *trusted* authority is responsible to collect, aggregate and present all the ratings [8]. To address this core limitation, *referral networks* [4,9] have recently been proposed as a decentralized rating systems based on software agents. Although in theory this agent-based approach might look very promising for enabling the SOC vision, real-world referral technologies and systems are still missing. Indeed, only simulations have been discussed in literature to study some performance indicators, such as effectiveness and efficiency [4]. Design guidelines to build real-life applications have also been outlined, but the point is that referral networks are still far from being considered a convincing technology coping with real-life scenarios. This gap between theory and practice represents the leading motivation underlying the paper. Indeed, if we are not able to provide agent-based systems for real-life referral networks, any hype about theoretical and mathematical rigor becomes pointless.

The Contribution of this Paper. In this paper we investigate this gap from an inter-agent communication point of view, which represents one of the key features of agent-based distributed systems. The contributions of our analysis are threefold. Firstly, we highlight the main inter-agent communication requirements needed to cope with real-life agent-based referral networks (Section 2). Secondly, we consider the standard language for agent communication released by the FIPA consortium (FIPA ACL) and we show that, although it represents the widely recommended ACL in the construction of multi-agent systems (MAS), it is not suitable for supporting the intrinsic openness and dynamism of referral networks (Section 3). This conclusion is derived from the fact that FIPA ACL does not fulfill the mentioned requirements. As a result, we claim that this is a practical impediment to the realization of real-world agent-based referral networks. Finally, we intuitively and briefly show that the requirements are satisfied by FT-ACL, an advanced agent communication language recently proposed for open and dynamic MAS (Section 4). Section 5 concludes the paper summing up its main contributions.

2   Agent-Based Referral Networks

The key idea behind referral networks ([9,4]) envisions an *online community* representing a set of interacting members (people, businesses or other organizations). Members provide services as well as referrals for services to each other. Referrals may be provided proactively or in response to requests. This should be realized by means of *software agents* (agents for short), helping members manage their interactions.

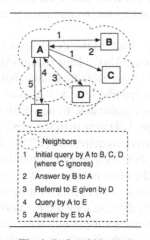

Fig. 1. Referral Network

Agents may represent different members and assist them in evaluating services and referrals provided by others, maintaining contact lists, and deciding or suggesting whom to contact for different services. Agents organize themselves into communities. Agents in the same community are called *neighbors*. Communities are dynamically formed according to the model that each agent maintains of some other agents. This model is usually based on two aspects: the *party's expertise* (ability to provide correct services) and *sociability* (ability to produce accurate referrals).

Fig. 1 shows an example of referral system for selecting an online service. Agent *a* sends a request for information about who provides a specific service to its neighbors *b*, *c* and *d*. Agent *c* autonomously decides to ignore the request and it does not reply. In contrast, agents *b* and *d* both answer to *a*'s request but in two different ways. Indeed, in referral systems an answer can be a referral to another member (as *d*'s answer) or even oneself (as *b*'s answer), in which case there would be some more interaction to actually provide the service. According to *d*'s referral, agent *a* decides to forward the query to agent *e*. Again, *e* could reply with some referrals or proposing itself.

2.1 Basic Inter-agent Communication Requirements for Referral Networks

To cope with real-life referral networks, several agent communication related issues must be addressed. The basic needs to enable agents to collaborate with each other in a referral network can be grouped into three main communication requirements (CR):

[CR1] Dynamic Service Registration: agents must be able to dynamically register and unregister their interests and services, *capabilities* in short, in the referral network.

[CR2] Dynamic Service Querying: agents must be able to dynamically query the overall network or a virtual community for a specific service.

[CR3] Robustness: agents must be able to collaborate despite possible run-time failures of some interacting members of the network.

All these communication requirements are based on the main assumption underlying the rationale of referral networks:

[A1] Distributed Rating System: there is no central authority responsible for managing agents interaction, registration and failures.

Back to the example of Fig. 1, agent *a* asks agents *b*, *c* and *d* for a particular service. This at least requires that agent *a* knows agents *b*, *c* and *d*, although in practice it is reasonable to assume that agent *a* will query the neighbors that do actually provide a specific service if *a* knows them (that is, agent *a* knows that agents *b*, *c* and *d* are somehow able to deal with the service). Therefore, to be reached by someone and to provide their own services, agents must previously register their capabilities in the network (requirement [CR1]). In this way, sooner or later they will be queried by someone about their specific capabilities and from that point on they will be able to interact with the other members in the system (forming and/or participating in communities). In the same way, agents must be able to unregister a capability from the system, for instance in the case they are no more able to provide or rate a specific service. In other words, since online communities are formed according to agent interactions and evaluations of such interactions, agents must be able to register their interests so that they become reachable and they can start to interact each others, forming their own communities.

Fig. 1 motivates requirement [CR2] too. Indeed, an agent that is looking for a service, such as agent *a*, must be able to ask their neighbors or the overall network for a specific service. The former situation requires some previous interaction with the other members of the community, so that a can decide which members to keep as its neighbors. The latter situation concerns the circumstance of a new agent registered in the system. In this case the agent does not belong to any community and it still has not formed its own community, at least until it receives some queries from the other agents. In this specific situation the agent must be able to act proactively (querying the network about the service it is looking for) instead of remaining idle until a sufficient set of messages have been received.

Requirement [CR3] is motivated by the intrinsic openness and asynchrony of a referral network, where (according to the SOC vision) the number of agents is supposed to dynamically change. In such environment, robustness plays a crucial role since agents may become unavailable suddenly due to various reasons, for instance because the machine on which the agent process is running crashes due to hardware and/or software faults. Thus, agents must be able to collaborate despite possible dynamic failures of the interacting peers. Back to the example of Fig. 1, if one agent crashes, say agent b, than agent a should not endlessly wait for b's answer.

The above requirements represent the key desiderata for agent communication in referral networks. In particular, this means that the ACL adopted by the software agents to interact must support these requirements. In the rest of the paper we will show that the standard ACL (FIPA ACL) fails to achieve this goal, which is instead attained by a recently proposed ACL, namely FT-ACL.

3   The Bad News: The Failure of the Standard (FIPA ACL)

FIPA Agent Communication Language (FIPA ACL) [10] is the standard language for agent communication released by the FIPA standardization consortium. It represents the widely recommended speech act based ACL in the construction of multi-agent systems. An exhaustive description of such language is outside the scope of the paper and interested readers may consult the FIPA ACL communicative acts library specification [10] to this aim. Instead, what we would like to point out here is that the FIPA ACL is not suitable for supporting agent communication in agent-based referral networks. In particular, we claim that FIPA ACL is still an impediment to the actual realization of large, dynamic and open multi-agent systems where the number of agents is not supposed to be known a priori and it can dynamically change at run-time. Intuitively, the main reason lies in the fact that referral networks can substantially be seen as agent-based Peer-to-Peer (P2P) systems where virtual communities are formed according to agents' preferences (indeed, neighbors can be thought as *agents' favorite peers* in a P2P jargon). These kinds of systems are not completely supported by FIPA ACL because their basic communication needs require more powerful communication primitives. To motivate this claim, let us consider the communication requirements highlighted in Section 2.1 and show that FIPA ACL does not satisfy any of them.

To fulfill requirement [CR1] under the assumption [A1] a broadcast primitive is needed. For instance, when an agent joins the network for the first time, it has no friends to which send its interests or service advertisements. Moreover, it is reasonable to assume that the agent does not know any other agent in the network. Since no central authority is available and all FIPA communicative acts requires at least one explicit receiver, a non-FIPA primitive is therefore needed to register the agent in the system.

The same remark is valid for requirement [CR2]. Let us suppose that the agent was able to join the network (by means of a non-FIPA communicative primitive) and, looking for a service, it wants to query the other agents. Some FIPA ACL messages do actually have a recipient field that is a set of recipients, so messages can easily be multicast. But the point here is: to which peers should the agent send the message if, being new in the system, it has not interacted with anyone yet and consequently it has no friends? How should this fixed list of agents be defined? From a technical point of view, it is worth noting that in FIPA there is no middleware support for multicasting to all agents registered to provide a given service. Therefore, the required service cannot be used as parameter for determining this specific list. A possibility could be sending a proxy message to a known registry agent by means of the *proxy* FIPA ACL communicative act, but no single central entry point is available in the network where to send this request (assumption [A1]). How the agent might select and trust another peer for this purpose? Again, the fundamental lack of FIPA ACL leads to the need of more powerful communication primitives.

Finally, requirements [CR3] is not fully satisfied since FIPA communicative acts do not provide any form of failure handling. Indeed, in the FIPA model of communication, failure handling can be expressed only at the *interaction protocol (IP) level*. For instance, the FIPA request IP handles one kind of failure, namely when an agent, say B, fails in its attempt to fill the request from another agent, say A. Another example are the several FIPA interaction protocols, such as the FIPA Contract Net IP Specification: at any point in the IP, the initiator of the IP may cancel the interaction protocol by initiating a specific FIPA Cancel meta protocol. This protocol is substantially based on a *failure* communicative act sent as a reply of a request. The intended meaning is to tell another agent that an action was attempted but the attempt failed. Of course, this approach is not sufficient to support fault tolerant communication in a very large agent-based open system. This is evident considering crash failures only: how a crash of an interacting agent should be handled in this model? For instance, how can an initiator of the FIPA Contract Net IP handle a crash of one or more bidding agents? Here, both the FIPA Cancel meta protocol and the *failure* communicative act are useless, because there is no partner to interact with. The partner crashed and therefore it is not possible to start any "recovery" protocol with him. On the other hand, the initiator must be able to react to this failure, for instance not waiting an answer to a specific query forever. It is worth noting and not surprisingly that our claim is supported by all the FIPA IP specifications[1], where the following sentence is reported: *"real world issues such as the effects of cancelling actions, asynchrony, abnormal or unexpected IP termination, nested IPs, and the like, are explicitly not addressed here."*

Table 1 summarizes the key points discussed so far. The main result of this analysis is that, from an inter-agent communication point of view, programming FIPA agents for referral networks is a complex task that needs adequate programming skills and tools in order to be carried out successfully. In particular, programmers must rely on the underlying implementation language and platform for all the basic communication

---

[1] Available at http://www.fipa.org/repository/ips.php3

needs. This proves the uselessness of the current FIPA ACL specification to cope with real-life referral systems. We claim that this gap between theory and practice represents one of the main reasons of the unsuccessful adoption of referral networks in practice. How these systems can be built if agents interact with each other by means of a communication language that is not able to support the basics communication needs of such systems? Generalizing this critique to distributed systems (such as P2P systems), this also explains why only few people are currently able to contribute to the development of agent-based distributed systems [11]. The good news is that we do not need to invent a new technology, as we will show in the next Section. We therefore advocate the need of a review of the current FIPA specifications in order to take this critique into account.

Table 1. Why FIPA ACL Fails to Support the Inter-Agent Communication Requirements [CR1-3]

Requirement	Motivation
[CR1] Dynamic Service Registration	No broadcast or content-based primitive available
[CR2] Dynamic Service Querying	No broadcast or content-based primitive available
	No middleware support for content-based multicasting to registered agents
[CR3] Robustness	No sufficient failure handling, just a protocol based on a *failure* primitive meaning that some previous attempt failed

4   The Good News: The Technology Is Already There (FT-ACL)

FT-ACL is an advanced speech act based ACL with a formal definition of its concurrent semantics [12,13]. Intuitively, the key strength of FT-ACL with respect to FIPA ACL lies in its being specifically designed for *open* and *dynamic* asynchronous MAS (*i.e.,* where agents can dynamically join or leave the system and the number of agents is not supposed to be known at priori), resulting in a language that fits naturally with real-world open systems such as referral networks. Moreover, FT-ACL is the only ACL that deals with dynamic *crash* failures of the interacting agents. It is not surprising that the inter-agent communication requirements listed in Section 2.1 represent some of the main *concurrent features* that FT-ACL supports.

For space limitations, we do not provide a comprehensive introduction of FT-ACL. Readers interested in the language specification and semantics, as well as in its implementation can refer to the FT-ACL literature ([11,12,13,14,15]). However, it is worth stressing that FT-ACL has been fully implemented on top of the JXTA P2P platform [16] and consequently each FT-ACL primitive have been successfully implemented in real-life distributed applications. Details on such implementation can be found in [14,11], where scalability issues are also discussed, showing that the architecture supporting FT-ACL scales well when the number of agents grows.

Table 2 summarizes the main contribution of FT-ACL for supporting agent communication in referral networks. Each agent communication requirement is satisfied by means of specific FT-ACL primitives. In particular, requirement [CR1] is satisfied by means of the dynamic FT-ACL primitives *register* and *unregister*. The implementation

514   N. Dragoni

Table 2. How FT-ACL Supports the Inter-Agent Communication Requirements [CR1-3]

Requirement	Supported by FT-ACL
[CR1] Dynamic Service Registration	*register* and *unregister* content-based primitives (anonymous interaction protocol)
[CR2] Dynamic Service Querying	*ask-everybody* primitive for content-based queries (anonymous interaction protocol) *ask-one* primitive for point-to-point queries
[CR3] Robustness	success and failure continuations in primitives

of such primitives supports an anonymous interaction protocol [13] based on the *ask-everybody* and *ask-one* FT-ACL primitives. These primitives make FT-ACL able to fulfill requirement [CR2]. Indeed, agents registers in the system by means of the content-based FT-ACL primitive *register*. As a result, they become dynamically reachable by *ask-everybody* multicast queries executed by the other agents in the system. One-to-one communication (needed for instance by an agent to query a neighbor instead of a set of agents) can be performed by using the FT-ACL *ask-one* primitive.

It is worth noting that the FT-ACL primitives *register*, *unregister* and *ask-everybody* do not require an explicit receiver but their implementation is capabilities-based. This is in accordance with assumption [A1], since it also means that no central authority is needed to register and search for services. This is one of the key advantages of FT-ACL over FIPA ACL. The simplicity of realizing inter-agent communication in referral networks by means of FT-ACL should not be surprisingly. As pointed out at the beginning of Section 4, this is specifically due to the design principles of FT-ACL.

Finally, the requirement [CR3] is straightforwardly satisfied by FT-ACL thanks to its fault tolerant primitives. As already mentioned, fault tolerance represents one of the distinguishing features of FT-ACL, allowing to specify open MAS where agents collaborate despite possible failures. For instance, thanks to the fault tolerant ask primitives, several concurrent properties such as liveness and termination have been proved also in presence of dynamic crash failures of the recipient agents [13,15]. For space limitations, in this paper we omit a specific discussion on how fault-tolerant protocols can be specified by means of FT-ACL. However, interested readers may consult the FT-ACL related literature for a detailed treatment of these topics.

5 Conclusion

In this paper we have investigated the gap between theory and practice of agent-based referral networks from the point of view of agent communication, since it represents one of the key features of such systems. The technical contributions of our analysis have been threefold. Firstly, we have highlighted the main agent communication requirements needed to cope with real-life agent-based referral networks. These requirements represent the desiderata for agent communication in open and dynamic referral networks. Secondly, we have shown that the standard language for agent communication released by the FIPA standardization consortium (FIPA ACL) is not suitable for supporting the intrinsic openness and dynamism of referral networks, resulting to be a practical impediment to the realization of real-world agent-based referral networks. This claim has been derived from the fact that FIPA ACL does not fulfill the mentioned communication requirements. Finally, we have briefly discussed how these requirements can be easily satisfied by FT-ACL, an advanced agent communication language recently proposed for open and dynamic multi-agent systems.

References

1. Papazoglou, M., Georgakopoulos, D.: Service-Oriented Computing. Comm. of the ACM 46(10), 25–65 (2003)
2. Dayal, S., Landesberg, H., Zeisser, M.: Building trust on-line. McKinsey Quarterly (October 2001), http://www.mckinseyquarterly.com
3. Liu, C., Marchewkaa, J., Lub, J., Yub, C.: Beyond concern: a privacy–trust–behavioral intention model of electronic commerce. Information & Management 42(1), 127–142 (2004)
4. Yolum, P., Singh, M.: Engineering Self-Organizing Referral Networks for Trustworthy Service Selection. IEEE Trans. on Systems, Man, and Cybernetics 35(3), 396–407 (2005)
5. Adomavicius, G., Tuzhilin, E.: Toward the next generation of recommender systems: A survey of the state-of-the-art and possible extensions. IEEE Trans. on Knowledge and Data Engineering 17, 734–749 (2005)
6. Wang, Y., Vassileva, J.: A review on trust and reputation for web service selection. In: Proc. of ICDCS, Washington, DC, USA. IEEE, Los Alamitos (2007)
7. Josang, A., Ismail, R., Boyd, C.: A survey of trust and reputation systems for online service provision. Decision Support Systems 43(2), 618–644 (2007)
8. Dragoni, N.: Toward trustworthy web services - approaches, weaknesses and trust-by-contract framework. In: Proc. of WI/IAT Web Privacy and Trust Workshop (WPT 2009), Milano, Italy. IEEE, Los Alamitos (to appear 2009)
9. Singh, M., Yu, B., Venkatraman, M.: Community-based service location. Comm. of the ACM 44(4), 49–54 (2001)
10. FIPA Consortium: FIPA Communicative Act Library Specification (2002), http://www.fipa.org/ Document number: SC00037J
11. Gaspari, M., Guidi, D.: Facilitating agent development in open distributed systems. In: Dastani, M.M., El Fallah Seghrouchni, A., Leite, J., Torroni, P. (eds.) LADS 2007. LNCS (LNAI), vol. 5118, pp. 243–260. Springer, Heidelberg (2008)
12. Dragoni, N.: Fault tolerant knowledge level inter-agent communication in open multi-agent systems. Technical Report [PhD Thesis] UBLCS-2006-5, Dep. of Computer Science, Univ. of Bologna (2006)
13. Dragoni, N., Gaspari, M.: Crash failure detection in asynchronous agent communication languages. Autonomous Agents and Multi-Agent Systems 13(3), 355–390 (2006)
14. Dragoni, N., Gaspari, M., Guidi, D.: A Reasoning Infrastructure to Support Cooperation of Intelligent Agents on the Semantic Grid. International Journal of Applied Intelligence 25, 159–180 (2006)
15. Dragoni, N., Gaspari, M., Guidi, D.: An acl for specifying fault tolerant protocols. Applied Artificial Intelligence 21(4), 361–381 (2007)
16. Gong, L.: Jxta: A network programming environment. IEEE Internet Computing 5, 88–95 (2001)

SADE: A Development Environment for Adaptive Multi-Agent Systems

Menggao Dong[*], Xinjun Mao, Junwen Yin, Zhiming Chang, and Zhichang Qi

Dept. of Computer Science and Technology, National University of Defense Technology,
Changsha, Hunan Province, P.R.China, 410073
{mgdong,xjmao,jwyin,zmchang,qzc}@nudt.edu.cn

Abstract. This paper presents SADE, a software supporting environment for developing and running self-adaptive multi-agent systems (MAS). SADE consists of four parts: an adaptive mechanism, a programming language SADL, a reusable software package and supporting software tools. The adaptive mechanism is based on the organization metaphor to analyze and implement self-adaptation of MAS. In our approach, self-adaptation of agent is realized as the changes of roles that agent plays in MAS organization by executing four atomic adaptation operations: "join", "quit", "activate" and "deactivate". SADL is presented to describe the adaptive strategies that express how agents in MAS adapt to the changes of the situated environment. It enables developers to describe self-adaptation explicitly and separate the functional behaviors from adaptation behaviors of agents, thus simplifying the development and maintenance of complex adaptive MAS. SADE also provides a reusable software package that encapsulates the elementary functionalities of self-adaptation, such as the adaptive mechanism, etc. In order to support the development, deployment and execution of adaptive MAS, a compiler and editor for SADL, the architecture of self-adaptive agent and its execution engine have been developed. The technical details of SADE are introduced and a case is studied to illustrate our approach.

Keywords: Multi-agent systems, self-adaptation, dynamic binding mechanism, development environment.

1 Introduction

More and more applications are built on the open, dynamic and heterogeneous environment, in which self-adaptation of software systems is necessary and desirable to accommodate environment changes and to satisfy design objectives. Examples of such applications include traditional embedded system, telephone switch systems, and other business services that require 7×24 availability, etc. However, due to the complexity of the situated environment and dynamic adjustment of system structure and behavior, self-adaptive systems are complex systems that usually go beyond the

---

[*] The first author is a PhD student of Department of Computer Science, National University of Defense Technology.

J.-J. Yang et al. (Eds.): PRIMA 2009, LNAI 5925, pp. 516–524, 2009.

capabilities of traditional abstractions and mainstream technologies of software engineering, such as object-oriented and component-based methodologies [1].

Agent technology is considered as an appropriate and powerful paradigm to develop complex and dynamic distributed systems [2]. It provides high level abstractions and capabilities to deal with autonomy, situatedness, openness, etc. In the past decade, many efforts and progresses have been made in the literature of agent-oriented software engineering (AOSE). However, the lack of effective and easy-to-use agent-oriented programming languages and supporting environment has hampered its wide acceptance and adoption in industry.

In this paper, we present an adaptive mechanism and corresponding supporting environment to construct and execute adaptive MAS. Our approach separates programming concerns of functional behaviors and adaptation behaviors, which can effectively simplify the development and maintenance of complex adaptive MAS. The remainder of the paper is organized as follows. Section 2 introduces the relevant mechanism, framework and language to support to construct the adaptive MAS. In section 3, SADE is described from three layers. Section 4 introduces how to develop the adaptive MAS with SADE, and a case is studied. The comparisons with related work are made in section 5. Lastly, the conclusions and future works are discussed.

2 Constructing Adaptive MAS

In this section we firstly examine an example to illustrate the basic characteristics of adaptive agents. In an e-commerce system on the Internet, each user acts as an agent that can play various roles such as visitor, buyer or seller according to its intention. The environment in which an agent is situated is open and dynamic, because new agents may enter the system and existing agents may leave the system spontaneously. Moreover, the services provided by agents may change from time to time. In the system, agents adapt to the changes of its environment can be performed by changing its roles in the system. For example, after agent Tom logs into the system, he may first play the visitor role to browse goods and services in the system. When he finds the goods he wants to buy, he may quit the visitor role and join the buyer role in order to get the desired goods. An agent adapts to the changes of its environment can also be performed by leaving a role temporarily and then returning to the role. To develop such application, the mechanism, language facility and supporting technical framework to describe and implement self-adaptation should be proposed.

2.1 Dynamic Binding Mechanism

In our approach, a multi-agent system is considered as an organization, which consists of a number of roles that stand in certain relationships and participate in various interactions with each other. In such an organization, an agent is situated in its environment and plays the roles of the organization. Role is the abstract characterization of the behaviors and the environments of agents.

In order to meet the design objectives and adapt to the environment changes, an agent should adjust its roles that it plays. The adaptation and adjustment of the agent can be performed by the following four atomic adaptation operations: join, quit, activate and deactivate. Adaptive agent can join or quit a role, and consequently, it obtains or loses the structural and behavioral features defined by the role. The status of a role bound by an agent is either active or inactive, and can be switched by the agent's action activate or deactivate. A formal definition of dynamic binding mechanism can be found in [7].

2.2 Technical Framework

Self-adaptive agent is a special kind of agent that can adjust its structure and behavior to adapt to the changes of their environment. The environment of an agent includes the system context (e.g. network bandwidth and the resources) and the other agents that can affect the agent in the system. In our approach, the situated environment of agent is abstracted and encapsulated as agents. Therefore, we can view the environment of an agent uniformly as the subset of the agents in MAS. The environment changes are specified as the occurrences of the environment events.

The environment event is composed by three parts: event type, event source and event constraint. Therefore, EnvironmentEvent = ⟨Type, Source, Constraint⟩. According to the interaction scope of agent with its environment, the environment event can be divided into three types: SERVICE, AGENT and ROLE. Table 1 shows the type and meaning of the various environment events.

Fig. 1 depicts our technical framework to construct self-adaptive agent based on SADE. A program of adaptive multi-agent system consists of three parts: role module, agent module and adaptive strategy. Role is the elementary module unit that encapsulates its environment and the behavior. Agent module implements the dynamic binding mechanism. The self-adaptation of agent is described by adaptive strategies.

Table 1. The type and meaning of environment event

Type	Meaning	Example
SERVICE	Changes of service provided by agents	⟨SERVICE, "Sell_Books", "AI"⟩
AGENT	Changes of states, behaviors and lifecycle state of a particular agent	⟨AGENT, "Tom", "AgentState"⟩
ROLE	Changes of states, behaviors and lifecycle state of the agents that bound to the role	⟨ROLE, "Buyer", "RoleState"⟩

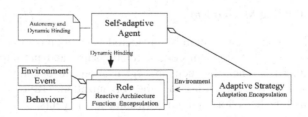

Fig. 1. Technical framework to construct self-adaptive agents

```
<Program> ::= ("package" <PackageName> ";")?
    ("import" ((<PackageName> "." "*") | ((<PackageName> ".")? <RoleClassName>)) ";")*
    "use" ((<PackageName> ".")? <AgentClassName> ";")
    "program" <ProgramName> "{" (<InitStrategy>)? (<AdaptiveStrategy>)+ "}" <EOF>
<AdaptiveStrategy> ::= "strategy" <StrategyName> "{" (<AdaptiveRule>)+ "}"
<AdaptiveRule> ::= "when" "(" <EventExpression> ")" "{" ( <IfStatement> | <AdaptationStatement>)* "}"
<IfStatement> ::= "if" "(" <StateExpression> ")" "{" (<AdaptationStatement> )? "}"
    ("else if" "(" <StateExpression> ")" "{" (<AdaptationStatement> )? "}" )* ("else" "{" (<AdaptationStatement> )? "}")?
```

Fig. 2. Part of SADL Syntax

2.3 SADL: Self Adaptation Description Language

In order to explicitly describe the self-adaptation of MAS, we present SADL as a self-adaptation description language. Fig. 2 shows the part of SADL syntax. EventExpression is the description of environment event each of which has name and parameters. StateExpression describes the state of adaptive agent. AdaptiveStatement describes how an agent adapts to environment changes by taking actions (e.g., join, quit, activate and deactivate) to adjust its structure and behaviors.

3 SADE: Self-adaptive Agent Development Environment

To support the development, deployment and execution of self-adaptive multi-agent systems, we developed Self-adaptive Agent Development Environment (SADE) based on JADE [10]. Fig. 3 shows the whole framework of SADE with three layers: fundamental layer, running layer and development layer. Fundamental layer is based on the fundamental facilities of JADE and supports agents that are situated in heterogeneous environment to communicate with each other.

In running layer, SADE provides several functional modules for compiling, loading and executing strategies, transporting environment event and monitoring system, etc.

Event service is a very important part of SADE. To implement event service, we extend the content of ACLMessage from string to object, and supply the subscriber and publisher of event. In SADE, various changes of environment are encapsulated

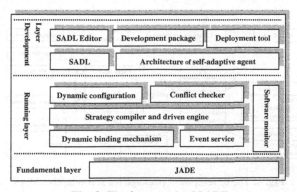

Fig. 3. The framework of SADE

into various message classes (such as AgentPropertyMessage, RoleBehaviorMessage and ServiceMessage, etc.). The instances of the message classes will be as the contents of ACLMessage and transported among agents.

Dynamic binding mechanism acts as the fundamental mechanism to construct adaptive agents. When an agent joins a role, the agent will get the instance of the role class, and obtain the role's behaviors. And then the agent will add the behaviors into its behavior list. In this way, the agent owns the behaviors of the role. It is worthy to note that the agent will also get the environment events defined in the role when it joins the role. To perceive the environment changes, the agent will load the subscribers according to the environment events automatically.

Compiler and execution are responsible for compiling and executing SADL programs. The developer compile the SADL program to adaptive strategy class, which is further complied into Java bytecodes. When all programs including roles and agents are complied as Java bytecodes, the SADE running platform is responsible for loading and execution of the adaptive multi-agent system.

Dynamic configuration supports the adaptive strategy to be loaded dynamically. An agent situates in environment which is changing continually and unpredictably, so it should have the ability of loading new strategy that can deal with new environment changes by using dynamic configuration.

Software monitor is used for monitoring the states and running information of the adaptive agents in an application so that the manager or maintainer can observe the states of application and understand whether the application is running normally.

Development layer provides a strategy description language, reusable components and tools for developing and deploying self-adaptive MAS.

SADL Editor is an Eclipse plug-in, which is designed to help application developer code SADL programs. To implement SADL Editor, we use the techniques of Java reflection, code tracking and syntax coloring.

Tools for self-adaptive software deployment are used for deploying the application system to target node. To execute the program developed on SADE rightly, we should configure the strategy configuration file and deploy the codes of roles, agents and strategies to the platform.

Development package for self-adaptive MAS provides the specifications of programming self-adaptive software and supports the design and development of self-adaptive MAS, Fig. 4 shows the part of the package.

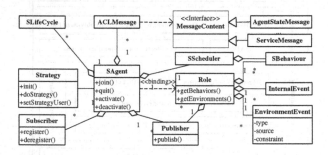

Fig. 4. The development package for self-adaptive MAS

4 Programming Adaptive MAS

The development of adaptive multi-agent systems mainly consists of the following steps, as shown in Fig. 5. In the design phase, the developer should identify the roles and agents for implementing the system according to results of the requirement description and analysis. When designing the roles, the developer should define the internal events and environment events of the role, and design the functional behaviors. When designing the agents, the developer should define the properties explicitly. Based on the roles and agents, developer can define the adaptive strategies with SADL for each adaptive agent.

In the implementation phase, the roles and agents are developed by inheriting the base classes Role and SAgent. When developing the roles, the developer should define the functional behaviors and the environment event by creating some instances of EnvironmentEvent. When developing the agents, the developer should set the parameters about the adaptive strategy.

To design and implement the case described in section 2 using SADE, we should identify and design a number of roles firstly. The attributes and behaviours of each role should be defined. Fig. 6 depicts the class diagram of roles.

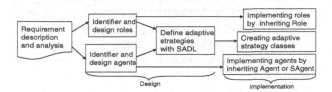

Fig. 5. The development process of a self-adaptive MAS

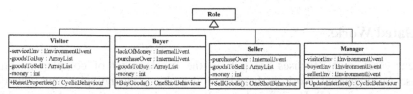

Fig. 6. The class diagram of roles of e-Commerce System

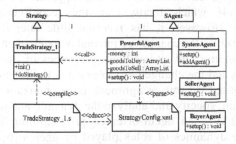

Fig. 7. The Agent class diagram

Secondly, a number of agents can be identified and designed. PowerfulAgent is a self-adaptive agent. The most important work in implementing self-adaptive agent is to define what adaptive strategy the self-adaptive agent will use. Fig. 7 depicts the class diagram of agents.

Finally, the adaptive strategy (TradeStrategy_1.s) can be defined by SADL. Fig. 8 shows the part of the screenshot of defining the adaptive strategy in the SADL Editor.

```
1 package examples.tradingSystem.strategies;
2 import examples.tradingSystem.roles.*;
3 //PowerfulAgent uses the strategy
4 use examples.tradingSystem.agents.PowerfulAgent;
5 program TradeStrategy_1 {
6     //Agent joins Visitor initially
7     InitStrategy { join(Visitor); }
8     strategy Wait {//Agent waits for service occurrence
9         when (SERVICE_EVENT(Sell, Book)) {
10             deactivate(Visitor); join(Buyer); } }
11    strategy Buy {
12        //Agent binds to various role for buying goods
13        when (INTERNAL_EVENT(LackOfMoney, Buyer)) {
14            if (self.goodsToBuy.length > 0
15                && Seller@UNBOUND) {
16                deactivate(Buyer); join(Seller);
17            }
18        }
```

Fig. 8. The part of adaptive strategy of PowerfulAgent defined by SADL

5 Related Works

In recent years, many focuses are put on the development of complex adaptive systems. An important work is based on the object technologies and adaptive reflection mechanism [3]. However, due to the static characteristics of objects and the lack of flexible support to dynamic re-classification of objects, they are not suitable for the dynamic and open environment. Another approach is based on adaptive software architecture [4] which focuses on the reconfiguration of software architecture at runtime. However, it has received little attention about how the software entity adapts itself to the changes of internal or external environment.

We believe the autonomy and situatedness properties of agents can deal well with the self-adaptation and the changed environments. In the past years, a number of mechanisms [5,6] based on role assignment and organization metaphors have been presented to explain, specify and analyze the dynamic and adaptive aspects of multi-agent systems. 2APL, an agent-oriented programming language, extends 3APL and captures the dynamics of roles played by agents [6]. However, 2APL does not consider how to describe the adaptive strategies that support agents adapting to the changes of the situated environment. Another important work is the dynamic caste mechanism [8] and programming language SLABSp [9]. In these agent-oriented programming languages, the functional behaviors are tangled with adaptation behaviors together. Such approaches make it more difficult and complicated to construct and maintain complex adaptive multi-agent systems. RoleX [11] is an interaction infrastructure, which enables Java agents to assume and use roles at runtime dynamically. It performs the bytecode manipulation to assume roles. However, this way is not so natural and easy for implementing and debugging MAS.

6 Conclusions

Adaptive system is a kind of complex system that is widespread in many applications. Up to now, it is still a challenge to develop such system in a systematic way. In this paper, we present an adaptive mechanism which is based on organization metaphors and corresponding supporting environment to construct complex adaptive systems. We program complex adaptive MAS by separating concerns of functional logic and adaptive logic. In this way, application programmers can focus on different aspects of complex adaptive multi-agent systems, therefore the efficiency of developing the complex systems can be improved.

We have successfully developed a supporting environment called SADE, and based on SADE, a number of adaptive applications have been implemented, such as e-commerce system, garbage cleaner, interest management system. The practices and case studies show that the proposed approach to programming adaptive MAS is feasible, the dynamic binding mechanism is effective, SADL is simple, easy-to-use and robust, and the developed software systems are maintainable. However, there are still several problems that should be dealt with in further. (1) More ways that agent senses environment should be studied. (2) The correctness and consistency of self-adaptation strategy should be checked at design time, etc.

Acknowledgements

The authors gratefully acknowledge the financial support from High-Tech 863 Program of China under granted number 2007AA01Z135, Natural Science Foundation of China under granted number 60773018.

References

1. Zambonelli, F., Van Dyke Parunak, H.: Towards a paradigm change in computer science and software engineering: a synthesis. The Knowledge Engineering Review 18(4), 329–342 (2003)
2. Jennings, N.R.: An Agent-based Approach for Building Complex Software Systems. Communication of ACM 44(4), 35–41 (2001)
3. Yoder, J.W., Balaguer, F., Johnson, R.: Architecture and design of adaptive object models. In: Proc. of the Technology Presentation at the 2001 Conference on Object-Oriented Programming Systems, Languages, and Applications. ACM Press, New York (2001)

4. Garlan, D., Cheng, S.W., Huang, A.C.: Rainbow: Architecture-based self-adaptation with reusable infrastructure. Comput. 37(10), 46–54 (2004)
5. Odell, J., Parunak, H.V.D., Brueckner, S., Sauter, J.: Temporal aspects of dynamic role assignment. In: Giorgini, P., Müller, J.P., Odell, J.J. (eds.) AOSE 2003. LNCS, vol. 2935, pp. 201–213. Springer, Heidelberg (2004)
6. Dastani, M., Mol, C., Steunebrink, B.: Modularity in agent programming languages: An illustration in extended 2apl. Technical Report (2008)
7. Mao, X., Shang, L., Zhu, H., Wang, J.: The Adaptive Casteship Mechanism for Developing Multi-Agent Systems. International Journal of Computer Applications in Technology (IJCAT) 31(1/2), 17–34 (2008)
8. Zhu, H.: SLABS: A Formal Specification Language for Agent-Based Systems. International Journal of Software Engineering and Knowledge Engineering 11(5), 529–558 (2001)
9. Wang, J., Shen, R., Zhu, H.: Towards Agent Oriented Programming Language with Caste and Scenario Mechanisms. In: Proc. of International Joint Conference on Autonomous Agents and Multiagent Systems, pp. 1297–1298. ACM Press, New York (2005)
10. Bellifemine, F., Caire, G., Poggi, A., Rimassa, G.: JADE: A white paper. Telecom Italia Lab Journal EXP 3(3), 6–19 (2003)
11. Cabri, G., Ferrari, L., Leonardi, L.: Injecting roles in Java agents through run-time bytecode manipulation. IBM Systems Journal 44(1), 185–208 (2005)

Recursive Adaptation of Stepsize Parameter for Non-stationary Environments

Itsuki Noda[1]

[1] Information Technology Research Institute
National Institute of Advanced Industrial Science and Technology
1-1-1 Umezono, Tsukuba, Ibaraki 305-8568, Japan
i.noda@aist.go.jp
[2] School of Information Science
Japan Advanced Institute of Science and Technology, Japan
[3] Department of Systems Innovation, The University of Tokyo, Japan

Abstract. In this article, we propose a method to adapt stepsize parameters used in reinforcement learning for non-stationary environments. When the environment is non-stationary, the learning agent must adapt learning parameters like stepsize to the changes of environment through continuous learning. We show several theorems on higher-order derivatives of exponential moving average, which is a base schema of major reinforcement learning methods, using stepsize parameters. We also derive a systematic mechanism to calculate these derivatives in a recursive manner. Based on it, we construct a precise and flexible adaptation method for the stepsize parameter in order to maximize a certain criterion. The proposed method is also validated by several experimental results.

1 Introduction

Although reinforcement learning is expected to be useful open problem like real world problems, most of the works assume that statistic models of rewards and noises of the environment for agents is stationary during and after learning. In such a case, it is reasonable that a stepsize parameter α is monotonically decreased to 0 through learning in the following temporal difference(TD) learning algorithm in order to estimate the expected values of the states or actions (Q-value) [1].

$$Q_{t+1}(state_t, act_t) = (1 - \alpha)Q_t(state_t, act_t) + \alpha(r_t + \gamma \max_{act'} Q_t(state_{t+1}, act'))(1)$$

After the Q-values seem to be sufficiently near the true expected values, the agents generally stop learning and behave on the basis of the fixed Q-value. An important assumption here is that the true expected values are constant during and after learning [2].

On the other hand, in common real world problems, especially the problems on open and multiagent systems, the environment may change gradually or rapidly. For example, market systems such as the stock market and foreign exchange can

J.-J. Yang et al. (Eds.): PRIMA 2009, LNAI 5925, pp. 525–533, 2009.

be affected by both agents' behavior and various other fundamental conditions. Therefore, it is difficult to suppose that the true expected rewards of states or actions are stationary. Instead, agents in such an environment should continue learning to adapt to changes in the environments. In this case, since we cannot decrease the stepsize parameter α monotonically, we control it such that it is capable of meeting the changes in the environment.

In order to adapt to such dynamic and non-stationary environments, [3] proposed a method, called optimal stepsize algorithm (OSA), to control stepsize parameters in order to minimize noise factors on the basis of the relationships among the stepsize parameter, noise variance, and changes in learning values. [4] also proposed a framework to accumulate error variance to find out the suitable learning parameters. In both works, the focus is only on minimizing estimation errors, in which the effect of the changes in the stepsize parameter on the learning processes is ignored.

For this issue, we focus on the effects of the changes in the stepsize parameter, and extend the learning process to estimate the effects. On the basis of the estimation, we can construct a method to adjust the stepsize parameter in order to optimize any criteria calculated from estimated values like ($Q(s, a)$ in eq. (1).

2   Exponential Moving Average and Stepsize Parameter

2.1   Exponential Moving Average

Here, we simplify eq. (1) as follows;

$$\tilde{x}_{t+1} = (1 - \alpha)\tilde{x}_t + \alpha x_t, \tag{2}$$

where x_t and $\tilde{x}_t$ are the actual observed value (for example, received reward r_t) and the corresponding expected value, respectively, that are updated through discrete time line t. α is a *stepsize parameter*, which indicates whether the agent regards recent observed values x_t as important, or the agent should take a long-term average so as to calculate the true expected value ($\tilde{x}_t$). This equation is called as *exponential moving average* (EMA).

2.2   Recursive Exponential Moving Average

Suppose that we should adjust α to minimize a certain criteria $f(\tilde{x}_t)$. In this case, a simple way is to find $\frac{\partial f}{\partial \alpha} = \frac{\partial f}{\partial \tilde{x}_t} \cdot \frac{\partial \tilde{x}_t}{\partial \alpha}$. To do this, we try to extract the derivatives of the expected value $\tilde{x}_t$ using the stepsize parameter α, and construct a method to adapt α according to a given sequence of observation $\{x_t\}$.

First, we introduce the following *recursive exponential moving average* (REMA) $\xi_t^{\langle k \rangle}$ by applying eq. (2) recursively:

$$\xi_t^{\langle 0 \rangle} = x_t$$

$$\xi_{t+1}^{\langle 1 \rangle} = \tilde{x}_{t+1} = (1 - \alpha)\tilde{x}_t + \alpha x_t$$

$$\xi_{t+1}^{\langle k \rangle} = (1 - \alpha)\xi_t^{\langle k \rangle} + \alpha \xi_t^{\langle k-1 \rangle} = \alpha \sum_{\tau=0}^{\infty} (1 - \alpha)^\tau \xi_{t-\tau}^{\langle k-1 \rangle}. \tag{3}$$

With regard to REMA, we can state the following lemma and theorem.

Lemma 1. *The first partial derivative of REMA $\xi_t^{\langle k \rangle}$ by α is given by the following equation:*

$$\frac{\partial \xi_t^{\langle k \rangle}}{\partial \alpha} = \frac{k}{\alpha}(\xi_t^{\langle k \rangle} - \xi_t^{\langle k+1 \rangle}). \tag{4}$$

(See section A for the proof.)   □

Theorem 1. *The k-th partial derivative of EMA $\tilde{x}_t$ $(= \xi_t^{\langle 1 \rangle})$ is given by the following equation:*

$$\frac{\partial^k \tilde{x}_t}{\partial \alpha^k} = (-\alpha)^{-k} k! (\xi_t^{\langle k+1 \rangle} - \xi_t^{\langle k \rangle}). \tag{5}$$

(See section B for the proof.)   □

2.3 Gradient Descent Adaptation of Stepsize Parameter Using Higher-Order Derivatives and REMA

Because theorem 1 provides the derivatives of $\tilde{x}_t$ by α, we can construct algorithms to optimize a certain criterion, for example, mean square errors, by gradient descent/ascent methods. An important aspect of theorem 1 is that it can provide derivatives of any order. Therefore, we can form more precise gradient descent/ascent methods. We refer to such methods that use higher-order derivatives given by REMA as *recursive adaptation of stepsize parameters* (RASP).

Suppose that $\Delta \tilde{x}_t$ is the change in $\tilde{x}_t$ when α changes by $\Delta \alpha$. In this case, $\Delta \tilde{x}_t$ can be represented by Taylor expansion and theorem 1 as follows:

$$\Delta \tilde{x}_t = \sum_{k=1}^{\infty} \frac{1}{k!} \frac{\partial^k \tilde{x}_t}{\partial \alpha^k} \Delta \alpha^k = \sum_{k=1}^{\infty} (-1)^k \left(\frac{\Delta \alpha}{\alpha}\right)^k (\xi_t^{\langle k+1 \rangle} - \xi_t^{\langle k \rangle}). \tag{6}$$

Further, generally, $\Delta \xi_t^{\langle k \rangle}$ for any k can be estimated by the first Taylor expansion and lemma 1 as follows: [1]

$$\Delta \xi_t^{\langle k \rangle} = \Delta \alpha \frac{\partial \xi_t^{\langle k \rangle}}{\partial \alpha} \simeq k \left(\frac{\Delta \alpha}{\alpha}\right) (\xi_t^{\langle k \rangle} - \xi_t^{\langle k+1 \rangle}). \tag{7}$$

These expansions indicate that RASP exhibits the following features.

1. We can approximate the precise changes in the estimation value $\tilde{x}_t$ even for a large $\Delta \alpha$, using higher-order derivatives calculated by REMA. Therefore, we can change α rapidly.

---

[1] We can also use a higher-order Taylor expansion to utilize higher-order derivatives as shown in the appendix.

2. We can also calculate $\Delta\xi_t^{\langle k\rangle}$ by a modification of α, using the derivatives of $\xi_t^{\langle k\rangle}$. Therefore, the values of the variables that are affected by the changes in α are kept precise.

Of course, it is impossible to calculate infinite higher-order derivatives. Instead, we can set upper limit of k large enough to achieve the required precision. Because the calculation of REMA itself is very simple, the cost to calculate higher-order derivatives is small.

The following procedure details the use of RASP to minimize the square error between the expected value $\tilde{x}_t$ and the actual observation x_t. (We call this procedure RASP-MSE.)

Initialize: $\forall k \in \{0 \dots k_{\max} - 1\} : \xi^{\langle k\rangle} \leftarrow x_0$
while forever **do**
    Let x be an observation.
    for $k = k_{\max} - 1$ to 1 **do**
        $\xi^{\langle k\rangle} \leftarrow (1 - \alpha)\xi^{\langle k\rangle} + \alpha\xi^{\langle k-1\rangle}$
    end for
    $\xi^{\langle 0\rangle} \leftarrow x, \delta \leftarrow \xi^{\langle 1\rangle} - x$
    Calculate $\frac{\partial\xi^{\langle 1\rangle}}{\partial\alpha}$ by eq. (5).
    for $k = 1$ to $k_{\max} - 1$ **do**
        Calculate $\Delta\xi^{\langle k\rangle}$ by eq. (6) and eq. (7).
        $\xi^{\langle k\rangle} \leftarrow \xi^{\langle k\rangle} + \Delta\xi^{\langle k\rangle}$
    end for
    calculate a new α according to δ and $\frac{\partial\xi^{\langle 1\rangle}}{\partial\alpha}$.
end while

---

3   Experiments

3.1   Exp.1: Learning Best α for Noise Reduction

In the first experiment, we show that the above procedure to adapt α yields the best stepsize parameter value for noise reduction that is determined by eq. (8).

Figure 1 shows the results of the adaptation of α through the learning of observation sequences $\{x_t\}$ that consist of random walk sequences $\{s_t\}$ and noise $\{\epsilon_t\}$ as follows: $x_t = s_t + \epsilon_t$, where average and standard deviation of ϵ_t are 0 and σ_ϵ, respectively. The random walk sequence $\{s_t\}$ is defined as $s_{t+1} = s_t + v_t$, where v_t is a random value with average 0 and standard deviation σ_v. In this case, the best value of α can be derived from given σ_ϵ and σ_v as follows:

$$\alpha = \frac{-\gamma^2 + \sqrt{\gamma^4 + 4\gamma^2}}{2}, \tag{8}$$

where $\gamma = \frac{\sigma_v}{\sigma_\epsilon}$.

Each curve in the graph of Figure 1 shows the changes in α through the learning of expected value $\tilde{x}_t$ by eq. (2) and adaptation of α by RASP-MSE.

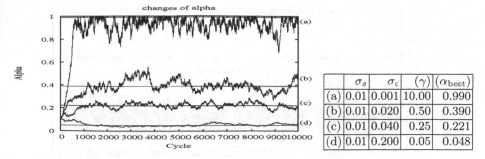

Fig. 1. Exp.1: Changes in α through the Learning of Observed Value Using the Various Ratios of Standard Deviations of Random Walk and Noise (γ)

The horizontal axis in the graphs indicates the learning (and adaptation) cycle, while the vertical axis represents the value of α. Further, the horizontal line in each graph indicates the best stepsize parameter (α_{best}) as calculated by eq. (8). As shown in these graphs, α approaches the best value and is then consistent through learning. Note that α does not converge to the best value because of the noise factors added in the observed value. Fortunately, the perturbation is large only when α is relatively large; in this case, the effect of α changes slowly, so that the behavior of the learning does not change drastically even α changes with a large step.

3.2   Exp.3: Square-Waved True Value

EMA is used in general reinforcement learning, for example, eq. (1), because it can reduce noise and yield a value that approaches the stationary true value. In the second experiment, we suppose that the true value is almost stationary but does change occasionally. In such a case, the learning mechanism needs to detect the changes in the true value. In the actual experiment, we use a sequence of true values $\{s_t\}$ that follows a square wave over time.

Figure 2 shows the result of an experiment to adapt α by RASP-MSE in the EMA learning of $\tilde{x}_t$ when the true value s_t alternates between 0.0 and 0.5 every 1000 steps. In this experiment the standard deviation of noise ϵ_t is 5.0. (a) shows the changes in α, and (b), in x_t, $\tilde{x}_t$, and s_t through learning. (c) shows a result of the case that we apply OSA [3] to the same problem for the comparison.

(b) indicates that RASP-EMA reduces the large noise factor and at the same time can follow the changes in the true value. Compared with (c), we found that following the true value is more precise by RASP-EMA than by OSA. Actually, the average square error of $\tilde{x}_t$ from x_t in (b) is 1.192, while the error in (c) is 2.496. Corresponding changes in α in (a) shows that α approaches zero almost all the times but is relatively large at the time when the true value s_t changes ($t = 1000, 2000, \ldots$). From the meaning of α in EMA ($\tilde{x}_t$ follows the previous observed value x_t when α is large, and $\tilde{x}_t$ becomes a long-term moving average of x_t when α is small), the change in α shown in (a) indicates that RASP-MSE

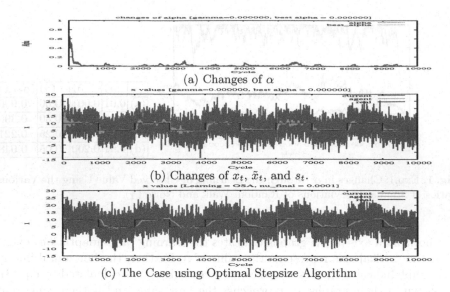

(a) Changes of α

(b) Changes of x_t, $\tilde{x}_t$, and s_t.

(c) The Case using Optimal Stepsize Algorithm

Fig. 2. Exp.3: Learning Square-waved True Value s_t

detects the timing of changes in s_t and lets an agent regard the recent observation as plausible: On the other hand, RASP-MSE lets the agent use the long-term smoothed value when the environment is stationary. In other words, RASP-MSE can control the features of learning by EMA in accordance with the changes in the environment.

4   Discussion and Summary

In this article, we derive the relations between stepsize parameter α and expected value $\tilde{x}_t$ acquired by EMA, and provide a method called RASP that calculates the higher-order derivatives of $\tilde{x}_t$ by α. We also propose a procedure called RASP-MSE that adjusts α suitably for given observed data both to reduce noise factors in the observation and to follow the changes in the environment. Experiments illustrate the functionality and performance of RASP-MSE for adjusting the stepsize parameters as shown in theorems and lemmas.

The main feature of RASP is that we can obtain derivatives $\partial\tilde{x}_t/\partial\alpha$. Therefore, we can apply it to various optimization applications that require EMA. For example, it can not only be applied to situations where the minimization of estimation error is desired, but also to the learning of decision making directly, for example, back-propagations in neural networks. Thus, it can be said that RASP has more potential than the other adaptation mechanisms of stepsize parameters such as OSA [3].

The stochastic gradient adaptive (SGA) stepsize method [5] is identical to RASP-MSE if we use only the first-order derivative. As we can calculate higher-order derivatives, the adaptation based on RASP can be more quick and precise.

There are many other works on speed-up of reinforcement learning. Ahmadi et. al. tried to apply domain knowledge to selection of feature set to speed up the learning [6]. Abstracting feature and state spaces is also a major method to speed up and scale up the learning [7]. RASP can be combine to these works to increase adaptability to the changes of environment.

There still several open issues. For example, we should apply RASP-MSE to TD learning and multiagent learning, which may not follow the assumption of random walk. Also, we need to utilize higher-order derivatives to calculate the best stepsize instead to change it gradually.

Acknowledgments. This work was supported by JSPS KAKENHI 21500153.

References

1. Sutton, R.S., Barto, A.G.: Reinforcement Learning: An Introduction. MIT Press, Cambridge (1998)
2. Even-dar, E., Mansour, Y.: Learning rates for q-learning. Journal of Machine Learning Research 5 (December 2003)
3. George, A.P., Powell, W.B.: Adaptive stepsizes for recursive estimation with applications in approximate dynamic programming. Machine learning 65(1), 167–198 (2006)
4. Sato, M., Kimura, H., Kobayashi, S.: TD algorithm for the variance of return and mean-variance reinforcement learning (in japanese). Transactions of the Japanese Society for Artificial Intelligence 16(No. 3F), 353–362 (2001)
5. Douglas, S.C., Mathews, V.J.: Stochastic gradient adaptive step size algorithms for adaptive filtering. In: Proc. International Conference on Digital Signal Processing, pp. 142–147 (1995)
6. Ahmadi, M., Taylor, M.E., Stone, P.: IFSA: Incremental feature-set augmentation for reinforcement learning tasks. In: The Sixth International Joint Conference on Autonomous Agents and Multiagent Systems (May 2007)
7. Schoknecht, R., Riedmiller, M.: Speeding-up reinforcement learning with multi-step actions. In: Dorronsoro, J.R. (ed.) ICANN 2002. LNCS, vol. 2415, pp. 813–818. Springer, Heidelberg (2002)

Appendix

A   Proof of Lemma 1

First, we show the following lemma.

Lemma 2

$$\xi_{t+1}^{\langle k \rangle} = \alpha^2 \sum_{\tau=0}^{\infty} \tau (1 - \alpha)^{\tau-1} \xi_{t-\tau}^{\langle k-2 \rangle}. \tag{9}$$

$\square$

Proof
Suppose that

$$\eta_{t+1}=\alpha^2 \sum_{\tau=0}^{\infty} \tau(1-\alpha)^{\tau-1}\xi_{t-\tau}^{\langle k-2\rangle}=\alpha^2 \left[1(1-\alpha)^0\xi_{t-1}^{\langle k-2\rangle} + 2(1-\alpha)^1\xi_{t-2}^{\langle k-2\rangle} + 3(1-\alpha)^2\xi_{t-3}^{\langle k-2\rangle} + \ldots\right].$$

Then, we can obtain the following equation:

$$(1-\alpha)\eta_t = \alpha^2 \left[1(1-\alpha)^1\xi_{t-2}^{\langle k-2\rangle} + 2(1-\alpha)^2\xi_{t-3}^{\langle k-2\rangle} + 3(1-\alpha)^3\xi_{t-4}^{\langle k-2\rangle} + \ldots\right].$$

This can be rewritten as follows:

$$\eta_{t+1} - (1-\alpha)\eta_t = \alpha^2 \sum_{\tau=0}^{\infty}(1-\alpha)^\tau \xi_{t-1-\tau}^{\langle k-2\rangle} = \alpha\xi_t^{\langle k-1\rangle}.$$

Finally, we can obtain the recurrence formula: $\eta_{t+1} = (1-\alpha)\eta_t + \alpha\xi_t^{\langle k-1\rangle}$. This formula is the same as the one for $\xi_t^{\langle k\rangle}$. Therefore, if $\eta_0 = \xi_0^{\langle k\rangle}$, η_t is identical to $\xi_t^{\langle k\rangle}$ for all t. Therefore, we can obtain eq. (9). ∎

Using this lemma, we can prove Lemma 1 as follows:
In the case of $k = 1$, we can obtain the following equation:

$$\frac{\partial \xi_t^{\langle 1\rangle}}{\partial \alpha} = \frac{\partial}{\partial \alpha}\left[\alpha\sum_{\tau=0}^{\infty}(1-\alpha)^\tau x_{t-\tau-1}\right] = \frac{1}{\alpha}(\xi_t^{\langle 1\rangle} - \xi_t^{\langle 2\rangle}).$$

Therefore, eq. (4) is satisfied when $k = 1$.
Suppose that eq. (4) is satisfied for any $k < k'$. Then, we can calculate the k'-th derivative as follows:

$$\frac{\partial \xi_t^{\langle k'\rangle}}{\partial \alpha} = \sum_{\tau=0}^{\infty}(1-\alpha)^\tau \xi_{t-\tau-1}^{\langle k'-1\rangle} - \alpha\sum_{\tau=0}^{\infty}\tau(1-\alpha)^{\tau-1}\xi_{t-\tau-1}^{\langle k'-1\rangle} + \alpha\sum_{\tau=0}^{\infty}(1-\alpha)^\tau \frac{\partial}{\partial \alpha}\xi_{t-\tau-1}^{\langle k'-1\rangle}$$

$$= \frac{1}{\alpha}\xi_t^{\langle k'\rangle} - \frac{1}{\alpha}\xi_t^{\langle k'+1\rangle} + (k'-1)\sum_{\tau=0}^{\infty}(1-\alpha)^\tau \xi_{t-\tau-1}^{\langle k'-1\rangle} - (k'-1)\sum_{\tau=0}^{\infty}(1-\alpha)^\tau \xi_{t-\tau-1}^{\langle k'\rangle}$$

$$= \frac{k'}{\alpha}(\xi_t^{\langle k'\rangle} - \xi_t^{\langle k'+1\rangle}).$$

As a result, eq. (4) holds for any $k > 0$. ∎

B   Proof of Theorem 1

In the case of $k = 1$, we can obtain the following equation:

$$\frac{\partial \tilde{x}_t}{\partial \alpha} = \frac{\partial}{\partial \alpha}\xi_t^{\langle 1\rangle} = \frac{1}{\alpha}(\xi_t^{\langle 1\rangle} - \xi_t^{\langle 2\rangle}) = (-\alpha)^{-1}(\xi_t^{\langle 1\rangle} - \xi_t^{\langle 2\rangle}).$$

Therefore, eq. (5) is satisfied when $k = 1$.

Suppose that eq. (5) is satisfied for any $k < k'$. Then, we can calculate the k'-th derivative as follows:

$$\frac{\partial^k \tilde{x}_t}{\partial \alpha^k} = \frac{\partial}{\partial \alpha} \frac{\partial^{k-1} \tilde{x}_t}{\partial \alpha^{k-1}} = \frac{\partial}{\partial \alpha} \left[(-\alpha)^{-(k-1)} (k-1)! (\xi_t^{\langle k \rangle} - \xi_t^{\langle k-1 \rangle}) \right]$$

$$= -(k-1)(-1)^{-(k-1)} \alpha^{-k} (k-1)! (\xi_t^{\langle k \rangle} - \xi_t^{\langle k-1 \rangle})$$

$$+ (-1)^{-(k-1)} \alpha^{-(k-1)} \left[\frac{\partial}{\partial \alpha} \xi_t^{\langle k \rangle} - \frac{\partial}{\partial \alpha} \xi_t^{\langle k-1 \rangle} \right]$$

The first and second terms inside the brackets in the right hand side of this equation are $\frac{k}{\alpha}(\xi_t^{\langle k \rangle} - \xi k + 1_t)$ and $\frac{k-1}{\alpha}(\xi_t^{\langle k-1 \rangle} - \xi k_t)$, respectively. Therefore,

$$\frac{\partial^k \tilde{x}_t}{\partial \alpha^k} = (-1)^{-(k-1)} \alpha^{-k} (k-1)!$$

$$\times \left[-k \xi_t^{\langle k+1 \rangle} + (k + (k-1) - (k-1)) \xi_t^{\langle k \rangle} + ((k-1) - (k-1)) \xi_t^{\langle k-1 \rangle} \right]$$

$$= (-1)^{-(k-1)} \alpha^{-k} (k-1)! \left[-k \xi_t^{\langle k+1 \rangle} + k \xi_t^{\langle k \rangle} \right]$$

$$= (-1)^{-k} \alpha^{-k} k! (\xi_t^{\langle k+1 \rangle} - \xi_t^{\langle k \rangle}) = (-\alpha)^{-k} k! (\xi_t^{\langle k+1 \rangle} - \xi_t^{\langle k \rangle}).$$

As a result, eq. (5) holds for any $k > 0$.   ∎

Furthermore, the m-th derivatives of general REMA $\xi_t^{\langle k \rangle}$ by α can be shown using the same inductive method:

$$\frac{\partial^m \xi_t^{\langle k \rangle}}{\partial \alpha^m} = \frac{k}{\alpha^m} \sum_{i=0}^{m} (-1)^i \frac{m!}{i!(m-l)!} \frac{(k+i-1)!}{(k+i-m)!} \xi_t^{\langle k+i \rangle}.$$

Mechanism Design Simulation for Healthcare Reform in China

Guanqun Liang[1], Hirofumi Yamaki[2], and Huanye Sheng[1]

[1] Department of Computer Science and Engineering of Shanghai Jiao Tong University
Shanghai, China
liang_guanqun@yahoo.com.cn, hysheng@mail.sjtu.edu.cn
[2] Information Technology Center Nagoya University Nagoya, Japan
yamaki@itc.nagoya-u.ac.jp

Abstract. We present a new insurance system for healthcare reform to meet the medical demand and alleviate the cost burden in China. China healthcare reform is complex where unlike most countries' uniform system; it has two branches: urban health insurance and new rural cooperative medical. The equity and efficiency of the two medical healthcare systems are discussed in this paper. We use multi-agent based computational mechanism design simulation to analyze the healthcare insurance's coverage, service and treatment cost of the people. A summary of the recent medical healthcare reforms undertaken in China is also discussed. Research results indicate that our novel hybrid healthcare insurance system formed by merging parts of the two branches can improve equity without compromising efficiency.

Keywords: Multi-agent system; Computational mechanism design; Healthcare system.

1 Introduction

China citizens' basic healthcare insurance system mainly consists of two explicit programs, urban health insurance and New Rural Cooperative Medical (NRCM) [1]. China's two healthcare systems have limited the equity and efficiency of the whole system thus covering only 70% of the population. Another important factor is that the patient is the major contributor for medical costs. By 2005, almost 56% of all healthcare bills were paid by patients [2]. Other countries healthcare systems such as for US, Europe and Japan, the major contributors are either the government or medical insurance companies [3]. China goal is to reduce the percentage cost patients.

Considerable researches on healthcare systems have dealt mostly with statistical methods [4, 5]. Some have approached the issue from a psychological view [6]. We design a multi-agent system based on computational mechanism method [7, 8], which can remedy the realistic insufficiency [9]. Bounded rationality [10, 11] elements are used in our model. The agents do not know the other agents' strategies but deduces the reasons about them from the model's primitives [12]. One goal of the mechanism is to maximize the aggregate contribution by players to a system, while another is to

J.-J. Yang et al. (Eds.): PRIMA 2009, LNAI 5925, pp. 534–541, 2009.

maximize the total social welfare of all the agent players. Patients will change their strategies to insurance and hospitals or medical providers [13].

The remainder of the paper is organized as follows: Section 2 describes the model, and discusses the settings of the mechanism. Section 3 describes the results and the evaluation of the result. Section 4 discusses the model and gives further exploration, and finally we provide the conclusions in Section 5.

2 Theoretical Analysis

2.1 Model

Four types of agents in our multi-agent based healthcare reform mechanism design are patient, healthcare insurance fund manager, fiscal budget manager and healthcare provider. A set of these autonomous and rational agents $N = \{1, 2, \cdots, i, \cdots, n\}$ each hold private information θ_i about its preferences. θ_i is not known by the mechanism or any other agent. Agent i with θ_i has utility function $u_i(\theta_i, r)$ for result $r \in \delta$, where δ is the set of all possible results that depend on its own and the outcome chosen by the mechanism. All agents report expressions to the mechanism, denoted by their θ_i.

So the healthcare reform can be expressed by a mechanism $M = (N, \Sigma, g)$ that includes agents strategy space Σ and outcome rule $g(\delta)$ for $\delta=(\delta_1, \delta_2, \cdots, \delta_n) \in \Sigma_N$. A strategy $s_i(\theta_i) \in \Sigma$ defines the agent's action choice in the mechanism for all possible type θ_i. Agent i selects strategy in Σ. In our mechanism, all agents are bounded rationality. They will try to find the best utility strategy in their ability.

We define the agent choice function $f: A \rightarrow \delta$, which describes the desired outcome. A is the set of actions available to agent. In order to achieve efficiency and maximize the total utility gained of all agents:

$$f(A)=argmax_{r \in \delta} \sum_{i \in N} u_i(\theta_i, r) \tag{1}$$

All types of agents have some properties which are known, such as:

- Maximize utility: Agents will prefer better outcomes.
- Bounded Rationality: Agent's calculation ability cannot be beyond its capacity.
- Budget restricted: Agent payment cannot exceed their cost capacity.
- Individual rationality: Each agent has nonnegative utility. The mechanism cannot force the agent to participate in the system and the agent will quit the system because of negative utility.

First, we discuss the fiscal budget manager agent. The fiscal budget manager agent has one special property. We look at this special property as a special kind of social welfare (SW) to measure the implementation of government's wide coverage policy. Many of the poor are not covered by the basic healthcare insurance, thus improving the coverage is one of the most urgent and important tasks. If agent i is an inpatient and low income person, agent i may become bankrupt while not covered by any medical insurance. So the fiscal budget manager agent plays a pivotal role by establishing the required budget for equitable policy.

Patient agent is more complex than the fiscal budget agent. Patient agents are not restricted to pure strategy and incentive. Our medical healthcare mechanism assumes that the agents know their preferences over different outcomes, and the mechanism is to get the agents to reveal their information. The patient cost depends on two parameters, one is the disease and the other is the choice of the hospital.

The third important agent type is healthcare insurance fund agent. Almost all countries use healthcare insurance as a useful way to reduce the patient economic risk.

The fourth part is hospital agent. Three types of hospitals exist. They are big integrated hospital agent, middle size or community hospital and clinic or small hospital. The same type agents provide the same level service and offer similar cost.

We give a definition of the multi-agent based healthcare mechanism.

Definition 1. n-player, normal-form mechanism in the medical mechanism $G = \{N, A_i, u_i\}$:

- $N = \{1, \cdots, n\}$ is the set of agents.
- $A_i = \{a_{i1}, \cdots, a_{im}\}$ is the set of actions available to agent i, where m is the number of available actions for agent i. Agent's actions depend on his strategy set $\Sigma_{i \in N}$. $a = (a_1, \cdots, a_n)$ to denote a profile of actions, for all agents in one simulation round. Also, let $a_{-i} = (a_1, \cdots, a_{i-1}, a_{i+1}, \cdots, a_n)$ denote this same profile excluding the action of agent i, so that (a_i, a_{-i}) forms a complete profile of actions.
- $u_i : A_1 \times \cdots \times A_n \rightarrow r$ is the utility function for each agent i. It maps a profile of actions to a value. Agents will calculate their u_i in each simulation round then evaluate the action taken in this round according to the u_i.

A multi-agent based healthcare mechanism $M = (N, \Sigma, g(\delta))$ is such a system, where N agents use Σ as strategy sets to pursuit the optimal results under the outcome rule g. $g(\delta)$ is restricted by medical background.

So the solution to the system is drawn as:

Definition 2. Our multi-agent based healthcare mechanism solution is said to implement its outcome function in dominant strategies as a function o: $\theta_1 \times \theta_2 \times \theta_3 \times \cdots \times \theta_n \rightarrow \delta$. This means for any agent $i \in N$, and for any strategy $\theta_i \in \Theta$, there are $s_i(\theta_i)$ and $s_i(\theta_i^*) \in \Sigma$, we have expected utility $E^*_{utility}(\theta_i^*, (s_i(\theta_i^*), o(\theta_1 \times \theta_2 \times \theta_3 \times \cdots \times \theta_i^* \times \cdots \times \theta_n))) \geq E_{utility}(\theta_i, (s_i(\theta_i), o(\theta_1 \times \theta_2 \times \theta_3 \times \cdots \times \theta_i \times \cdots \times \theta_n)))$.

2.2 Mechanism Settings and Agent Strategy

To describe our notion of one period, we refer to the sequence of triples (*strategy, action, utility*) as stage n of the run.

Agent's strategy is to search the best action as equation in (1). The strategy maps the action he takes. All agents learn from their past simulation rounds and results.

The agent's strategy at round $t+1$ is affected by the utility of the early time t:

$$A(t+1)=argmax(U_{i,Si}(A(t))) \qquad (2)$$

$$A(t) = \sum_{t=0}^{t} \sum_{i=1}^{N} A_{i,s_i(t)}^{u(t)} \qquad (3)$$

If agent i plays action $A(t)$ in period t and receives utility $U_i^t(A)$. Agent also can give new estimate for the action set A using learning [14]. We show that, at each stage most agents will have learned a best reply to the environment; a suitable parameter λ is used for incremental changes. We formally describe our agent learning as:

$$argU_i^{t+1}(A) = argU_i^{t-1}(A) + (1+\lambda^t)\,argU_i^t(A) \tag{4}$$

The parameter λ^t area is $0 < \lambda^t < 1$ which controls the evaluation adjustment after one period. In this paper we set the control parameter $\lambda \in \{0, 0.1, 0.2, 0.3\}$. That means if an agent gets much higher utility than average utility from an action from A.

$$\begin{cases} \lambda = 0.3 & \text{if top 10\%} \\ \lambda = 0.2 & \text{if top 10\% to 20\%} \\ \lambda = 0.1 & \text{if top 20\% to 30\%} \\ \lambda = 0 & \text{else} \end{cases} \tag{5}$$

In our mechanism M, agents use strategies that we denote $s_i(\theta_i, t)$, for $s_i(\theta_i, t) \in \Sigma$, where $A(s_i(\theta_i, t))$ is multiplied by parameter λ, in equation (4). Thus, if the agent calculates that it can get more utility from a strategy result of $s_i(\theta_i, t)$, it assigns a higher value to the strategy with parameter λ by (5).

The agents learn their strategy and action as follows: If $t = 0$, $s_i(t)$ is chosen Σ without history reference. If t is nonzero, $s_i(t)$ will be searched in Σ where $s_i(t) = argmax_{s \in \Sigma} U$. Otherwise, $s_i(t) = max\{argmax_{s \in \Sigma} U, (1+\lambda)*s_i(t-1)\}$, where $\lambda \in (5)$. Its action evaluation is updated to the highest value. Table 1. displays the algorithm.

Table 1. Algorithm for patients choose strategy in the mechanism

---

$t = t_0$ /* t_0 is the start time */
$s(t) \leftarrow$ **for all** Strategy Σ choose one **then**
stack push $s(t_0)$
do measure utility
if is the highest utility that the agent finds **then**
stack.push $\leftarrow s(t)$
else stack.pop
if stack empty **then**
$s(t+1) \leftarrow$ **for all** Strategy Σ search one
else $s(t+1) \leftarrow s(t-1)$ /* stack top equals $s(t-1)$ */
update utility

In our medical healthcare system fiscal budget manager agent pays equal attention to the equity (we look it as social welfare, SW) and the budget (efficiency). If the equity index decreases, the agent will adjust its society strategy and afford more to help the poor patients who do not be covered by any healthcare insurance. The total social welfare of result r when agents have private type θ_i is denoted as $SW(\theta_i, r)$.

$$SW(\theta_i, r) = \Sigma_i u_i(\theta_i, r) \tag{6}$$

Using equation (6), we can describe the medical mechanism expected efficiency.

After the available healthcare fiscal budget has been used up, if more patient agents need help, a small ε is subtracted from the SW, for every patient agent who needs extra insurance. Now we set $\varepsilon=1\% * SW$, $\varepsilon'=2\% * SW$. We want to use this to show the intent that the SW dropped if the society is not even.

Insurance fund manager agent is similar with fiscal budget manager agent, but they have different strategies and utility functions from other type agents. This type of agent's income mostly is from citizen premium and urban employer premium which cover the patient's medical costs during their illness. Of course its utility can be negative if too many patients exist. In our model, we simplified to the basic two styles as urban healthcare insurance and NRCM. Insurance fund agent recommends the most suitable type to patient agent [15]. These two mechanisms have different premiums and medical cost percentage cover.

Patient agent has two indexes to evaluate the result from the healthcare mechanism, these two are the service the patient gets from hospital and its cost. We now try to combine these two together. Only consistent data can be added together. In our mechanism the hospitals are divided into three levels. These levels map to a number. We set the integrated hospital service equals 80 point, middle hospital service equals 60 point and clinic or small hospital service equals 40 point. The Gaussian distribution is used to make the number more realistic. The following equations show formal expression.

$$Point = \begin{cases} 80*Gaussian(0,40) & \text{Integrated Hospital} \\ 60*Gaussian(0,30) & \text{Middle size Hospital} \\ 40*Gaussian(0,20) & \text{Clinic} \end{cases} \tag{7}$$

Then each patient agent will get a service evaluation point, however, this cannot be added directly to the cost point relating to the payment to the hospital. More steps will be needed to standardize the data for the purpose summation. The following equations give the algorithm.

$$Temp_i = (P_i - P_{average})/S \tag{8}$$

$$Z_i = Temp_i*100 + 500 \tag{9}$$

$$Z_i = Z_i * (1+\lambda) \tag{10}$$

Where P_i is the point of agent$_i$, $P_{average}$ is the average of all the agent point, and S is the points' standard variance. In equation (9), we keep Z_i positive and maintain the order of points in the whole point set. If at a specific time agent$_i$ has a positive λ utility parameter. We use $Z_i = Z_i * (1+\lambda)$ to set the new Z_i.

The agent's cost in hospital is done in a similar way. After this, we get a new patient's hospital cost array C_i for each agent. The following equation is used to get the evaluation number.

$$Agent_i \ evaluation \ point = Z_i/C_i \tag{11}$$

From the evaluation result, mechanism designers have some basic rules to compare with other medical mechanism.

All the simulation data in this paper is actual data from National Bureau of Statistics of China [2, 16] and Ministry of Health of the People's Republic of China [17]. Data are scale-down to be computable. In our multi-agent based computational healthcare mechanism system, there are 2000 patient agents, 1 insurance fund agent with urban and rural two strategies, 1 fiscal budget manager agent caring insurance coverage as equity, 3 medical provider agent of three different levels.

3 Results and Evaluation

3.1 Results

A graph of patient agents average cost for different strategies are shown in Fig.2 for pure NRCM, pure urban healthcare insurance and our new designed model. Fig.2a is that the mechanism sets no demand to attend the urban healthcare insurance. The average cost is RMB 154.83. Fig.1b is opposite, and all patients use urban healthcare insurance. The patient cost rises to RMB 161.31. Fig.2c simulates what cost is needed in our new mechanism. Patients are allowed to choose freely accroding their strategies. Fig.2c shows the result of our learning hybrid medical mechanism. It is less than both of the two pure insurance as RMB 147.34. This mechanism keeps advantages of both the NRCM and urban health insurance. The simulation results from the simulation indicate that there is a cost reduction and improved efficiency if our model is adopted.

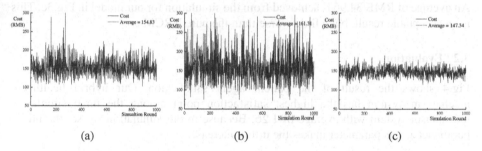

(a)   (b)   (c)

Fig. 1. Simulation results of patient average cost in 3 types of medical health care mechanism. (a) shows the result of new rural cooperative medical average cost. (b) is the urban health insurance result. Our learning hybrid mechanism is (c).

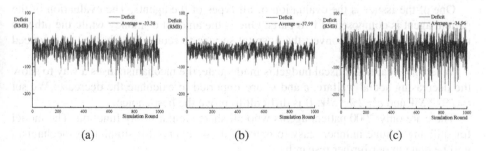

(a)   (b)   (c)

Fig. 2. Simulation results of healthcare insurance fund agent's deficit in 3 types of medical healthcare mechanism. (a) is the new rural cooperative medical average deficit. (b) shows the result of the urban health insurance. Our learning hybrid mechanism is (c).

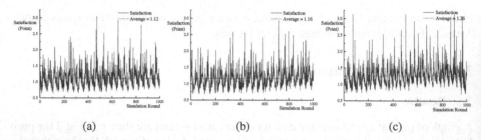

(a)   (b)   (c)

Fig. 3. Simulation results of the patient agent satisfaction point. (a) is the satisfaction point of new rural cooperative medical. (b) shows the result of the urban health insurance. Patient satisfaction point in our learning hybrid mechanism is (c).

Fig.3 shows the fiscal budget burden. Fig.3b shows that the highest deficit will be experienced if all patients use urban healthcare insurance shown in Fig.2b. In Fig.3a, NRCM pays 70% of the medical costs subject to a top limit of RMB 20,000 each year. Urban healthcare insurance does not have such top restriction. The rural patient pays 30% of the medical bills and any amount above the insurance limit where applicable. An average of RMB 34.96 is achieved from the simulation for our model in Fig.3c. This is an acceptable result, but a little worse than the pure NRCM.

3.2 Evaluation

Fig.4 shows the result of the patient agent satisfaction. Our hybrid healthcare mechanism system has the highest satisfaction point among the three simulation mechanism system with average of 1.26. Because in our simulation we set the utility parameter λ, this parameter makes the utility increase.

4 Discussions

There are some further issues that merit exploration.

One of the issues is the evaluation of all types of the agents. The evaluation of the patient agent is composed of two parts. One is the amount of money while the other is the level of service. To convert the hospital service to score needs however may need further research work.

Where the healthcare fiscal budget is inadequate, the mechanism uses a way to show the decreasing social welfare. ε and ε' are imported to calculate the decrease. We set $\varepsilon=1\% * SW$ and $\varepsilon'=2\% * SW$. It is difficult to prove the best choice.

There are only 2000 patient agents who all share similar utility function. The model for utilizing a huge number, easy to enter and quit agents for simulation mechanism will be done in our further research.

Another restriction of our results is that our agents only learn pure strategies. In reality, a person choosing the hospital or insurance company is affected by all kinds of factors. If all these factors are included, all agents will not act as simply as in our simplified medical mechanism.

5 Conclusions

Two types of healthcare insurance mechanisms are not suitable to Chinese citizens. By use of multi-agent based computational theory method, a simulation to evaluate the two mechanisms was undertaken. A novel hybrid mechanism by merging parts of the two branches in particular has been designed and discussed. This learning hybrid healthcare insurance mechanism proves social equity and efficiency as well.

References

1. Ministry of Health: An analysis report of national health services survey in 2008. Center for Health Statistics and Information, Beijing (2008)
2. National Bureau of Statistics of China: China Health Yearbook 2006. National Bureau of Statistics of China, Beijing (2006)
3. Ward, S.: Demographic: Factors in the Chinese Healthcare Market. Nature Reviews Drug Discovery (May 2008)
4. Kwon, S.: Payment system reform for healthcare providers in Korea. Health Policy and Planning 18(1), 84–92 (2003)
5. Eggleston, K., Hsieh, C.: Healthcare payment incentives: a comparative analysis of reforms in Taiwan, Korea and China. Alied Health Economics and Health Policy, 31-14 (2004)
6. Erev, I., Barron, G.: On adaptation, maximization, and reinforcement learning among cognitive strategies. Psychological review 112(4), 912–931 (2005)
7. Parkes, D.C.: Computational mechanism design. In: Lecture notes of Tutorials at 10th Conf. on Theoretical Aspects of Rationality and Knowledge (TARK-2005), Institute of Mathematical Sciences, University of Singapore (2008)
8. Parkes, D.C., Lyle, H.: Ungar: Learning and adaption in multi-agent systems. In: Proc. AAAI 1997 Multi-agent Learning Workshop, Providence, USA (1997)
9. Nisan, N., Ronen, A.: Algorithmic Mechanism Design. In: Proceedings of the 31st ACM Symposium on Theory of Computing, pp. 129–140 (1999)
10. Aumann, R.J.: Rationality and Bounded Rationality. Games And Economic Behavior 21, 2–14 (1997)
11. Rubinstein, A.: Modeling Bounded Rationality. MIT Press, Cambridge (1998)
12. Parkes, D.C.: On Learnable Mechanism Design. In: Collectives and the Design of Complex Systems, pp. 107–131. Springer, Heidelberg (2004)
13. Dutta, P.K.: Strategies and games. MIT Press, Cambridge (1999)
14. Friedman, E.J., Shenker, S.: Learning and implementation on the internet (1998), http://www.icir.org/shenker/decent.ps
15. Kraus, S.: Negotiation and cooperation in multi-agent environments. Artificial Intelligence 94, 79–97 (1997)
16. National Bureau of Statistics: China statistical yearbook 2008. National Bureau of Statistics of China, Beijing (2008)
17. Ministry of Health: China health statistical yearbook 2008. Ministry of Health, Beijing (2008)

Case Learning in CBR-Based Agent Systems for Ship Collision Avoidance

Yuhong Liu[1], Chunsheng Yang[2], Yubin Yang[3], Fuhua Lin[4], and Xuanmin Du[5]

[1] Merchant Marine College of Shanghai Maritime University, Shanghai 200135, China
[2] Institute for Information Technology, National Research Council, Canada
[3] State Key Laboratory for Novel Software Technology, Nanjing University, China
[4] School of Computing and Information Systems, Athabasca University, Canada
[5] Shanghai Marine Electronic Equipment Research Institute, Shanghai 201108, China

Abstract. With the rapid development of case-based reasoning (CBR) techniques, CBR has been widely applied to real-world applications such as agent-based systems for ship collision avoidance. A successful CBR-based system relies on a high-quality case base. Automated case creation technique is highly demanded. In this paper, we propose an automated case learning method for CBR-based agent systems. Building on techniques from CBR and natural language processing, we developed a method for learning cases from maritime affair records. After reviewing the developed agent-based systems for ship collision avoidance, we present the proposed framework and the experiments conducted in case generation. The experimental results show the usefulness and applicability of case learning approach for generating cases from the historic maritime affair records.

Keywords: Case-based reasoning, multi-agent system, ship collision avoidance, maritime affair records, case learning, case base management/updating.

1 Introduction

Human error is one of the most important factors in maritime accidents. In particular, it was a root of ship collision avoidances. To improve the navigation safety and avoid human error, an amount of research work [1-6] has focused on developing intelligent systems for collision avoidance. Yang et al. [4] developed a rule-based expert system based on the navigators' experiences and applied it to an integrated navigation system as a decision-making support system for collision avoidance. Similarly, the authors in [2] [3] developed an intelligent decision support system for ship collision avoidance. These intelligent systems were developed based on rule-based reasoning techniques. The rules were created or obtained from traffic regulations, or encounter scenarios, or navigation theories. Therefore, such rules cannot fully mimic the human's ship-handling behavior and experience, which is the most important factor in ship-handling for collision avoidance. This is why it is difficult to apply these research results to practical navigation systems.

J.-J. Yang et al. (Eds.): PRIMA 2009, LNAI 5925, pp. 542–551, 2009.

To overcome the shortcomings in rule-based reasoning systems, we have started to look into applying Case-Based Reasoning (CBR) and agent techniques to ship collision avoidance [15][17][18]. CBR is one of the reasoning paradigms and is a feasible and efficient way to the problems which are difficult to be solved with traditional methods such as model-based reasoning. CBR-based approach has been widely applied to different real-world applications such as diagnostic, design, and decision-making support [7-12]. Moreover, we are also looking into applying agent techniques to ship collision avoidance as well. A ship, navigating in an open and dynamic environment, can be looked as a rational and intelligent agent. Ships with navigators can detect the changes of the environment, collect the information of other ships, judge the dangerous degree of current situation, make decisions by using some knowledge, and take actions to avoid the collision with other ships or obstacles. To facility this research, we have developed a multi-agent system for ship collision avoidance by using agent and CBR techniques. The agent in this system [17] was implemented with CBR-based decision-making support for collision avoidance [18].

When we develop a CBR-based system for any applications, a significant challenge that faces us is case generation. Without a high-quality case base, it is impossible for a CBR-based system to function well for solving the given problems. It is a challenge because different domain applications require different approaches for case generation. For example, the authors in [16] developed a methodology to automatically generate cases from the historic maintenance database for diagnostic CBR systems. In this study, we looked into the historic maritime affairs records which were collected in navigation over many years. These records reflect either instructive and successful cases or edifying and failing cases. These cases are a valuable resource to generate cases for CBR-based collision systems. To this end, we have collected many famous maritime cases from Asia and Europe from 1976 to 2006. These cases are documented in an unstructured text format and in different language, mainly in Chinese. To efficiently generate cases from these unstructured text records, we developed a framework, focusing on Chinese text format, by using techniques from natural language processing (NLP) and CBR. In this paper, we present the developed techniques and some preliminary results.

The next section gives an overview on the developed CBR-based multi-agent system for ship collision avoidance; following that, we mainly present a framework for generating cases from maritime affair records; Section 4 introduces the experiments along with some preliminary results; the final section is conclusions and future work.

2 Overview of the Developed CBR-Based Agent Systems

In order to conduct the research for collision avoidance, we developed a multi-agent system [17] for simulating real navigation environments. It consists of two types of agents: control agent and function agent. The control agent contains system agent and union agent; and function agent is either ship agent or VTS (Vessel Traffic Service) agent. In general, the control agents manage the function agents, including information maintenance, agent communication, task partition and assignment, resource distribution and administration, conflict reconcilement, etc. The function agent performs CBR-based reasoning for collision avoidance by using the information from control agents and the environment data.

The function agents such as Ship agent and VTS agent are implemented following the BDI (Beliefs, Desires, and Intentions) model [19]. A BDI agent is a particular type of bounded rational software agent, imbued with particular mental attitudes, such as Beliefs, Desires and Intentions. The BDI model has some philosophical basis in the Belief-Desire-Intention theory of human practical reasoning. We applied CBR to BDI model for modeling human reasoning on collision avoidance. With the help of CBR, the architecture of CBR-based Ship agent and VTS agent is designed as shown in Figure 1. Basically, a CBR-based BDI agent implemented consists of two types of components: BDI function components and CBR function components. BDI function components such as communication, action trigger, model base, provide ability to interact with other agents. CBR function components consist of three main components for performing CBR reasoning: problem description, case bases, and case learning. The problem description component creates a description for a collision situation based on real-time navigation data. These data include static information (such as ship type, ship length and sea gauge), dynamic information (such as course, speed and position), and navigation information (such as the relative course and speed, azimuth, distance, DCPA, TCPA, encounter situation, and collision risk). Case base stores cases with a given presentation and an index structure. Once a collision problem is defined from the problem description component, a case retrieval algorithm is used to retrieve similar cases from the case base. The case with maximal similarity is selected as the proposed solution for the current collision problem. The case learning component is a core of CBR-based agent system. The main task is to automatically generate cases from maritime affaire records or a real-time ship-handling simulation. We will present this component in detail in the following Section.

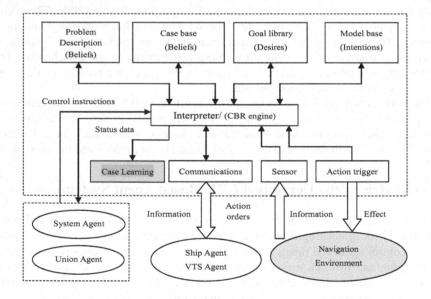

Fig. 1. The detail design of the CBR-based agent system

3 Case Learning

To make CBR function well for collision avoidance, a high-quality case base is required. Cases can be generated either in running time or at the initial stage of system development. For collision avoidance it is not feasible to generate cases in running time because of cost and safety. In our previous work [18], we proposed to create cases from ship-handling simulators. By analyzing the ship-handling trajectories we can create some cases for designated encountering cases. Another feasible and effective way to generate cases is using maritime affaire records collected in the navigation history. This section presents a framework to automatically generate cases from historic maritime affair records. We first give some preliminaries for a collision avoidance case based on navigation practice. Then we present the proposed framework for case learning.

3.1 Preliminaries

Ship collision avoidance is a dynamic process having a close connection with the sea, the ship, the human, and the environment, and involving much information and changes during a period. In order to describe our framework, we first give out some definition on ship encountering situation, viewpoint of navigation, maritime affair data, case and case base.

Definition 1. Encounter Scene (ES): A well-defined data structure. It is used to record the environment information (EI), the basic information (BI) of each ship, the relative information (RI) between own ship and each target ship and the proposed actions (PA) at a given time point. That is:

$$ES = < EI, BI, RI, PA > \tag{1}$$

Definition 2. View Point (VP): During the ship collision avoidance, we label one of the encountering ships as the own ship (OS) and the others as target ships (TS). And then we select a time point T and record the encounter scene (ES) at this moment. VP is denoted as:

$$VP = < OS, TS, T, ES > \tag{2}$$

Definition 3. Case base (CB): A case (c) is defined as $c = \{ p_c, s_c, m_c \}$. P_c denotes a set of problem attributes, which describes a collision problem, and a set of VP; S_c is a set of solution attributes, either a single action or several actions for avoiding a collision; m_c contains all attributes related to case base maintenance, including redundancy, inconsistency, success times, collision times, successful actions, and failed actions. Let CB denote a case base, where $CB \supseteq \{ c_1, c_2 ......, c_i, ..., c_n \}$.

Definition 4. Maritime Affair Database (MD): For a given maritime affair record noted as md_i, it contains implicitly or explicitly environment description (ED) (sea state, weather condition, and visibility), ship information description (SID) (encounter ships, ship name, type, length, draft, cargos and operation condition), and the collision or collision avoidance procedure description (PD) (the dynamic operation process and ship-ship relative information). For the collected maritime affair data, we denote it as a database, **MD**, where $MD \supseteq \{md_1, md_2 \ldots\ldots, md_i, \ldots, md_q\}$.

3.2 The Method of Case Base Creation

From the above definitions, our task is to create a CB from a given MD. The task of automating the case base creation is accomplished by the following three processes:

- Identifying a collision problem and its solutions
- Creating a template case
- Updating a case base

A. Identifying a collision problem and its solutions

The task of this process is to find p_c and the solution s_c for a given **md_i** in **MD**. In this work, the collected **MD** is unstructured Chinese text. Such Chinese text format makes the work more complicated. Unlike English or other western languages, Chinese is character based, not word based. There are no "blank spaces" serving as word boundaries in Chinese sentences [20] [21]. In order to obtain ED, SID and PD information from a given **md_i**, we first conduct Chinese word segmentation, and then perform semantic analysis according to a selected view point (VP).

The Chinese word segmentation separates a maritime affair record into three different paragraphs and extracts necessary information for ED, SID and PD. The algorithm for the Chinese word segmentation is shown in Table 1. It relies on a domain dictionary (*DicBase*) and a text tree (*TextTree*). The *DicBase* contains the main vocabulary for a collision avoidance problem. It is created based on the following principles: (1) The vocabulary is arranged in the sequence of WordKindSet= <noun, verb, adjective, adverb, conjunction, pronoun, preposition, auxiliary, quantifier, numeral>; (2) The words having same initial character are arranged in length sequence from long to short; (3) Each word in the vocabulary is appended a numerical value to express its occurrence frequency. A higher frequency is associated with a larger value. The *TextTree* is generated by paragraph segmentation, sentence segmentation and node segmentation. The three paragraphs corresponding to the ED, SID, and PD respectively are segmented. The sentence segmentation is based on the original text sentence and the segmentation tag is the five punctuations, ".", ",", ":", "?" and "!". The node segmentation is based on the kind of the character strings. There are five kinds of characters which are considered, NodeKindSet = <Chinese, English, number, special symbol, quotation mark>. Only the Chinese need to be segmented furthermore, and the other four kinds of character strings can be treated as a solid semantic unit and do not need more treatment.

This is an FMaxMatch and BMaxMatch algorithm. It runs in both forward and backward directions using the final word list as the references. Some domain knowledge is used in the algorithm to improve the segmentation efficiency. The outputs of FMaxMatch and BMaxMatch are stored in a static database, *SegBase*. The differences between the FMaxMatch and BMaxMatch outputs indicate the positions where the overlapping ambiguities occur. To avoid the ambiguity in segmentation, three rules are used to remove the ambiguity in our algorithm. The first rule is to remove overlapping ambiguity. The algorithm detects it and dispels it by selecting the

Table 1. Algorithm for Automatic Segmentation

INPUT: TextTree, DicBase;

OUTPUT: SegBase;

INITIALIZATION: NodeCount=0; DicCount=0; SegCount=0; SegFlg=FALSE; DelWord ←NULL;

　　　　　　 RemainWord ←NULL;

BEGIN:
```
    WHILE (TextTree[NodeCount] is not NULL) DO
    { InBuffer ← TextTree[NodeCount]; NodeCount++;
        IF InBuffer.Kind ∈ {English, Number, Symbol and quotation }
        ELSE {   WHILE ( Infuffer.Words is not NULL) DO
        {   DicCount=0; SegFlg=FALSE;
            WHILE (DicBase[DicCount] is not NULL]) DO
            {   IF (InBuffer.Words == DicBase[DicCount])
                THEN {    SegBase[SegCount] ← InBuffer.;
                                SegCount++; SegFlg=TRUE;
                                nBuffer ← DelWord;
              } ELSE DicCount ++;
            }
        IF (SegFlg==FALSE)  THEN {
            FMaxMatch: DelWordPro (LastOne, InBuffer, RemainWord, DelWord);
            BMaxMatch: DelWordPro (FirstOne, InBuffer, RemainWord, DelWord);
            IF (RemainWord is NULL) THEN
            {    SegBase[SegCount] ← InBuffer.;
                 SegBase[SegCount].Kind= unknown;
                 SegCount++;
            } ELSE InBuffer ← RemainWord;
            }
        }
      }
    }
END
```

---

words with higher occurrence frequency as the segmentation result or selecting the words manually. The second rule is to remove combination ambiguity by assigning a high priority to a combined string. The third rule is to deal with an unrecorded ambiguity string which is detected as *SegBase.Kind*. For an unrecorded ambiguity string, the "unknown" will be assigned to *SegBase.Kind*.

B. Creating a template case

Having P_c and S_c from the previous process, this process creates a potential case, $c_{tmp} = \{p_{ctmp}, s_{ctmp}, m_{ctmp}\}$ (where $p_{ctmp} \equiv p_c$, $s_{ctmp} \equiv s_c$; m_{ctmp} is to be determined). A potential case is a structured case representation, which might be added to a case base as a new case or be merged with the other cases based on the case base maintenance policies. These policies are presented in the following section.

C. Updating the case base

In ship navigation, an encounter situation (collision case) might occur many times, and the avoiding action may be either the same or different. In such a case, we expect to create a single case to restore these experiences rather than multiple cases. Therefore, we need a sophisticated approach to manage the case base when we add a potential case to an existing case base. The main goal of this algorithm is to determine the attributes of m_c for a given temporary case. The first step is to determine whether the potential case could be a new case. We check the redundancy or inconsistency of the potential case against the existing case base. If a case is not against any case in the existing case base, this case could be a new case. We add it to the case base. Otherwise, we move on to the second step that conducts case base management for the existing case base if we find a case (c_i) that is similar to c_{tmp}. This includes updating an existing case in the case base, deleting a case, and merging multiple cases into a new case. This operation is realized by updating the attributes for m_c. If we detected a similar case (c_i) in the existing case base against the potential case c_{tmp}, i.e., $p_{ci} \approx p_{ctmp}$ [1] and $s_{ci} \approx s_{ctmp}$, then m_{ci} will be updated to reflect the effect of the repair action applied to the problem. If c_{tmp} is a positive case, then we increase the count of successful repair actions of m_{ci} otherwise we increase the count of unsuccessful repair actions of m_{ci}. In the same way, if we detected a similar case (c_i) against case c_{tmp}, which has similar problem descriptions but different solutions, i.e., $p_{ci} \approx p_{ctmp}$ and $s_{ci} \approx! s_{ctmp}$, we will update the existing case by adding the new solution to it, so that, the case will become more powerful for solving the similar problem in the future.

4 Experiments

We implemented a case-learning component using the proposed method with the support of the CBR engine in our developed multi-agent system in a VC++ platform. We conducted some experiments for creating cases from the collected maritime affair records.

We have collected 60 collision avoidance cases from maritime affairs record books [22, 23]. These records were written in Chinese and cover a time from 1972 to 2006. Most of the records contain full information in unstructured Chinese text format. From the collision records, we could extract necessary information for creating cases: including, ES (EI, BI, RI, PA), VP (OS, TS, T, ES), and actions taken for collision avoidance, or reason analysis for collisions. Among 60 cases, 50 collision cases took place in Europe and were collected in Lloyd's Report, and 10 cases were from China. Most of collision or collision avoidance took place in near coast and shallow water area. From the encounter situation, most of the cases are two ship collisions. Only five cases are related to multiple ship collisions. From the viewpoint of encounter relationships, 12 cases are heading collisions; 26 cases are crossing collisions; 10 cases are overtaking collisions; and 10 cases are out navigating route in shallow water

---

[1] $\approx$ means that two items are similar. It is computed with the nearest neighbor algorithm in our system.

area. From the viewpoint of navigation environments, 27 cases happened in an invisible weather; and 33 cases were under visible weather. We created electronic version for these records in the Chinese text format. We provided these electronic documents to our developed case learning system and created cases automatically. At the end, we generated 48 cases successfully. Some cases were created from several collision cases because those cases might contain similar encountering situation and navigating environment and took the similar action for avoiding the collisions. The interesting fact is that only two collision cases do not contain all necessary information for generating the cases.

5 Conclusion and Future Work

In this paper, we started from an overview on the developed CBR-based agent system for collision avoidance. We introduced a method for automatic case generation, which was developed using techniques from Chinese Language Processing and CBR. Even though the proposed method is built on Chinese language processing techniques, it is easy to move on to English or other western language. We also presented the experiments conducted for case learning from the collected 60 collision cases along with some results. The experimental results show that the proposed method can provide a useful and effective means for case creation in CBR-based collision avoidance systems.

Although the proposed method can be used to generate the valuable cases from historic maritime affair records, the created cases have to be evaluated carefully before they are applied to CBR-based collision avoidance systems. As mentioned, we have incorporated the evaluation tool into the multi-agent systems. This tool is capable of evaluating the ship-handling results by analyzing the trajectories. Therefore, we can evaluate the case by conducting ship-handling simulation with the created cases. From the ship-handling results we can evaluate the case quality by analyzing the collision avoidance trajectories. Using ship-handling simulation is a cost effective way for evaluating the cases. Some work is ongoing; we will report the results in other paper. Furthermore, some uncertainties in case presentation and case learning still need to be studied in future.

Acknowledgments

This research is supported by Shanghai Leading Academic Discipline Project (S30602) and Shanghai Maritime University project (2009130). Part of work was done while Dr. Yuhong Liu visited the National Research Council Canada in 2007.

References

1. Sato, Y., Ishii, H.: Study of collision-avoidance system for ships. Control Engineering Practice 6, 1141–1149 (1998)
2. Liu, Y., Yang, W.: The structure Design of an Intelligent Decision Support System for Navigation Collision Avoidance. In: IEEE The Third International Conference on Machine Learning and Cybernetics, August 2004, vol. 1, pp. 302–307 (2004)

3. Liu, Y.: A design and Study on Intelligence Collision Prevention Expert System for Navigation. Ph.D. thesis, Harbin Engineering University, china (July 1999)
4. Yang, C.: An Expert System for Collision Avoidance and Its Application. Ph.D. thesis, Hiroshima University, Japan (September 1995)
5. Hwang, C.: The Integrated Design of Fuzzy Collision Avoidance and H∞- Autopilots on ships. The Journal of navigation 55(1), 117–136 (2002)
6. Liu, Y., Du, X., Yang, S.: The Design of a Fuzzy-Neural Network for Ship Collision Avoidance. In: Yeung, D.S., Liu, Z.-Q., Wang, X.-Z., Yan, H. (eds.) ICMLC 2005. LNCS (LNAI), vol. 3930, pp. 804–812. Springer, Heidelberg (2006)
7. Watson, I., Marir, F.: Case-Base Reasoning: A Review. Knowledge Engineering Review 9(4) (1994)
8. Yang, C., Orchard, B., Farley, B., Zaluski, M.: Automated Case Base Creation and Management. In: Proceedings of International Conference on Industrial & Engineering. Applications of Artificial Intelligence & Expert System (IEA/AIE 2003) (June 2003)
9. Therani, M., Zhao, J., Marshall, B.: A case-based reasoning framework for workflow model management. Data & Knowledge Engineering 50, 87–115 (2004)
10. Avesani, P., Ferrari, S., Susi, A.: Case-Based Ranking for Decision Support Systems. In: Ashley, K.D., Bridge, D.G. (eds.) ICCBR 2003. LNCS (LNAI), vol. 2689, pp. 35–49. Springer, Heidelberg (2003)
11. McSherry, D.: Similarity and Compromise. In: Ashley, K.D., Bridge, D.G. (eds.) ICCBR 2003. LNCS (LNAI), vol. 2689, pp. 291–305. Springer, Heidelberg (2003)
12. Nordlund, J., Schafer, H.: Case-Based Reasoning in a support System. Master's thesis, UMEA University, Sweden (April 2006)
13. Liu, Y., Hu, S.: An Evaluation System for Single-Target Ship Collision Avoidance Based on Data Fusion. Navigation of China 65(4), 40–45 (2005)
14. Liu, Y., Liu, H.: Case Learning Based on Evaluation System for Vessel Collision Avoidance. In: The Proceedings of IEEE The Fifth International Conference on Machine Learning and Cybernetics, August 2006, vol. 4, pp. 2064–2069 (2006)
15. Liu, Y., Wen, M., Du, Z.: A case Learning Model for Ship Collision Avoidance Based on Automatic Text Analysis. In: The Proceedings of IEEE The Fifth International Conference on Machine Learning and Cybernetics, Baoding, China (July 2009)
16. Yang, C., Farley, B., Orchard, B.: Automated Case Creation and Management for Diagnostic CBR Systems. International Journal of Applied intelligence 28(1), 17–28 (2008)
17. Liu, Y., Yang, C., Du, X.: Multi-agent Planning for Ship Collision Avoidance. In: The Proceedings of IEEE International Conferences on Cybernetics & Intelligent Systems (CIS) and Robotics, Automation & Mechatronics (RAM) (CIS-RAM 2008), Chengdu, China (June 2008)
18. Liu, Y., Yang, C., Du, X.: A CBR-Based Approach for Ship Collision Avoidance. In: Nguyen, N.T., et al. (eds.) IEA/AIE 2008. LNCS (LNAI), vol. 5027, pp. 687–697. Springer, Heidelberg (2008)
19. Rao, A.S., Georgeff, M.P.: Modeling Rational Agents within a BDI-Architecture. In: Proceedings of the 2nd International Conference on Principles of Knowledge Representation and Reasoning, pp. 473–484 (1991)
20. Gong, H., Gong, C., Zhou, C.: Chinese word segmentation system research. Journal of Beijing Institute of Machinery 19(3), 52–61 (2004)

21. Qiu, J., Wen, T., Zhou, L.: Research of Chinese Automatic Segmentation and Content Analysis Method. Journal of The China Society For Scientific and Technical Information 24(3), 309–317 (2005)
22. China MSA (Maritime Safety Administration). Typical water traffic accident cases. China Communications Press, pp. 1–89 (October 2007)
23. Zhao, J., Wang, F.: The collision regulations and cases, pp. 560–685. Dalian Maritime University Press (March 1997)

An Adaptive Agent Model for Emotion Reading by Mirroring Body States and Hebbian Learning

Tibor Bosse[1], Zulfiqar A. Memon[1,2], and Jan Treur[1]

[1] Vrije Universiteit Amsterdam, Department of Artificial Intelligence
De Boelelaan 1081, 1081 HV Amsterdam, The Netherlands
[2] Sukkur Institute of Business Administration (Sukkur IBA),
Airport Road Sukkur, Sindh, Pakistan
{tbosse,zamemon,treur}@few.vu.nl
www.few.vu.nl/~{tbosse,zamemon,treur}

Abstract. In recent years, the topic of emotion reading has increasingly received attention from researchers in Cognitive Science and Artificial Intelligence. To study this phenomenon, in this paper an adaptive agent model is presented with capabilities to interpret another agent's emotions. The presented agent model is based on recent advances in neurological context. First a non-adaptive agent model for emotion reading is described involving (preparatory) mirroring body states of the other agent. Here emotion reading is modelled taking into account the Simulation Theory perspective as known from the literature, involving the own body states and emotions in reading somebody else's emotions. This models an agent that first develops the same feeling, and after feeling the emotion imputes it to the other agent. Next the agent model is extended to an adaptive model based on a Hebbian learning principle to develop a direct connection between a sensed stimulus concerning another agent's body state (e.g., face expression) and the emotion recognition state. In this adaptive agent model the emotion is imputed to the other agent before it is actually felt. The agent model has been designed based on principles of neural modelling, and as such has a close relation to a neurological realisation.

Keywords: agent model, emotion reading, cognitive, theory of mind, adaptive.

1 Introduction

In the Simulation Theory perspective on emotion reading (or Theory of Mind) it is assumed that a person uses the facilities involving the own mental states that are counterparts of the mental states attributed to another person; e.g., [12]. For example, the state of feeling pain oneself is used in the process to determine whether the other person has pain. More and more neurological evidence supports this perspective, in particular the recent discovery of mirror neurons that are activated both when preparing for an action (including a change in body state) and when observing somebody else performing a similar action.; e.g., [10], [15], [17], [25], [26], [27] and [29]. Mirror neurons usually concern neurons involved in the preparation of actions or body states. By [8] such preparation neurons are attributed a crucial role in generating

J.-J. Yang et al. (Eds.): PRIMA 2009, LNAI 5925, pp. 552–562, 2009.

and feeling emotional responses. In particular, using a 'body loop' or 'as if body loop', a connection between such neurons and the feeling of emotions by sensing the own body state is obtained; see [8] or the formalisation presented in [4]. Taken together, the existence of mirror neurons and Damasio's theory on feeling emotions based on (as if) body loops provides strong neurological support for the Simulation Theory perspective on emotion reading.

An extension of this idea was adopted by assuming that the (as if) body loop is processed in a recursive manner: a positive feedback loop based on reciprocal causation between feeling state (with gradually more feeling) and body state (with gradually stronger expression). This cycle is triggered by the stimulus and ends up in an equilibrium for both states. In [5] and [19] a non-adaptive cognitive emotion reading model based on a recursive body loop was presented, formalised in the hybrid modelling language LEADSTO [3]. In [6] it was shown how this hybrid causal model can be extended to obtain an adaptive cognitive emotion reading model. The adaptation creates a shortcut connection from the sensed stimulus (observed face) to the imputed emotion, bypassing the own emotional states.

In the current paper an adaptive agent model is presented for similar mindreading phenomena, but instead of a causal modelling approach, a more neurological point of departure is explored by using a neural network structure which is processed using generic principles for neural activation and Hebbian learning. In this way the obtained agent model stays more close to the neurological source of evidence and inspiration.

The structure of this paper is as follows. First, the basic emotion reading agent model is introduced. Next, it is shown how the agent model can be made adaptive, by adopting a Hebbian learning principle that enables the agent to strengthen the connections between neurons. For both the basic agent model and the adaptive agent model, some simulation results are shown, and different variations are discussed. The paper is concluded with a discussion.

2 A Neural Agent Model for Emotion Reading

In this and the next section the agent model to generate emotional states for a given stimulus is introduced. It adopts three important concepts from [8] theory of consciousness: an *emotion* is defined as 'an (unconscious) neural reaction to a certain stimulus, realised by a complex ensemble of neural activations in the brain', a *feeling* is 'the (still unconscious) sensing of this body state', and a *conscious feeling* is what emerges when 'the organism detects that its representation of its own body state has been changed by the occurrence of the stimulus' [8]. Moreover, the agent model adopts his idea of a 'body loop' and 'as if body loop', but extends this by making these loops recursive. According to the original idea, from a neurological perspective emotion generation roughly proceeds according to the following causal chain; see [4] and [8] (in the case of a body loop):

> sensing a stimulus → sensory representation of stimulus → (preparation for) bodily response → sensing the bodily response → sensory representation of the bodily response → feeling the emotion

For example, reading the acceptance email of your paper induces a smile, which by sensing it leads to a positive feeling. An 'as if body loop' uses a causal relation preparation for bodily response $\rightarrow$ sensory representation of the bodily response

as a shortcut in the neurological chain. In this case the smile itself may be suppressed, but the preparation for it still leads to the feeling. In the agent model used here an essential addition is that the body loop (or as if body loop) is extended to a recursive body loop (or recursive as if body loop) by assuming that the preparation of the bodily response is also affected by the state of feeling the emotion (also called emotional feeling):

feeling the emotion $\rightarrow$ preparation for bodily response

as an additional causal relation. For example, the positive feeling due to a smile strengthens the smile. The author in [9] also assumes such recursively used reciprocal causal connections:

> '... feelings are not a passive perception or a flash in time, especially not in the case of feelings of joy and sorrow. For a while after an occasion of such feelings begins – for seconds or for minutes – there is a dynamic engagement of the body, almost certainly in a repeated fashion, and a subsequent dynamic variation of the perception. We perceive a series of transitions. We sense an interplay, a give and take.' ([9] pp. 92).

Within the neural agent model presented here both the neural states for preparation of bodily response and the feeling are assigned a level of activation, expressed by a number, which is assumed dynamic. The cycle is modelled as a positive feedback loop, triggered by the stimulus and converging to a certain level of feeling and body state. Here in each round of the cycle the next body state has a level that is affected by both the level of the stimulus and of the emotional feeling state, and the next level of the emotional feeling is based on the level of the body state.

This neural agent model refers to activation states of (groups of) neurons and the body. An overall picture of the connection for this agent model is shown in Fig. 1. Here each node stands for a group of one or more neurons, or for an effector, sensor or body state. The nodes can be interpreted as shown in Table 1.

Table 1. Overview of the nodes involved

node nr	denoted by	Description
0	s	stimulus; for example, another agent's body state b'
1	$SS(s)$	sensor state for stimulus s
2	$SRN(s)$	sensory representation neuron for s
3	$PN(b)$	preparation neuron for own body state b
4	$ES(b)$	effector state for own body state b
5	$BS(b)$	own body state b
6	$SS(b)$	sensor state for own body state b
7	$SRN(b)$	sensory representation neuron for own body state b
8	$FN(f)$	neuron for feeling state f
9	$RN(s, f)$	neuron representing that s induces feeling f

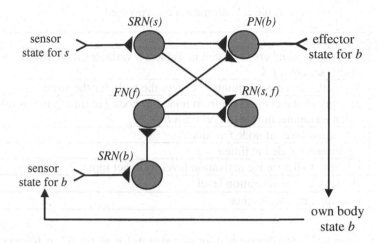

Fig. 1. Neural network structure of the agent model with body loop

In the neural activation state of $RN(s, f)$, the experienced emotion f is related to the stimulus s, which triggers the emotion generation process. Note that the more this neuron is strongly related to $SRN(s)$, the more it may be considered to represent a level of awareness of what causes the feeling f; this may be related to what by [8] is called a state of conscious feeling. This state that relates an emotion felt f to any triggering stimulus s can play an important role in the conscious attribution of the feeling to any stimulus s.

According to the Simulation Theory perspective an agent model for emotion reading should essentially be based on a neural model to generate the own emotions as induced by any stimulus s. Indeed, the neural agent model introduced above can be specialised in a quite straightforward manner to enable emotion reading. The main step is that the stimulus s that triggers the emotional process, which until now was left open, is instantiated with the body state b' of another agent, for example a facial expression of another agent. Indeed, more and more evidence is available that (already from an age of 1 hour), as an example of the functioning of the mirror neuron system [27], sensing somebody else's facial expression leads (within about 300 milliseconds) to preparing for and showing the same facial expression ([13] pp. 129-130). Within the network in Fig. 1., this leads (via activation of the sensory representation state $SRN(b')$) to activation of the preparation state $PN(b)$ where b is the own body state corresponding to the other agent's body state b'. This pattern shows how this preparation state $PN(b)$ functions as a mirror neuron. Next, via the recursive body loop gradually higher and higher activation levels of the own feeling state f are generated.

To formally specify the neural agent model, the mathematical concepts listed in Table 2 are used. The function g can take different forms, varying from the identity function $g(v) = v$ for the linear case, to a discontinuous threshold (indicated by β) step function with $g(v) = 0$ for $v < \beta$ and $g(v) = 1$ for $v \geq \beta$, or a continuous logistic threshold function based on $1/(1+exp(-\alpha(v-\beta)))$ with steepness α. For the connections between nodes of which at least one is not a neuron the connections have been made simple: weights 1 and g the identity function; so $w_{12} = w_{34} = w_{45} = w_{56} = w_{67} = 1$.

Table 2. Mathematical concepts used

concept	description
N	set of node numbers (as listed in Table 1); variables indicating elements of this set are i, j, k
N'	$N \backslash \{0\}$ the set of node numbers except the node for the stimulus s
$w_{ij}(t)$	strength of the connection from node i to node j at time t; this is taken 0 when no connection exists or when $i=j$
$y_i(t)$	activation level of node i at time t
$net_i(t)$	net input to node i at time t
g	function to determine activation level from net input
γ	change rate for activation level
η	learning rate for weights

The activation levels are determined for step size Δt for all $i \in N'$ as follows:

$$net_i(t) = \Sigma_{j \in N} \; w_{ji}(t) \; y_j(t)$$
$$\Delta y_i(t) = \gamma(g(net_i(t)) - y_i(t)) \; \Delta t$$

Note that for step size $\Delta t = 1$ and change rate $\gamma = 1$, the latter difference equation can be rewritten to

$$y_i(t+1) = g(net_i(t))$$

which is a well-known formula in the literature addressing simulation with neural models.

The agent model description in the form of a system of differential equations can be used for an analysis of equilibria that can occur. Here the external stimulus level for s is assumed constant. Moreover, it is assumed that $\gamma > 0$. In general putting $\Delta y_i(t) = 0$ provides the following set of equations for $i \in N'$:

$$y_i = g(\Sigma_{j \in N} \; w_{ji} \; y_j)$$

For the given network structure these equilibrium equations are:

$$y_1 = g(w_{01} \, y_0) \qquad y_2 = g(w_{12} \, y_1) \qquad y_3 = g(w_{23} \, y_2 + w_{83} \, y_8)$$
$$y_4 = g(w_{34} \, y_3) \qquad y_5 = g(w_{45} \, y_4) \qquad y_6 = g(w_{56} \, y_5)$$
$$y_7 = g(w_{67} \, y_6) \qquad y_8 = g(w_{78} \, y_7) \qquad y_9 = g(w_{29} \, y_2 + w_{89} \, y_8)$$

Taking into account that connections between nodes among which at least one is not a neuron have weight 1 and g the identity function, it follows that the equilibrium equations are:

$$y_2 = y_1 = y_0$$
$$y_7 = y_6 = y_5 = y_4 = y_3$$
$$y_8 = g(w_{78} \, y_7)$$
$$y_3 = g(w_{23} \, y_2 + w_{83} \, y_8)$$
$$y_9 = g(w_{29} \, y_2 + w_{89} \, y_8)$$

3   Example Simulations: Non-adaptive Emotion Reading

The numerical software environment Matlab has been used to obtain simulation traces for the agent model described above. An example simulation trace that results from this agent model with the function g the identity function is shown in Fig. 2. Here, time is on the horizontal axis, and activation levels of three of the neurons $SRN(s)$, $FN(f)$, and $RN(s,f)$ are shown on the vertical axis. As shown in this picture, the sensory representation of a certain stimulus s quickly results in a feeling state f, and a representation that s induces f. When the stimulus s is not present anymore, the activations of $FN(f)$ and $RN(s, f)$ quickly decrease to 0. The weight factors taken are: $w_{23} = w_{83} = w_{89} = 0.1$, $w_{78} = 0.5$ and $w_{29} = 0$. Moreover, $\gamma = 1$, and a logistic threshold function was used with threshold 0.1 and steepness 40.

For the values taken in the simulation of Fig. 2. The equilibrium equations are:

$$y_2 = y_1 = y_0$$
$$y_7 = y_6 = y_5 = y_4 = y_3$$
$$y_8 = g(0.5\,y_7)$$
$$y_3 = g(0.1\,y_2 + 0.1\,y_8)$$
$$y_9 = g(0.1y_8)$$

As the threshold was taken 0.1 it follows from the equations that for stimulus level $y_0 = 0$ all values for y_i are (almost) 0, and for stimulus level $y_0 = 1$ that all values for y_i are 1, which is also shown by the simulation in Fig. 2.

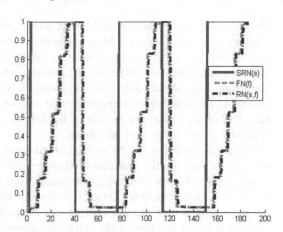

Fig. 2. Example simulation for an agent performing non-adaptive emotion reading

4   A Neural Agent Model for Adaptive Emotion Reading

As a next step, the neural agent model for emotion reading is extended by a facility to strengthen the direct connection between the neuron $SRN(s)$ for the sensory representation of the stimulus (the other agent's face expression) and the neuron $RN(s, f)$. A strengthening of this connection over time creates a different emotion reading process that in principle can bypass the generation of the own feeling. The learning principle to achieve such an adaptation process is based on the Hebbian learning principle that connected neurons that are frequently activated simultaneously strengthen their connecting synapse e.g., [1], [14], [11] and [28]. The change in strength for the connection w_{ij} between nodes $i, j \in N$ is determined (for step size Δt) as follows:

$$\Delta w_{ij}(t) = \eta\, y_i(t)y_j(t)(1 - w_{ij}(t))\, \Delta t$$

Here η is the learning rate. Note that this Hebbian learning rule is applied only to those pairs of nodes $i, j \in N$ for which a connection already exists.

558   T. Bosse, Z.A. Memon, and J. Treur

Also for the adaptive case equilibrium equations can be found. Here it is assumed that $\gamma, \eta > 0$. In general putting both $\Delta y_i(t) = 0$ and $\Delta w_{ij}(t) = 0$ provides the following set of equations for $i, j \in N'$:

$$y_i = g(\Sigma_{j\in N}\ w_{ji}\ y_j) \qquad\qquad y_i y_j(1 - w_{ij}) = 0$$

From the latter set of equations (second line) it immediately follows that for any pair $i, j \in N'$ it holds:

$$\text{either} \qquad y_i = 0 \text{ or } y_j = 0 \text{ or } w_{ij} = 1$$

In particular, when for an equilibrium state both y_i and y_j are nonzero, then $w_{ij} = 1$.

5 Example Simulations: Adaptive Emotion Reading

Based on the neural agent model for adaptive emotion reading obtained in this way, a number of simulations have been performed; for an example, see Fig. 3. As seen in this figure, the strength of the connection between $SRN(s)$ and $RN(s, f)$ (indicated by b which is in fact w_{29}) is initially 0 (i.e., initially, when observing the other agent's face, the agent does not impute feeling to this). However, during an adaptation phase of two trials, the connection strength goes up as soon as the agent imputes feeling f to the target stimulus s (the observation of the other agent's face), in accordance with the temporal relationship described above.

Note that, as in Fig. 2., the activation values of other neurons gradually increase as the agent observes the stimulus, following the recursive feedback loop discussed. These values sharply decrease as the agent stops observing the stimulus as shown in Fig. 3., e.g. from time point 40 to 76, from time point 112 to 148, and so on. Note that at these time points the strength of the connection between $SRN(s)$ and $RN(s, f)$ (indicated by b) remains stable. After the adaptation phase, and with the imputation sensitivity at high, the agent imputes feeling f to the target stimulus directly after occurrence of the sensory representation of the stimulus, as shown in the third trial in Fig. 3. Note here that even though the agent has adapted to impute feeling f to the

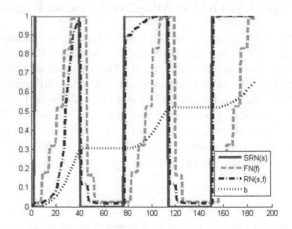

Fig. 3. Example simulation for an agent performing adaptive emotion reading

target directly after the stimulus, the other state property values continue to increase in the third trial as the agent receives the stimulus; this is because the adaptation phase creates a connection between the sensory representation of the stimulus and emotion imputation without eliminating the recursive feedback loop altogether. Note that when a constant stimulus level 1 is taken, an equilibrium state is reached in which $b = 1$, and all y_i are 1. The learning rate η used in the simulation shown in Fig. 3. is 0.02. In Fig. 4. a similar simulation is shown for a lower learning rate: 0.005.

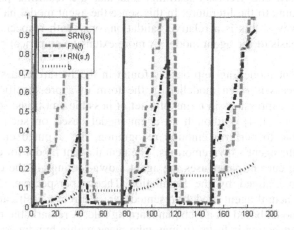

Fig. 4. Adaptive emotion reading with lower learning rate

6   Discussion

In recent years, an increasing amount of neurological evidence is found that supports the 'Simulation Theory' perspective on emotion reading, e.g., [10], [15], [16], [17], [25], [26], [29]. That is, in order to recognise emotions of other persons, humans exploit observations of these other persons' body states as well as counterparts within their own body. The current paper introduces a numerical agent model to simulate this process. This agent model is based on the notions of (preparatory) mirror neurons and a recursive body loop (cf. [8], [9]): a converging positive feedback loop based on reciprocal causation between mirror neuron activations and neuron activations underlying emotions felt. In addition, this agent model was extended to an adaptive neural agent model based on Hebbian learning, where neurons that are frequently activated simultaneously strengthen their connecting synapse (cf. [1], [11], [14] and [28]). Based on this adaptive agent model, a direct connection between a sensed stimulus (for example, another person's face expression) and the emotion recognition can be strengthened.

The agent model has been implemented in Matlab, in a generic manner. That is, the agent model basically consists of only 2 types of rules: one for propagation of activation levels between connected neurons, and one for strengthening of connections between neurons that are active simultaneously. These rules are then applied to all nodes in the network. To perform a particular simulation, only the initial activation levels and connection strengths have to be specified. Both for the non-adaptive and for the adaptive model, a number of simulations have been performed. These simulations indicated that the agent model is indeed sufficiently generic to simulate various patterns of adaptive emotion reading. An interesting challenge for the future is to extend the agent model such that it can cope with multiple qualitatively different emotional stimuli (e.g., related to joy, anger, or fear), and their interaction.

Validation of the presented agent model is not trivial. At least, this paper has indicated that it is possible to integrate Damasio's idea of body loop with the notion of mirror neurons and Hebbian learning, and that the resulting patterns are very plausible according to the literature. In this sense the agent model has been validated positively. However, this is a relative validation, only with respect to the literature that forms the basis of the agent model. A more extensive empirical evaluation is left for future work.

By other agent modelling approaches found in the literature, a specific emotion recognition process is often modelled in the form of a pre-specified classification process of facial expressions in terms of a set of possible emotions; see, for example, [7], [18], [23] and [24]. Although an agent model based on such a classification procedure is able to perform emotion recognition, the imputed emotions have no relationship to the agent's own emotions. The neural agent model for emotion reading presented in the current paper uses the agent's own feelings in the emotion reading process as also claimed by the Simulation Theory perspective, e.g., [12], [13]. Besides, in the neural agent model presented here a direct classification is learnt by the adaptivity model based on a Hebbian learning rule. A remarkable issue here is that such a direct connection is faster (it may take place within hundreds of milliseconds) than a connection via a body loop (which usually takes seconds). This time difference implies that first the emotion is recognised without feeling the corresponding own emotion, but within seconds the corresponding own emotion is in a sense added to the recognition. When an as if body loop is used instead of a body loop, the time difference will be smaller, but still present. An interesting question is whether it is possible to design experiments that show this time difference as predicted by the neural agent model.

Some other computational models related to mirror neurons are available in literature; for instance: a genetic algorithm model which develops networks for imitation while yielding mirror neurons as a byproduct of the evolutionary process [2]; the mirror neuron system (MNS) model that can learn to 'mirror' via self-observation of grasp actions [20]; the mental state inference (MSI) model that builds on the forward model hypothesis of mirror neurons [22]. A comprehensive review of these computational studies can be found in [21]. All of the above listed computational models and many others available in the literature are targeted to imitation, whereas the neural model presented here specifically targets to interpret somebody else's emotions.

In ([12], pp. 124-132) a number of possible emotion reading models from the Simulation Theory perspective are sketched and discussed. For his model 1 a generate and test process for emotional states was assumed, where on the basis of a hypothesised emotional state an own facial expression is generated, and this is compared to the observed facial expression of the other person. In the assessment of this model, the hypothesis generation process for a given observed face was considered as less satisfactory. Models 2 and 3 discussed in [12] are based on a notion of 'reverse simulation'. This means that for the causal relation from emotional state to (the preparation of) a facial expression which is used to generate the own facial expressions, also a reverse relation from prepared own facial expression to emotional state is assumed, which is used for the mind reading process. A point of discussion concerning these models is that it is difficult to fit them to the Simulation Theory perspective: whereas the emotional states and facial expression (preparation) states used for mindreading are the same as used for the own emotions and facial expressions, the causal relations between them used in the two cases are not the same. Model 4 is based on a so-called 'mirroring process', where a correlation between the emotional state of the other person and the corresponding own emotional state is assumed, based on a certain causal chain between the two. However, the relation of such a causal chain with the causal relations used to generate the own emotional states and facial expressions is not made clear.

The approach adopted in the current paper has drawn some inspiration from the four models sketched (but not formalised) in ([12] pp. 124-132). The recursive body loop (or as if body loop) introduced here addresses the problems of model 1, as it can be viewed as an efficient and converging way of generating and testing hypotheses for the emotional states. Moreover, it solves the problems of models 2 and 3, as the causal chain from facial expression to emotional state is not a reverse simulation, but just the causal chain via the body state which is used for generating the own emotional feelings as well. Finally, compared to model 4, the models put forward here can be viewed as an efficient manner to obtain a mirroring process between the emotional state of the other agent on the own emotional state, based on the machinery available for the own emotional states.

References

1. Bi, G., Poo, M.: Synaptic Modifications by Correlated Activity: Hebb's Postulate Revisited. Ann. Rev. Neurosci. 24, 139–166 (2001)
2. Borenstein, E., Ruppin, E.: The evolution of imitation and mirror neurons in adaptive agents. Cognitive Systems Research 6(3), 229–242 (2005)
3. Bosse, T., Jonker, C.M., van der Meij, L., Treur, J.: A Language and Environment for Analysis of Dynamics by Simulation. International Journal of Artificial Intelligence Tools 16, 435–464 (2007)
4. Bosse, T., Jonker, C.M., Treur, J.: Formalisation of Damasio's Theory of Emotion, Feeling and Core Consciousness. Consciousness and Cognition Journal 17, 94–113 (2008)
5. Bosse, T., Memon, Z.A., Treur, J.: Adaptive Estimation of Emotion Generation for an Ambient Agent Model. In: Aarts, E., Crowley, J.L., de Ruyter, B., Gerhäuser, H., Pflaum, A., Schmidt, J., Wichert, R. (eds.) AmI 2008. LNCS, vol. 5355, pp. 141–156. Springer, Heidelberg (2008)
6. Bosse, T., Memon, Z.A., Treur, J.: An Adaptive Emotion Reading Model. In: Proc. of the 31th Annual Conference of the Cognitive Science Society, CogSci 2009, pp. 1006–1011. Cognitive Science Society, Austin (2009)
7. Cohen, I., Garg, A., Huang, T.S.: Emotion recognition using multilevel HMM. In: Proc. of the NIPS Workshop on Affective Computing, Colorado (2000)
8. Damasio, A.: The Feeling of What Happens: Body, Emotion and the Making of Consciousness. Harcourt Brace (1999)

9. Damasio, A.: Looking for Spinoza. Vintage books, London (2004)
10. Ferrari, P.F., Gallese, V., Rizzolatti, G., Fogassi, L.: Mirror neurons responding to the observation of ingestive and communicative mouth actions in the monkey ventral premotor cortex. Eur. J. Neurosci. 17, 1703–1714 (2003)
11. Gerstner, W., Kistler, W.M.: Mathematical formulations of Hebbian learning. Biol. Cybern. 87, 404–415 (2002)
12. Goldman, A.I.: Simulating Minds: the Philosophy, Psychology and Neuroscience of Mindreading. Oxford University Press, Oxford (2006)
13. Goldman, A.I., Sripada, C.S.: Simulationist models of face-based emotion recognition. Cognition 94, 193–213 (2004)
14. Hebb, D.O.: The Organization of Behaviour. John Wiley & Sons, Chichester (1949)
15. Iacoboni, M.: Mirroring People. Farrar, Straus & Giroux, New York (2008)
16. Iacoboni, M.: Understanding others: imitation, language, empathy. In: Hurley, S., Chater, N. (eds.) Perspectives on imitation: from cognitive neuroscience to social science, vol. 1, pp. 77–100. MIT Press, Cambridge (2005)
17. Kohler, E., Keysers, C., Umilta, M.A., Fogassi, L., Gallese, V., Rizzolatti, G.: Hearing sounds, understanding actions: action representation in mirror neurons. Science 297, 846–848 (2002)
18. Malle, B.F., Moses, L.J., Baldwin, D.A.: Intentions and Intentionality: Foundations of Social Cognition. MIT Press, Cambridge (2001)
19. Memon, Z.A., Treur, J.: Cognitive and Biological Agent Models for Emotion Reading. In: Jain, L., et al. (eds.) Proc. of the 8th International Conference on Intelligent Agent Technology, IAT 2008, pp. 308–313. IEEE Computer Society Press, Los Alamitos (2008)
20. Oztop, E., Arbib, M.A.: Schema design and implementation of the grasp-related mirror neuron system. Biological Cybernetics 87(2), 116–140 (2002)
21. Oztop, E., Kawato, M., Arbib, M.: Mirror neurons and imitation: a computationally guided review. Neural Networks 19(3), 254–271 (2006)
22. Oztop, E., Wolpert, D., Kawato, M.: Mental state inference using visual control parameters. Cognitive Brain Research 22(2), 129–151 (2005)
23. Pantic, M., Rothkrantz, L.J.M.: Automatic Recognition of Facial Expressions and Human Emotions. In: Proceedings of ASCI 1997 conference, ASCI, Delft, pp. 196–202 (1997)
24. Pantic, M., Rothkrantz, L.J.M.: Expert System for Automatic Analysis of Facial Expressions. Image and Vision Computing Journal 18, 881–905 (2000)
25. Rizzolatti, G., Craighero, L.: The mirror-neuron system. Annu. Rev. Neurosci. 27, 169–192 (2004)
26. Rizzolatti, G., Fogassi, L., Gallese, V.: Neuro-physiological mechanisms underlying the understanding and imitation of action. Nature Rev. Neurosci. 2, 661–670 (2001)
27. Rizzolatti, G.: The mirror-neuron system and imitation. In: Hurley, S., Chater, N. (eds.) Perspectives on imitation: from cognitive neuroscience to social science, vol. 1, pp. 55–76. MIT Press, Cambridge (2005)
28. Wasserman, P.D.: Neural Computing: Theory and Practice. Van Nostrand Reinhold, New York (1989)
29. Wohlschlager, A., Bekkering, H.: Is human imitation based on a mirror-neurone system? Some behavioural evidence. Exp. Brain Res. 143, 335–341 (2002)

Agent Evacuation Simulation Using a Hybrid Network and Free Space Models

Masaru Okaya, Shigeru Yotsukura, Kei Sato, and Tomoichi Takahashi

Meijo University, Tenpaku, Nagoya, 468-8501, Japan
{m0930007,m0830040,m0840014}@ccmailg.meijo-u.ac.jp,
ttaka@ccmfs.meijo-u.ac.jp

Abstract. The simulation of a large number of people's evacuation behaviors is assumed to support the decision of rescue operations or prompt
planning for disaster mitigation. Simulations of agents at wide areas with
fine resolutions require a lot of computational resources and computer
powers. We propose a hybrid traffic simulation combining network and
area models to simulate agents' behaviors. This paper presents that a
hybrid traffic simulator had same results that have used all free space
models. This indicates that our system can simulate behaviors a huge
number of agents at wide areas with high resolutions by reasonable computational resources.

1 Introduction

It is difficult to make models for human behaviors in complex situations. Disaster
and rescue simulation is one of the issues, and involves a very large numbers of
heterogeneous agents in a hostile environment. Agent based simulations (ABS)
have been providing a paradigm to simulate it [1]. The ABS presents humans as
agents and simulates their behaviors in environments created by data from real
worlds and disaster simulators.

The simulation of a large number of people's evacuation behaviors is assumed
to support the decision of rescue operations or prompt planning for disaster mitigation. The movement of people happens at disasters are escape from a smoke-
filled room, evacuating from buildings or underground malls, moving outside to
refuges. Various systems of simulating human movements have been presented.
One of them is pedestrian simulation and crowd simulations [4] [7]. They simulate human movements in open spaces. The other simulation is traffic of cars in
downtown [2].

In a case of disaster and rescue simulations in cities, it is required to simulate
human movements inside buildings and outside of them, and the traffics of cars
including emergency vehicles. The modeling of space where agents move is different from the purposes of simulation or the available resources of computation.
For example, three dimensional geographical data and free space model are used
in indoor simulations [6] [3]. Outside wide area simulations use two dimensional
data and network model of roads [5]. In a case of simulations for outside area,

J.-J. Yang et al. (Eds.): PRIMA 2009, LNAI 5925, pp. 563–570, 2009.

the size of area is wide and the number of objects in the map is large, so it takes a lot of computational resources for simulations.

We propose a hybrid simulator that enables to simulate the behavior of agents on maps that are represented in a network model, free space model and combined one . By presenting crowded areas as free spaces and the places that human move smoothly by the network, the simulation of evacuation behaviors at wide area becomes possible. Section 2 describes traffic simulation in disaster and rescue simulations. Our proposed hybrid simulator is presented in Section 3, and the results of experiments are discussed in Section 4. Summary and discussions are in Section 5.

2   Human Movements in Disaster and Rescue Simulations

2.1   Rescue Scenarios

When earthquakes occur in urban areas, various types of causalities and accidents occur. These are related to one another. Collapsed buildings injure civilians and block roads with debris. The rescuers must rush the victims to hospitals, help civilians evacuate to safe areas, and prevent fires, if any, from spreading.

We consider following rescue scenarios, if disasters occur when students attend their lectures.(Figure 1)

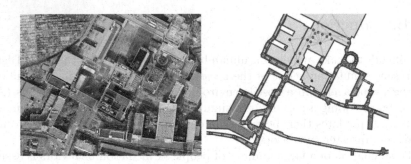

Fig. 1. Students evacuation task. (left: An image of our university by Google Map, right: A model used by our traffic simulator. Buildings and roads inside campus are modeled by free space and roads outside are represented by a network model.)

A. At outside buildings: Students evacuate from buildings. On the other hand, rescue teams rush to the buildings to rescue injured students. The students move to refuges and injured ones are transported to hospitals.
B. At inside buildings: Students go to the exits of classes, look for the emergency exit, and take the stairs to the ground floor. The rescue teams enter the buildings, go to rooms, and check whether there are some left there.
C. At outside and inside buildings: Around entrances of the buildings, there are many students and rescue teams. The crowded situations are to be simulated.

Simulation of scenario A corresponds to movements from a building inside campus to refuges outside campus. Scenario B is handled by house size simulations with three dimensional graphical models. Scenario C requires simulation at both inside and outside.

2.2 Related Works and Problems

ABS provides the paradigm that implement agents behaviors as results of their wills. The wills are for example, they want to go home, go to refuges, or search for their family. One of methods that involve the agent's will in a multi agent simulation system (MABS) is that MAS has a function of calculating their positions at every simulation step. A traffic simulation is a typical one. Most of traffic simulations are using a network model. The network model is consisted of edges and nodes, and the edges have lanes along that cars run. Methods for simulating behaviors using a free space model are used to simulate the movements of human in an open space, One crowd simulation is based on a force model by defining objects as points, lines and polygons. Other crowd simulation presents objects as arrays of cells, express the occupant agents as a cell, and simulate the behavior as Cellular Automata [8].

Casti showed that MABS traffic planners, TRANSIMS, simulated traffic patterns in Albuquerque, New Mexico, and was used to assess the impact of new road construction [2]. For pedestrian simulations, FreeWalk provides a social interaction platform [3]. Human participants and autonomous characters can socially interact with one another in a virtual city space. There are also commercial products [9].

The above systems can simulate the behaviors of agents, but they cannot take into eternal factors such as earthquakes, fires, and floods. There are systems that simulate the behaviors of agents under dynamically changing environments combined with disaster simulations. RoboCup Rescue Simulation (RCRS) was designed to simulate the behaviors of civilians, the operations of rescue teams, and disasters situations simultaneously at the Hanshin-Awaji earthquake disaster [5]. USARSim is a robot simulator developed based on the 3D game environment [6].

3   A Hybrid Model of Network and Free Space

Simulating evacuation behaviors at disaster situations requires follows:

1. Several types of agents such as persons and cars, are involved in the simulation. And they have different wills and their behaviors are not represented by one model. As a result, their movements are not similar ones when they are at the same situations.
2. When a huge number of agents move in area with limited space, traffic jam may occur there.
3. When the area of simulation is wide, the required resolution or dimension of the area varies according to the situations.

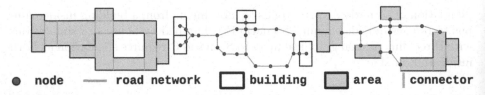

● **node** ——— **road network** ☐ **building** ☐ **area** | **connector**

Fig. 2. Map representation in different models (top: a free space model, center: a network model, bottom: area & network models)

We propose a hybrid traffic simulator that can simulate agents' behavior in wither a network model or a free space model. Using a free space model, it takes computational resources to simulate the behaviors of agents, while using a network model costs less computational resources. The hybrid traffic simulator can meet the above requirements by switching the models to present maps.

3.1 Specifications of Maps

Figure 2 shows maps represented by three models. The top one shows a free space model. The center one displays a network model and four builds are represented as nodes. The bottom one is a hybrid of network & free space models and some roads are represented as a form of free space models in addition to the buildings.

3.2 Simulations of the Behavior of Agents

Behavior simulation using network model: Under a network model, agents move along lanes that are components of edges. Collisions between different lanes are not taken into considerations in simulations. The destination that agents want to go and the route to it are represented as a node and a path of edges to the node. The position in an edge is calculated as following codes at every simulation step (Figure 3).

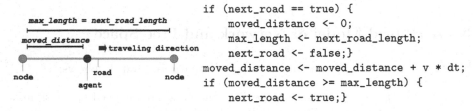

```
if (next_road == true) {
    moved_distance <- 0;
    max_length <- next_road_length;
    next_road <- false;}
moved_distance <- moved_distance + v * dt;
if (moved_distance >= max_length) {
    next_road <- true;}
```

Fig. 3. The position of agents in a network model. A wide road (edge) is consisted of several lanes. Agents are on one lane, if their positions (*moved_distance*) are different.

Behavior free space model: The movements of agents in free spaces are calculated with Helbing's physical force model [4]. The destinations of agents are given as $\mathbf{e}_i^0(t)$ in the following.

$$m_i \frac{dv_i}{dt} = m_i \frac{v_i^0(t)e_i^0(t) - v_i(t)}{\tau_i} + \sum_{j(\neq i)} f_{ij} + \sum_W f_{iW} \qquad (1)$$

where m_i represents a pedestrian i of mass, v_i^0 represents a certain desired speed, e_i^0 represents a certain direction, v_i represents a actual velocity, τ_i represents a certain characteristic time, j and W represent other pedestrians and walls, f_{ij} and f_{iW} represent interaction forces, and t is simulation time.

3.3   Results of Implementation

Figure 4 shows snapshots of agents' behaviors. The left figure is the movements of 300 agents from a right room (free space) to the left up position through the other space. Two spaces are connected via an access aisle presented as an edge of a network model. The connector node in Figure 2 between a free space and an edge works as ingress and egress points of agents. Each agent is displayed by a cycle with two arrows. The dark arrow shows the movement and the other light arrow is the force applied to them. The right figure shows the collisions of two groups of agents at the narrow aisle. The groups move to opposite directions.

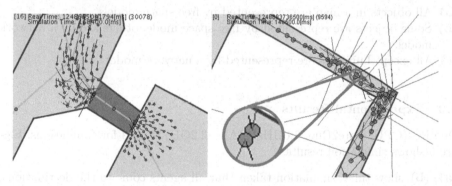

Fig. 4. Snapshots of simulations (light gray (pink) area: using free space model, gray area: using network model, white (green) line: road network used network model) left: agent movements from a free space to the other space via a road present in a network model. right: collisions of agents at narrow space.

4   Evacuation Simulations

4.1   Rescue Scenarios and Experiment Environments

Rescue scenarios: Followings are experiment rescue scenarios described in section 2.1.

- A large number ($n = \{100, 300, 600, 900\}$) of students move from a right up building to a left bottom building in Figure 5.
- A number (30) of rescue teams move in the opposite direction, from the left bottom building to the right up building.

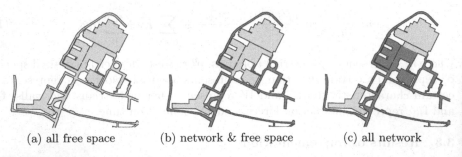

(a) all free space   (b) network & free space   (c) all network

Fig. 5. Experiment maps of three models (light gray (pink) area: simulation is done by free space model. gray area: network model is used in the simulation.)

The times of agents of student group and rescue team group to move are measured in simulation time and wallclock time.

Experiment environments: The simulations are executed at three models of maps (Figure 5).

(a) All objects in a map are represented by free space models.
(b) Some objects are represented by free space mode, others are by a network model.
(c) All except buildings are represented by a network model.

4.2   Experimental Results

One PC (CPU: Core2Duo, 3.0GHz, RAM: 3.2GB) is used for simulations. Figure 6 shows simulation results.

(a), (b) show times simulation taken that all agents come to the destinations, respectively in simulation time and wall clock time. The times become less as the portions that are represented in the network model are increased. It is interesting that rescue team takes more time than students in the case of free space than in the case of network model.

It makes sense to take longer time to get through against large oppositely-directed flow of a pedestrian than usual. This feature can be found in free space model and hybrid model. It shows that hybrid model can simulate fine resolution as free space model one.

(c), (d) show the average times needed for student agents and rescue team agents to move, respectively. When the number of students agents the simulation time to move increased. The increases show the collisions among agents causes traffic jams.

(e), (f) show histograms of arrival times for 300 and 900 students, respectively. The arrival times among three models correlate each other. The peak times between the 300 student case and 900 student case are almost the same. The late ones of 900 student case take more time than the 300 student case.

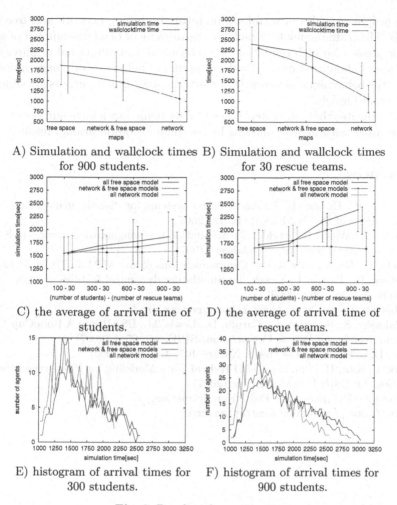

A) Simulation and wallclock times   B) Simulation and wallclock times
for 900 students.   for 30 rescue teams.

C) the average of arrival time of   D) the average of arrival time of
students.   rescue teams.

E) histogram of arrival times for   F) histogram of arrival times for
300 students.   900 students.

Fig. 6. Results of experiments

These show that (1) our hybrid evacuation simulation model presents similar results of free space model ones, , and (2) crowd situations are presented in space model. And these show possibility that setting parameters of them will give reasonable results with less computational resources.

5 Discussion and Summary

The simulation of a large number of people's evacuation behaviors is assumed to support the decision of rescue operations or prompt planning for disaster mitigation. Agent based simulations (ABS) have been providing a paradigm to simulate situations that are difficult to model. Simulations of many agents at wide areas with fine resolutions require a lot of computational resources and computer powers.

We propose an idea of a traffic simulator combining network and free space models. The traffic simulator simulates the movement of a large number of agents at wide areas with high resolutions by reasonable computational resources. The experiments show that our method can simulate behaviors of a huge number of agents, the behavior causes crowded situations, and similar outputs are simulated for different models.

This indicates that our system can simulate behaviors a huge number of agents at wide areas with high resolutions by reasonable computational resources.

References

1. Fiedrich, F., Burghardt, P.: Agent-based systems for disaster management. Communications of the ACM 50(3), 41–42 (2007)
2. Casti, J.L.: Would-Be World: How Simulation is Changing the Frontiers of Science. John Wiley and Sons Inc., Chichester (1997)
3. Ishida, T.: Digital City Kyoto. Communications of the ACM 45(7), 76–81 (2002)
4. Helbing, D., Farkas, I., Vicsek, T.: Simulating dynamical features of escape panic. Nature 407, 487–490 (2000)
5. RoboCup Rescue, http://www.robocuprescue.org/
6. Balakirsky, S., Scrapper, C., Carpin, D., Lewis, M.: USARSim: A RoboCup Virtual Urban Search and Rescue Competition. SPIE, vol. 6561 (2007)
7. Low, D.J.: Following the crowd. Nature 407, 465–466 (2000)
8. Park, I., Kim, H., Jun, C.: 2D-3D Hybrid Data Modeling for Fire Evacuation Simulation. In: ESRI User Conference (2007)
9. Quadstone Paramics Ltd., PedestrianSimulation, http://www.pedestrian-simulation.com/

Designing Agent Behaviour in Agent-Based Simulation through Participatory Method

Patrick Taillandier[1,2] and Elodie Buard[3,4]

[1] IRD, UMI UMMISCO 209,
32 avenue Henri Varagnat, 93143 Bondy, France
[2] IFI, MSI, UMI 209,
ngo 42 Ta Quang Buu, Ha Noi, Viet Nam
patrick.taillandier@gmail.com
[3] COGIT IGN, 2/4 avenue Pasteur,
94165 Saint-Mandé, France
[4] UMR Géographie Cités,
13 rue du Four, 75006 Paris, France
elodie.buard@ign.fr

Abstract. Agent-based simulation has demonstrated its usefulness for the modelling of complex systems. However, the simulation widely depends on the agent behaviour designing. In order to facilitate the definition of such behaviour, we propose an approach based on a participatory method: a domain expert directly enters his knowledge about entities in a specific environment. In this paper, we propose to formalise the agent behaviour by using a combination of production rules and of a multi-criteria decision making method. An experiment, carried out in the domain of ecological simulation, is presented. This first experiment shows promising results for our approach.

Keywords: multi-agent simulation, agent behaviour design, participatory method, multi-criteria decision making, ecological simulation.

1 Introduction

Agent-based simulations are powerful tools to study complex systems. Indeed they enable to take into account not only different level of granularity but also the heterogeneity of the entities composing the system. A key point of these simulations concerns the designing of the agent's behaviour. Unfortunately, this task can be complex and fastidious. A recent approach to face this difficulty in the context of agent-based simulation consists in using participatory methods [6]. These methods propose to let human actors (e.g. domain experts) directly participate in the agent modelling process through their interactions in the simulation. In this paper, we propose an approach dedicated to the agent behaviour design based on a participatory method. Thus, we propose to let a human expert plays the role of an agent in the simulation and to analyse the logs produced in order to extract knowledge about the expert behaviour. In Section 2, the context of our work is introduced. Section 3 is

J.-J. Yang et al. (Eds.): PRIMA 2009, LNAI 5925, pp. 571–578, 2009.

devoted to the presentation of our agent behaviour design approach. Section 4 describes an application of our approach in the domain of ecological simulations. Section 5 concludes and presents the perspectives of this work.

2 Context

In this paper, we deal with agent behaviour design. For numerous complex systems, designing such behaviour is a complex task, in particular, when no formalised knowledge is available on the system studied. In this context, it becomes necessary to directly obtain the necessary knowledge from domain experts. Unfortunately, extracting this knowledge is often a fastidious and difficult task. To face this difficulty, an approach consists in using Machine Learning techniques. Indeed, these techniques enable to acquire general knowledge from examples. It is then possible to obtain knowledge about the agent behaviour by analysing examples of their behaviour. Two questions arise from the use of such approach: which data to use and how to learn the agent behaviour from these data. An approach to answer these questions consists in using the participatory paradigm. Based on this approach, [4] and [10] propose methods to learn expert decision criteria in the context of rescue simulation. More precisely, they propose methods to learn utility functions representing the agent behaviour by means of interactions between an expert and the system. In [4], the expert observes the behaviour of an agent and has the possibility to correct an action if not relevant. The agent takes into account this intervention to refine its behaviour. In [10], the expert directly takes the control of an agent. Here, the behaviour is learnt *a posteriori* in analysing the produced logs. In this paper, we propose to use the same general approach as in [10]. Thus, the agent behaviour is learnt in analysing the expert activities when this one takes the control of an agent. However, we refine the formalism representing the agent behaviour to get a more powerful tool. Indeed, in contrary to [4] and [10] where a weighted linear combination of criteria was used to represent the agent behaviour, we propose to use a combination of production rules and of a powerful multi-criteria decision making method. This new formalism brings about more complex and reliable agent behaviours. In this context, we put forward a new approach to learn the agent behaviour which is described in the next part.

3 Approach Proposed

3.1 General Agent Behaviour Design Approach

In this part, we carry out the designing of agent behaviours in multi-agent simulations. We define the agent behaviour as the function that the agent uses to choose, at each step of the simulation process, an action to apply between a set of possible actions. As stated in the introduction, we propose to learn this function by using a participatory method: an expert directly plays the role of an agent in the simulation and the behaviour of this one is learnt by analysis of the expert behaviour. Our general approach is composed of two stages: the first one consists in producing data concerning the behaviour of the human expert, the second one in analysing these data in order to learn about the expert behaviour. The method used for this second stage deeply depends on the formalism used to represent the agent behaviour. In Section 3.2, we describe the data gathering in the acquisition stage. As for the learning stage, in Section 3.3, we present the formalism we used to represent the agent behaviour and in Section 3.4 the learning method we propose.

3.2 Production of Data Concerning the Expert Behaviour

This stage, which consists in producing data representing the expert behaviour, is similar as the one presented in [10]. In order to produce these data, we propose to use a participatory method: an expert directly interacts in the simulation by playing the role of an agent. At each step of the simulation process, the action he chooses is logged. The actions can be of different types. Typically, some actions can refer to displacement toward an objective, other to communications, other to the modification of the environment, and so on. We propose to characterise the actions of each type by sets of criteria. We assume that, for each type of actions, a set of criteria is defined to characterise the actions of this type and that a set of criteria is defined to characterise the state of the agent.

3.3 Formalisation of the Agent Behaviour

In this paper, we propose to solve the action choice problem by decomposing it into two sub-problems. Indeed, instead of directly choosing the action that is the most relevant between the complete set of actions, the agent will choose, in a first step, the type of action that is relatively more appropriate in regards with its state, then, in a second step, the action of this type that is the most relevant. The interest of this decomposition is to reduce the complexity of the agent behaviour design problem.

Concerning the action type choice problem, we propose to formalise the knowledge used to make this choice by a set of production rules. The advantage of this kind of representation is to be easily interpretable by domain experts and thus to facilitate its validation and update.

For the choice of the most relevant of the action type considered, we propose to formulate the problem as a multi-criteria decision making problem. The goal is to choose, according to criteria specific to the selected action type, the action that is the most relevant. In the literature, numerous approaches are proposed to solve this type of multi-criteria decision making problems. In this work, we propose to use a method based on the ELECTRE methods [8]. The ELECTRE methods are well-established multi-criteria decision making methods based on partial aggregation. They enable to make a decision from incomparable criteria [2]. These methods were used with success to solve numerous problems [9]. Their principle is to compare the possible actions by pair. These methods analyses the possible outranking relation (noted S) existing between two actions. An action outranks another if this one is at least as good as the other one.

Our decision making method requires defining several parameters for each criterion:

- The *weight* of the criterion: importance of the criterion in the action choice.
- The *preference threshold*: represents the threshold from which the difference between two criterion values allows to prefer one action over another.
- The *indifference threshold*: represents the threshold from which the difference between two criterion values is considered significant.
- The *veto threshold*: represents the threshold from which the difference between two criterion values disqualifies the action that obtained the smaller value.

A last parameter to define is the cutting level of the fuzzy relation λ. It defines the reference threshold for the action comparison. The higher this threshold, the more the establishment of the relation A_1SA_2 requires unanimity from the criteria concerning the fact that the action A_1 is superior to the action A_2.

The first step of our method consists in computing, for each pair of actions (A_1, A_2) and for each criterion j, the concordances $c_j(A_1SA_2)$ and $c_j(A_2 S A_1)$ between the two actions as well as the discordances $d_j(A_1SA_2)$ and $d_j(A_2SA_1)$. The concordance and the discordance are computed from the difference of values of the criterion j for the two actions. We note A^j, the value of the criterion j for the action A. Figure 2 illustrates how to compute the concordance and the discordance values from the difference of values of the actions for the criterion j.

The second step of our method consists in computing, for each pair of actions (A_1, A_2), the *concordance indexes* $C(A_1SA_2)$ and $C(A_2SA_1)$ between the two actions. These indexes represent the mean concordance obtained for the whole criterion set weighted by the criterion weight. It enables to estimate the part of criteria for which an action is at least as good as another one. Let w_j be the weight of criterion j. For two actions A_1 and A_2, the global concordance index is equal to:

$$C(A_1SA_2) = \frac{\sum\limits_{j \in \{criterion\}} w_j \times c_j(A_1SA_2)}{\sum\limits_{j \in \{criterion\}} w_j} \qquad (1)$$

The third step consists in computing, for each pair of actions (A_1, A_2), the *credibility indexes* $\rho(A_1 S A_2)$ and $\rho(A_2 S A_1)$ between the two actions. The credibility indexes are computed as follows:

$$\rho(A_1SA_2) = C(A_1SA_2) \times \prod\limits_{j \in \{i \in \{criterion\}/d_i(A_1SA_2) > C(A_1SA_2)\}} \frac{1 - d_j(A_1SA_2)}{1 - c(A_1SA_2)} \qquad (2)$$

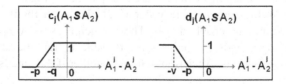

Fig. 1. Computation of the concordance and of the discordance

This index represents the degree with which the action A_1 is at least as good as the action A_2. It corresponds to the *concordance index* weaken by the possible effect of the veto.

The fourth step consists in establishing, according to the values of the *credibility indexes*, the relation between each pair of actions (A_1, A_2). There are four types of possible relations:

- $\rho(A_1SA_2)<\lambda$ and $\rho(A_2SA_1)<\lambda \Rightarrow A_1PA_2$: means that the actions are incomparable.
- $\rho(A_1SA_2)\geq\lambda$ and $\rho(A_2SA_1)<\lambda \Rightarrow A_1PA_2$: means that the action A_1 is better than A_2.
- $\rho(A_1SA_2)<\lambda$ and $\rho(A_2SA_1)\geq\lambda \Rightarrow A_2PA_1$: means that the action A_2 is better than A_1.
- $\rho(A_1SA_2)\geq\lambda$ and $\rho(A_2SA_1)\geq\lambda \Rightarrow A_1IA_2$: means that the two actions are as good.

The last step consists in selecting the best action among the action set. For each action A_1 belonging to the action set *Act*, we compute the preference index $P(A_1)$ that represents the number of times this action was preferred over another action minus the number of times another actions was preferred over this action.

$$P(A_1) = \left|\left\{A_2 \in Act \: / \: A_1PA_2\right\}\right| - \left|\left\{A_2 \in Act \: / \: A_2PA_1\right\}\right| \qquad (3)$$

The action selected is the one that maximises the preference index.

3.4 Learning of the Agent Behaviour

Learning of the action type selection rules. The goal of this step is to learn rules that define, according to the agent state (characterised by a set of criteria), the type of actions that is the most relevant to apply. We remind that we have gathered data concerning the expert behaviour. These data are composed of a set of example (s_{ag}, A_s, a_{exp}) with s_{ag} the agent state, and a_{exp} the action the expert chose to apply when he had to choose between the action set A_s. It is thus easy to build, from these data, a learning set for the action type selection. The attributes are the criteria charactering the agent state. The value is the action type chosen by the expert. Several algorithms can be used to learn rules from such learning set. In this paper, we propose to use the RIPPER algorithm. This one enables to learn relevant rules and has a good generalisation power [5].

Learning from the parameter values of the ELECTRE I method. We propose to formulate the problem of the definition of the best values for the ELECTRE I method parameters as a minimisation problem. We define a global error function that represents the inadequacy between the agent behaviour (and thus the ELECTRE I method parameters values) and the expert behaviour. The goal of this step is to find the parameter values enabling to minimise the global error.

Let P be the current set of utility functions. Let (s_{ag}, A_s, a_{exp}) be an example representing that the expert chose to apply the action a_{exp} when he had to choose between the action set A_s and when the agent state is s_{ag}.

We define the function $error((s_{ag}, A_s, a_{exp})\ P)$ that determines, for an example (A_s, a_{exp}), if the agent behaviour induced by the parameter value P is compatible with the expert behaviour, i.e. if the action applied by the expert behaviour would have been applied taking into account the parameter values. If the agent behaviour is compatible, $error((s_{ag}, A_s, a_{exp}), P) = 0$, otherwise, $error((s_{ag}, A_s, a_{exp}), P) = 1$.

The global error function proposed corresponds to the sum of all errors obtained for each example of the data set *Data*:

$$Error(Data, P) = \sum_{(A_s, a_{exp}) \in Data} error((s_{ag}, A_s, a_{exp}), P) \tag{4}$$

The aims of this step is to find the set of parameter values that minimises *Error(Data,P)*. The size of the search space will be most of time too high to carry out a complete search. Thus, it will be necessary to proceed by incomplete search. In this context, we propose to use a metaheuristic to find the best weight assignment. We propose to use genetic algorithms [7] which are particularly effective when the search space is well-structured as it is in our search problem.

4 Case Study

4.1 Case Study Context

The national park of Hwange. In this case study, we study the link between elephant populations and available natural resources. Indeed, the activity of elephants during the day is often related to the utilisation of these resources. Making decision concerning the resources implies to understand the impact of natural resources on the animal populations. In this context we propose to study the activities of elephant populations in the Hwange National Park, located in Zimbabwe. This park presents one of the highest elephant densities of the world [3]. The low availability of water during the dry season has lead to the installation of water pumps. The issue of the park manager is to manage these pumps, in particular to define the flow of the pumps to maintain the elephant demography neither too high nor too low.

Implemented simulation. In this work, we chose to develop our simulation with the GAMA platform [1]. This platform provides a complete modelling and simulation development environment for building spatially explicit multi-agent simulations. The main advantage of this platform is the simplicity to define a model with it. In our simulation, the environment is represented by a grid. We defined six types of cells: void space, grass, bush, forest, natural water tap and pump water tap. We modelled each group of elephant by an agent. An *elephant group* agent represents a group of elephants composed of 20 to 30 elephants. The behaviour of an *elephant group* agent depends on its state and its perceptions. At each step of the simulation, each *elephant group* agent chooses an objective, then a cell to carry out this objective. We defined four objectives for this agent: *Eating, Drinking, Bathing* and *Sleeping*. In the context of our agent behaviour design approach, the objectives represent the action types. Thus, we have four possible action types. Concerning the target cells, they represent the possible actions: for each step of the simulation, each possible target cell is an action.

4.2 Test Protocol

As a test protocol, we propose to use our approach to learn the behaviour of the *elephant group* agent from a set of examples (the *learning set*) and then to compare

Table 1. *Error rate* obtained on the *learning* and *test* set by the behaviour defined "manually" by the expert and the behaviour defined by our approach

Example set	Behaviour defined "manually" by the expert	Behaviour defined by our approach
Learning set	0.27	0.19
Testing set	0.31	0.25

the learnt behaviour with a behaviour defined by an ecologist expert on another set of examples (the *testing set*). The expert chosen is studying the elephant behavior in the park. He knows the field features and how the elephant move according to attraction points such as water or vegetation. The *learning set* and the *testing set* are composed of 50 examples that represent various situations. For each defined behaviour, we compute on both example sets the *rate of errors*, i.e. the number of actions chosen by the agent (with the considered behaviour) that are different from the ones chosen by the expert.

4.3 Results

As shown on Table 1, the behaviour defined by our approach has obtained better results than the one defined "manually" by the expert. Indeed, the error rates obtained with our approach are lower than the ones obtained with the behaviour defined "manually" by the expert on both example sets. Another advantage of our approach concerns its simplicity to define the agent behaviour. Indeed, with our approach, the expert has just to play the role of an agent in the simulation. In contrary, the "manual" definition of the behaviour requires a long and fastidious tuning process. We can note that even if our approach get good results, these results are not perfect (the error rates are not null). An explanation is the lack of criteria to characterise the agent state and the different actions. Indeed, in our experiment, we only used simple criteria that did not allow to understand some complex decisions made by the expert. In order to learn a more accurate behaviour, additional criteria are needed.

5 Conclusion

In this paper, we presented an approach dedicated to the designing of agent behaviour through the participation of expert playing the role of the agents in the simulation. Our approach is based on the logging of the expert behaviour when this one is confronted to predefined scenarios and on the extraction of knowledge from logs analysis. We proposed to formalise the agent behaviour by using a combination of production rules and of a multi-criteria decision making method. This formalism enables to design complex agent behaviours. We presented a first experiment in the context of ecological simulations that shows promising results for our approach. Indeed, this experiment showed that our approach allow to easily and quickly design a relevant agent behaviour, better than one defined "manually" by an expert. Further experiments need to be carried out in order to study the effectiveness and the limitations of our approach compared to the real world. Our approach is based on the use of one particular supervised learning algorithm and one optimisation algorithm. An interesting study could be to test different algorithms and to compare the results with the ones obtained with chosen algorithms. Taking initial knowledge into account could be the last perspective of this work. Indeed, for some applications where experts have some reliable pieces of formal knowledge, it could be interesting to take into account these pieces in the agent behaviour design process. These pieces of knowledge could allow agents to learn better behaviours.

References

1. Amouroux, E., Chu, T.-C., Boucher, A., Drogoul, A.: GAMA: an environment for implementing and running spatially explicit multi-agent simulations. In: PRIMA (2007)
2. Ben Mena, S.: Introduction aux méthodes multicritères d'aide à la décision. Biotechnol. Agro. Soc. Environ. 4(2), 83–93 (2000)
3. Blanc, J.J., Barnes, R.F.W., Craig, G.C., Douglas-Hamilton, I., Dublin, H.T., Hart, J.A., Thouless, C.R.: Changes in elephant numbers in major savanna populations in eastern and southern Africa. Pachyderm 38, 19–28 (2005)
4. Chu, T.Q., Boucher, A., Drogoul, A., Vo, D.A., Nguyen, H.P., Zucker, J.D.: Interactive Learning of Expert Criteria for Rescue Simulations. In: PRIMA, Hanoi, pp. 127–138 (2008)
5. Cohen, W.: Fast effective rule induction. In: Proceedings of the Twelfth International Conference on Machine Learning, pp. 115–123 (1995)
6. Guyot, P., Drogoul, A., Honiden, S.: Power and negotiation: lessons from agent-based participatory simulations. In: AAMAS, pp. 27–33 (2006)
7. Holland, J.H.: Adaptation in Natural and Artificial Systems. University of Michigan Press, Ann Arbor (1975)
8. Roy, B.: The outranking approach and the foundations of ELECTRE methods. Theory and Decision 31 (1991)
9. Taillandier, P.: Knowledge diagnosis in systems based on an informed tree search strategy: application to cartographic generalisation. In: CSTST Student Workshop, Cergy-Pontoise (Paris), France, pp. 589–594 (2008)
10. Taillandier, P., Chu, T.Q.: Using Participatory Paradigm to Learn Human Behaviour. In: ICKSE, Hanoi, Viet Nam (2009)

Influence of Social Networks on Recovering Large Scale Distributed Systems

Wei Ren, Yang Xu, Jinmei Luo, and Liying Guo

School of Computer Science & Engineering
University of Electronic Science and Technology of China
Chengdu, Sichuan 610054, China
wren.uestc@gmail.com, xuyang@uestc.edu.cn

Abstract. Network Topology has been shown as a key factor on influencing system performance even under the same coordination algorithm. Although many distributed algorithm designs have been proved to be feasible to make up some functions in the large scale distributed systems as claimed, for example, recovering the network from link or node failures, they may significantly change the network topology which has never been tested. Therefore, their influences on the overall system performance are unknown. In this paper, we have made an initial effort to find how a standard network recovery policy, such as MPLS algorithm, may change the network in terms of network congestions and shifts of network topologies. Those interesting discoveries are helpful to predict their influences on system performance and in turn to be useful for new algorithm design.

Keywords: Large-Scale Distributed Systems, Network Recovery, Node Failure, Link Failure, Social Networks.

1 Introduction

With the development of information technology, large scale distributed system design has been a booming research field. Its applications have been successfully applied to the domains such as military, aeronautics, commercial services and scientific research. In these applications, distributed systems are always organized as a social network where each node only maintains direct connections with a few of the others. When the network is organized as a social network topology, it is a key factor on influencing the system performance and has been intensively studied in the disciplines of computer science, physics, economics and physiology. For example, large scale distributed networks such as citation graphs [1], Internet [2], hyperlinks in web [3], ad hoc networks [4] are benefited from the characteristics of social networks — *small world effect* [5] and *scale free phenomenon* [6]. Xu learned that the same coordination algorithm may lead to huge different performances when the social network topologies vary [7]. Scerri mathematically analyzed how different social networks may affect the team in the coordination of information sharing, sensor fusion and task allocation [8]. Gaston took a bottom-up research on network

J.-J. Yang et al. (Eds.): PRIMA 2009, LNAI 5925, pp. 579–586, 2009.

formation and found the incomplete network social structure varies decentralized adaptation strategies [9].

The effects of social networks are popular, but not all distributed algorithms are tested under different social network topologies. Although their feasibility on claimed operations [10] have been proved, the effects may be different on different topologies. Therefore the exact system performance is unpredictable. In this paper, we made our initial efforts for this issue and chose network recovery as a sample operation because network failures, including link failures and node failures, are inevitable in a large scale distributed system. We simulated a series of large scale distributed systems with different social network topologies. A popular restoration of re-routing mechanism-MPLS (Multi-Protocol Label Switching) [11] is implemented to recover link and node failures. To simulate a physical network, in those experiments, the communication capabilities of each link or node are limited. The experiment results are presented in two major sections: influences on system efficiency and changes on network topologies.

In the first section, communication data from failure nodes or links has to be redirected and they may cause congestions on existing links or nodes. We investigated on the number of new congested links or nodes which will hurt system performance. By comparing the influences on different networks, we found that a random network is more likely to be congested if more links are failed, while a small-world network is the least likely. On the other hand, a scale-free network appears to be more vulnerable to node congestions, while a grid network is the most robust.

In the second section, we tested how the network topology may be changed from network recover operations. We have found that most network topologies are immune to the network recovery when the congestions are not so bad. However, when the number of congested links and nodes becomes high, network topologies may be significantly changed, especially when the network is organized as a scale-free network or a small-world network. From our previous experience, those changes in topologies probably result a significant effect on system's overall performances [7].

2   Modeling Network

The network topology of a large scale distributed system is defined as an undirected graph $G = (V, E)$, where $V = \{1, 2, \cdots, N\}$, $N = |V|$, is the nonempty set of all nodes. E denotes the set of edges between nodes. An edge that connects the nodes i and j is written as $(i, j) \in E$, and i and j are called neighbors. Function $n : V \to E$ defines the set of all neighbors of a specific node. i.e., $n(i) = \{b, j, l\}$ represents the neighbors of node $i : b, j$ and l. In order to study the influence of network recovery on a large scale distributed system, different network models would be proposed. In this paper we model some topologies of systems based on social networks: a random network, a grid network, a small-world network, and a scale-free network. Preliminary studies have found that network topologies play an important role in the fundamental properties, i.e., network diameter, average distance between nodes, cluster, degree distributions, and so on. For the purpose of this paper, we mainly focus on the following fundamental properties to describe the difference between the models above.

- Degree: The degree of node i is: $d(i) = |n(i)|$.
- Average degree: $\bar{d} = \dfrac{1}{N} \sum_{i \in V} n(i)$ is the average degree of all nodes in the network.
  In a social network, each node only connects with a few of the others, therefore $\bar{d} \ll |V|$.
- Degree distribution: describes the $p(k) = \Pr[d = k]$ defined as a fraction of nodes (the number of such nodes is d) with the degree k.
- Distance: the distance of any pairs of nodes $< i, j >$ is called $dis\tan ce(i, j)$ defined as the number of hops in the shortest path between two nodes. Specifically, $dis\tan ce(i, j) = 1$, if $(i, j) \in E$.
- Network diameter: The diameter of the graph G is defined as $\arg\max(D)$ $where$ $D = \{dis\tan ce(i, j) \mid i, j \in E\}$.
- Sub-graph: Let G' be the sub-graph of G, $G' = (V', E')$, where V' is the set of nodes on the all shortest paths between the pairs of nodes $< i, j >$, and $E' \subset E$.
- Transition nodes: Let $s(i)$ be the set of neighbor nodes that can transmit the flow from node i, and $s(i) \subset (n(i) \cap G')$.
- Transition paths: Let $path(i)$ be the set that records all the pairs of neighbor nodes $< s, t >$ that communicate data via i, and $s, t \in n(i)$.

Different social network topologies can be described according to these properties. A random network follows a Poisson distribution of the degree distribution. Most nodes in a grid network have the same degree. A small world network has a generalized binomial degree distribution and has much shorter average distance than that of grid networks. Moreover, some typical large scale distributed systems such as Internet and hyperlinks in web posses the *scale free phenomenon*, a power law distribution: $p(k) \propto k^{-r}$ ($2 < r < 3$). Some researchers found an interesting formula: $\arg\max(D) \propto \ln\ln N$ [12], which means the average distance may decrease as the network grows [13]. This formula precisely reflects small world effect as well. Figure 1 shows the four social network topologies we are interested in our research.

To simulate a physical network, we define the rate of communication through $(i, j) \in E$ is $f(i, j)$ and its predefined max-flow is F_{max} , which is a constant. Therefore, the bandwidth for any of the link is set. $f(i, j)$ can't be more than its bandwidth or the link will be jammed. Please note, if $f(i, j) = 0$, there is no communication in (i, j) and it is called as a backup link that may be used for future

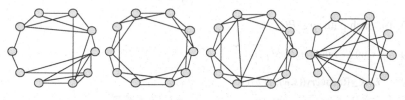

Fig. 1. Topologies: Random network, Grid network, Small-world network, Scale-free network

communications [14]. In addition, we define $r(i)$ is the amount of communication through node i. $r(i)$ can't be more than $C_{\max}(i)$, the max allowed bandwidth capability through node i, otherwise the node is jammed too. Node i's capacity defined as $C_{\max}(i) = \lambda \times d(i) \times F_{\max}$ where $0 < \lambda < 1$ is a constant so that its capability is proportional to the degree of the node.

3 Network Recovery Algorithm

When it comes to link failures and node failures, we use a popular network recovery policy—MPLS algorithm. Related LSR (Label Switch Path) would perform *the restoration of re-routing mechanisms* to maintain the communication between nodes once failed spots are discovered. Algorithm 1 briefly shows how a failed link (i, j) is recovered (we supposed there is a social sequencing according to nodes' ID that $i \prec j$) and the amount of restored data flow is $f(i, j)$. By assuming that each node is able to get the global state of the network, node i can easily find all the alternatives shortest path to j, and w is all the transition nodes $s(i)$.

Algorithm1: *Link* _ Recovery$((i, j), f(i, j))$

(1) find all transition nodes $s(i)$

(2) for each node $w \in s(i)$

(3)   *SendData*$(w, f(i, j)/|s(i)|)$;

(4) end for

Algorithm 2 briefly shows how a failed node i is recovered. The communication through a node is composed of several streams from different links. Each stream p through a node i, is written as a unique path $\{..., s, i, w, ...\}$ *where* $s \prec w$. The amount of p is written as $f(p)$. Therefore, to recover node failure i, algorithm 2 first enumerate all the stream $P(i)$ and each p can be routed through the link failure algorithm (algorithm 1) if we supposed there has been a link of (s, w) whose amount of communication is $f(p)$.

Algorithm2: *Node* _ Recovery(i)

(1) $P(i) \leftarrow EnumerateStream(i)$; $// \; c(i) = \sum_{p \in P(i)} f(p)$

(2) for each path $p \in P(i)$

(3) $(s, w) \leftarrow FindNeigbors(p, i)$;

(4)   *Link* _ Recovery$((s, w), f(p))$;

(5) end for

Although MPLS algorithm can effectively enhance recovery efficiency, network congestion can't be avoided due to the limited physical communication capacities of the links and nodes. We define the conditions of network congestion as follows:

1. Link (i, w) is congested by an additional recover flow μ

$$link\_congestion(i, w) = (F_{max} - (\mu + f(i, w))) < 0?true: false;$$

2. Node i is congested by an additional stream μ.

$$node\_congestion(i) = (C_{max}(i) - (\mu + r(i))) < 0?true: false;$$

4 Network Performances on Different Network Topologies

In this section, we investigate how network recovering operation may create node or link congestions when it is organized as different social network topologies: random networks, scale-free networks, grid networks and small-world networks. System size is $N = 1000$, average degree of each node $\bar{d} = 6$, and maximum allowed link overload is $F_{max} = 10$. The results are evaluated according to newly congested links and congested nodes by varying the ratio of failed links ($Ratio\_link$), the ratio of failed nodes ($Ratio\_node$), and the ratio of average communication of each link $f(i, j)$ ($Ratio\_flow$). Moreover, in this experiment, additional 15% backup links that communication flow isn't presented. We assume the amount of communication for each link is randomly set. The experiment results are based on 100 runs.

4.1 Link Failure Recovery

In this subsection, we examined the number of congested links and congested nodes when MPLS fixed link failures. We fix the average communication of each link $f(i, j)$ as 50% of the F_{max} ($Ratio\_flow = 0.5$). In Figure 2, we varied the number of link failures to be fixed from 0.5% to 5% of the whole network. Figure 2.a shows that network recovery operation leads to congested links and congested links presents the trend of rapid increase with the slow increase of $Ratio\_link$ .We can find that random network appears to the largest number of congested links while the small-world network appears to the least number of congested links.

The experiment results in Figure2.b show that excluding the grid network, network recovery operation on failed links will lead to node congestions. Apparently, scale-free networks appear to the largest number of congested nodes in any settings. The reason is that the stability of hub-nodes which have large bandwidth (proportion to its degree). Therefore, the other nodes with limited bandwidth are prone to be jammed.

4.2 Node Failure Recovery

In this subsection, we investigate the network performances after MPLS recovering node failures. In figure 3, we varied the failed nodes in the network from 0.5% to 5% when $Ratio\_flow = 0.5$ and found the congested links increased quickly and congested nodes slowly increased. As our expected, scale free networks made heavy congested

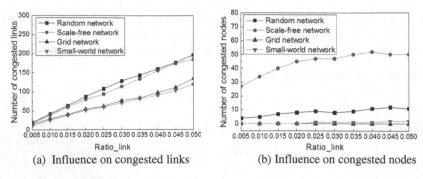

(a) Influence on congested links   (b) Influence on congested nodes

Fig. 2. Influence of network recovery on network congestion based on varying *Ratio _ link*

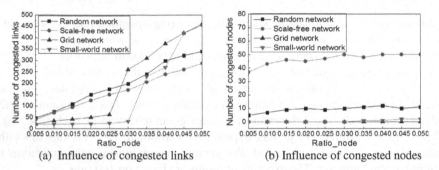

(a) Influence of congested links   (b) Influence of congested nodes

Fig. 3. Influence of network recovery on network congestion based on varying *Ratio _ node*

nodes. However, although random networks and scale free networks have more number of congested links when the failed nodes are sparse, small world and grid networks create about 40% more congested links when failed nodes are more than 3.5%.

5   Influence on Network Topology

In this section, we verify if network recovery operation would lead to the changes of social network topologies. Similar experiment settings are kept as section 4 for network failure recovery. However, we set $C_{max}(i)=\lambda \times F_{max}$ where $\lambda > 1$ is a constant and node capability is fixed. We have found that the changes of network topologies are not significant if the congestions are not so serious, while the topologies are destroyed if network breaks. In this experiment we pickup two settings: *Ratio _ link* = 0.02 and *Ratio _ flow* = 0.7 ; *Ratio _ link* = 0.035 and *Ratio _ flow* = 0.5 , so that the shifts of network topologies are distinct, but the networks in most runs are connected (very few disconnected networks are excluded). The experiment results are shown as degree distribution. Each graph represents one type of social network, and consists of three curves with three settings: the original network topology without any failures (normal), the network topology after network recovery while 15% backup links presented (m>0) and the network topology after network recovery without any backup links (m=0).

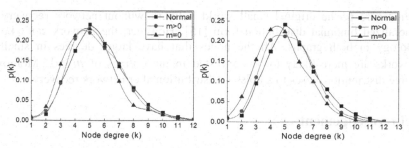

Fig. 4. Influence of network recovery on random network. (a) *Ratio_link* = 0.035 , *Ratio_flow* = 0.5 (b) *Ratio_node* = 0.03 , *Ratio_flow* = 0.5 .

Figure 4 shows how a random network topology shifts on two different settings. Although the random network topology is kept and its distribution still follows a Poisson distribution, the distribution clearly shifts left after the link failure or node failure recoveries (more distinct when $m = 0$). Therefore, its average degree is decreased in this condition.

Figure 5 shows the scale free network significantly changed. In both graphs, the scale free networks are losing their power law distribution and are more and more close to a Poisson distribution as random networks. In the settings of $m = 0$ (blue lines), almost all the hub nodes with very high degrees are disappeared. The reason is that hub nodes are easily jammed if it does not have much higher communication capacities.

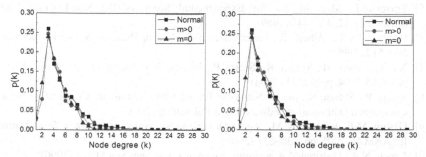

Fig. 5. Influence of network recovery on scale-free network. (a) *Ratio_link* = 0.03 , *Ratio_flow* = 0.5 (b) *Ratio_node* = 0.01 , *Ratio_flow* = 0.5 .

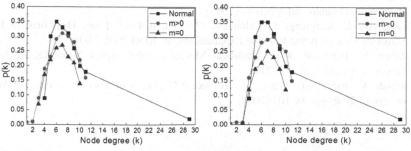

Fig. 6. Influence of network recovery on small-world network. (a) *Ratio_link* = 0.04 , *Ratio_flow* = 0.5 (b) *Ratio_node* = 0.03 , *Ratio_flow* = 0.5 .

In figure 6, the original small world network without network recovery has a generalized binomial distribution form [15]. However, the network can't keep this topology in both graphs. All the nodes that have larger degrees in small-world networks are more likely to be congested in the settings of $m \geq 0$. Moreover, its degree distribution closes to a Poisson distribution after network recovery.

Acknowledgement

This research has been sponsored in part by National Natural Science Foundation of China 60905042 and Foundation of University of Electronic Science and Technology of China for young scientists.

References

[1] Price, D.J.: Networks of Scientific Papers. Science 149(3683), 510–515 (1965)

[2] Bononi, L., Bracuto, M., D'Angelo, G., Donatiello, L.: Exploring the Effects of Hyper-Threading on Parallel Simulation. In: DS-RT 2006, pp. 257–260 (2006)

[3] Broder, A., Kumar, R., Maghoul, F., Raghavan, P., Rajagopalan, S., Stata, R., Tomkins, A., Wiener, J.: Graph Structure in the Web. Computer Networks 33(1) (2000)

[4] Musolesi, M., Hailes, S., Mascolo, C.: An Ad Hoc Mobility Model Founded on Social Network Theory. In: MSWiM 2004, pp. 20–24 (2004)

[5] Travers, J., Milgram, S.: An Experimental Study of the Small world Problem. Sociometry 32, 425–443 (1969)

[6] Barabasi, A.-L., Albert, R.: Emergence of Scaling in Random Networks. Science 286, 509–512 (1999)

[7] Xu, Y., Lewis, M., Sycara, K., Scerri, P.: Information Sharing in Very Large Teams. In: AAMAS 2004, pp. 12–21 (2004)

[8] Scerri, P., Sycara, K.: Social Networks for Effective Teams. In: Cooperative Networks: Control and Optimization. Edward Elgar Publishing (2008)

[9] Gaston, M.E. des Jardins, M.: Agent-Organized Networks for Dynamic Team Formation. In: AAMAS 2005, pp. 230–237 (2005)

[10] Lynch, N.A.: Distributed Algorithms. Morgan Kaufmann, San Mateo (1996)

[11] Sharma, V., Hellstrand, F.: Framework for Multi-protocol Label Switching (MPLS)-Based Recovery[S]. RFC 3469 (2003)

[12] Cohen, R., Havlin, S., Ben-avraham, D.: Structural Properties of Scale-Free Networks. Handbook of Graphs and networks (2003)

[13] Leskovec, J., Kleinberg, J., Faloutsos, C.: Graphs Over Time: Densification Laws, Shrinking Diameters and Possible Explanations. In: KDD 2005 (2005)

[14] Albert, R., Barab´asi, A.-L.: Statistical Mechanics of Complex Networks. Review of Modern Physics 74, 47–97 (2002)

[15] Mahdi, K., Farahat, H., Safar, M.: Temporal Evolution of Social networks in Paltalk. In: iiWAS 2008, pp. 98–103 (2008)

Dynamic Evolution of Role Taxonomies through Multidimensional Clustering in Multiagent Organizations*

Ramón Hermoso, Holger Billhardt, and Sascha Ossowski

Centre for Intelligent Information Technologies (CETINIA)
University Rey Juan Carlos Madrid (URJC), Spain
{ramon.hermoso,holger.billhardt,sascha.ossowski}@urjc.es

Abstract. This paper addresses the problem of exploring how organizational structures may evolve over time using the information from the agents' trust models. We present a mechanism based on clustering techniques capable of detecting behavioural patterns in organizational multi-agent systems, thereby identifying new roles that dynamically extend the role taxonomy. We present experimental results showing that this extension leads to an improvement of the agents' decision making processes when compared to static organizational structures.

1 Introduction

Endowing Multi-Agent Systems (MAS) with an organizational flavour has been extensively studied in recent years. It is commonly accepted that MAS designed with organizational structures allow tackling complex problems from an easier perspective [7]. These organizational structures are usually conceived as static design patterns that regulate agent behaviour. Nevertheless, lately the importance of openness and dynamics in MAS is growing, calling for structures that dynamically adapt over time to changing circumstances [2]. In addition, most of the work about organizations in MAS is centred on macro-level issues [5] while the questions of how autonomous agents in open systems deal with them appears to be secondary. Even if we assume that agents do not transgress organizational prescriptions, it is important to notice that, by definition, autonomous agents should always be given a certain freedom of choice. When agents are not able to perform a task by themselves, the need of finding a good counterpart to delegate the task becomes a key problem.

We claim that in decision making (DM) processes for selecting partners agents may make their choice supported on three different types of information, namely: *i)* past own experience; *ii)* opinions from neighbours (reputation); and *iii)* other "organizational" information sources. The first two types have already been

---

* STUDENT PAPER. The present work has been partially funded by the Spanish Ministry of Education and Science under project TIN2006-14630-C03-02 and by the Spanish project "Agreement Technologies" (CONSOLIDER CSD2007-0022, INGENIO 2010).

J.-J. Yang et al. (Eds.): PRIMA 2009, LNAI 5925, pp. 587–594, 2009.

widely studied in many works [6,9]. Some other works [4] have studied how organizational information influences agents' selections, especially when no direct experiences – or not reliable enough – have been collected before.

We deal with this third type of information aforementioned, namely how agents can use organizational structures to better determine "good" partners to interact with, especially if no valuable direct experiences are available to reason about. We show that agents cannot only exploit existing organizational structures, in particular, role taxonomies, to determine trustworthy candidates to interact with, but we also put forward a mechanism that makes use of the information managed by the agents' trust models so as to create and evolve role taxonomies. We claim that this taxonomy evolution provides agents with more precise information, helping them to make better decisions such as to decide which other agents to interact with. We propose an adaptive mechanism that evolves role taxonomies by using a multidimensional clustering algorithm to capture behavioural patterns among agents.

2   Organizational Structures for Agent's DM

The environment we use to describe the mechanism presented in this work is based on Task-oriented Multi-Agent Systems (T-MAS) which can be specified as follows:

Definition 1. *A T-MAS is a tuple* $TM=\langle \mathcal{A}_g, \mathcal{X}, \mathcal{T}, \mathcal{U} \rangle$, *where:*

- $\mathcal{A}_g$ *is a set of agents participating in the MAS; we assume each agent* $a \in \mathcal{A}_g$ *has an utility function* $\mathcal{U}_a : Ag \times \mathcal{T} \rightarrow R$, *where* Ag *is the delegated agent that performs the task* $\mathcal{T}$;
- $\mathcal{X}$ *is the environmental state space;*
- $\mathcal{T}$ *is a set of tasks that can be performed by agents;*
- $\mathcal{U} : \mathcal{X} \rightarrow R$ *is the system utility function;*

The functioning of a T-MAS is as follows (at each time step): i) a task is assigned to each agent $a_1 \in \mathcal{A}_g$; ii) if an agent a_1 cannot perform the task by itself it reassigns (delegates) the tasks to another agent $a_2 \in \mathcal{A}_g$; and iii) agents a_2 performs the task and a_1 obtains a utility from the performance. Furthermore, we assume that the utility obtained by an agent at a certain time step is equivalent to the agent's perception on the fulfilment of the delegated task to another agent. Note that this definition of individual utility allows for *subjective* utility functions. In this sense, $\mathcal{U}_a(b, t)$ represents the subjective perception of agent a on how well agent b performs task t. Notice that an agent may delegate a task to itself if considers that it is the more qualified agent to carry it out.

2.1   Organizational Information

We are particularly interested in how organizational information may help agents to agree faster on "good" task distributions in a T-MAS. Many organizational concepts can be found in the MAS literature: *roles* [8], *interactions* [3], or *norms* [1] are just some of them. The mechanism presented in this paper is based on the use of the concepts *role* and *role specialization taxonomy*. We conceive roles from the point of view of an observer, i.e. as a set of *expectations* regarding the behaviour of agents performing certain actions. This means that a role generates by itself some public expectations over certain actions that agents playing it should accomplish.

Definition 2. *Let* $TM = \langle \mathcal{A}_g, \mathcal{X}, \mathcal{T}, \mathcal{U} \rangle$ *be a T-MAS and let* $\mathcal{R}$ *be a set of role identifiers. A role in* TM *is a pair* $\langle r, \mathcal{E} \rangle$ *where* $r \in \mathcal{R}$ *is the role name; and* $\mathcal{E} = \{t_1, ..., t_n\}$, *where* $t_1, ..., t_n \in \mathcal{T}$ *is a finite set of tasks.*

The intended semantics of a role $\langle r, \mathcal{E} \rangle$ is that the agents playing the role r are qualified to perform the tasks in the set $\mathcal{E}$ in the sense that they are "skillful" for those tasks.

Definition 3. *Let* $TM = \langle \mathcal{A}_g, \mathcal{X}, \mathcal{T}, \mathcal{U} \rangle$ *be a T-MAS. A role specialization taxonomy in* TM *is a structure* $\mathcal{RT} = (R, \rhd_r)$ *consisting of a set* R *of roles in* TM *and a partial ordering* $\rhd_r$ *on* R, *such that:*

1. $\exists r_{root} = \langle r_r, \mathcal{E}_r \rangle \in R :$

$$\mathcal{E}_r = \mathcal{T} \wedge \forall r \in R : (r = r_{root} \vee r \rhd_r r_{root})$$

2. $\forall \langle r_1, \mathcal{E}_1 \rangle, \langle r_2, \mathcal{E}_2 \rangle \in R : \langle r_1, \mathcal{E}_1 \rangle \rhd_r \langle r_2, \mathcal{E}_2 \rangle \Leftrightarrow$

$$\mathcal{E}_{r_1} \subseteq \mathcal{E}_{r_2} \quad \wedge \tag{1}$$

$$\forall t \in \mathcal{E}_{r_1} : \frac{\sum_{a \in ag(r_1)} \sum_{b \in \mathcal{A}_g} \mathcal{U}_a(b,t)}{|ag(r_1)| \cdot |\mathcal{A}_g|} > \frac{\sum_{a \in ag(r_2)} \sum_{b \in \mathcal{A}_g} \mathcal{U}_a(b,t)}{|ag(r_2)| \cdot |\mathcal{A}_g|},$$

where $ag(r)$ *denotes the set of agents playing role* r.

A role specialization taxonomy structures the roles by establishing a specialization relation $\rhd_r$ based on the skills of the agents playing those roles; that is, given two different roles $r_1, r_2 \in R$ then $r_1 \rhd_r r_2$ iff. there is a subset of tasks from r_2 on which agents playing role r_1 perform better, on average, than agents playing role r_2. The hierarchy contains a top role - the root of the taxonomy $\langle r_{root}, \mathcal{E}_{root} \rangle$ - which contains all tasks and is not a specialization of any other role. This is consistent with the assumption that every agent can perform every task. We can assume that every agent in a T-MAS plays at least the top role.

2.2   A Trust Model for Agent's DM

A trust model is usually used to endow agents with an internal representation of information about others in order to better choose partners to interact with in any DM process. In the context of a T-MAS, we use the notion of trust model as a mechanism that drives the agent to choose the most trustworthy agent to which it can delegate a given task. Trust models aims at calculating expectations on other agents on particular situations, by either using past information gathered through the time – based on past interactions – or inferring using opinions from third party using their own previous assessments. As we have aforementioned roles represents expectations on different tasks available in the system. This paper combines semantics of both, trust models and role meaning. The main contribution of the work is twofold: i) building role taxonomies containing on the expectations that the agents participating in the T-MAS are currently calculating during their execution in the T-MAS; and, ii) agents may make use of the created role taxonomies in order to tune up their own expectations on different situations. These two processes are executed in parallel and continuously repeat during the T-MAS lifetime.

Next algorithm describes how an agent a uses the information provided by a role specialization taxonomy $\mathcal{RT}$ together with its own experience about previously delegated tasks in order to select an appropriate agent to which it can delegate a given task t.

1. $r = mostSpecializedRolesForTask(t)$
2. $\mathcal{A}_x = agentsPlayingRoles(r)$
3. $bestAgent = localTrustEvaluation(\mathcal{A}_x, r, t)$
4. $delegate(t, bestAgent)$

For the calculation of trust values $t_{a\rightarrow\langle a_i,r_k\rangle} \in [0..1]$, we assume that agents store their past experiences in their internal structure in form of confidence values $c_{a\rightarrow\langle a_i,r_k\rangle}$, denoting the recompiled confidence an agent a has in agent a_i playing role r_k . If agent a does not store any confidence values for the agent a_i (i.e., $c_{a\rightarrow\langle a_i,\_\rangle}$) or if all confidence values for agent a_i are for roles r_j which have no similarity to the role r_k (i.e., $sim(r_j,r_k) = 0$) then the value of $t_{a\rightarrow\langle a_i,r_k\rangle}$ is set to the default value 0.5. In any other case, $t_{a\rightarrow\langle a_i,r_k\rangle}$ is calculated by the following equation:

$$t_{a\rightarrow\langle a_i,r_k\rangle} = \frac{\sum\limits_{\langle a_i,r_j\rangle\in IS_a} c_{a\rightarrow\langle a_i,r_j\rangle} \cdot sim(r_j,r_k)}{\sum\limits_{\langle a_i,r_j\rangle\in IS_a} sim(r_j,r_k)} \qquad (2)$$

where sim is a similarity function on roles and IS_a represents a's internal structure, that is, the set of confidence values it stores. We use similarity function from [4].

3   Evolution of Role Taxonomies

We argue that creation of new roles has to be based on trust that other agents have on a specific role - that is similar to say "on the agents playing that role in the system". Trust is a subjective measure, since not all agents neither have to share the same preferences in the system nor have to use the same trust model.

Our mechanism tries to build a source of information - role taxonomy - from subjective individual assessments of trust.

We propose to use clustering methods to capture behavioural patterns of agents performing tasks. The idea is to identify groups of agents that perform a set of tasks better than others and to reflect such cases in form of a new role. In order to do this we assume that agents store confidence values $c_{a \to \langle a_i, t \rangle}$, representing agent a's recompiled experience on how well agent a_i performs a task t (from its particular point of view). Such confidence values are similar to the ones presented in Section 2.2. Let $TM = \langle \mathcal{A}_g, \mathcal{X}, \mathcal{T}, \mathcal{U} \rangle$ be a T-MAS. The confidence values stored by agents provide a means to represent agents as a point in the n-dimensional vector space formed by all possible tasks $t \in \mathcal{T}$ in the T-MAS where n is the number of tasks in $\mathcal{T}$. In particular, each agent a_i can be represented as a tuple $\hat{a} = (c_1, c_2, ..., c_n)$ where c_k is defined as follows:

$$c_k = \frac{\sum\limits_{a \in \mathcal{A}_g} c_{a \to \langle a_i, t_k \rangle}}{|\mathcal{A}_g|} \qquad (3)$$

We can denote the set of vector representations of agents – e.g., the trust space formed by agents – by $TS = \{\hat{a} = (c_1, c_2, ..., c_n) | a \in \mathcal{A}_g\}$. In a similar way, given a role $r_k \in \mathcal{R}$, we can define a trust space for the agents that have ever played that role: $TS_{r_k} = \{\hat{a} = (c_1, c_2, ..., c_n) | a \in \mathcal{A}_g \text{ and } a \text{ enacts } r_k\}$.

A trust space TS_{r_k} can be subdivided into groups of agents such that those groups fulfil the requirements of Definition 3, that is, they can be considered as agents that specialize the role r_k. It is important to note that the role taxonomy evolution depends on the group of agents performing within the system. Thus, changes in the group of members of the system will entail different evolutions for the role structure.

3.1   Trust-Based Multidimensional K-Means

To specialize roles - create new roles in the role taxonomy - we apply the K-means clustering algorithm, where k represents the number of clusters to be created in each execution. Let TM be a T-MAS with a set of roles R and a role specialization taxonomy $\mathcal{RT} = (R, \rhd_r)$. In order to evolve the role taxonomy, the clustering algorithm is applied to each set TS_{r_j} with $r_j \in R$ and r_j being a leaf in the taxonomy $\mathcal{RT}$. On each execution, the algorithm returns a set of k clusters. A cluster centroid represents the expected behaviour of all the agents belonging to it and the whole cluster represents a pattern of behaviour for all the agents included.

The possible clusters returned by the algorithm are candidates for the creation of new roles. However, considering Definition 3 in order to include a new role in the taxonomy we need to guarantee that any new role r_x fulfil the ordering $\rhd_r$ with the role from which it is extended. In particular, we process the clusters and only convert it into a new role r_x if the agents enacting r_x provide a better performance (on average) on at least one of the tasks of the role it extends. Furthermore, when deciding whether a cluster should form a new role or not, the mechanism applies two additional criteria: (a) we do not create roles with "bad" behaviours. We apply a threshold θ such that a new role is only created if the tasks it specializes have at least an expected value of θ. For the experiments we will use $\theta = 0.7$. In general, this value should always be defined as higher than 0.5 since the latter usually represents total uncertainty; (b) in most of the cases we would want to create new roles if, in fact, they may have a "long" life. That is, most of the times there is no much sense on creating roles when only an agent may play it. Would make sense to create role *Surgeon* if only one agent in the world could play it? For that reason, we include another threshold, called Υ that determines the minimum number of agents that a cluster must include to convert the have the possibility of converting the cluster into a new role. In our experiments, we use $\Upsilon = 3$.

In this work we tackle the problem of creating new roles forming a taxonomy based on agents experience and trust assessments. In this context there are other issues that are important such as: i) specifying when the mechanism should be launched. So far, we consider that the mechanism executes periodically; ii) defining in the mechanism dynamics the possibility of removing roles besides creating new ones; and iii) modifying existing roles what would entail re-allocating agents that were enacting those roles and defining policies to allocate agents when these join the system for the first time. Although we consider these as key issues to study we do not cover them in this paper.

4   Experiments

In this section we explain the domain we have used to test our mechanism. It is based on Information Retrieval (IR) systems and consists of a group of agents that make queries to others in order to obtain some relevant documents. We assume that agents are cooperative, *i.e.* requested agents have the duty of replying every incoming query. We instance our scenario as follows: i) let $\mathcal{A}_g$ be a set of rational agents in a IR network; ii) let $\mathcal{Q} \equiv \mathcal{T}$ be a set of queries that agents receive; iii) let $\mathcal{D}$ be a set of available documents in the IR network; $|D|$ will denote the number of documents in the system. Given these definitions we can define an agent's individual utility function as: $\mathcal{U}_{a_x} : \mathcal{A}_g \times \mathcal{Q} \rightarrow R$, that represents the utility function for agent a_x with regards to a requested query in $\mathcal{Q}$ performed by an agent in $\mathcal{A}_g$ to whom the query was delegated. In order to endow with more heterogeneity to the population of agents participating in the experiments we will include what we call ABNORMAL agents. Those agents will share an individual utility function that sub-estimates the shared individual utility shared by what we call NORMAL agents. We will use an aggregation function to measure the overall utility of the system. Some considerations that should be taken into account are: *i)* agents send each query to only one other agent. An agent can only delegate in only one other agent (including itself); *ii)* an agent cannot attend simultaneously more than one query; *iii)* although a T-MAS consists on a group of agents performing tasks, in this instance we have created a task-delegation scenario for IR, where agents are assigned tasks - queries - and they need to find any other agent to delegate the query and so obtain the relevant documents; and *iv)* a top role is needed to run the system. We use a root role to initialize the role taxonomy. Next roles are created following the clustering mechanism.

The system bootstrapping is described as follows: *i)* documents have to be assigned among agents following the function: $assignDocs : \mathcal{A}_g \times \mathcal{D} \rightarrow \{0, 1\}$, allowing for the same document to be distributed to different agents; *ii)* at every time step (σ) a query is assigned to every agent: $assignQuery : \mathcal{A}_g \times \sigma \rightarrow \mathcal{Q}$ following an uniform distribution. Note that queries have a random name and have no semantics; *iii)* we assume that agents receiving queries need to find another agent to delegate (possibly itself); *iv)* in order to find a good agent to delegate the query, they will ask the system for the more specialized role in the role taxonomy for the specific task; *v)* once the system replies with the "best" role according to the role taxonomy, the agent will select its partner using its trust model from among those agents that have the ability to play that role.

The set $\mathcal{D}$ of documents has been collected from Yahoo webpage.The base set-up we have used for different tests, namely TEST0, TEST1 and TEST2 is: $\theta = 0.5$, with 100 agents, 500 documents per agent and 30000 query instances out of 20 different types of queries. The only parameter that changes is the % of *abnormal agents* with values 0 (TEST 0), 30% (TEST 1), 55%(TEST 2) respectively for the three tests. The results are the average of 5 different runs with the same setup. The algorithm of clustering has been used in a cyclical way every 1000 queries over the total. For every test we have compared how evolve the system using three different scenarios: *i) Basic*: in this scenario agents use their own experience to choose an individual to request for a query, utilising the trust model used to make the decision presented in Section 2.2; *ii) Evolving*: in this scenario agents use the same trust model than in (i) but the system also runs the clustering mechanism to learn new roles; and *iii) Evolved*: in this scenario agents use the information provided by the role taxonomy to choose counterparts. The results of the experiments performed show how our clustering mechanism improve the overall utility of the system. As it was expected when using an already evolved taxonomy agents can use this information from the very first delegation process, thus achieving more utility than in any other case. The more the number of agents injected in the system the more sharp decrease is in agents' utility caused by the subjectivity of their utility functions.

5   Related Work and Conclusions

Much work has been done in the field of trust and reputation mechanisms to endow agents with more information when making decisions [6]. The difference with our approach is that those mechanisms have not been embedded in other mechanisms as we have done with the clustering mechanism for extending role taxonomies. Moreover, those approaches do not take advantages of organizational structures as we do. There is also much literature about re-organization in MAS [10], but none of them have included trust mechanisms as a support for re-organizing organizational structures. It is the use of trust given by agents what allows the system to re-organize the role taxonomy. On the other hand, once role taxonomy is reliable, trust models that use this structure to infer the behaviour of other agents improve their selections as well. In [2] adaptive methods for structural adaptation in organizations are proposed, but they differs from ours in the sense they re-organise the system from the point of view of agents relationships, and not from a global perspective, changing information observable to any agent, such as role taxonomies.

In this work we have proposed a mechanism for T-MAS that help agents to select counterparts to interact with. The mechanism evolves role taxonomies using trust-related information from the agents in the system. We show in the experiments that the use of evolving taxonomies enhance the utility obtained by agents through the time. We are currently working in additional modifications for the mechanism presented in this work to endow it with more functionality. For example, it is necessary to allow agents join and leave from the system. This could be interesting to study since set out the possibility of removing roles when re-organizing the system (for example if no agent enacts a specific role any more). We are also working on policies to let the system decide when to adapt the system at run-time.

References

1. Boella, G., Torre, L., Verhagen, H.: Introduction to normative multiagent systems. Computational & Mathematical Organanization Theory 12(2-3), 71–79 (2006)
2. Deloach, S.A., Oyenan, W.H., Matson, E.T.: A capabilities-based model for adaptive organizations. Autonomous Agents and Multi-Agent Systems 16(1), 13–56 (2008)
3. Ferber, J., Gutknecht, O., Michel, F.: From agents to organizations: An organizational view of multi-agent systems, pp. 443–459 (2004)
4. Hermoso, R., Billhardt, H., Centeno, R., Ossowski, S.: Effective use of organisational abstractions for confidence models. In: O'Hare, G.M.P., Ricci, A., O'Grady, M.J., Dikenelli, O. (eds.) ESAW 2006. LNCS (LNAI), vol. 4457, pp. 368–383. Springer, Heidelberg (2007)
5. Hübner, J.F., Sichman, J.S., Boissier, O.: Moise+: Towards a structural, functional, and deontic model for MAS organization. In: AAMAS 2002, pp. 501–502 (2002)
6. Huynh, T.D., Jennings, N.R., Shadbolt, N.R.: FIRE: An integrated trust and reputation model for open multi-agent systems. In: Proceedings of the 16th European Conference on Artificial Intelligence, ECAI (2004)
7. Omicini, A., Ossowski, S.: Objective versus subjective coordination in the engineering of agent systems. In: Klusch, M., Bergamaschi, S., Edwards, P., Petta, P. (eds.) Intelligent Information Agents. LNCS (LNAI), vol. 2586, pp. 179–202. Springer, Heidelberg (2003)
8. Partsakoulakis, I., Vouros, G.: Roles in MAS – Managing the Complexity of Tasks and Environments, pp. 133–154. Kluwer Academic, Dordrecht (2004)
9. Luke Teacy, W.T., Patel, J., Jennings, N.R., Luck, M.: Travos: Trust and reputation in the context of inaccurate information sources. Autonomous Agents and Multi-Agent Systems 12(2), 183–198 (2006)
10. Wang, Z.-g., Liang, X.-h., Zhao, Q.-p.: Adaptive mechanisms of organizational structures in multi-agent systems (2006)

Adaptation and Validation of an Agent Model of Functional State and Performance for Individuals

Fiemke Both[1], Mark Hoogendoorn[1], S. Waqar Jaffry[1], Rianne van Lambalgen[1], Rogier Oorburg[2], Alexei Sharpanskykh[1], Jan Treur[1], and Michael de Vos[2]

[1] Vrije Universiteit Amsterdam, Department of Artificial Intelligence,
De Boelelaan 1081, 1081 HV Amsterdam, The Netherlands
{fboth,swjaffry,rm.van.lambalgen,sharp,treur}@few.vu.nl
[2] Force Vision Lab, Barbara Strozzilaan 362a,
1083 HN Amsterdam, The Netherlands
{rogier,michael}@forcevisionlab.nl

Abstract. Human performance can seriously degrade under demanding tasks. To improve performance, agents can reason about the current state of the human, and give the most appropriate and effective support. To enable this, the agent needs a model of a specific person's functional state and performance, which should be valid, as the agent might otherwise give inappropriate advice and even worsen performance. This paper concerns the adaptation of the parameters of the existing functional state model to the individual and validation of the resulting model. First, human experiments have been conducted, whereby measurements related to the model have been performed. Next, this data has been used to obtain appropriate parameter settings for the model, describing the specific subject. Finally, the model, with the tailored parameter settings, has been used to predict human behavior to investigate predictive capabilities of the model. The results have been analyzed using formal verification.

Keywords: Agent model, functional state, validation.

1 Introduction

In demanding working circumstances the quality of the tasks performed by a human might be severely influenced (see e.g. [4]). Especially when tasks are performed in a critical domain, such effects are highly undesired. To improve task performance in such situations, personal assistant agents (cf. [7,10,8]) can be used to monitor the activities of the human, and intervene in case needed. Interventions could for example take the form of assigning (part of) the tasks to other humans, or give advice regarding the performance of the task.

One crucial element in the support given by a personal assistant agent is that it should be given in appropriate circumstances: the agent should have an awareness of the state of the human. In [1] a dynamical model has been presented that describes the cognitive workload experienced by humans, given knowledge of the human's characteristics in combination with the tasks that need to be performed. The model is

J.-J. Yang et al. (Eds.): PRIMA 2009, LNAI 5925, pp. 595–607, 2009.

quantitative, based upon mostly qualitative theories from Psychology, but was not validated yet using human experiments. The primary focus of this paper is to develop and implement an approach for the tuning of the parameters of this human functional state model to a specific person and validating the model. The overall process has been performed by taking a number of steps. First of all, an experiment with 31 human subjects has been conducted where the subjects had to perform a task with different amounts of workload. Each subject was given two conditions. Using the empirical data obtained from this experiment, parameter estimation techniques have been deployed to find appropriate parameter settings for the model to accurately describe the subject's behavior in one of the conditions. Thereafter, these settings have been used to predict the behavior of the subject in the other condition. Finally, properties that relate to the functional state model have been verified against the empirical data as well.

This paper is organized as follows. First, the functional state model is briefly explained. Thereafter, the setup of the experiment and the results of parameter adaptation are shown. Next, the verification of properties against the empirical data, and finally the paper is concluded and future work is discussed.

2   The Agent Model for Functional State and Performance

The agent model for the Functional State (FS) of a human represents the dynamical state of a person when performing a certain task. States such as experienced pressure and motivation of the person are predicted, but also the performance quality and the amount of generated effort to the task.

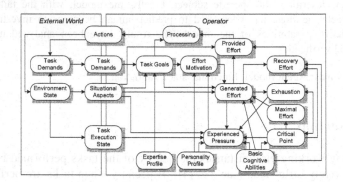

Fig. 1. Agent Model for a Human's Functional State

The model is based on two different theories: 1) the cognitive energetic framework [6], which states that effort regulation is based on human resources and determines human performance in dynamic conditions; 2) The idea, that when performing sports, a person's generated power can continue on a *critical power* level without becoming more exhausted [5]. In the FS model critical power is represented by the critical point: the amount of effort someone can generate without becoming more exhausted, influenced by the cognitive abilities of a person.

As input the FS model uses external factors and personal factors. The external factors task demands and environment state are influenced by the external world (e.g. demands of the task, environmental noise). The personal factors are determined by a person's task expertise, cognitive abilities and personality (e.g. optimal experienced pressure). In addition, a person's expertise is taken into account. These inputs are used to determine a person's dynamical state. In addition, it determines the relation of this state to the human's actions with respect to the task that influence the Task Execution State (e.g. performance quality). An example equation of the model is:

$$E(t+\Delta t) = E(t) + [Pos(\eta \cdot (GE(t)-CP(t))) - \pi \cdot RE(t)] \cdot \Delta t$$

Here exhaustion (E) builds up or reduces over time. When the generated effort (GE) is above the critical point (CP), exhaustion increases, otherwise exhaustion decreases depending on the level of recovery effort (RE). Parameters η and π determine the amount of increase or decrease. The function $Pos(x)$ in this formula is defined as the maximum of x and 0.

$$GE(t+\Delta t) = GE(t) + \beta \cdot (CCE(t)-GE(t)) \cdot \Delta t$$

In the temporal relation for generated effort the previous generated effort is taken into account, as well as a current contribution CCE. Here β is a flexibility parameter; it determines how much of the new generated effort is affected by the current contribution.

$$EP(t+\Delta t) = EP(t) + [\mu 1 \cdot Pos(EPC(t) \cdot (1-EP(t)) - \mu 2 \cdot Neg(EPC(t) \cdot EP(t))] \cdot \Delta t$$

The temporal relation for experienced pressure (EP) is based on the previous experienced pressure and a change value (EPC). Parameter μ determines the influence of the change value.

Furthermore, the model includes a number of instantaneous relations. For more details on the model, see [1].

3 Experimental Setup

First, an overview of the software environment and its participants is given. The main part of the experiment is a simulation-based training environment which combines a shooting task and a calculation task. Thereafter, the procedure of the experiment is explained. A more detailed version can be found in Appendix A: http://www.few.vu.nl/~wai/PRIMA/appendix_A.pdf. Finally, a description is given of how data from the experiment has been used as input for the functional state model.

3.1 Simulation-Based Training Environment and Participants

In the experiment the main task is a task where the goal is to get as many points as possible by eliminating hostile objects. Objects (friends and enemies) are falling down in different locations with different speeds. The purpose is to shoot the enemies before they hit the ground. Shooting at a missile is done by a mouse click at a specific location; the missile explodes exactly at the location of the mouse click. When an object is within a radius of 50 pixels of the explosion, the object is destroyed. The number of points a participant receives for hitting an enemy is proportional to the proximity of the explosion. When a participant shoots a friend or when an enemy reaches the bottom of the screen, points are lost. When a friendly object reaches the bottom of the screen points are gained. Next to each object, a calculation is written on the screen. A correct calculation indicates that the object is friendly and should not be shot. An incorrect calculation indicates that the object is an enemy and should be shot before it reaches the bottom of the screen. For a demo of the simulation-based training environment, see http://www.forcevisionlab.nl/demo/missilecommand.swf.

In the study 31 persons participated (18 males, 13 females, of which 25 students). They ranged in age from 17 to 57 years with a mean age of 26 years. The experiment took approximately 1 hour for which participants received a voucher of 10 euro. In addition, there was a voucher of 100 euro for the participant with the best score.

3.2 Procedure

For the experiment a 2 factor within subjects design was used. Two different conditions within each participant were tested. In [1] two scenarios were simulated using the model. Scenario 1 started with a low task level and continued with a high task level. Scenario 2 started with a high task level and continued with a low task level. As these scenarios showed realistic results they were used for this experiment. Condition was counterbalanced over participants to correct for a possible order effect; participants with an odd number started with condition 2 (high-low) and even numbered participants started with condition 1 (low-high).

Participants started the experiment by filling out a personality questionnaire with questions from the NEO-PI-R and the NEO-FFI [3]; with these questions some aspects of each participant's personality were measured, to serve as input for the personality profile of the FS model. Neuroticism and extraversion were measured with the NEO-FFI. With the NEO-PI-R vulnerability (part of neuroticism) and ambition (part of conscientiousness) were measured.

After the questionnaire, participants performed three small tests each consisting of 30 trials which were equal between participants. These tests served as input for model validation (see the next subsection for the explanation thereof). The instructions for each test were shown on the screen. Participants started with a simple choice Reaction Time test (choice-RT), where a square was presented either left or right from a fixation cross at the centre of the screen. Participants had to react with either the left arrow (when the square was presented left) or the right arrow (when the square was presented right). The second test was a task where calculations were presented similar to the calculations in the calculation task of the experiment. Like in the experiment, participants had to choose whether the calculation was correct (left arrow) or incorrect (right arrow). The third small test (mouse-RT) was another Reaction Time task; here a circular target was presented somewhere on the screen. Participants had to react quickly and precisely by clicking with the mouse as close as possible to the centre.

After the three small tasks, participants practiced during 3 minutes for the experiment described in the previous subsection. The goal of the practice task was familiarize with the shooting and calculation tasks. After practice the participants started the experiment with either condition 1 or condition 2, which both took 15 minutes.

3.3 From Experiment Data to Functional State Model

In order to validate the model, data from the experiment was used to calculate the values of several concepts of the FS model, namely personality profile, basic cognitive abilities (BCA) and expertise profile, following theories from Psychology [9,12,13,14]. To determine the exact influence of the experimental data (e.g. personality test results that were scaled between 0 and 1, and the results of the three small tests) on these concepts additional parameters are introduced. This brings the number of parameters that should be estimated to 27. For the precise mathematical equations used, see http://www.few.vu.nl/~wai/PRIMA/appendix_D.pdf.

Furthermore, from the experiment data the task demands can be calculated by looking at the number of contacts that have to be handled. Although the scenarios were the same for all participants, the calculated task demands could differ due to the performance quality. Therefore, Task Demands were calculated per time window per participant. According to the model, task demands and the expertise profile together contribute to task level.

$$TaskLevel = (1.5 - Exp) \cdot TaskD \tag{1}$$

In the experiment, performance quality was measured in terms of efficiency and effectiveness. Efficiency represented the number of missiles necessary to shoot an enemy. Effectiveness was dependent on how close to the object the missile exploded (explosion fraction) and whether an enemy or friend was shot. In case of an enemy being shot:

$$Effectiveness = (1 + explosion\_fraction)/2.0 \tag{2}$$

Effectiveness was 0 when a friend was shot or an enemy landed. When a friend landed, effectiveness was 1. Using effectiveness and efficiency, the task execution state was calculated:

$$ObjTES = (0.25 \cdot efficiency + 0.75 \cdot effectiveness) \cdot 2 \tag{3}$$

4   Adapting Parameters to an Individual

This section presents the results of parameter estimation for the FS model using two methods: a gradient-based approach and an approach based on probabilistic search.

4.1 Gradient-Based Parameter Estimation

To perform parameter estimation, a method based on the maximum likelihood principle has been applied [15]. In line with this principle a likelihood function of the measurement data and the unknown parameters is defined. This function is essentially the probability density function of the measurement data given the parameter values $p(z|\theta)$. Furthermore, it was assumed that the measurements contained noise which is zero-mean and has a Gaussian distribution. The measurement data were represented by the random, normally distributed variable z. Such an assumption is often made for dynamic systems in many areas. The parameter vector, which makes the likelihood function most probable to obtain the measurements z ($\hat{\theta}_{ML}$ which maximizes the likelihood function) is called the maximum likelihood estimate; it is obtained by minimizing the error function:

$$E(\theta) = \frac{1}{2} \cdot \sum_{i=1}^{N} (z_i - y_i)^T \cdot R^{-1} \cdot (z_i - y_i) + \frac{N}{2} \cdot \ln |R| \qquad (5)$$

Here the measurements obtained are discrete time, N is the number of measurements, R is the measurement noise covariance matrix. The estimate of R is obtained as:

$$\hat{R} = \frac{1}{N} \cdot \sum_{i=1}^{N} (z_i - \hat{y}_i) \cdot (z_i - \hat{y}_i)^T \qquad (6)$$

The maximum likelihood estimates are consistent, asymptotically unbiased and efficient [15].

The calculation of the maximum likelihood estimate is performed iteratively. The estimate value at the $(k+1)$ iteration is determined as:

$$\hat{\theta}_{ML}^{k+1} = \hat{\theta}_{ML}^{k} + [\nabla_\theta^2 E(\theta)]^{-1} \cdot [\nabla_\theta E(\theta)] \qquad (7)$$

Here the first gradient is defined as:

$$\nabla_\theta E(\theta) = \sum_{i=1}^{N} \left[\frac{\partial y_i}{\partial \theta}\right]^T \cdot R^{-1} \cdot (z_i - y_i) \qquad (8)$$

For the functional state model the expressions for the partial derivatives w.r.t. the parameters (i.e., sensitivity coefficients) have been obtained analytically (see Appendix B: http://www.few.vu.nl/~wai/PRIMA/appendix_B.pdf).

The analytical determination of the second gradient is more involved, therefore a Gauss-Newton numerical approximation has been used for it:

$$\nabla_\theta^2 E(\theta) = \sum_{i=1}^{N} \left[\frac{\partial y_i}{\partial \theta}\right]^T \cdot R^{-1} \cdot \left[\frac{\partial y_i}{\partial \theta}\right] \qquad (9)$$

Such an approximation does not cause a significant error in the parameter estimate. Furthermore, the use of the second gradient speeds up the convergence of the estimation process significantly.

The state values of the system were calculated by numerical integration of the model equations using the 4th order Runge-Kutta method, which has proven to be both accurate and stable. The estimation error is calculated in each iteration as root mean square error:

$$err = \sqrt{\sum_{i=1}^{N} \frac{(z_i - \hat{y}_i)^2}{N}} \qquad (10)$$

The parameter adaptation procedure based on the maximum likelihood principle has been implemented using the following algorithm:

Algorithm: ML-PARAMETER-ADAPTATION

Input: Initial values of the parameters θ^1, maximal number of iterations itmax; satisfactory error value err_sat; matrix of the input values U; matrix of the output values Z

Output: Maximum likelihood estimate θ_{ML}

1   i=1
2   Until i ≤ itmax perform steps 3-7
3   Calculate the current state of the system using the model
      equations
4   Calculate the output root mean square error err^j using (10).
5   if err ≤ err_sat, then $\theta_{ML} = \theta^i$; **exit** endif.
6   if i < itmax, then
  6a Calculate the noise covariance matrix R using (6)
  6b Calculate the sensitivity coefficients $\partial y / \partial \theta$
  6c Calculate the first and second gradients using the formulae
          (8) and (9) respectively.
  6d Calculate the parameter values for the next iteration θ^{i+1} using (7)
      endif
7   i = i+1
8   Find the minimum error err^m in $\{err^j | i=1..itmax\}$; then
        $\theta_{ML} = \theta^m$; **exit**.

The algorithm was implemented in the Matlab 7 environment. The worst case complexity is estimated as $O(NN \cdot |\theta| \cdot M)$, where NN is the number of integration points, $|\theta|$ is the number of the estimated parameters, M is the number of outputs. The execution of an iteration took less than 2 sec on an average PC.

4.2 Simulated Annealing

The Simulated Annealing method uses a probabilistic technique to find a parameter setting. In this method a random parameter setting is chosen as the best available parameter setting at the start. Then a displacement is introduced into these settings to generate a neighbor of the current parameter settings in the search space. If this neighbor is found to be a more appropriate representation of the observed human behavior then it is marked as the best known parameter setting, otherwise a new neighbor is selected to evaluate its appropriateness. The displacement in the parameter settings depends on the temperature, in case the temperature is higher, the steps will become larger. The temperature at a certain time point for the parameter settings is defined as follows

$$Temperature = computational\text{-}budget\text{-}left \cdot error \tag{11}$$

Here the computational budget is the number of neighbors to be tested for better approximation. The displacement in the parameter for example γ was derived from the following equations selecting any one at random.

$$\gamma = \gamma + Temperature \cdot (1-\gamma) \cdot random\_no\_between[0,1] \tag{12a}$$

$$or \; \gamma = \gamma - Temperature \cdot \gamma \cdot random\_no\_between[0,1] \tag{12b}$$

The method is described as follows:

Algorithm: SA-PARAMETER-ADAPTATION

Input: Initial randomly selected values of the parameters θ^1, computational budget C; observed human behaviour B;
Output: Best estimate of parameter settings θ_{BE}
1   $\theta_{BE} = \theta^1$
2   while C ≥ 0 perform steps 3-8
3   Choose a random parameter setting θ in neighbourhood of θ_{BE} using equation (11 and 12a, 12b).
4   Calculate the output root mean square error err for θ using (10).
5   Calculate the output root mean square error err_{BE} for θ_{BE} using (10).
6   if err ≤ err_{BE}, then θ_{BE} = θ; err_{BE} = err; endif.
7   Decrease C;
8   Temperature = C * err_{BE};
9   **output** θ_{BE}.

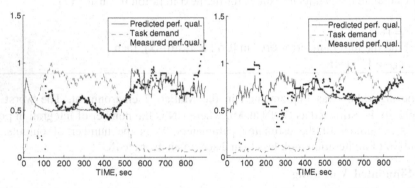

Fig. 2. Empirical data and the estimated output performance quality for subject 37 for condition1 (left) and condition 2 (right)

In Figure 2 the performance quality for subject 37 is shown with the computational budget set to 10000 (i.e. the C in the algorithm specified above) and 900 seconds of empirical data. Here it should be noted that the graph represents the curve generated with parameter settings producing minimum root mean square error found till the end of computational budget. The algorithm has been implemented in C++ and applied to the functional state model. If C is computational budget, then the worst case complexity of the method can be expressed as O(C·B), where B is the number of observed behaviors. Here it could be observed that computational complexity of this method is independent of the number of parameters.

4.3   Results of the Estimation

The gradient-based and simulated annealing methods have been applied for the estimation of 30 parameters of the functional state model (see Appendix C:

http://www.few.vu.nl/~wai/PRIMA/appendix_C.pdf). The estimation has been performed for 31 subjects, for both experimental conditions. The initial setting of the parameters has been taken from [1]. This setting is grounded partially in the psychological literature; furthermore it ensures the desired properties of the modeled system. Figure 2 illustrates the empirical data and the estimated output performance quality for subject 37 for both conditions.

The estimation by both methods showed similar behavioral patterns in the output of the model. However, the gradient-based method has a better precision in comparison to the simulated annealing. The root mean square errors calculated in both parameter estimation methods are given in Table 1. To evaluate the quality of estimation also other measures have been used. In particular, the Cramer-Rao bounds provide a useful measure of relative accuracy of the estimated parameters [15]. This measure sets a lower bound on the standard deviation of the estimators:

$$\sigma_\theta \geq \sqrt{I^{-1}(\theta)} \qquad (13)$$

Here $I(\theta)$ is the information matrix:

$$(I(\theta))_{ij} = E \left| \frac{\partial^2 \log p(z \mid \theta)}{\partial \theta_i \partial \theta_j} \right| \qquad (14)$$

Table 1. Root mean square errors of estimation by the gradient-based (GB) and simulated annealing (SA) methods for all subjects in both experimental conditions

Error range		< 0.1	[0.1, 0.25)	[0.25, 0.4)	> 0.4
Subjects in condition 1	G	21	11-20, 22, 24-41	-	-
	B				
	S		40	11, 12, 22, 24-26, 30, 32-39, 41	13-18, 20, 21, 28, 29, 31
	A				
Subjects in condition 2	G	12, 15, 18, 27, 30	11, 13, 14, 16, 17, 19, 22, 24-26, 28, 32-41	29, 31	-
	B	20, 21, 23,			
	S	32	17, 26, 30, 31, 34. 35, 37, 40	12, 27, 38, 41	11, 13-16, 18-23, 25, 28, 29, 33, 36, 39
	A				

For efficient estimation the equality holds. Furthermore, for the maximum likelihood method, $I(\theta) = \nabla^2_\theta E(\theta)$, which also needs to be calculated for (9); thus no additional computation effort for the evaluation of this measure is required. Using this measure at least 57% (70% in the best case) of the estimated parameters have been identified as accurate for all subjects in both conditions (relative standard deviation (rsd) ≤ 5%). Other parameters, although less accurate (5% < rsd < 40%) still have a degree of confidence.

Another useful criterion for judging the quality of the estimates is the correlation coefficients among the estimates calculated as:

$$c_{\theta_i \theta_j} = \frac{(I(\theta)^{-1})_{ij}}{\sqrt{(I(\theta)^{-1})_{ii} \cdot (I(\theta)^{-1})_{jj}}} \qquad (15)$$

Only one significant correlation between the parameters A and ϕ has been identified.

Table 2. Prediction errors of estimation by the GB and SA methods for all subjects in condition 1 using the estimated parameters from condition 2

Error range	< 0.1	[0.1, 0.25)	[0.25, 0.4)	> 0.4
GB	21	12-20, 22, 24-30, 34-40	11, 31, 32, 41	33
SA	-	17, 26, 31, 32, 37, 40	12, 13, 22, 25, 28, 30, 34, 35, 38, 41	11, 14-16, 18-21, 29, 33, 39

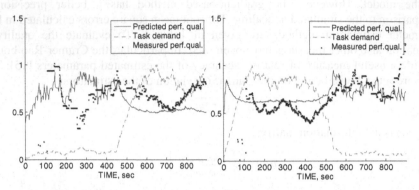

Fig. 3. Predicted dynamics for subject 37 in condition 1 using the estimated parameters from condition 2 (left) and in setting 2 using the parameters from setting 1 (right)

The prediction quality was determined by comparing the root mean square errors for both conditions. For most of the subjects (84%) in the GB estimation, prediction errors (Table 2) differ from the estimation errors (Table 1, subjects in condition 1) insignificantly (less than 10%). Furthermore, also cross-validation was performed, in which data from one of the settings were used for parameter estimation and data from the other setting were used for validation (Figure 3).

5   Verification of Properties

This section focuses on logical verification, another approach which has been used to validate the model. The idea is that properties are identified that are entailed by the FS model, and these properties are verified against the empirical data that has been obtained. In order to conduct such an automated verification, the properties have been specified in a language called TTL (for Temporal Trace Language, cf. [2]) that features a dedicated editor and an automated checker. This predicate logical temporal language supports formal specification and analysis of dynamic properties, covering both qualitative and quantitative aspects. TTL is built on atoms referring to *states* of the world, *time points* and *traces*, i.e. trajectories of states over time. In addition, *dynamic properties* are temporal statements that can be formulated with respect to traces based on the state ontology Ont in the following manner. Given a trace γ over state ontology Ont, the state in γ at time point t is denoted by state(γ, t). These states can be related to state properties via the formally defined satisfaction relation denoted by the infix predicate |=, i.e., state(γ, t) |= p denotes that state property p holds in trace γ at time t. Based on these statements, dynamic properties can be formulated in a formal manner in a sorted first-order predicate logic, using quantifiers over time and traces and the usual first-order logical connectives such as ¬, ∧, ∨, ⇒, ∀, ∃. For more details on TTL, see [2].

Three main properties have been identified that follow from the FS model. The first property specifies that performance quality decreases in case a task level in a certain range is experienced:

P1(min_level, max_level, d, x)
*If at time point t1 the task level is tl and the performance quality pq, and tl is in the range [min_level max_level], and until t1+d the task level does not cross these boundaries, then there exists a time point t2> t1 at which the performance quality is at most x * pq.*
P1(min_level, max_level, d, x) ≡
∀γ:TRACE, t1:TIME, pq1:REAL
  [state(γ, t1) |= has_value(performance_quality, pq1) &
  ∀tl:REAL, t':TIME ≥ t1 & t' ≤ t1 + d
   [state(γ, t') |= has_value(task_level, tl) ⇒
    [tl ≤ max_level & tl ≥ min_ level]]
  ⇒ ∃t2:TIME > t1, pq2:REAL
   [state(γ, t2) |= has_value(performance_quality,pq2) &pq2 ≤ x * pq1]

This property has been verified using the following values: min_level is set to 20% above BCA, max_level is set to the highest task level encountered in the experiment, the duration d is set to 60 time steps (i.e. a minute real time), and x is set to 1 (i.e. performance quality should never go up, but can remain the same). These settings follow the model: in case a task level above BCA is experienced, the human becomes exhausted, and the quality can no longer go up. Results show that this property is satisfied in **60%** of the empirical traces.

The second property concerns the opposite: in cases where there is a task level between certain boundaries, the performance quality should be at least as high as before the period (note that the formal form has been omitted for the sake of brevity):

P2(min_level, max_level, d, x)
*If at time point t1 the task level is tl and the performance quality pq, and tl is in the range [min_level, max_level], and until t+d the task level does not cross these boundaries, then there exists a time point t2> t1 at which the performance quality is at least x * pq.*

Using the following settings: max_level at 20% below BCA, min_level is set to 0 and d and x the same as for the previous property, this property is satisfied in 45% of the cases. In case a task level is experienced which is somewhat below the highest task level that can be handled without exhaustion building up (i.e. the BCA), then the performance will get better, or at least stay the same (as there is no exhaustion).

The final property which has been verified concerns performance quality being higher for cases whereby there is a lower task level:

P3(low_level, high_level)
In case the task level at a time point t1 is tl1, and at a time point t2 the task level is tl2, and tl1 > high_level and tl2 < low_level, then there exists a time point t' > t1 and there exists a time point t'' > t2 such that the performance quality at time point t' is lower than the performance quality at time point t''.

Using a low_level of 20% below BCA, and a high_level of 20% above the cognitive abilities, this property is satisfied in 60.7% of the cases. The property complies with the model, because a task level beyond BCA results in exhaustion leading to a worsened performance, which is not the case for a task level far below BCA. In total, 25.0% of the cases comply with properties P1, P2, and P3.

6 Discussion and Conclusions

To reason about the human behavior and support possibilities personal assistant agents often use (cognitive) models. To ensure that support is provided by agents in a timely and knowledgeable manner, such models should be accurate and validated. This paper contributes an approach to validate the FS model.

In the Experiment, the participants were very motivated to perform well on the main task. This was not only due to the reward; they were also enthusiastic about the task itself. In order to keep the learning effect to a minimum and to maintain the participants' concentration, every participant performed only two sessions of the 15 minute session. However, precision of parameter estimation will increase when measurements of more within-subject conditions are taken.

The results obtained for the parameter adaptation are satisfactory. However, a number of parameters (35% in average) were evaluated as less accurate, and, therefore, less reliable. Partially this can be explained by a large overall number of parameters being estimated. Most of the less precise parameters have a weak relation to the measured output (e.g., noise sensitivity). Furthermore, since the empirical data were collected based on irregular events (i.e., actions of humans), some intervals contained an insufficient amount of information for estimation. Despite this, as shown in the paper, the models with estimated parameters demonstrated good predictive capabilities in the cross-validation, which is a strong indicator of the model validity.

The trends as predicted by the model have also been verified against the empirical material. The results show that a reasonable percentage of the traces satisfy each of these individual properties. The combination of all three properties is however only satisfied in 25% of the cases, which can mainly be attributed to the aforementioned collection based on irregular events, making the data more prone to sudden changes.

The topic of model validation received much attention in the areas of Psychology and Social Science. In particular, a validation approach from [16] distinguishes the validation phases similar to the ones considered in the paper (e.g., conceptual and operational validation); however, the precise elaboration of the phases is focused largely on social processes, not relevant for our work. Furthermore, examples of model validation are found in psychology, e.g. on the subject of visual attention [11], however often no parameter estimation is involved.

In the future research the considered parameter adaptation methods will be extended for the case of real-time adaptation, which accounts for human learning. Furthermore, a personal assistant agent will be implemented that is able to monitor and balance the functional state of the human in a timely and knowledgeable manner.

References

1. Bosse, T., Both, F., van Lambalgen, R., Treur, J.: An Agent Model for a Human's Functional State and Performance. In: Jain, L., et al. (eds.) Proceedings of International Conference, IAT 2008, pp. 302–307. IEEE Computer Society Press, Los Alamitos (2008)
2. Bosse, T., Jonker, C.M., Meij, L., van der Sharpanskykh, A., Treur, J.: Specification and Verification of Dynamics in Agent Models. International Journal of Cooperative Information Systems 18(1), 167–193 (2008)
3. Costa Jr., P.T., McCrae, R.R.: Revised NEO Personality Inventory (NEO-PI-R) and the NEO Five-Factor Inventory (NEO-FFI) professional manual (Psychological Assessment Resources). Odessa, FL (1992)
4. Hancock, P.A., Williams, G., Manning, C.P., Miyake, S.: Influence of task demand characteristics on workload and performance. The International Journal of Aviation Psychology 5(1), 63–86 (1995)
5. Hill, D.W.: The critical power concept. Sports Medicine 16, 237–254 (1993)
6. Hockey, G.R.J.: Compensatory control in the regulation of human performance under stress and high workload: a cognitive-energetical framework. Biological Psychology 45, 73–93 (1997)
7. Kozierok, R., Maes, P.: A Learning Interface Agent for Scheduling Meetings. In: Proceedings of the 1st International Conference on Intelligent User Interfaces, pp. 81–88 (1993)
8. Maheswaran, R., Tambe, M., Varakantham, P., Myers, K.: Adjustable autonomy challenges in personal assistant agents: A position paper. In: Proceedings of the AAMAS 2003 Workshop on Agents and Comp. Autonomy, pp. 187–194 (2003)
9. Matthews, G., Deary, I.J.: Personality traits. Cambridge University Press, Cambridge (1998)
10. Mitchell, T., Caruana, R., Freitag, D., McDermott, J., Zabowski, D.: Experience with a Learning Personal Assistant. Communication of the ACM 37(7), 81–91 (1994)
11. Parkhurst, D., Law, K., Niebur, E.: Modeling the role of salience in the allocation of overt visual attention. Vision Research 42(1), 107–123 (2002)
12. Plomin, R., Spinath, F.M.: Genetics and general cognitive ability. Trends in Cognitive Science 6(4), 369–176
13. Rose, C.L., Murphy, L.B., Byard, L., Nikzad, K.: The role of the Big Five personality factors in vigilance performance and workload. European Journal of Personality 16, 185–200 (2002)
14. Salgado, J.F.: The five factor model of personality and job performance in the European community. Journal of Applied Psychology 82(1), 30–43 (1997)
15. Sorenson, H.W.: Parameter estimation: principles and problems. Marcel Dekker, Inc., New York (1980)
16. Yilmaz, L.: Validation and verification of social processes within agent-based computational organization models. Computational and Mathematical Organization Theory 12, 283–312 (2006)

A Cooperation Trading Method with Hybrid Traders

Satoshi Takahashi[1] and Tokuro Matsuo[2]

[1] Graduate School of System and Information Engineering
University of Tsukuba
takahashi2007@e-activity.org
[2] Graduate School of Science and Engineering
Yamagata University
matsuo@tokuro.com

Abstract. We present a new trading scheme in e-commerce in which end-users behave both buyers and sellers. We define hybrid traders as new users, analyze their trading models, and develop a trading mechanism. In our trading scheme, hybrid traders forge coalition formations to purchase items, since hybrid traders do not have enough money purchase extensive items. We create an incentive for coalitions using a side payment policy. We propose a side payment value decision mechanism based on the coalition's contribution. Also, in multiple-item trading, we discuss the strategy analyses.

1 Introduction

This paper proposes a trade model and mechanism in which users make coalition formations in electronic commerce, which is one of most important research areas not only for economics but also for information science and business administration [1] [2]. In the markets in which end-users positively participate such as Internet auctions and group-buys, there is a business model where end-users purchase to sell items in the same market. In this model, an end-user behaves like a seller, purchasing items for resale to obtain pecuniary profit. There are also such adjusted markets as the Internet auction market and the group-buy market in which end-users can easily participate. Consumers can simply be sellers like a company.

We define such end-users as hybrid traders [3] [4]. We analyse markets in which hybrid traders forge coalition formations. We create an incentive for hybrid traders to participate in cooperation by employing a side payment policy in which a proposer pays part of its profit to cooperative hybrid traders as rewards. If hybrid traders are rational, they have an incentive to participate in cooperation depending on the side payment's value. They also get side payments by participating in the cooperation.

When introducing a side payment policy to our trading model, the problem of an efficient profit allocation method for proposers must be confronted. We give two cases of the problem. One is that we give participation probability depending on side payment value to hybrid traders and calculate an optimal side payment value by simulation. The other is that we calculate the side payment value based on the contributions of cooperators. In the latter case, we analyze budget allocation strategies in multiple-item transaction.

J.-J. Yang et al. (Eds.): PRIMA 2009, LNAI 5925, pp. 608–615, 2009.

2 Preliminaries

2.1 Hybrid Traders and a Volume Discount Mechanism

We define end-users as hybrid traders who are both buyers and sellers in e-commerce. They do not consume the items but sell them for profit on Internet shops that they themselves opended. In e-marketplaces, since their costs are almost zero, hybrid traders are able to trade on Internet auction sites without knowledge and know-how. This is an advantage for hybrid traders.

We set the conditions of hybrid traders. Hybrid traders do not have enough money to purchase a large quantity of items, since they are general end-users. Hybrid traders can purchase in quantity by cooperating with each other, because on the Internet, negotiation between users is easy. A larger-scale community can be formed compared with actual community formation. Therefore, hybrid traders can gather cooperators easily and purchase items cheaper.

Since hybrid traders purchase all items with a volume discount, the item price is reduced based on quantity. Their price functions are step-functions. When the quantity of an item increases, the price goes down.

Hybrid traders allocate the items based on a percentage of investing. We assume n hybrid traders. Let $q = \{q_i | i = 1, ..., n\}$ be a set of the allocation of items for hybrid traders and b_i be a set of hybrid trader i's investing budget. Then, the allocation for hybrid trader i is calculated using the following formula:

$$q_i = Q \cdot \frac{b_i}{\sum_{j=1}^{n} b_j}$$

Q is the number of purchased items.

2.2 Side Payment Policy

Hybrid traders can purchase more and more items by cooperating with each other than by individual trading, because purchasing items more cheaply is possible when the scale of the coalition is larger. Therefore, we have to create an incentive for cooperation with other hybrid traders.

In a side payment policy, the proposer pays a reward of the cooperating relationship to the cooperators. Setting an appropriate side payment value does encourage effective cooperation, and the proposer's utility becomes the maximum.

If the proposer pays all the utility as side payment value to the cooperators, the proposer's utility becomes zero, and there is no incentive for proposer cooperation. The side payment value must be paid from the utility of increased cooperation. Let U be a proposer's utility when the proposer creates a cooperation, and let U' be the utility when the proposer trades individually. Side payment value S is defined by an interval $[0, U - U']$. $U - U'$ is the pure utility the proposer gets from cooperation.

2.3 Model

We show our trading model. Hybrid traders participate in special community sites for making cooperation. Let $H = \{1, ..., i, ..., n\}$ be a set of hybrid traders, and let

$B = \{b_i | i \in H, b_i \geq 0\}$ be a set of hybrid traders' budgets. Let $G = \{a_1, ..., a_j, ..., a_m\}$ be a set of tradable items that are sold by a volume discount mechanism based on trading quantity. Let $v_{a_j}(\omega)$ be the price of the item a_j, where ω shows the item quantity variable given by $\{\omega | \omega \in N\}$. We define the volume discount rate as follows:

$$\forall \omega, \omega' \text{ such that } \omega > \omega'$$
$$\frac{v_{a_j}(\omega) - v_{a_j}(\omega')}{\omega - \omega'} > 0, \forall j$$

Let p_{i,a_j} be the price at which hybrid trader i sells item a_j. The price is based on individual value.

Assumption 1. Since hybrid traders do not have enough money to purchase a lot of items, they cannot satisfy their demands. Sufficient money is defined as when a hybrid trader gets a large enough volume discount when he/she trades individually.

Assumption 2. The item is priced based on a volume discount mechanism. The volume discount depends on the item and the seller's type, and the rate is not same. The seller strongly tries to sell items as volume discount to get space for purchasing new items.

Assumption 3. Utility u_{i,a_j} in which hybrid trader i sold the item a_j is defined by $p_{i,a_j} - v_{a_j}(\omega)$. Since this utility is a quasi-linear utility, it is assumed [5]. Also, the hybrid traders' utilities are not reduced when they purchase an item. A hybrid trader tries to purchase as many items as possible within her budget.

Assumption 4. Hybrid traders have types $t = \{t_1, ..., t_k\}$ about coalition formation. They decide issues of participation and budget based on their types. The incentive to participate in cooperation is stronger when the side payment value is larger.

Assumption 5. Hybrid traders sell items by hopeful prices. In this paper, we do not assume risks of sales.

3 Single Item Tradings

In this section, we discuss trading in which hybrid traders are given participation probability based on side payment value. There is one proposer in this trading scheme, and we consider single item trading.

Hybrid traders purchase the item based on the following protocols:

Step 1. A hybrid trader proposes purchasing the item and paying the side payment value. Other hybrid traders decide cooperation based on the proposed trade.

Step 2. The proposer gathers budgets from cooperators and purchases the proposed item. He/She allocates the purchased item to cooperators based on their investments.

Step 3. Hybrid traders sell the allocated item to end-users at self-responsibility.

Step 4. The proposer pays side payments to cooperators based on their investments.

Side payment value S is decided by side payment rate s decided by the proposer in $Step1$ i.e. $S = s \cdot (u - u')$. The proposer's strategy is to decide appropriate side payment rate s. Hybrid traders make a decision about participating in the cooperation based on the

Table 1. Relationship of price and quantity

Quantity	$
1 - 5	7
6 - 10	5.5
11 -	3

side payment rate. Therefore, they have participation probability function $f(\cdot)$, which is based on the side payment rate. Rational hybrid trader participation probabilities increase when the side payment rate becomes larger. Namely, the proposer can make a large coalition formation if the side payment rate is nearly 100%. But then the proposer's utility decreases, causing a disadvantage for the proposer. Consequently, our system decides the optimal side payment rate for the proposer and remakes the trading protocol.

3.1 Examples

We consider n-hybrid traders. Hybrid trader i proposes purchasing item a_j, and then the item price is $v_{a_j}(\omega)\{\omega|\omega \in N\}$. Each hybrid trader has participation probability $f(s)$ based on side payment rate s, and then we give subsets $H'(t_k) \subseteq H$ in which hybrid traders have type t_k. The number of hybrid traders who have the same type is defined by each subset's element count. The number of all hybrid traders is as follows:

$$|H| = \sum_{k=1}^{k} |H'(t_k)|$$

When the side payment rate is $\hat{s}$, the number of participation n^* is shown as follows:

$$n^* = \sum_{k=1}^{k} f(\hat{s}) \cdot |H'(t_k)|$$

Therefore, the proposer can decide the side payment rate using the number of hybrid traders who participate in the cooperation. Then, side payment value S_i for hybrid trader i is decided from interval $0 \leq S_i \leq u_{i,a_j} - u'_{i,a_j}$, which is the difference between the proposer's cooperated utility $u_{i,a_j} = p_{i,a_j} - v_{a_j}(\omega) * Q_{i,a_j}$ and the proposer's individually purchasing utility u'_{i,a_j}. Q_{i,a_j} is the allocation for hybrid trader i when the cooperation purchases the item a_j. A specific side payment value is calculated by the side payment rate in utility increase $s_i * (u_{i,a_j} - u'_{i,a_j})$.

3.2 Side Payment Decision by Simulation

Our system ran a trading simulation to calculate the optimal side payment rate. We considered three types of hybrid traders in which hybrid traders have the participation probability of each type when the side payment rate is changed between $0\% \leq s \leq 100\%$. $Type1$ shows nonlinear monotone increasing participation probability. $Type2$ shows quadric participation probability, which has a maximum value of 50%. $Type3$ shows linear participation probability.

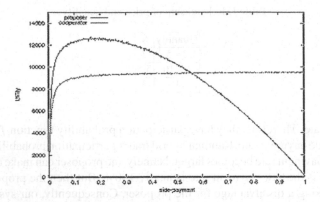

Fig. 1. Average utility of the proposer and the cooperators

In the simulation, we set the hybrid traders' budget is between \$20, 000 and \$200, 000 at random, and change the side payment rate between $0\% \leq s \leq 100\%$. We show simulation result in Fig. 1, where the cooperators' average utility became larger than the proposer's one in $50\% \leq s \leq 60\%$. This shows that the side payment is increasing, and the proposer's utility is decreasing. Therefore, the side payment rate should be decided by an interval below 60%, and the optimal side payment rate is 20% when the proposer's average utility is maximum. The proposer's utility becomes maximum when our system calculates the optimal side payment rate in the simulation.

In our protocol, the proposer cannot get enough volume discount when he/she proposes a low side payment rate, since the proposer can decide any side payment rate. Adversely if the proposer proposes a high side payment rate, his/her utility decreases. Consequently, we use a dynamic mechanism in which our system decides the optimal side payment rate for the proposer in every trading simulation. This mechanism changes the protocol and is shown as follows.

Step 1. Our system decides an optimal side payment rate in each trading simulation.
Step 2. The proposer chooses the rate, and negotiates with other hybrid traders about cooperation.
Step 3. Other hybrid traders deterine their participation in cooperation based on comparing the proposed side payment rate and their evaluated rate.

There are two advantages in this dynamic mechanism. One is that the proposer can decide an optimal side payment rate for efficient trading. The other is that, since the system calculates the side payment rate with each trading, it can exclude pernicious users whose only purpose is to get the side payments.

4   Discussion

4.1   A Decision Method of the Side Payment

We change the side payment decision method which is based on a hybrid trader's contribution. Side payment value S is given by $0 \leq S \leq u - u'$. The proposer's utility is converted into utility per unit item.

$$u - u' = (p - v(\omega)) - (p - v(\omega'))(\omega \geq \omega')$$
$$= v(\omega') - v(\omega)$$

This shows the cooperation's effect per unit item, and its effect per each cooperator is as follows:

$$\underset{i \in C_{a_j}}{u} - \underset{i \notin C_{a_j}}{u'} = \underset{i \notin C_{a_j}}{v_{a_j}(\omega')} - \underset{i \in C_{a_j}}{v_{a_j}(\omega)} = \frac{S_i}{q_{i,a_j}}$$

Here, C_{a_j} is a cooperation group for purchasing item a_j, q_{i,a_j} is hybrid trader i's allocated items and $Q_{a_j} = \sum_{i \in C_{a_j}} q_{i,a_j}$ is all of their purchased item.

Hybrid trader i's side payment value S_i can be defined by the difference of item price when hybrid trader i do not participate in the cooperation and the price when he/she does participate. Then side payment value S satisfies interval $0 \leq S \leq u - u'$.

No cooperator can receive the side payment value as long as a volume discount is not generated by investments. Therefore, cooperators have an incentive to invest more and more.

4.2 Multiple Items Tradings

We discuss a trading scheme that uses a side payment value decision method based on contribution. In this scheme, there are two or more proposers, and hybrid traders can purchase multiple items. The following descriptions are additional definitions when we expand to multiple items tradings.

Definition 2. Their types classify hybrid traders into several groups. The hybrid traders in the group propose their purchasing plan. Then the hybrid traders who do not propose cannot participate in any cooperation. The proposed item is not purchased when there is no cooperator for the item proposed in the group.

Definition 3. Hybrid traders have strategies for cooperation negotiation.

Strategy 1: Mutual cooperation strategy: The side payment value is counterbalanced when the proposer participates in the cooperator's proposed coalition. This strategy does not generate the side payment value.

Strategy 2: Side payment strategy: The proposers pay the side payment value for cooperation.

Next we analyze the hybrid trader's strategies and consider a hybrid trader's maximum purchasing utility problem.

$$(P) \begin{vmatrix} \max & \sum_{i \in H} \sum_{j=1}^{m} u_{i,a_j} \\ \text{subject to } & u_{i,a_j} = v_{a_j}(1) - v_{a_j}(\omega_{a_w}) \\ & \sum_{j=1}^{m} v_{a_j}(\omega) \cdot q_{i,a_j} \leq \sum_{i \in H} b_i \\ & q_{i,a_j} \geq 0 \qquad\qquad j = 1, ..., m \\ & \omega_{a_j} = \sum_{i \in H} q_{i,a_j} \end{vmatrix}$$

We introduce the following an assumption:

$$v_{a_1}(1) > v_{a_2}(1)$$
$$v_{a_1}(\omega_1) < v_{a_2}(\omega_2)$$

We compare the volume discount rates of items a_1 and a_2.

$$\frac{v_{a_1}(\omega_1)}{v_{a_1}(\omega_1 + \omega')} > \frac{v_{a_2}(\omega_1)}{v_{a_2}(\omega_1 + \omega')}$$

When hybrid trader 1 allocates his/her budget as $b_1 = b^1 + b^2 (b^1 = b^2)$, based on Strategy 1, the hybrid trader 1's utility is shown as follows:

$$u_{i,a_1,a_2} = \{v_{a_1}(1) - v_{a_1}(\omega_{a_1})\} \cdot q_{1.a_1}$$
$$+ \{v_{a_2}(1) - v_{a_2}(\omega_{a_2})\} \cdot q_{1.a_2}$$

When the budget allocation is changed to $b^1 > b^2$, the utility is as follows:

$$u'_{i,a_1,a_2} = \{v_{a_1}(1) - v_{a_1}(\omega_{a_1} + q_{1,a_1})\} \cdot (q_{1.a_1} + q_{1,a_1})$$
$$+ \{v_{a_2}(1) - v_{a_2}(\omega_{a_2} - q_{1,a_2})\} \cdot (q_{1.a_2} - q_{1,a_2})$$

Then, the item a_1's volume discount rate is larger than item a_2's.

$$\frac{v_{a_1}(\omega_{a_1}) - v_{a_1}(\omega_{a_1} + q_{1,a_1})}{v_{a_2}(\omega_{a_2}) - v_{a_2}(\omega_{a_2} - q_{1,a_2})} > 0$$

An assumption and this formula show that allocating a big budget to item a_1 increases the utility. Therefore, the purchasing utility satisfies the following formula:

$$u_{i,a_1,a_2} \leq v_{a_1}(1) - v_{a_1}(\omega'_{a_1}), \omega_{a_1} << \omega'_{a_1}$$

Then an item price $v_{a_1}(\omega'_{a_1})$ is when hybrid trader i allocates his/her budget to purchasing item a_1.

When hybrid trader i proposes to purchase item a_1, hybrid trader i should not use strategy 1 for the cooperator who proposes a_2, since his/her utility is decreased. If other hybrid traders do not change their strategies, allocating his/her budget to purchase a_1 is an optimal strategy for hybrid trader i.

The same argument follows when the assumption is changed:

$$\frac{v_{a_1}(\omega_1)}{v_{a_1}(\omega_1 + \omega')} < \frac{v_{a_2}(\omega_1)}{v_{a_2}(\omega_1 + \omega')}$$

In this case, it is better for hybrid trader i to use strategy 1 for the cooperator who proposes a_2. Consequently, hybrid traders decide their strategies by comparing the volume discount rates of items.

Hybrid traders use strategy 2, if the volume discount rate of the proposed item is larger than the cooperator's proposal. Hybrid traders use the strategy 1 if the volume discount rate of the proposed item is smaller than the cooperator's proposal.

5   Conclusion

In this paper, we discussed a cooperative trading in an electronic commerce employed hybrid traders. In our trading model, hybrid traders try to cooperate with each other to purchase item cheaply by volume discount. We introduced a side payment policy as an incentive for cooperating with each other. We also proposed two situations for optimizing side payment value.

In situation 1, we proposed a decision method of side payment value by simulation in which hybrid traders are given their participation probabilities based on the side payment rates. If the situation has complete information of each hybrid trader, our system can decide the optimal side payment rate using a dynamic mechanism in which we add the simulation to our mechanism.

In situation 2, we proposed a new decision method of the side payment value using cooperators' contributions. In the method, our system decides the side payment value without a proposer's decision making. A decided side payment value agrees with the side payment definition in the elicitation process. Also we set out the decision making condition of choosing hybrid traders' strategies by comparing items' volume discount rates in multiple items trading.

Acknowledgment

We thank Prof. Maiko Shigeno of Tsukuba University for helpful discussions.

References

1. Yamamoto, J., Sycara, K.: A stable and efficient buyer coalition formation scheme for e-marketplaces. In: Proceedings of the fifth international conference on autonomous agents, pp. 576–583 (2001)
2. Li, C., Sycara, K.: Algorithm for combinatorial coalition formation and payoff division in an electronic comerce. In: Proc. of the first international joint conference on Autonomous Agents and Multi Agent Systems (AAMAS 2002), pp. 120–127 (2002)
3. Takahashi, S., Matsuo, T.: Negotiation process based on hybrid trader with side payment. In: Proc. of International Conference on Knowledge Information, Creativty Support Systems (2007)
4. Takahashi, S., Matsuo, T.: An approach to efficient trading model of hybrid traders based on volume discount. In: IEA/AIE 2008, New Challenges in Applied Intelligence Technologies, Studies in Computational Intelligence, vol. 134, pp. 45–54 (2008)
5. Milgrom, P.: Putting Auction Theory to Work. Cambridge University Press, Cambridge (2004)

GPGCloud: Model Sharing and Execution Environment Service for Simulation of International Politics and Economics

Yoshiki Kato[1,*], Hirofumi Yamaki[2], and Yuki Asai[1,*]

[1] Nagoya University Graduate School of Information Science
{yoshikik,asai}@net.itc.nagoya-u.ac.jp
[2] Information Technology Center, Nagoya University
yamaki@itc.nagoya-u.ac.jp

Abstract. Simulation-based studies have attracted the attention of researchers of social science like politics and economics, and many findings are given in those domains through simulations. In spite of successful results, it has long been pointed out that there are relatively high bars for those researchers to newly adopt these approaches. We consider that one of them is the large cost related to programming, which is not only learning it but also understanding other researchers' work represented both in their papers and in their codes. Another is the cost for introducing and managing computer systems required to perform efficient researches. We propose a system, GPGCloud, which helps users to share their simulation models with others, to cope with the programming related cost. It also provides an easy access to a large computation environment that allows them to simultaneously perform a number of simulation runs based on their models, which reduces the cost on managing large computers. We implemented a prototype of GPGCloud, which consists of several parts built on top of well-known open-source softwares. This paper describes the design and the implementation of the system.

1 Introduction

Computer simulations are popularly used by researches in several fields in recent years. In research domains of politics and economics, the method is considered as one of effective research tools as typically shown in Axelrod's famous work[1]. Our goal is to promote the simulation-based researches in social science, especially the domains of international politics and economics.

Generally, it requires various skills, especially in programming, for researchers in those domains to create simulation models. One might consider they could hire engineers and have them implement simulation models based on their idea. But, from our experience, it is often inefficient, because the internal logic of such models reflects the hypotheses that they make in the process of research

---

* Student.

J.-J. Yang et al. (Eds.): PRIMA 2009, LNAI 5925, pp. 616–623, 2009.

and is inevitably changed as their studies proceed. This makes the process of implementing systems very costly. From this point of view, we consider that it is preferable for the researchers to create and modify their own simulation models easily and freely by themselves.

As well as acquiring programming skills, the execution of simulation, which tends to require a large amount of time, can be a cost for those researchers. For example, a simulation study typically requires a huge number of runs with different sets of parameters, to estimate the behavior of targets. In other cases, models are very large, and each run requires a long time to finish.

Our approach to these problems is as follows. First, we promote the sharing of simulation models among researchers in the domains by providing supports, which is similar to, but not the same as, those often found in open-source development community. Second, we implement a system where researchers can easily run their simulation models in massive computing environment.

Below, we describe our system, "GPGCloud," which is designed and implemented to achieve our goal.

2   Promoting Simulation Studies by GPGCloud

In this chapter, we introduce existing approaches to problems in performing simulation-based studies in politics and economics, and then, we explain ours.

2.1   Existing Approaches

To reduce a cost of creating models or modifying them, various simulators are proposed, such as Swarm[2], Repast[3], artisoc[4], SOARS[5], GPGSiM[6], and so on. In particular, GPGSiM successfully achieves both freedom and effectiveness, avoiding too much load to users. GPGSiM also provides a number of simulation models that are well-known in the target domains, and users can utilize them in order to build their own models by modifying them. However, this approach has its limits, that a single project cannot implement and provide all the models considered in a domain. There should be a mechanism to collect, accumulate, and provide models developed by users in a somewhat autonomous fashion.

As for the cost of managing computational environment, there have been simulators providing computation services as well as simulation programs, such as International Futures[1]. Users of such simulators specify parameters to run the provided simulation model, but it is not allowed to run their own models. For individual researchers to run their original models, it is required to prepare their own environment from scratch.

2.2   GPGCloud

Based on the above analysis, we designed and implemented *GPGCloud*, that offers the following two services, (a) Repository service to share models among

---

[1] http://www.ifs.du.edu/

researchers, and (b) Computation service to run a large number of simulations simultaneously.

Model Repository Service

Fundamentally, researchers do not always implement their original models from zero. Rather, they often read preceding papers, understand the ideas, and implement their own version of simulator using the models described on the paper to validate the result, in order to then modify them to derive their original results and explore the implication. The cost in this process can be minimized, by reducing the implementation tasks.

Our approach is to provide repositories to share codes. Several similar services already exist to cope with this kind of issues, for example, SourceForge[2], OpenABM[3].

Viewed from our perspective, the former is mainly for engineers and software developers and is complex for our intended users. The latter is more focused on the domains similar to those we focus on, but, in contrast to the former, it provides little functions to computationally support users. Thus, we decided to create a new system that fits our purpose.

Computation Service

Recently, a group of services referred as Cloud Computing[7] have proliferated in the marketplace, such as Google App Engine[4], Amazon EC2(Amazon Elastic Compute Cloud)[5], and Salesforce.com[6]. Inspired by these, we endeavored to design our system to allow the researchers to utilize such environment as if it were just an extension of their PCs. As you can see, the name of the service is taken from them.

Similar approaches have already taken in some academic projects. Sim-PETEK[8] is among them, where simulations are simultaneously run in a grid computing environment. The grid in Sim-PETEK is implemented based on standardized protocols, which enables users to easily apply the system to their simulation-based studies. Though the layer of provided services is different from ours, its underlying concept is not far from ours.

When a large-scale computer is applied to simulation-based studies, it is often the case that a very large and complex simulation with many types of components interacting each other is run, and preceding works that consider the combination of large computers and simulations tend to assume such scenarios. However, especially in the research domain we focus on, simulation models are usually not very large, but a number of runs are required to go through the parameter space. Both GPGCloud and Sim-PETEK are designed to handle such cases, and thus the task generation to achieve efficient experiments is far more important than handling interactions in a large complex system, which has been focused on in usual massively agent-based simulation works.

---

[2] http://sourceforge.net/
[3] http://www.openabm.org/site/
[4] http://code.google.com/intl/en/appengine/
[5] http://aws.amazon.com/ec2/
[6] http://salesservice.com

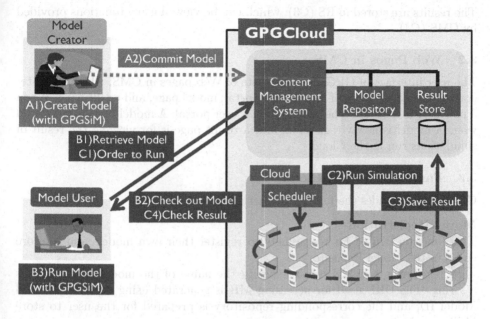

Fig. 1. GPGCloud: Components and Usage

3 Design of GPGCloud

3.1 Concept of GPGCloud

Components and usage of GPGCloud are shown in Fig. 1.

GPGCloud consists of four main components: the Content Management System (CMS), the Model Repository (MR), the Result Store (RS), and the Cloud. CMS implements the user interface. MR is for storing codes, while RS is for result data. The Cloud consists of computers connected by high-speed channels and runs a number of simulations simultaneously.

We divide users into two categories: model creators and model users. This categorization is just for convenience of explanation, and a user can be both a model creator and a model user.

A model creator creates his/her models using GPGSiM (A1), and registers them via CMS (A2). Registered models are stored in MR, and any user can view and download them.

A model user runs simulations using models stored in MR, where there are two scenarios. One is the case where simulations are run in the computer owned by him/her, and the other is the one where they are run in the Cloud.

In the former, he/she searches a model from CMS (B1), then downloads the corresponding code from MR (B2), and runs the code using GPGSiM in his/her computer (B3).

In the latter, he/she requests to run models via CMS (C1), and specifies parameters so that simulations are executed in the Cloud simultaneously (C2).

The results are stored in RS (C3), which can be viewed using functions provided by CMS (C4).

3.2 Web Pages in CMS

The user interface of GPGCloud consists of Web pages in CMS, which are categorized into three types of pages: user portal, model page, and result page. When a new user is registered, he/she is given a user portal. A model page is generated when a model is newly registered, and a result page is for viewing the result of simulations run in the Cloud.

3.3 Functions in GPGCloud

GPGCloud provides the following functions.

Model Registration

This function is used for researchers to register their own models and to store codes in the Model Repository.

In registering a model, a user specify the name of the model and its ID as a string. The URL used for accessing MR is generated using the User ID and Model ID, and the corresponding repository is prepared for the user to store his/her codes.

Model Derivation

As discussed before, many researchers make derived models by modifying those created in the preceding works to inherit features of them.

When "Create Derived Model" button in a model page is pushed by a user, he/she is asked on the name and the ID of a derived new model, then a new set of model page and repository are created based on it, and the contents of the page is copied from the original page to the new. At the same time, the model is copied to his/her repository from original one, so he/she can modify the model to his/her research.

Execution of Simulations in the Cloud

Another important objective of GPGCloud is to provide large-scale computation for executing large number of simulations simultaneously to support the researchers.

Users request to run simulations in GPGCloud via the model pages of the models they want to run. When the "Run in the Cloud" button in a model page is pushed, a page for specifying parameters is shown. When values are input and "Run" button is pushed, tasks are generated and are sent to the scheduler in the Cloud to be simultaneously executed on VMs that reside on processors in the Cloud. After they are finished, the results are stored in the RS, which users access via corresponding result pages.

Result Management

This function is for managing the result data stored in RS, and is provided in result pages. The results generated in the Cloud are listed in those pages, and the date of each run and the parameters are shown. Users read them on Web pages, or download the data to analyze them using their client software.

Other Functions
GPGCloud also has functions which are Model/User Search and Page Editing. Users can search models/users, and edit pages they own.

4 Implementation of GPGCloud

4.1 Components

Based on the design discussed in Section 3, we implemented a prototype of GPGCloud.

AS for CMS, we used an open source content management system, Plone[7], as the base system, and added some mechanisms needed to achieve our purpose.

As for MR and RS, we introduced Subversion[8] which is also an open source product and is widely used to implement software repositories. Since the authorization policies are different between MR and RS, they are implemented separately.

The Cloud mainly consists of Java Virtual Machines (JavaVMs) and the Scheduler. Each VM is stand-alone in this prototype, since, in the intended usage, communications among VMs are not needed. We disable the communication functions of each VM mainly for security reasons. The Scheduler generates jobs based on user requests and specified parameters and assigns them to VMs.

4.2 Functions and Resource Allocation

Model Registration/Derivation
When a user creates a new original model, he/she pushes the "Model Registration" button in his/her user portal. And, when he/she creates a new derived model, he/she pushes the "Create Derived Model" button in an existing model page. CMS checks for conflicts, and, if any, returns an error to the user. Otherwise, CMS generates a URL for the model in MR. After the directory is created, CMS generates the model page for the new model. When the user commits the codes to MR using the given URL, they are compiled and are run once, to check whether the model is runnable in the Cloud.

Simulation Execution in the Cloud/Result Management
When a user requests to run simulations based on a model via the corresponding model page, CMS confirms that the specified revision of the model stored in MR is runnable. If the model is runnable, CMS generates a form to input parameters.

Scheduler in the Cloud receives the URL and the revision number of the model, the specified parameters, and the time stamp. Scheduler creates jobs based on these informations, and assigns them to each VM after scheduling.

---

[7] http://plone.org/
[8] http://subversion.tigris.org/

When a VM receives a job, it fetches the codes of the model according to the URL and the revision number from MR. Then, it runs a simulation on GPGSiM using the parameters specified in the job, and stores the result to RS.

Other Functions
We use the features of Plone for Page Editing and Searching as they are.

Resource Allocation
One simulation is run on one Java VM, and thus the memory and the CPU allocated to the VM is dedicated to the simulation.

We currently use the First-In-First-Out (FIFO) scheme to generate and send jobs from Scheduler to Java VMs in GPGCloud mainly for simplifying the implementation. Each simulation is executed in the allocated VM to its end without being interrupted, unless it is terminated by using more time than a limit which is defined beforehand. This termination based on the time limit is for preventing jobs from failing to finish by program errors such as infinite loops.

5   Conclusion

Our objective is to increase the circle of researchers who perform simulation-based studies in the domains of global economics and politics. Two types of costs impede this: the cost for creating models and that for managing computing environments. GPGCloud is aimed at reducing these problems by providing the support for sharing models and the easy-to-use large computing environment.

In GPGCloud, users register their models, create derived models from those registered by others, and describe the models they own. By using this environment, researchers can make use of codes written in preceding works by skilled ones as well as their results, which helps them make original contributions at lower cost.

GPGCloud runs a large number of simulations with relatively small models, and users easily make use of the computational power. They download and analyze the results stored in the system. This particular design is based on the actual needs from researchers who are not experts in parallel computing but still have needs for the help of such environment. We found the notion of cloud computing very beneficial in the particular domains we aim to support.

Though we provide supports for users to share models, we feel this is not sufficient, in that the intended users still tend to fail to utilize existing codes largely because of the shortage of programming skills needed in understanding and modifying codes. We now plan to apply several techniques from knowledge engineering, especially meta-data related ones. By marking up the codes, the correspondence between models and papers about it can be handled by computers, so that they provide more advanced support than that an general programming environment can, to help the researchers make use of the outcome from earlier works and concentrate on their own contribution to their research domains.

Acknowledgments

We thank the members of the project "Simulation Analysis of Global Orders based on the Concept of Global Public Goods," especially, Mr. Muneyoshi Saito in Mathematical Systems, Inc., Prof. Makoto Sejima in Osaka International University and Prof. Kazuo Yoshida in Kyoto University, for fruitful discussions. We also thank Mr. Hidenori Muramatsu in Nagoya University for his contribution to our system.

This work was supported by Grant-in-Aid for Scientific Research of MEXT (Grant-in-Aid for Scientific Research(S)) "Simulation Analysis of Global Orders based on the Concept of Global Public Goods"(17103002).

References

1. Axelrod, R.: The Complexity of Cooperation: Agent-based Models of Competition and Collaboration. Princeton University Press, Princeton (1997)
2. Minar, N., Burkhart, R., Langton, C., Askenazi, M.: The swarm simulation system: A toolkit for building multi-agent simulations. Working Paper 96-06-042 (1996)
3. North, M.J., Collier, N.T., Vos, J.R.: Experiences creating three implementations of the repast agent modeling toolkit. ACM Transactions on Modeling and Computer Simulation 16 (January 2006)
4. Kozo Keikaku Engineering, Inc.: MAS Community, http://mas.kke.co.jp (in Japanese)
5. Tanuma, H., Deguchi, H., Shimizu, T.: Soars: Spot oriented agent role simulator: Design and implementation. In: Post-Proceeding of the AESCS International Workshop 2004 (2004)
6. Saito, M., et al.: GPGSiM: A new simulation environment for international politics and economics. In: Summer Computer Simulation Conference 2009 (2009)
7. Vouk, M.A.: Journal of computing and information technology. CIT 16 (April 2008)
8. Bozagac, D., Karaduman, G., Kara, A., Alpdemir, M.: Sim-PETEK: A parallel simulation execution framework for grid environments. In: Summer Computer Simulation Conference 2009 (2009)

Creating and Using Reputation-Based Agreements in Organisational Environments*

Roberto Centeno[1], Ramón Hermoso[1], and Viviane Torres da Silva[2]

[1] Centre for Intelligent Information Technologies (CETINIA)
University Rey Juan Carlos Madrid (URJC), Spain
{roberto.centeno,ramon.hermoso}@urjc.es
[2] Universidade Federal Fluminense (UFF), Brazil
viviane.silva@ic.uff.br

Abstract. Reputation mechanisms have been developed during last few years as valid methods to allow agents to better select partners in organisational environments. In most of works presented in the literature, reputation is summarised as a value, typically a number, that represents an opinion sent by an agent to another about a certain third party. In this work, we put forward a novel concept of *reputation-based agreement* in order to support the reputation definition, as well as, some desirable properties about it. We define a reputation service that collects opinions from agents, so creating *agreements* over *situations*. This service will also be in charge of presenting the information by using different *informative mechanisms*. Finally, a case study is presented in order to exemplify our work.

1 Introduction

Reputation mechanisms have been proved to be successful methods to build multi-agent systems where agents' decision-making processes to select partners are crucial for the system functioning [4][5][8]. In this work we propose to endow organisations with a reputation service that may help agents to make decisions when they do not have enough relevant stored information.

On the other hand, an *agreement* is usually defined as a meeting of minds between two or more parties, about their relative duties and rights regarding current or future performance. Around this concept new paradigms have been emerged [1] oriented to increase the reliability and performance of agents in organisations by introducing in such communities these well-known human social mechanisms. With this in mind, we propose a novel approach for the meaning of reputation. From a global point of view, a *reputation-based agreement* is a meeting point on the behaviour of an agent, participating within an organisation,

---

* The present work has been partially funded by the Spanish Ministry of Education and Science under project TIN2006-14630-C03-02 (FPI grants program) and by the Spanish project "Agreement Technologies" (CONSOLIDER CSD2007-0022, INGENIO 2010).

J.-J. Yang et al. (Eds.): PRIMA 2009, LNAI 5925, pp. 624–631, 2009.

with regard to its reputation. Agreements are evaluated by aggregating opinions sent by participants about the behaviour of agents. We also define some interesting properties that describe different types of agreements. Besides, information about reached agreements will be provided to agents by using the concept of informative mechanism [2].

The paper is organised as follows: Section 2 formalises the reputation service, supported by the idea of reputation-based agreements. In Section 3 we illustrate all concepts introduced by means of a case study. Section 5 discusses some related work and, finally, summarises the paper and presents the future work.

2 Reputation Service Based on Reputation-Based Agreements

As we have previously pointed out, the current work faces with the task of formalising a reputation service working on organisational multi-agent systems. We adhere the definition of organisation given in [3]. Summarising, an organisation is defined as a tuple $\langle \mathcal{A}g, \mathcal{A}, \mathcal{X}, \phi, x_0, \varphi, \{\mathcal{ON}^{om}, \mathcal{R}^{om}\}\rangle$ where $\mathcal{A}g$ represents the set of agents participating within the organisation; $\mathcal{A}$ is the set of actions agents can perform; $\mathcal{X}$ stands for the environmental states space; ϕ is a function describing how the system evolves as a result of agents actions; x_0 represents the initial state of the system; φ is the agents' capability function describing the actions agents are able to perform in a given state of the environment; $\mathcal{ON}^{om}$ is an organisational mechanism based on organisational norms; and $\mathcal{R}^{om}$ is an organisational mechanism based on roles that defines the positions agents may enact in the organisation (see [3] for more details).

The dynamics of the reputation service is threefold: *i)* agents within an organisation have to send their opinions about *situations* in which they have been involved; *ii)* the reputation service aggregates all opinions received from agents, creating *reputation-based agreements*; and *iii)* information about the agreements reached within the organisation is provided to agents by using different informative mechanisms [2]. In following sections we explained each task in detail.

2.1 How Agents Send Their Opinions

Along the lifetime of an agent within an organisation, it is involved in several different *situations*. A situation is defined as a tuple $\langle \mathcal{A}g, \mathcal{R}, \mathcal{A}, T \rangle$, that represents an agent $\mathcal{A}g$, playing the role $\mathcal{R}$, while performing the action $\mathcal{A}$, through a time period T. Agents usually evaluate those situations in order to compile reliable information that allows them to predict the result of future situations. Situations are evaluated from an agent's individual point of view and, at any time, the agent can send its opinion about a particular situation to the reputation service. We call this information *reputation information message* and it is formalised as follows:

Definition 1. *A reputation information message* $\mathcal{R}_{ag_i \in \mathcal{A}g}^{info}$ *is a tuple, representing an opinion sent by the agent* ag_i *to the reputation service containing an evaluation about a particular situation,* $\mathcal{R}_{ag_i}^{info} = \langle Sit, RepVal \rangle$,

Where ag_i stands for the agent, which sends the opinion; Sit is the situation being evaluated; and $RepVal$ represents the evaluation the agent is sending about the situation (typically a number).

2.2   Creating Reputation-Based Agreements

In this section we intend to face the task of giving a novel approach for the meaning of reputation, from a centralised point of view, tackling this concept as a partial agreement about a certain situation. When the reputation service receives reputation information messages from agents, it aggregates them creating what we have called *reputation-based agreements*. That is, the aggregation of all the opinions regarding a particular situation is *'per se'* what set of agents – as a whole – actually think about the aforesaid situation. Thus, a reputation-based agreement represents the consensus reached in the reputation opinions space sent by a set of agents about a particular situation. Formally:

Definition 2. *A reputation-based agreement π for a particular situation, is a tuple $\langle Sit, \mathcal{A}g, RepVal, t \rangle$*

Where Sit stands for the situation about which the agreement is reached; $\mathcal{A}g$ is the set of agents that contributed to the agreement; $RepVal$ represents the reputation value – whatever its representation is (qualitative, quantitative, etc.) – reached as consequences of all opinions sent about the situation; and t stands for the time when the agreement was reached. Therefore, an agreement means a global opinion that a set of agents have on a certain situation. This agreement, as we put forward in next section, can be used as a generalist expectation for a situation in which agents have no (or little) previous information about.

The reputation service requires a function that is able to aggregates information reputation messages sent by agents. The aim of such a function is to create agreements from reputation opinions that agents send to the service by means of reputation information messages. We formally define the function as follows:

Definition 3. *Let f_π be a function that given all the reputation information messages sent by agents and a particular situation creates a reputation-based agreement for that situation: $f_\pi : |\mathcal{R}^{info}_{ag_i \in \mathcal{A}g}| \times Sit \rightarrow \Pi$*

Where $|\mathcal{R}^{info}_{ag_i \in \mathcal{A}g}|$ stands for the set of reputation information messages received by the reputation service; Sit is the set of situations; and Π represents the set of reputation-based agreements.

As aggregation function the module might use any function that is able to aggregate values without any modification. For instance, it is possible to use a simple function to calculate the average of all opinions or a more elaborated function that aggregates the opinions by means of complex calculation.

2.3   Reputation-Based Agreements: Properties

From previous definitions – definitions 2 and 3 – it is possible to define some desirable properties about reputation-based agreements. These properties should be taken into account when agreements are created and may also provide useful extra information when informing about different issues.

Property 1. *A reputation-based agreement π is* **complete** *iff. all agents participating in an organisation, at time t, contribute to reach that agreement:*

$$\pi^* \Leftrightarrow \begin{cases} \mathcal{O} = \langle \mathcal{Ag}, \mathcal{A}, \mathcal{X}, \phi, x_0, \varphi, \{\mathcal{ON}^{om}, \mathcal{R}^{om}\} \rangle \ \wedge \\ \pi = \langle Sit, \mathcal{Ag}', RepVal, t \rangle \ \wedge \\ (\mathcal{Ag} = \mathcal{Ag}') \end{cases}$$

That is, given a time t every participant $ag \in \mathcal{Ag}$ in the organisation $\mathcal{O}$ has necessarily sent a reputation information message indicating its opinion about the situation concerning the agreement $(\mathcal{Ag} = \mathcal{Ag}')$. The more complete agreements are in the system, the more reliability the information will be supposed to offer.

Property 2. *A reputation-based agreement π is* α-**consistent** *iff. the reputation value of π differs, at most, $1 - \alpha$ from the reputation value sent by every agent that contributed to reached that agreement:*

$$\pi^\alpha \Leftrightarrow \begin{cases} \pi = \langle Sit, \mathcal{Ag}, RepVal, t \rangle \ \wedge \\ \forall ag \in \mathcal{Ag} \ [\forall r \in Rep_{ag}^{info}[(r = \langle Sit_i, RepVal_i \rangle) \ \wedge \\ (Sit_i = Sit) \ \wedge \ (|RepVal_i - RepVal| \leq 1 - \alpha)]] \end{cases}$$

This property represents how agents sending their opinions about a situation agree in a certain aspect. So, the higher α is, the more similar the opinions are.

Property 3. *A reputation-based agreement π is* **full** *iff. it is complete and 1-consistent:* $\pi^\phi \Leftrightarrow (\pi^* \ \wedge \ \pi^\alpha \ \wedge \ \alpha = 1)$

In the case α is 1 means that all agents have the same opinion about a given situation. This property is very desirable when seeking reputation-based agreements, because the more agents contribute to the agreement, the stronger validity the latter gets. Thus, the likelihood of capturing what is actually happening in the organisation tends to be higher.

Property 4. *A reputation-based agreement π is* $\mathcal{R}$-**consistent** *iff. all the agents contributing the agreement play the same role in the system:*

$$\pi_{\mathcal{R}} = \langle Sit, \mathcal{Ag}, RepVal, t \rangle \Leftrightarrow \forall ag \in \mathcal{Ag} \ play(ag, \mathcal{R})$$

where $\mathcal{R}$ stands for the role the consistency is based on, $\mathcal{Ag}$ is the set of agents that contribute to reach the agreement, and $play : \mathcal{Ag} \times \mathcal{R} \rightarrow [true, false]$ is a function that returns *true* if the agent $\mathcal{Ag}$ plays the role $\mathcal{R}$.

This property is useful in cases in which a new agent, joining an organisation, wants to know what other agents – that are executing in the organisation and playing the same role to it is, think about a given situation. For instance, someone who is thinking of *buying* something would like to know which are the opinions of those who have previously played the role *buyer*.

Property 5. *A reputation-based agreement π is* $\mathcal{R}$-**complete** *iff. is $\mathcal{R}$-consistent and is complete for all the agents that play the role $\mathcal{R}$ at time t:*

$$\pi_{\mathcal{R}}^* = \langle Sit, \mathcal{A}g', RepVal, t \rangle \Leftrightarrow \begin{cases} \pi_{\mathcal{R}} \wedge \mathcal{O} = \langle \mathcal{A}g, \mathcal{A}, \mathcal{X}, \phi, x_0, \varphi, \{\mathcal{ON}^{om}, \mathcal{R}^{om}\} \rangle \wedge \\ \forall ag \in \mathcal{A}g \ (play(ag, \mathcal{R}) \rightarrow ag \in \mathcal{A}g') \end{cases}$$

Property 6. *A reputation-based agreement* π *is* $\mathcal{R}$-**full** *iff. is* $\mathcal{R}$-*complete and is 1-consistent:* $\pi_{\mathcal{R}}^{\phi} \Leftrightarrow (\pi_{\mathcal{R}}^* \wedge \pi^{\alpha} \wedge \alpha = 1)$

2.4 Providing Information about Reputation-Based Agreements

In this section, we deal with the problem of how the reputation service may provide such information. To that end, we part from the notion of *informative mechanism* [2]. Those types of mechanisms are in charge of providing some kind of information to agents in order to regulate a multi-agent system. Thus, an *informative mechanism* $\Gamma : \mathcal{S}' \times \mathcal{X}' \rightarrow \mathcal{I}$ is a function that given a partial description of an internal state of an agent (S') and, taking into account the partial view that the service has of the current environmental state ($\mathcal{X}'$), provides certain information ($\mathcal{I}$). We adhere this definition to create mechanisms over the agreements for different situations, creating information valuable for participants in the organisation. We formally define them as follows:

Definition 4. *An informative mechanism providing information about reputation-based agreements is:* $\Gamma_{\Pi} : Sit \times \mathcal{X}' \rightarrow \mathcal{I}_{\Pi}$

Where $Sit, \mathcal{X}'$ are already defined and $\mathcal{I}_{\Pi}$ stands for the information provided by the mechanism by using the set of agreements Π reached over the situation Sit.

We have chosen a very general definition about information in order to cover all possible types of information the reputation service could offer taking into account the reputation-based agreements reached. The information provided may consist of a ranking sorting the best agents for a particular situation, such as $\langle \_, \mathcal{R}, \mathcal{A}, \_ \rangle$, created from the agreements reached for that situation, a value representing the reputation value for a situation, reached as consequence of the agreement for that situation, information about the properties of the agreement reached for a particular situation, if it is full, complete, etc.

3   Case Study: Pubs Area

In this section, we illustrate the proposed model by means of a simple case study. The scenario we use involves four different agents: *Anna, John, Jessica* and *Albert*. In this organisation agents can *order* and *delivery* drinks. That organisation is created with the aim of getting in touch pubs' owners and providers of drinks. Thus, agents join the organisation playing the roles of *pub* and *provider*, representing a pub's owner and a company provider of drinks, respectively. In our particular example, agents are playing the following roles: *Anna - pub, John - pub, Jessica - pub* and *Albert - provider*.

In this scenario, agents representing pubs' owners are interested in collaborating sharing information about providers, because the pubs are situated in the same area and they collaborate each other so as to foster the attraction customers to that area. That is, although they try to maximize their own benefit, one of their goals is to foster the pubs area where they are, even if that entails to exchange information about drink providers.

Therefore, after several interactions among them – performing actions of ordering and delivering different types of drinks – *Anna* decides to make public her opinion about *Albert* as provider. Thus, she uses the reputation information messages to send to the reputation service her opinion, as follows:

$$\mathcal{R}_{Anna}^{info} = \langle\langle Albert, provider, \_, \_\rangle, 0.8\rangle$$

This information shows that *Anna* has had bad experiences while she was ordering drinks to *Albert* (0.8) because *Albert* almost never violates contracts and offers low prices. Similarly, *John* and *Jessica* send their opinions about *Albert* as providers, by using the following reputation information messages:

$$\mathcal{R}_{John}^{info} = \langle\langle Albert, provider, \_, \_\rangle, 0.7\rangle \; ; \; \mathcal{R}_{Jessica}^{info} = \langle\langle Albert, provider, \_, \_\rangle, 0.9\rangle$$

It seems that both *John* and *Jessica* agree that *Albert* is a reliable provider.

When the reputation service receives this information, it is able to create reputation-based agreements by using a function that aggregates the reputation information messages. Let us suppose that it aggregates the messages by calculating the average of reputation values sent by agents over exactly the same situation[1]:

$$f_\pi(Sit) = \frac{\sum_{i=1}^n \mathcal{R}_{ag_i}^{info} = \langle Sit, RepVal_i\rangle}{n}$$

Thus, from the set of messages sent by the agents, the reputation service can create two reputation-based agreements regarding to two different situations:

$$\pi_1 = \langle\langle Albert, provider, \_, \_\rangle, \{Anna, John, Jessica\}, 0.8, t\rangle$$

π_1 represents that there exists an agreement within the organisation regarding to *Albert* as *provider* – regardless the action he performs – is evaluated as 0.8, and such an agreement is reached by the collaboration of *Anna*, *John* and *Jessica*, at time t.

In order to provide information about agreements the reputation service makes available three different informative mechanisms:

- $\Gamma_\Pi^1(\langle Ag, \mathcal{R}, \_, \_\rangle)$ given a situation where an agent and a role are specified, returns meta-information[2] about the reputation-based agreement reached regarding that situation;
- $\Gamma_\Pi^2(\langle Ag, \mathcal{R}, \_, \_\rangle)$ given a situation where an agent and a role are specified, returns the reputation-based agreement reached. In particular, it returns the reputation value in the agreement of that situation;

---

[1] It could be used whatever other function that is able to aggregate the information received from agents.

[2] With meta-information we mean the α-consistency of the agreement, if it is full, complete, etc.

- $\Gamma_\Pi^3(\langle \_, \mathcal{R}, \_, \_ \rangle)$ given a situation specifying a role, returns a ranking of agents playing the role, sorted by the reputation value they have as consequence of the reputation-based agreements reached until the current time t.

Let us suppose that a new pub is opened in the same area by *Alice*, so she joins the organisation playing the role *pub*. Since she is looking for a drinker *provider*, a ranking of "best" providers would be a great solution to select the best one. She can thus use Γ_Π^3: $\Gamma_\Pi^3(\langle \_, provider, \_, \_ \rangle)$. Lets suppose that by using this information *Alice* knows that there exists an agreement within the organisation showing that *Albert* is among the best providers. But, how good is him?. To answer this question *Alice* queries the informative mechanism Γ_Π^2 as follows:

$$\Gamma_\Pi^2(\langle Albert, provider, \_, \_ \rangle) \Rightarrow 0.8$$

In addition, she would like to know if the agents that have testified about *Albert*'s behaviour have similar opinions about him. So, she performs the following query:

$$\Gamma_\Pi^1(\langle Albert, provider, \_, \_ \rangle) \Rightarrow \pi^{0.9}$$

With this information *Alice* knows that all opinions sent about *Albert* are coincident because of the reputation-based agreement reached is 0.9-consistent ($\pi^{0.9}$).

4   Related Work

As stated before, one of the main advantages of having a centralised reputation service is that it decreases the cost and makes it feasible for an agent to know a more consistent reputation about another agent based on numeral experiences. In the case of distributed mechanisms (such as [5][8]), the agent itself would need to participate in several interactions with the given agent and also to ask other agents for their experiences with others. In the case of a centralised mechanism, the agent can easily get information about the reputation showing the behaviour of other agents within the system. In [9], Sabater et al. present a centralised reputation mechanism that is incorporated as a service in Electronic Institutions (EIs). From a global perspective, this work has many similarities with ours, since uses also a reputation service in an organisational environment (EIs). However, the authors do not focus on how to exploit the collected information as agreements that can be presented to agents in different ways.

In [6] the authors present an approach to create rankings able not only to provide the most trustful agents but also a probabilistic evidence of such reputation values. Those rankings are also computed by a centralised system by aggregating the reputations reported by the agents. This approach could be complementary to ours, since that paper focuses on defining the ranking algorithms and ours focuses on describing the mechanism that allows to receive the reputation information and to provide the already evaluated agreements (for instance by using rankings). Another work that could be also complementary to the approach presented here, is the one presented in [7]. They describe the algorithm *NodeRanking* that creates rankings of reputation ratings. Therefore, our reputation service could use this algorithm so as to provide information about the reputation-based agreements reached within the organisation.

5   Conclusions

Summarising, this work puts forward a novel approach of reputation-based agreement concept by supporting on a reputation service that creates reputation-based agreements as aggregations of opinions sent by participants within an organisation. Besides, we also define some desirable properties that can be derived and should be taken into account when providing the information they contain. Furthermore, we also propose to provide agents with useful information by means of informative mechanisms. Finally, we illustrate how the reputation-based agreements works in a collaborative domain where agents are interested in sharing their opinions. In future work we plan to experimentally test our approach by implementing a case study presented here, as well as, running several experiments comparing our approach with similar ones. We also intend to investigate new properties about reputation-based agreements to provide agents participating in an organisation with more useful information. Finally, we plan to extend the concept of reputation-based agreement by creating agreements aggregating "similar" situations, so we must go into the concept of similar situations in depth.

References

1. Carrascosa, C., Rebollo, M.: Modelling agreement spaces. In: Proc. of WAT@IBERAMIA, pp. 79–88 (2008)
2. Centeno, R., Billhardt, H., Hermoso, R., Ossowski, S.: Organising mas: A formal model based on organisational mechanisms. In: SAC, pp. 740–746 (2009)
3. Centeno, R., Torres da Silva, V., Hermoso, R.: A reputation model for organisational supply chain formation. In: Proc. of COIN@AAMAS, pp. 33–48 (2009)
4. Dellarocas, C.: Reputation Mechanisms. In: Handbook on Economics and Information Systems. Elsevier, Amsterdam (2005)
5. Huynh, T., Jennings, N., Shadbolt, N.: Fire: An integrated trust and reputation model for open multi-agent systems. In: Proc. of ECAI, pp. 18–22 (2004)
6. Ignjatovic, A., Foo, N., Lee, C.: An analytic approach to reputation ranking of participants in online transactions. In: Proc. of WI-IAT, pp. 587–590. IEEE Computer Society, Los Alamitos (2008)
7. Pujol, J., Sangüesa, R., Delgado, J.: Extracting reputation in multi agent systems by means of social network topology. In: Proc. of AAMAS, pp. 467–474. ACM, New York (2002)
8. Sabater, J., Sierra, C.: Reputation and social network analysis in multi-agent systems. In: AAMAS, pp. 475–482 (2002)
9. Sabater-Mir, J., Pinyol, I., Villatoro, D., Cun, G.: Towards hybrid experiments on reputation mechanisms: Bdi agents and humans in electronic institutions. In: Proc. of CAEPIA, vol. 2, pp. 299–308 (2007)

Directory Service in the Language Grid for System Integration

Daisuke Yanagisawa[1,*], Takuya Furuta[2], and Hirofumi Yamaki[3]

[1] Graduate School of Information Science, Nagoya University
yanagi@net.itc.nagoya-u.ac.jp
[2] Hitachi, Ltd.
furuta@net.itc.nagoya-u.ac.jp
[3] Information Technology Center, Nagoya University
yamaki@itc.nagoya-u.ac.jp

Abstract. To develop a multilingual application based on the Language Grid, developers need to fill semantical gaps that exist among multilingual resources and software that are developed for different objects by various organizations. Authors have proposed a metadata-based approach, based on which the *Language Grid Facilitator* (LGF) is developed as a directory service that provides computational supports, and is aimed at helping developers who implement parallel text applications.

To cope with the increase of computational costs resulting from logical or semantical calculation performed in the LGF, we divided queries into two parts. One of them encodes static knowledge about the semantical gaps between resources and applications, and can be cached and indexed for better performance. A prototype was implemented, and experimental results have shown that our approach successfully reduced the computational cost while helping users to specify fine-grained conditions needed in the development of parallel text applications.

1 Introduction

The Language Grid is a service infrastructure that provides a unified access interface to multilingual services, that consist of language processing software, such as machine translators and morphological analysers, and language resources, such as dictonaries and parallel texts, which are provided by different organizations. Multilingual applications connected to the Language Grid provide their users with multilingual functionalities by using or integrating these software and resources. When implementing such applications, developers have to choose appropriate services and fill semantical gaps among these services which result from their varying backgrounds.

In the context of parallel text applications which we focus on in this paper, this issue typically appears in choosing proper texts to be shown in a given category. For example, two language resources, which both are for disaster damage prevention, may have completely different category hierarchy, and texts in one

---

* Student.

J.-J. Yang et al. (Eds.): PRIMA 2009, LNAI 5925, pp. 632–640, 2009.

category in one resource do not fit in the category with the same name in the other resource. A category name, "Earthquake Information," is for texts that forecast earthquakes and their possible damages in one, while it is for information about life after an earthquake in the other. If a developer does not consider these gaps, his/her application may show categories that include confusingly mixed set of parallel texts, which we consider unfavorable.

To help developers of multiligual applications, we have proposed metadata-based scheme [1], and have designed a vocabulary and a reference category set to be used in integrating parallel-text resources and applications.

In this paper, we present the *Language Grid Facilitator* (LGF) which is aimed at providing computational support to them based on the metadata approach. The LGF is a directory service that accumulates metadata of language resources and performs searches in them.

Though metadata-based approaches allow users to specify fine-grained conditions to choose resources, they tend to require relatively large computational cost. Through analysing queries, we found that the large part of those queries encode the knowledge to fill the semantical gaps discussed above, and thus seldom change if the combination of the application and the resource is fixed. We separate this static parts from queries and cache them in the LGF so that they can be indexed beforehand for better performance. We call this part of a query as *local knowledge*. By doing so, the size of each query is reduced and also the processing time is shortened.

We implemented a prototype of the LGF and measured the performance. Results shows that the above local-knowledge approach successfully improves the search performance.

2   Language Grid

The Language Grid is a service infrastructure where multilingual application developers are able to use language processing software such as machine translation and language resources such as parallel texts. By using the Language Grid, we are able to combine language resources and language processing software, and implement new multilingual application easily.

Fig. 1 shows the outline of the Language Grid system. For convenience, we call both language processing software and language resource as *language service* in this section. Each language service is administrated by its maintainers, and each multilingual application is managed by its providers. And, these applications provide multilingual functionalities to users using language services. Multilingual applications communicate with language services using SOAP [2]. During this communication, the Language Grid Core Node authenticates, authorizes, and monitors multilingual applications.

Here, we give the definitions of a *parallel text resource* and a *parallel text service*. In this paper, we refer an organized set of parallel texts provided by an individual or an organization as a parallel text resource. For example, the set of parallel texts used in the translation system by the Aichi International

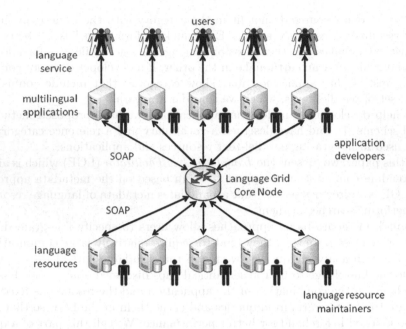

Fig. 1. Outline of the Language Grid

Association and the Multilingual Disaster Information System Consortium[1] is called the MDIS parallel text resource.

A parallel text service is a Web service that wraps a parallel text resource. For instance, the MDIS parallel text service is a Web service which contains the MDIS parallel text resource, and which returns parallel texts from it according to received requests.

3   System Integration of Multilingual Services Using Metadata

3.1   Issues in Integrating Language Services with Categories

During system integration on the Language Grid, multilingual application developers search elements that suit for their application from a number of language resources. They made this search with keyword search and category search.

Language resources and multilingual applications may use different category structures. Application developers need to fill the gap when they integrate systems. It is difficult to associate a category structure of a language resource with a category structure of multilingual application.

The gap is serious in parallel text applications. These applications have user interfaces which shows parallel texts in appropriate categories to a domain of

---

[1] http://www.aia.pref.aichi.jp/mlis/

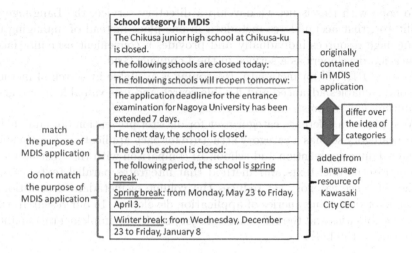

Fig. 2. Integrated Category in Trial Experiment

each application. For example, the Multilingual Disaster Information System (MDIS) [2] and the Language Grid Playground [3] have such interfaces. Fig. 2 shows an instance seen in a trial experiment to integrate the parallel text resource of Kawasaki City CEC [3] into MDIS. Four parallel texts at the top are originally contained in MDIS application, while five at the bottom are added from the language resource of Kawasaki City CEC. The upper two parallel texts from Kawasaki City CEC match the purpose of MDIS application, but the lower three do not because these ones contain the word of spring break or winter break. These differences are caused by the contrast of a purpose of language resources and the way of thinking about category classification of different designers.

As just described, it is difficult to appropriately classify parallel texts into categories which are correctly categorized in other applications because these categories are designed by different points of view. From the trial, we figured out that it is hard by using only simple matching of categories and keyword search provided by the parallel text service interface in the Language Grid [4]. Because of this, we introduce metadata system integration. It enables application developers to select appropriate parallel texts.

3.2 Approach for System Integration

It is hard to integrate applications and language resources with different structures of categories. If the developer of each application must specify the correspondence between categories of the application and of language resource one by one, the cost as a whole will be the number of language resources times that of applications.

---

[2] http://www.aia.pref.aichi.jp/mlis/
[3] http://www.langrid.org/playground/kawasaki-parallel.html

To cope with this issue, we develop a directory service, the Language Grid Facilitator, that accumulates metadata in one place instead of managing them in language resources individually and provides a convenient user interface for application developers as a service in the Language Grid.

We used RDF [5] for metadata. Reasoning is available in search of metadata. Reasoning enables advanced and flexible search and it is valuable in integrating of multilingual systems.

We designed a reference category set for disaster prevention domain. The reference category set has a category structure for each application domain such as disaster damage prevention and school. In comparison with the existing method to integrate parallel texts, our method that integrates parallel texts according to the reference category set reduces the volume of metadata description and the time for describing queries of application developers. In our research, we use these vocabularies and the reference category set in the implementation and the evaluation of the LGF.

4   The Language Grid Facilitator

4.1   Directory Service

The LGF accumulates metadata about various elements of language resources in a single RDF store using unified metadata vocabulary, and provides search functionality, that do not require knowledge about metadata, for users. RDF store accumulates RDF triples and provide search functions.

We describe the outline of system integration with the LGF below.

1. Administrators of the LGF annotate metadata about language resources and elements of language resources using RDF and unified metadata vocabulary. They put them into the RDF store of the LGF.
2. A multilingual application sends a search query to the LGF. The LGF generates a SPARQL [6] query based on the search query and searches the RDF store.
3. The LGF returns the result to the application. This result contains the URIs of the elements of language resources, the URIs of language resources which includes these elements, and the URLs of the services of these language resources.
4. The application requests elements of language resources based on the search result.
5. A language resource returns requested elements to the application.

4.2   Search Function

The LGF is aimed at supporting application developers by providing a sophisticated search functions that are built on top of metadata technologies. However, it is not easy for those who are not specialized in metadata to use directly such interfaces as SPARQL-based queries.

Instead, the LGF provides multiple types of search interfaces that implements search methods which are useful in developing multilingual applications. We call a certain meaningful set of search methods as a *profile*, and the LGF implements a number of profiles so that it supports different kinds of applications.

Profiles are composed of *primary profiles* and *sub profiles*. Primary profiles contain classes of language resources (e.g., dictionaries, translations, parallel texts, etc.). Sub profiles contain searching methods (e.g., category search, metadata search, etc.) in each primary profile.

In the Language Grid, primary profiles are selected from parallel text, machine translation, dictionary etc. They enable application developers to represent search conditions depending on a function of applications.

By this design policy, we are able to extend and upgrade function by adding and modifying profiles as units. And we ensure some degree of freedom in the design of the LGF because modifications of design inside of a profile do not propagate a impact of itself. In this paper, we only implement a parallel text profile. But, we plan to study and implement other profiles, to deal with the increase of the types of language resources in the Language Grid.

On the other hand, sub profiles mean each search function. To improve precision of search using metadata, detailed metadata vocabulary is required. But if a metadata vocabulary is too detailed, it becomes difficult to annotate metadata and represent search query. It is required to understand metadata vocabulary and to represent with query description languages like SPARQL. To tackle this, we designed sub profiles of each function for easy understanding.

Currently, elements of sub profile for parallel texts have designed. Designed classes are *category search*, *sender search*, *receiver search*, *grammar tag search*, *discourse tag search* and *belonging resource search*. It allows more than one sub profiles in one search query. It is possible to represent more detailed search queries by combining sub profiles with set operations, whose input uses conjunctive canonical form to represent a combination of search conditions.

4.3 Local Knowledge

When considering metadata sub profiles, it is observed that queries from an application to the LGF tend to share some sentences, which typically reflect some conceptual structure about the application itself, such as a part of its ontology or taxonomy.

Since this part is often relatively large, it is effective to separate it from the rest and cache it for better performance. We call this part as the *local knowledge* of the application.

We describe the usage of the local knowledge below. First, the application divides its query into the two parts: the local knowledge that does not change in multiple queries, and the rest that changes. The latter part is sent to the LGF, while the local knowledge is stored as an XML file that is available via HTTP and only its URL is sent to the LGF. When receiving the query, the LGF checks if it already has the local knowledge, and, if not, it fetches the data by the URL and cache it. If the cached local knowledge is available, it is used without

```
<localcategory uri="http://example.com/Category/Earthquake">
  <refcategory>...../ReferenceCategory/Disaster/Earthquake</refcategory>
  <refcategory>...../ReferenceCategory/Timing/AfterDisaster</refcategory>
</localcategory>
```

Fig. 3. An Example of Local Knowledge

any transmission. After obtaining the local knowledge, it is combined with the rest part, and then the search is performed. In addition to caching, the local knowledge is indexed into the RDF store, which achieves better performance.

Fig. 3 is an example of local knowledge. This list shows `http://example.com/Category/Earthquake` is a category of multilingual application and this category matches the intersection of the reference category `http://.../ReferenceCategory/Disaster/Earthquake` and the reference category `http://.../ReferenceCategory/Timing/AfterDisaster`. With this local knowledge, we are able to reduce a query. Developers can use simple queries with local knowledge instead of complicated queries with the reference category set.

5   Evaluation

The performance of the LGF is critical to the usability of applications. We implemented the mechanism that previously described and evaluated its performance. In implementation, we used JDK 1.6.0_07. Also, we built a server executing the LGF (LGF server) and a server to store local knowledge. We implemented a program that communicates with the LGF. Then, we measured response time querying the LGF server.

We assumed a parallel text application, and examined the relationship between the execution time and the number of parallel texts. Using metadata sets generated randomly based on the vocabulary and the categories designed in [1]. We assumed that each parallel text is annotated with three triples, and measured the performance in the cases where the number of parallel texts is 1000, 5000, and 10000. For each run, queries are sent 10 times, and length of time to process them were recorded.

As shown in the Table 1, in the case of 10,000 parallel texts, the first execution time is 11,000 ms, and for the queries after that, the average is 2,875 ms, which is shorter than the first. This tendency holds in any case we observed. We believe

Table 1. The Number of Parallel Texts and the Execute Time

Number of Parallel Texts	Execution Time(msec)	
	1st	from 2nd to 10th (average)
1,000	3,578	1,016
5,000	6,469	1,625
10,000	11,000	2,875

that this is because of the time required to fetch local knowledge, putting it into the RDF store, and establishing connection with AllegroGraph in the first access.

In an actual parallel text resource, the number of parallel texts included in a parallel text resource is usually at most 1,000. We suppose that the number of language resources accessed by an application is up to 10, and we believe the scenario that the RDF store keeps triples of 10,000 parallel texts is a reasonable assumption. It depends on applications whether described performance is sufficient or not, but, we believe that it is possible to process it within a practicable length of time by using local knowledge.

6   Conclusion

In this paper, we proposed the LGF that is a directory service that manages metadata for integrating language resources. The LGF accumulates metadata of language resources on the RDF store and mediates metadata search in multilingual applications.

We introduced search profiles. A profile consists of a primary profile that corresponds to the class of language resources and sub profiles corresponds to classes of search conditions such as category search.

Since a profile provides useful search functionality for application developers, compared with RDF format, developers can describe queries easily.

Then, we introduced local knowledge to reduce execution time. Search queries sent from applications contain search conditions and conceptual structures that are unique to each application. Conceptual structures are not basically modified because they express ideas of application design. We separated this structure from search query as local knowledge. This approach shortens the size of search query. And, we reduced execute time by caching local knowledge in the LGF.

We made experiments that assumed actual case with prototype of the LGF. As a result, the first execution time is 3,200 ms, and the average from second to tenth is 1,000 ms. It shows that caching local knowledge is effective in reducing execution time.

Even though Language Grid supports various classes of language resources and language processing software such as bilingual dictionaries, current implementation of the LGF supports only parallel texts. We hope to design and implement other classes of language resources in the future.

References

1. Takeuchi, I., Yamaki, H., Ukai, M.: Development of a metadata authoring environment for Language Grid. IEICE Tech. Rep. 108(441), 97–102 (2008) (in Japanese)
2. Mitra, N.: SOAP Version 1.2. W3C Recommendation, August 9 (2003)
3. Sakai, S., Gotou, M., Murakami, Y., Morimoto, S., Morita, D., Tanaka, M., Ishida, T.: Language grid playground: light weight building blocks for intercultural collaboration. In: IWIC 2009: Proceeding of the 2009 international workshop on Intercultural collaboration, pp. 297–300. ACM, New York (2009)

4. Gotou, M., Yamaki, H., Yanagisawa, D., Ukai, M., Tanaka, M., Ishida, T.: Resource Sharing by Multilingual Expression Services. In: IEEE Asia-Pacific Services Computing Conference (APSCC 2008), pp. 470–475 (2008)
5. Klyne, G., Carroll, J., McBride, B.: Resource Description Framework (RDF): Concepts and Abstract Syntax. W3C Recommendation (2004)
6. Prud'hommeaux, E., Seaborne, A.: SPARQL Query Language for RDF. W3C Recommendation (2008)

SBDO: A New Robust Approach to Dynamic Distributed Constraint Optimisation

Graham Billiau and Aditya Ghose

Decision Systems Lab
University of Wollongong
NSW, Australia
{gdb339,aditya}@uow.edu.au

Abstract. Here we introduce a novel algorithm for continual optimisation of dynamic distributed constraint optimisation problems. By using techniques derived from argumentation for communication the algorithm does not need to use an ordering over the variables. The lack of a hierarchy allows the algorithm to efficiently solve dynamic problems, as well as be completely asynchronous, fault tolerant and anytime. However it prevents an ordered search, making the algorithm incomplete.

1 Introduction

Dynamic Distributed Constraint Optimisation Problems (DynDCOP's) are an important variation of Distributed Constraint Optimisation Problems (DCOP's) that are not well explored. DynDCOP's take into account that in the real world the problem being solved is very rarely static. They change over time as new information is discovered or current information becomes obsolete. Current DCOP algorithms, such as ADOPT [1], ADOPT-ng [2], BnB-ADOPT [3], DPOP [4] and NCBB [5] are unsuitable for solving DynDCOP problems, as they rely on the variables being ordered in a preprocessing stage, which would have to be repeated every time the problem changes. Algorithms such as DynDBA [6] and DynAWC [7] solve distributed dynamic CSP's. DynCOAA [8] solves DynDCOP's but using a entirely different technology – ant colony optimisation.

None of the above algorithms take into account the possibility that the agents in the network may fail. There are many reasons why an agent may fail, and it is particularly important to account for this in dynamic algorithms, which may be expected to run continually for a long duration.

In order to overcome these problems we present a new algorithm for solving DynDCOP's called Support Based Distributed Optimisation (SBDO) that is completely asynchronous, anytime, fault tolerant and does not require the re-computation of variable orderings every time the problem undergoes change (such as the addition/deletion of variables, constraints or objectives).

SBDO addresses distributed optimisation problems where the problem-solving knowledge (constraints) as well as the objectives are distributed across a set of agents. As with many other proposals in the area, we make the simplifying

J.-J. Yang et al. (Eds.): PRIMA 2009, LNAI 5925, pp. 641–648, 2009.
© Springer-Verlag Berlin Heidelberg 2009

assumption that each agent corresponds to a single decision variable, i.e., the agent is able to autonomously decide on the value of that variable. This does not lead to a loss of generality, since a variable could represent a sub-problem with multiple underlying decision variables (the Cartesian product of whose domains would constitute the domain of this higher-level variable). We assume the existence of a global objective function that the collection of agents seeks to optimise, but we require that it must be possible to decompose this function into agent-specific objective functions such that if each agent were to optimise its local objective function, the resulting global solution would be optimal.

Each objective function must return a real value that is proportionate to how good the partial solution is, a utility value, such that a better solution returns a higher utility value. The utility values returned by all of the objective functions must be comparable.

To increase the generality of the algorithm shared objectives can be used as well as local objectives. Shared objectives are used when a (sub)objective can not be decomposed to include only the variables of one agent. In this case the objective can be shared between the agents which together control the variables used in the objective. The objective is evaluated by any of the agents that share it as soon as that agent knows the assignment to all the variables in the objective. The utility returned by the shared objective is added to the utility of the agents local objective. If the agent does not have enough information to evaluate the objective it is ignored and only the agents local objective is used.

It is trivial to convert soft or valued constraints to shared objectives. The objective function is defined by the values in the constraint and the agents/variables that it is shared between are the agents/variables involved in the constraint.

Many real world problems include hard constraints as well as a global objective. To ensure that any solution produced by SBDO satisfies all the hard constraints they are handled differently to objectives. Nogood's with justifications [9] are used as they allow us to guarantee that any solution generated will satisfy all the hard constraints while also allowing for changes in the problem. (This is demonstrated in [10].)

Due to the dynamic nature of the input problem the algorithm never terminates (detecting that the network of agents has reached a quiescent state, or detecting that the problem is over-constrained are in themselves insufficient as terminating criteria, since new inputs from the environment, in the form of added or deleted variables/constraints/objectives might invalidate them). In dynamic settings, we view SBDO as an anytime algorithm, which the user can 'interrupt' at any time (allowing for a certain duration since the last change to the problem during which the solution may be inconsistent) to obtain the current near-optimal solution. The duration during which the solution may not be consistent is the period required for the obsolete nogood's to be removed and utility values updated throughout the network. As with anytime algorithms SBDO is pre-emptivly schedulable (it saves state when interrupted, and resumes from the saved state). As with anytime algorithms, the solution quality is monotonically non-decreasing (see also Section 3 on evaluation results).

However if the algorithm is deployed in a static environment detecting that
the network has reached a quiescent state is sufficient to detect termination. This
can be achieved by taking a consistent global snapshot using algorithms such as
ChandyLamport [11]. The algorithm will also terminate if it detects that there
is no solution to the problem.

For correct operation all that is required is that messages are never lost.

SBDO is in part inspired by techniques used in formal argumentation, where
the notion of an argument is used to encode alternate points of view. A range
of techniques have been developed in formal argumentation theory for identifying the set of winning arguments, given a base set of arguments. Every partial
assignment in SBDO, annotated with a utility value (called an isgood, to be
described in detail later) is similar to an argument (for the receiving agent to
take on a value consistent with the isgood). The sequence of variable-value assignments in an isgood may be viewed as a justification. As in argumentation,
the agent receiving these (potentially competing) arguments must pick the winning argument (ie., isgood). An argument may attack/defeat other arguments.
Arguments are represented as <justification, conclusion> pairs. Each agent also
attempts to send stronger arguments over time to attempt to influence their
neighbours.

2   Support Based Distributed Optimisation

Support Based Distributed Optimisation is an extension to Support Based Distributed Search [10].

In order to optimise the solution, as well as to prevent cycles forming SBDO
uses a global total ordering over the set of partial solutions. To determine this
ordering first the total utility of the partial solution is considered, with higher
values preferred. If they are equal the size of the partial solution is considered,
with larger solutions preferred. If they are equal an arbitrary total ordering is
used (hash functions can provide this total ordering). Whenever we refer to one
isgood being better than another in this paper it is with respect to this ordering.

An isgood is an ordered partial solution ie. a sequence of triples consisting of
the agent identifier, the assignment(s) to that agents variable(s) and the utility
value returned by that agents local objective. It is written as

$$\langle (agent, assignment, utility), ... \rangle,$$

where *utility* is the utility of the *assignment* to *agent*. Each agent must be a
neighbour of the agent immediately before it in the isgood. Isgood's are the main
message used for communication between agents and roughly means "I've taken
the value ... because ...". The total utility of an isgood is the sum of the utilities
of all the assignments within it.

In order to guarantee that any solution generated satisfies all the hard constraints nogood's with justifications [9] are used. A nogood is a partial solution
that is proven to not be part of any global solution, ie. a collection of assignments

that together violate one or more constraints. When an agent sees a partial solution that is a superset of one of the nogood's it knows about it can immediately reject that partial solution. When a nogood is created the set of all hard constraints that are violated are added to the nogood. These constraints form the justification of the nogood. Whenever a constraint is removed from the problem the justifications of all nogood's are checked, if they contain the constraint then that nogood is also deleted.

Because only the current value of each agent is communicated to other agents it is easy to modify the algorithm to solve problems with continuous or infinite domains. Each agent selects it's own value and communicates it to the other agents exactly as for finite domains. However nogood's must be modified to exclude a range of values, instead of a single value.

Because there is no hierarchy between the agents and it is a local search algorithm, each agent is free to change its own assignment at any time. This allows agents in different parts of the problem to act independently. Even neighbouring agents can act independently as they are not waiting on a message from a child or parent.

That the algorithm is fault tolerant follows from the algorithm being completely asynchronous. This allows all the other agents to continue solving when one or many of the agents fail, it is just that the value assigned to the failed agent can not be changed. When the agent is restarted it will be able to quickly rebuild its state information from the messages sent to it by other agents.

Cyclic behaviour is a problem that plagues distributed algorithms. It occurs when a cycle of agents form which oscillate between two or more sets of assignments. In most algorithms it is prevented by having a total order over the agents. So one agent can not cause the value of a higher ranked agent to change. In order to prevent cyclic behaviour in SBDO a total order over the partial solutions is used instead. There are two parts to the cyclic behaviour prevention, first is the greedy selection of its new view and second is the constant attempt to increase the length of isgood's sent to neighbours. Because any cycle must be finite and we constantly increase the length of isgood's, eventually an isgood will include all the agents in the cycle. If the values in the cycle violate a constraint then a nogood will be generated to break the cycle. Otherwise the greedy selection of its new view will cause all the agents to converge to the best solution within the cycle.

The selection of which agent to use as the support and the ordering over partial solutions are critical to the performance of this algorithm. If agents change their support often then it is easier for the algorithm to escape from local optima, but it is just as likely to get stuck in a worse local optima as a better one and it will take longer to converge on a solution. While if agents change their support rarely the algorithm will converge to a solution quickly, but will not explore much of the search space.

There are three basic types of changes to the environment that must be communicated to the SBDO agents. They are a hard constraint has changed, an objective has changed and an agent has been added/removed. These messages are assumed to be sent by the environment to all agents that are affected by the change, but they could be sent by one of the agents instead.

A change to the hard constraints is handled by the add constraint and remove constraint messages. Modifying constraints is achieved by first removing the old constraint then adding the modified constraint. Adding constraints is easy, the constraint is simply added to the agents known constraints. Removing constraints is harder, as the justification of all nogood's must be updated. Then the constraint can be removed from the agents known constraints.

A change to the objectives, whether local or shared, is handled by the add objective and remove objective messages. Modifying objectives is achieved by first removing the old objective then adding the modified one. Both adding and removing objectives is easy, the objective is added or removed from the agents known objectives, then the agent re-evaluates its own assignment and updates its neighbours as normal.

A change to the agents involved is handled implicitly by the other environment messages. When an agent no longer has any links to one of its neighbours, that agent is no longer a neighbour. Similarly once an agent has no links to any other agents it is effectively removed from the problem. Agents are added to the problem by creating a link between them and another agent. In the process they are then also a neighbour of that agent.

When the environment decides that one agent in the problem is no longer required it sends a terminate message to that agent, which causes the agent to shutdown gracefully. Similarly if the environment decides that the algorithm has finished it can send a different terminate message which will cascade through the network, causing the entire algorithm to shutdown gracefully.

2.1   Algorithm

The basic steps each agent takes are quite simple, First it processes all the messages in its message queue. Then it decides what value to assign to its own variable. Last it sends all of its neighbours a message telling them what value it has chosen.

Processing messages starts with all of the nogood's received. Nogood's are processed first in case they are later rendered obsolete by a message from the environment and because one of them might be a sub-set of one of the isgood's in the message queue. When a nogood is received it is added to the set of all known nogood's, then all the received isgood's must be rechecked to see if there is still a valid assignment to this agents own variable. If there isn't a nogood is created and sent back to the agent that sent the isgood. This will force the sender to change their value in the next iteration. Next all messages from the environment are processed. The order within this group doesn't matter, but they may affect how the isgood's are processed Finally the received isgood's are processed. First the received isgood's are updated with this most recent isgood, then it checks if there is a valid assignment to its own variable. If there isn't a nogood is created and sent back to the agent that sent the isgood. This will force the sender to change their value in the next iteration.

While the processing of most messages from the environment is straight forward, removing constraints requires special mention. When a constraint is removed from the problem all of the nogood's that were generated because of that constraint must also be removed. This is made more difficult because it is possible for the nogood message to arrive after the remove constraint message that makes it obsolete.

In order to ensure they are all deleted each agent must also maintain a store of all the nogood's it has sent and who it sent them to. Then when a remove constraint message is received by an agent it checks its sent nogood store to see if any of its neighbours must be notified. If any of the nogood's have the removed constraint as part of their justification they are now obsolete and the agents neighbour must be notified. To notify the neighbour this agent sends a constraint removed message (this is different to the remove constraint message) with the constraint that has been removed and the total number of nogood's sent to that agent that are made obsolete.

When an agent receives the constraint removed message it must go through its store of received constraints and delete any that have this constraint as part of their justification. For each one that is deleted the counter of total obsolete nogood's in the constraint removed message is decremented. When the counter reaches zero all of the obsolete nogood's have been deleted and the constraint removed message can be deleted. The agent must also check its own store of sent nogood's to see if any of its neighbours must be notified of the change. This is exactly as above. If an agent receives two or more constraint removed messages for the same constraint the counters are simply added together.

Now that the agent has the most recent information about its environment it can choose the best assignment to its own variable. First it updates its own view. This must be called now in case the agents support has changed its value since the last iteration or if the environment has changed significantly.

Updating the agents view is very simple, first it takes the isgood sent by the agents support and greedily adds an assignment to its own variable, ensuring that the resulting partial solution does not violate any constraints. It then checks to see if using this as its world view will defiantly cause cyclic behaviour. Using this partial solution will defiantly cause cyclic behaviour if all of the following hold, the new and old solutions have assignments to the same variables, the old solution is better than the new solution, the new solution is out of date and the old solution is not out of date.

After the agent has updated its own view it then checks to see if one of the other agents would make a better support than the current one. To do so it picks the best isgood out of all of the isgood's it has received, then compares it with its view. If the isgood is better then it changes its support to the agent which sent the best isgood and then has to update its view again. If its view is better than it keeps its current support.

The agent can then tell all its neighbours that it has changed its value. First it checks to see if it needs to send an update to this neighbour. If the assignment to our its variable does not conflict with the last isgood it received from that neighbour and its view has not changed significantly since the last message then there is no need to send another one. Then it checks to see if it has received a message from this neighbour after we finished processing messages this iteration. If it did it delays sending a message to this neighbour until it has processed the message. Every time an isgood is sent to this neighbour it tries to make it longer than the last message sent to this neighbour. This is required to prevent cyclic behaviour as well as provides a stronger argument to the neighbour so it is more likely to change its value. It then takes the appropriate length tail of its view to use as the isgood, except if that isgood contains an assignment to this neighbour. If that is the case then the isgood is shortened further so that there isn't a reference to this neighbour in it. This is because each variable can only be assigned a value once in an isgood. Once it has the final isgood it can calculate the utility its objective function gives to the isgood, the finally it sends the isgood to this neighbour and updates its list of sent isgood's.

Table 1 shows the messages that are exchanged when solving the following CSP.

$$\mathcal{V} = \{1, 2, 3, 4, 5\}$$
$$\mathcal{D}_i = \{\alpha, \beta, \gamma\}$$
$$\mathcal{C} = \{1 \neq 2, 2 \neq 3, 3 \neq 1, 1 \neq 4, 4 \neq 5\}$$

Table 1. Messages sent in a sample run of SBDO

From	To	message	
1	2,3,4	$\langle (1, \alpha) \rangle$	Agents 1 and 5 announce their values, other agents could also announce their values.
5	4	$\langle (5, \beta) \rangle$	
2	1,3	$\langle (2, \gamma) \rangle$	Agents 2 and 3 pick 1 as their support and agent 4 picks 5 as it's support. They then announce the values they have chosen.
3	1,2	$\langle (3, \beta) \rangle$	
4	1,5	$\langle (4, \alpha) \rangle$	
4	5	$\langle (5, \beta), (4, \alpha) \rangle$	As agent 1 is inconsistent with agent 4, 4 sends a stronger isgood to 1.
1	2,3,4	$\langle (4, \alpha), (1, \beta) \rangle$	Agent 1 is then convinced to change its value and so selects 4 as support.
3	1,2	$\langle (1, \beta), (3, \gamma) \rangle$	Agent 3 is then inconsistent and so changes its value.
2	1,3	$\langle (1, \beta), (2, \gamma) \rangle$	The values of agents 2 and 3 are then inconsistent so they attempt to convince the other to change.
3	1,2	$\langle (4, \alpha), (1, \beta), (3, \gamma) \rangle$	
2	1,3	$\langle (4, \alpha), (1, \beta), (2, \gamma) \rangle$	Finally agent 2 convinces 3 to change its value and the solution is consistent.
3	1,2	$\langle (4, \alpha), (1, \beta), (2, \gamma), (3, \alpha) \rangle$	

3 Conclusion

By using a simple form of argumentation for communication we were able to create an algorithm that can solve dynamic distributed constraint optimisation problems. It also has the advantages of being completely asynchronous, anytime and fault tolerant. However it sacrifices completeness.

The efficiency of the algorithm still needs to be properly evaluated against similar algorithms.

References

1. Modi, P.J., Shen, W.M., Tambe, M., Yokoo, M.: Adopt: asynchronous distributed constraint optimization with quality guarantees. Artificial Intelligence 161, 149–180 (2005)
2. Silaghi, M.C., Yokoo, M.: Nogood based asynchronous distributed optimization (adopt-ng). In: AAMAS 2006: Procedings of the fifth international joint conference on Autonomous agents and multiagent systems, pp. 1389–1396. ACM, New York (2006)
3. Yeoh, W., Felner, A., Koenig, S.: Bnb-adopt: an asynchronous branch-and-bound dcop algorithm. In: AAMAS 2008: Procedings of the 7th international joint conference on Autonomous agents and multiagent systems, Richland, SC, International Foundation for Autonomous Agents and Multiagent Systems, pp. 591–598 (2008)
4. Petcu, A., Faltings, B.: Dpop: A scalable method for multiagent constraint optimization. In: IJCAI 2005, Edinburgh, Scotland, August 2005, pp. 266–271 (2005)
5. Chechetka, A., Sycara, K.: No-commitment branch and bound search for distributed constraint optimization. In: AAMAS 2006: Proceedings of the fifth international joint conference on Autonomous agents and multiagent systems, pp. 1427–1429. ACM, New York (2006)
6. Mailler, R.: Comparing two approaches to dynamic, distributed constraint satisfaction. In: AAMAS 2005: Proceedings of the fourth international joint conference on Autonomous agents and multiagent systems, pp. 1049–1056. ACM, New York (2005)
7. Schiex, T., Verfaillie, G.: Nogood recording for static and dynamic constraint satisfaction problem. International Journal of Artifical Intelligence Tools 3(2), 187–207 (1994)
8. Mertens, K.: An Ant-Based Approach for Solving Dynamic Constraint Optimization Problems. PhD thesis, Katholieke Universiteit Leuven (December 2006)
9. Schiex, T., Verfaillie, G.: Nogood recording for static and dynamic constraint satisfaction problems. In: Proceedings of Tools with Artificial Intelligence, 1993. TAI 1993, November 1993, pp. 48–55 (1993)
10. Harvey, P., Chang, C.F., Ghose, A.: Support-based distributed search: a new approach for multiagent constraint processing. In: AAMAS 2006: Proceedings of the fifth international joint conference on Autonomous agents and multiagent systems, pp. 377–383. ACM, New York (2006)
11. Chandy, K.M., Lamport, L.: Distributed snapshots: Determining global states of distributed systems. ACM Transactions on Computer Systems 3(1), 63–75 (1985)

Evacuation Planning Assist System with Network Model-Based Pedestrian Simulator

Tomohisa Yamashita, Shunsuke Soeda, and Itsuki Noda

National Institute of Advanced Industrial Science and Technology,
Aomi 2-41-6, Koto-ku, Tokyo 135-0064, Japan
{tomohisa.yamashita,shunsuke.soeda,I.Noda}@aist.go.jp

Abstract. In this paper, we analyzed the influence of time required to begin coping behaviors of managers in chemical terrorism. In order to calculate the damage of chemical attacks in a major rail station, our network model-based pedestrian simulator was applied with hazard prediction systems of indoor gas diffusion. Our analysis was used for enlightening the managers of the rail station in a tabletop exercise held by Kitakyushu City Fire and Disaster Management Department.

1 Introduction

CBR terrorisms caused by chemical(C) and biological(B) agents and radioactive(R) materials are nonselective attacks on crowds in urban areas. These hazardous materials might be sprinkled, vaporized, or spread with an explosion. A first responder of these accidents, such as a fire protection and police agencies of municipalities, has to prepare practical plans of coping behaviors against CBR terrorism, but they do not have much experience and knowledge of CBR terrorism. Therefore, useful tools supporting to make plans is required to estimate and illustrate the damage done by CBR attacks.

With our evacuation planning assist system, a user can estimate the damage caused by CBR terrorism. These disasters, which are likely to be caused in urban areas, have many characteristics different from natural disasters. These disasters are caused intentionally, which means we must prepare for the worst; there are still few case that CBR terrorism were actually conducted, which means we still know little about what damage will be caused by such terrorism; unlike natural disasters, these disasters are not always harmful to some of the urban infrastructure, which means that they could be utilized for more efficient evacuation.

In this paper, we explain our evacuation planning assist system, and share with an example of practical use of our system. We dealt with coping behaviors against chemical attack in a major rail station because of a request from the Fire and Disaster Management Department of Kitakyushu City. In our simulation, we revealed the relationship between the time required to begin coping behaviors of the managers and the damage of passengers. Our analysis was used for enlightening the managers of the rail station in a tabletop exercise held by the Fire and Disaster Management Department of Kitakyushu City.

J.-J. Yang et al. (Eds.): PRIMA 2009, LNAI 5925, pp. 649–656, 2009.

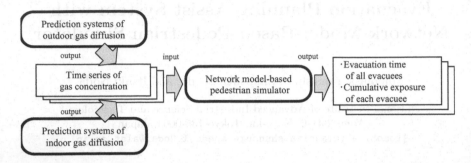

Fig. 1. Outline of dataflow of the evacuation planning assist system

2 Evacuation Planning Assist System

Our evacuation planning assist system consists of three components; a pedestrian simulator constructed by Advanced Industrial Science and Technology (AIST), a prediction system of outdoor gas diffusion by Mitsubishi Heavy Industries (MHI), and a prediction system of indoor gas diffusion by Advancesoft. At first, the prediction systems of indoor and outdoor gas diffusion calculate concentration of hazardous gases. The output of these systems is time series of gas concentration in designated areas. Then, the pedestrian simulator calculates evacuation time of all evacuees and cumulative exposure of each evacuee with time series of gas concentration. Outline of dataflow of the evacuation planning assist system is shown in Fig. 1.

2.1 Pedestrian Simulator

Various kinds of pedestrian simulators have been developed for various purposes. Pan roughly classified them into three categories; fluid and particle systems, matrix-based systems, and emergent systems [5]. However, all of these systems are two dimensional systems, which allow pedestrians to move around two dimensionally. Unlike other pedestrian simulators, our simulator simplifies traffic lines by representing it with a graph model - a model with links and nodes (Fig. 2). The paths where the pedestrians move around are represented as links, and these links are connected at nodes. As the pedestrians could move only along the links, our model is more one dimensional than two dimensional.

This approach has often been used in traffic simulators [1], but not for pedestrian simulators. We chose the network based-model for our simulator, as we need a high speed simulator dealing with evacuation behaviors of many evacuees on the macroscopic side. Network based-model is not suitable for simulating many pedestrians evacuating large space precisely, but could be used to reveal bottlenecks and evocation time quickly as well as to compare a lot of evacuation plans. Appearance of a network-based pedestrian simulator are shown in Fig. 3.

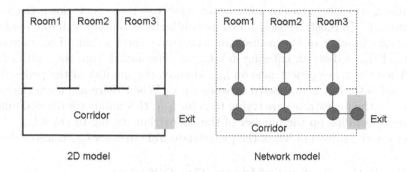

Fig. 2. 2D model and network model

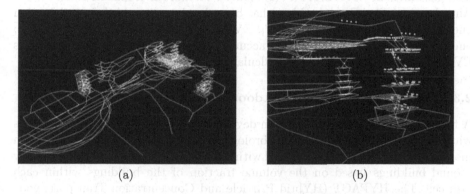

(a)   (b)

Fig. 3. 3D views of our network-based model pedestrian simulator

The speed of a pedestrian is calculated from the density of the crowd on the link. Each link has a width and a length, which is used to calculate the area of the link. Then, the density of the crowd on the link could be calculated from the number of the pedestrians on the link. Speed V_i of the pedestrian on link i is calculated from the following formula;

$$V_i = \begin{cases} V_f, & d_i < 1 \\ d_i^{-0.7945}V_f, & 1 \le d_i \le 4 \\ 0, & d_i > 4 \end{cases} \qquad (1)$$

where V_f represents free flow speed of the pedestrians, which is the speed of the pedestrian when not in a crowd, and d_i represents the density of the pedestrians on link i. The exception to this formula is the pedestrian on the head of a crowd on the link. For this pedestrian, V_f is used regardless of how the link is crowded. Note that when the density of a link exceeds 4 pedestrians/m^2, all the pedestrian on the link cannot move except for the one who is on the head of the crowd.

Confluences - where two or more paths meet together - slow down the speed of pedestrian. To illustrate slow-down by confluence, we used a simple model of limiting the number of the pedestrian who could enter a link. The maximum number of the pedestrian entering link l_{out} is determined from the width of the link. When there are pedestrians on l_{out} already, the number of the pedestrians that could enter l_{out} is decreased at some ratio. When there are more than two links where the pedestrians are trying to enter l_{out}, this number is divided among the links depending on the number of the pedestrians trying to enter l_{out}. Also, in this case, the total number of the pedestrians able to enter l_{out} is also reduced.

2.2   Prediction Systems of Indoor Gas Diffusion

For prevention or reduction of these disasters, a hazard prediction systems of indoor gas diffusion "EVE SAYFA" (Enhanced Virtual Environment Simulator for Aimed and Yielded Fatal Accident) has been developed to aid their anticipation and the evaluation of the safety [2,7]. EVE SAYFA has two simulation models; one is EVE SAYFA 3D with highly accurate 3-dimensional model. The other is EVE SAYFA 1D with high-speed calculating 1-dimensional network model.

2.3   Prediction Systems of Outdoor Gas Diffusion

A hazard prediction system has been developed for CBR attacks in urban areas with the use of the mesoscale meteorological model, RAMS and its dispersion model HYPACT. RAMS is equipped with an optional scheme to simulate airflow around buildings based on the volume fraction of the buildings within each grid cell. The HYPACT (HYbrid PArticle and Concentration Transport) code is an atmospheric diffusion code that can be coupled to RAMS. The developed simulation system, called MEASURES, consists of HYPACT, RAMS and an airflow database [3,4].

3   Simulation

3.1   Simulation Settings

With our evacuation planning assist system, we dealt with an chemical attack in a major rail station because of a request from the Fire and Disaster Management Department of Kitakyushu City. In our simulations, the chemical attack with chloropicrin is set to be taken place in the station yard of the conventional line. Gas diffusion in the station yard is calculated with the prediction system of indoor gas diffusion, EVE SAYFA 1D. The move and the damage of about 9000 passengers is calculated with our pedestrian simulator. The amount of exposure of chloropicrin of the passenger is calculated as product of the concentration of chloropicrin and the time spent in the area. The influence of exposure of chloropicrin [6,8] on the passenger's behavior is described in table 1.

This rail station is a complex facility. There are 4 kinds of facilities; a conventional line, a new bullet train line, a monorail, and a hotel. Each facility has

Table 1. The influence of exposure of chloropicrin

amount of exposure $(mg \cdot min/m^3)$	1	200	1,000	2,000	20,000
Influence on behavior	pain in the eye & throat	nausea & headache	breathing trouble	lethal dose 50%	lethal dose 100%
Implementation in pedestrian simulation	decrease in speed (-40%)	decrease in speed (-90%)	stop	stop	stop
damage level	mild	moderate	severe	severe	severe

Table 2. Coping behaviors of the managers and the times required for them

Manager		Coping behavior	Time required to begin(min) quick	slow
Conventional line	1	detecting chemical attack	5	10
	2	reporting to the fire department and the other managers	3	6
	3	shutting down the trains	3	6
	4	ordering an evacuation to the passengers	3	6
New bullet train line	5	ordering an evacuation to the passengers	3	6
	6	shutting down the trains	3	6
Monorail station	7	ordering an evacuation to the passengers	5	6
	8	shutting down the trains	3	6
Hotel	9	ordering an evacuation to the guests	3	6
Fire and Disaster Management Department	10	rescuing insured passengers	20	30

a manager. We assume following 10 coping behaviors of the managers and the times required to begin these coping behaviors described in table 2. The times required to begin these coping behaviors has a influence on the damage of the passengers because the beginning of evacuation of the passengers is also delayed if the beginning of these coping behaviors is delayed. The sequence of the coping behaviors is shown in Fig. 4. For example, the manager of the new bullet train line has two coping behaviors; (5) ordering an evacuation to the passengers, and (6) shutting down the trains. Each coping behavior is set to have two kinds of the time required. For example, if coping behavior 5 (ordering an evacuation to the passengers) is begun quickly, the time required to begin is 3 minutes. Otherwise (begun slowly), the time required is 6 minutes.

The number of all evacuation scenarios is 1024 because the number of combination of the times required to begin 10 coping behaviors is 2^{10} (=1024). We calculate the damage of about 9000 passengers in 1024 evacuation scenarios. In our pedestrian simulation, each passenger walks around normally, from/to outside of the station from/to platforms, until the attack is detected and alarm is given. After ordering an evacuation to the passengers, the passengers evacuate through the route directed by station staffs.

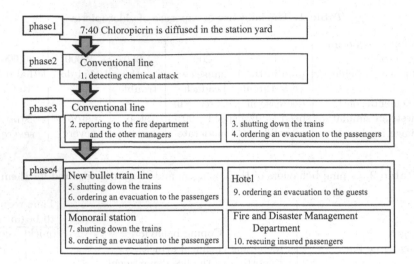

Fig. 4. The sequence of the coping behaviors

3.2 Simulation Result

The result of our simulation is shown in Figs. 5~7.

In Fig. 5, the graph shows the number of the severe victims in 1024 scenarios. Based on the number of the severe victims, there are 5 characteristic clusters. In each cluster, the scenarios has the same tendency of coping behavior 1 and 4. In the scenarios of cluster 1-1, both (1) detecting chemical attack and (4) ordering an evacuation to passengers of the conventional line are begun quickly. In the scenarios of cluster 1-2, (1) detecting is begun quickly, and (4) ordering an evacuation is begun slowly. In the scenarios of cluster 1-3a and 1-3b, (1) detecting is begun slowly, and (4) ordering an evacuation is begun quickly. The difference between cluster 1-3a and 1-3b is coping behavior 10. In the scenarios in cluster 1-3a, (10) rescuing insured passengers by Fire and Disaster Management Department is begun slowly. On the other hand, in the scenarios in cluster 1-3b, (10) rescuing is begun quickly. In the scenarios of cluster 1-4, both (1) detecting and (4) ordering an evacuation are begun slowly. Therefore, it is confirmed that both (1) detecting, (4) ordering an evacuation, and (10) rescuing insured passengers are more important to decrease the severe victims.

In Fig. 6, the graph shows the number of the moderate victims in 1024 scenarios. Based on the number of the severe victims, there are 4 characteristic clusters. The number of victims in cluster 2-1 is less than that of other clusters. There is not so much difference among the number of the victims of cluster 2-1, 2-2, and 2-3. Therefore, it is confirmed that (1) detecting and (4) ordering an evacuation are more important to decrease the moderate victims.

In Fig. 7, the graph shows the number of the mild victims in 1024 scenarios. Based on the number of the severe victims, there are 4 clusters. The number of mild victims in cluster 3-1 is more than that in cluster 3-2. However, the

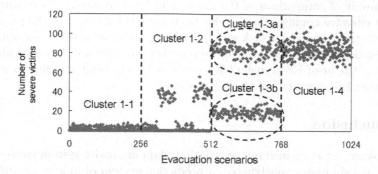

Fig. 5. The number of the severe victims

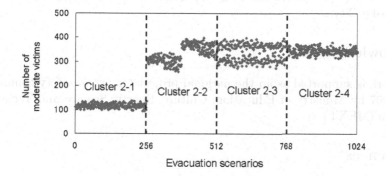

Fig. 6. The number of the moderate victims

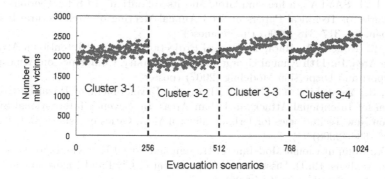

Fig. 7. The number of the mild victims

amount of all victims in cluster 1-1, 2-1, and 3-1 is equal to that in cluster 1-2, 2-2, and 3-2. Therefore, Therefore, it is confirmed that (1) detecting is important to decrease the damage of the passengers.

As a result of comparison of the damage in 1024 scenarios, we confirm that the most effective coping behaviors for decreasing the damage of the passengers are i) detecting chemical attack and ii) ordering an evacuation to passengers of the conventional line. In a tabletop exercise held by Fire and Disaster Management Department of Kitakyushu City, our simulation result was shared with for enlightening the managers of the rail station.

4   Conclusion

In this paper, we explained our evacuation planning assist system consisting of a pedestrian simulator constructed, a prediction system of indoor gas diffusion, and a prediction system of outdoor gas diffusion. Chemical attack in a major rail station in Japan is taken up as an example of practical use of our system because of a request from the Fire and Disaster Management Department of Kitakyushu City.

Acknowledgment

This work is supported as an the national project for urban safety commenced from 2007 by Ministry of Education, Culture, Sports, Science and Technology of Japan (MEXT).

References

1. Burmeister, B., Haddadi, A., Matylis, G.: Application of Multi-Agent Systems in Traffic and Transportation. Software Engineering 144(1), 51–60 (2002)
2. Nara, M., Kato, S., Huang, H., Zhu, S.W.: Numerical analysis of fire on disasters with "EVE SAYFA", a fire simulator, and its validation? LES for thermal plume. Summaries of Technical Papers of 2006 Annual Meeting of Architectural Institute of Japan, pp. 317–318 (2006) (in Japanese)
3. Ohba, R., Kouchi, A., Hara, T.: Hazard Projection System of Intentional Attack in Urban Area. In: 11th Annual George Mason University, Conference on Atmospheric Transport and Dispersion Modeling (2007) (poster)
4. Ohba, R., Yamashita, T., Ukai, O., Kato, S.: Development of Hazard Prediction System for Intentional Attacks in Urban Areas. In: Seventh International Symposium on New Technologies for Urban Safety of Mega Cities in Asia (USMCA 2008), pp. 687–696 (2008)
5. Pan, X.: Computational Modelling of Human and Social Behaviours for Emergency Egress Analysis. Ph.D. Dissertation, Department of Civil and Environmental Engineering, Stanford University (2006)
6. http://en.wikipedia.org/wiki/Chloropicrin
7. http://venus.iis.u-tokyo.ac.jp/english/Research/field-e/evesayfa/index.html
8. http://www.workcover.nsw.gov.au/Documents/Publications/AlertsGuidesHazards/DangerousGoodsExplosivesFireworksPyrotechnics/chloropicrin_fact_sheet_1371.pdf

Author Index